W9-BKM-717

MAGILL'S ENCYCLOPEDIA OF SOCIAL SCIENCE

PSYCHOLOGY

MAGILL'S ENCYCLOPEDIA OF SOCIAL SCIENCE

PSYCHOLOGY

Volume 2
Data description – Meditation and relaxation

Editor
Nancy A. Piotrowski, Ph.D.
University of California, Berkeley

Project Editor
Tracy Irons-Georges

SALEM PRESS, INC.
Pasadena, California
Hackensack, New Jersey

Editorial Director: Christina J. Moose
Project Editor: Tracy Irons-Georges
Copy Editor: Leslie Ellen Jones
Assistant Editor: Andrea E. Miller
Acquisitions Editor: Mark Rehn
Photograph Editor: Philip Bader
Research Supervisor: Jeffry Jensen
Production Editor: Cynthia Beres
Page Design/Graphics: James Hutson
Layout: Eddie Murillo

∞ The paper used in these volumes conforms to the American National Standard for Permanence of Paper for Printed Library Materials, Z39.48-1992 (R1997).

Some of the updated and revised essays in this work originally appeared in *Magill's Survey of Social Science: Psychology,* edited by Frank N. Magill (Pasadena, Calif.: Salem Press, Inc., 1993).

Library of Congress Cataloging-in-Publication Data

Magill's encyclopedia of social science: psychology/ editor, Nancy A. Piotrowski.
    p. cm.
Includes bibliographical references and index.
ISBN 1-58765-130-0 (set : alk. paper) — ISBN 1-58765-131-9 (v. 1 : alk. paper) —
ISBN 1-58765-132-7 (v. 2 : alk. paper)— ISBN 1-58765-133-5 (v. 3 : alk. paper) —
ISBN 1-58765-134-3 (v. 4 : alk. paper)
1. Psychology—Encyclopedias. I. Piotrowski, Nancy A.

BF31 .M33 2003
150'.3—dc21

2002151146

Fourth Printing

PRINTED IN THE UNITED STATES OF AMERICA

Table of Contents

MAGILL'S ENCYCLOPEDIA OF SOCIAL SCIENCE

PSYCHOLOGY

D

Data description

TYPE OF PSYCHOLOGY: Psychological methodologies
FIELDS OF STUDY: Descriptive methodologies; experimental methodologies; methodological issues

Data description refers to how the results from research studies are organized, summarized, and characterized statistically.

KEY CONCEPTS
- bar graph
- frequency polygon
- grouped frequency distributions
- histogram
- interquartile range
- line graph
- mean
- median
- mode
- negatively skewed distributions
- positively skewed distributions
- range
- semi-interquartile range
- simple frequency distributions
- standard deviation
- variance

INTRODUCTION

Almost all research investigations involve studying a sample of individuals randomly selected from a population with the goal of applying what is learned from the sample to all the individuals who constitute the population. A critical part of this enterprise entails organizing, summarizing, and characterizing the data collected from the sample in meaningful ways. To accomplish this aim, researchers use statistical procedures and graphing techniques. Among these techniques are frequency distributions, measures of central tendency, and measures of variability. In addition, the numbers that constitute research data have different meanings. This is reflected in the scales of measurement to which numbers adhere.

SCALES OF MEASUREMENT

Not all numbers are created equal. Different numbers have different meanings and thus have different characteristics. For example, the number 24 on the back of a baseball player's jersey does not indicate that the player is twice as good as another player who wears the number 12. On the other hand, $24 does indicate twice as many dollars as $12. To differentiate these characteristics, one must understand the scale of measurement to which numbers adhere.

There are four scales of measurement. In ascending order, they are nominal, ordinal, interval, and ratio. Each scale has all the characteristics of the preceding scale plus one additional unique characteristic. Numbers that adhere to the nominal scale simply represent different categories or groups, such as the numbers 1 or 2 to indicate the gender of a research subject. The ordinal scale has the characteristic of different categories but also reflects relative magnitude or degree of measurement, such as ranking photographs from 1 to 5 based on their aesthetic qualities. Both features of separate categories and relative magnitude are reflected in the next scale, the interval scale, with the added characteristic that the distances between successive numbers on the scale are of equal interval. Temperatures on either the Celsius or Fahrenheit scale would be examples of an interval scale of measurement. Finally, numbers that adhere to the ratio scale of measurement reflect the three characteristics of the interval scale along with an absolute zero point, with a value of 0 representing the absence of the measurement. The variables, for example, of time, height, or body weight all would adhere to the ratio scale of measurement. In a research context, knowing the scale of measurement to which numbers adhere will have an impact on the type of statistical procedure used to analyze the data.

ORGANIZING DATA

At the completion of any research study, the data collected need to be organized and summarized in ways that allow the researcher to identify trends or other interesting consistencies in the results. One of the techniques for organizing and summarizing data, especially large sets of data, is the frequency distribution. Frequency distributions allow the researcher to tabulate the frequencies associated with specific response categories and also allow for the data to be summarized and characterized in a more manageable fashion. The organized frequency data are then presented in table form, with the response categories organized in ascending or descending order. Organizing the results in such a manner will facilitate making interpretations from and conclusions about the data.

Generally speaking, there are two types of frequency distribution: simple frequency distribution and grouped frequency distribution. These two types of frequency distribution are constructed identically, with one exception. The simple frequency distribution entails categorizing frequencies for each and every possible response category or score (symbolized X), while grouped frequency distributions combine specific categories or specific scores into groups called class intervals. Grouping frequencies into class intervals has the advantage of making data sets with wide-ranging categories or scores easier to manage and thus easier to summarize. However, doing so does come with a price. By grouping categories or scores together, the researcher loses some specificity with regard to the number of frequencies associated with particular categories or scores.

Much information can be gleaned from a frequency distribution table. Apart from listing the scores or response categories and their frequencies (symbolized as f), frequency distributions often contain columns indicating the percent of the total frequency each particular frequency represents (symbolized as % f), the cumulative frequency counts (symbolized as cum f) and their associated percents (symbolized as % cum f), the products of each pair of f × X terms (symbolized as fX), and the products of each pair of f × X² terms (symbolized fX²). Each of these two latter columns, along with the frequency

Figure 1. Simple Frequency Distribution

X (height)	f	% f	cum f	% cum f	fX	fX²
72	1	2%	1	2%	72	5,184
71	0	0%	1	2%	0	0
70	1	2%	2	4%	70	4,900
69	2	4%	4	8%	138	9,522
68	1	2%	5	10%	68	4,624
67	4	8%	9	18%	268	17,956
66	5	10%	14	28%	330	21,780
65	10	20%	24	48%	650	42,250
64	9	18%	33	66%	576	36,864
63	7	14%	40	80%	441	27,783
62	5	10%	45	90%	310	19,220
61	3	6%	48	96%	183	11,163
60	1	2%	49	98%	60	3,600
59	0	0%	49	98%	0	0
58	1	2%	50	100%	58	3,364
$\Sigma = 50$					$\Sigma = 3,224$	$\Sigma = 208,210$

column, is summed (indicated by the capital Greek letter Σ). These sums are then used in calculating the values of the mean and the standard deviation.

An example of the use of a frequency distribution can be seen in the case of a researcher interested in determining the frequencies with which heights (in inches) present in a sample of fifty subjects. (The number of subjects in a research study is indicated by N.) Each subject's height measurement might be presented in the simple frequency distribution in figure 1.

Organizing the data in this manner allows the researcher to make sense of the data by identifying the most frequent (65 inches) and least frequent (59 inches and 71 inches) height, the percent of the total associated with each height category, and by recording the cumulative frequencies and their associated percentages. Moreover, by examining the values in the "f" column, the manner in which the heights are distributed over the various categories can be easily ascertained. In this distribution, for example, the greatest number of frequencies are associated with height categories that lie toward the middle range of scores, while very few frequencies are associated with heights that lie at either the upper or lower ends of the range of height scores. This type of distribution is called a bell-shaped curve or a normal distribution and is often a characteristic of psychological and behavioral data.

MEASURES OF CENTRAL TENDENCY

Because research data represent large sets of numbers, it is desirable, in fact necessary, to summarize these data in order to facilitate making sense of them. In an attempt to accomplish this goal, researchers calculate summary statistics that provide one value whose purpose is to reflect the general characteristics of the data. The most frequently used summary statistics are called measures of central tendency, and they include the mean or arithmetic average, the median or middle point of the distribution, and the mode or the most frequently encountered score in the distribution.

The calculations for the mean, median, and mode are quite simple. Adding all the scores together and dividing by the number of scores in the distribution obtains the mean. In the simple frequency distribution above, the sum of all the scores is indicated by ΣfX, while the number of scores is reflected in the Σf term. Thus, the mean for this set of data is $3{,}224 \div 50$, or 64.48 inches. The median or middle point of this distribution of fifty scores lies somewhere between the twenty-fifth and twenty-sixth scores. Since this point in the distribution does not have an actual score associated with it, the convention is to estimate the value of this score by averaging the twenty-fifth and twenty-sixth scores. It just so happens that the twenty-fifth and twenty-sixth scores in the above distribution both have values of 64 inches, therefore making the median $(64 + 64) \div 2$, or 64 inches. Lastly, since the mode is the most frequently exhibited score in the distribution, its identification in the above simple frequency distribution is obtained by looking down the "f" column and determining the largest frequency and its associated height score. By doing so, the mode for this distribution is determined to be 65 inches.

The measures of central tendency are not only useful for using a single value to characterize large data sets but also helpful in identifying the shape of the distribution. For example, it is known that distributions whose mean, median, and mode values are all the same (or similar) most likely are normal distributions. Distributions whose mean value is larger than its median value are most likely to be positively skewed. Positively skewed distributions are those that have the majority of their frequencies toward the lower end of the range of scores. In contrast, when the median value of a distribution exceeds the mean value, then the majority of scores fall at the upper end of the range of scores and the distribution is described as being negatively skewed.

Of the three measures of central tendency, the mean is the most frequently used. However, the use of this statistic will depend on the shape of the distribution and the scale of measurement to which the scores adhere. The mean should be used when working with either interval or ratio data and also when the distribution is approximately normal and does not contain many excessively extreme scores at either end of the distribution. The last criterion is important because the presence of extreme scores in the distribution can severely distort the value of the mean. For this reason, government statistics that summarize income or house prices, for example, typically report median values. When the mean is inappropriate to use, the median is the statistic of choice, as long as the data adhere either to the ordinal, interval, or ratio scale. The mode can be used with any scale of measurement and is typically the statistic of choice with nominal data.

MEASURES OF VARIABILITY

Although measures of central tendency are useful statistics, they only reflect one aspect of the data. Another important feature of the data is the amount of spread or dispersion that exists among the scores. This dimension is reflected in another class of statistics called measures of variability.

The most straightforward measure of variability is the range. (It should be noted that the range is not used with nominal data.) The range sample reflects how far apart two extreme scores in the distribution are from each other. In its simplest form, the range is calculated by subtracting the least value from the greatest value. In the height data above, the range would equal 14 inches (that is, 72 inches minus 58 inches). A variant of the range is the interquartile range, and its calculation entails taking a difference between the scores that lie at the twenty-fifth and seventy-fifth percentiles. Again, using the height data, it can be seen in the "cum f" column that the scores that lie at the twenty-fifth and seventy-fifth percentiles are 66 and 63, respectively; thus the interquatile range would equal 3 inches. Another variant of the range is called the semi-interquartile range, and its calculation is the interquartile range divided by 2. For the height data, the semi-interquartile range would be 1.5 inches. The range, or one of its variants (typically the semi-interquartile range), is used as the measure of variability when the median is used as the measure of central tendency.

The utility of the ranges as measures of variability is quite limited, since their calculations involve using only two scores from the distribution. The variance and standard deviation, on the other hand, use all the scores in their calculations and thus are better measures, but they do require that the data fit either the interval or ratio scale of measurement. The variance is obtained by applying the following formula to the data: $[\Sigma X^2 - ((\Sigma X)^2 \div N)] \div N$. Thus, the variance for the height data discussed above would be equal to $[208,210 - (3,224^2 \div 50)] \div 50$ or 6.53 inches. (Note, a mathematically equivalent formula is $[\Sigma(X - mean)^2] \div N]$.) The standard deviation is simply the square root of the variance and

its value would be 2.56 inches. Of these two measures of variability, the standard deviation is the one almost always used and it is reported when the appropriate measure of central tendency is the mean.

The variance and standard deviation are important in a number of ways. First, the variance represents a measurement that reflects the average squared dispersion between each score and the mean of the distribution. (Note, mathematically, squaring the difference between the score and the mean when calculating the variance or standard deviation is necessary to avoid always obtaining a quotient of 0.) Second, the variance can be interpreted as an estimate of the margin of error when using the mean to predict the value of a randomly selected individual's score from the population. For example, based on the sample of fifty subjects presented in the frequency distribution above, the height of a randomly selected person from the population would be 64.48 ± 6.53 inches. Another example of a variance measure would be the margin of error that accompanies the results of most public opinion polls. Finally, the standard deviation is used in calculating a standardized score, also known as a z-score. A standardized score is equal to the squared difference between the score and the mean divided by the standard deviation (that is, $z = (X - mean)^2 \div$ standard deviation). Standardized scores are helpful in comparing the relative performance of scores that come from different populations and samples, and are also used in determining various proportions of the population associated with different regions of the normal distributions. For example, 68.26 percent of the scores in a normal distribution will fall within ± 1 z-score unit (or ± 1 standard deviation unit) from the mean while 95.44 percent will fall within ± 2 z-score units (± 2 standard deviation units).

GRAPHS

It has been said that a picture is worth a thousand words. This is also true when it comes to research data. Researchers very often will present their data or summary statistics calculated from their data in graphic form. There are a variety of ways to do this. Frequency data are often displayed via a frequency polygon, bar graph, or histogram. All three of these types of graphs plot the frequency data as a function of the score categories on a set of X,Y axes, as is illustrated in figures 2, 3, and 4.

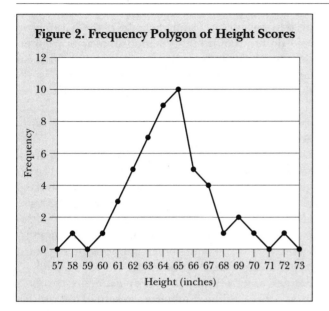

Figure 2. Frequency Polygon of Height Scores

sides of the curve are anchored to the X-axis. This is accomplished by starting the X-axis off with the score below the lowest score in the data set and ending the X-axis with the score above the highest score. There are no frequencies associated with these two X values, thus the curve is anchored to the X-axis.

Data derived from an experiment, on the other hand, are usually plotted using a line graph. A line graph typically plots the mean of some measure (called the dependent variable) as a function of the variables (called the independent variables) studied in the experiment. Also included in a line graph are T-bars that extend from the mean. The T-bars represent each plotted mean's measure of variability, often expressed in terms of ± 1 standard deviation unit. Line graphs do, however, require that the data be derived from either an interval or ratio scale of measurement. Experimental data that are either ordinal or nominal in nature should be plotted using a bar graph.

Apart from the obvious differences in their look, these three graphs differ in another way. Frequencies associated with either the nominal or ordinal scale of measurement should be plotted using a bar graph, while data that reflect some quantifiable measurement (that is, quantitative data) can be plotted using either a frequency polygon or a histogram. It is the convention to use a frequency polygon, rather than a histogram, when there is a large range of scores to be plotted on the X-axis. Another important feature of frequency polygons is that the left- and right-hand

The example of a line graph provided in figure 5 presents fictitious data for illustration purposes. The relationship expressed in this graph is the effect of number of alcoholic drinks (one independent variable) on the number of words recalled (the dependent variable) in both male and female subjects (a second independent variable). The mean values for each of the eight groups of subjects are plotted along with their standard deviations, represented by the T-bars that extend upward and downward from each point in the graph. In this set of fic-

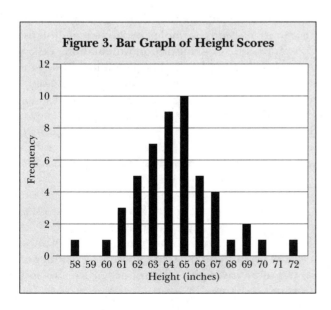

Figure 3. Bar Graph of Height Scores

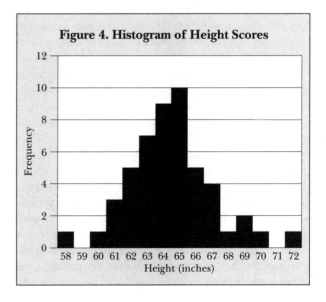

Figure 4. Histogram of Height Scores

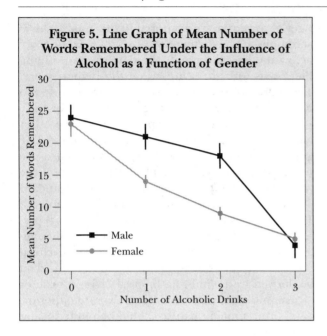

Figure 5. Line Graph of Mean Number of Words Remembered Under the Influence of Alcohol as a Function of Gender

of the groups are similar), while nonparametric tests do not require that these assumptions are met. Analyzing research data with inferential statistical tests is a critical component of the scientific process that enables researchers to identify cause-and-effect relationships in nature.

SOURCES FOR FURTHER STUDY

Bruning James L., and B. L. Kintz. *Computational Handbook of Statistics*. 3d ed. Glenview, Ill.: Harper-Collins, 1987. This book provides a step-by-step guide to the calculations for many statistical tests.

Heiman, Gary W. *Basic Statistics for the Behavioral Sciences*. 3d ed. Boston: Houghton Mifflin, 2000. A very good introduction to the various statistical procedures used in research.

Keppel, Geoffrey. *Design and Analysis: A Researcher's Handbook*. 2d ed. Englewood Cliffs, N.J.: Prentice Hall, 1982. This book, which emphasizes the mathematical bases of statistics, is recommended only to those who already have a strong background in statistics.

Siegel, Sidney. *Nonparametric Statistics for the Behavioral Sciences*. New York: McGraw-Hill, 1956. Although old, this book is the quintessential guide to nonparametric statistical testing.

Spatz, Chris. *Basic Statistics: Tales of Distributions*. 7th ed. Belmont, Calif.: Wadsworth/Thomson Learning, 2001. Another very good introduction to the various statistical procedures used in research.

Anthony C. Santucci

titious data, it can seen that, on average, female subjects were more adversely affected by either one or two alcoholic drinks, but showed the same degree of memory impairment as male subjects when three alcoholic drinks were administered.

INFERENTIAL STATISTICS

All the methods thus far described are descriptive in nature. That is, they simply describe, summarize, and illustrate the trends that exist in the data. Many other statistical procedures exist that enable researchers to make inferences about the population at large based on sample data. These procedures are referred to as inferential statistics. Essentially, the goal of all inferential statistics is to establish, within a specific probability of certainty, whether groups of subjects performed differently and whether these differences are attributable to the effects of the independent variable being studied in the investigation.

Inferential statistical tests fall into two broad categories, depending on whether two groups or more than two groups of subjects were studied. Further, each broad category is subdivided into two subcategories called parametric and nonparametric tests. Parametric tests are used when certain assumptions about the population from which the subjects were selected can be safely made (that is, the population is normally distributed and the population variances

SEE ALSO: Animal experimentation; Archival data; Case-study methods; Complex experimental designs; Experimental psychology; Experimentation: Ethics and participant rights; Experimentation: Independent, dependent, and control variables; Field experimentation; Hypothesis development and testing; Observational methods; Quasi-experimental designs; Sampling; Scientific methods; Statistical significance tests; Survey research: Questionnaires and interviews; Within-subject experimental designs.

Death and dying

TYPE OF PSYCHOLOGY: Developmental psychology
FIELDS OF STUDY: Aging; classic analytic themes and issues; stress and illness

Death is a universal human experience that, for most of history, has been primarily the province of religion and philosophy. It has, however, increasingly been a concern of social scientists; perhaps, more than has been previously realized, death has important things to teach both scientists and laypersons about human existence.

KEY CONCEPTS
- chronic illnesses
- death anxiety
- defense mechanisms
- denial
- five-stage theory
- syndrome

INTRODUCTION

Although death is a universal phenomenon, it is a topic which has come late to psychology and the other social sciences. Authors, scholars, theologians, and ordinary people have dealt with death since the beginning of recorded history—and certainly before that. Dealing with death in a scientific way is, to a large extent, a product of the twentieth century.

The reasons for the scientific neglect of death are manifold. It is a complex idea, and one against which most people build defense mechanisms (psychological strategies, generally unconscious, which the personality uses as a defense against anxiety). The scientist might argue that death is not an empirical fact (that is, the type of knowledge that relies on information which comes through the senses, as opposed to relying on logical or rational processes), in the sense that no one can experience death first-hand in order to study it or write about it. Sigmund Freud, the founder of psychoanalysis, said that no one can imagine his or her own death, and that does seem to be true; if one tries to imagine oneself dead, one still seems to be around, in some sense, doing the imagining.

Some scholars have distinguished between the death state and the death event. The death state (what it is like to be dead) is essentially a religious or philosophical issue. It would seem not to be amenable to empirical study, although the impact of death on other people and the impact of thoughts about death while one is still alive can be studied. The death event, on the other hand, is, to some degree at least, a part of life. It is possible to study how, why, and where people die. It is possible to study the

process of dying and to study grief and bereavement.

It has also become necessary, particularly in recent years, to ask difficult questions about death: questions about when physical death actually occurs, about humane treatment for the dying patient, about the "right to die," about children and the best way to answer their concerns about death, and about how best to help people deal with their grief. Most of these questions generally cannot be answered by science alone. Almost all deal with ethical, religious, and social issues as well as with scientific information.

It has been argued that America is a "death-denying" culture. Even though aspects of death are around all the time, Americans live most of the time as if death were not a reality. Ernest Becker argued in his classic book *The Denial of Death* (1973) that American lives are organized around the fear and denial of death. His often-convincing, although primarily philosophical, argument is augmented by research such as that of psychologists at Princeton University who studied undergraduates, most of whom did not admit having much conscious death anxiety (an emotional apprehension or vague fear caused by thinking about or facing the fact of death). Yet by a word-association test, measures of galvanic skin response (a biological electrical current in the skin assumed to be related to levels of psychological anxiety), and response latency (the time between the presentation of a stimulus word and the response from the subject), researchers collected data that clearly showed that these college students responded to words related to death with greater emotional intensity than to equivalent words drawn from other topic areas.

EMERGING UNDERSTANDING OF DEATH

If the United States is a death-denying society, it is nevertheless apparent that in the latter part of the twentieth century some people became willing to look at death more clearly; this is demonstrated in the behavioral and social sciences. In research, books, articles, and in many other ways, interest in death and dying, and closely related topics, has multiplied enormously.

In 1944, Erich Lindemann did a systematic study of the grief reactions of individuals who had lost a close relative; many of his subjects were relatives of those who died in the tragic 1942 Cocoanut Grove nightclub fire in Boston that killed almost five hundred people. He was particularly interested in studying the differences between what he called "normal" grief and the "abnormal" reactions he saw in some of the survivors. He concluded from his study that acute grief is a definite syndrome (a combination of behaviors or symptoms which together may be signs of illness or pathology) with psychological and somatic symptomatology. In his description of normal grief, he said: "Common to all is the following syndrome—sensations of somatic distress occurring in waves lasting from 20 minutes to an hour, a feeling of tightness in the throat, choking with shortness of breath, need for sighing, an empty feeling in the abdomen, lack of muscular power, and an intense subjective distress described as tension or mental pain." Lindemann then pointed out the pathologies of grief, many of which are the intensification, elongation, or absence of the symptoms of normal grief.

Lindemann was a pioneer in the attempt to bring death into the arena of science, and since his time there have been thousands of studies, the creation of several organizations (such as the Association for Death Education and Counseling) and journals (such as *Omega*), and the publishing of dozens of books (including textbooks) in the area of death and dying.

As an example of how science grows by building on the work of others, it was soon found that Lindemann had not contacted his bereaved subjects soon enough. Therefore, he had missed a stage of grief which seems to be almost universal: a period of shock, numbness, and denial in which the bereaved person acts as if nothing had happened for a few hours or even days—sometimes even longer in abnormal grief.

STAGES OF DYING

One of the major pieces of evidence that many people were indeed interested in the subject of death was the remarkable popularity of a book published in 1969. It was titled *On Death and Dying* and was written by Elisabeth Kübler-Ross, a physician who had come to the United States from Switzerland. Perhaps the best-known aspect of Kübler-Ross's book, based on her informal research, was her outline of a series of stages which she had found that many dying patients go through. She had become convinced that modern medicine, in its efforts to keep the patient alive, treated dying patients in ways that were often inhumane. She found that very little was known about the psychology of the dying person; she pointed out that there were no courses on death and dying in medical schools or, for all practical purposes, anywhere else at the time.

Kübler-Ross interviewed several hundred persons who were dying of chronic illnesses—generally long-term illnesses, such as heart disease and cancer, which are the major causes of death in older Americans. She found that dying patients, for the most part, go through five stages in the terminal period of their lives. The first stage is one of denial: "This isn't really happening. Someone has made a mistake. I am not really going to die." In most people, the probable reality of the diagnosis eventually replaces the denial with a sense of anger: "Why me? Why now?" Generally the anger is displaced onto the most available candidate—a physician, a family member, a nurse, a clergyperson, God. The real object of the anger is death, but it is difficult to express anger toward what is really an abstract and ill-defined concept. The third stage is one of bargaining: "If only I don't die, or at least if my life is extended, then I will change my ways." It generally becomes clear that the bargaining is not going to work, and the fourth stage is depression. Kübler-Ross describes it as "a sense of great loss." Losses of any kind are one of life's major difficulties, and death is the ultimate loss of everything. Finally, the fifth stage that Kübler-Ross observed is the stage of acceptance. This is not the same as saying that the patient now wants to die or is looking forward to death. Kübler-Ross describes this stage as "almost void of feelings." It is the acceptance of the inevitability of what is about to happen.

Kübler-Ross's five-stage theory has come under criticism, as most theories do. Edwin Shneidman, one of the first professionals to be called "thanatologists" because they specialize in working with the dying and the grieving, stated that in his experience he rarely sees the neat progression through the five stages that Kübler-Ross enumerates. Many other people in the field believe that the five-stage theory is too simplistic for the way things happen in the real world. (Kübler-Ross herself agree that the five-stage theory does not apply to all dying people.) Undoubtedly, factors such as the length of the terminal illness, the religious beliefs of the dying person, the amount of support, and even the age of the patient

Death rituals, such as burial, play an important psychological role for survivors. (CLEO Photography)

may make a difference in the way people deal with their dying. Nevertheless, a framework such as the five stages, if not held too literally, seems to be a great aid for many who have to support or work with someone who is dying.

THE DEATH SYSTEM

Turning from the individual to the society, it is easy to see many places where death plays an important role in social life. Robert Kastenbaum has characterized this as the "death system." Just as society has many systems to deal with essential functions, such as the economic system, the educational system, and the transportation system, society must also deal with death on a daily basis. The death system would include, among other matters, all that is involved with the disposition of the dead body: the funeral arrangements, the cemetery, the church or other religious organization. A large number of people are involved, in one way or another, full-time or part-time, in this aspect of the death system. Although the funeral business has taken its share of criticism, some of it undoubtedly deserved, it fills

a need that the majority of people in Western society seem to have.

The death system also has other functions. Already noted is the care of the dying, which involves a large part of the health care system in the United States, as well as family and friends, and organizations such as hospice. One might also include in the death system the many aspects of society which are involved in trying to prevent death, from police officers to the national Centers for Disease Control in Atlanta to the hurricane warning center to the manufacturer of railroad crossing signals. Actually, few people in the United States do not have at least a peripheral connection to the death system. Many florists, for example, say that half or more of their business is the provision of flowers and wreaths for funerals and for cemetery plots.

MODERN RELATIONSHIPS WITH DEATH

Richard Kalish, among others, has pointed out a number of reasons for the contemporary interest in the social sciences in the study of death and dying. It is fairly easy to identify a number of factors that have increased concern about this topic. For example, more lives were lost in the twentieth century in warfare than in any other period of history. The presence of thermonuclear weapons continues to be a realistic concern for the peoples of the world. The increase in the number and influence of the elderly is also undoubtedly a factor. Most of the elderly die of heart disease, cancer, or other chronic illnesses in which death takes place over a period of time. This has led to a different kind of acquaintance with death, in comparison to times not so long ago when death came more commonly as the result of a short acute illness.

Closely related to the previous point are the advances in medical technology which allow some people with chronic illnesses to be kept alive on life-support systems when their brains, and thus their personalities, are no longer functioning. Because of such scientific advances, serious questions arise as to when death really occurs and as to what decisions ought to be made about that situation, legally, morally, and psychologically.

Undoubtedly, the impact of television has profoundly influenced society in its attitudes toward death and dying. For several decades, television has brought death "up close and personal," in both real-life and fictional situations. The effect of all this death on television (as well as in motion pictures) has yet to be fully studied or understood by psychologists or other social scientists.

A more sanguine reason for the increased interest in death and dying is that, perhaps, society is becoming more humane in its attempt to deal with these issues. There is a concern for "dying with dignity" and for a "good death" (the original meaning of the term "euthanasia"). The hospice movement has grown rapidly in the attempt to give the dying (particularly those dying from chronic illnesses) more choices about their own dying and the opportunity to live out their final days in a way not so different from the way in which they lived the rest of their lives. Social scientists may be coming to realize that death has something important to teach humankind about human existence.

SOURCES FOR FURTHER STUDY

Becker, Ernest. *The Denial of Death.* 1973. Reprint. New York: Free Press, 1997. A strong book on the power of death both for the individual and within a culture. Written, to a large extent, from a psychoanalytic standpoint. Not easy to read without some background in psychology or anthropology.

Cohen-Almagor, Raphael. *The Right to Die with Dignity: An Argument in Ethics, Medicine, and the Law.* New Brunswick, N.J.: Rutgers University Press, 2001. An even-handed overview of the controversies surrounding physician-assisted suicide and the right to choose death in the face of terminal illness.

Feifel, Herman, ed. *The Meaning of Death.* New York: McGraw-Hill, 1959. One of the original books which stimulated interest in death and dying. Contains essays by writers such as Carl Jung, Paul Tillich, and Robert Kastenbaum, as well as articles reporting empirical studies. Generally reads well and contains myriad interesting and thoughtful ideas.

Kastenbaum, Robert. *Death, Society, and Human Experience.* Boston: Allyn & Bacon, 2000. A textbook for classes on the sociology of death and dying, bringing together perspectives from the humanities, social sciences, and psychology.

Kessler, David. *The Needs of the Dying: A Guide for Bringing Hope, Comfort, and Love to Life's Final Chapter.* New York: HarperCollins, 2000. Written by a leader in hospice care. Explains the common emotions and psychology of the dying and offers suggestions for dealing with death.

Kübler-Ross, Elisabeth. *On Death and Dying.* 1969. Reprint. New York: Charles Scribner's Sons, 1997. A popular book which had a major impact on the general public. It reads well and is not only interesting but also of practical help to many who are dealing with the issue of dying.

Mitford, Jessica. *The American Way of Death.* New York: Simon & Schuster, 1963. A polemical look at the funeral business. This book made many Americans aware of excesses and shoddy practices, which eventually led to a number of changes—some because of government regulation. However, the reader needs to be aware that it is quite one-sided.

_____. *The American Way of Death Revisited.* New York: Alfred A. Knopf, 1998. Mitford's follow-up to her 1963 classic traces changes in the funeral industry over the intervening thirty-odd years. Ironically, a posthumous publication.

Tomer, Adrian, ed. *Death Attitude and Older Adults.* New York: Brunner/Mazel, 2001. A collection of essays studying current practice in dealing with death from the perspectives of gerontology, thanatology, and general psychology.

James Taylor Henderson

SEE ALSO: Aging: Physical changes; Aging: Theories; Coping: Terminal illness; Emotions; Grieving; Stress-related diseases; Suicide; Teenage suicide.

Decision making

TYPE OF PSYCHOLOGY: Cognition
FIELDS OF STUDY: Cognitive processes

Because decision making is such a common and important human activity, it appears in theories of behavior in nearly every area of psychology. Behavioral decision researchers have been able to explain a variety of behaviors in terms of the cognitive processes involved in making decisions.

KEY CONCEPTS
- descriptive theory
- heuristic
- normative theory
- preference
- rationality
- utility

INTRODUCTION

Much of what people do—with the exceptions of reflexive and habitual behavior—results from the cognitive processes of deciding. Even a minor decision, such as whether to drive the car, take the bus, or walk to work, involves the coordination of many complex processes. In making this choice, one might take into consideration one's perception of the weather, guilt about contributing to smog, feeling of physical energy, goal of obtaining more exercise, memory of a recent bus trip, desire for company, or judged likelihood of working late. Even such a relatively minor decision can be difficult to make because there are numerous considerations, and some favor one alternative while remaining considerations favor other alternatives. In addition, the decision maker cannot know all relevant information, so there is uncertainty about the outcomes of important events.

A major goal of decision research is to understand the rules that people use in choosing alternatives. This often means gaining insight into the decision processes that are used when no alternative is clearly preferred. In order to accomplish this, it is necessary to understand what is meant by a rule and to identify different potential rules for selecting one of a set of alternative courses of action. Some rules are heuristics, or strategies for simplifying choice that limit the evaluation of alternatives. Heuristics can be very efficient. In the example about choosing the mode of transportation to work, if one used a heuristic, one might consider only the amount of time available for getting to work. Such a simplistic analysis of the problem can, however, lead to a poor decision. In other words, the employee might have more regrets after using this heuristic than would be the case if he or she had made a more careful analysis of the alternatives.

DECISION THEORIES

Decision theory has a long history of identifying normative procedures for decision making. These procedures tell people what rules they should follow in making decisions. A standard rule is to take into account two dimensions for each decision alternative: likelihood and utility. This principle, which is embodied in subjective expected utility theory, is intended to maximize the personal value of one's anticipated outcomes. A person may be given a choice between a 50 percent chance of winning $100 and a certain $2. The first alternative has an expected outcome of $50 (calculated by 50 percent of $100 = $50), since that is what one would expect to win on average if one played this game many times. The other alternative has an expected outcome of $2 (calculated by 100 percent of $2 = $2). Subjective expected utility theory indicates that one should choose the first alternative, the 50 percent chance of $100, because it has a higher expected outcome. This choice is called "rational" in the sense that it is the choice that is likely to maximize earnings.

The cognitive approach to decision making emphasizes an understanding of the ways in which various factors influence the choices that people make in reality—regardless of whether they follow normative principles. In contrast to the normative approach, the cognitive approach is focused on description of the actual processes that people use. A person may be given a 30 percent chance of $100 or a certain $20. Calculations based on likelihood and value dictate that one should choose the first alternative, since its anticipated outcome of $33 (30 percent of $100 = $33) is more than $20. Many people, however, simply do not want to take the risk of receiving nothing with the first alternative. They prefer the security of knowing that they will receive $20 to the uncertainty of getting $100 or nothing. The possibility of an additional $10 is not worth the risk. This is not necessarily "irrational." As this example shows, normative decision theory cannot predict what many or even most people will choose. For this reason, psychologists have become increasingly interested in examining the processes that people actually use to make decisions.

ILLUSIONS AND HEURISTICS
Of particular interest in the cognitive approach to decision making are those factors that lead to miscalculations of likelihood or utility, since they will ultimately contribute to undesirable outcomes. Psychologists Amos Tversky and Daniel Kahneman revolutionized the field of decision making by identifying factors that contribute to poor decision making. Some of these may be called "cognitive illusions," because they lead a decision maker to a judgment that is in fact a distortion of reality. One type of judgment that is often affected by such illusions concerns likelihood estimation, the chance of an event leading to a particular outcome.

Another type of judgment that is susceptible to illusionary distortion is the estimation of quantity or frequency. In making these estimations, people often use heuristics. In a heuristic for estimating quantity called "anchoring and adjustment," one takes any available number as an initial starting point or anchor and then adjusts it to arrive at an estimate. For example, one might predict tomorrow's temperature by taking today's temperature and adjusting downward for forthcoming rainfall. Although heuristics can be more efficient than the careful and comprehensive analysis of relevant information, they can also be misleading.

Illusions and heuristics can be detrimental to good decision making because they lead the decision maker to a distorted view of the problem and available alternatives. It is often possible to develop procedures for improving the decision-making process. Elaborate technologies have been developed to assist people in making decisions in nearly every area. Sometimes it is instructive, however, merely to understand the processes that people use and to know their limitations. It must be kept in mind that evaluating the quality of decisions is very difficult. One reason is that some decisions that are made with great care, thought, and objectivity can still have very disappointing outcomes. On other occasions, luck can operate to bring favorable outcomes despite poor decision processes. The ultimate key to improving human judgment and decision making is research that integrates normative and descriptive theories.

EXPECTANCY, UTILITY, AND MOTIVATION
The principles of subjective expected utility theory have been applied in a wide variety of problem areas. A distinction between expectancy and utility can be quite useful. For example, two people who choose to continue to smoke may do so for different reasons. One may truly believe that he has a high chance of developing a serious disease such as lung cancer. He may anticipate great medical advances, however, and expect that lung cancer will be only a mild problem by the time he is diagnosed with it. Though the expectation of a negative outcome is high, the outcome is not particularly negative to this individual. Another person may be convinced that lung cancer is—and will continue to be—a painful, expensive, deadly disease. Despite the fact that this outcome has great negative utility for this person, she may continue to smoke because her expectation is that she will not develop lung cancer. Each of these individuals is influenced by different factors. Understanding how the decision to smoke or to quit is made can assist health advocates—and tobacco advertisers—to influence these decisions.

One of the areas in which subjective expected utility principles have been highly influential is that of motivation. While early theories of motivation viewed behavior as the result of basic drives or personality traits, subsequent theories emphasized the way in which people thought about their options. From this perspective, it is meaningless to label someone "unmotivated." Everyone is motivated, in the sense that all people have time and effort to give to activities. People choose how much time and effort to give to each of the various options open to them: work, leisure, and family activities. Employees who do little or no work do not necessarily lack "drive" or have flawed personalities. They have simply decided to spend their time and effort on other things. This does not excuse or overlook the workers' lack of productivity, but it does suggest methods to alter their lack of performance. The key is to understand their judgments of the utilities of outcomes from working and their perceived likelihood of obtaining these outcomes by choosing to put time and effort into work activities. Thus, the study of decision making is important to organizational efforts to enhance productivity.

BIASES IN DECISION MAKING

In one sense, it is easy to observe instances of illusions and heuristics that lead to biases in decision making in real life. Bad decisions seem to be everywhere. As noted, however, decisions that turn out badly may sometimes result from badly made decisions. People are accustomed to judging the actions of others and will label them irrational if it appears that they are choosing alternatives with inferior outcomes for themselves. During the Persian Gulf War of 1991, the American media frequently concluded that Saddam Hussein was "irrational" because he chose not to withdraw from Kuwait by the United Nations deadline. Though it is tempting to label an enemy "irrational," it is wise to keep in mind a serious problem in determining irrationality in a decision maker. It is exceedingly difficult to assess the utility of any alternative for the decision maker. By American standards, it would have been better for the Iraqis to withdraw from Kuwait before suffering enormous loss of life—and eventual forced withdrawal from Kuwait—so it seemed that Hussein could not possibly be evaluating the alternatives realistically. Either he did not understand the potential magnitude of his human and economic losses from a failure to withdraw or he did not understand the virtual certainty of losing the war. Hussein may, however, have understood both perfectly and simply have attached different utilities to the outcomes anticipated from withdrawal versus war. Perhaps from Saddam Hussein's perspective the loss of life could be offset easily by the opportunity to show himself to the Arab world as someone who "stood up" to the international community, if only briefly.

Scientific investigations of biases in decision making require that the investigator prove that a given alternative is superior to the one that is chosen by most people. This is often done by means of mathematics or statistics. In one demonstration of the representativeness bias, people are given a brief personality sketch of "Linda" and asked to determine how likely it is that Linda is a member of various categories. Most people tend to judge Linda as more likely to be a bank teller and a feminist than merely a bank teller. In fact, however, there must be at least as many bank tellers as there are feminist bank tellers, since the category "bank teller" will contain all feminist bank tellers as well as all nonfeminist bank tellers. The illusion comes from the erroneous conclusion that because Linda's personality traits represent both the occupation of a bank teller and the political perspective of a feminist, she is more likely to be both than one or the other. Research such as this helps to determine how people can jump to conclusions and misjudge someone. Overestimating the likelihood that a person belongs to two categories diminishes one's ability to estimate appropriately the expected utilities of alternatives for decisions about that person.

DECISIONS IN THE WORKPLACE AND DAILY LIFE

Numerous forces have come together to fuel the study of human decision making as a cognitive process. One of these is the coming of the information age. With the transition from a production economy to a service economy, workers are no longer seen as people who engage in only physical work. Workers at all levels deal with information and decisions. It is no longer possible to attribute all the difficulty of making decisions to insufficient information. Decision makers are often overloaded and overwhelmed by information. The real problem they face is knowing which information to select and how to integrate it into the decision-making process.

Within psychology, two areas of study that have had a great impact on behavioral decision making are perception and quantitative psychology. Both Kahneman and Tversky did extensive work in the area of perception before becoming interested in studying the cognitive processes in human judgment and decision making. Many other behavioral decision researchers began their studies in quantitative psychology or statistics. The primary objective in this area is to learn how to make decisions under uncertainty using the laws of probability. Since this is what people routinely face in the course of their work and daily lives, there are many intriguing parallels between statistics and behavioral decision making.

Advances in understanding the rationality of human decision making were furthered, ironically, by economic theories that assumed rationality on the part of human decision makers. Psychologists who conducted empirical studies of people had data to show that many choices that people make do not follow rational economic models. For example, standard economic theory predicts that people will choose the option that maximizes their own payoff. Yet people often prefer a plan that they deem fair to everyone over one that is financially superior for themselves. Behavioral decision theory attempts to understand the way in which people actually make decisions—not the way that formal models say that they should.

SOURCES FOR FURTHER STUDY

Connolly, Terry, Hal R. Arkes, and Kenneth R. Hammond, eds. *Judgment and Decision Making: An Interdisciplinary Reader*. 2d ed. New York: Cambridge University Press, 1999. A collection of essays focusing on practical applications in public policy and legal fields, as well as theoretical critiques, research agendas, and new directions.

Hastie, Reid, and Robyn M. Dawes. *Rational Choice in an Uncertain World*. Thousand Oaks, Calif.: Sage Publications, 2001. A social-psychological perspective on judgment and decision processes. Highly interesting content and style for all audiences. Includes thoughtful discussions of controversial applications. Nontechnical and concise. Chapters can be read individually or out of order.

Plous, Scott. *The Psychology of Judgment and Decision Making*. New York: McGraw-Hill, 1993. An introductory textbook that uses the reader's own decisions as a heuristic tool for explaining the psychology of decision making.

Russo, J. Edward, and Paul J. H. Shoemaker. *Decision Traps*. New York: Doubleday, 1989. Superb and colorful coverage of cognitive processes in decision making. Balance of research and applications. Examples are well-chosen, memorable illustrations of major concepts. Particularly relevant to the businessperson but will appeal to all.

Slovic, Paul, Sarah Lichtenstein, and Baruch Fischhoff. "Decision Making." In *Steven's Handbook of Experimental Psychology*, edited by Richard C. Atkinson et al. 2d ed. New York: John Wiley & Sons, 1988. A comprehensive review of the field of decision making. Traces the origins of subjective expected utility theory as well as other decision theories. Brief and well-written explanations of different perspectives in the field. Ties decision making to other areas of experimental psychology.

Tversky, Amos, and Daniel Kahneman. "Judgment Under Uncertainty: Heuristics and Biases." *Science* 185 (1974): 1124-1131. A classic paper written for the general scientific and lay community. The authors illustrate various judgment heuristics in thought-provoking fashion. This article is not intended to be a balanced view of human "rationality"; it emphasizes the cognitive limitations of human decision makers.

Janet A. Sniezek

SEE ALSO: Artificial intelligence; Cognitive development: Jean Piaget; Cognitive maps; Computer models of cognition; Consumer psychology; Group decision making; Logic and reasoning; Problem-solving stages; Problem-solving strategies.

Defense reactions
Species-specific

TYPE OF PSYCHOLOGY: Learning
FIELDS OF STUDY: Aggression; biological influences on learning; nervous system

All animal species employ maneuvers and deceptive tactics to protect themselves from conspecific competitors, predators, and parasites. These defensive reactions include alarm calls, flocking or herding, mimicry, bluffing, displays, and aggressive counterattacks. Defensive mechanisms vary from species to species, but some defensive tactics are common throughout the animal kingdom.

KEY CONCEPTS
- alarm
- competition
- display

- dominance hierarchy
- flocking
- mimicry
- pheromone
- predation
- prey density
- saturation

INTRODUCTION

All living organisms live within complicated food and energy webs in which energy is transferred from organism to organism through consumption. Plants convert energy from sunlight to manufacture organic nutrients. Herbivorous animals eat plants to obtain this energy, and carnivorous animals eat herbivores and other carnivores to obtain the same energy. Within an animal species, individuals compete with one another for available food and natural resources in order to survive; in the process, they establish dominance hierarchies in which dominant individuals overpower subordinates. Among different species, interactions occur that lead to predation (an interspecific interaction in which the individuals of one animal species hunt and kill members of another species for food), disease, and parasitism; in each case, one species is feeding on another species.

Intraspecific competition and interspecific predation and parasitism represent two principal animal behaviors important to the evolution of life. Each species possesses an innate (instinctive) drive to survive and to continue the transmission of its deoxyribonucleic acid (DNA) in space and time. Within the food webs of the living environment, each species evolves specific adaptations for survival that enable it to carve out a particular habitat, or place to live, and niche, or occupation, in the environment. Since the food webs of life on Earth are circular, the evolution of competition and predation are necessary for life to continue. All species will become predators (hunters) of certain other species and will simultaneously be prey (the hunted) for certain different species.

LEARNED AND GENETIC ADAPTATIONS

In order to survive, each species possesses specific adaptations for hunting its prey and for defending itself from predators. Defensive mechanisms come in many different varieties. Some very effective defense mechanisms are highly conserved be-

tween different species; other defenses are unique to only one or a few species. Of these defenses, some are instinctive, occurring automatically because of biochemical changes within individual animals, whereas others are learned from environmental experiences. Learned defensive mechanisms are prevalent in highly social mammal and bird species.

Intraspecific competition occurs among individuals of a given population or group and among different populations or groups. Within a population, the social structure is either genetically or behaviorally conditioned to construct castes or dominance hierarchies in which dominant individuals are superior to more subordinate individuals. The social insects (such as ants, termites, bees, and wasps), whose behavior is almost exclusively genetic in nature, construct their societies, or hives, around castes which have specific jobs to perform. Such societies revolve around a central, fertile queen, sterile female workers, and male drones. Workers are subdivided into several specializations, such as hunting for food and defending the hive. Soldier workers have specialized body structures for attacking intruders; furthermore, they release pheromones (hormonal attractants) from their bodies at the sign of danger to attract other soldier workers to the region of intrusion.

DOMINANCE HIERARCHIES

Within the highly social and intelligent mammal and bird species, populations either migrate in bands or groups or set up individual adjacent territories that are heavily defended by the owner. In either of these situations, learned dominance hierarchies are established in which stronger individuals outcompete weaker individuals, thereby establishing a "pecking order" (as it is called for chickens) of precisely ranked dominant individuals to progressively more subordinate individuals. The dominant individuals possess the best territory, the most food, and the most mates. The most dominant individuals also have the best protection from predators, because their territories are central and therefore are shielded by the territories of more subordinate individuals. Consequently, the most subordinate individuals have the worst territories, poor food, few if any mates, and poor protection from predators, which usually attack outskirt territories. These territories are maintained by constant fighting between males, especially during the breeding season. Males vocalize and present visual displays (visual dances or series of movements or gestures by individuals to communicate such things as dominance, aggression, and courtship to other individuals) to force their opponents to submit; submission is routine, and few encounters are fatal.

PREDATOR-PREY INTERACTIONS

In interspecific predator-prey interactions, the prey utilize a variety of quick-response defenses. One of the most common defenses is the flocking or herding defense. When a predator approaches a group of prey and is identified, the discovering prey individual announces danger by a vocalization (an alarm call), specific movement, and/or the release of chemical pheromones to warn the other members of the group. The prey group response is instantaneous, with all members contracting into a dense mass. A predator is less likely to succeed in capturing a prey individual during an attack on a compact group than when the prey individuals are scattered. Furthermore, the predator may sustain personal physical damage in an attack on a compact group, which easily could turn upon the predator. Most predators are far more successful at capturing very young, old, or sickly individuals that are isolated or located at the poorly defended outskirts of a prey group. Some predators, such as hawks, falcons, and wolves, do make repeated passes at compact groups in sometimes successful attempts at panicking individuals and thereby scattering the group. Flocking behavior is a very effective defense that is utilized by bees, fish, tadpoles, most bird species, and most mammal species. Prey species usually utilize excellent vision, hearing, and sense of smell.

The dynamics of predator-prey interactions can be complicated, although numerous mathematical models of such relationships have been developed that enable researchers to make predictions concerning future interactions in natural populations. Predator-prey interactions are important for the stability and survival of both predator and prey populations. Without prey, predators would die; however, without predators, prey populations would grow unchecked until they exceeded the available resources in the environment, ending in a massive population crash in which many individuals would die. Such occurrences have been thoroughly documented in many species, including moose, deer, rabbit, and even human populations. Defensive mechanisms are important to all species in order to ensure the survival of enough members of each species population to reproduce and continue the transmission of the species' genetic information. Perfect defense, however, could be as detrimental to the population as no defense. Numerous mathematical ecologists have developed impressive models of animal population growth based upon predator-prey interactions. Among the most famous models are those that were developed by Alfred Lotka and Vito Volterra, and they still are in use. Such models are of critical importance to the study of human overpopulation.

ANIMAL DEFENSE MECHANISMS

Other species-specific defense mechanisms include camouflage, mimicry (an inherited or behavioral defense phenomenon in which an individual of a species either looks dangerous to its predators or can exaggerate its appearance to fool a predator), predator saturation (a defensive mechanism in some animal species in which a prey animal population synchronizes its growth so that it becomes too large for predators to consume any significant fraction of the population), and long-term incubation. Most species have adaptations in skin and fur coloration in order to blend in with their particular environment. For example, albino hares and squirrels predominate in areas which have snow for a good portion of the year, whereas the same species in more temperate climates usually have a grayish-brown coloration. Zebras have a striped pattern that enables them to blend with tall grass; many mammalian predators (lions, wild dogs) are color-blind. Some species (the chameleon, for example) can alter their body color to their background through biochemical changes in their skin. Some lizard species simply discard body parts, such as their tails, when captured by predators.

Müllerian mimicry is a phenomenon used by moths and butterflies to defend themselves from bird predators. A few butterfly species with bright orange-black wings are poisonous; several dozen nonpoisonous species have coevolved bright black and orange or yellow wings and are therefore less likely to be eaten, since birds learn avoidance very quickly from only a few encounters with the poisonous varieties. Some species of fish, birds, and mammals have short, rapid bursts of reproduction, so that their predators are overwhelmed, or saturated, by the high prey densities. In both of these instances, some prey are eaten. The thirteen- and seventeen-year periodic locust species of North America combat predation by burrowing underground for many years before surfacing and reproducing within only a few weeks.

IMPLICATIONS FOR HUMAN SOCIETY

The study of species-specific defensive reactions is of intense interest to animal behavior researchers. Research into such behavior enables them to understand how highly adaptive and elaborate defenses have evolved in animal species over the past five hundred million years. These studies also have potential impact upon the psychology of human behavior. Humans are very territorial animals and exhibit considerable competitive behavior, including interpersonal conflicts and aggression. Consequently, defense mechanism studies are strongly applicable to the study of human conflict, social tensions, and warfare. Furthermore, species-specific defense mechanisms are also of interest to medicine, since humans, while being the apparently dominant species on Earth, are subject to predation, particularly from parasitic bacterial, fungal, and viral diseases.

The explosion of human technological growth during the past century has included medical advances that have eradicated many diseases which once were major killers of humans. Medicine has been a tremendous artificial defense mechanism developed by the intelligence of the human species. It has defeated dozens of bacterial, fungal, and viral predators and parasites of humans. Because of these advances, humans live longer and better lives, human birthrates have soared, and human death rates have declined; however, the elimination of human predators has produced some very serious problems. One such problem is overpopulation. The explosive human population growth is approaching the planet's carrying capacity (the available food and resources). Some areas of the world, most notably Asia and Africa, have already seen human overpopulation far above the carrying capacity; the result has been devastating famines and millions of deaths. Furthermore, medical science is taxed by the appearance of new mutated viral and bacterial predators to replace the eradicated ones. The hu-

man immunodeficiency virus (HIV), which causes acquired immunodeficiency syndrome (AIDS), is an example. Furthermore, certain diseases, such as cholera, are on the rise worldwide. Life on Earth is very homeostatic (self-regulatory); it contains mechanisms for keeping populations of all species in check.

Leaving the microscopic scale, humans and other primates defend themselves from competitors and very large predators in much the same fashion. Humans have territories that each territory-holder defends. Furthermore, several dominant males may group to attack intruders and other predators. There can be no doubt that such behavior has evolved into the large armies that different countries have amassed to defend their territorial borders. The structure of many such armies is somewhat reminiscent of mammalian dominance hierarchies. The frontline soldiers who face the brunt of an opponent's attack usually are individuals who are less equipped and trained. They are sometimes called "cannon fodder." Better-trained, more dominant individuals follow; they are more likely to survive hostile encounters with the enemy.

Species-specific defensive behaviors are also applicable to human behavior in terms of social and personal relationships. Complex human societies are rigidly structured along territorial lines, with laws to regulate the behaviors of individuals. Cross-sections through American cities reveal the segregation of the poor from the middle class from the rich, the segregation of black from white from Hispanic. Individuals in each of these groups construct physical, social, and legal barriers to defend themselves from competition from outsiders. With overpopulation and competition for resources, individuals and countries resort to mechanical weapons ranging from handguns to semiautomatic rifles to atomic bombs. Stress, inequality, and mistrust of others involve biological reactions that have evolved over hundreds of millions of years.

Each of the approximately one million animal species on Earth has evolved through the endurance of predator-prey interactions. Understanding how species defend themselves can be of great importance in helping endangered species to survive and in controlling the overpopulations of species and the spread of disease. It also can help humankind to alleviate many of its own species' social problems.

UNDERSTANDING ECOSYSTEMS

The study of species-specific defense mechanisms is of considerable interest to animal behaviorists and psychologists because of their implications for human behavior. All animal behaviors can be influenced by endogenous (instinctive) or exogenous (environmental) factors. Endogenous behaviors include imprinting and biochemical changes within the body of the individual that enable one to recognize events or situations instantaneously for survival. Behaviors such as recognizing danger are critical for survival and therefore must be instinctive. Within the intelligent and highly social mammals and birds, a period of learning during infancy enables the development of exogenous behaviors from experiences in one's immediate environment. Such learned behaviors are of equal importance in such species.

The study of species-specific defensive reactions allows scientists to uncover the intricacies of species interactions within the environment. In any given ecosystem (such as a forest, grassland, ocean, or desert) populations of thousands of different species are linked by intricate food webs. The destruction of the environment or the extinction of any one species can have irreparable effects upon all the other species within the ecosystem. The defensive mechanisms of most species can work only so well.

SOURCES FOR FURTHER STUDY

Andrewartha, Herbert George. *Introduction to the Study of Animal Populations.* 2d ed. Chicago: University of Chicago Press, 1971. This tremendous resource book for ecologists and animal behaviorists was written by one of the foremost authorities in animal behavior research. Andrewartha defines the parameters of animal population growth, including predator-prey interactions and species defense mechanisms, in the first part of the book. He devotes the second portion of the book to experimental methods and set-ups for gathering research data on animal populations. Describes all concepts with great clarity, even the mathematics and graphing of data.

Klopfer, Peter H., and Jack P. Hailman. *An Introduction to Animal Behavior: Ethology's First Century.* 2d ed. Englewood Cliffs, N.J.: Prentice-Hall, 1974. Klopfer and Hailman provide an excellent presentation of animal behavior research and the major theories describing the evolution of species' behaviors. Chapter 7, "The Social Life of Animals," explores social behavior in mammals and birds, including descriptions of competition and dominance hierarchies. Chapter 11, "How Is Behavior Controlled?", describes specific adaptations of various species to environmental stimuli, including danger. Extremely well written and referenced.

Krebs, Charles J. *Ecology: The Experimental Analysis of Distribution and Abundance.* 5th ed. Reading, Mass.: Addison-Wesley, 2000. This well-organized, information-packed introduction to ecology was written by a leading ecologist and represents an outstanding reference for both scientist and layperson. Numerous factors that influence animal and plant populations are described, including predator-prey interactions and defense mechanisms. Hundreds of species interactions are cited with clearly explained mathematical models. Chapters 5, "Factors Limiting Distributions: Interrelations with Other Organisms," 12, "Species Interactions: Competition," and 13, "Species Interactions: Predation," exhaustively cover offensive and defensive behaviors.

Lorenz, Konrad. *On Aggression.* Translated by Marjorie Kerr Wilson. New York: Harcourt, Brace & World, 1966. This excellent survey of aggressive animal behavior, written by a Nobel laureate and pioneer in behavior research, is aimed at the layperson. Lorenz clearly outlines the evolution of animal behavior and the adaptiveness of aggressive behavior. He cites several species interactions, illustrating both offensive and defensive animal behaviors. Also addresses aggression within the context of human behavior, stressing the need for human control of aggressive behaviors for our own survival.

Manning, Aubrey, and Marian Stamp Dawkins. *An Introduction to Animal Behavior.* 5th ed. New York: Cambridge University Press, 1998. A concise presentation of theory and experimentation in animal behavior research. Describes major behavior theories and relevant experimental work from the biological research. Chapter 3, "Stimuli and Communication," describes animal species' responses and adaptations to environmental stimuli, including displays, mimicry, and responses to danger. Chapter 5, "Conflict Behavior," describes various offensive and defensive mechanisms used by different species in both competition and predator-prey interactions.

Wilson, Edward O. *Sociobiology: The New Synthesis.* 1975. 25th anniversary edition. Cambridge, Mass.: Harvard University Press, 2000. This mammoth work, written by one of the world's leading entomologists and animal behaviorists, is a revival of an important theory in animal behavior and evolutionary research. Wilson clearly and exhaustively cites hundreds of detailed studies of various social animal species to drive home key points. Describes offensive and defensive behavioral mechanisms plus other behaviors.

David Wason Hollar, Jr.

SEE ALSO: Animal experimentation; Ethology; Imprinting; Instinct theory; Learning; Preparedness.

Dementia

TYPE OF PSYCHOLOGY: Cognition; memory; psychopathology

FIELDS OF STUDY: Aging; cognitive processes; depression; interpersonal relationships; social perception and cognition; thought

Dementia is a chronic progressive brain disorder that may occur as a result of various events. Dementia is the loss of cognitive and social abilities to the degree that they interfere with activities of daily living (ADLs). Dementia may or may not be reversible.

KEY CONCEPTS
- activities of daily living (ADLs)
- cognition
- delirium
- depression
- memory loss
- pseudodementia

INTRODUCTION

Dementia is usually characterized as a gradual, progressive decline in cognitive function that affects speech, memory, judgment, and mood. However, it may also be an unchanging condition that results from an injury to the brain. Initially, individuals may be aware of a cognitive decline, but over time they no longer notice. The insidious and pro-

gressive nature of dementia may make early diagnosis difficult because cognitive changes may appear as only slight declines in memory, attention, and concentration or rare episodes of inconsistencies in behavior that are attributed to aging. Over time, increased confusion and irritability in unfamiliar environments, poor judgment, difficulty in abstract thinking, and personality changes may be seen.

Delirium is a transient alteration in mental status that is a common feature of dementia. Signs and symptoms of delirium develop over a short period of time. Once the underlying causes of delirium, such as medical problems, stress, and medications, are identified and ministered to, delirium can be reversed. Visual and auditory hallucinations, paranoia, and delusions of persecution may be observed. Memory loss is another symptom of dementia. People with dementia often forget how to perform activities of daily living (ADLs), such as dressing, cleaning, and cooking, that they have been performing for years. They may repeatedly ask the same questions, have the same conversations, forget simple words, or use incorrect words when speaking. They may become disoriented to time and place and become lost in familiar surroundings. Problems with abstract thinking may make solving math problems and balancing a checkbook impossible. People with dementia may misplace items and be unable to find them because the items were put in unaccustomed places. Mood swings and drastic personality changes, such as sudden, unexpected swings from calm and happiness to tears and anger, are not uncommon in those with dementia.

Depression may be mistaken for dementia. Symptoms of depression include feelings of profound sadness, difficulty in thinking and concentrating, feelings of despair, and apathy. Severe depression brings with it an inability to concentrate and a poor attention span. As the person with dementia tries to conceal memory loss and cognitive decline, appetite loss, apathy, and feelings of uselessness may ensue. In combined dementia and depression, intellectual deterioration can be extreme. An older adult who is depressed may also show signs of confusion and intellectual impairment even though dementia is not present. These individuals are identified as having pseudodementia. Depression, alone or in combination with dementia, is treatable.

DSM-IV-TR Criteria for Vascular Dementia (DSM code 290.4x)

Development of multiple cognitive deficits manifested by both memory impairment (impaired ability to learn new information or recall previously learned information) and one or more of the following cognitive disturbances:

- aphasia (language disturbance)
- apraxia (impaired ability to carry out motor activities despite intact motor function)
- agnosia (failure to recognize or identify objects despite intact sensory function)
- disturbance in executive functioning (planning, organizing, sequencing, abstracting)

Cognitive deficits each cause significant impairment in social or occupational functioning and represent significant decline from previous level of functioning

Focal neurological signs and symptoms (such as exaggeration of deep tendon reflexes, extensor plantar response, pseudobulbar palsy, gait abnormalities, weakness of an extremity) or laboratory evidence indicative of cerebrovascular disease (such as multiple infarctions involving cortex and underlying white matter) judged to be etiologically related to disturbance

Deficits do not occur exclusively during course of a delirium

Code based on predominant features:
- With Delirium (DSM code 290.41): Delirium superimposed on dementia
- With Delusions (DSM code 290.42): Delusions as predominant feature
- With Depressed Mood (DSM code 290.43): Depressed mood (including presentations meeting full symptom criteria for Major Depressive Episode) as predominant feature; separate diagnosis of Mood Disorder Due to a General Medical Condition not given
- Uncomplicated (DSM code 290.40): None of the above predominates in current clinical presentation

Specify if with Behavioral Disturbance

PREVALENCE AND IMPACT

Dementia may occur at all ages, but its incidence increases with advanced age. Dementia is most frequent in those older than age seventy-five. There are an estimated 600,000 cases of advanced dementia in the United States, and milder degrees of altered mental status are very common in the elderly. The prevalence of dementia increases from 1 percent at age sixty to 40 percent at age eighty-five. The expense of long-term care at home or in a nursing facility has been estimated at $40 billion per year for people age sixty-five and older. The prevalence of dementia is expected to continue to increase as a result of increased life expectancy and an aging population of baby boomers. Many of the problems caused by dementia are due to memory loss.

CAUSES

Dementia may be reversible or irreversible. Reversible causes include brain tumors, subdural hematoma, slowly progressive or normal-pressure hydrocephalus; head trauma; endocrine conditions (such as hypothyroidism, hypercalcemia, hypoglycemia); vitamin deficiencies (of thiamin, niacin, or vitamin B_{12}); thyroid disease; ethanol abuse; infections; metabolic abnormalities; effects of medications; renal, hepatic, and neurological conditions; and depression. Irreversible dementia is more common in the elderly. Irreversible causes of dementia include diseases of the brain such as Alzheimer's, Parkinson's, Pick's, Creutzfeldt-Jakob, and Huntington's diseases; human immunodeficiency virus (HIV) infection; vascular dementia; and head trauma.

TYPES OF DEMENTIA

Alzheimer's disease is the most common form of dementia and is responsible for 50 percent of all dementias. No direct cause has been identified, but it is thought that viruses, environmental toxins, and family history are involved. Definitive diagnosis of Alzheimer's disease can only be made on autopsy when neurofibrillary tangles are found in the brain.

Vascular dementia is less common after age seventy-five. It is estimated that 8 percent of individuals over sixty years old who have a stroke develop dementia within one year. Early treatment of hypertension and vascular disease may prevent further progression of dementia.

Parkinson's disease is an insidious, slow, progressive neurological condition that begins in middle to late life. It is characterized by tremor, rigidity, bradykinesia, and postural instability. Dementia is also present in 20 percent to 60 percent of those with Parkinson's disease. It is characterized by diminishing cognitive function, diminishing motor and executive function, and memory impairment.

Lewy body disease is similar to Alzheimer's disease. Visual hallucinations and Parkinson-like features progress quickly. Lewy bodies are found in the cerebral cortex. Patients exhibit psychotic symptoms and have a sensitivity to antipsychotic medications.

Pick's disease and other frontal lobe dementias are rare and are identified by changes in personality and emotions, executive dysfunction, deterioration of social skills, inappropriate behavior, and language problems. Pick's disease is most common between ages fifty and sixty. It progresses rapidly and may be accompanied by apathy, extreme agitation, severe language difficulties, attention deficits, and inappropriate behavior. Pick's disease can only be confirmed on autopsy when Pick's inclusion bodies are found.

Another disorder that can lead to progressive dementia is Huntington's disease, a genetic disorder that usually occurs in middle age. The basal ganglia and subcortical structures in the brain are affected, causing spasticity in body movements. Personality, memory, intellect, speech, and judgment are altered.

Creutzfeldt-Jakob disease (spongiform encephalopathy) is a rare and fatal brain disorder caused by a virus that converts protein into infectious, deadly molecules. Early symptoms may be memory loss and changes in behavior. Creutzfeldt-Jakob disease progresses into mental deterioration, muscle spasms, weakness in the extremities, blindness, and coma.

RISK FACTORS AND DIAGNOSIS

Risk factors for dementia include a family history of dementia, head trauma, lower educational level, and gender (females are more prone to

dementia). Alcohol and drug abuse, infections, cardiovascular disease, and head injuries are also causes for the development of dementia.

The criteria in the American Psychiatric Association's *Diagnostic and Statistical Manual of Mental Disorders: DSM-IV-TR* (rev. 4th ed., 2000) for the diagnosis of dementia require the presence of multiple cognitive deficits in addition to memory impairment.

DSM-IV-TR Criteria for Dementia Due to Other General Medical Conditions (DSM code 294.1x)

Development of multiple cognitive deficits manifested by both memory impairment (impaired ability to learn new information or recall previously learned information) and one or more of the following cognitive disturbances:
- aphasia (language disturbance)
- apraxia (impaired ability to carry out motor activities despite intact motor function)
- agnosia (failure to recognize or identify objects despite intact sensory function)
- disturbance in executive functioning (planning, organizing, sequencing, abstracting)

Cognitive deficits each cause significant impairment in social or occupational functioning and represent significant decline from previous level of functioning

Evidence from history, physical examination, or laboratory findings that disturbance is direct physiological consequence of one of the following general medical conditions:
- Dementia Due to HIV Disease (DSM code 294.1)
- Dementia Due to Head Trauma (DSM code 294.1)
- Dementia Due to Parkinson's Disease (DSM code 294.1)
- Dementia Due to Huntington's Disease (DSM code 294.1)
- Dementia Due to Pick's Disease (DSM code 290.10)
- Dementia Due to Creutzfeldt-Jakob Disease (DSM code 290.10)
- Dementia Due to [General Medical Condition not listed above] (DSM code 294.1), such as normal-pressure hydrocephalus, hypothyroidism, brain tumor, vitamin B deficiency, intracranial radiation

Deficits do not occur exclusively during course of a delirium

Code based on presence or absence of clinically significant behavioral disturbance:
- Without Behavioral Disturbance (DSM code 294.10): Cognitive disturbance not accompanied by any clinically significant behavioral disturbance
- With Behavioral Disturbance (DSM code 294.11): Cognitive disturbance accompanied by clinically significant behavioral disturbance such as wandering or agitation

The diagnosis of dementia is based on cognitive deficits that are severe enough to cause impairment in occupational or social functioning and must represent a decline from a previous level of functioning. The nature and degree of impairment are variable and often depend on the particular social setting of the individual. Standardized mental status tests are a baseline for evaluation for dementia. Examples of some short tests are the Mini-Mental Status Test, the Blessed Information-Memory-Concentration Test, and the Short Portable Mental Status Questionnaire. A standardized mental status test score should be used to confirm the results of a history and physical examination. Standardized mental status tests should not be the single deciding factor for the diagnosis of dementia. Some tests such as blood evaluations, urinalysis, chest radiography, carotid ultrasound, Doppler flow studies, electroencephalogram, lumbar puncture, and computed tomography (CT) scans of the head are done in relation to the presenting symptoms.

TREATMENT

The goals of treating dementia are improving mental function and maintaining the highest level of function possible. Many families care for family members with dementia at home. A structured home environment and established daily routines are important as the person with dementia begins to experience difficulty learning and remembering new activities. Establishing simple chores to enhance a sense of usefulness, such as watering plants, dusting, and setting the table, are helpful. It is essential to provide a safe home environment. This includes maintaining uncluttered surroundings and removing potentially dangerous items such as matches, lighters, knives, scissors, and medications. In later stages of dementia, stoves, ovens, and other cooking items may need to be disabled to prevent fires. Clocks, calendars, television, magazines, and newspapers are good ways to help to keep those with dementia oriented. As functioning decreases, nursing home placement may be necessary.

It is important that the families who care for members with dementia at home are made aware of community services that can assist them in locating support groups and social service agencies to access day care, counseling, home, day, respite care, and group therapy services.

PHARMACEUTICAL THERAPIES

Successfully treating some of these causes of dementia may reverse the condition: brain tumors; subdural hematoma; slowly progressive or normal-pressure hydrocephalus; head trauma; hypothyroidism; hypercalcemia; hypoglycemia; deficiency of thiamine, niacin, or vitamin B_{12}; thyroid disease; ethanol abuse; infections; metabolic abnormalities; effects of medications; renal, hepatic, and neurological conditions; and depression.

Nerve growth factor, antioxidant therapy, and other drugs are being investigated for the management of dementia. Psychotrophic medications such as carbamazepine, desipramine, haloperidol, lorazepam, and thioridazine are used to control symptoms of agitation, anxiety, confusion, delusions, depression, and hallucinations in patients with dementia. Unfortunately, some of the medications used to improve patients' quality of life may not work, worsen memory deficits, or cause neurological effects such as irreversible tremors (tardive diskinesia).

It is important to reduce cerebrovascular risk factors such as hypertension, diabetes, smoking, hyperlipidemia, and coronary artery disease in patients with vascular dementia. Dementia resulting from neurologic conditions (Parkinson's disease, normal-pressure hydrocephalus, brain lesions, carotid artery disease) requires a neurological workup. Dementia related to a hereditary condition requires referral for genetic counseling.

SOURCES FOR FURTHER STUDY

Epstein, David, and James Gonnor. "Dementia in Elderly: An Overview." *Generations* 23, no. 3 (1999): 9-17. Presents an overview of various types of dementia and their treatments.

Rabins, Peter V., Constantine G. Lyketsos, and Cynthia Steele. *Practical Dementia Care.* New York: Oxford University Press, 1999. Written primarily for medical professionals. Covers definitions, evaluation, diseases causing dementia, care for the patient and the family, treatment options, terminal care, and ethical and legal issues.

Schindler, Rachel. "Late-Life Dementia." *Geriatrics* 55, no. 10 (2000): 55-57. Discusses American Psychiatric Association guidelines for detecting and treating dementia.

Teitel, Rosette, and Marc Gordon. *The Handholder's Handbook: A Guide to Caregivers of People with Alzheimer's or Other Dementias.* New Brunswick, N.J.: Rutgers University Press, 2001. A guide to practical and emotional issues for caregivers of dementia patients. Chapters provide checklists of topics that caregivers should deal with or cover as they adjust to their role.

Sharon Wallace Stark

SEE ALSO: Aging: Cognitive changes; Aging: Physical changes; Alzheimer's disease; Brain damage; Brain structure; Coping: Chronic illness; Hallucinations; Parkinson's disease; Support groups.

Denial

TYPE OF PSYCHOLOGY: Cognition; consciousness; developmental psychology; emotion; motivation; psychopathology; stress

FIELDS OF STUDY: Cognitive processes; coping; personality assessment; psychodynamic and neoanalytic therapies; social motives; stress and illness

Denial is a cognitive mechanism in which aspects of reality are kept out of conscious awareness. It can serve as a defense against painful emotions or result from neurological impairment. It has an important emotional function in managing trauma and in coping with severe physical illness, particularly cancer.

KEY CONCEPTS
• alienation
• anosodiaphoria
• anosognosia
• confabulation
• disavowal
• negation
• repression

INTRODUCTION

The term "denial" originally described a psychological defense in which aspects of reality were kept out of a subject's consciousness. In the strict sense, the person who denies something acts as if it does not exist. For example, a person with cancer looks in the mirror at a large facial tumor, blandly claims to see nothing there, does not seeks medical care, and does not attend to the wound.

TYPES OF DENIAL

Over time, the term has been broadened and refined, and related terms introduced. "Disavowal" is essentially a synonym, translated from Sigmund Freud's use of the German word *Verleugnung*. Denial and disavowal include internal emotions; for example, unacceptable anger toward a parent who died. There is also denial of the emotional meaning of external events, such as the failure by Jews in the Warsaw Ghetto to recognize the relevance to them posed by Nazi genocide in other areas, even as they recognized the facts of what was happening. One can deny personal relevance, urgency, dangerousness, emotion, or information. In each example, the subject has an unconscious emotional motivation for not allowing something into awareness.

To some degree, all defenses help a person avoid awareness of some part of the self or external reality. To this extent, denial is the cornerstone of the ego's defensive functions. In denial, however, the excluded idea or feeling is not available to the subject in any form. In contrast, related ego defenses allow greater conscious and preconscious awareness of the avoided elements.

"Repression" is a related term for a psychological defense in which an emotionally charged fact is temporarily ignored and held out of consciousness but can emerge easily. For example, a student who knows he has bad grades on a report card may "forget" to bring home his school backpack containing the grades. However, he will be aware of a nagging feeling of something amiss and instantly remember that he has left it at school when questioned.

Similarly, "negation" refers to a defense in which a fact is allowed into consciousness, but only in the negative. An example would be someone who states, "I'm not jealous. I really admire all that she has." By allowing the possibility of jealousy but negating one's connection to it, denial of the emotion is maintained. In contrast, in true denial the idea of jealousy could not be allowed in consciousness at all.

Denial functions to prevent the individual from becoming overwhelmed by the threatening aspects of a situation. If the emotional impact of something is too great, it is initially kept out of awareness. Patients diagnosed with a terminal illness typically respond with denial when they first receive this news. After the destruction of the World Trade Center towers in 2001, some Americans denied the facts of the huge buildings' collapse into dust, maintaining hope of survivors being found far beyond what could be medically expected, in order to soften the impact of that magnitude of loss.

Denial can be adaptive or maladaptive. Adaptive denial allows a person to function in a situation of unavoidable pain or danger. Maladaptive denial worsens functioning because action is needed on the denied elements. For example, in Roberto Benigni's film *La Vita é Bella* (1997; *Life Is Beautiful*, 1998), a father and son are in a German concentration camp in World War II. The father translates German commands incorrectly for his son, making up a game in which they must do certain things truly demanded by the Germans to get a big prize. By denying the danger and the meaning of the subjugation they face, he protects his son from overwhelming fear, humiliation, and anger. His denial is also adaptive because his son is still able to function as he must to survive. Ultimately, however, the father's denial becomes maladaptive for him. He becomes too wrapped up in the story to accommodate a changing situation and makes mistakes which result in his death.

Common examples of adaptive denial include disavowal of one's eventual death or the degree of risk in daily behaviors such as driving a car. Common examples of maladaptive denial include a substance abuser's refusal to see a problem or a teenager's denial of the risk in experimental behavior. In empirical studies, for example, smokers rate the health risk of smoking, especially for themselves, lower than do nonsmokers.

NEUROLOGY OF DENIAL

Denial can also result from neurological impairment. Anosognosia is a phenomenon common to patients with right hemispheric stroke in which they fail to recognize (neglect), or seem indifferent to anything located to their left. This can be visual—objects held up, words, or their own body parts—as well as tactile or auditory. For example, they will not shave the left side of the face, forget to wear a left shoe, or read only "girl" if shown the word "schoolgirl." Alienation is an extreme version of this, in which patients fail to recognize their own body parts. Shown their left arm, they may say, "Yes, it is attached to my left shoulder, but it is not mine," or, "That is your arm, doctor." They maintain this view

even when confronted. For example, when asked, "Is this not your wedding ring on this hand?" they may answer, "Yes, doctor. Why are you wearing my ring?" Anosodiaphoria is a related syndrome in which the patient recognizes he or she is paralyzed but denies the emotional significance of the inability to move.

Denial and neglect of this type are most often associated with lesions of the right inferior parietal lobule, a brain area thought important in the circuitry of the general arousal response that allows people to attend to stimuli from the opposite side. The cingulate gyrus and right thalamus have also been associated with this deficit. That these lesions are part of more global self-awareness and arousal circuits, however, is demonstrated by the disease of Korsakoff's syndrome. In Korsakoff's syndrome, caused by alcoholism, there is no discrete brain lesion. The individual loses the ability to form new memories and will confabulate, that is, make up stories about his or her life and also make up answers to questions, while appearing to deny any awareness that the stories are not true. Anton's syndrome is another denial syndrome, associated with bilateral occipital blindness, in which the individual believes and acts as if he or she is not blind.

The use and consequences of denial in cancer patients have been extensively studied. The majority of the studies suggest that people with heavier use of denial as a personality trait have an increased risk of breast, melanoma, and other cancers. Such people show increased levels of physical stress, such as blood pressure changes, when confronted with disturbing stimuli, but they are more likely not to report feeling upset. Chronic stress such as this, particularly linked to anger, is likely connected to changes in immune function and other physical events that compromise tumor suppression. Such people also tend to delay going to the doctor for diagnosis and treatment, further worsening prognosis.

In contrast, patients who deny their emotional reactions while in the state of recent diagnosis of cancer tend to have complied with treatment and report less emotional distress when evaluated months later. Their denial helps them not be overwhelmed by the traumatic news that they have cancer. Thus it appears that, in cancer patients, denial as a reaction to an acute threat promotes physical and mental health, while denial as a general coping strategy does not.

HISTORY OF DENIAL

Psychoanalyst Sigmund Freud (1856-1939) first described the concept of disavowal, or *Verleugnung*, in 1923, in developing his notions of infantile sexuality. He said that children see a little girl's lack of a penis but "disavow" this fact and believe they see one anyway. He believed children later accept that the girl lacks a penis but are traumatized by this awareness, which Freud linked to female penis envy and male castration anxiety. Freud described a similar disavowal in writing about the fetishist in 1927. He believed fetishists choose a fetishistic object to replace a penis and thereby deny female castration in external reality but also experience anxiety if the object is not available, showing internal awareness of castration.

Freud believed that all human capacity to say "no" was fueled by the death instinct. He linked denial to three other types of "saying no": projection, negation, and repression. Because disavowal most rejects external reality, however, he thought that it "split the ego" and was the first step toward psychosis. It was also the most extreme form of negation.

Anna Freud (1895-1982) also wrote about denial as a basic defense that was normal in children but not in adults. René Spitz (1887-1974) described a developmental course to the infant's ability to say no. He took the infant who closes his eyes or falls asleep in an intensely stimulating or upsetting environment as the prototype for later forms of denial. Head-shaking and hiding behind a parent are later forms of denial. Spitz thought that denial expressed in this way was the first abstract thought of the infant because it involves imagining an alternative option to the current reality. He also noted its positive role in promoting independence, both in infants and in adolescents.

Contemporary theorists such as Theodore Dorpat and Charles Brenner have refined notions of the psychological mechanism of denial and its subtypes and have struggled to distinguish how it differs from and underlies other psychological defenses. Others have studied the effects of denial in different populations, such as cancer patients. In everyday clinical practice, psychoanalysts and psychologists work with individual patients to determine when denial must be broken through to promote the individual's self-acceptance and mental and physical health, and when denial should not be confronted to avoid overwhelming a person with painful feelings. In this ongoing work, the understanding of denial remains at the core of the understanding of human coping and defense.

SOURCES FOR FURTHER STUDY

Edelstein, E. L., D. L. Nathanson, and A. M. Stone, eds. *Denial: A Clarification of Concepts and Research*. New York: Plenum, 1989. This collation of articles presented by psychoanalysts, neurologists, and oncologists at an international conference is a comprehensive evaluation of denial from a variety of theoretical and historical perspectives. Suitable for the graduate and postgraduate student.

Freud, Anna. *The Ego and the Mechanisms of Defense*. Vol. 2 in *The Complete Works of Anna Freud*. New York: International University Press, 1971. A classic work on psychoanalytic views of defense mechanisms including a chapter on denial. Suitable for the levels of undergraduate student and above.

Kreitler, S. "Denial in Cancer Patients." *Cancer Investigation* 17, no. 7 (1999): 514-534. An extensive review of denial in cancer patients and empirical studies of the health consequences of denial.

Elizabeth Haase

SEE ALSO: Ego defense mechanisms; Emotions; Freud, Anna; Freud, Sigmund; Guilt; Psychoanalytic psychology and personality: Sigmund Freud.

Depression

TYPE OF PSYCHOLOGY: Psychopathology
FIELD OF STUDY: Depression

The study of depression has focused on biological underpinnings, cognitive concomitants, stress and coping style precursors, and interpersonal context.

KEY CONCEPTS

- bipolar disorder
- major depressive episode
- manic episode
- unipolar depression

INTRODUCTION

Almost everyone gets "down in the dumps" or has "the blues" sometimes. Feeling sad or dejected is clearly a normal part of the spectrum of human emotion. This situation is so common that a very important issue is how to separate a normal "blue" or "down" mood or emotion from an abnormal clinical state. Most clinicians use measures of intensity, severity, and duration of these emotions to separate the almost unavoidable human experience of sadness and dejection from clinical depression.

Depression is seen in all social classes, races, and ethnic groups. It is so pervasive that it has been called "the common cold of mental illness" in the popular press. It is approximately twice as common among women as it is among men. Depression is seen among all occupations, but it is most common among people in the arts and humanities. Famous individuals such as U.S. president Abraham Lincoln and British prime minister Winston Churchill had to cope with depression; Churchill called the affliction "the black dog." More recently, United States senator Thomas Eagleton and astronaut Edwin "Buzz" Aldrin were known to have bouts of serious depression.

Of all problems that are mentioned by patients at psychological and psychiatric clinics, some form of depression is most common. It is estimated that approximately 25 percent of women in the United States will experience at least one significant depression during their lives. Contrary to a popular misconception that depression is most common among the elderly, it is actually most common in twenty-five- to forty-four-year-olds. About 10 percent of the college population report moderate depression, and 5 percent report severe depression. Suicidal thoughts are common in depressive clients. In long-term follow-up, it has been found that approximately 15 percent of depressed individuals eventually kill themselves. Alternatively viewed, approximately 60 percent of suicides are believed to be caused by depression or by depression in association with alcohol abuse. As has been vividly portrayed in the media, teenage suicide in the United States is increasing at an alarming rate.

The role of family or genetic factors in depression was addressed long ago by Robert Burton in

Depression in one partner can place serious strain on a relationship. (CLEO Photography)

The Anatomy of Melancholy (1621), in which he noted that the "inbred cause of melancholy is our temperature, in whole or part, which we receive from our parents" and "such as the temperature of the father is, such is the son's, and look what disease the father had when he begot him, his son will have after him." More than 350 years later, the role of family factors in depression was addressed in a major collaborative study in the United States. In what was called the National Institute of Mental Health Collaborative Study of the Psychobiology of Depression, a large number of standardized instruments were developed to assess prevalence and incidence of depression, life histories, psychosocial stressors, and outcome of depression. The family members of depressed persons were assessed along with the depressed individual. It was found that bipolar depression was largely confined to relatives of individuals with bipolar disorder. Unipolar depression, however, was common among relatives of both unipolar- and bipolar-depressed individuals. The different patterns of familial transmission for bipolar and unipolar disorders strengthen the general conviction that these two disorders should be kept distinct from each other.

One explanation for increased vulnerability to depression in close relatives of depressed individuals is an inherited deficiency in two key components of brain chemistry: norepinephrine and serotonin, both of which are neurotransmitters. If depressions could be reliably subtyped according to the primary neurotransmitter deficiency, the choice of antidepressant medication would logically follow. Research is conflicting, however, on whether there is one group of depressed individuals who are low in norepinephrine and normal in serotonin and another group of depressives who are low in serotonin and normal in norepinephrine. Future developments in the study of neurotransmitters may have practical implications for the matching of particular pharmacotherapy interventions with particular types of depression. Evidence does indicate that for many depressed patients, substantial alteration in neurotransmitter activity occurs during their depression. This altered activity may directly mediate many of the disturbing symptoms of depression.

COGNITIVE AND STRESS THEORIES
A different approach to understanding depression has been put forward by cognitive theorists. Accord-

ing to Aaron Beck, in *Cognitive Therapy and the Emotional Disorders* (1976), cognitive distortions cause many if not most of a person's depressed states. Three of the most important cognitive distortions are arbitrary inference, overgeneralization, and magnification and minimization. Arbitrary inference refers to the process of drawing a conclusion from a situation, event, or experience when there is no evidence to support the conclusion or when the conclusion is contrary to the evidence. For example, an individual concludes that his boss hates him because he seldom says positive things to him. Overgeneralization refers to an individual's pattern of drawing conclusions about his or her ability, performance, or worth based on a single incident. An example of overgeneralization is an individual concluding that she is worthless because she is unable to find her way to a particular address (even though she has numerous other exemplary skills). Magnification and minimization refer to errors in evaluation that are so gross as to constitute distortions. Magnification refers to the exaggeration of negative events; minimization refers to the underemphasis of positive events.

According to Beck, there are three important aspects of these distortions or depressive cognitions. First, they are automatic—that is, they occur without reflection or forethought. Second, they appear to be involuntary. Some patients indicate that these thoughts occur even though they have resolved not to have them. Third, the depressed person accepts these thoughts as plausible, even though others would clearly not view them in the same manner.

While there is ample empirical support for the association of depression and negative cognitive factors such as cognitive distortions, irrational beliefs, and negative statements about oneself, research that demonstrates the ability of cognitive variables to predict subsequent depression is just beginning. It appears that a cognitive vulnerability plays a role in symptom formation for at least some individuals and in the maintenance of ongoing episodes of depression for many, if not all, depressed persons.

Yet another approach to understanding depression focuses on stress and coping. James Coyne, in a 1991 article, suggests that depression may be understood as a failure to cope with ongoing life problems or stressors. It has been hypothesized that coping effectively with problems and stressors can lessen the impact of these problems and help prevent them from becoming chronic. Depressed patients show slower recovery if they display poor coping skills. Avoidance coping strategies appear to be particularly likely in depression and are one example of poor coping. Depressed persons also show elevated levels of emotion-focused coping strategies, such as wishful thinking, distancing, self-blame, and isolation. These strategies also tend to be ineffective. While most forms of coping are impaired during an episode of depression, only self-isolation, an interpersonal avoidance strategy, appears to be an enduring coping style of persons vulnerable to depression. Thus, coping processes appear to change for the worse during an episode of depression, and poor coping helps to maintain the episode. In particular, depressed persons appear likely to avoid problem situations and to engage in strategies with a low likelihood of resulting in problem resolution or an enhanced sense of personal control.

Interpersonal approaches to understanding depression are related to stress and coping models but highlight the interpersonal environment as particularly important in depression. There is considerable evidence that low levels of social support are related to depression. Perhaps the relationship between social support and depression results from the fact that depressed persons do not seek social support; however, there is also evidence that poor social support leads to or maintains depressive symptomatology. In particular, evidence links the absence of close relationships with the development of depressive symptomatology. Accordingly, the work on general social support and depression can be seen as pointing in the direction of direct consideration of intimate relationships and their role in depression. Since the strongest family ties are usually in the marital relationship, it is natural to look to the marital relationship for particularly powerful opportunities to provide social support. Indeed, there is considerable evidence of an association between marital discord and depression. It had been expected by some that the association between marital discord and depression would be greater for women than men; however, it is generally equivalent between sexes when one looks across studies. Indeed, the risk of having a major depressive episode is approximately twenty-five times higher for both males and females if they are in a discordant marital relationship than if they are in a nondiscordant marital relationship.

TREATMENT METHODS

There are a number of ways to understand depression, and each approach appears to have something to offer. Given the distressing nature of depression, it is not surprising that these differing approaches have led in turn to several effective ways of treating depression.

Pharmacological interventions for unipolar depression have sometimes been held to normalize a genetically determined biochemical defect; the evidence, however, does not support this extreme biological characterization of unipolar depression. Yet neurotransmitters may directly mediate many of the behaviors affected in depression (for example, sleep, appetite, and pleasure), and neurotransmitter level and activity are disturbed as a concomitant of many episodes of depression. Hence, the use of antidepressant agents that influence neurotransmitter level or activity should be helpful in reducing or eliminating symptoms of depression even if the disturbance in neurotransmitter level or activity is itself the result of environmental or cognitive changes. In addition, there is considerable direct evidence that antidepressants can be useful in the treatment of depression in many cases. In controlled trials, both more recently developed and older forms of antidepressants provided improvement rates of 66 to 75 percent, in contrast to placebos, which showed improvement rates of 30 to 60 percent. Exactly for whom they will work, however, and exactly how or why they work are still not entirely clear.

A second effective approach to the treatment of depression can be found in cognitive therapy. It has become clear that altering cognitions and behavior in a cognitive behavioral format can relieve an ongoing episode of depression and may reduce the likelihood of relapse further than the use of psychopharmacology alone. Thus, cognitive processes are, at a minimum, reasonable targets of intervention in the treatment of many depressed patients. In addition, cognitive therapy appears to work well at decreasing depressive symptomatology even in the context of ongoing marital discord. Thus, for many depressed patients, interventions targeted at altering dysfunctional, negative automatic thoughts are likely to be useful.

Finally, interpersonal psychotherapy (IPT) has been developed by Gerald Klerman. This successful approach emphasizes abnormal grief, interper-

Depression in Children

Possible signs:

- frequent sadness, tearfulness or crying
- feelings of hopelessness
- withdrawal from friends and activities
- lack of enthusiasm or motivation
- decreased energy level
- major changes in eating or sleeping habits
- increased irritability, agitation, anger or hostility
- frequent physical complaints such as headaches and stomachaches
- indecision or inability to concentrate
- feelings of worthlessness or excessive guilt
- extreme sensitivity to rejection or failure
- pattern of dark images in drawings or paintings
- play that involves excessive aggression directed toward oneself or others or that involves persistently sad themes
- recurring thoughts of death and suicide or self-destructive behavior

Source: National Mental Health Association (NMHA) factsheet "Children's Mental Health Matters: Depression and Children."

sonal disputes, role transitions, loss, and interpersonal deficits, as well as social and familial factors. Results of a large, multicenter collaborative study conducted by the National Institute of Mental Health (NIMH) indicated that IPT can work as well as antidepressant medication for many depressed patients. In addition, earlier research indicated that IPT can improve the social functioning of depressed patients in a manner not typically produced by antidepressant medications alone. Given the interpersonal problems which are often part of a depressive episode, these improvements in social functioning and interpersonal environment appear to be particularly important for depressed persons. In a related development, marital therapy has been tested as a treatment for depressed persons who are maritally discordant, and it appears to be successful.

FROM MELANCHOLY TO PROZAC

The identification of depression as a recognizable state has a very long history. Clinical depression was described as early as the eighth century B.C.E. in the biblical descriptions of Saul. During the fourth century B.C.E., Hippocrates coined the term "melancholy" to describe one of the three forms of mental

illness he recognized. Later, Galen attempted to provide a biochemical explanation of melancholy based on the theory of "humors." Indeed, repeated descriptions and discussions of depression are present from classical times through the Middle Ages and into modern times.

The first comprehensive treatment of depression in English was provided by Timothy Bright's *Treatise of Melancholia* (1586). In 1621, Robert Burton provided his own major work on depression, *The Anatomy of Melancholy.* Most of the credit for developing the modern understanding of affective disorders, however, is given to Emil Kraepelin, a German psychiatrist. It was in Kraepelin's system that the term "depression" first assumed importance.

Since classical times, there has been debate about whether depression is best considered an illness or a response to an unhappy situation. Indeed, it is obvious to the most casual observer that sadness is a normal response to unhappy events. Even now, there is less than complete agreement on when fluctuations in mood should be considered pathological and when they are within normal limits. To help resolve this problem, diagnostic criteria have been developed, and structured interview procedures are often used to determine whether a particular individual should be considered depressed.

In the American Psychiatric Association's *Diagnostic and Statistical Manual of Mental Disorders: DSM-IV-TR* (rev. 4th ed., 2000), a common diagnostic tool, unipolar depression is divided into the categories Dysthymic Disorder, Major Depressive Disorder-Single Episode, and Major Depressive Disorder-Recurrent, while bipolar depression is divided into Bipolar I Disorder, Bipolar II Disorder, Cyclothymic Disorder, and Bipolar Disorder Not Otherwise Specified (NOS). In most articles, the term "depression" refers to unipolar depression only. Because unipolar depression is much more common than bipolar depression, it is likely that it will continue to attract a larger share of research attention in the future.

Throughout history, models of depression have become increasingly sophisticated, progressing from Hippocrates' theory that depression was produced by an excess of black bile to modern biochemical, cognitive, coping, stress, and interpersonal models. In the future, even more sophisticated models of depression may provide guidance for the next great challenge facing clinical psychology: reversing the trend in Western societies toward ever-increasing rates of depression.

SOURCES FOR FURTHER STUDY
Beach, Stephen R. H., E. E. Sandeen, and K. D. O'Leary. *Depression in Marriage.* New York: Guilford, 1990. Summarizes the literature on basic models of depression. Provides the basis for understanding the important role of marriage in the etiology, maintenance, and treatment of depression.

Beck, Aaron T. *Cognitive Therapy and the Emotional Disorders.* 1976. Reprint. New York: New American Library, 1979. Clearly lays out the basics of the cognitive model of depression. An important start for those who wish to understand the cognitive approach more thoroughly.

Burns, David D. *Feeling Good: The New Mood Therapy.* Rev. ed. New York: Avon Books, 1999. Provides a very entertaining and accessible presentation of the cognitive approach to depression. Presents basic results and the basics of cognitive theory, as well as a practical set of suggestions for getting out of a depression.

Coyne, James C., ed. *Essential Papers on Depression.* New York: New York University Press, 1985. Includes representatives of every major theoretical position advanced between 1900 and 1985. Each selection is a classic presentation of an important perspective. This source will acquaint the reader with the opinions of major theorists in their own words.

Coyne, James C., and G. Downey. "Social Factors and Psychopathology: Stress, Social Support, and Coping Processes." *Annual Review of Psychology* 42 (1991): 401-426. This influential essay ties together stress and coping with interpersonal processes to provide a deeper understanding of the nature of depression. Also provides an account of advances in the way both depression and interpersonal processes related to depression may be studied.

Kleinman, Arthur, and Byron Good. *Culture and Depression.* Berkeley: University of California Press, 1985. This exceptional volume examines the cross-cultural research on depression. Authors from anthropology, psychiatry, and psychology attempt to address the diversity that exists across cultures in the experience and expression of depression.

Paykel, Eugene S. *Handbook of Affective Disorders.* 2d ed. New York: Guilford, 1992. Provides comprehensive coverage of depression, mania, and anxiety in relation to depression. Includes detailed descriptions of symptoms, assessment procedures, epidemiology, and treatment procedures.

Solomon, Andrew. *The Noonday Demon: An Atlas of Depression.* New York: Charles Scribner's Sons, 2000. Solomon, who suffered serious depression himself, provides an insightful investigation of the subject from multiple perspectives of history, psychology, literature, psychopharmacology, law, and philosophy.

Stahl, Stephen M. *Essential Psychopharmacology of Depression and Bipolar Disorder.* New York: Cambridge University Press, 2000. Up-to-date coverage of the rapidly expanding options in drug treatments for depression.

Stephen R. H. Beach

SEE ALSO: Abnormality: Biomedical models; Abnormality: Psychological models; Bipolar disorder; Clinical depression; Cognitive behavior therapy; Cognitive therapy; Coping: Social support; Drug therapies; Emotional expression; Emotions; Mood disorders; Seasonal affective disorder; Suicide; Teenage suicide.

Depth and motion perception

TYPE OF PSYCHOLOGY: Sensation and perception
FIELDS OF STUDY: Vision

Depth and motion perception are key aspects of visual perception. They aid in form recognition and play an important role in visually guided navigation.

KEY CONCEPTS
- apparent motion
- biological motion
- corollary discharge theory
- corresponding points
- fusion
- induced motion
- monocular cues for depth
- optic array
- random-dot stereograms
- stereopsis

INTRODUCTION

A person looking at the view from a high vantage point can easily perceive that some objects in the landscape below are closer than others. This visual discrimination appears to require no apparent skill; the information is contained in the light entering the eyes that was reflected off the objects making up that scene. This light is focused onto the back of the eyes by the cornea and the lens of the eye. Once it reaches the back of the eye, the light is reflected onto the two-dimensional surface of the retina and causes a variety of retinal cells to fire, yet the observer perceives the scene in three dimensions. Furthermore, in spite of the presence of two separate physical retinal images, only one visual object is perceived. These phenomena are so natural that they occasion no surprise, instead people are surprised only if they have trouble determining depth or if they see double. Yet the opposite—single vision from two distinct retinal images—is the truly remarkable phenomenon that requires an explanation.

PERCEPTION OF A SINGLE FUSED IMAGE

The process that results in one percept arising from two retinal images is known as fusion. The physiological hypothesis of fusion is founded on the structures and functions of the visual pathways and is supported by increasing amounts of neuroanatomical and neurophysiological evidence. It represents the mainstream of thought in physiological optics today. The phenomenon of fusion, then, is based on a relationship between points on the two retinas. For every point on the left retina, there is a corresponding point on the right retina. Corresponding points are the pairs of anatomical locations, one from each retina, that would overlap if one retina could be slid on top of the other retina. So, for example, if the foveae of the two eyes are both focused on the same object, A, the images in each eye cast by A are said to lie on corresponding points on the two reti-

A National Aeronautics and Space Administration scientist administers a test for perceptual motor skills in 1973. (Hulton Archive)

nas. Similarly, any other object producing images in the two eyes that are equidistant from the fovea in each eye is also said to be stimulating corresponding points. All these objects will be at about the same distance as A. This hypothesis states that corresponding points are anatomically connected and that these connections form a final common pathway, or fusion center. For sensory fusion to occur, the images not only must be located on corresponding retinal areas but also must be sufficiently similar in size, brightness, and sharpness to permit sensory unification.

SPECIFIC QUALITIES OF DEPTH PERCEPTION

Perception of depth is created by various depth cues which signify the three-dimensionality of a scene from the two-dimensional information on the retina. Many of these cues are monocular depth cues, meaning that they give information about depth in a scene even if the observer is using only one eye. The cues include overlap, shadowing, relative brightness, and aerial perspective. Visual experience in these cases depends on the transfer of light from an object in the real world to the eye of the observer. These cues depend on characteristic ways that light travels to the eye, or ways in which it interacts with the medium through which it passes. In other cases, size and object relations provide information about depth. These cues include relative size, familiar size, perspective, and texture gradients. Monocular depth cues are used by artists to create the impression of depth in their artwork. However, it is rare that a painting is mistaken for an actual scene, because there are some cues that cannot be used in pictures.

One of these cues involves changes that come about in the pattern of retinal simulation as the result of motion. These cues include motion parallax and optical expansion. Objects closer to a moving observer than the fixation point would appear to move much faster than those further away from the fixation point. Thus, motion also provides information about depth.

Finally, there are certain cues for distance and depth which arise from the physical structure of visual systems. These physiological cues to depth include convergence (the turning in of the eyes as objects approach the face) and binocular disparity.

The problem of how the third dimension is perceived has been a point of debate for many noted philosophers, especially the empiricists. It has been suggested that different angles of inclination of the eyes (convergence) and different degrees of blurring of the image and strain in the muscles of the lens (accommodation) are the primary cues. There is, however, another potentially important perceptual source of information about relative distance for animals with binocularly overlapping fields of vision.

This other cue is binocular or retinal disparity, which is based on the fact that the two eyes see the world from slightly different positions, creating two different views of the world. If the two eyes are focused on an object, A, the images in each eye cast by A are said to lie on corresponding points on the two retinas as described earlier.

The images cast by a nearer or more distant object, B, will fall on noncorresponding or disparate points on the two retinas, and the amount or degree of disparity will depend upon the differences in depth between A and B. Thus, if the brain can compute the degree of disparity, this will give precise information about the relative distances of objects in the world.

It is possible to manipulate binocular disparity under special viewing conditions to create a strong depth impression from two-dimensional pictures. If pairs of pictures are presented dichoptically to each eye of what that eye would see if an actual object in depth were presented, a strong depth effect is achieved. The stereoscope, invented by Sir Charles Wheatstone in 1833, operates on this principle. Two photographs or drawings are made from two slightly different positions, the distance being the separation of the two eyes, approximately 63 millimeters. The stereoscope presents the left picture to the left eye and the right picture to the right eye so that they combine to result in a convincing three-dimensional perception of the scene. Wheatstone was the first to realize that horizontally displaced pictures presented in this fashion produced stereopsis, or binocular depth perception.

Although the disparity created by presenting a different view to each eye creates depth in stereoscopic pictures, most stereoscopic pictures also contain other depth information in addition to disparity. Monocular cues such as linear perspective, overlap, or relative size may contribute to the depth effect. Vision psychologist Bela Julesz, however, created the illusion of depth by using a stereoscope with random dot patterns, which contain no depth information other than disparity. The patterns are constructed by first generating two identical random dot patterns with a computer and then shifting a subset of the dots horizontally on one of the patterns. The effect of shifting one section of the pattern in this way is to create disparity, which causes the perception of depth when the patterns are viewed through a stereoscope. The shifted dot pattern is perceived as a small square floating above the background. When viewed monocularly, each pattern gives a homogeneously random impression without any global shape or contour. A central square is seen floating above the background when the two views are combined in a stereoscope. Thus, even with no other depth information present, retinal disparity can cause the perception of depth.

How does the brain use the disparity information provided by images that fall on noncorresponding positions on the retinas of the two eyes? There are many binocular neurons in the visual cortex of the cat that are sensitive to small differences in retinal disparity. There are also disparity selective cells in monkeys. Tuned excitatory cells respond strongly to a single disparity (usually near zero) and weakly for any other disparity. The tuning width of these cells along the dimension of disparity is very narrow. Tuned inhibitory cells respond well at all depths except on or near the fixation plane. Finally, near and far cells respond strongly to stimuli in front of or beyond the fixation plane, respectively, but little if at all to the opposite stimuli. There is a "functional architecture" for binocular disparity in the feline visual cortex, with horopter-coding cells being located near the boundaries of ocular dominance columns and "near-and-far" cells predominating at the interior of the columns. These neurophysiological findings in cats and monkeys can be extrapolated to human depth perception as well.

A further question of interest is whether stereopsis is processed by neural streams associated with the parvocellular or the magnocellular layers of the lateral geniculate nucleus. Evidence in support of a parvocellular component to stereopsis has been reported. Monkeys with lesions in the parvocellular layers of the lateral geniculate nucleus showed disruptions in fixations of random-dot stereogram stimuli, particularly for fine dot arrays. Magnocellular lesions seemed to have little or no effect. This suggests that the parvocellular stream is needed to process stereopsis when the stimuli are presented in fine dot arrays as in random-dot stereograms.

MOTION PERCEPTION

An essential quality that distinguishes all animals from plants is their capacity for voluntary movement. Animals move to find mates, shelter, and food, and to avoid being eaten themselves. However, the ability to move brings with it the requirement to sense movement, whether to guide one's progress through the world or to detect the movement of other mobile animals such as approaching predators. For sighted animals, this means sensing movement in the retinal image.

The need to sense retinal motion, and sense it as quickly as possible, places great demands on the visual system. Movement is characterized by subtle but highly structured changes in retinal illumination over space and over time. To sense movement very early in processing, the visual system relies on specialized neural processes. These processes make use of information about localized changes of image intensity over time. This representation effectively isolates those parts of the image that contain movement. However, to code the direction of movement, this temporal change information must be combined with information about spatial change-intensity edges. Increases of intensity over time come from image regions that contain spatial edges that are, for example, bright on the left and dark on the right. Decreases over time were associated with edges of opposite contrast polarity. These space-time pairings signify motion from left to right. A reversal of polarity either in the temporal signal or in the spatial signal would signify motion in the opposite direction.

The medial temporal area in the visual cortex is thought to be very important for motion perception because 90 percent of neurons in this area are directionally sensitive and damage to this area impairs ability to detect the direction of movement. How can the brain tell the difference between object motion and eye movement? Corollary discharge theory proposes that information about eye movement is provided by signals generated when the observer moves, or tries to move, the eyes. A motor signal travels from the brain to the eye muscles to move the eyes. The image moves across the retina and creates a sensory movement signal. If the sensory movement signal reaches the cortex, motion of the object is perceived. If only the eyes move, the corollary discharge signal, a copy of the motor signal, is transmitted to a hypothetical structure (the comparator) that receives both the corollary discharge signal and the sensory movement signal. This cancels the sensory movement signal so that object motion which does not really exist is not perceived. There is a growing body of psychophysical and physiological evidence supporting corollary discharge theory; however, researchers still do not completely understand the processes involved.

Perception of movement can be determined by how things move relative to one another in the environment as well. J. J. Gibson coined the term "optic array" to refer to the structure created by the surfaces, textures, and contours of the environment. He believed that what was important about the optic array is the way it changes when an observer moves or when something in the environment moves. A local disturbance in the optic array indicates that the object causing the disturbance is moving. A global disturbance in the optic array indicates that the observer is moving through the environment, which is stationary.

Perception of movement can even assist in the perception of three-dimensional forms. Several studies have demonstrated just how much information can be derived from biological movement. Actors were dressed in black and small lights were attached to several points on their bodies, such as their wrists, elbows, shoulders, hips, and feet. Films were made of the actors in a darkened room while they were performing various behaviors, such as walking, jumping, dancing, and lifting both a light and a heavy box. Even though observers who watched the films could only see a pattern of moving lights against a dark background, they could readily perceive the pattern as belonging to a human, could identify the behaviors in which they were engaged and could even tell the actors' genders.

There are also instances in which the perception of movement exists even though no movement is actually occurring. A person who sits in a darkened room and watches two small lights that are alternately turned on and off perceives a single light moving back and forth between two different locations rather than a light turning off at one location and then on at the other. This response, known as the phi phenomenon, is an example of apparent motion. Theater marquees and moving neon signs make use of this phenomenon. Instead of seeing images jumping from place to place, people perceive smooth movement in a particular direction. This ability to perceive movement across "empty space" was the basis for the creation of the first motion pictures in the late 1800's. This phenomenon may also explain some unidentified flying object (UFO) sightings related to flashing lights on radio towers. A related phenomenon, called induced motion, occurs when a person sitting in a train or bus feels that the vehicle has begun to move when actually the vehicle next to it has moved. The movement of one object induces the perception of movement in another object.

SOURCES FOR FURTHER STUDY

Bruce, Vicki, Patrick Green, and Mark A. Georgeson. *Visual Perception: Physiology, Psychology and Ecology.* 3d ed. Hove, East Sussex, England: Psychology Press, 1996. This graduate-level textbook contains detailed information on both depth and motion perception. Highly recommended as a specialized source of information on this topics.

Gibson, James J. *The Ecological Approach to Perception.* Boston: Houghton Mifflin, 1979. This very readable book fully describes the ecological theory by the theoretician himself. The ecological approach has become increasingly recognized as one of the important theories of perception.

Goldstein, E. Bruce. *Sensation and Perception.* 6th ed. Pacific Grove, Calif.: Wadsworth Group, 2002. This college-level textbook contains several chapters relevant to depth and motion perception. It is very up to date, readable and filled with beautiful illustrations.

Gregory, Richard L. *Eye and Brain: The Psychology of Seeing.* 5th ed. Princeton, N.J.: Princeton University Press, 1997. This relatively inexpensive paperback has established itself as an essential introduction to the basic phenomena of visual perception. Gregory offers clear explanations, excellent illustrations and writes with wit and style.

Johansson, G. "Visual Motion Perception." *Scientific American* 232 (1975): 76-89. This original article describes the first biological motion studies.

Julesz, Bela. *Foundations of Cyclopean Perception.* Chicago: University of Chicago Press, 1971. This is the definitive source of information on random dot stereograms (RDS). It contains everything from detailed descriptions of Julesz's original experiments using RDS to multiple red/green anaglyphs with a pair of stereoglasses included to add to the fun.

Sekuler, Robert, and Randolph Blake. *Perception.* 4th ed. New York: McGraw-Hill, 2001. This college-level textbook provides a good introduction to the structure and function of the sensory systems. The authors emphasize perception in a real-world context by relating concepts to everyday experiences.

Cynthia O'Dell

SEE ALSO: Nearsightedness and farsightedness; Pattern recognition; Pattern vision; Sensation and perception; Senses; Vision: Brightness and contrast; Vision: Color; Visual system.

Development

TYPE OF PSYCHOLOGY: Developmental psychology
FIELDS OF STUDY: Adolescence; behavioral and cognitive models; infancy and childhood

Developmental theories allow psychologists to manage and understand the enormous body of data on behavioral development from infancy through old age. Theories of development focus on many different issues and derive from many perspectives and periods in history. All, however, are concerned with explaining stability and change in human behavior as individuals progress through their lives.

KEY CONCEPTS
- behaviorism
- emergent process
- heuristic
- "organic lamp" theory
- psychodynamic theory

INTRODUCTION

Developmental theory has changed greatly over time. The theories of societies at various times in history have emphasized different aspects of development. The Puritans of the sixteenth and seventeenth centuries, for example, focused on the moral development of the child; they believed that Original Sin was inherent in children and that children had to be sternly disciplined in order to make them morally acceptable. In contrast to this view was the developmental theory of the eighteenth century French philosopher Jean-Jacques Rousseau, who held that children were born good and were then morally corrupted by society. Sigmund Freud (1856-1939) was interested in psychosexual development and in mental illness; his work therefore focused on these areas. John B. Watson (1878-1958), B. F. Skinner (1904-1990), and Albert Bandura (born 1925) worked during a period when the major impetus in psychology was the study of learning; not surprisingly, this was the focus of their work.

As developmental theorists worked intently within given areas, they often arrived at extreme positions, philosophically and scientifically. For example, some theorists focused upon the biology of behavior; impressed by the importance of "nature" (genetic or other inherited sources) in development, they may have neglected "nurture" (learning and other re-

sources received from the parents, world, and society). Others focused upon societal and social learning effects and decided that nurture was the root of behavior; nature has often been relegated to subsidiary theoretical roles in physiological and anatomical development. Similar conflicts have arisen concerning developmental continuity or discontinuity, the relative activity or passivity of children in contributing to their own development, and a host of other issues in the field.

These extreme positions would at first appear to be damaging to the understanding of development; however, psychologists are now in a position to evaluate the extensive bodies of research conducted by adherents of the various theoretical positions. It has become evident that the truth, in general, lies somewhere in between. Some developmental functions proceed in a relatively stepwise fashion, as Jean Piaget (1896-1980) or Freud would hold; others are much smoother and more continuous. Some development results largely from the child's rearing and learning; other behaviors appear to be largely biological. Some developmental phenomena are emergent processes (any process of behavior or development that was not necessarily inherent in or predictable from its original constituents) of the way in which the developing individual is organized, resulting from both nature and nurture in intricate, interactive patterns that are only beginning to be understood. These findings, and the therapeutic and educational applications that derive from them, are only comprehensible when viewed against the existing corpus of developmental theory. This corpus in turn owes its existence to the gradual construction and modification of developmental theories of the past.

THEORETICAL QUESTIONS AND PROPERTIES

Theoretical perspectives on development derive from a wide variety of viewpoints. Although there are numerous important theoretical issues in development, three questions are central for most theories. The first of these is the so-called nature-nurture question, concerning whether most behavioral development derives from genetics or from the environment. The second of these issues is the role of children in their own development: Are children active contributors to their own development, or do they simply and passively react to the stimuli they encounter? Finally, there is the question of whether development is continuous or discontinuous: Does development proceed by a smooth accretion of knowledge and skills, or by stepwise, discrete developmental stages? Current perspectives within developmental psychology represent very different views on these issues.

Useful developmental theories must possess three properties. They must be parsimonious, or as simple as possible to fit the available facts. They must be heuristically useful, generating new research and new knowledge. Finally, they must be falsifiable, or testable: A theory that cannot be tested can never be shown to be right or wrong. Developmental theories can be evaluated in terms of these three criteria.

PSYCHODYNAMIC THEORIES

Arguably, the oldest developmental theoretical formulation in use is the psychodynamic model, which gave rise to the work of Erik Erikson (1902-1994), Carl G. Jung (1875-1961), and, as its seminal example, the theory of Sigmund Freud. Freud's theory holds that all human behavior is energized by dynamic forces, many of which are consciously inaccessible to the individual. There are three parts to the personality in Freud's formulation: the id, which emerges first and consists of basic, primal drives; the ego, which finds realistic ways to gratify the desires of the id; and the superego, the individual's moral conscience, which develops from the ego. A primary energizing force for development is the libido, a psychosexual energy that invests itself in different aspects of life during the course of development. In the first year of life (Freud's oral stage), the libido is invested in gratification through oral behavior, including chewing and sucking. Between one and three years of age (the anal stage), the libido is invested in the anus, and the primary source of gratification has to do with toilet training. From three to six years, the libido becomes invested in the genitals; it is during this phallic stage that the child begins to achieve sexual identity. At about six years of age, the child enters latency, a period of relative psychosexual quiet, until the age of twelve years, when the genital stage emerges and normal sexual love becomes possible.

Freud's theory is a discontinuous theory, emphasizing stage-by-stage development. The theory also relies mainly on nature, as opposed to nurture; the various stages are held to occur across societies and with little reference to individual experience. The theory holds that children are active in their own development, meeting and resolving the conflicts that occur at each stage.

The success of psychodynamic theory has been questionable. Its parsimony is open to question: There are clearly simpler explanations of children's behavior. The falsifiability of these ideas is also highly questionable because the theories are quite self-contained and difficult to test. Psychodynamic theory, however, has proven enormously heuristic—that is, having the property of generating further research and theory. Hundreds of studies have set out to test these ideas, and these studies have significantly contributed to developmental knowledge.

BEHAVIORIST THEORIES

In contrast to psychodynamic theories, the behaviorist theories pioneered by John B. Watson and B. F. Skinner hold that development is a continuous process, without discrete stages, and that the developing child passively acquires and reflects knowledge. For behaviorists, development results from nurture, from experience and learning, rather than from nature. The most important extant behaviorist theory is the social learning theory of Albert Bandura, which holds that children learn by watching others around them and imitating others' actions. For example, Bandura demonstrated that children were far more inclined to commit violent acts (toward a toy) if someone else, particularly an adult, committed the acts first. The children were especially disposed to imitate if they perceived the acting individual as powerful or as rewarded for his or her violent actions.

ORGANIC LAMP THEORIES

The behaviorist theories are relatively parsimonious and heuristic. They are also testable, and it has been shown that, although many of the findings of the behaviorists have stood the test of time, there are developmental findings that do not fit this framework. To understand these findings, one must turn to the so-called organic lamp theories. This term comes from the fact that within these theories, children are seen as active contributors to their own development, and certain developmental processes are held to be "emergent": As fuel combusts to produce heat and light in a lamp, hereditary and environmental factors combine in development to produce new kinds of behavior. This framework was pioneered by Kurt Goldstein and Heinz Werner, but the most significant extant organic lamp theory is the cognitive development theory of Jean Piaget.

PIAGET'S CONTRIBUTIONS

Piaget's theory involves a discontinuous process of development in four major stages. The sensorimotor stage (birth to two years) is followed by the preoperational stage (two to seven years), the concrete operational stage (seven years to adolescence), and the formal operational stage (adolescence to adulthood). During the sensorimotor stage, the child's behavior is largely reflexive, lacking coherent conscious thought; the child learns that self and world are actually different, and that objects exist even when they are not visible. During the preoperational stage, the child learns to infer the perspectives of other people, learns language, and discovers various concepts for dealing with the physical world. In the concrete operational stage, the ability to reason increases, but children still cannot deal with abstract issues. Finally, in formal operations, abstract reasoning abilities develop. The differences between the four stages are qualitative differences, reflecting significant, discrete kinds of behavioral change.

Piaget's theory is not entirely accurate; it does not apply cross-culturally in many instances, and children may, under some experimental circumstances, function at a higher cognitive level than would be predicted by the theory. In addition, some aspects of development have been shown to be more continuous in their nature than Piaget's ideas would indicate. Yet Piaget's formulation is relatively parsimonious. The various aspects of the theory are readily testable and falsifiable, and the heuristic utility of these ideas has been enormous. This theory has probably been the most successful of the several extant perspectives, and it has contributed significantly to more recent advances in developmental theory. This progress includes the work of James J. Gibson, which emphasizes the active role of the organism, embedded in its environment, in the development of perceptual processes; the information processing theories, which emphasize cognitive change; and the ethological or evolutionary model, which emphasizes the interplay of developmental processes, changing ecologies, and the course of organic evolution.

MODERN-DAY APPLICATIONS

Developmental theory has been important in virtually every branch of medicine and education. The psychoanalytic theories of Sigmund Freud were the foundation of psychiatry and still form a central core for much of modern psychiatric practice. These theories are less emphasized in modern clinical psychology, but the work of Freud, Erikson, Jung, and later psychodynamicists is still employed in many areas of psychotherapy.

The behavioristic theories have proved useful in the study of children's learning for educational purposes, and they have considerable relevance for social development. An example is seen in the area of media violence. Bandura's work, and other research stemming from social learning theory, has repeatedly demonstrated that children tend to imitate violent acts that they see in real life or depicted on television and in other media, particularly if the individuals who commit these acts are perceived as powerful or as rewarded for their actions. Although this is disputed, especially by the media, most authorities are in agreement that excessive exposure to televised violence leads to real-world violence, largely through the mechanisms described by social learning theorists. Social learning theory has contributed significantly to an understanding of such topics as school violence, gang violence, and violent crime.

INTERPLAY OF NATURE VERSUS NURTURE

The organic lamp views have provided developmentalists with useful frameworks against which to understand the vast body of developmental data. Work within the Piagetian framework has shown that both nature and nurture contribute to successful development. One cannot, for example, create "superchildren" by providing preschoolers with college-level material. In general, they are simply not ready as organisms to cope with the abstract thinking required. On the other hand, the work of researchers on various Piagetian problems has shown that even very young children are capable of complex learning.

Organic lamp theory has demonstrated the powerful interplay between biological factors and the way in which children are reared. An example is seen in the treatment of Down syndrome, a chromosomal condition that results in mental retardation. The condition occurs when there are three chromosomes, rather than two, at the twenty-first locus. Clearly, this is a biological condition, and it was believed to be relatively impervious to interventions that come from the environment. It has now been shown, however, that children afflicted with Down syndrome develop much higher intelligence when reared in an intellectually stimulating environment, as opposed to the more sterile, clinical, determined environments typically employed in the past. The child's intellect is not entirely determined by biology; it is possible to ameliorate the biological effects of the syndrome by means of an environmental intervention. This type of complex interplay of hereditary and environmental factors is the hallmark of applied organic lamp theory.

The most important application of developmental theory generally, however, lies in its contribution to the improved understanding of human nature. Such an understanding has considerable real-world importance. For example, among other factors, an extreme faith in the nature side of the nature-nurture controversy led German dictator Adolf Hitler to the assumption that entire races were, by their nature, inferior and therefore should be exterminated. His actions, based on this belief, led to millions of human deaths during World War II. Thus, one can see that developmental theories, especially if inadequately understood, may have sweeping applications in the real world.

SOURCES FOR FURTHER STUDY

Gollin, Eugene S., ed. *Developmental Plasticity: Behavioral and Biological Aspects of Variations in Development.* New York: Academic Press, 1981. Excellent coverage of important theoretical issues in modern developmental psychology. Accessible to college or graduate students with some background in psychology and/or biology.

Lerner, Richard M. *On the Nature of Human Plasticity.* New York: Cambridge University Press, 1984. Insightful discussion of modern theory in developmental psychology and some historic antecedents. Emphasis on biological issues. Accessible to advanced students, graduate students, or professionals.

Miller, Patricia H. *Theories of Developmental Psychology.* 4th ed. New York: Worth, 2001. Excellent, comprehensive treatment of developmental theory. Describes extant theories in detail and discusses commonalities and dissimilarities. Accessible to the layperson with some background in psychology.

Piaget, Jean. *Biology and Knowledge.* Chicago: University of Chicago Press, 1971. This is a seminal summary of Piagetian theory that contains more general information and information concerning theory construction than do Piaget's other, more specific works. Readily accessible to the college student or the advanced high school student.

Shaffer, David Reed. *Developmental Psychology: Childhood and Adolescence.* 6th ed. Belmont, Calif.: Wadsworth, 2001. Good general textbook on developmental psychology, with an excellent basic treatment of theoretical issues in development. Accessible to the college or high school student.

Siegler, Robert S. *Emerging Minds: The Process of Change in Children's Thinking.* New York: Oxford University Press, 1998. Proposes a methodology of describing change as children's cognitive processes evolve.

Matthew J. Sharps

SEE ALSO: Adolescence: Cognitive skills; Aging: Cognitive changes; Attachment and bonding in infancy and childhood; Behaviorism; Cognitive development theory: Jean Piaget; Developmental methodologies; Ego psychology: Erik Erikson; Gender-identity formation; Physical development: Environment versus genetics; Psychosexual development.

Developmental disabilities

TYPE OF PSYCHOLOGY: Developmental psychology
FIELDS OF STUDY: Childhood and adolescent disorders; cognitive development; infancy and childhood; organic disorders

Developmental disabilities are conditions that result in substantial functional limitations. They manifest themselves in childhood and persist throughout the life span, requiring a continuum of medical, educational, and social services.

KEY CONCEPTS
- activities of daily living (ADLs)
- individual education plan (IEP)
- individual family service plan (IFSP)
- medically fragile
- mental retardation
- pervasive developmental disorder (PDD)

INTRODUCTION

The concept of developmental disabilities was first introduced in the Developmental Disabilities Services and Facilities Construction Act of 1970. Subsequently, the Developmental Disabilities Assistance and Bill of Rights Act of 1990 defined developmental disabilities. The term "developmental disability" means a severe, chronic disability of a person five years of age or older that is attributable to a mental or physical impairment or a combination of both. The disability must manifest itself before the person reaches the age of twenty-two and be expected to continue indefinitely. It results in substantial functional limitations in three or more areas of major life activity including self-care, receptive and expressive language, learning, mobility, self-direction, capacity for independent living, and economic self-sufficiency. The inclusion of the requirement of substantial functional limitations in three or more major life areas forms the basis for provision of services to individuals with severe impairments.

The American Psychiatric Association does not use the term "developmental disabilities." However, it does identify pervasive developmental disorders (PDD) in its diagnostic manual. The description of these disorders and their manifestations in many ways overlaps the definition of developmental disabilities.

The terms "developmental disabilities" and "mental retardation" are often used as if they were synonymous. However, there are important distictions as well as areas of overlap. The President's Committee on Mental Retardation uses the definition developed and utilized by the American Association on Mental Retardation and generally understood by the Arc-USA (a national organization for people with mental retardation and related developmental disabilities and their families). Developmental disabilities covers more disabilities than those encompassed under mental retardation. Developmental disabilities focuses on severe and chronic disabilities, while mental retardation includes a large number of individuals functioning at the mild level of cognitive impairment who require little or no support in adulthood. However, mental retardation does account for 70 percent of the people who are developmentally disabled. The term "medically fragile" is sometimes used to describe those vulnerable individuals whose complex medical needs can seriously compromise their health status.

POSSIBLE CAUSES

There are a multitude of etiologies for developmental disabilities. The cause can be prenatal, perinatal, or postnatal. Risk factors for developmental disabilities can be biological, environmental, or a combination of both. Genetics plays a role in conditions, such as Tay-Sachs disease and other inborn errors of metabolism, Klinefelter's syndrome, Fragile X syndrome, and Down syndrome, that typically lead to developmental disability. Genetic causes may be chromosomal abnormalities, single gene defects, or multifactorial disorders. For example, autism appears to have a genetic component that interacts with developmental factors.

A number of conditions in the prenatal environment may increase the likelihood that a child will be born with the potential for a developmental disability. Fetal alcohol syndrome, for example, is completely preventable if pregnant women do not drink alcohol. Women who have sufficient amounts of folic acid in their diets reduce the risk of having a child with a neural tube defect that can result in a developmental disability.

Smoking during pregnancy, use of certain drugs such as cocaine or heroin, poor maternal nutrition, and extremes of maternal age greatly increase the chances of fetal brain damage and/or premature delivery and low birth weight. Babies with low birth weights are three times more likely than normal-weight babies to have developmental disabilities. Approximately 61 percent of premature infants have a developmental disability of some kind.

Children may later be at risk through environmental causes such as lead poisoning, inadequate nutrition, infections, nonstimulating environments, abuse, neglect, and traumatic brain injury.

DIAGNOSING DEVELOPMENTAL DISABILITIES

Developmental disabilities are defined in terms of what an individual can or cannot do rather than in terms of a clinical diagnosis. They affect the typical processes in a child's growth, particularly the maturation of the central nervous system. For this reason, early identification is important. The potential exists for an improved outcome if children are provided with education and habilitation. Prenatal diagnostic techniques may be appropriate for at-risk pregnancies. If a fetus is affected, the physician is better able to plan the delivery and for special care during the newborn period.

DSM-IV-TR Criteria for Pervasive Developmental Disorders

ASPERGER'S DISORDER (DSM CODE 299.80)

Qualitative impairment in social interaction, manifested by at least two of the following:
- marked impairment in use of multiple nonverbal behaviors (eye-to-eye gaze, facial expression, body postures, gestures)
- failure to develop peer relationships appropriate to developmental level
- lack of spontaneous seeking to share enjoyment, interests, or achievements with others
- lack of social or emotional reciprocity

Restricted, repetitive, and stereotyped patterns of behavior, interests, and activities, manifested by at least one of the following:
- preoccupation with one or more stereotyped and restricted patterns of interest abnormal in either intensity or focus
- apparently inflexible adherence to specific, nonfunctional routines or rituals
- stereotyped and repetitive motor mannerisms (hand or finger flapping, complex whole-body movements)
- persistent preoccupation with parts of objects

Symptoms cause clinically significant impairment in social, occupational, or other important areas of functioning

No clinically significant general delay in language

No clinically significant delay in cognitive development or development of age-appropriate self-help skills, adaptive behavior (other than in social interaction), and curiosity about environment

Criteria for another specific pervasive developmental disorder or schizophrenia not met

AUTISTIC DISORDER (DSM CODE 299.00)

Six or more criteria from three lists

1) Qualitative impairment in social interaction, manifested by at least two of the following:
- marked impairment in use of multiple nonverbal behaviors
- failure to develop peer relationships appropriate to developmental level
- lack of spontaneous seeking to share enjoyment, interests, or achievements with others
- lack of social or emotional reciprocity

2) Qualitative impairments in communication, manifested by at least one of the following:
- delay in, or total lack of, development of spoken language, not accompanied by attempts to compensate through alternative modes of communication such as gesture or mime
- in individuals with adequate speech, marked impairment in ability to initiate or sustain conversation
- stereotyped and repetitive use of language or idiosyncratic language
- lack of varied, spontaneous make-believe play or social imitative play appropriate to developmental level

3) Restricted, repetitive, and stereotyped patterns of behavior, interests, and activities, manifested by at least one of the following:
- preoccupation with one or more stereotyped and restricted patterns of interest abnormal in either intensity or focus
- apparently inflexible adherence to specific, nonfunctional routines or rituals
- stereotyped and repetitive motor mannerisms
- persistent preoccupation with parts of objects

Delays or abnormal functioning in at least one of the following areas, with onset prior to age three:
- social interaction
- language as used in social communication
- symbolic or imaginative play

Symptoms not better explained by Rett's Disorder or Childhood Disintegrative Disorder

(continued)

Newborn screening is another way in which to identify conditions that can result in developmental disabilities if untreated. The Apgar test is administered by the medical staff in the delivery room at one minute, five minutes, and, if there are complications, at ten and fifteen minutes after birth. It measures the effects of various complications of labor and birth and determines the need for resuscitation. The test assesses physical responsiveness, development, and overall state of health using a scale of five items rated from 0 to 2. A low Apgar score at birth can signal the potential for a developmental disability.

Measurement of head circumference is a useful tool for predicting whether an infant is likely to have a neurodevelopmental impairment such as

CHILDHOOD DISINTEGRATIVE DISORDER (DSM CODE 299.10)

Apparently normal development until at least age two, with age-appropriate verbal and nonverbal communication, social relationships, play, and adaptive behavior

Clinically significant loss of previously acquired skills before age ten in at least two of the following areas:
- expressive or receptive language
- social skills or adaptive behavior
- bowel or bladder control
- play
- motor skills

At least two of the following abnormalities of functioning:
- qualitative impairment in social interaction (impairment in nonverbal behaviors, failure to develop peer relationships, lack of social or emotional reciprocity)
- qualitative impairments in communication (delay or lack of spoken language, inability to initiate or sustain conversation, stereotyped and repetitive use of language, lack of varied make-believe play)
- restricted, repetitive, and stereotyped patterns of behavior, interests, and activities, including motor stereotypies and mannerisms

Symptoms not better explained by another specific pervasive developmental disorder or schizophrenia

RETT'S DISORDER (DSM CODE 299.80)

Apparently normal prenatal and perinatal development, apparently normal psychomotor development through first five months after birth, and normal head circumference at birth

Onset of all the following after the period of normal development:
- deceleration of head growth between five and forty-eight months of age
- loss of previously acquired purposeful hand skills between five and thirty months of age, with the subsequent development of stereotyped hand movements
- loss of social engagement early in course (although often social interaction develops later)
- poorly coordinated gait or trunk movements
- severely impaired expressive and receptive language development, with severe psychomotor retardation

microcephaly. A blood test screening can be done for phenylketonuria (PKU), congenital hypothyroidism, galactosemia, maple syrup urine disease, homocystinuria, and biotinidase deficiency. Early detection of these conditions and appropriate intervention may reduce the severity of the resulting disability.

An older child can be referred to a developmental pediatrician for assessment of a developmental disability if the child has not attained expected age-appropriate developmental milestones, exhibits atypical development or behavior, or regresses to a previous level of development. Correcting for prematurity in developmental testing is necessary. An instrument commonly used is the Denver Developmental Screening Test. The more severely affected a child is, the clearer is the diagnosis, since an individual's failure to meet developmental milestones may represent a short-term problem that resolves over time as the child "catches up." Even readily identifiable indicators of potential disability do not always result in expected delays.

Related issues such as feeding, elimination, and cardiorespiratory problems; pressure sores; and infection control are also considered as part of the diagnosis. Screening for lead poisoning and/or psychological testing may be recommended.

At whatever age the person is referred, a multidisciplinary evaluation attempts to establish a baseline of the present level of performance, including both skills and deficits. Activities of daily living (ADLs) such as bathing, eating, and dressing are widely used in assessing this population. Needing assistance with ADLs becomes an important criterion for determining eligibility for public and private disability benefits. An appraisal is made of those deficits that can remediated and those that require accommodation. The predictive accuracy of the diagnosis improves with the individual's age.

Language development is another predictor variable. Individuals with developmental disabilities may have little or no apparent intent to communicate and may not understand that they can affect their environment through communication.

Though developmental disabilities by definition are severe, it is possible that a child not previously identified could be detected by routine public school prekindergarten screening.

THE DEVELOPMENTALLY DISABLED POPULATION

The Administration on Developmental Disabilities of the United States Department of Health and Human Services estimates that there are four million Americans with developmental disabilities. Data specific to the incidence and prevalence of developmental disabilities are difficult to obtain because of the various etiologies present in this population. Conditions which often fall under the umbrella of developmental disability include mental retardation, autism, epilepsy, spinal cord injury, sensory impairment, traumatic brain injury, and cerebral palsy.

Though developmental disabilities can be associated with neurological damage, many of the conditions resulting in a developmental disability do not result in lowered intellectual functioning. Persons with developmental disabilities are estimated to comprise 1.7 to 1.8 percent of the population. This percentage has risen markedly since the mid-1970's for two reasons: increased life span for older individuals with disabilities and a greater number of children and adolescents surviving conditions that previously would have been fatal. The number of students diagnosed with autism has grown dramatically, from approximately 5,500 in the 1991-1992 school year to nearly 55,000 in 1998-1999.

Between 200,000 and 500,000 people in the United States over the age of sixty may have some form of developmental disability. Some of these individuals present special problems as they age. Those with epilepsy appear to be at greater risk for osteoporosis, while those with Down syndrome seem to begin the aging process earlier than others.

TREATMENT OPTIONS

The person with a developmental disability needs a combination of interdisciplinary services that are individually planned and coordinated and of lifelong or extended duration throughout the life cycle. Because the causes and manifestations of developmental disabilities are so varied, each affected person is unique and requires an individualized approach to treatment and training. Each disability has specific needs that must be addressed and accommodations that must be provided.

When a defect has been identified prenatally, fetal treatment may be possible in order to prevent developmental disability. Some inborn errors of metabolism respond to vitamin therapy given to the mother. Bone marrow transplants and fetal surgery have also been performed.

Services for children from birth to two years old provide special education as well as access to specialists in the areas of speech and physical therapy, psychology, medicine, and nursing. Assistive technology, physical adaptations, and case management are also offered. Medical management, monitoring, and consultation may be the responsibility of a developmental pediatrician.

Early intervention may be home-based, or the child can be enrolled in a center with a low child-to-teacher ratio. In either case, an Individual Family Service Plan (IFSP) is developed which includes a statement of the child's present level of development, the family's concerns, priorities, and resources, major outcomes to be achieved, and the specific early intervention services to be provided; identification of the coordinator responsible for implementing the plan; and procedures for transition to preschool.

Among the equipment used in treating the child may be positioning devices, wheelchairs, special car restraints, amplification devices, and ambulation aids. Some children may require gastronomy tubes, tracheostomy tubes, cardiorespiratory monitors, nasogastric tubes, ventilators, bladder catheters, splints, or casting. They may be placed on antiepileptic medication, antispasticity drugs, antireflux medications, antibiotics, respiratory medications, or medications to influence mood and behavior.

The Individuals with Disabilities Education Act mandates comprehensive educational services for children from three through twenty-one years of age. Services are offered in a continuum of settings that are individually determined. These settings may include hospitals, residential facilities, separate day schools, homes, and public schools. Children are ideally placed in what the law refers to as "the least restrictive environment." An Individual Education Plan (IEP) replaces the IFSP.

ADLs are a prime focus of the educational program. The goal is to promote independence in such areas as eating, drinking, dressing, toileting, grooming, and tool use, which, in turn, fosters self-esteem.

Facilitating language acquisition and communicative intent are critical to any intervention program. Many developmentally disabled individuals will need numerous stimulus presentations before acquiring a rudimentary vocabulary. For those children who continue to be nonverbal, alternative communication systems such as sign language, use of pictures, and communication boards are introduced to enable communicative interaction. Computers with interface devices such as switches or touch-sensitive screens may be introduced to children with cerebral palsy.

Children with developmental disabilities exhibit challenging behaviors more often than typically developing children. After previously unrecognized medical conditions are ruled out as causes, positive behavioral supports at home and in school and/or traditional behavior management programs aim at producing comprehensive change in those challenging behaviors. Drugs that affect central nervous system function can also be helpful in treating disruptive behaviors.

Newer treatment approaches include neurodevelopmental therapy and sensory integration therapy. Neurodevelopmental therapy is widely used by physical and occupational therapists. It emphasizes sensorimotor experience to facilitate normal movement and posture in young developmentally disabled children with cerebral palsy or other, related disorders. Sensory integration is a normal process in which the child's central nervous system organizes sensory feedback from the body and the environment and makes appropriate adaptive responses. Sensory integration therapy uses controlled sensory input to promote those adaptive responses.

Adults with developmental disabilities are living longer than ever before. Most have the ability to live happy, productive lives in their communities. One component of treatment is transition planning. The Developmental Disabilities Act of 1984 emphasizes the importance of employment of persons with developmental disabilities and offers guidelines for providing supported employment services. Other transition issues include sexuality, social integration, recreation, and community residential options. Medical and physical care plans are necessary since long-term consequences of therapeutic interventions may occur. Movement disorders can result from the prolonged use of neuroleptic medications, while bone demineralization may be secondary to the chronic use of certain anticonvulsants.

HISTORY OF TREATMENT

Services for people now referred to as having a developmental disability began in the United States in 1848 in Boston. The philosophy of early schools was to cure the "deviant." However, by 1877 a unidisciplinary medical model replaced the educational model and emphasized providing shelter and protection to this population. Later, the interest in Mendelian genetics led to a change in focus to protecting society from those whose disabilities were considered hereditary. By 1926, twenty-three states had laws requiring mandatory sterilization of the developmentally disabled on the books, and between 1925 and 1955 over fifty thousand involuntary sterilizations occurred in the United States. In the 1950's, parents began to organize opportunities for individuals with developmental disabilities within public school systems.

Treatment evolved from the medical model to a multidisciplinary approach in which a physician consulted with members of other disciplines. Later, an interdisciplinary model emerged in which professionals from each discipline gathered together to discuss their individual assessments and decide jointly on a plan of care. More recently, a transdisciplinary approach has been developed in which professionals, along with the individual concerned and the family, work together equally to identify needs, plan care, implement interventions, and evaluate progress.

Though the term "developmental disabilities" was not used in it, PL 94-142, the Education for All Handicapped Children Act of 1975, mandated a free, appropriate, public education for children who could be considered developmentally disabled. The Education of the Handicapped Act Amendments of 1986 extended early identification and intervention services under the auspices of the public schools to identified children three to five years of age and those at risk for developmental disabilities. This legislation was reauthorized as the Individuals with Disabilities Education Act (IDEA) of 1990. Guarantees of equal protection under the law were extended to adults with developmental disabilities by the Americans with Disabilities Act (ADA) of 1990.

The years since 1970 have been a period of remarkable growth and achievement in services for individuals with developmental disabilities. Cultural, legal, medical, and technological advances have occurred. Services now include protection and advocacy systems under the auspices of state councils on developmental disabilities; university centers involved in education, research, and direct service; training in self-determination; and family supports. At the heart of this growth has been a transformation from a system of services provided primarily in institutions to one provided primarily in local communities. There has been a movement away from segregation and toward integration following what has been called the principle of normalization.

SOURCES FOR FURTHER STUDY

Batshaw, Mark L., ed. *Children with Disabilities*. Baltimore: Paul H. Brooks, 1997. Serves as a primer on developmental disabilities for educators, therapists, psychologists, social workers, health care professionals, and child advocates. Families can find useful information on medical and rehabilitation aspects of developmental disabilities.

Copeland, Mildred E., and Judy R. Kimmel. *Evaluation and Management of Infants and Young Children with Developmental Disabilities*. Baltimore: Paul H. Brookes, 1989. The authors present clear and concise descriptions of selected developmental disabilities illustrated with photographs and sketches. Discussion of assessment and management is geared to teachers and parents.

Dowrick, Peter W. "University-Affiliated Programs and Other National Resources." In *Handbook of Developmental Disabilities*, edited by Lisa A. Kurtz, Peter W. Dowrick, Susan E. Levy, and Mark L. Batshaw. Gaithersburg, Md.: Aspen, 1996. Provides a listing of referral sources by region and by state.

McLaughlin, P. J., and Paul Wehman, eds. *Mental Retardation and Developmental Disabilities*. Austin, Tex.: Pro-Ed, 1996. Leaders in the field discuss developmental disabilities from a life-span perspective. Eight individual chapters deal with specific conditions considered developmental disabilities. Services and program issues are reviewed.

Roth, Shirley P., and Joyce S. Morse, eds. *A Life-span Approach to Nursing Care for Individuals with Developmental Disabilities*. Baltimore: Paul H. Brookes, 1994. Though written for nurses, this book gives the general reader a foundation of information regarding developmental disabilities from a quality-of-life perspective.

Gabrielle Kowalski

SEE ALSO: Abnormality: Biomedical models; Autism; Birth: Effects on physical development; Childhood disorders; Down syndrome; Mental retardation; Physical development: Environment versus genetics; Prenatal physical development; Psychobiology; Reflexes in newborns.

Developmental methodologies

TYPE OF PSYCHOLOGY: Developmental psychology
FIELDS OF STUDY: Adulthood; infancy and childhood; methodological issues

Developmental methodologies describe how information about age-related changes in people's physical growth, thought, and behavior is collected and interpreted. Sound methodologies are essential for describing accurately the course of life-span development, comparing people with different environmental and biological backgrounds, predicting developmental patterns, and explaining the causes of positive and negative outcomes in development.

KEY CONCEPTS
• cohort
• control
• generalizability
• research designs
• research methods

INTRODUCTION

Developmental methodologies have as their purpose the investigation of questions about age-related changes throughout the life span, and they include both a variety of research methods and the designs within which these methods are applied. The overarching framework for developmental methodologies is the scientific process. This process embodies systematic rules for testing hypotheses or ideas about human development under conditions in which the hypotheses may be supported or refuted. This process also requires that research be done in such a way that it can be observed, evaluated, and replicated by others.

Data collected through developmental methodologies can be characterized as descriptive, correlational, or experimental. Descriptive data simply describe a variable—for example, the average age of the adolescent growth spurt. Correlational data provide information on relationships between variables, such as the association between newborn size and the amount of smoking a mother did during pregnancy. Experimental data result from the careful manipulation of one variable to discover its effect on another, and only in experimental studies can cause-and-effect relationships among variables be inferred. For example, experimental studies demonstrate that training techniques can cause an improvement in the memory performance of persons in late adulthood.

RESEARCH CATEGORIES

Developmental research methods are commonly separated into three general categories. One of these categories is observational methods, in which researchers observe people as they go about their lives. The settings for such research can be homes, schools, playgrounds, nursing homes, and so on. Observational research may be quite subjective, as in diary studies in which the researcher writes down observations and impressions in a free-flowing manner. The extensive cognitive developmental model of Jean Piaget had its beginnings in hypotheses which emerged from diary studies of his children. On the other hand, observational research may be very rigorous and systematic; researchers carefully define what and how they will observe and record, and then train data collectors before any formal observations are made. Videotaping of children's language samples, which are then carefully segmented and analyzed, is an example of this systematic approach.

The second category, self-report methods, is generally more intrusive than observational research. It involves asking questions of participants and may take the form of interviews, questionnaires, or standardized tests. Interviews may be free-flowing or highly structured, with predetermined questions and sequence. The famous studies of sexual behavior by Alfred Kinsey, for example, utilized carefully planned interview techniques. Questionnaires and standardized tests are usually structured with both questions and response categories provided. Questionnaires are often used to gather descriptive information such as size of family or educational level, as well as opinions on a variety of social issues. Standardized tests are used to assess a great variety of information, including measured intelligence, vocational interests, and self-concept.

The third category of developmental methods involves experimentation. Experimentation can occur in natural settings where individuals may not be aware that they are participating in research, such as in situational studies of children's moral behavior. It can also occur in laboratories where individuals may be unaware of their participation or fully aware of the artificiality of the setting and even the study's intent. Research using a complex apparatus to study newborn perception is one example of the former, while research using nonsense syllables in memory tasks to assess age differences in free recall is an example of the latter.

RESEARCH METHODS AND DESIGNS

Research methods can be compared according to their generalizability and their ability to control participants' selection, experiences, and responses. Generalizability refers to the extent to which research results are applicable to people beyond those who participated in the study. Generally, methods that are more intrusive and contrived provide the greatest opportunity for control—the extent to which a researcher can regulate who participates in a study, what the participants experience, and how the participants respond. Thus, laboratory experimentation often is associated with high levels of control. For the same reasons, however, questions are raised regarding the applicability to the real world of data collected in the artificiality of a laboratory. Thus, observation in natural settings is often associated with high levels of generalizability. Both control and generalizability are desirable and are sought in developmental research regardless of method.

In order to assess whether age-related changes exist, developmental research methods are applied within larger frameworks of research designs which require that data be collected at two or more points in developmental time. These designs permit inquiry into whether behavior is the result of maturational changes associated with age changes, such as the emergence of language in infancy; the effect of the immediate social context, such as a nation at war; or the effect of historical events which affected everyone born at about the same time (a group known as a cohort, a term which means an identifiable group of people that has a common association), such as growing up during the Great Depression. Two of the most common designs are cross-sectional and longitudinal designs. In cross-sectional designs, data are collected on different cohorts at the same time. These designs permit an examination of age differences in behavior; however, they cannot separate out the effects of different life experiences between cohorts. In longitudinal designs, data are collected on the same cohort a number of times. These designs permit an examination of developmental trends for individuals; however, they cannot separate out the effects of social change, since no comparison can be made to a group not experiencing the social context. An alternative to cross-sectional and longitudinal designs are sequential designs, in which data are collected on a number of cohorts a number of times. These designs are able to reveal the effects of age, cohort, and social context. Because of the difficulties of administering these complex designs and their expense, sequential designs are least often applied, even though they provide the most useful developmental information.

Regardless of the research methods or designs utilized, developmental methodologies must account for the complexity of human development. They must control for multiple variables, such as age, cohort, social context, socioeconomic class, gender, educational level, and family structure. They must take into account the culture of the participants, and they must protect against bias in formulating the research hypothesis, applying the methods, and interpreting the data collected.

Developmental methodologies are applicable to literally any developmental question, from conception to death. Resultant data permit description of current status, comparison between groups, prediction of developmental patterns, and explanation of the causes of developmental outcomes. Description, comparison, prediction, and explanation all contribute to a better understanding of development, which in turn permits the fostering of social settings that promote healthy development, as well as intervention to prevent potential developmental problems or to counter developmental problems already in existence.

NEWBORN RESEARCH

Research on the competencies of newborns provides one demonstration of the relationship between understanding and therapeutic intervention. Observational research of newborns and young infants indicates a cyclical relationship in infant attention when the infant is interfacing with a caregiver. This cycle is one of activation, discharge, and then recovery when the infant withdraws its attention. Caregivers who adjust their behavior to their infants' rhythms by entering into interaction when their infants are responsive and slackening off when their infants withdraw attention experience a greater amount of time in which the infant looks at them than do caregivers who either attempt to force their own rhythms on their infants or continuously bombard their infants with stimulation.

Psychologists are applying this understanding as part of an overall intervention program with premature infants who enter the world at risk for physical, social, and intellectual impairments. Premature newborns require greater stimulation than full-term newborns before they respond; however, they also are overwhelmed by a level of stimulation to which full-term newborns respond very positively. This narrow range of tolerance can disrupt the relationship between a parent and the premature infant. In experimental research, parents of premature newborns have been trained to imitate everything their infants do, and by so doing follow their infants' rhythms. This training helps parents remain within the narrow tolerance of their infants and increases the amount of positive interaction both experience. This, in turn, contributes positively to healthy social development of this high-risk group of infants.

TELEVISION STUDIES

Research on the developmental effects of television provides a demonstration of the relationship between understanding and influences on social policy. Beginning in the mid-1950's with a series of inquiries and hearings sponsored by a Senate subcommittee on juvenile delinquency, followed by a Surgeon General's report and associated Senate hearings in the early 1970's and a major National Institute of Mental Health report in the early 1980's, questions about the effect of violent programming on children have been raised in the public domain. Consequently, public efforts have emerged to control the amount and timing of violence on television and to regulate the number and content of television commercials targeted at children. Central to the national debate and social policies surrounding television content has been the application of developmental methodologies.

Significant research in this area emerged in the early 1960's with the now-classic "Bobo" doll studies of Stanford University psychologist Albert Bandura. In a series of experimental laboratory studies, nursery school children observed a variety of televised models behaving aggressively against an inflatable punching-bag clown. Later, when their play behavior was observed in a controlled setting, children clearly demonstrated imitation of specific aggressive behaviors they had viewed. Additional experimental laboratory studies have been conducted; however, they have been consistently criticized for their artificiality. Consequently, field experiments have emerged in which the experimental variables have been actual television programs, and the effects have been assessed on spontaneous behavior in natural settings, such as playgrounds.

Since experimental studies require systematic manipulating of variables for their effects to be observed, and since the manipulations of levels and types of aggression and other relevant variables such as home violence are either unethical or impractical, numerous correlational studies have also been conducted. Most of these have assessed the relationship between the amount of violence viewed and subsequent violent behavior, violent attitudes, or perceptions of violence in the real world. Many of these studies have applied longitudinal or sequential designs covering many years, including one longitudinal study which covered a span of twenty-two years from childhood into adulthood. These studies have controlled multiple variables including age, educational level, and initial level of aggressive behavior. Although not all studies have supported a causal link between television violence and aggressive behavior and attitudes, the large majority of laboratory experimental, field experimental, and correlational studies indicate that children do learn antisocial and aggressive behavior from televised violence and that some of them may directly imitate such behaviors. The effects depend on the characteristics of the viewers and the settings.

Not only have developmental methodologies been used after the fact to discover the effects of television programming, they have also been applied proactively to develop prosocial children's programming, and then to evaluate the effects of those prosocial programs on children's development. The program *Sesame Street*, for example, has as its foundation research into child development, attention, and learning. In fact, one of its objectives has been to act as an experimental variable, intervening into homes in which children are economically and educationally disadvantaged. Although researchers have had limited access to those high-risk homes, both experimental research and correlational longitudinal research support the effectiveness of *Sesame Street* in developing early academic skills, school readiness, positive attitudes toward school, and positive attitudes toward people of other races.

EVOLUTION OF RESEARCH

Today's developmental methodologies have their origins in the nineteenth century, with its advances in science and medicine, the emergence of the fields of psychology and psychoanalysis, and developments in measurement and statistics. Developmental psychological research and methodologies often emerged to deal with concrete social problems. With compulsory education bringing approximately three-quarters of all American children into classrooms at the beginning of the twentieth century, social concerns were focused primarily on child health, education, and social welfare. Consequently, the first major research into child intellectual, social, and emotional development also occurred during this period, and developmental psychology began to consolidate as a distinct discipline of psychology.

The universal draft of World War I required assessment of multitudes of older adolescent and young adult men with vast differences in education, health status, and social and emotional stability. Standardized testing became the tool to evaluate these men, and it has remained a major tool in developmental methodologies, as well as in other disciplines of psychology. Following the war, efforts to understand these individual differences led to the first major longitudinal studies, which were focused on descriptions of normative growth and predictions of developmental patterns; some of these studies have followed their participants and next generations for more than fifty years.

In the two decades following World War II, the baby boom and national anxiety over falling behind the Soviet Union in science and technology rekindled efforts dampened during the war years in the disciplines of developmental and educational psychology. Of particular interest were methodologies in applied settings such as school classrooms, focused on learning and academic achievement. Also during this period, greater accessibility to computers permitted increases in the complexity of developmental research methods and designs, and of resultant data analyses. Complex sequential designs, intricate correlational techniques, and multiple-variable techniques became much more frequently used in research.

Heightened awareness of economic and social inequalities in the United States following the Civil Rights movement led to many carefully designed educational, health, social, and economic interventions into communities that are economically at risk. The interventions were part of developmental methodologies in which experimental, correlational, and descriptive data were collected longitudinally to assess their outcomes. Head Start educational programs are one prominent example.

In more recent decades, with changes in family structure, developmental methodologies have been applied to questions about single parenting, day care, and "latch-key" children. With substance abuse, developmental methodologies have been applied to questions about prenatal development in wombs of addicted mothers, postnatal development of infants born drug-addicted, and developmental intervention for drug-related disabilities in many of these infants. With more adults living longer and healthier lives, developmental methodologies have been applied to questions about learning and memory, self-esteem, and life satisfaction among persons in late adulthood. Clearly, developmental methodologies will continue to be relevant as long as people are motivated to understand and nurture healthy life-span development and to intervene into social problems.

SOURCES FOR FURTHER STUDY

Miller, Scott A. *Developmental Research Methods.* 2d ed. Upper Saddle River, N.J.: Prentice Hall, 1997. A guidebook for psychology students, covering how to devise, carry out, and report on a research project. Provides an overview of developmental methodologies and advises on how to choose the appropriate method for the topic being investigated.

Mussen, Paul Henry, ed. *Handbook of Research Methods in Child Development.* New York: John Wiley & Sons, 1960. Commissioned by the Committee on Child Development of the National Academy of Sciences, this handbook continues to be a classic. Although dated in its applications, it provides conceptual and theoretical underpinnings for a variety of developmental methodologies. Includes many chapters written by quite eminent developmental psychologists.

Nielsen, Joyce McCarl, ed. *Feminist Research Methods: Exemplary Readings in the Social Sciences.* Boulder, Colo.: Westview Press, 1990. Challenges the traditional scientific method, including traditional developmental methodologies. Argues that Western cultural and masculine biases are pervasive in research assumptions and process, and provides alternative methodologies. Janet Shibley Hyde's critique of developmental research into cognitive sex differences is particularly relevant. Advanced reading level.

Sears, Robert R. "Your Ancients Revisited: A History of Child Development." In *Review of Child Development Research.* Vol. 5, edited by E. M. Hetherington. Chicago: University of Chicago Press, 1975. A well-respected developmental psychologist, himself a participant in a longitudinal study from childhood, reviews the founding of the field in a readable and interesting chapter. Places developmental research and methodologies in the context of changes in society's needs and priorities. Discusses influences from other fields of study including anthropology and psychoanalysis.

Sommer, Barbara B., and Robert Sommer. *A Practical Guide to Behavioral Research: Tools and Techniques.* 5th ed. New York: Oxford University Press, 2001. A jargon-free, understandable introduction to behavioral research. Further describes observational, self-report, and experimental research methods and descriptive, correlational, and experimental data analyses.

Triandis, H. C., and A. Heron, eds. *Basic Methods.* Vol. 4 in *Handbook of Cross-Cultural Psychology: Developmental Psychology.* Boston: Allyn & Bacon, 1981. Presents conceptual basis for cross-cultural developmental research and research methodologies. Clearly demonstrates the potential and limitations of adapting Western developmental methodologies to the study of non-Western peoples. Presents a variety of research areas including language, memory, Piagetian cognitive structures, and personality development.

Wolman, Benjamin B., ed. *Handbook of Developmental Psychology.* Englewood Cliffs, N.J.: Prentice-Hall,

1982. A comprehensive handbook, the first ten chapters of which focus on research methods and theories. Surveys a variety of developmental methodologies, and demonstrates the relationship between theoretical models and methodologies applied. Includes a chapter on ethics and regulation of research with children.

Michael D. Roe

SEE ALSO: Data description; Experimentation: Independent, dependent, and control variables; Scientific methods; Hypothesis development and testing; Observational methods.

Diagnosis

TYPE OF PSYCHOLOGY: All
FIELDS OF STUDY: All

Diagnosis is a process whereby an assessor evaluates symptoms and signs of illness or abnormality in order to be able to determine the type of problem present. This can be done using interviews, observation, and formal testing instruments or procedures.

KEY CONCEPTS
- assessment
- associated features
- course
- criteria
- differential diagnosis
- interviewing
- screening
- signs
- symptoms

INTRODUCTION

The word "diagnosis" is derived from two Greek roots: *dia*, which means "to distinguish," and *gnosis*, which means "knowledge." It is most often understood to be a noun, but from the perspective of a psychologist or a person assessing an afflicted individual, it is seen as a process whereby one understands the condition of the person affected. It is also important to remember that diagnosis is not a one-time event but is ongoing. For example, diagnoses may shift. Changes can be noted in terms of signs (the observable indications of mental health

problems) and symptoms (the problems reported by clients indicating their discomfort, notice of changes, or abnormality in their way of being). In some ways, diagnosis has no discrete end but consists of different observation points in time when the progress of a disorder is evaluated.

SCREENING

The goal of diagnosis is to arrive at information that can be communicated and used to aid in the treatment of the person with the mental and/or physical health problem. In the United States, mental health diagnoses are typically based on the framework presented in the American Psychiatric Association's *Diagnostic and Statistical Manual of Mental Disorders* (DSM), which is updated periodically. In order to be diagnosed with a particular mental disorder, individuals go through a systematic evaluation to determine whether they satisfy the diagnostic criteria, (the conditions necessary to qualify for a disorder), as described in the DSM.

Often, this process begins when individuals or their significant others notice symptoms and seek the consultation of a professional. At that time, the professional will begin a series of systematic inquiries, ruling possible conditions in and out of consideration, in order to determine how best to proceed with further diagnostic work. In some cases, a preliminary step called screening may be undertaken. Screening is a relatively brief procedure in which the signs and symptoms that have the highest association with specific mental health conditions are asked about in order to determine whether a more thorough evaluation is necessary.

Typically, screening results in a person being placed into one of two categories: possibly having the condition of concern or mostly likely not having the condition. Those individuals in the former category receive more thorough evaluations. Those who are judged as unlikely to have the condition do not receive more thorough evaluations immediately but instead may be invited to continue their own observations of symptoms and/or to begin another path of diagnostic inquiry.

For those performing the screening, the primary goal is to identify those individuals who may have the problem. It is also important, however, to not rule out individuals for further evaluation who might actually have the condition of concern but do not appear to do so during the screening. In technical terms, the first group is known as true positives: individuals who are screened as likely to have the condition and who actually have it. The second group is known as false negatives: individuals who are screened as not having the condition but actually do have it.

Screening tests increase in their usefulness if they are not overly sensitive and do not produce too many false positives: people who screen positive but who actually do not have the condition. It is important to minimize false positives because some diagnostic procedures, such as magnetic resonance imaging (MRI), are expensive. Additionally, some diagnostic procedures can be invasive, such as injection dye procedures used to observe different organ systems in action. Minimizing false positives in screening saves money for healthcare providers but, more important, also saves potential pain, suffering, and anxiety for individual clients.

Finally, screening also increases in usefulness when it can effectively identify true negatives: individuals who are screened as not having the problem and who in fact do not. The sooner these individuals are identified, the more quickly they can be referred onward to other professionals for evaluation or considered for other diagnostic possibilities.

ASSESSMENT

In general, screening is important because it is often brief and can be applied to a large number of people with little effort, saving expensive time on evaluation and yet efficiently identifying individuals who may be most likely to have a formal mental health condition. It is much less costly than the next step in a diagnostic workup after being screened as positive: the process of assessment, a lengthier process in which detailed information is gathered in a systematic way about the patient's probable condition. Assessment procedures may include formal diagnostic interviewing, in which the psychologist or clinician asks a step-by-step series of questions to get a clear picture of what the symptoms are and how they developed. Interviewing can be used to assess not only the individual affected but also family members or significant others, as sometimes these individuals have valuable information related to the history or development of the symptoms. These informants can also be helpful if the individual is not able or willing to speak or to describe the condition.

Assessment procedures may also include the use of paper-and-pencil questionnaires, surveys, or checklists about symptoms. They may include observation by the psychologist in interpersonal interactions or under certain other conditions. They may also include formal medical tests, such as blood tests, urine toxicology, and tests of psychomotor performance.

Overall, assessment procedures seek to reveal the course of the symptoms present, or how they have changed over time. Assessment also seeks to show how the most prominent symptoms relate to both one another and to less prominent symptoms. This is particularly important to a process called differential diagnosis, in which disorders that may appear alike in some features are diagnostically separated from one another in order to determine if one or more conditions are present.

If, in the process of assessment, it is found that the number, severity, and duration of the individual's symptoms and signs meet the diagnostic criteria, or standards of required evidence to warrant a diagnosis, then a diagnosis is rendered. If the signs and symptoms are all present but fall short of being present in the right number, severity, or duration, then the condition might be thought of as subclinical. This would mean that although the symptoms do not meet the formal criteria necessary to warrant a diagnosis, they are problematic and may still require some clinical observation and attention.

Finally, sometimes a client may have one disorder that is clearly present but also what might be called leftover symptoms that do not seem to fit. In some cases, these symptoms may be what are known as associated features, or symptoms associated with disorders but not part of the disorder in a formal diagnostic way. For example, many people who suffer from agoraphobia also experience symptoms of depression. In some cases, these individuals also qualify for a diagnosis of depression. In other cases, they are experiencing depressed mood more as a consequence of having agoraphobia, and the depression is an associated feature. Once these aspects of a diagnosis are understood, the information can be put to use.

IMPORTANCE

Diagnoses are important because of the information that they convey. They are important in facilitating effective communication among professionals, as well as for effective treatment planning. The diagnostic terminology of the DSM allows professionals to communicate clearly with one another about their clients' conditions. This communication helps to direct clients to the proper treatment and also ensures continuity of care when clients switch treatment providers. For example, a client who is traveling or is outside his or her regular locale may need assistance and seek out another healthcare provider. The new provider would be greatly aided in helping the client by communication with the regular provider about the individual and his or her condition. A proper assignment could then be reached to create a useful treatment strategy.

On another level, standard diagnoses are useful because they also allow for important communication between clinicians and researchers in psychology. This is most true when new symptoms are emerging and the need arises for developing new treatment strategies. When the mental health community uses the same language about signs and symptoms in the study of specific conditions, medical and psychological knowledge can advance much more efficiently.

More practically, diagnostic information is important to treatment because diagnostic information is needed to justify treatment financially. When a client meets formal diagnostic criteria for a disorder, the healthcare provider can administer services and justify the treatment to insurance agencies and others interested in the financial management of mental health problems. Diagnoses may also help such agencies to discover trends in which treatments work and where disorders tend to be developing (the focus of the field of epidemiology) or to recognize gaps in services, such as when people with certain disorders suddenly disappear from the mental healthcare system.

Even more important, however, standard diagnoses and thorough diagnostic procedures allow for good communication among professionals, their clients, and the families of those affected by mental illness. Communicating diagnostic information effectively to the client and family members or significant others is likely to help with the management of the problem. The better that all involved understand the symptoms and prognosis (expectations for the effects of the condition on future functioning), the more likely everyone is to assist with treat-

ment compliance. Further, it can be very helpful to families to learn that their loved ones have formal diagnoses. Mental health conditions can create chaos and misunderstanding, and improvements in relationships may occur if families and significant others are able to place problematic symptoms in perspective. Rather than attributing symptomatic behavior to personal irresponsibility or problems of character, family members and friends can see the symptoms as reflecting the illness. Although this understanding does not make everything perfect, it may help facilitate a more effective problem-solving strategy for the affected person and significant others.

CONTEXT

Diagnosis is a process most often associated with a visit to see a primary care physician, but primary care physicians are not the only ones who perform this work. Licensed and certified professionals of many types gather diagnostic information and render diagnoses. Psychiatrists and psychologists predominate in the area of mental health diagnoses, but social workers, educational counselors, substance abuse counselors, criminal justice workers, social service professionals, and those who work with the developmentally disabled also gather mental health diagnostic information and use it in their work.

Over time, the process of assessment has been separated from the actual diagnostic decision, so that assistants and helpers may be the ones gathering and organizing the symptom-related information in order to present it to the expert diagnostician who has the authority to render the diagnosis. This shift has occurred as a matter of financial necessity in many cases, as it is more expensive to use experts for time-intensive information gathering than it is to use such assistants. Increasing effort has also been focused on developing more accurate diagnostic screening and assessment instruments to the same end. If time can be saved on assessment by using screening, so that only very likely cases receive full symptom assessment, then valuable medical resources will be saved. Further, if paper-and-pencil or other diagnostic procedures can be used to better describe symptoms in a standardized manner, then even the time of diagnostic assistants can be saved.

On one hand, such advances may allow more people to be treated in an efficient manner. On the other hand, some complain that people can fall through the cracks and be missed on a screening, and consequently continue to suffer. This situation may be particularly likely for individuals who are not often included in the research upon which the screening instruments are designed, such as women and minorities. Similarly, others suggest that these processes put too much paper between the client and the healthcare provider, creating barriers and weakening therapeutic relationships.

In considering cultural practices and understandings of the doctor-patient relationship, this effect is even more important, as many cultural groups see the social nature of this relationship as a critical piece of the treatment interaction. While efficiency and saving money are important, it must be recognized that those goals are culturally bound and are choices that are being made. They are not the only way for the art and science of diagnosis to proceed.

It is also important for diagnosticians to recognize cultural differences in terms of the way in which symptoms are experienced, expressed, and understood. For some, mental health disorders may be seen as expressions of underlying spiritual problems; for others, they may be seen as disharmonies among elements in the universe or environment; and for others, they may be seen as extensions of physical problems. Each of these perspectives is a valid way of understanding such conditions, and it is only good training that includes attention to cultural variation in diagnostic procedures and practice that will allow diagnosticians to function effectively.

It should also be noted that culture is not limited to a client's racial background or ethnicity; it also varies by characteristics such as gender, age, sexual orientation, socioeconomic status, and locale. Increasingly, diagnosticians are being forced to grapple with such diversity so as to improve diagnostic procedures and client care. Such characteristics are important to diagnosis not only because of differences in perspectives on illness but also because of differences in the prevalence of illnesses in various groups. This distinction is particularly important when considering medical conditions that might be associated with psychological disorders. In some cases, medical problems may mimic psychiatric disorders; in other cases, they may mask, or cover up, such disorders. Because some disorders are more common in certain populations—such as among women, people of color, and elders—knowledge of such prevalence differences is important to the process of differential diagnosis.

Culture is also an important consideration in diagnosis because the information gathered is transmitted socially. Knowledge of diagnoses is exchanged among professionals, researchers, clients, and their families. Diagnoses have social meaning and can result in those carrying the diagnosis being stigmatized. As crucial differences exist in the degree of stigmatization in different cultures, the delivery of such important mental health information deserves thoughtful consideration, good planning, and follow-up to ensure that all parties involved are properly informed.

SOURCES FOR FURTHER STUDY

American Psychiatric Association. *Diagnostic and Statistical Manual of Mental Disorders: DSM-IV-TR.* Rev. 4th ed. Washington, D.C.: Author, 2000. The standard text outlining the major mental health disorders diagnosed in the United States.

Beutler, Larry E., and Mary L. Malik. *Rethinking the DSM: A Psychological Perspective.* Washington, D.C.: American Psychological Association, 2002. Offers some critiques of the dominant diagnostic framework used in the United States, the *Diagnostic and Statistical Manual of Mental Disorders* (DSM).

Castillo, Richard J. *Culture and Mental Illness: A Client-Centered Approach.* Belmont, Calif.: Wadsworth, 1997. Discusses how cultural issues fit into the diagnostic process and the understanding of mental health and illness.

Seligman, Linda. *Diagnosis and Treatment Planning in Counseling.* 2d ed. New York: Plenum, 1996. Connections between diagnosis and treatment planning are highlighted in this text, with case examples for illustration.

Shea, Shawn Christopher. *Psychiatric Interviewing: The Art of Understanding—A Practical Guide for Psychiatrists, Psychologists, Counselors, Social Workers, and Other Mental Health Professionals.* 2d ed. Philadelphia: W. B. Saunders, 1998. The skills of interviewing as a means of establishing a therapeutic relationship and the basis for forming diagnostic impressions are reviewed from a perspective that is useful for a variety of mental health practitioners. Also allows nonprofessionals to see how interviewing is structured and leads to diagnoses.

Simeonsson, Rune J., and Susan L. Rosenthal, eds. *Psychological and Developmental Assessment: Children* with Disabilities and Chronic Conditions. New York: Guilford, 2001. This text focuses on issues important to the diagnosis of mental health and other behavioral disorders in children.

Trzepacz, Paula T., and Robert W. Baker. *Psychiatric Mental Status Examination*. New York: Oxford University Press, 1993. The mental status examination is one of the foundations of any psychiatric diagnosis. This book describes these procedures for assessing the appearance, activity level, mood, speech, and other behavioral characteristics of individuals under evaluation.

Nancy A. Piotrowski

SEE ALSO: Assessment; Confidentiality; *Diagnostic and Statistical Manual of Mental Disorders* (DSM); *International Classification of Diseases* (ICD); Madness: Historical concepts; Mental health practitioners; Observational methods; Psychopathology; Sampling; Scientific methods; Survey research: Questionnaires and interviews.

Diagnostic and Statistical Manual of Mental Disorders (DSM)

DATE: Originated in 1952
TYPE OF PSYCHOLOGY: Psychopathology
FIELDS OF STUDY: All

The DSM is a book compiled by the American Psychiatric Association that describes all currently identified mental health problems that may receive a formal medical diagnosis in the United States.

KEY CONCEPTS
- axes
- category
- clinical significance
- continuum
- course
- criteria
- differential diagnosis
- prevalence
- specifiers
- subtypes
- v-code

INTRODUCTION

The *Diagnostic and Statistical Manual of Mental Disorders* (DSM) is the primary classification scheme used to describe mental disorders identified in psychiatric practice in the United States; it is revised periodically. The manual provides a standardized definition and a numerical code for each of the mental disorders described. These codes are currently designed so that the majority of the DSM is consistent with the *International Classification of Diseases* (ICD), which is published by the World Health Organization (WHO). Whereas the ICD is used internationally, the DSM is used primarily in the United States, representing an American perspective on the classification of mental illness.

The 2000 text revision of the DSM features descriptions of general classification areas of mental health problems. These areas include disorders usually first diagnosed in infancy, childhood, or adolescence; delirium, dementia, and amnestic and other cognitive disorders; mental disorders due to a general medical condition not elsewhere classified; substance-related disorders; schizophrenia and other psychotic disorders; mood disorders; anxiety disorders; somatoform disorders; factitious disorders; dissociative disorders; sexual and gender-identity disorders; eating disorders; sleep disorders; impulse control disorders not elsewhere classified; adjustment disorders; personality disorders; and other conditions that are the focus of clinical attention.

With the exception of the last general area, all other areas mentioned are known mental disorders that manifest themselves with identifiable behavioral, biological, cognitive, emotional, intrapersonal, social, or other features. The latter area, however, refers to problems that are not mental disorders but issues that, while considered normal problems of everyday life, may be addressed in treatment. For example, bereavement is covered under this area. It is not a mental disorder but a natural reaction to the death of a significant other that may require treatment in order to help comfort the affected person. Only if the bereavement extends over such a lengthy period of time that it becomes more problematic is an actual disorder diagnosed. These problems of everyday life are usually coded with a special designation typically called a v-code, so that they may be identified as a problem other than a formal mental disorder.

TYPES AND SYMPTOMS

Within all other areas of disorders mentioned, many types of disorders are listed. Each of these types is discrete, meaning that it is unique relative to the other disorders in that area. In this way, each disorder may be thought of as a category, or grouping, into which the symptoms of concern either fit or do not fit. While there may be a continuum, or range, of symptom severity within any category, the severity is less important in rendering a diagnosis than making sure that the type and number of necessary symptoms are present.

Each specific symptom helps to define each unique mental disorder. In some cases, the same symptom may be identified as part of several different disorders. For example, depressed mood is a symptom associated with several mood disorders. For a particular disorder to be identified, the symptoms must occur in particular groupings, particular numbers of groups, or with specific consequences. When such conditions are met, an individual's symptoms will be described as meeting the diagnostic criteria for a particular disorder. Diagnostic criteria are standard elements that must be included in a group of symptoms to allow for a judgment of its presence or absence. Some disorders are composed of multiple types of symptoms, such as behaviors, thoughts, and feelings. An individual might be required to have particular types of disrupted behaviors, thoughts, and feelings in order to qualify for a given disorder. If only disrupted behavior and feelings are present, but not thoughts, the diagnostic criteria would not be met.

Some disorders also have subtypes, or slight but unique variations that are individually identified, often because specific subtypes demand different treatment strategies. Subtypes may be defined by certain subsets of the overall list of symptoms making up the disorder. For example, schizophrenia has several specific subtypes that have slightly different features but are unique enough to warrant their own categorical identification. These subtypes include the paranoid, disorganized, catatonic, undifferentiated, and residual types. Other disorders are denoted as having additional slight variations through the means of diagnostic specifiers, or distinctions of variation with a particular type of disorder for one or more symptoms. An example would be bulimia nervosa, an eating disorder that has a purging and a nonpurging type identified by a specifier.

In general, each disorder demonstrates clinical significance, meaning that the disorder is causing distress or impairment judged to be important enough to warrant treatment in the eyes of the professional evaluator. Individual mental disorders are known to have specific sets of symptoms and a specific course, or pattern of development of the disorder over time. The course of a disorder provides a picture of how the symptoms might be expected to evolve. Each disorder also has a known prevalence, or incidence rate, and is formally distinguished from similar disorders through a process called differential diagnosis.

Finally, in the DSM system, disorders are typically noted in a specific format. This format is similar to an outline that has five major pieces. Each of the five pieces of the outline is called an axis and represents a particular type of information related to mental health disorder diagnosis. Individual axes are noted as Axis I, Axis II, Axis III, Axis IV, and Axis V, and they contain specific types of information. Axis I lists v-code conditions and most of the mental health disorders. Axis II lists personality disorders and mental retardation. Axis III lists general medical conditions. Axis IV lists psychosocial and environmental stressors. Axis V is where the evaluator gives a Global Assessment of Functioning (GAF), or overall rating of how impaired the individual is by the current set of symptoms, as well as a rating of how well the individual has functioned over the last year.

IMPORTANCE

It is important to have standard diagnostic definitions for two major reasons: effective communication and treatment planning. The diagnostic terminology of the DSM allows professionals to communicate clearly with one another about their clients' symptoms. It also allows clinicians and researchers to communicate in their efforts to develop new interventions or to investigate emerging symptoms. Similarly, the DSM nomenclature allows professionals to communicate with insurance agencies and others interested in the financial management of mental health problems. Standard diagnoses also allow for good communication among professionals, their clients, and the families of those afflicted. More generally, standard diagnoses facilitate the matching of problems to treatments. This process is similar in other areas of medicine. For example, stomach pain is a common symptom, but depending on the other symptoms present at the same time, it might be treated with either chicken soup (for indigestion or overnight flu) or surgery (for appendicitis). The difference depends on the diagnosis.

HISTORY

As long as there has been healthcare, there has been a need for some sort of classification system to describe different mental health conditions. The first attempt to describe mental health problems in the United States occurred in the 1840 census, when officials tried to track the presence or absence of problems characterized by mental deficiency, such as insanity or idiocy. Forty years later in another census, seven categories of problems were included. In the ensuing seventy years, as mental hospitals increased in number and psychiatric conditions related to war garnered attention, the beginnings of the DSM took shape.

The DSM has evolved in the years since its original edition, published in 1952. It was followed by a second edition, DSM-II, in 1968; a third edition, DSM-III, in 1980; a revised third edition, DSM-III-R, in 1987; a fourth edition, DSM-IV, in 1994; and a text revision, DSM-IV-TR, in 2000. The manual is an evolving document because knowledge about psychiatric disorders grows daily. Between the original version of the DSM and DSM-II, for example, recognition increased concerning the need for explicit definitions of the conditions described so as to promote diagnostic reliability. Between DSM-II and DSM-III, an effort was made to coordinate the DSM with the ICD system. With DSM-III-R, changes were made to incorporate findings from statistical research. Similarly, DSM-IV updated the manual with an even greater emphasis on statistical data, clinical usefulness, and test characteristics such as reliability and validity. With DSM-IV-TR, changes were made to bring the manual into even better alignment with the ICD, as well as to allow for updated information regarding prevalence and biological data relevant for diagnosis.

CONTEXT

The DSM is evolving to incorporate culture and the diversity of presentations of mental health disorders. Because ways of expressing and understanding symptoms have definite cultural traditions, over time there has been increasing integration of the DSM with the ICD system and increasing attention to the impact of culture on diagnosis. An example is the addition of an appendix that presents an outline of how to think about cases, taking culture into account, as well as a glossary describing culture-bound syndromes (syndromes specific to cultural groups), taking into consideration a culture's understanding of the world, symptoms (how and why they are expressed), and expectations concerning treatment.

A trend in both the clinical and research literatures suggests increased recognition of diversity within some disorders currently identified. For example, with bipolar disorder, it appears that the pattern and intensity of periods of mania and depression may be important in terms of treatment management. With alcohol dependence, the presence or absence of physiological dependence is relevant to the odds of preventing the client's return to substance use. In such cases, consideration is being given to developing finer diagnoses that are more complex, to allow for more precise diagnoses and, consequently, more accurate and effective treatment management. Such advances in diagnostic precision will ultimately benefit those seeking treatment and facilitate the advancement of knowledge.

SOURCES FOR FURTHER STUDY

American Psychiatric Association. *Diagnostic and Statistical Manual of Mental Disorders: DSM-IV-TR.* Rev. 4th ed. Washington, D.C.: Author, 2000. The manual used by professionals to diagnose all recognized mental disorders in the United States.

Helzer, J. E., and J. J. Hudziak. *Defining Psychopathology in the Twenty-first Century: DSM-V and Beyond.* Washington, D.C.: American Psychiatric Association, 2002. This book critiques the DSM-IV-TR and outlines the probable directions for growth and advancement in the next version.

Maj, Mario, Wolfgang Gaebel, Juan José Lopez-Ibor, and Norman Sartorius, eds. *Psychiatric Diagnosis and Classification.* New York: John Wiley & Sons, 2002. This book critiques the DSM and ICD approaches to diagnosis. It also attempts to place diagnosis in a context so that it is understood as consisting of more than medical terms and as more of a process than a conclusion.

Spitzer, Robert L., Miriam Gibbon, Andrew E. Skodol, Janet B. W. Williams, and Michael B.

First, eds. *DSM-IV-TR Casebook: A Learning Companion to the "Diagnostic and Statistical Manual of Mental Disorders, Fourth Edition, Text Revision."* Washington, D.C.: American Psychiatric Association, 2002. This book gives examples of disorders and their presentation in real life. Designed to help professionals with differential diagnosis.

World Health Organization. *The ICD-10 Classification of Mental and Behavioral Diseases: Clinical Descriptions and Diagnostic Guidelines.* Albany, N.Y.: Author, 1992. This book presents the tenth revision of the *International Statistical Classification of Diseases and Related Health Problems* (ICD-10), focusing on mental and behavioral diseases. It represents the best international thinking on how psychiatric disorders can be conceptualized and is a companion to the DSM-IV-TR.

Nancy A. Piotrowski

SEE ALSO: Assessment; Diagnosis; *International Classification of Diseases* (ICD); Mental health practitioners; Psychopathology.

Disaster psychology

TYPE OF PSYCHOLOGY: Emotion; sensation and perception; social psychology; stress
FIELDS OF STUDY: Anxiety disorders; attitudes and behavior; coping; depression; interpersonal relations; problem solving; social perception and cognition; stress and illness

Disaster psychology examines how emotional trauma can be assessed and treated during emergencies and investigates disaster-related conditions such as post-traumatic stress disorder.

KEY CONCEPTS
- catastrophes
- emergency
- mass casualties
- relief workers
- shock
- survivors
- trauma
- unpredictability
- victims
- witnesses

INTRODUCTION

Disaster psychology responds to unpredictable events by aiding victims and witnesses of natural and artificial catastrophes, such as earthquakes, tornadoes, hurricanes, airplane crashes, toxic spills, industrial accidents, fires, explosions, terrorism, and school shootings, which often involve mass casualties. The American Red Cross (ARC) estimates that 350 to 400 national disasters requiring external emergency aid occur annually in the United States.

Mental health professionals use their skills to help trauma survivors and relief workers cope with the drastic changes and shock associated with tragedies. Many mental health professionals consider disaster service a social responsibility. Even though people may not have obvious physical wounds, they usually suffer emotional pain. Disaster mental health personnel often serve as media contacts to educate the public about ways to resume normalcy.

Short-term crisis mental health services assess the psychological status of affected populations, provide grief counseling, and initiate individual and community recovery. They provide emotional support when relatives identify bodies at morgues. Volunteers help victims who temporarily suffer survivor guilt, anxiety, mood swings, sleeping disturbances, social withdrawal, and depression by reassuring them that they are reacting normally to abnormal, unexpected, and overwhelming situations which have disrupted their lives and that heightened emotions will eventually lessen.

Long-term disaster psychology recognizes how catastrophes can result in some participants having post-traumatic stress disorder and other delayed or chronic reactions such as nightmares and flashbacks, which are sometimes triggered by disaster anniversaries or sirens. Therapists also deal with disaster-related conditions such as substance abuse, irrational fears, and self-mutilation.

In addition to providing practical services, some disaster psychologists conduct research to develop more effective methods to help people during disasters. Procedures are developed to be compatible with varying coping styles for adults and children. Disaster psychologists often conduct workshops and conferences to teach techniques based on prior experiences to mental health relief workers, health professionals, and community leaders. Preparation and planning for future disasters are important components of disaster psychology. Disaster mental health providers educate representatives of schools, municipalities, humanitarian organizations, and corporations about disaster readiness.

Disaster mental health professionals create educational materials to inform people about how to cope with disasters. Most disaster psychology literature addresses how disasters make people feel vulnerable and helpless and suggest practicing psychological skills to acquire some control during volatile situations. For example, after the September 11, 2001, terrorist attacks on the United States, many disaster psychological pamphlets emphasized how to keep in perspective the actual personal risks of unknown threats such as anthrax contamination and biological warfare.

HISTORICAL DEVELOPMENT

Mental health professionals developed disaster psychology methods based on medical triage techniques and practical experiences with disasters. Several notable disasters were crucial to establishing disaster mental health services. In 1942, 491 people died in Boston's Cocoanut Grove nightclub fire. Erich Lindemann investigated how survivors reacted emotionally. Disaster mental health authorities often cite Lindemann's trauma and stress study as the fundamental work addressing disaster crisis theory. Pioneers in this emerging field utilized studies of military and civilian reaction to war-related stress and anxiety.

A 1972 dam collapse resulted in the flooding of Buffalo Creek in West Virginia, causing 125 deaths. Approximately five thousand people became homeless. When survivors sued the dam's owner, attorneys hired mental health consultants, who collected information about the psychological impact of this disaster on the community. That information was evaluated twenty years later, when investigators conducted a follow-up psychological study of survivors. The 1974 Disaster Relief Act stated that Federal Emergency Management Agency (FEMA) emergency funds could be used for mental health services. The 1979 Three Mile Island nuclear meltdown revealed the need for mental health disaster services to be better coordinated and focused.

One decade later, the ARC emphasized that coordinated professional mental health response procedures comparable to medical health response plans were crucial. Often, ARC nurses who were not qualified to provide psychological services encountered

disaster victims and relief workers in need of such help. The situation was exacerbated by the succession of major disasters in 1989: the Sioux City, Iowa, airplane crash in July; Hurricane Hugo in the Caribbean and southeastern United States in September; and the Loma Prieta earthquake in the San Francisco Bay area in October.

Psychologists who assisted airplane crash survivors and victims' families suggested that the American Psychological Association (APA) work with the ARC to establish a national plan for the training of disaster mental health personnel. Mental health teams were assigned to accompany ARC relief workers when Hurricane Hugo occurred. These volunteers were already exhausted when the San Francisco earthquake occurred, yet instead of returning home, relief personnel were asked to transfer to San Francisco. Unfamiliarity with inner city and ethnic cultures, language barriers, and long-duration service assignments intensified relief workers' stress. The need for mental health services for relief workers became apparent.

PROFESSIONAL ORGANIZATION

Although mental health professionals provided disaster services throughout the twentieth century, disaster psychology emerged as a professional field during the 1990's. In 1990, the APA financed a California Psychological Association disaster response course. The ARC assisted with the class. Tornadoes in Illinois in the spring of 1991 prompted the Illinois Psychological Association to respond to the ARC's request for mental health services. The first community request for disaster mental health services occurred after a tornado devastated Sherwood, North Dakota, in September, 1991. Citizens sought help for their children in coping with the damage and casualties.

The ARC established the Disaster Mental Health Services (DMHS) by November, 1991, and issued guidelines for training, certification, and service. Psychologists attending ARC disaster training began offering courses in their regions. The APA agreed to collaborate with the ARC the next month. Representatives of the APA and ARC decided that the APA's Disaster Response Network (DRN) would prepare psychologist volunteers to offer free mental health services to survivors and relief workers at disaster scenes. After Hurricane Andrew hit Florida in 1992, approximately two hundred DRN psychologists helped survivors with the ARC. The APA has es-

DSM-IV-TR Criteria for Acute Stress Disorder (DSM code 308.3)

Exposure to a traumatic event in which both of the following were present:
- experiencing, witnessing, or confronting an event or events involving actual or threatened death or serious injury, or a threat to the physical integrity of self or others
- response involving intense fear, helplessness, or horror

Either while experiencing or after experiencing the distressing event, three or more of the following dissociative symptoms appear:
- subjective sense of numbing, detachment, or absence of emotional responsiveness
- reduction in awareness of surroundings
- derealization
- depersonalization
- dissociative amnesia

Traumatic event persistently reexperienced in at least one of the following ways:
- recurrent images
- thoughts
- dreams
- illusions
- flashback episodes

- sense of reliving the experience
- distress on exposure to reminders of traumatic event

Marked avoidance of stimuli arousing recollections of trauma (thoughts, feelings, conversations, activities, places, people)

Marked symptoms of anxiety or increased arousal (difficulty sleeping, irritability, poor concentration, hypervigilance, exaggerated startle response, motor restlessness)

Disturbance causes clinically significant distress or impairment in social, occupational, or other important areas of functioning or impairs ability to pursue necessary tasks (such as obtaining necessary assistance or mobilizing personal resources by telling family members about experience)

Disturbance lasts a minimum of two days and a maximum of four weeks and occurs within four weeks of traumatic event

Disturbance is not due to direct physiological effects of a substance or general medical condition

Not better accounted for by Brief Psychotic Disorder, and not merely an exacerbation of a preexisting Axis I or Axis II disorder

---

tablished task forces to evaluate mental health response to various catastrophes.

The American Psychiatric Association sponsors a Committee on Psychiatric Dimensions of Disaster (CPDD), formed in 1993 after three years of development as a task force. Members of this committee create educational information to help psychiatrists provide disaster-related services. The committee seeks to advance the field of disaster psychiatry through training and research to determine scientific methods to provide optimum psychiatric treatment for disaster victims. Members distribute materials to district branches to aid local response to potential disaster situations. In addition to publishing brochures and creating audiotapes and videotapes, the American Psychiatric Association also posts information addressing disaster topics for the public on its Web site (http://www.psych.org).

The American Psychiatric Association's emergency services and disaster relief branch cooperates with other mental health groups and emergency services to prepare professionals to respond appro-

priately and effectively to psychological aspects of disasters. Multiorganization conferences in 1995 and 1996 clarified mental health professionals' roles during disasters and approved American Psychiatric Association goals. The American Psychiatric Foundation established a fellowship to pay branch members' tuition at the introductory disaster psychiatry course presented at the annual American Psychiatric Association meeting. Psychiatrists often feel limited by the ARC prohibition of psychiatrists prescribing medications while acting as ARC volunteers. Some mental health professionals formed local groups to intervene during disaster relief. Disaster Psychiatry Outreach (DPO; http://www.disasterpsych.org/) was established after the 1998 Swissair Flight 111 crash as an effort to provide better disaster mental health services in the New York City vicinity. Most DPO volunteers are qualified to prescribe medications for survivors and their families. Ethical and legal concerns specific to disaster mental health services provided by any source include abandonment of victims and soliciting patients.

DISASTER PROCEDURES

At a disaster scene, mental health professionals aid medical emergency workers to identify people who are behaving irrationally. Disaster psychologists help people deal with losses of family members and homes or with injuries. Specific emotional issues might include disfigurement, loss of body parts, and exposure to grotesque scenes. Psychologists soothe disaster victims undergoing sudden surgical processes.

Most disaster survivors and relief workers are resilient to permanent emotional damage. Volunteers advise people who seem likely to suffer psychiatric disorders due to the disaster to seek professional treatment. People in denial who ignore disaster-induced psychological damage can develop disorders such as post-traumatic stress disorder (PTSD), which can have a detrimental effect on social and professional interactions. The fourth edition of the American Psychiatric Association's *Diagnostic and Statistical Manual of Mental Disorders* (1994, DSM-IV) was the first to classify acute stress disorder (ASD), which has symptoms resembling PTSD but lasts only a few days to several weeks within one month of trauma. ASD is distinguished from PTSD by the presence of dissociative symptoms beginning either during the disaster or soon after.

Disaster mental health professionals introduce new methods such as critical incident stress management (CISM) and critical incident stress debriefing (CISD) based on experiences and research. CISM was created to help emergency personnel who undergo stages of demobilization, defusing, debriefing, and education. Debriefing helps people voice their experiences and often provides group support from colleagues. Relief workers immersed in such stressful situations as recovering bodies often seek counseling. Twenty percent of the 1995 Oklahoma City bombing emergency workers received psychological attention. After the September 11, 2001, terrorist attacks, counselors reported that approximately two thousand emergency workers sought their services.

Research topics include evaluation of how PTSD is related to disasters or how heroes react to public attention, disaster-stimulated life changes such as marriage or divorce, stress reactions of secondary victims who are not directly affected by disasters, and variables such as gender, religious affiliation, and ethnicity. Children, adolescents, and elderly victims have unique needs during and after disasters. Other possible research groups include the homeless, the handicapped, and those medically or mentally ill at the time of the disaster. Researchers utilize computer and technological advances to enhance studies of data and model disaster scenarios.

Internationally, academic programs, symposiums, and conferences explore disaster-related metal health topics. The University of South Dakota's Disaster Mental Health Institute (http://www.usd.edu/dmhi/) offers a comprehensive curricula of undergraduate and graduate disaster psychology courses to train ARC-approved disaster mental health personnel.

SOURCES FOR FURTHER STUDY

Austin, Linda S., ed. *Responding to Disaster: A Guide for Mental Health Professionals.* Washington, D.C.: American Psychiatric Press, 1992. This collection, edited by a psychiatrist who has served during disasters, includes essays addressing fundamental concerns such as community reaction to tragedies and disaster planning, in addition to case studies of disaster mental health interventions.

Everly, George S., Jr., and Jeffrey T. Mitchell. *Critical Incident Stress Management (CISM): A New Era and Standard of Care in Crisis Intervention.* 2d ed. Ellicot City, Md.: Chevron, 1999. This volume explains how to help emergency workers avoid emotional problems and burnout because of disaster stresses and supplements the authors' other guides discussing relief workers' mental health.

Fullerton Carol S., and Robert J. Ursano, eds. *Posttraumatic Stress Disorder: Acute and Long-Term Responses to Trauma and Disaster.* Washington, D.C.: American Psychiatric Press, 1997. Applying their psychological expertise about military personnel to disaster scenarios, the authors investigate how survivors' reactions to devastating situations can influence different aspects of their lives.

Gist, Richard, and Bernard Lubin, eds. *Response to Disaster: Psychosocial, Community, and Ecological Approaches.* Philadelphia: Brunner/Mazel, 1999. Designed for disaster relief personnel, the writers in this collection provide technical explanations of trauma theories, analyze how disasters affect various demographic groups, and criticize some applications of disaster treatments.

Jacobs, Gerard A. "The Development of a National Plan for Disaster Mental Health." *Professional Psychology: Research and Practice* 26, no. 6 (1995): 543-549. Discusses disasters that motivated mental health and relief organizations to create an effective network of disaster mental health professionals to plan, serve, research, and educate for emergencies.

Norwood, Ann E., Robert J. Ursano, and Carol S. Fullerton. "Disaster Psychiatry: Principles and Practice." *Psychiatric Quarterly* 71, no. 3 (2000): 207-226. Experts in the field who have both practical and theoretical disaster experiences outline basic procedures for disaster mental health services to help both individuals and communities prepare, cope, and recover.

Raphael, Beverley, and John P. Wilson, eds. *Psychological Debriefing: Theory, Practice, and Evidence.* New York: Cambridge University Press, 2000. The editors address the controversy of whether debriefing trauma victims reduces the occurrence of PTSD. Presenting both pro and con arguments, this anthology guides mental health professionals to understand that debriefing is a complex process which varies according to patients' needs and can be detrimental in some cases.

Ursano, Robert J., Brian G. McCaughey, and Carol S. Fullerton, eds. *Individual and Community Responses to Trauma and Disaster: The Structure of Human Chaos.* New York: Cambridge University Press, 1994. Lead editor Ursano was the first American Psychiatric Association CPDD chairman. Essays focus on both standard psychological concerns as PTSD and specialized topics such as the impact of disasters on relief workers' spouses.

Elizabeth D. Schafer

SEE ALSO: American Psychiatric Association; American Psychological Association; Anxiety disorders; Clinical interviewing, testing, and observation; Community psychology; Coping: Social support; Cultural competence; Death and dying; Depression; Emotions; General adaptation syndrome; Health psychology; Internet psychology; Media psychology; Mental health practitioners; Post-traumatic stress disorder; Psychology: Fields of study; Stress; Stress: Behavioral and psychological responses; Stress: Physiological responses; Stress-related diseases; Support groups.

Dix, Dorothea

BORN: April 4, 1802, in Hampden, Maine
DIED: July 17, 1887, in Trenton, New Jersey

IDENTITY: American social reformer
TYPE OF PSYCHOLOGY: Emotion; motivation
FIELDS OF STUDY: Attitudes and behavior, prejudice and discrimination

Dix was a pioneer in the reform of conditions for housing and treating the mentally ill.

Dorothea (originally Dorothy) Lynde Dix was born in a small village on the Massachusetts frontier, then part of Maine. Alienated from her family, she ran away to her grandmother in Boston at age twelve and, by fourteen, had opened the first of several schools. Influenced by her father's Methodist evangelicalism and a growing circle of Boston Unitarians, she hoped to influence the young through moral education, teaching, and providing an example of rigorous self-control (especially repression of emotion), self-sacrifice, and social activism. She published her first educational book, *Conversations on Common Things*, in 1824.

In 1841, she viewed for the first time the treatment of the mentally ill, often chained in poorhouses and jails with inadequate food, clothing, and sanitation. She then made her life's work the establishment of institutions where her principles of moral education could be used to reintroduce the mentally ill to society. Beginning in Massachusetts, she toured facilities throughout eastern, midwestern, and southern states and wrote "memorials" to legislators. She became the most successful political lobbyist of her time. Her proposal to grant millions of acres of public land to states for the establishment of mental institutions was passed by Congress in 1854 but vetoed by President Franklin Pierce. Her activities led to the funding of thirty-two mental hospitals as well as other institutions, and, during her travels abroad between 1854 and 1856, she played a major role in changing European attitudes. She published *Remarks on Prisons and Prison Discipline in the United States* in 1845; her other publications included "memorials" on prisons and the mentally ill, collections of hymns and moral tales for children, and meditations.

Her fame led to her appointment as Superintendent of Union Army Nurses at the outbreak of the Civil War; her strict standards and independence created enemies among nurses and government officials, and her authority was undermined. After the war, despite failing health, she attempted to continue her activities. She eventually settled in a private suite in the state hospital in Trenton, New Jersey, the first hospital built through her efforts. She died there in 1887.

SOURCES FOR FURTHER STUDY

Brown, Thomas J. *Dorothea Dix: New England Reformer.* Cambridge, Mass.: Harvard University Press, 1998. Brown examines legends of family abuse and alcoholism in Dix biographies, explores Dix's life in terms of her dual roles as conservative Victorian lady and social activist, and presents a detailed account of her activities as Congressional lobbyist and international reformer.

Gollaher, David. *Voice for the Mad: The Life of Dorothea Dix.* New York: Free Press, 1995. General biography with a detailed account of Dix's activities in individual states.

Herstek, Amy Paulson. *Dorothea Dix: Crusader for the Mentally Ill.* Berkeley Heights, N.J.: Enslow, 2001. Simply written general biography in the Historical American Biographies series; contains a chronology of major events in Dix's life and a brief bibliography.

Betty Richardson

SEE ALSO: Educational psychology; Madness: Historical concepts; Moral development.

Domestic violence

TYPE OF PSYCHOLOGY: Psychopathology
FIELDS OF STUDY: Adulthood; aggression

Domestic violence refers to all forms of abuse which occur within families, including child abuse, elder abuse, and spouse abuse. The term came into common usage in the 1970's to emphasize wife abuse. Domestic violence (wife abuse) is explained by several psychologically based theories which in turn propose different solutions.

KEY CONCEPTS
- battered woman syndrome
- cycle of violence
- domestic violence
- family systems theory
- feminist psychological theory
- learning theory
- post-traumatic stress disorder
- psychoanalytic theory
- systems theory
- wife abuse

INTRODUCTION

Domestic violence is difficult to measure since there are no agreed-upon standards as to what it is. In addition, most domestic violence occurs in private, and victims are reluctant to report it because of shame and fear of reprisal. Its scope is also difficult to determine, and society's reluctance to acknowledge it results in only estimates of the number of rapes, robberies, and assaults committed by family members and other relatives, such as spouses, former spouses, children, parents, boyfriends, and girlfriends.

In the 1970's, publicity about domestic violence, and more specifically wife abuse, made the public aware that many women did not live in peace and security in their own homes. Through the usage of the terms "abuse," "woman abuse," "battering," "partner abuse," "spouse abuse," "intimate violence," "family violence" and "relationship violence," feminists made the public aware of the problem. As a result of the publicity, women were identified as the most likely victims of domestic violence.

The selection of a name for the behavior will have implications for treatment choices. In addition, the term "domestic violence" removes the issue from a societal perspective, which condones, reinforces, and perpetuates the problem. Domestic violence minimizes the role of gender and places the relationship in the dominant spot. As a result, the choice of a name offers varying perspectives, which differentially view the persons involved, the nature of the problem, and possible solutions.

Abused women in a domestic violence situation are confronted with several types of abuse, namely economic abuse, physical abuse, psychological/emotional abuse, and sexual abuse. Economic abuse results when the financial resources to which a woman is legally entitled are not accessible to her. Examples of economic abuse include being prevented from seeking employment even if qualified to do so, as well as being denied access to needed education, which would aid the woman in securing better employment.

Physical abuse is the major way that men control the behavior of women. Abused women have likened psychological or emotional abuse to brain-washing. Little research has been done on this type of abuse because it is difficult to record. The abused woman is terrorized, isolated, and undermined by her abuser. Psychological or emotional abuse allows men to avoid the legal effects of physical abuse, since they can frighten women without touching them. Five common emotional abuse methods include isolation, humiliation and degradation, "crazy-making" behavior, threats to harm the woman and those she loves, and suicidal and homicidal threats.

Sexual violence was reported by 33 percent to 59 percent of the battered women in a study by Angela Browne published in 1987. Since 1992, it has been legal in all fifty states for a woman to charge her husband with rape. Historically, rape was thought of as intercourse forced on someone other than the wife of the accused. As a result, a woman could not legally accuse her husband of rape.

POSSIBLE CAUSES

Four theories, each of which has a psychological basis, attempt to explain wife abuse. Each of the theories has a unique perspective regarding the causes of wife abuse. The four theories are family systems theory, feminist psychological theory, learning theory, and psychoanalytic theory.

The first theory, family systems theory, includes the application of systems theory to all current family therapy approaches. Systems theory stresses mutual influences and reciprocal relationships between the individual members and the whole, as well as vice versa. In family systems theory, abuse is seen as a feature of the relationship between the abused wife and her husband. Underlying the abusive behavior, both the abused wife and her husband have a frail sense of self. When they marry or establish a relationship, a battering routine or system unfolds. Several factors lead the man to have a drive for power and control over the woman. These factors include social conditions, the need for control, intimacy fears, and lack of awareness of his own conflicts regarding dependency. The abused woman, in turn, has a limited range of coping behaviors, dependency conflicts, a history of childhood family violence, and other psychosocial traits which are similar to those of the man. Change is prevented from occurring and the dysfunctional interpersonal behavior patterns continue as a result of the unwritten expectations that control these behaviors. Change is blocked by the use of violent behavior.

The second theory, feminist psychological theory, is based on the work of American feminist psychologist Lenore Walker. She believes that the behaviors of abused women are coping behaviors developed as a result of living in a brutal environment.

Walker first theorized the concept of learned helplessness as used in relation to abused women. The abused woman can do nothing to stop the violence. The woman's chief concern is survival. However, survival comes with consequences. Several of the consequences include passively giving in to her abuser, becoming an observer of her own abuse through the process of disassociation, and waiting for days to seek medical care because she may distort the reality of the abuse. In addition, women's helplessness is reinforced by society in two ways. First, women learn to respond passively to abuse through gender-role socialization. Second, women's ability to control their lives is thwarted through the interrelated effects of sexism, discrimination, and poverty.

Walker has described a cycle of violence that unfolds in the individual relationship. The woman yields to the batterer's demands in the first stage in order to keep small episodes from increasing. However, over time these small episodes increase and accumulate. The woman also begins to withdraw from family and friends because she does not want them to know what is going on as the family tension increases. As time passes, the woman withdraws from the batterer as well, because she realizes that her efforts to prevent further development of the violence are futile. The batterer, in turn, becomes more and more angry because he fears that he is losing control of his wife. He then explodes, in the second stage. The third stage quickly follows; the batterer is characterized as being placid and there is a pause in the abusive behaviors. The man promises the woman that he will change, brings her gifts, and is extremely regretful. He changes back into the man she originally loved and is at his most defenseless state.

In order to explain the behaviors of women who have been frequently abused, Walker developed the theory of the battered woman syndrome, which she sees as a variant of post-traumatic stress disorder (PTSD). The key behaviors of anxiety, cognitive distortion, and depression can on one hand help a woman to survive her abuse. On the other hand, they can interfere with her ability to change her life situation by using appropriate methods.

The third theory is learning theory, incorporating both social learning theory and cognitive behavioral therapy. Social learning theorists stress the occurrence of modeling and the reinforcements received for abusive behavior. Cognitive behavioral theorists stress the internalization of beliefs that support abusive behavior. Boys may internalize the belief that they should be in charge by learning abusive behaviors from male role models, ranging from their fathers to media stars. Girls internalize the belief that they are helpless and weak, by learning passively from their role models. Later adult behaviors are hindered by the earlier learned behaviors and internalized messages.

The fourth theory, psychoanalytic theory, focuses on intrapersonal pathology. Abused women and abusing men feel that early life experiences shape

Mehola Shah, a counselor at the Asian Women's Center in New York City, listens to a woman who has been a victim of domestic abuse. (AP/Wide World Photos)

the particular pathological personality. The battered woman develops beliefs and behaviors that are dysfunctional in adulthood, although they are based in childhood experiences with cruel persons. The women do not resist the abuse. They submit to the abuse because they fear offending the stronger male and also because they think of themselves as deserving abuse. The women choose abusive men and may even touch off the abusive behavior, because of their strong feelings of worthlessness. Passive-aggressive, psychopathic, obsessive-compulsive, paranoid, and sadistic are some of the labels given to violent men who have experienced severe and traumatic childhood abuse episodes themselves. Men learn that violence gets them what they want and also allows them to feel good about themselves, in spite of their childhood experiences of abuse both as victims and as observers.

DIAGNOSING DOMESTIC VIOLENCE

Six factors have been identified as increasing a woman's chances of being in an abusive relationship: age, alcohol use, childhood experience with violence, race, relationship status, and socioeconomic factors.

A person's risk of being abused or being an abuser increases among adolescents. Research has discovered high levels of abuse among dating couples. However, the rate of violence among dating couples falls below that of couples who are married or cohabitating if controlled for age.

Clinical samples in which women are asked to describe their husbands' drinking patterns have provided the basis for the opinion that men beat their wives when they are drunk. Researchers have found that from 35 to 93 percent of abusers are problem drinkers. Better controlled studies have found that in only 25 percent of the cases was either partner drinking at the time of the abuse.

Individuals are more likely to be an abused woman or an abusive man if they were abused as a child. It is less clear that a relationship exists between witnessing wife abuse as a child and experiencing it as an adult. Researchers have found that men are more likely to become adult abusers if they observed domestic violence as boys. The data are inconclusive regarding a woman's chance of being abused if she observes domestic violence as a child. Men who observed domestic violence between their parents are three times more likely to abuse their wives. Sons of the most violent parents have a rate of wife abuse 1,000 percent greater than sons of nonviolent parents.

African American and Latino families have above-average rates of wife abuse. Abuse rates for African Americans are four times the rate of white Americans and twice the rate of other minorities. There are twice as many Latina women abused as non-Latina white women. Socioeconomic factors can explain these differences. According to data from a 1980 survey, African Americans earning $6,000 to $11,999 annually (approximately 40 percent of all African American respondents) had higher rates of wife abuse than comparably earning white Americans, while they had lower rates than white Americans in all other socioeconomic levels. When age, economic deprivation, and urban residence are controlled, then the differences between Latina and non-Latina white Americans vanish.

Legally married couples have half the amount of violence as cohabiting couples. It is felt that cohabiting couples may allow conflict to escalate because they are less invested in the relationship, more likely to struggle over autonomy and control issues, and more isolated from their social networks.

Domestic violence is more common in families with fewer economic resources, though it is found in all socioeconomic levels. Higher rates of wife abuse have been found in families where the man works in a blue-collar job or is unemployed or underemployed and the family lives at the poverty level.

THE ABUSED POPULATION

Male partners severely assault over 1.5 million married and cohabiting women each year. Of women treated in hospital emergency rooms, 22 percent to 35 percent are there because of symptoms related to abuse. Approximately 20 percent to 25 percent of all women are abused at least once by a male partner. Victims of boyfriends tend to be young (sixteen to twenty-four years old), while victims of current or former spouses are likely to be older (twenty to thirty-four years old). Women in families with incomes over $50,000 are four times less likely to be abused than are women in families with annual incomes of less than $20,000.

TREATMENT OPTIONS

The four theories of domestic abuse also provide several treatment options for the psychologist.

Family systems theory prescribes marital counseling to bring about change in the marital system and to identify dysfunctional patterns. Partners are each responsible for changing the way they relate to each other and for the specific behaviors that contribute to the violence.

Walker describes three levels of intervention in terms of feminist psychological theory. Primary prevention changes the social conditions that directly and indirectly contribute to the abuse of women. Examples would include eliminating rigid gender-role socialization and reducing levels of violence in society. Secondary intervention encourages women to take control of their lives and to break the cycle of violence. Examples include crisis hot lines as well as financial and legal assistance. A shelter where the women will slowly regain their ability to make decisions for themselves and where they will be safe is an example of tertiary intervention. At this level, women have been totally victimized and are unable to act on their own.

Learning theory stresses that the partners be given opportunities to learn and be rewarded for a new range of actions and underlying beliefs. It is felt that intervention should teach the partners how they have learned and been rewarded for their present behaviors. As a result, the intervention moves beyond a pathological framework. Other approaches, mainly from a cognitive-behavioral perspective, strive to change dysfunctional thoughts, teach new behaviors, and eliminate the abuse. This approach works with couples and with abusive men in a group.

Psychoanalytic theory stresses long-term, corrective, individual psychotherapy. The end result of the therapy would be to help the abused woman to break the cycle of violence. She would learn to avoid choosing men who re-create her familiar and unhappy childhood by their violent behavior.

HISTORY OF TREATMENT

Domination of women by men has a long history. Early Roman law gave men absolute power over their wives. However, it is not clear if they had the power to put their wives to death. Physical force was their chief means of control. As the Roman Empire declined, men's right to control women continued to be supported by church doctrine.

The "rule of thumb" was born in English common law, which stated that men had the right to beat their wives as long as the weapon they used was "a rod no bigger than their thumb." Early U.S. judicial decisions supported the right of men to beat their wives. The government's hands-off policy and the legal sanction to a husband's right to control the behavior of his wife were the two major impacts of the court rulings. The first wave of feminists in the nineteenth century briefly exposed the existence of wife abuse and made some efforts to criminalize it. This state of affairs continued until the 1970's, when the second wave of feminism exposed the public to the abuse that many women experienced in their own homes. The battered women's movement identified two key concerns: first, to create a society that no longer accepted domestic violence and second, to provide safe, supportive shelter for all women who were abused.

Sources for Further Study

Ammerman, Robert T., and Michel Hersen, eds. *Assessment of Family Violence: A Clinical and Legal Sourcebook*. New York: John Wiley & Sons, 1992. Leading figures in the field of family violence review a decade of research and examine strategies and measures relevant to assessment of the problem. They also comment on treatment planning and legal requirements. Other areas of concern include epidemological models, intervention planning, and standards of practice.

Browne, Angela. *When Battered Women Kill*. New York: Free Press, 1987. A study based on interviews with 250 physically abused women, 42 of whom had killed their batterers, shows how "romantic idealism" drives the early stages of the abusive relationship. Obsessive "love" continues along with the abuser's need to physically control the woman. In addition, coping and survival strategies of the battered women are presented.

Buttell, Frederick P. "Moral Development Among Court-Ordered Batterers: Evaluating the Impact of Treatment." *Research on Social Work Practice* 11, no. 1 (2001): 93-107. Court-ordered participants in a cognitive-behavioral group treatment program for batterers were studied regarding changing their levels of moral reasoning. The control group consisted of thirty-two adult men with an average age of thirty-two years, 84 percent of whom African American, who were ordered into a standard group treatment program. The major finding was that the current treatment program was ineffectual in changing batterers' moral reasoning.

Goetting, Ann. *Getting Out: Life Stories of Women Who Left Abusive Men*. New York: Columbia University Press, 1999. Sixteen women shared their stories with the author, who organized them into seven categories, including women of privileged backgrounds, children, two-timing batterers, family and friends to the rescue, shelter life, positive workings of the system, and the impacts of loss and death. A very readable book.

Gondolf, Edward W., and Robert J. White. "Batterer Program Participants Who Repeatedly Reassault: Psychopathic Tendencies and Other Disorders." *Journal of Interpersonal Violence* 16, no. 4 (2001): 361-380. Psychopathic tendencies were studied in 580 men from four batterers' programs. The men had assaulted their partners many times in spite of arrests for domestic violence and being referred to batterer counseling programs. The major conclusion was that men who had abused their partners many times were no more likely to have a psychopathic disorder than other men.

Jones, Loring, Margaret Hughes, and Ulrike Unterstaller. "Post-traumatic Stress Disorder (PTSD) in Victims of Domestic Violence: A Review of the Research." *Trauma Violence and Abuse* 2, no. 2 (2001): 99-119. An analysis of data from the literature focusing on the interplay between post-traumatic stress disorder (PTSD) and being a battered woman. The authors identified three major objectives of the study as well as seven major findings, chief of which is that PTSD symptoms are consistent with the symptoms of battered women.

Krishman, Satya P., Judith C. Hilbert, and Dawn Van Leeuwen. "Domestic Violence and Help-Seeking Behaviors Among Rural Women: Results from a Shelter-Based Study." *Family and Community Health* 24, no. 1 (2001): 28-38. A study conducted on a sample of predominantly Hispanic women living in rural communities that focused on their help-seeking behaviors, including those at a rural domestic violence shelter. One major finding was that a high percentage of the Hispanic subjects had thought about and/or attempted suicide.

Pellauer, Mary. "Lutheran Theology Facing Sexual and Domestic Violence." *Journal of Religion and Abuse* 2, no. 2 (2000): 3-48. The author argues that Martin Luther was theologically ambivalent on the issues of wife battering and child abuse and seemed to be confused between the ideas of sexuality and sexual violence. She ends her essay with a review of the themes for a Lutheran response to domestic violence, as well as making several recommendations for action based on further analysis of Luther's writings and teachings.

Smith, Darcy M., and Joseph Donnelly. "Adolescent Dating Violence: A Multi-systemic Approach of Enhancing Awareness in Educators, Parents, and Society." *Journal of Prevention and Intervention in the Community* 21, no. 1 (2001): 53-64. Mental health professionals have hesitated to report that adolescents are the fastest-growing at-risk segment of the population. One in eight high school students and one in five college students will be involved in abusive relationships. In 1993, six hundred teenage girls were murdered by their boyfriends. Useful prevention and treatment strategies are also presented.

Walker, Lenore E. *The Battered Woman Syndrome*. New York: Springer, 1984. A readable volume in which the author reports the results of a research project to identify key psychological and sociological factors that make up the battered woman syndrome. In addition, she tested eight specific theories about battered women and also gathered relevant data about battered women.

Carol A. Heintzelman

SEE ALSO: Aggression; Aggression: Reduction and control; Anger; Battered woman syndrome; Child abuse; Codependency; Family life: Adult issues; Family life: Children's issues; Rape and sexual assault; Separation and divorce: Adult issues; Separation and divorce: Children's issues; Violence and sexuality in the media; Violence by children and teenagers.

Down syndrome

TYPE OF PSYCHOLOGY: Psychopathology

FIELDS OF STUDY: Childhood and adolescent disorders

Down syndrome (DS), a congenital condition linked to a specific chromosomal error, has received significant attention from physicians and other health professionals, educators, psychologists and other providers of human services, and researchers from a variety of disciplines. Early identification and intervention, special education, vocational education, and supportive services in adulthood contribute to an increasingly favorable prognosis for persons with DS.

KEY CONCEPTS
- chromosome 21
- trisomy 21
- translocation
- mosaicism

INTRODUCTION

Down syndrome (DS) is a clinical condition present at birth that is characterized by certain distinctive physical features, varying degrees of delay in different developmental domains, and an extra chromosome 21 in the individual's genetic structure. The condition was first identified as a clinical entity in 1866 by an English physician, John Langdon Down, who also described its characteristic features. Because of a superficial physical resemblance between persons who had these features and Mongolians, Down labeled the syndrome "mongolism," and those who had it "mongols" or "mongoloids." These labels persisted until the latter half of the twentieth century, when "Down syndrome" became the preferred designation.

Many physical features have been ascribed to Down syndrome, but the most common characteristics are a face that looks round when viewed from the front but appears flat in profile; brachycephaly or a slightly flattened back of the head; eyes that slant slightly upward, with prominent epicanthic folds; a short, broad neck; thin lips and a mouth cavity slightly smaller than average while the tongue is slightly larger; hands that tend to be broad, with short fingers, of which the littlest sometimes has only one joint instead of the usual two and may be slightly curved toward the other fingers (clinodactyly), and the palm may have only one crease going across it or two creases that may extend right across it; feet that tend to be stubby, with a wide space between the first and second toes, where a short crease on the sole begins; hypotonia or low muscle tone, so that limbs and necks are often floppy; and weak reflexes.

Slower than average development that may result in developmental deficits is characteristic of persons with DS. The extent of developmental delay varies

Nurses and other health care professionals can offer both medical and emotional support to people with Down syndrome. (PhotoDisc)

among individuals and within the same individual across different developmental domains. Among individuals, the degree of the developmental lag or deficit is influenced by the type of DS and by environmental factors. Within the same individual, the highest levels of development are usually attained in the physical or social domains, while the lowest tends to be in language.

At least three types have been identified. Trisomy 21, characterized by an extra chromosome 21 in every cell, is the most common (95 percent). Translocation, wherein an extra part of chromosome 21 is attached to another chromosome in every cell, is found in 4 percent of individuals with DS. Mosaicism, the rarest type (1 percent), is distinguished by a mixture of cells, some of which have an extra chromosome 21 whereas others are normal. The first two types tend to be similar with respect to physical features and degree of intellectual limitation. Those who have a mosaic type tend to have milder form of the condition.

Associated Features and Disorders

Down syndrome is often associated with mental retardation. Studies of intellectual development in persons with DS prior to the 1900's reported that for individuals with DS, intelligence quotient (IQ) scores fell within the "idiot" or, in current terminology, "profound mental retardation" range. During the first half of the twentieth century, similar studies found that 50 to 75 percent of persons with DS tested had IQ scores ranging from 20 to 50; the average IQ score was 20 to 35, indicative of severe mental retardation. Those early studies recruited their samples mainly from institutions. Subsequent studies that drew their samples from the entire population yielded higher IQ scores. The majority of children and adults with DS tested had IQ scores falling within 30 to 50, with the group average between 40 and 50, classifiable as moderately retarded. Studies in the 1960's found that 5 to 10 percent of older children and adults with DS had IQ scores indicative of mild mental retardation and were considered "educable." By the mid-1970's, studies included former participants in early intervention programs and as much as 33 to 50 percent of older children and adults with DS attained IQ scores in the mild mental retardation range. Some had IQ scores within the dull-normal range, and a few in the normal range.

Many infants with DS (40 to 50 percent) are born with congenital heart disease. Lower proportions have congenital anomalies of the gastrointestinal tract (5 to 12 percent) or congenital cataracts (3 percent). In childhood, some start having convulsive seizures (8 percent). About 15 to 20 percent of older adults with DS exhibit what seem to be clinical signs of Alzheimer's disease.

PREVALENCE

Down syndrome occurs approximately once in 700-1,100 births. It is found in all ethnic groups. Slightly more males than females have received this diagnosis, for reasons yet unknown. Children with DS have been born to women of any age. Two-thirds are born to mothers under thirty-five years and one-fifth of all children with DS are born to mothers under twenty-five years of age. The risk of having a child with DS increases with the mother's age at the time of conception, particularly after the age of thirty-five years.

ETIOLOGY

John Langdon Down thought that the syndrome he had identified was due to a reversion to a primitive Mongolian ethnic stock. This etiological hypothesis was repudiated soon after by his son, Reginald Down, also a physician. The hypothesis that DS might be caused by a chromosomal abnormality was first advanced in 1932 but was not confirmed until 1959, with the discovery of an extra chromosome 21 in children with DS. Later, geneticists found other chromosomal abnormalities, translocation and mosaicism, in children who had DS. In all three cases, faulty cell division accounts for the chromosomal error.

PRENATAL SCREENING AND DIAGNOSIS

Prenatal screening for DS can be done using a combination of either three or four tests. The triple test includes tests for alpha-feroprotein (AFP), estriol, and human chorionic gonadotropin (hCG). These three tests together with a test for inhibin comprise the quad test. Approximately 60 to 80 percent of fetuses with Down syndrome can now be identified through either the triple or the quad test and consideration of the mother's age.

The most commonly used techniques in prenatal diagnosis of Down syndrome are amniocentesis, chorionic villus sampling (CVS), and ultrasonography. Compared to amniocentesis, CVS can be performed much earlier in pregnancy and produces results more quickly because chromosomal studies can be performed immediately. Studies show that the risk associated with CVS is slightly but not significantly greater than that of amniocentesis. The latest technique, developed in the 1990's, is fluorescent in situ hybridization (FISH). Appropriate caution is needed in prenatal diagnosis of Down syndrome because certain techniques may involve some risk to the mother and/or fetus. Siegfried M. Pueschel states that prenatal diagnosis is indicated when screening tests reveal that AFP and estriol levels are low and hCG and inhibin levels are significantly increased; the mother is thirty-five years of age or older; paternal age is approximately fifty years or older; the couple has a child with Down syndrome or other chromosomal abnormality; the parent has a balanced chromosome translocation; or the parent has a chromosome disorder.

COURSE OF THE DISORDER

Many studies have reported a decrease in IQ of individuals with DS with increasing age. This does not imply that intellectual development has stopped or reversed its course. As discussed by Cliff Cunningham, the IQ decline is an artifact of how IQ is calculated. Some studies suggest that persons with DS who have higher IQ scores continue to develop intellectually well into their twenties and possibly up to their late thirties. Those with much lower IQ scores reach a plateau much earlier and their intelligence remains in the severe mental retardation range.

Research has shown that children with DS go through the same steps in language acquisition and acquire the same linguistic structures or language rules as normally developing children, but they do so at a slower pace. Also, periods when their progress occurs at a near normal rate (around four to seven years of age) are followed by periods when very little progress occurs. After years of a developmental plateau, growth in linguistic structures may take place again in late adolescence. Because children and adolescents with DS seem unable consistently to maintain and apply the linguistic rules that they have already acquired, their ultimate language levels are low. Within this population, there are variations in rate of development and in the ultimate level of language attainment associated with differences in general intelligence, environment, and other factors. There is also variability in development within different language domains. Receptive vocabulary tends to be greater than expressive vocabulary. There are longer delays in development of language production than in language comprehension, and in acquisition of syntax compared to acquisition of lexical or vocabulary skills. Last, some evidence suggests that in children with DS, the understanding of language use in social interaction and communication may be greater than that suggested by their actual levels of grammatical development, and that they use nonverbal behaviors to augment their verbal communications. Despite the slow progress and somewhat low levels of ultimate attainment, the language of persons with DS is meaningful, relevant, and communicative.

Soon after birth, infants with DS are able to engage in reciprocal interactions with their parents by using social signaling behaviors such as smiling, eye contact, and vocalization. These social behaviors emerge with only minor delays and distortions. There are individual differences among infants and parents in their abilities to enter into these early social interactions. Parental differences in resilience (that is, in coming to terms emotionally with having an infant who has DS) imply differences in readiness for reciprocal social interactions with their infants. In general, the development of infant-mother attachment in children with DS follows the same sequence observed in normally developing children, but proceeds at a slower rate.

Similarly, the social skills of children with DS emerge in the same sequence but lag behind those of their peers without DS. This is evident in the development of mutual gaze behavior, social play, and communication skills. Although this lag can affect peer relations, it has been noted that mutual social and language adaptation can take place between children with and without DS, leading to more social interactions. In adolescence and adulthood, persons with DS may have fewer friends than they would like and interact with those they have less frequently than their peers without DS. This is partly due to lack of opportunity, since they are dependent on parents and other adults to take them to places and events that promote friendship development. Often, their friendships are restricted to those persons with DS and others whom they encounter at school and at work. Many refer to persons with whom they have professional relationships (such as social workers) as friends.

Treatment and Prognosis

There are no effective medical interventions that can "cure" Down syndrome. Still, comprehensive, high-quality medical care from birth onward remains essential to promote the physical growth and development, as well as maintain the health, of this population. Research has shown that cognitive, linguistic, and social development of young children with DS can be improved significantly through early identification and intervention, including physical and speech therapy. For older children, adolescents, and adults in this population, special education, vocational training, and supportive services in adulthood have produced marked increases in educational, occupational, and social skills, and in overall adaptation to the community. Family involvement is an essential ingredient for the success of these various approaches.

Home-rearing, parent advocacy, public policies and programs that provide an array of services including special education, and supportive communities have markedly improved the outcomes for this population. Increasingly, more adults with DS are able to attain self-sufficiency or partial self-sufficiency, to hold jobs or work in sheltered workshops, to live independently or in group homes, and, in general, to live as well-functioning members of their communities.

Sources for Further Study

Cicchetti, Dante, and Marjorie Beeghly, eds. *Children with Down Syndrome: A Developmental Perspective.* New York: Cambridge University Press, 1990. For graduate students and professionals interested in the development of children with Down syndrome, this book's in-depth treatment of theory and research on the topic remains unmatched.

Cunningham, Cliff. *Understanding Down Syndrome: An Introduction for Parents.* Cambridge, Mass.: Brookline Books, 1996. An internationally recognized researcher on the development of children with

Down syndrome provides parents with an excellent research-based overview that is written with clarity, sensitivity, and practical applications.

Pueschel, Siegfried M. *A Parent's Guide to Down Syndrome: Toward a Brighter Future.* Baltimore, Md.: Paul H. Brookes, 2001. A comprehensive guide to different aspects of Down syndrome, this book is a particularly good resource for the information about etiology, prenatal screening and diagnosis, and the physical, medical, and health-related features.

Felicisima C. Serafica

SEE ALSO: Abnormality: Biomedical models; Developmental disabilities; Intelligence; Mental retardation; Physical development: Environment versus genetics; Prenatal physical development.

Dreams

TYPE OF PSYCHOLOGY: Cognition; consciousness
FIELDS OF STUDY: Classic analytic themes and issues; cognitive processes; sleep; thought

Dreams are the series of images, thoughts, and feelings that occur in the mind of the sleeping person. Dreams are usually confused with waking reality while they are occuring. Distinctive neurological phenomena are associated with the production of dreams, and diverse psychological experiences are conveyed in dreaming.

KEY CONCEPTS
- D-sleep
- latent content
- manifest content
- NREM sleep
- REM sleep
- S-sleep
- sleep mentation

INTRODUCTION

Humans spend roughly one-third of their lives sleeping, and laboratory research indicates that at least a third of the sleep period is filled with dreaming. Thus, if a person lives seventy-five years, he or she will spend more than eight of those years dreaming.

People throughout the millennia have pondered the meaning of those years of dreaming, and their answers have ranged from useless fictions, to psychological insights, to the mark of God.

Some of the earliest known writings were about dreams. The *Epic of Gilgamesh*, written around 3500 B.C.E., contains the first recorded dream interpretation. An Egyptian document dating to the Twelfth Dynasty (1991-1786 B.C.E.) called the Chester Beatty Papyrus (named after its discoverer) presented a system for interpreting dreams. The biblical book of Genesis, attributed to Moses, who is claimed to have lived between 1446 and 1406 B.C.E., records a dream of Abimelech (a contemporary of Abraham and Sarah) from a period that appears to antedate the Twelfth Dynasty. Other classics of antiquity, such as the *Iliad* and *Odyssey* of Homer (c. eighth century B.C.E.), the *Republic* of Plato (427-347 B.C.E.), and *On the Senses and Their Objects*, written by Aristotle (384-322 B.C.E.), grappled with discerning the meaning of dreams. Artemidorus Daldianus (c. second century C.E.) provided a comprehensive summary of ancient thinking on dreams in his famous book, *Oneirocritica* (the interpretation of dreams).

To better understand dreaming, it must be distinguished from related phenomena. If the person is fully awake and perceives episodes departing from natural reality, the person is said to have experienced a vision. Experiencing an unintended perceptual distortion is more properly called a hallucination. A daydream is a purposeful distortion of reality. In the twilight realm of dreamlike imagery occurring just before falling asleep or just before becoming fully awake, hypnagogic or hypnopompic reverie, respectively, are said to occur. Dreams occur only in the third state of consciousness—being fully asleep. Another distinction is needed to differentiate between the two types of psychological phenomena that occur when a person is in this third realm of consciousness. Dreams have the attributes of imagery, temporality (time sequence), confusion with reality, and plot (an episode played out). Those subjective experiences that occur during sleep and are lacking in these attributes can be labeled as sleep mentation.

TYPES OF DREAMS

Just as there are different types of dreamlike experiences, there are different kinds of dreams. While there will be shortcomings in any effort toward classifying dreams, some approximate distinctions can be made in regard to sleep stage, affect (feelings and emotions), reality orientation, and dream origin.

When people fall asleep, brain activity changes throughout the night in cycles of approximately ninety minutes. Research with the electroencephalograph (which records electrical activity) has demonstrated a sequence of four stages of sleep occurring in these cycles. The first two stages are called D-sleep (desynchronized EEG), which constitutes essential psychological rest—consolidation of memories and processing of thoughts and emotions. The other two stages, which constitute S-sleep (synchronized EEG), are necessary for recuperation from the day's physical activity—physical rest. S-sleep usually disappears during the second half of a night's sleep. Dreaming occurs in both S-sleep and D-sleep but is much more likely to occur in D-sleep.

A further distinction in the physiology of sleep is pertinent to the type of dreaming activity likely to occur. During stage one sleep there are often accompanying rapid eye movements (REM) that are not found in other stages of sleep. Researchers often distinguish between REM sleep, where these ocular movements occur, and non-REM (NREM) sleep, in which there is an absence of these eye movements. When people are aroused from REM sleep, they report dreams a majority of the time—roughly 80 percent—as opposed to a minority of the time—perhaps 20 percent—with NREM sleep. Furthermore, REM dreams tend to have more emotion, greater vividness, more of a plot, a greater fantastical quality, and episodes that are more likely to be recalled and with greater clarity.

The prevalence of affect in dreams is linked with people's styles of daydreaming. Those whose daydreams are of a positive, uplifting quality tend to experience the greatest amount of pleasant emotionality in their dreams. People whose daydreams reflect a lot of anxiety, guilt, and negative themes experience more unpleasant dreams. While most dreams are generally unemotional in content, when there are affective overtones, negative emotions predominate about two-thirds of the time. Unpleasant dreams can be categorized into three types. Common nightmares occur in REM sleep and are caused by many factors, such as unpleasant circumstances in life, daily stresses, or traumatic experiences. Common themes are being chased, falling, or reliving an aversive event. Night terrors are most likely to occur in stage four sleep and are characterized by sudden wakening, terror-stricken reactions, and disorientation that can last several minutes. Night terrors are rarely recollected. An extreme life-threatening event can lead to post-traumatic stress disorder (PTSD). Recurring PTSD nightmares, unlike other nightmares and night terrors, are repetitive nightmares in which the sufferer continues to relive the traumatic event. Furthermore, PTSD nightmares can occur in any stage of sleep.

DREAMS AND REALITY

The reality level of dreams varies in terms of time orientation and level of consciousness. Regarding time orientation, dreams earlier in the night contain more themes dealing with the distant past—such as childhood for an adult—while dreams closer toward waking up tend to be richer in content and have more present themes—such as a current concern. The future is emphasized in oneironmancy, the belief that dreams are prophetic and can warn the dreamer of events to come. A famous biblical story exemplifies this: Joseph foretold seven years of plenty followed by seven years of famine after hearing about Pharaoh's dream of seven fat cows devoured by seven lean cows.

The unconscious mind contains material that is rarely accessible or completely inaccessible to awareness. The personal unconscious may resurrect dream images of experiences that a person normally cannot voluntarily recall. For example, a woman may dream about kindergarten classmates about whom she could not remember anything while awake. The psychologist Carl Jung proposed that dreams could sometimes include material from the collective unconscious—a repository of shared human memories. Thus, a dream in which evil is represented by a snake may reflect a universal human inclination to regard snakes as dangerous.

When waking reality rather than unconscious thoughts intrude upon dreaming, lucid dreams occur. Lucid dreams are characterized by the dreamer's awareness in the dream that he or she is dreaming. Stephen LaBerge's research has revealed that lucid dreams occur only in REM sleep and that people can be trained to experience lucidity, whereby they can exercise some degree of control over the content of their dreams. Such explorers of dreams have been called oneironauts.

ORIGINS AND SIGNIFICANCE

Theories about the origins of dreams can be divided into two main categories: naturalistic and supernaturalistic. Proponents of naturalistic theories of dreaming believe that dreams result from either physiological activities or psychological processes. Aristotle was one of the first people to offer a physiological explanation for dreams. His basic thesis was that dreams are the afterimages of sensory experiences. A modern physiological approach to dreaming was put forth in the 1970's by J. Allan Hobson and Robert McCarley. According to their activation-synthesis theory, emotional and visual areas of the brain are activated during REM sleep, and the newly alerted frontal lobe tries to make sense of this information plus any other sensory or physiological activity that may be occurring at that time. The result is that ongoing activity is synthesized (combined) into a dream plot. For example, a man enters REM sleep and pleasant memories of playing in band during school are evoked. Meanwhile, the steam pipes in his bedroom are banging. The result is a dream in which he is watching a band parade by with the booming of bass drums ringing in his ears. Hobson does not believe that, apart from fostering recent memories, dreams have any psychological significance.

Plato believed that dreams do have psychological significance and can reveal something about the character of people. More recent ideas about the psychological origins of dreams can be divided into symbolic approaches that emphasize the hidden meanings of dreams and cognitive perspectives that stress that dreaming is simply another type of thinking and that no deep, hidden motives are contained in that thinking. The most famous symbolic approach to dreaming was presented by Sigmund Freud in his book *The Interpretation of Dreams* (1900). For Freud, the actual dream content is meaningless. It hides the true meaning of the dream, which must be interpreted. David Foulkes, in *Dreaming: A Cognitive-Psychological Analysis* (1985), proposed a contrary perspective. His cognitive approach to dreaming states that dreams are as they are remembered and that it is meaningless to search for deep meanings. Foulkes proposes that randomly activated memories during sleep are organized into a comprehensible dream by a "dream-production system."

The final category of dreams represents the most ancient explanation—dreams may have a supernatural origin. Often connected with the supernatural approach is the belief that God or supernatural beings can visit a person in a dream and heal that person of physical illnesses. This belief is called dream incubation and was widely practiced by the ancient Greeks beginning around the sixth century B.C.E. Several hundred temples were dedicated to helping believers practice this art. Spiritual healing, not physical healing, is the theme presented in the numerous references to dreaming in the Bible: over one hundred verses in nearly twenty chapters. The Bible presents a balanced picture of the origins of dreams. God speaks through dreams to Abimelech in the first book of the Old Testament (Genesis 20:6) and to Joseph in the first book of the New Testament (Matthew 1:20). However, Solomon (Ecclesiastes 5:7) and Jeremiah (23:25-32) warn that many dreams do not have a divine origin.

DREAM CONTENT

Dream content varies depending on stage of sleep and time of night. Research has also revealed that characteristics of the dreamer and environmental factors can influence the nature of dreams.

Three human characteristics that influence dreams are age, gender, and personality. It has been found that children are more likely to report dreams (probably because they experience more REM sleep) and their dreams are reported to have more emotional content, particularly nightmarish themes. Elderly people report more death themes in their dreams. Male dreams have more sexual and aggressive content than female dreams, which have more themes dealing with home and family. Women report that they dream of their mothers and babies more when they are pregnant. Introverts report more dreams and with greater detail than extroverts. Psychotic individuals (those with severe mental disorders), depressed people, and those whose occupations are in the creative arts (musicians, painters, and novelists) report more nightmares. Schizophrenics and severely depressed people provide shorter dream reports than those of better mental health. It is also reported that depressed people dream of the past more than those who are not depressed.

Environmental factors occurring before and during sleep can shape the content of dreams. What people experience prior to falling asleep can show up in dreams in blatant, subtle, or symbolic forms. People watching movies that evoke strong emotions tend to have highly emotional dreams. In fact, the greater the emotionality of a daily event, the greater the probability that the event will occur in a dream during the subsequent sleep period. Those who are wrestling mentally with a problem often dream about that problem. Some have even reported that the solutions to their problems occurred during the course of dreaming. The German physiologist Otto Loewi's Nobel Prize-winning research with a frog's nerve was inspired by a dream he had. Sometimes events during the day show up in a compensatory form in dreams. Thus, those deprived of food, shelter, friends, or other desirables report an increased likelihood of dreaming about those deprivations at night.

Events occurring during sleep can be integrated into the dream plot as well. External stimuli such as temperature changes, light flashes, and various sounds can be detected by the sleeping person's senses and then become part of the dream. However, research indicates that sensory information is only infrequently assimilated into dreams. Internal stimulation from physiological activities occurring during sleep may have a greater chance of influencing the nature of dreams. Dreams about needing to find a bathroom may be caused in part by a full bladder. Similarly, nighttime activation of the vestibular system (which controls the sense of balance), the premotor cortex (which initiates movements), and the locus coeruleus (which plays a role in inhibiting muscles during sleep so that dreams are not acted out) perhaps can stimulate the production of dreams about falling, chasing, or being unable to move, respectively.

DREAM INTERPRETATION

There is a plethora of books about dream interpretation offering many different, and often contradictory, approaches to the subject. With so many different ideas about what dreams mean, it is difficult to know which approach is more likely to be successful.

A few principles increase the probability that a dream interpretation approach will be valid. First, the more dream content recalled, the better the opportunity to understand its meaning. Most people remember only bits and pieces of their dreams and serious efforts to interpret dreams require serious efforts by people to remember their dreams. Second, the more a theme recurs in a series of dreams, the greater the likelihood that the theme is signifi-

cant. Dream repetition also helps in interpretation: Content from one dream may be a clue to the meaning of other dreams. Finally, the focus of dream interpretation should be the dreamer, not the dream. In order to understand the dream, one must spend time and effort in knowing the dreamer.

There are many scholarly approaches to dream interpretation. Three theories are particularly noteworthy due to their influence on the thinking of other scholars and their utility for clinical application. Each perspective emphasizes a different side of the meaning of dreams.

Sigmund Freud proposed that dreams are complementary to waking life. His basic thesis was that many wishes, thoughts, and feelings are censored in waking consciousness due to their unsuitability for public expression and are subsequently pushed down into the unconscious. This unconscious material bypasses censorship in dreaming by a process in which the hidden, "true" meaning of the dream— the latent content—is presented in a disguised form—the manifest content. The manifest content is the actual content of the dream that is recalled. To interpret a dream requires working through the symbolism and various disguises of the manifest content in order to get to the true meaning of the dream residing in the latent content. For example, Jane's manifest content is a dream in which she blows out candles that surround a gray-headed man. The candles might symbolize knowledge and the gray-headed man may represent her father. The latent content is that Jane resents her father's frequent and interfering advice. Thus, blowing out the candles represents Jane's desire to put an end to her father's meddling.

Carl Jung proposed that dreams could be understood at different levels of analysis and that the essential purpose of dreams was compensatory. By compensatory, Jung meant that dreams balance the mind by compensating for what is lacking in the way a person is living life. For example, the timid Christian who is afraid to speak up for his or her beliefs with atheistic colleagues dreams of being a bold and eloquent evangelist. Jung believed that four levels of analysis could be used to help dreamers gain insight into their dreams. His general rule guiding the use of these levels is that recourse to analysis at deeper levels of consciousness is only warranted if the dream cannot be adequately understood from a more surface level of examination. To illustrate, a man has a dream in which he steps into a pile of manure. At the conscious level of analysis, it may be that he is dreaming about a recent experience—no need to posit symbolic interpretations. Looking into his personal unconscious, an image from his childhood may be evoked. Recourse to the cultural level of consciousness would examine what manure symbolizes in his culture. It could be a good sign for a farmer in an agrarian world, but a bad sign for a politician in an industrialized society. In some cases, it may be necessary to look at the dream from the perspective of the collective unconscious. Manure might be an ancient, universal image that symbolizes fertility. Could the man be questioning whether or not he wants to be a father?

Zygmunt Piotrowski developed a theory of dream interpretation based on projective techniques. For Piotrowski, in a dream about another person, that person may actually represent a facet of the dreamer's own mind. The more the dream figure is like the dreamer and the closer the proximity between the figure and the dreamer in the dream, the greater the likelihood the dreamer is projecting him- or herself (seeing in others what is really in the self) into that dream figure. For instance, a woman may dream she is walking with her closest friend but that friend is ignoring everything she is saying to her. An interpretation according to Piotrowski's system could be that the dreamer is actually dealing with the fact that she is not a good listener.

Dreams may be complementary, compensatory, or projective, useless fictions or avenues of insight, products of the brain or a touch from God. Many credible answers have been proposed, but it is hard to believe that there is a single explanation for every instance of dreaming. Perhaps the best answer is that dreams reveal many different things about many different dreamers—biologically, psychologically, socially, and spiritually.

SOURCES FOR FURTHER STUDY

Dement, William C. *The Promise of Sleep*. New York: Random House, 1999. One of the pioneers in sleep research presents a comprehensive overview of sleep for the general public. Chapters 13 and 14 specifically deal with dreaming, while research pertinent to dreaming is also found in other chapters.

Farthing, G. W. *The Psychology of Consciousness*. Englewood Cliffs, N.J.: Prentice Hall, 1992. In a scholarly book emphasizing research on various aspects of consciousness, Farthing examines dreaming in three chapters and related phenomena in two other chapters.

Freud, Sigmund. *The Interpretation of Dreams*. Translated by Joyce Crick, edited by Ritchie Robertson. New York: Oxford University Press, 2000. This is the classic book that outlined Freud's theory of the mind and revolutionized thinking about dreams. Probably the single best book ever written about dreaming.

Hall, James A. *Patterns of Dreaming*. Boston: Shambhala, 1991. James Hall looks at dream interpretation from a Jungian perspective with an emphasis on clinical application. This intellectually sound book contains excellent historical background and well-rounded coverage of different approaches toward dream interpretation, including a brief look at Piotrowski's system.

Kallmyer, J. D. *Hearing the Voice of God Through Dreams, Visions, and the Prophetic Word*. Harre de Grace, Md.: Moriah Press, 1998. This book is an excellent source for a spiritual examination of dreaming.

Paul J. Chara, Jr.

SEE ALSO: Analytical psychology: Carl G. Jung; Archetypes and the collective unconscious; Consciousness: Altered states; Freud, Sigmund; Hallucinations; Jung, Carl G.; Psychoanalytic psychology and personality: Sigmund Freud; Sleep.

Drives

TYPE OF PSYCHOLOGY: Motivation
FIELDS OF STUDY: Motivation theory

A drive is a state influenced by an animal's need; the animal is motivated to reduce tension or to seek a goal. Drive theory is concerned with the nature of the internal forces that compel an animal to behave.

KEY CONCEPTS
- drive
- drive reduction
- law of effect
- need
- reinforcement

INTRODUCTION

One goal of science is to understand, predict, or manipulate natural events. A scientist may start by observing an event of interest and measuring it as precisely as possible to detect any changes. In experimental research, scientists systematically manipulate various other events to see whether the event of interest also varies. In survey research, various events are measured to see whether they vary with the event of interest. Understanding is achieved when the relationship between the event of interest (the dependent variable) and other events (independent variables) is established. One can then predict and/or manipulate the event of interest. A theory provides a guideline to organize the variables into a system based upon common properties. To a psychologist, the dependent variable is the behavior of all animals and humans. The independent variable (also called a determinant) may be any other variable related to behaviors. Psychological research aims to discover the determinants of certain behavior; some of them are motivational variables. The field of motivation examines why particular behavior occurs, why it is so strong, and why it is so persistent.

A drive is a process related to the source of behavioral energy originating from within the body that is created by disturbances in homeostasis (a state of systemic equilibrium). A homeostatic imbalance creates a state of need for certain stimuli from the environment which can restore the balance. For example, abnormal body temperature and hyperosmolality of the body fluid (electrolyte concentration outside cells that is higher than that of the intracellular fluid, resulting in cell dehydration) are disturbances in homeostasis. The homeostatic balance can be restored through two means. Physiological means such as vasodilation, sweating, and panting serve to reduce body temperature; concentration of electrolytes in the urine by the kidneys reduces hyperosmolality. Second, behavioral means such as taking off clothes, turning on an air conditioner, and drinking cold liquid lower body temperature; drinking water would also result in reducing the hyperosmolality. One may examine a case of homeostatic imbalance in detail to illustrate how the two means function to restore the balance.

When the body fluid volume is reduced (hypovolemia) because of loss of blood or of body fluid from intense sweating, the body responds immediately by vasoconstriction, reducing urine volume (through vasopressin release), and conserving sodium (through aldosterone release). Those are physiological means that will restore the blood pressure and prevent circulatory failure. Eventually, however, the body must get back the lost fluid from the environment via behavior (seeking water and drinking) to achieve long-lasting homeostasis. The physiological means are immediate and effective, but they are only stopgap measures. Behavior is the means with which the animal interacts with its environment to get back the lost resource.

DRIVE, REINFORCEMENT, AND LEARNING

The concept of drives is very important to the theories of Clark L. Hull, a neo-behaviorist. According to Hull, a drive has at least two distinct functions as far as behavioral activation is concerned. Without drives there could be no reinforcement and thus no learning, because drive reduction is the reinforcement. Without drives there could be no response, for a drive activates behavioral potentials into performance. Drive theory maintains that a state named "drive" (or D) is a necessary condition for behavior to occur; however, D is not the same as the bodily need. D determines how strongly and persistently a behavior will occur; it connects the need and behavior. This distinction between need and drive is necessary because, while the state of need serves as the source of behavior, the intensity of behavior is not always related to the intensity of need. Need can be defined as a state of an organism attributable to deprivation of a biological or psychological requirement, related to a disturbance in the homeostatic state.

There are cases in which the need increases but behavior does not, or in which the need remains but behavior is no longer manifested. Prolonged deprivation, for example, may not result in a linear or proportional increase in behavior. A water-deprived animal may stop drinking even before cellular dehydration is restored to the normal state; the behavior is changing independent of homeostatic imbalance. Cessation of behavior is seen as being attributable to drive reduction.

Hull uses D to symbolize drive and sHr (H is commonly used to denote this, for convenience) to symbolize a habit which consists of an acquired relationship between stimulus (S) and response (R). It represents a memory of experience in which certain environmental stimuli and responses were followed by a reward. An effective reward establishes an S-R relationship; the effect is termed reinforcement. One example of an H would be an experience of maze stimuli and running that led to food. H is a behavioral potential, not a behavior. Food deprivation induces a need state that can be physiologically defined; then D will energize H into behavior. The need increases monotonically with hours of deprivation, but D increases only up to three days without food. A simplified version of the Hullian formula for a behavior would be "behavior = HD," or "performance = behavioral potential energizer." The formula indicates that learning, via establishing behavioral potential, and D, via energizing the potential, are both necessary for performance to occur. This is a multiplicative relationship; that is, when either H or D is zero, a specific performance cannot occur.

ROLE OF FREUD'S "ID"

Sigmund Freud proposed, in his psychoanalytical approach to behavioral energy, that psychic energy is the source of human behaviors. The id is the reservoir of instinctual energy presumed to derive directly from the somatic processes. This energy is unorganized, illogical, and timeless, knowing "no values, no good or evil, no morality" (according to Freud in 1933). The id operates according to the pleasure principle, using the primary process to discharge its energy as soon as possible, with no regard for reality. When the discharge is hindered by reality, however, the ego handles the situation according to the reality principle, using a secondary process to pursue realistic gratification. The ego mediates between the id on one hand and reality on the other.

Freud thus conceptualized the id to be the energy source and the ego to manage behavior in terms of reality. Learning is manifested in the way the ego manages behavior for gratification under the restriction of the environment and the superego. In this model, the drive is seen as the energizer of behavior. The similarity between the Freudian and Hullian concepts of drive is obvious. Food deprivation would generate homeostatic imbalance, which is the somatic process, and the need, which is similar to the energy of the id. The organism cannot obtain immediate gratification because of environmental constraints to obtain food, so behavior is generated to negotiate with the environment. Drive is much like the ego, since it energizes the behavioral potentials into behaviors to seek reality gratification, which is equivalent to drive reduction. The concept of pleasure and behavioral changes commonly appears in various theories that incorporate a subtle influence of Freudian thought.

DEPRIVATION AND INCENTIVE MOTIVES

In one classic experiment, Carl J. Warden studied the persistence of behavior as a function of various sources, including the strength of a drive, using an apparatus called a Columbia obstruction box. He demonstrated that a rat without food would cross an electrified grid to reach a goal box that held food. When the rat was immediately brought back from the goal box to the start box, it would cross the grid again and again. The number of grid crossings was positively related to the number of days without food for up to three days. From the fourth day without food, however, the number of crossings slowly decreased. When baby rats were placed in the goal box, a mother rat would cross the grid repeatedly. When a male or female rat was placed in the goal box, a rat of the opposite sex would cross repeatedly. The number of crossings by the male rat was positively related to the duration it spent without a female companion.

These animals were all manifesting the effect of different drives: hunger, maternal instinct, or sex. It was shown that the maternal drive was associated with the greatest number of crossings (twenty-two times in twenty minutes), followed by thirst (twenty times), hunger (seventeen), female sex drive (fourteen), male sex drive (thirteen), and exploration (six). Warden demonstrated that various internal forces, created by deprivation and hormonal state, and external forces, created by different goal objects, together determine the grid-crossing behavior. The level of deprivation induces drive motivation; the reward in the goal box induces incentive motivation. In this example, the focus is on drive motivation.

If one were to place a well-trained rat into a maze, it might or might not run to the goal box. Whether it would run, how fast it would run, and how well (in terms of errors) it would run would depend upon whether the subject were food-deprived. With food deprivation, the well-trained rat would run to the goal box with few errors. If it had just been fed, it would not run; it would simply wander, sniff at the corner, and go to sleep. The environmental stimulus (the maze) is the same; the rat's behavior is different because the internal force—the drive created by food deprivation—is different. A need state produces D, and D then triggers behavior. The behavior that will occur is determined jointly by the past experience of learning, which is termed H, as well as stimuli, S, from the environment. An inexperienced rat, without the H of maze running, will behave differently from a well-trained rat in a maze. D is an intervening variable: It connects need and behavior, so one must consider both the source (need) and the consequence (behavior) to define D. When D is zero, there will be no maze running, no matter how well-trained the rat is. On the other hand, if there is no H (training), the proper maze-running behavior will not occur, no matter how hungry the rat is. An animal must be exposed to a maze when hungry to learn to negotiate the various turns on the way to the goal box containing food. Without food deprivation (and the resultant D), the animal would not perform even if it could; one cannot tell whether an animal has the knowledge to run the maze until one introduces a D variable. H is a potential of behavior, and D makes the potential into the observable reality of performance. Motivation turns a behavior on.

These ideas can be applied to countless real-life examples. If a person is not very good at playing tennis (has a low H), for example, no matter how motivated (high D) he is, he will not be able to beat a friend who is an expert at the game. If a person is very good at tennis (high H) but does not feel like playing (low D), perhaps because of a lack of sleep, she will not perform well. The same situation would apply for taking a test, delivering a speech, or running a marathon.

PUZZLE-BOX LEARNING

In another experiment involving drive, Edward L. Thorndike put a cat into a puzzle box. The cat attempted to get out via various behaviors (mewing, scratching, and so on). By chance, it stepped on a plate that resulted in the door opening, allowing the cat to escape. The cat was repeatedly returned to the box, and soon it would escape right away by stepping on the plate; other, useless behaviors were no longer manifested. The source of D in this case was the anxiety induced by confine-

ment in the box, which could be measured by various physiological changes, such as heart rate and hormonal levels. Escaping would make the anxiety disappear; D is reduced. D reduction results in an increase in the probability that the behavior immediately preceding it (stepping on the plate) will recur. Thorndike describes this puzzle-box learning as trial and error, implying a blind attempt at various means of escape until one happens to work. He states that a "satisfying effect" will create repetition, calling this the law of effect; the essence of the satisfying effect appears to be drive reduction. A five-stage learning cycle is then complete: It consists of need, drive, behavior, drive reduction, and behavior repetition.

CENTRAL MOTIVE STATE

The question of how a habit (H) is formed and how it is stored in the brain is a lively research topic in the psychobiology of learning, memory, and cognition, as well as in neuropsychology, which deals with learning deficit and loss of memory. Drive and reinforcement are important variables that determine whether learning will succeed and whether past learning will be manifested as behaviors. Research on hunger and thirst forms one subfield of psychobiology.

If D is the common energizer of various behaviors, then all sources of D—hunger, thirst, sex, mothering, exploration—should have something in common physiologically. The so-called central motive state is hypothesized to be such a state. It is known that arousal is common to the sources of D. Research involves biological delineation of the sources of D; researchers are studying the mechanisms of hunger, for example. There has been insufficient attention paid to the physiological processes by which hunger may motivate various behaviors and by which drive reduction would serve as a reinforcement in learning. Extreme lack of motivation can be seen in some depressed and psychotic patients, which results both in a lack of new learning and in a lack of manifesting what is already known. The neuronal substrates of this "lack of energy" represent one problem under investigation in the area of drive and motivation.

SOURCES FOR FURTHER STUDY

Amsel, Abram. *Mechanisms of Adaptive Behavior: Clark Hull's Theoretical Papers, with Commentary.* New

York: Columbia University Press, 1984. An annotated collection of Hull's theoretical work on drives and behavior.

Bolles, Robert C. *Theory of Motivation.* 2d ed. New York: Harper & Row, 1975. This standard text in motivation reviews the concepts of motivation and drive and present pros and cons of the drive concept.

Freud, Sigmund. *New Introductory Lectures on Psychoanalysis.* New York: W. W. Norton, 1933. Freud explains his theory of the workings of the id, ego, and superego. His concept of behavioral energy is described in this book.

Hull, Clark Leonard. *Principles of Behavior.* New York: Appleton-Century, 1943. This bible of the Hullian neobehavioristic theory delineates the concepts of D and H and the philosophical bases of behavioral study. The theory has excited many students into studying psychology.

Pfaff, Donald W., ed. *The Physiological Mechanisms of Motivation.* New York: Springer-Verlag, 1982. Various authors describe the physiological substrates of different sources of drive and motivation in terms of the nervous system, hormones, and body fluid parameters.

Stellar, James R., and Eliot Stellar. *The Neurobiology of Motivation and Reward.* New York: Springer-Verlag, 1985. Eliot Stellar, one of the best-known theorists in biopsychology of motivation, along with his son, describes how biological antecedents of motivation can be found to explain various behavior.

Warden, Carl John. *Animal Motivation: Experimental Studies on the Albino Rat.* New York: Columbia University Press, 1931. This was the first research attempting to compare different sources of drive using various reward substances.

Sigmund Hsiao

SEE ALSO: Hunger; Incentive motivation; Instinct theory; Motivation; Sex hormones and motivation; Thirst.

Drug therapies

DATE: The 1950's forward
TYPE OF PSYCHOLOGY: Biological bases of behavior; psychopathology; psychotherapy

FIELDS OF STUDY: Anxiety disorders; depression; models of abnormality; nervous system; organic disorders; personality disorders; schizophrenias; sexual disorders; stress and illness; substance abuse

Psychotropic drugs have revolutionized the treatment of mental illness. Many disorders including anxiety, depression, and schizophrenia may be treated effectively with these modern drugs. However, the use of psychotropic drugs has created new problems, both for individuals and for society.

KEY CONCEPTS
- antianxiety drugs
- antidepressant drugs
- antipsychotics
- mood stabilizers
- neurotransmitters
- psychopharmacology
- psychostimulants
- psychotropic

INTRODUCTION

Before 1950, no truly effective drug therapies existed for mental illness. Physicians treated patients with mental illness with a combination of physical restraints, blood-letting, sedation, starvation, electric shock, and other minimally effective therapies. They used some drugs for treatment, including alcohol and opium, primarily to calm agitated patients. Interest in drug therapy in the early twentieth century was high, based on the rapidly increasing body of chemical knowledge developed during the late nineteenth century. Researchers in the first half of the twentieth century experimented with insulin, marijuana, antihistamines, and lithium with varying success. The term "psychopharmacology," the study of drugs for the treatment of mental illness, dates to 1920.

In 1951, a French scientist, Paul Charpentier, synthesized chlorpromazine for use in reducing surgical patients' anxiety and the prevention of shock during surgery. Physicians noted its calming effect and began to use it in psychiatry. Previously agitated patients with schizophrenia not only became calmer, but their thoughts became less chaotic and they became less irritable. Chlorpromazine was truly the first effective psychotropic drug (that is, a drug exerting an effect on the mind) and is still used today.

The discovery of chlorpromazine ushered in a new era in the treatment of psychiatric illness. Pharmaceutical companies have developed and introduced dozens of new psychotropic drugs. Many long-term psychiatric treatment facilities have closed, and psychiatrists have released the vast majority of their patients into community-based mental health care. Patients with mental health problems are treated on an outpatient basis, with brief hospitalizations for stabilization in some cases. Treatment goals are no longer simply to sedate patients or to protect themselves and others from harm, but to provide them with significant relief from their symptoms and to help them function productively in society. As scientific knowledge about the brain and its function increases, researchers are able to create drugs targeting increasingly specific areas of the brain, leading to fewer adverse side effects.

This psychotherapeutic drug revolution has had some negative consequences, however. Drug side effects range from annoying to life threatening. Community mental health treatment centers have not grown in number or received funding sufficient to meet the needs of all the patients released from long-term care facilities. Many mentally ill patients have fallen through the cracks of community-based care and live on the streets or in shelters for the homeless. In addition, some physicians and patients have come to expect a "pill for every ill" and fail to utilize other, equally or more effective treatment methodologies. Researchers estimate that 15 percent of the population of the United States receives a prescription for a psychotropic drug each year, greatly adding to the nation's health care costs. The majority of these prescriptions are written by generalist physicians rather than by psychiatrists, raising concerns about excessive or inappropriate prescribing. Some people abuse these drugs, either by taking their medications in excess of the amount prescribed for them or by obtaining them illicitly. Studies have shown that prescription drug abuse causes more injuries and deaths than abuse of all illicit drugs combined. Feminist scholars have pointed out that physicians tend to prescribe psychotropic drugs more readily for women than for men.

Despite the negative effects, psychotropic drugs are extremely important in the provision of health care, not only for those people traditionally thought of as mentally ill, but for people with chronic pain,

serious medical illness, loss and grief, and those who have experienced traumatic events.

HOW PSYCHOTROPIC DRUGS WORK

To understand how these mind-affecting drugs work, it is necessary to understand a little of how the brain works. The brain is made up primarily of neurons (nerve cells) that form circuits controlling thoughts, emotions, physical activities, and basic life functions. These nerve cells do not actually touch one another but are separated by a gap called a synapse. An electrical impulse moves along the neuron. When it reaches the end, it stimulates the release of chemicals called neurotransmitters into the synapse. These chemicals then fit into receptors on the next neuron and affect its electrical impulse. The neurotransmitters act by either causing the release of the electric impulse or inhibiting it so the neuron does not fire. Any neurotransmitter left in the synapse is then reabsorbed into the original neuron. This process is called reuptake.

Problems can arise in one of two ways: either too much or too little neurotransmission. Too much transmission may occur when the neuron fires in the absence of a stimulus or when too many neurotransmitters attach to the receptors on the far side of the synapse (the postsynaptic receptors). Too little transmission can occur when too few neurotransmitters attach to these postsynaptic receptors. The primary neurotransmitters involved in mental illnesses and their treatment are dopamine, serotonin (5-HT), norepinephrine, and gamma-amino butyric acid (GABA).

ANTIDEPRESSANT DRUGS

Some scientists believe that depression is caused by insufficient norepinephrine, serotonin, and/or dopamine in the synapse. Others theorize that depression has to do with the number and sensitivity of postsynaptic receptors involved in the neuron's response. Drugs for the treatment of depression come in four major classes: the monoamine oxidase inhibitors (MAOIs), the tricyclic antidepressants, the selective serotonin reuptake inhibitors (SSRIs), and "other." None of these drugs is addictive, although patients need to be weaned from them slowly to avoid rebound depression or other adverse effects.

MAOIs were the first modern antidepressants. Monoamine oxidase is an enzyme that breaks down serotonin, norepinephrine, and dopamine. Inhibiting the enzyme increases the supply of these neurotransmitters. MAOI drugs available in the United States include phenelzine and tranylcypromine. These drugs are not used as commonly as are the other antidepressants, mostly because of their side effects. However, they are used when other treatments for depression fail. In addition, they may be used to treat narcolepsy, phobias, anxiety, and Parkinson's disease. Common side effects include drowsiness, fatigue, dry mouth, and dizziness. They may also cause orthostatic hypotension (a drop in blood pressure when arising) and sexual dysfunction. Most important, the MAOIs interact with tyramine-containing foods, such as hard cheese, red wine, and smoked or pickled fish. Consuming these foods along with an MAOI can cause a hypertensive crisis in which the patient's blood pressure rises to potentially deadly levels. Patients taking MAOIs must also avoid other drugs which stimulate the nervous system to avoid blood pressure emergencies.

The tricyclic antidepressants were introduced in 1958. They all inhibit the reuptake of neurotransmitters but differ in which one is involved. Some affect primarily serotonin, some norepinephrine, and some work equally on both. Tricyclics commonly available in the United States include amitriptyline, imipramine, doxepin, desipramine, nortriptyline, amoxapine, protriptyline, and clomipramine. Primarily used for depression, these drugs may also be helpful in the treatment of bed-wetting, agoraphobia (fear of being out in the open) with panic attacks, obsessive-compulsive personality disorder, chronic pain, nerve pain, and migraine headaches. An important treatment issue is that it takes two to three weeks of drug therapy before the depressed patient feels much improvement in mood and energy. During this time, the side effects tend to be the most bothersome, leading patients to abandon the treatment before it becomes effective. Another important treatment issue is that tricyclic antidepressants are highly lethal in overdose. Common side effects include dry mouth, blurred vision, constipation, urinary retention, orthostatic hypotension, weight gain, sexual dysfunction, cardiac problems, and jaundice. Some of the tricyclics are highly sedating, and so may be useful in patients who are having difficulty sleeping. On the other hand, a patient who is already feeling sluggish and sleepy may benefit from a tricyclic that is less sedating. Any antidepressant may precipitate mania or hypomania in a patient with a predisposition to bipolar (manic-depressive) disorder. Elderly patients may be at increased risk for falls or confusion and memory impairment when taking tricyclics and should be started on very low doses if a tricyclic is indicated.

The newer selective SSRIs have several advantages over the tricyclics: They are much less lethal in overdose, are far safer in the elderly, and do not cause weight gain. They work, as the name implies, by decreasing serotonin reuptake, thereby increasing the amount of neurotransmitter available at the synapse. Like the tricyclics, SSRIs may need to be taken for several weeks before a patient notices significant improvement in mood and energy level. SSRIs available in the United States include fluoxetine, sertraline, fluvoxamine, paroxetine, trazodone, nafazodone, and venlafaxine. In addition to depression, the SSRIs are used for treatment of bulimia nervosa and obsessive-compulsive disorder. Possible side effects include nausea, diarrhea, nervousness, insomnia, anxiety, and sexual dysfunction.

Other drugs used in the treatment of depression include mianserin, maprotiline, and bupropion. The mechanisms by which these drugs work are not clear, but they may be useful in patients for whom the other antidepressants do not work or are contraindicated.

MOOD STABILIZERS

Some patients who have depression also have episodes of elevated mood and erratic, uncontrolled behavior. These patients are diagnosed with bipolar disorder, formerly known as manic-depression. The underlying cause for this disorder is unknown, but there is a strong genetic predisposition. Evidence suggests it is due to overactivity of the neurotransmitters. Treatment for bipolar disorder consists of mood-stabilizing drugs. These drugs control not only the "highs" but also the episodes of depression.

Lithium is a naturally occurring mineral that was observed to calm agitated behavior as long ago as ancient Egypt. Its usefulness as a mood stabilizer was first scientifically established in the 1940's and it was approved in 1970 for use in the United States. It is effective not only in stabilizing the mood during a manic episode but also in the prevention of future episodes. A significant problem with the use of lithium is that the dose at which it becomes effective is quite close to the dose which produces toxicity, characterized by drowsiness, blurred vision, stagger-ing, confusion, irregular heart beat, seizures, and coma. Patients taking lithium must therefore have blood drawn on a regular basis in order to determine drug levels. Patients who have poor kidney function should not take lithium because it is excreted pri-marily through the urine. Lithium's side effects in-clude nausea, diarrhea, tremor of the hands, dry mouth, and frequent urination.

Drugs usually used for the treatment of seizures may also help stabilize mood in bipolar patients, usually at lower doses than would be used for sei-zure control. These include carbamazepine, dival-proex, gabapentin, lamotrigine, and topiramate. It is believed that these drugs increase the amount of GABA at the synapse. GABA has a calming or inhibi-tory effect on the neurons. Side effects of these medications include dizziness, nausea, headaches, and visual changes.

PSYCHOSTIMULANTS

Attention-deficit hyperactivity disorder (ADHD) is found in both children and adults. Children with ADHD have difficulties at school because of im-pulsivity and inattention. The underlying cause of ADHD is extremely complex and the ways in which drugs used to treat it work are equally complex. The most successful treatments are with drugs that actu-ally stimulate the central nervous system. Drug ther-apy is most effective when combined with behavioral treatments. The most commonly used psychostim-ulants are methylphenidate and pemoline, but am-phetamines are sometimes used as well. Formerly, depressed patients were treated with amphetamines and similar compounds; occasionally this use is still found. These stimulant drugs do improve school performance; however, they may cause growth retar-dation in both height and weight. They may also cause insomnia and nervousness. Importantly, these drugs may be abused, leading ultimately to addic-tion, paranoia, and severe depression during with-drawal.

ANTIANXIETY DRUGS

These drugs are central nervous system depressants. Many of these antianxiety drugs or anxiolytics are, in higher doses, also used as sedative-hypnotics, or calming and sleep-inducing drugs. They seem to act by enhancing the effect of GABA in the brain. The earliest of these depressant drugs included chloro-

form, chloral hydrate, and paraldehyde, and they were used for anesthesia and for sedation.

Barbiturates were introduced in Germany in 1862 and were widely used for treatment of anxiety and sleep problems until the 1960's. Barbiturates are still available today, including pentobarbital, secobarbital, amobarbital, and phenobarbital. Their major adverse effect is respiratory depression, par-ticularly when used in combination with alcohol, an-other central nervous system depressant. With the advent of the safer benzodiazepines, use of the bar-biturates has declined steadily.

Benzodiazepines are used for two major prob-lems: anxiety and insomnia. Anxiety disorders appro-priate for this kind of treatment include generalized anxiety disorder, panic disorder, obsessive-compulsive disorder, phobic disorder, and dissociative disorder. The benzodiazepines commonly used for anxiety include alprazolam, chlordiazepoxide, clonazepam, clorazepate, diazepam, lorazepam, and oxazepam. For most of these disorders, however, behavioral, cognitive, group, and social therapy, or one of these therapies plus medication, are more effective than medication alone. Benzodiazepines used for in-somnia include estazolam, flurazepam, midazolam, quazepam, temazepam, and triazolam. Benzodiaz-epines may also be used to prevent the development of delirium tremens during alcohol withdrawal. Pa-tients become tolerant to the effects of these drugs, meaning they have the potential for physical de-pendency and addiction. In addition, benzodiaze-pines interact with many other drugs, including alcohol. Their use should be limited to brief peri-ods of time, particularly in the treatment of in-somnia. Long-term treatment for anxiety should be monitored carefully by the health care provider. Elderly people are more likely to suffer adverse ef-fects (such as confusion or falls) from benzodiaz-epine use.

Another drug developed for treatment of anxiety is buspirone. Propranolol and atenolol, usually used to treat high blood pressure, are useful in treating stage fright or performance anxiety, and clonidine, another blood pressure medication, is successfully used in treatment of anxiety. Nonbenzodiazepine sleep agents include zolpidem and zaleplon.

ANTIPSYCHOTIC DRUGS

Formerly known as "major tranquilizers" or "neu-roleptics," the antipsychotic drugs have revolutionized the treatment of schizophrenia and other psychoses. The underlying cause of psychosis is not known, but it is thought to be related to the neurotransmitter dopamine. Most of the antipsychotics block the dopamine receptors in the brain. The older antipsychotic drugs include thorazine, thioridazine, perphenazine, trifluoperazine, fluphenazine, thiothixene, and haloperidol. These older drugs treat the so-called positive symptoms of schizophrenia—hallucinations and delusions—but they have little effect on the "negative" symptoms—withdrawal, poor interpersonal relationships, and slowing of the body's movement. They also have multiple serious side effects including severe muscle spasm, tremor, rigidity, shuffling gait, stupor, fever, difficulty speaking, blood pressure changes, restlessness, and involuntary movements of the face, trunk, arms, and legs. Some of these are treatable using other drugs but some are neither treatable nor reversible. In an effort to overcome these problems, newer antipsychotics have been developed. The first of these was clozapine, which was successful in treating about one-third of the patients who did not respond to other antipsychotic drugs. While it had fewer of the serious side effects listed above, a small percentage of patients experience a severe drop in the white blood cells, which puts them at risk for serious infection. For this reason, patients on clozapine must be followed with frequent blood counts. Other newer antipsychotics include risperidone, olanzapine, and quetiapine. In addition to fewer of the serious side effects, the newer antipsychotics seem to have some effect on the negative symptoms.

SOURCES FOR FURTHER STUDY

Breggin, David, and Peter Cohen. *Your Drug May Be Your Problem: How and Why to Stop Taking Psychiatric Drugs.* Cambridge, Mass.: Perseus, 2000. A controversial book making an important argument that too many people are taking psychiatric medications and suffer serious side effects from those drugs. The authors give specifics about how to withdraw from drugs safely.

Drummond, Edward H. *The Complete Guide to Psychiatric Drugs: Straight Talk for Best Results.* New York: John Wiley & Sons, 2000. Covers the current state of knowledge about psychiatric illness, what medications may be helpful, how to decide whether medication might be useful, managing side effects, and nondrug therapies.

Gorman, Jack M. *The Essential Guide to Mental Health: The Most Comprehensive Guide to the New Psychiatry for Popular Family Use.* New York: St. Martin's Press, 1998. Covers psychiatric illness, how to search for a psychiatrist, drugs, and over-the-counter remedies.

_____. *Essential Guide to Psychiatric Drugs.* New York: St. Martin's Press, 1998. Contains detailed descriptions of the psychiatric medications available in the U.S. including uses, adverse effects, cost, dosages, and research findings. Written in a straightforward style for the layperson, but also useful to clinicians.

Kramer, Peter D. *Listening to Prozac: A Psychiatrist Explores Antidepressant Drugs and the Remaking of the Self.* New York: Penguin, 1997. An examination of the growing use of drugs in the treatment of mental illness, with discussion of the implications of this practice, both positive and negative.

Olson, James. *Pharmacology Made Ridiculously Simple.* Miami: MedMaster, 1998. A brief and straightforward explanation of the general principles of pharmacology. Enhanced by excellent diagrams and tables.

Rebecca Lovell Scott

SEE ALSO: Behavior therapy; Behavioral family therapy; Brief therapy; Cognitive behavior therapy; Cognitive therapy; Couples therapy; Gestalt therapy; Group therapy; Music, dance, and theater therapy; Observational learning and modeling therapy; Person-centered therapy; Play therapy; Psychotherapy: Children; Psychotherapy: Effectiveness; Psychotherapy: Goals and techniques; Psychotherapy: Historical approaches; Rational-emotive therapy; Reality therapy; Shock therapy.

Dyslexia

TYPE OF PSYCHOLOGY: Language
FIELDS OF STUDY: Childhood and adolescent disorders

Dyslexia is often defined as severe reading disability in children of otherwise average or above-average intelligence; it is thought to be caused by neuropsychological problems. Dyslexia frustrates afflicted children, damages their self-image, produces grave maladjustment in many cases, and decreases their adult contributions to society.

KEY CONCEPTS
- auditory dyslexia
- brain dysfunction
- computed tomography (CT) scan
- dysgraphia
- electroencephalogram (EEG)
- kinesthetic imprinting
- imprinting
- phonology
- self-image
- visual dyslexia

INTRODUCTION

The ability to read quickly and well is essential for success in modern industrialized societies. Several researchers, including Robert E. Valett, have pointed out that an individual must acquire considerable basic cognitive and perceptual-linguistic skills in order to learn to read. First, it is necessary to learn to focus one's attention, to concentrate, to follow directions, and to understand the language spoken in daily life. Next, it is essential to develop auditory and visual memory with sequencing ability, word-decoding skills, a facility for structural-contextual language analysis, the ability to interpret the written language, a useful vocabulary that expands as needed, and speed in scanning and interpreting written language. Valett has noted that these skills are taught in all good developmental reading programs.

Yet 20 to 25 percent of the population of the United States and many other industrialized societies, people who otherwise possess at least average intelligence, cannot develop good reading skills. Many such people are viewed as suffering from a neurological disorder called dyslexia, a term that was first introduced by a German ophthalmologist, Rudolph Berlin, in the nineteenth century. Berlin meant it to designate all those individuals who possessed an average or above-average performance intelligence quotient (IQ) but who could not read adequately because of an inability to process language symbols. Others reported children who could see perfectly well but who acted as though they were blind to the written language. For example, they could see a bird flying but were unable to identify the word "bird" written in a sentence.

Although the problem has been redefined many times over the ensuing years, the modern definition of dyslexia is still fairly close to Berlin's definition. The American Psychiatric Association's *Diagnostic and Statistical Manual of Mental Disorders: DSM-IV-TR* (rev. 4th ed., 2000) labels this condition "reading disorder" and defines it as reading achievement substantially below that expected given chronological age, measured intelligence, and age-appropriate education that interferes significantly with academic achievement or activities of daily living requiring reading skills.

BRAIN DEVELOPMENT

Two basic explanations have evolved for dyslexia. Many physicians propose that it is caused by either brain damage or brain dysfunction. Evolution of the problem is attributed to accident, to disease, or to faults in body chemistry. Diagnosis is made by the use of electroencephalograms (EEGs), computed tomography (CT) scans, and other related technology. After such evaluation, medication is often used to diminish hyperactivity and nervousness, and a group of physical training procedures called patterning are used as tools to counter the neurological defects.

In contrast, many special educators and other related researchers believe that the problem is one of dormant, immature, or undeveloped learning centers in the brain. The proponents of this concept encourage the correction of dyslexic problems by emphasized teaching of specific reading skills to appropriate individuals. While such experts also agree that the use of appropriate medication can be of value, they lend most of their efforts to curing the problem by a process called imprinting, which essentially trains the dyslexic patient through use of often-repeated, exaggerated language drills.

Another interesting point of view is the idea that dyslexia may be at least partly the fault of the written languages of the Western world. Rudolph F. Wagner has pointed out that children in Japan exhibit an incidence of dyslexia that is less than 1 percent. One explanation for this, say Wagner and others, is that the languages of the Western world require reading from left to right. This characteristic is absent in Japanese—possibly, they suggest, making it easier to learn.

A number of experts, among them Dale R. Jordan, recognize three types of dyslexia. The most common type—and the one most often identified as dyslexia—is visual dyslexia: the lack of ability to translate observed written or printed language into meaningful terms. The major difficulty here is that afflicted people see certain letters backward or upside down. The result is that, to them, a written sentence is a jumble of letters whose accurate translation may require five times as much time as would be needed by an unafflicted person.

> ## DSM-IV-TR Criteria for Reading Disorder (DSM code 315.00)
>
> Reading achievement, as measured by individually administered standardized tests of reading accuracy or comprehension, substantially below that expected given chronological age, measured intelligence, and age-appropriate education
>
> Disorder interferes significantly with academic achievement or activities of daily living requiring reading skills
>
> If a sensory deficit is present, reading difficulties exceed those usually associated with it

AUDITORY DYSLEXIA AND DYSGRAPHIA

The other two problems viewed as dyslexia are auditory dyslexia and dysgraphia. Auditory dyslexia is the inability to perceive individual sounds of spoken language. Despite having normal hearing, auditory dyslexics are deaf to the differences between certain vowel or consonant sounds; what they cannot hear, they cannot write. Dysgraphia is the inability to write legibly. The basis for this problem is a lack of the hand-eye coordination required to write legibly.

Usually, a child who suffers from visual dyslexia also exhibits elements of auditory dyslexia. This complicates the issue of teaching such a student, because only one type of dyslexic symptom can be treated at a time. Also, dyslexia appears to be a sex-linked disorder; three to four times as many boys have it as do girls. In all cases, early diagnosis and treatment of dyslexia are essential to its eventual correction. For example, if treatment begins before the third grade, there is an 80 percent probability that dyslexia can be corrected. When dyslexia remains undiscovered until the fifth grade, this probability is halved. If treatment does not begin until the seventh grade, the probability of successful treatment is only 3 to 5 percent.

ASSESSMENT METHODS AND TREATMENT

Preliminary identification of the dyslexic child often can be made from symptoms that include poor written schoolwork, easy distractibility, clumsiness, poor coordination and spatial orientation, confused writing and/or spelling, and poor left-right orientation. Because nondyslexic children can also show many of these symptoms, the second step of such identification is the use of written tests designed to pick out dyslexic children. These include the Peabody Individual Achievement Test, the Halstead-Reitan Neuropsychological Test Battery, and the SOYBAR Criterion Tests. Many more personalized tests are also available.

Once conclusive identification of a dyslexic child has been made, it becomes possible to begin a corrective treatment program. Most such programs are carried out by special-education teachers in school resource rooms, in special classes limited to children with reading disabilities, and in schools that specialize in treating the disorder.

One often-cited method is that of Grace Fernald, which utilizes kinesthetic imprinting, based on a combination of "language experience" and tactile stimulation. In this popular method, the child relates a spontaneous story to the teacher, who transcribes it. Next, each word unknown to the child is written down by the teacher, and the child traces its letters over and over until he or she can write that word without using the model. Each word learned becomes part of the child's word file. A large number of stories are handled this way. Many variants of the method are in use. Though it is quite slow, many anecdotal reports praise its results. (Despite this, Donald K. Routh pointed out in 1987 that the method had never been subjected to a rigorous, controlled study of its efficacy.)

A second common method utilized by special educators is the Orton-Gillingham-Stillman method, developed in a collaboration by teachers Anna Gillingham and Essie Stillman and the pediatric neurologist Samuel T. Orton. The method evolved from Orton's conceptualization of language as developing from a sequence of processes in the nervous system that end in unilateral control by the left cerebral hemisphere. He proposed that dyslexia arises from conflicts, which need to be corrected, between this hemisphere and the right cerebral hemisphere, usually involved in the handling of nonverbal, pictorial, and spatial stimuli.

Consequently, the method used is multisensory and kinesthetic, like Fernald's; however, it begins with the teaching of individual letters and phonemes, and progresses to dealing with syllables, words, and sentences. Children taught by this method are drilled systematically to imprint a mastery of phonics and the sounding out of unknown written words. They are encouraged to learn how the elements of written language look, how they sound, how it feels to pronounce them, and how it feels to write them down. Donald Routh has pointed out that the Orton-Gillingham-Stillman method is as laborious as that of Fernald. It is widely used and appreciated, however, and believed to work well.

Another method that merits brief discussion is the use of therapeutic drugs in the treatment of dyslexia. Most physicians and educators propose the use of these drugs as a useful adjunct to the training of dyslexic children who are easily distracted and restless or who have low morale because of embarrassment resulting from peer pressure. The drugs used most often are the amphetamine Dexedrine and methylphenidate (Ritalin).

These stimulants, taken in appropriate doses, lengthen the time period during which some dyslexic children function well in the classroom and also produce feelings of self-confidence. Side effects of overdose, however, include lost appetite, nausea, nervousness, and sleeplessness. Furthermore, there is the potential problem of drug abuse. Despite this, numerous sources (including both Valett and Jordan) indicate that stimulant benefits far outweigh any possible risks when the drugs are utilized carefully and under close medical supervision. Other, less dependable therapies sometimes attempted include special diets and the use of vitamins and minerals.

One other important aspect of the treatment of dyslexia is good parental emotional support, which helps children cope with their problems and with peer pressure. Useful aspects of this support include a positive attitude toward the afflicted child; appropriate home help for the child that complements efforts undertaken at school; encouragement and praise for achievements, without recrimination when repeated mistakes are made; and good interaction with special-education teachers assigned to a child.

RESEARCH

The identification of dyslexia more than one hundred years ago, which resulted from the endeavors of the German physician Rudolf Berlin and of W. A. Morgan, in England, launched efforts to find a cure for this unfortunate disorder. In 1917, the Scottish eye surgeon James Hinshelwood published a book on dyslexia, which he viewed as being a hereditary problem, and the phenomenon became better known to physicians. Attempts at educating dyslexics, as recommended by Hinshelwood and other physicians, were highly individualized until the endeavors of Orton and coworkers and of Fernald led to more standardized and soon widely used methods.

Furthermore, with the development of a more complete understanding of the brain and its many functions, better counseling facilities, and the conceptualization and actualization of both parent-child and parent-counselor interactions, the prognosis for successful dyslexic training has improved significantly. Also, a number of extensive studies of dyslexic children have been carried out and have identified dyslexia as a complex syndrome composed of numerous associated behavioral dysfunctions related to visual-motor brain immaturity. These include poor memory for details, easy distractibility, poor motor skills, letter and word reversal, and the inability to distinguish between important elements of the spoken language.

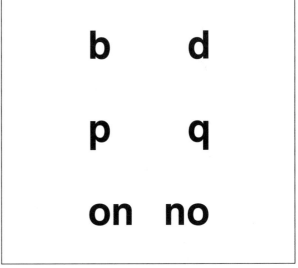

Dyslexia may make it difficult to distinguish letters and words that are mirror images of each other.

A particularly extensive and useful study was carried out by Edith Klasen and described in her book *The Syndrome of Specific Dyslexia: With Special Consideration of Its Physiological, Psychological, Testpsychological, and Social Correlates* (1972). The Klasen study identified the role of psychoanalytical interventions in the treatment of some dyslexic subjects, and it pointed out that environmental and socioeconomic factors contribute relatively little to occurrence of dyslexia but affect the outcomes of its treatment.

It is the endeavors of special education that have made the greatest inroads into treatment of dyslexia. Further advances in the area will undoubtedly be made, as the science of the mind grows and diversifies and as the contributions of the psychologist, physician, physiologist, and special educator mesh together more effectively.

SOURCES FOR FURTHER STUDY

Hoien, Torliev, and Ingvar Lundberg. *Dyslexia: From Theory to Intervention.* Norwell, Mass.: Kluwer, 2000. Presents European research in the causes and treatment of dyslexia, much of it presented in English for the first time.

Reid, Gavin. *Dyslexia: A Practitioner's Handbook.* 2d ed. New York: John Wiley & Sons, 1998. A review of dyslexia research and teaching practices for educators. Includes a review of resources for classroom strategies.

Reid, Gavin, and Janice Wearmouth. *Dyslexia and Literacy: An Introduction to Theory and Practice.* New York: John Wiley & Sons, 2002. Covers recent theoretical and practical approaches to dyslexia in both psychological and pedagogical contexts.

Snowling, Margaret J. *Dyslexia: A Cognitive Developmental Perspective.* 2d ed. New York: Basil Blackwell, 2000. Covers many aspects of dyslexia, including its identification, associated cognitive defects, the basis for development of language skills, and the importance of phonology. Also contains many references.

West, Thomas G. *In the Mind's Eye: Visual Thinkers, Gifted People with Dyslexia and Other Learning Difficulties, Computer Images, and the Ironies of Creativity.* Updated ed. Amherst, N.Y.: Prometheus Press, 1997. Argues that the rise of computer technology favors visual over verbal thinkers, decreasing the difficulties faced by dyslexics and others with verbal learning disorders.

Sanford S. Singer

SEE ALSO: Attention; Brain damage; Brain specialization; Brain structure; Language; Learning disorders; Peabody Individual Achievement Test (PIAT).

E

Eating disorders

TYPE OF PSYCHOLOGY: Psychopathology
FIELDS OF STUDY: General constructs and issues

Eating disorders include a group of eating and weight disturbances, including anorexia nervosa, bulimia nervosa, and binge-eating disorder, associated with underlying psychological problems.

KEY CONCEPTS
- anorexia nervosa
- binge-eating disorder
- bulimia nervosa
- eating disorder
- obesity

INTRODUCTION

Eating disorders were identified as early as ancient Rome, when banqueters gorged themselves, then induced vomiting. Some of the early female Christian saints were anorexic. However, eating disorders only emerged as an area of social and medical concern in the second half of the twentieth century.

Persons with eating disorders have a distorted body image and unrealistic ideas about weight. Although they are found primarily among young, middle- to upper-middle-class, well-educated Caucasian women, eating disorders increasingly affect and may be overlooked in men, older women, and persons of color. No single factor appears to be the cause of eating disorders, with social, cultural, psychological, genetic, biological, and physical factors all playing a part. Treatment may include hospitalization for nutritional monitoring and for stabilization in persons with serious medical complications or who are at risk for suicide. Regardless of the setting, treatment is best carried out by a multidisciplinary team, including a primary care physician or psychiatrist, a psychotherapist, a nutritionist, and, if appropriate, a family therapist.

Eating disorders are best thought of as problems involving body weight and distorted body image on a continuum of severity. The most serious is anorexia nervosa, a disorder characterized by weight loss greater than or equal to 15 percent of the body weight normal for the person's height and age. Bulimia nervosa is usually found in persons of normal weight and is characterized by consumption of large amounts of food followed by self-induced vomiting, purging with diuretics or laxatives, or excessive exercise. Binge-eating disorder, found usually in persons with some degree of overweight, is characterized by the consumption of large amounts of food without associated vomiting or purging. Other, milder, forms of eating disorders are at the least serious end of the continuum. Obesity may or may not be part of this continuum, depending on the presence or absence of underlying psychological problems. About one-third of obese persons have binge-eating disorder.

POPULATION AT RISK

Women constitute 90 percent of people diagnosed with eating disorders—eight million adolescent and young adult women in the United States alone. The majority of these are Caucasian (95 percent) and from middle- to upper-middle-class backgrounds. Research in the latter part of the twentieth century indicated that adolescent and young adult women were most likely to be affected; however, these disorders are now found in girls as young as nine and in older women. By the end of the twentieth century, eating disorders were also increasingly identified in women from other ethnic and socioeconomic groups. These disorders are most likely underreported in men and seem to affect gay men disproportionately. Also at risk are men with certain professions or avocations such as jockeys, dancers, body builders, and wrestlers, in which weight and body shape are an issue.

CAUSES OF EATING DISORDERS

No single cause has been identified for eating disorders. However, it is important to note that nearly all eating disorders begin with dieting to lose weight. Because these disorders are found almost exclusively in the developed world, where food is plentiful and where thinness in women is idealized, it appears that social and cultural factors are important contributors. Some theorists believe that cultural values of independence and personal autonomy rather than interdependence and the importance of human relationships contribute to eating pathology. Still others point to the changing and contradictory societal expectations about the roles of women as a contributing factor.

Studies suggest a genetic predisposition to eating disorders, particularly in those persons who engage in binge eating and purging behaviors. Their family histories typically include higher than expected numbers of persons with mood disorders and substance abuse problems. Dysfunctions in the pathways for the substances that transmit messages in the brain, the neurotransmitters, are thought to play a role in the development and maintenance of eating disorders, although these dysfunctions are not sufficient to explain the entire problem by themselves. The psychological theories about the causes of eating disorders postulate that individuals with underlying feelings of powerlessness or personal inadequacy attempt to cope by becoming preoccupied with their body's shape and size. Finally, the incidence of sexual abuse is higher among persons with eating disorders, particularly bulimia nervosa, than among those in the general population.

Eating disorders seem to develop in three stages. Stage 1 involves the period from the time a child is conceived until the onset of a particular behavior that precipitates the eating disorder. During this stage, individual psychological, personal, and physical factors, plus family, social, and cultural factors, place the person at increased risk. Individual risk factors include a personal history of depression, low self-esteem, perfectionism, an eagerness to please others, obesity, and physical or sexual abuse. Family risk factors include a family member with an eating disorder or a mood disorder and excessive familial concern for appearance and weight. Social and cul-

tural issues include emphasis on the cultural ideal of excessive thinness, leading to dissatisfaction with the body and dieting for weight loss. Young women who are dancers, runners, skaters, gymnasts, and the like may be particularly susceptible to this kind of cultural pressure.

Stage 2 involves the factors which actually precipitate the eating disorder. Some identified precipitating factors include onset of puberty, leaving home, new relationships, death of a relative, illness, adverse comments about weight and body appearance, fear of maturation, the struggle for autonomy during the midteen years, and identity conflicts.

Stage 3 involves the factors which perpetuate the eating disorder. These can be cognitive distortions, interpersonal events, and/or biological changes related to starvation.

ASSOCIATED MEDICAL PROBLEMS

Women with anorexia nervosa stop menstruating. Anorexics may also have abdominal pain, constipation, and increased urination. The heart rate may be slow or irregular. Many develop downy, dark body hair (lanugo) over normally hairless areas. They may have bloating after eating and swelling of the feet and lower legs. Low levels of potassium and sodium and other imbalances in the body's electrolytes can lead to cardiac arrest, kidney failure, weakness, confusion, poor memory, disordered thinking, and mood swings. The death rate for anorexics is high: About 5 percent will die within eight years of being diagnosed and 20 percent within twenty years.

Self-induced vomiting can lead to erosion of tooth enamel, gum abscesses, and swelling of the parotid glands in front of the ear and over the angle of the jaw. About one-third of women with bulimia have abnormal changes in their menstrual cycles. Some bulimics consume so much food in such a short period of time that their stomachs rupture. More than 75 percent of these individuals die. Use of ipecac and laxatives can lead to heart damage. Symptoms include chest pain, skipped heartbeats, and fainting, and these heart problems can lead to death. In addition, bulimics are at increased risk for ulcers of the stomach and small intestine and for inflammation of the pancreas.

One commonly overlooked problem is the "female athletic triad," a combination of disordered eating, loss of menstruation, and osteoporosis. This can lead to fractures and permanent loss of bone minerals.

ANOREXIA NERVOSA

The diagnosis of anorexia nervosa is made in persons who have lost 15 percent or more of the body weight that is considered normal for their height and age and who have an intense and irrational fear of gaining weight. Even with extreme weight loss, anorexics perceive themselves as overweight. Their attitude toward food and weight control becomes obsessive and they frequently develop bizarre or ritualistic behaviors around food, such as chewing each bite a specific number of times. Anorexics minimize the seriousness of their weight loss and are highly resistant to treatment.

The two basic types of anorexia nervosa are the restricting type and the binge-eating/purging type. The restricting type is characterized by an extremely limited diet, often without carbohydrates or fats. This may be accompanied by excessive exercising or hyperactivity. Up to half of anorexics eventually lose control over their severely restricted dieting and begin to engage in binge eating. They then induce vomiting, use diuretics or laxatives, or exercise excessively to control their weight. People who are in the binge-eating/purging group are at greater risk for medical complications.

As the weight loss in either type reaches starvation proportions, anorexics become more and more preoccupied with food; they may hoard food or steal. They also experience sleep abnormalities, loss of interest in sex, and poor concentration and attention. In addition, they slowly restrict their social contacts and become more and more socially isolated. In general, anorexics of the binge-eating/purging type are likely to have problems with impulse control and may engage in substance abuse, excessive spending, sexual promiscuity, and other forms of compulsive behavior. This group is also more likely to attempt suicide or to hurt themselves than others with eating disorders.

BULIMIA NERVOSA

Persons who have bulimia nervosa are similar in behavior to the subset of anorexics who binge and purge, but they tend to maintain their weight at or near normal for their age and height. They intermittently have an overwhelming urge to eat, usually associated with a period of anxiety or depression, and can consume as many as 15,000 calories in a relatively short period of time, typically one to two hours. Binge foods are usually high calorie and easy to digest, such as ice cream. The binge eating provides a sense of numbing of the anxiety or relief from the depression. Failing to recognize that they are full, bulimics eventually stop eating because of abdominal pain, nausea, being interrupted, or some other non-hunger-related reason. At that point, psychological stress again increases as they reflect on the amount they have eaten. Most bulimics then induce vomiting, but some use laxatives, diuretics, severe food restriction, fasting, or excessive exercise to avoid gaining weight.

Bulimics tend to be secretive, binge eating and purging when alone. These episodes may occur only a few times a week or as often as several times a day. As with binge-eating/purging anorexics, bulimics are likely to abuse alcohol and other drugs, make suicidal gestures, and engage in other kinds of impulsive behavior such as shoplifting. Because of the electrolyte imbalances and other adverse consequences of repeated vomiting or the use of laxatives or diuretics, bulimics are at risk for multiple serious medical complications which, if uncorrected, can lead to death.

BINGE-EATING DISORDER

The American Psychiatric Association has developed provisional criteria for binge-eating disorder in order to study this disorder more completely. The criteria include compulsive and excessive eating at least twice a week for six months without self-induced vomiting, purging, or excessive exercise. That is, binge-eating disorder is bulimia nervosa without the compensatory weight-loss mechanisms. For this reason, most binge eaters are slightly to significantly overweight. In addition to the eating problems, many binge eaters experience relationship problems and have a history of depression or other psychiatric disorders.

OTHER EATING DISORDERS

Anorexia and bulimia nervosa and binge-eating disorder have strict diagnostic criteria set forth by the American Psychiatric Association. However, these three do not cover the entire spectrum of disordered eating patterns. Those people who induce vomiting after consuming only a small amount of food, for example, or those who chew large amounts of food and spit it out rather than swallow it, do not fit the diagnosis of bulimia. For such persons, a diagnosis of "Eating Disorder, Not Otherwise Specified" is used.

PREVALENCE OF EATING DISORDERS

Anorexia nervosa is the rarest of the eating disorders, affecting fewer than 1 percent of adolescent and young women (that is, women ages thirteen to twenty-five) and a tiny proportion of young men. Bulimia nervosa, on the other hand, affects up to 3 percent of teenage and young adult women and about 0.2 percent of men. Even more of this age group, probably 5 percent, suffer from binge-eating disorder. In obese patients, fully one-third meet the criteria for this disorder. Binge eating is the most common eating disorder in men, although more women actually have this disorder. Eating Disorders, Not Otherwise Specified, are even more common.

TREATMENT

Treatment of persons with eating disorders can take place in an inpatient or an outpatient setting. Hospitalization is indicated for patients with severe malnutrition, serious medical complications, an increased risk of suicide, and those who are unable to care for themselves or have failed outpatient treatment.

The first step in the treatment of anorexics must be restoring their body weight. This may require hospitalization. A system of carefully structured rewards for weight gain is often successful. For example, the gain of a target amount of weight may be tied to being allowed to go outside or having visits from friends. Once the anorexic is nutritionally stabilized, individual, family, cognitive-behavioral, and other therapies are indicated to address issues specific to the individual.

The first step in the treatment of bulimics is a comprehensive medical evaluation. Bulimics are less likely than anorexics to require hospitalization. As with anorexia nervosa, treatment includes individual, family, and cognitive-behavioral therapies. In addition, group therapy may be helpful. Cognitive-behavioral therapies are effective in the treatment of bulimia nervosa. Patients are taught to recognize and analyze cues that trigger the binge-purge cycle. Once analyzed, they are taught to reframe these thoughts, feelings, and beliefs to more adaptive and less destructive ones, thus altering the cycle.

Outpatient care should be carefully coordinated among a multidisciplinary team: an experienced health care practitioner to monitor the patient's medical condition, a therapist to address psychological and emotional issues, a family therapist to deal with control and other issues within the family, and a nutritionist to develop and monitor a sensible meal plan.

Medications may be a helpful adjunct in some cases, particularly in those eating-disordered patients who have an additional psychiatric diagnosis such as major depression or obsessive-compulsive disorder. Simply gaining weight usually improves mood in anorexics, but antidepressants (particularly the selective serotonin-reuptake inhibitors or SSRIs) may help not only with depression but also with the obsessive-compulsive aspects of the anorexic's relationship with food.

Several different antidepressants (including monoamine oxidase inhibitors, the tricyclics amitriptyline and desipramine, and high-dose fluoxetine, an SSRI) are associated with fewer episodes of binge eating and purging in bulimic patients, in addition to treating anxiety and depression. These drugs have not been studied extensively in the treatment of binge-eating disorder, however.

PREVENTION OF EATING DISORDERS

Prevention measures should include education about normal body weight for height and techniques used in advertising and the media to promote an unrealistic body image. Parents, teachers, coaches, and health care providers all play a role in prevention. Parents, coaches, and teachers need to be educated about the messages they give to growing children about bodies, body development, and weight. In addition, they need to be aware of early signs of risk. Health care providers need to include screening for eating disorders as a routine part of care. Specific indicators include dieting for weight loss associated with unrealistic weight goals, criticism of the body, social isolation, cessation of menses, and evidence of vomiting or laxative or diuretic use.

SOURCES FOR FURTHER STUDY

Arenson, Gloria. *A Substance Called Food.* 2d ed. Boston: McGraw-Hill, 1989. Presents a variety of perspectives on eating, including the physiological and the transpersonal. Particularly useful in providing self-help advice and treatment modalities.

Examines the compulsiveness of food addiction and sees behavior modification as a means of addressing the addictive behavior.

Battegay, Raymond. *The Hunger Diseases.* Northvale, N.J.: Jason Aronson, 1997. Addresses the emotional hunger that, the author contends, underlies all eating disorders, from anorexia to obesity.

Bruch, Hilde. *The Golden Cage: The Enigma of Anorexia Nervosa.* Reprint. Cambridge, Mass.: Harvard University Press, 2001. A classic work by a pioneer in the field of eating disorders. Portrays the development of anorexia nervosa as an attempt by a young woman to attain a sense of control and identity. Discusses the etiology and treatment of anorexia from a modified psychoanalytic perspective.

Brumberg, Joan J. *Fasting Girls: The History of Anorexia Nervosa.* Rev. ed. New York: Vintage, 2000. Outlines the history of anorexia nervosa. Examines the syndrome from multiple perspectives while leaning toward a cultural and feminist perspective. A well-researched and very readable work.

Gordon, Richard. *Eating Disorders: Anatomy of a Social Epidemic.* 2d rev. ed. New York: Blackwell, 2000. A survey of current clinical practice in dealing with eating disorders, as well as thorough coverage of their history and social context.

Hirschmann, Jane R., and Carol H. Munter. *When Women Stop Hating Their Bodies: Freeing Yourself from Food and Weight Obsessions.* New York: Fawcett, 1997. A follow-up to the authors' *Overcoming Overeating* (1988), reviews the psychological basis for compulsive eating and provides alternative strategies to persons who have an addictive relationship with food. Presents convincing arguments against dieting and proposes that self-acceptance, physical activity, and health are more appropriate long-term solutions to the problem of overeating.

Sacker, Ira M., and Marc A. Zimmerman. *Dying to Be Thin: Understanding and Defeating Anorexia Nervosa and Bulimia.* Updated ed. New York: Warner Books, 2001. A practical approach, written by two medical doctors, to understanding the sources and causes of eating disorders and how to overcome them. Includes a guide to resources, treatment clinics, and support groups.

Schwartz, Hillel. *Never Satisfied: A Cultural History of Diets, Fantasies, and Fat.* New York: Free Press, 1986. Schwartz, a historian, looks at diets and eating from the perspective of American social and cultural history. Begins with the first weight watchers, in the early nineteenth century; examines how "shared fictions" about the body fit with various reducing methods and fads in different eras.

Rebecca Lovell Scott

SEE ALSO: Anorexia nervosa and bulimia nervosa; Anxiety disorders; Depression; Hunger; Obesity; Obsessive-compulsive disorder.

Educational psychology

TYPE OF PSYCHOLOGY: Learning
FIELDS OF STUDY: Cognitive learning

Educational psychology is a diverse and dynamic discipline aimed at facilitating human learning through effective instruction.

KEY CONCEPTS
- cognitive skill induction
- educational task
- far transfer
- interactive models
- metacognition
- near transfer
- problem solving

INTRODUCTION

Teaching is a complex undertaking involving decision making at many levels as well as a diversity of skills. From kindergarten to college, teachers are involved in designing curricula, planning lessons, selecting texts, evaluating the products of learning, and monitoring a full range of action within the classroom. The choices are many, and effective teaching demands additional expertise in terms of the delivery of instruction. Indeed, the teacher functions both as a theorist, objectively analyzing the situation of learning and methods of instruction, and as a practitioner, in the more spontaneous delivery of instruction in an attempt to inspire young minds.

Teaching is the deliberate facilitation of learning; learning is a relatively permanent change in behavior or the gaining of a new perspective on or insight into a problem. Learning may take place without teaching. For example, children seem to acquire language without specific instruction. Teaching, on the other hand, may or may not be effective in stimulating learning. It is the goal of educational psychology to facilitate effective instruction to foster human learning.

Educational psychology, a diverse scientific discipline, attempts to apply psychological principles to understand, predict, and influence classroom learning. Just as teaching and learning are ongoing processes, so is educational psychology an evolving enterprise. Researchers search for dependable answers to many practical educational questions. They ask which teaching methods are most effective, as well as which methods work best for particular students. They examine whether grades are effective motivators (and again, for which students they are effective). They look at whether holding a student back a grade has positive or negative effects on subsequent performance. Research in educational psychology is often inconclusive because of the complexity of the questions, discrepancies in terminology, and/or faulty methodologies. For this reason, research is replicated; sound educational practice is based on well-supported trends. Educational psychology is a continually developing discipline, integrating theoretical perspectives with practical concerns.

LEARNING MODELS

In 1979, James Jenkins devised an interactive model for learning researchers that can be used as a guide to understanding classroom learning in terms of both personal and environmental (outside the person) factors. This tetrahedral model posits that learning is influenced by four types of variables: characteristics of the learner (beliefs, skills, energy level, and so on), characteristics of the teacher (voice, gender, attitude), criterion of evaluation (for example, whether the work is for a grade), and characteristics of the task (such as whether it is written or verbal, and whether it is timed). The interplay of these four types of variables affects the quality of learning. In helping a child who apparently has difficulty with mathematics, a teacher familiar with the principles of the tetrahedral model might consider interventions such as changing the type of tests (timed tests might not be fair to some learners), changing the grading system, or even changing the lessons to include visual or diagrammatic materials to explain math principles. Often the solution focuses on

changing the learner, who is perhaps the hardest to change. Jenkins's model also serves as a framework for understanding how educational psychology is applied to classroom learning situations.

Student learning is complex, as are the variables that affect it. Learner and teacher characteristics, for example, include a variety of attributes. Some are stable or constant (sex, race, or ability). Others are consistent or generally stable, changing little over time or situation, such as attitudes, beliefs, and learning styles. Some learner and teacher attributes are unstable and likely to change, such as the level of arousal, anxiety, or mood. It is the more consistent variables that affect learning in general, are more easily measured, and are investigated more frequently. Among the most recently researched variables are perceptions of learners—about specific tasks, self, or others—which can be experimentally changed through a process of reorientation or instruction. Such variables are often found to affect students' willingness to engage or persist in learning, and consequently, to affect their school achievement. Along similar lines, the investigation of students' metacognition, or their management of their own thought processes, has inspired the development of effective remedial reading programs and revitalized instruction of study skills.

Other research on instruction in cognitive skills has focused on interventions to teach thinking, either through stand-alone programs (such as a course in philosophy or a unit on how to make valid inferences), instruction in processing skills in the context of subject matter teaming (such as measuring in science or problem-solving strategies in math), or instruction in problem solving during an authentic task, such as a computer simulation (of pioneer travel, for example) or a project (such as a scientific experiment). Results generally suggest that regardless of which of the three approaches is used, cognitive skill instruction is effective only if skills are taught explicitly and if skill assessment tasks are similar to tasks used in training (near transfer). Generalization of effects to distantly related assessment tasks (far transfer) diminishes with the degree of characteristics shared between assessment and training tasks.

APPLIED RESEARCH

In a 1972 study investigating how college students learn, Gordon Pask and others differentiated holist and serialist learning styles. Using a "teach-back" procedure, Pask had students create fictitious zoological taxonomies and then teach those classifications back to the experimenter. Serialists were characterized as remembering information in terms of lengthy strings of data. That is, bits of information were related sequentially and in a linear, step-by-step fashion. The serial style relies on memorization. Holists, on the other hand, remembered in terms of hierarchical relations, imaging the entire system of facts or principles in a more general manner; they focused on the big picture and fit details in later. The holist strategy was related to what Pask called "comprehension learning," with the serialist orientation reflective of "operational learning" (focusing on details and procedures). Pask also found that teaching materials could be structured in either a holist (meaningful) or serialist (memorization) fashion and were most effective when matched to the student's corresponding learning style.

In addition to investigating learner characteristics, researchers in educational psychology have explored how it is that teacher characteristics affect student learning. In particular, teachers' motivational beliefs, a fairly consistent variable, have been linked to teaching behaviors. In 1984, Carole Ames and Russell Ames identified three systems of teacher motivation based on specific values held by teachers that result in different perceptions, motivations, and teaching strategies. In the "ability evaluative" system, teachers tend to maintain their notions of self-worth by protecting their own positive notions of their ability. That is, teachers see their personal value as contingent on students' success. This results in blaming the student for failure and crediting themselves when students are successful. In the second system, the "moral responsibility" system, teachers primarily are concerned with the pupil. The resulting behaviors are the opposite of those associated with the ability evaluative orientation: blaming self for failures and crediting the student for success. In the "task mastery" condition, the task is of primary importance rather than a teacher's self-image. The focus is on accomplishing educational goals and fostering competence. Thus, from an interactionist perspective, teachers' beliefs about learning and about themselves are an integral part of the learning process.

The characteristics of the task are the third major type of variable affecting classroom learning and

are a primary area of concern for researchers. Attributes of the task might include the type of task: aural or visual, motor or verbal, comprehension or memorization, self-instructional or teacher-assisted. A major development in the area of self-instruction as related to learning tasks has been computer-aided instruction. In 1983, educational psychologists James Kulik, Robert Bangert, and George Williams reviewed numerous studies regarding the use of computers for instructional purposes in sixth- to twelfth-grade classrooms. They found that there were moderate benefits in terms of improvement on examinations and in reducing the amount of time needed for learning. Also, children taught with computers developed more positive attitudes toward computers than those who were taught in the traditional manner.

Finally, the type of evaluation has an effect on classroom learning. Perhaps the most common type of student evaluation is grading, assigning letter or number ratings to reflect the quality of student work. Although grades may be intended to function as incentives or motivators to encourage students to perform, it is unlikely that they do so. In a 2000 study, Robert Slavin found that grades are used for three primary functions: evaluation, feedback, and incentives. As a result, grades function as less than ideal motivators. Also, grades are given too infrequently for young children to see any relationship between their daily work and a grade received weeks later. Grades may be effective incentives for older students, however; studies comparing college students in graded versus ungraded classes have found that grades do function as an incentive.

PHILOSOPHICAL ROOTS AND CONTEMPORARY MODELS

Educational psychology draws on many resources to form well-grounded models. The philosophical roots of educational psychology lie in the early twentieth century work of William James and John Dewey. Both were scholars who shared a concern for the application of psychological principles in the classroom. James described the teacher's role as that of developing good habits and productive thinking in the student. Dewey, on the other hand, called for the transformation of education in terms of expanding the curriculum to include the needs of an increasingly industrial society. Dewey saw schools as agents of social change.

As the twentieth century progressed, psychology developed as a social science, and two major conceptions of learning were spawned: the Gestalt model and behaviorism. In the Gestalt view, learning is defined as a change in the perceptual process, or as understanding a problem in a new way—insight. In contrast, the behavioral view rests on the assumption of stimulus substitution: Existing responses became associated with new stimuli through the process of conditioning. The emphasis is on observed relationships—behaviors. Behaviorism had a profound influence on American education, in terms of both instruction and classroom management. For example, "time out," or removing a child from the stimuli of the existing environment to a quiet and boring place, has been used as a form of punishment.

Since 1975, cognitive psychology, with its emphasis on the processes of learning, has dominated the instructional scene. The advent of computer technology offered a model of information processing, and advances in military technology demanded that researchers consider how it is that humans carry out decision-making processes. More specifically, it was wondered how learners attend to, organize, store, and retrieve information. In a 2001 study, Margaret Gredler cited three reasons for increased emphasis on cognitive processes: Behaviorism was too limited in explaining human activity, learners had come to be viewed as active manipulators rather than as passive recipients of knowledge, and learners were viewed as interacting with environments. Prominent instructional models based on cognitive theory include Jerome Bruner's discovery learning, emphasizing the teacher's role in creating situations in which students can learn on their own, and, in contrast, David Ausubel's reception learning, which focuses on teacher-structured learning in the form of well-organized lessons. From an interactive perspective, discovery learning empowers the learner by positing the teacher as a facilitator, whereas reception learning empowers the teacher in controlling the learning situation. Finally, a model of teaming and teaching originating in Lev Vygotsky's cultural-historical theory of development emphasizes the development of a child's cognition through interaction with an adult who both models a skill and verbally mediates the child's encounter with the task until the child achieves independence at the task. From an interactive perspective, Vygotsky's model

might be seen to empower both teacher and learner in turn.

SOURCES FOR FURTHER STUDY

Gredler, Margaret E. *Learning and Instruction.* 4th ed. Englewood Cliffs, N.J.: Prentice-Hall, 2001. Gredler discusses the functions of learning theory as it applies to instruction, the history of the development of educational psychology, and seven contemporary views on learning and instruction. The presentation is concise and appropriate for secondary and college students.

Schmeck, Ronald R., ed. *Learning Strategies and Learning Styles.* New York: Plenum, 1988. Offers a timely selection of current thinking on student learning styles based on a variety of methodologies. Included are neuropsychological, cognitive, and affective perspectives. Well suited for college students as well as professionals.

Slavin, Robert E. *Educational Psychology.* 6th ed. Needham Heights, Mass.: Allyn & Bacon, 2000. Slavin offers a practical look at effective classroom practice based on recent research findings. The college-level text illustrates how research may directly affect classroom practice.

Snowman, Jack, Robert F. Biehler, and Curtis Bank. *Psychology Applied to Teaching.* 9th ed. Boston: Houghton Mifflin, 2000. A well-researched and timely look at classroom learning, this text emphasizes practical applications with real classroom situations. Especially useful for future teachers in secondary or college levels.

Ellen Lavelle;
updated by John F. Wakefield

SEE ALSO: Cognitive development: Jean Piaget; Cognitive maps; Concept formation; Cooperative learning; Learning; Prejudice reduction; Teaching methods.

Ego defense mechanisms

TYPE OF PSYCHOLOGY: Emotion; personality; psychopathology; psychotherapy

FIELDS OF STUDY: Anxiety disorders; models of abnormality; personality assessment; personality disorders; personality theory; classic analytic themes and issues; psychodynamic and neoanalytic models; psychodynamic therapies

The concept of ego defense mechanisms, originally a central feature of Sigmund Freud's psychoanalytic theory, came to be incorporated into the general body of knowledge in the fields of psychology and psychiatry during the last half of the twentieth century; ego defenses protect people from being overwhelmed by strong emotion and are crucial for psychological survival. However, when used maladaptively, they can result in the formation of psychiatric symptoms and psychopathology.

KEY CONCEPTS

- adaptation
- anxiety
- conflict
- psychoanalysis
- psychopathology
- repression
- suppression

INTRODUCTION

Ego defense mechanisms are complex, largely unconscious mental processes that protect people from becoming overwhelmed by strong emotions. Defense mechanisms protect the mind and nervous system just as the immune system protects the body, and they are essential for healthy functioning and adaptation. However, when they are used maladaptively, psychiatric symptoms can develop and result in psychopathology.

At birth, only rudimentary defenses are in place, so infants require substantial protection from external sources (caretakers) to protect them from becoming overwhelmed by internal and environmental stresses. Over the course of childhood and continuing into adulthood, however, increasingly complex defense mechanisms develop and are added to an individual's defense repertoire. As a result, each individual forms a personal defense system from which to automatically draw when emotions threaten to become too stressful. Some defenses work better in certain situations than others, so optimal adaptation in life is related to having more mature defenses, as well as flexibility in using them.

HISTORY

The phenomenon of defense mechanisms was not recognized until it was identified in the last decade of the 1800's by Sigmund Freud (1856-1939), the Austrian founder of psychoanalysis. Freud described defense mechanisms as discrete processes for managing emotion and instincts, but for more than twenty years, he interchangeably used the general term "defense" and the term for one specific defense mechanism named "repression," which resulted in considerable confusion among his readers. In 1936, however, Freud clarified that there were many defensive operations used by the ego and referred to the book his daughter, Anna Freud, a famous psychoanalyst in her own right, had just written entitled *Das Ich und die Abwehrmechanismen* (1936; *The Ego and the Mechanisms of Defense*, 1937). Building on this work, other researchers have since described additional defense mechanisms and have elucidated their roles as adaptive processes.

ANXIETY

In his seminal work, Sigmund Freud focused primarily on defense mechanisms in their role of protecting the ego from anxiety resulting from internal conflicts. A conflict is caused when two or more equally powerful influences cannot be satisfied at the same time. It is resolved when one of the influences prevails, but this often leads to frustration because one (or more) of the other goals is thwarted. Most internal conflicts involve the interactions of the id, ego, and superego. For example, one may have a strong id impulse to overeat, but one's superego may exert an equally powerful influence to remain thin. Thus, the sight of food may cause one to feel anxious without knowing why, because this conflict may be buried in the unconscious.

Conflicts may be either conscious or unconscious; according to Freud, all conflicts are accompanied by anxiety. Anxiety is an unpleasant emotional response that signals impending danger. It is anticipation of danger to be experienced in the future. Only the ego can feel anxiety, and this anxiety can be unbearable. It can occur in the absence of any objective external threat; even when a real threat exists, the emotional reaction is often much greater than warranted. For example, speaking in front of an audience is, in the real sense, not dangerous, but it can cause extreme anxiety in some people. Frequently, the threat that causes anxiety is unconscious, and the person may not be aware of the source.

Anxiety is a signal to take action, so it is both adaptive and self-regulating. That is, when faced with anxiety, the ego automatically attempts to reduce it, which at the same time should reduce the potential danger. In this regard, fear and anxiety are similar. For example, if a person is attacked, the person can fight the attacker or can run away. In both cases, the danger will be removed and the fear will subside. Since one of the main functions of the ego is to maintain survival, its typical response is to take actions which will protect itself and the organism. The ego responds in a defensive manner to all types of anxiety, no matter what their source. In the example above, the mode of reducing fear is overt—that is, it is easily observable (the person fights or runs away). In other situations, the actions taken by the ego to protect itself are said to be covert, which means they are not directly observable. These covert actions of protecting the ego from anxiety are called ego defense mechanisms. According to Freud, they operate at an unconscious level.

REPRESSION

Freud was especially interested in the process of repression, which begins when the ego fully separates itself from the id, but probably does not become fully operational until the phallic psychosexual stage of development. In repression, the ego blocks or diverts any ideas, thoughts, feelings, or urges that it finds unacceptable or anxiety producing. For example, a person might have a desire to have sex with his or her boss or teacher, but if this wish is totally unacceptable to the superego, it can be repressed into the unconscious. Allowing this wish to become conscious would result in punishment from the person's superego in the form of guilt, anxiety. or shame. In order to avoid this psychological response, the ego prevents the idea from ever becoming conscious. Although there is no memory of this impulse, it is never destroyed; in fact, it maintains all of its energy. It remains immediately under the level of awareness but has the potential to surface at any time. Because of this, the person may feel ill at ease or anxious but has no awareness concerning the origin of this distress. Furthermore, the repressed energy continues to seek expression, and it often escapes in a disguised form.

The most important disguised forms of repressed material are neurotic symptoms. According to Freud, repressed energy must be released if the organism is to remain healthy. As the ego puts more and more effort into repressing unacceptable drives, it becomes weaker; sooner or later, something has to give in. Symptoms serve as a compromise, because they al-

low the repressed ideas to be expressed indirectly in a disguised form, without arousing anxiety. The symptoms may be either psychological or physical. Physical symptoms are sometimes called conversion reactions, because the energy associated with the original repressed idea is converted into symptoms such as paralysis or even blindness; however, these symptoms are attributable to psychological causes, and there is no real organic impairment. Thus, Sigmund Freud delineated the manner in which repression can become maladaptive and result in psychopathology, a conceptualization that was extremely innovative for its time.

Freud hit upon the notion of repression when he noticed that his patients were resisting his attempts to help them. In this sense, repression is intimately linked to resistance. According to Freud, when he was using hypnosis to treat his patients, this resistance was hidden; however, as soon as the technique of free association replaced hypnosis, resistance was clearly evident, and psychoanalysis was born.

Freud's concept of repression (which he first called "defense") appeared in print in 1894. At that time, most of his patients were women who were suffering from an emotional disorder that was then called hysteria. Freud believed that hysteria was caused primarily by the repression of sexual impulses, and that it could be cured by means of a "talking" therapy. At the time, it was a giant leap for psychology, because the prevailing viewpoint of the nineteenth century was that emotional disorders were caused by organic or physical factors. Freud's theory emphasized a psychological cause and cure for emotional disorders, and thus opened a new area of exploration and set the stage for clinical psychology and psychiatry.

POST-FREUDIAN THEORIES

Freud wrote about various defense mechanisms in a number of his works, but his daughter Anna Freud is credited with bringing them all together in her book *The Ego and the Mechanisms of Defense*. In it, she describes the original nine defense mechanisms of repression, regression, undoing, isolation, turning against self, reaction formation, reversal, projection, and introjection. She also adds sublimation and displacement to these. Over the years, other defense mechanisms, such as denial, rationalization, identification, intellectualization, and idealization were added, along with new knowledge, such as the importance of defense with regard to other emotions, such as anger, and the differences between defenses due to the ages at which they first develop, as seen in Joseph Sandler's book, cowritten with Anna Freud, *The Analysis of Defense: The Ego and the Mechanisms of Defense Revisited* (1985).

In 1977, George E. Vaillant, a professor of psychiatry at Harvard University, published *Adaptation to Life*, a landmark study on the mental health and adaptation of a highly select group of male college graduates over a thirty-five-year period of adulthood. In his book, Vaillant documented important shifts in defensive styles during adult development, and also demonstrated that individual differences in the types of defenses utilized were dramatically related to variance between the best and worst outcomes, especially with regard to measures of social, occupational, and psychological adjustment. Vaillant believed that there were innumerable defenses, but he selected eighteen of what he thought were the most salient mechanisms and organized them into four levels according to their hypothesized maturity and importance with regard to the development of psychopathology:

Level 1. Psychotic Mechanisms (delusional projection, denial of external reality, and distortion)

Level 2. Immature Mechanisms (projection, schizoid fantasy or withdrawal, hypochondriasis, passive-aggressive behavior, and acting out)

Level 3. Neurotic Defenses (intellectualization, repression, displacement, reaction formation, dissociation)

Level 4. Mature Mechanisms (altruism, humor, suppression, anticipation, sublimation)

Level 1 defenses were noted as common in childhood prior to age five, in dreams of healthy individuals at all ages, and in psychotic types of psychopathology. Level 2 mechanisms were common in healthy children between the ages of three and fifteen, and in some types of adult psychopathology such as severe depression and personality disorders. Level 3 defenses were deemed common in healthy people of all ages after the age of three, in mastering acute adult stress, and in neurotic disorders. Level 4 defenses were listed as common in healthy individuals from age twelve on.

With regard to the study participants, Vaillant found that as adolescents, they were twice as likely to use immature defenses as mature ones, but by middle life, they were four times as likely to use mature defenses rather than immature ones. This developmental shift was not equally obtained by everyone, however. Rather, the thirty men with the best outcomes (termed "generative") had virtually stopped using immature mechanisms by midlife, with roughly equal use of neurotic and mature defenses. The men with the worst outcomes (termed "perpetual boys"), on the other hand, failed to show any significant shift in defenses after adolescence. Thus, Vaillant demonstrated that ego development, including maturation of defense mechanisms, was distinct from physical maturation as well as from cognitive or intellectual development, and that the level of defense maturation was directly related to life adjustment.

Vaillant was especially struck by the importance of suppression as an adaptive defense mechanism. He defined suppression as the conscious or subconscious decision to deliberately postpone attending to conscious conflicts or impulses, without avoiding them. This mechanism allows individuals to effectively cope with stress when it is optimal to do so. Vaillant delineated the evolution of this defense as beginning with denial before age five, followed by repression from five to adolescence, with suppression emerging during late adolescence and adulthood when defense maturation is optimal.

Thus, Vaillant helped to delineate better the relationship between the healthy and adaptive need for ego defense mechanisms and the psychopathological outcomes that occur when they are utilized maladaptively. Moreover, he demonstrated their development over time as part of the maturation process. Unfortunately, this study involved a highly select group of men and there were no women in this study, so generalizations to the larger population are difficult to make.

APPLICATIONS OF DEFENSE MECHANISMS

In spite of the difficulty with generalization, the body of information regarding defenses underscores the importance of teaching children and adolescents to utilize increasingly mature mechanisms. Research has shown that this can be done effectively with social and emotional literacy programs, for example, in school classrooms. This application primarily involves prevention and has been growing in use since about 1990.

Applications regarding interventions with individuals showing maladaptive defense use, on the other hand, have been utilized much longer than prevention. Sigmund Freud developed psychoanalysis at the turn of the twentieth century with this in mind, and other forms of psychotherapy have since evolved that also embrace the importance of defense mechanisms in the development of psychopathology.

One illustration from psychoanalytic theory provides some of the flavor of how complex this topic really is. Freud believed that many neurotic symptoms are associated with the sex drive. For example, a man with an unusually strong superego may repress all sexual impulses. Through the process of reaction formation, these impulses may be converted into compulsive handwashing. According to psychoanalytic theory, the symptoms serve as a substitute for the sexual gratification that he is not allowed to obtain in real life. This is an unconscious process, and the man has no idea of the connection between the symptoms and his sex drive. When a person's behavior is dominated by defense mechanisms, or symptoms become severe, there may be a need for psychotherapy. The goal of therapy is not to eliminate defense mechanisms, but rather to strengthen the ego so that it utilizes more mature processes and can respond to conflicts in a more adaptive and productive manner.

For example, one of the objectives of psychoanalytic therapy is to uncover repressed material that is responsible for the unconscious conflicts or symptoms, which in turn facilitates the development of suppression. In a sense, people relive their lives in the therapy room so the conflict can be traced to its origin. In order to help the patient do this, the psychoanalyst uses two major techniques within the important context of the therapeutic relationship. The first is called free association. This involves having the patient talk about anything and everything that enters his or her mind, no matter how trivial or embarrassing it may be. This technique is based on the idea that thoughts and ideas do not enter one's mind accidentally. There is usually an important reason for their appearance, and eventually thoughts that are related to the conflict are revealed. The second technique is interpretation, which can involve analyzing dreams, actions, feelings of the patient for the analyst, and so on. Freud was especially interested in dreams, the "royal road to the unconscious."

During sleep, ego defense mechanisms are weakened; therefore, many unconscious conflicts or desires may emerge—although still in a disguised form that needs to be interpreted by the therapist.

Although brief interventions can sometimes help people to cope better with life's stresses, therapy usually takes a long time, because maturation is generally a slow and complex process. Repression is especially difficult, because once material is repressed, the ego sets up a counterforce that prevents it from becoming conscious in the future. This counterforce is called resistance. It is responsible for a person unconsciously resisting treatment, as removing the symptoms only serves to return the ego to the original anxiety-producing conflict.

In the example above, once the resistance is overcome, the therapist may determine that the compulsive handwashing behavior is rooted in an unresolved Oedipus complex. In this case, the man's sexual attraction to his mother was repressed, and eventually all sexual impulses were treated in the same way. Giving careful consideration to timing, the therapist voices an interpretation, which is the method by which the unconscious meaning of a person's thoughts, behaviors, or symptoms is divulged. One interpretation is not enough to cure the patient, but a slow process of "working through," which involves many interpretations and reinterpretations, finally leads to insight. This last step occurs when a person fully understands and accepts the unconscious meaning of his or her thoughts and behaviors; at this point, the symptoms often disappear.

EXAMPLES OF SELECTED DEFENSE MECHANISMS

Regression involves reducing anxiety or other strong feelings by attempting to return to an earlier and less stressful stage of development and engaging in the immature behavior or thinking characteristic of that stage. The most basic type of regression is sleep, which occupies most of the time of infants. For example, in response to an anxiety-producing test, a person might sleep through the alarm and thus miss the test (and avoid anxiety). Another example of regression is a child engaging in behaviors such as thumb sucking when a new sibling is born, or the adult behavior of smoking, both of which have their roots in the oral stage of infancy. Regression is one of the first defense mechanisms to emerge: It begins in the first year of life.

Projection is when one first represses, then assigns one's own unacceptable or dangerous impulses, attitudes, or behaviors to other persons. For example, one blames others for one's failures. Freud believed that this occurs unconsciously, but some modern psychoanalysts believe that it can occur consciously as well. An example would be a married man with an unconscious desire to have an affair accusing his wife of having done so.

Denial occurs when the ego does not acknowledge anxiety-producing reality. For example, a person may not "see" that his marriage is falling apart and may behave as if nothing is wrong; a good student may "forget" that he failed a test in school. A form of psychotic denial is the example of a woman who continued to sleep with her husband's corpse for several days after he had died.

Rationalization occurs when the ego tries to excuse itself logically from blame for unacceptable behaviors. For example, a student declares that she failed a test because her roommate kept her up the night before, or a man gets drunk because he had such a "tough day" at the office.

Isolation is the process that separates unpleasant memories from emotions that were once connected to them. In this case, the ideas remain, but only in isolated form. For example, one might vividly remember a childhood situation of being spanked by one's father but not recall the intense negative feelings one had toward him at that time because such feelings would be painful. This defense mechanism probably begins to emerge in the anal psychosexual stage, but it fully develops between ages three and five.

Introjection is also called identification. It involves modeling or incorporating the qualities of another person, such as one's parents or teachers. Sometimes people do this with people that they fear; by doing so, the fear associated with them is reduced. Anna Freud calls this "identification with the aggressor." For example, little boys identify with their fathers in order to reduce the castration anxiety associated with the Oedipus complex. As a result, boys adopt the social, moral, and cultural values of the father, all of which become incorporated into the superego.

Reaction formation occurs when a person expresses a repressed unconscious impulse by its directly opposite behavior. Hate may be replaced by love, or attraction by repulsion. The original feeling is not lost, but it does not become conscious. For example, a reaction formation to strong sexual impulses may be celibacy, or a parent who unconsciously hates her child may "smother" it by being overly protective. Reaction formation is another defense mechanism that is closely related to repression.

Sublimation involves channeling the power of instincts and emotions into scientific or artistic endeavors such as writing books, building cities, doing research, or landing a person on the moon. Freud believed that sublimation was especially important for building culture and society.

Summary

Defense mechanisms were initially discovered and studied with regard to their role in psychiatric symptom formation when utilized maladaptively. Unfortunately, this led many people to believe that defense mechanisms themselves were dysfunctional, which is not true. As Vaillant and others have shown, defenses are necessary for adaptation, survival, and happiness, but some are more effective for different stages of life than others, and maturational shifts in the development of ego defenses can have profound effects on social, emotional, and occupational adjustment.

On the positive side, Freud's conceptualization of defense mechanisms led directly to his formulation of psychoanalysis, which was the first major personality theory and treatment method in psychology. Virtually all personality theories and treatment methods since then have been directly or indirectly influenced by the notions of defense and resistance. In addition, the concept of defense mechanisms has become an important part of Western language and culture.

Sources for Further Study

Appignanesi, Richard. *Freud for Beginners*. Illustrated by Oscar Zarate. New York: Pantheon Press, 1979. The authors describe this book as a "documentary comic book" about the world of Freud. Brief and easy to follow, it very simply reviews the major aspects of Freud's theory, such as the unconscious, sex drives, and dreams, in a picture format. It caricatures Freud's family, friends, and some of his patients. Although it is light and enjoyable, it must be supplemented by other works.

Freud, Anna. *The Ego and the Mechanisms of Defense.* Rev. ed. New York: International Universities Press, 1966. A short and relatively easy-to-read book written by Freud's daughter. She begins with a brief introduction to psychoanalysis and continues with a comprehensive review of all the ego defense mechanisms, which includes clear examples. Includes a short bibliography. Throughout the book, she notes original sources from her father's writing.

Freud, Sigmund. *The Standard Edition of the Complete Psychological Works of Sigmund Freud.* Edited by James Strachey. 24 vols. London: Hogarth Press, 1953-1974. Starting in 1953, all of Freud's written material was published in English in twenty-four volumes. Although more appropriate for advanced readers, all the volumes include an extensive bibliography and comprehensive footnotes which clarify the material very well. The volumes with subject matter related to ego defense mechanisms include *The Interpretation of Dreams* (vols. 4-5), *The Psychopathology of Everyday Life* (vol. 6), and *Inhibitions, Symptoms, and Anxiety* (vol. 20).

Sandler, J., with A. Freud. *The Analysis of Defense: The Ego and the Mechanisms of Defense Revisited.* New York: International Universities Press, 1985. This book provides short summaries that update different concepts related to defense mechanisms, but primarily includes transcripts of lengthy interviews with Anna Freud by Joseph Sandler on a variety of related topics.

Vaillant, G. E. *Adaptation to Life: How the Best and the Brightest Came of Age.* Boston: Little, Brown, 1977. This book provides details of the thirty-five years of research on the mental health, basic styles of adaptation, and developmental consequences of a select group of male college graduates. The importance of defense mechanisms for healthy adaptation is emphasized along with the psychopathological consequences with less-than-optimal maturation of defense mechanisms.

Salvatore Cullari;
updated by Carol A. Kusché

SEE ALSO: Abnormality: Psychological models; Anxiety disorders; Consciousness; Dreams; Ego, superego, and id; Psychoanalysis; Psychoanalytic psychology; Psychoanalytic psychology and personality: Sigmund Freud; Psychosexual development.

Ego psychology
Erik Erikson

DATE: The late 1930's forward
TYPE OF PSYCHOLOGY: Personality
FIELDS OF STUDY: Personality theory

Ego psychology, pioneered by Heinz Hartmann, Erik Erikson, Erich Fromm, Harry Stack Sullivan, and Karen Horney, provided a significant new reformation to the personality theory of Freudian psychoanalysis. Erikson's theory of the growth of the ego throughout the life cycle provided an especially important contribution to this movement.

KEY CONCEPTS
- ego
- id
- psychoanalysis
- unconscious
- psychosocial

INTRODUCTION

Ego psychology emerged in the late 1930's as a reform movement within psychoanalysis. Psychoanalysis, as developed by Sigmund Freud in the previous three decades, was an innovative approach to understanding psychological life. Freud developed the methodology and vocabulary to focus on the meaningfulness of lived experience. For Freud, the true meaning of an experience was largely unconscious. Dreams, slips of the tongue or pen, and symptoms provided examples of such unconscious layers of meaning. In psychoanalytic terminology, beneath the level of the conscious ego, there is an unconscious substructure (the id). Freud used the metaphor of an iceberg to relate these two levels, indicating that the conscious level is analogous to the small, visible tip of an iceberg that shows above the water, whereas the unconscious level is like its large, underwater, invisible mass. The ego, this small surface level of the personality, "manages" one's relations with the world beyond the psyche. The id, in contrast, is "intrapsychic" in the sense that it is not in a relation with the "outer" world beyond the psyche. Rather, the id draws its energy from the biological energy of the instinctual body (such as instincts for sex and aggression). In this traditional psychoanalytic theory, then, the conscious level of the person is rooted in, and motivated by, an unconscious level, as psychological life is ultimately rooted in biological forces.

Freudian psychoanalysis advanced psychology by legitimating the study of the meaningfulness of human actions, but it did so at the price of conceiving of conscious, worldly experience as being only a surface, subtended by unconscious, biological forces, mechanisms cut off from worldly involvement. By the late 1930's, some psychoanalysts had concluded this was too steep a price to pay. The first to formulate these objections systematically was Heinz Hartmann, whose writings between 1939 and 1950 advanced the argument for the autonomy of the ego as a structure of the personality independent of the domination of the unconscious id. It was Hartmann who gave to this protest movement the name "ego psychology."

In the next generation of analysts, this movement found its most articulate voices: Erich Fromm, Harry Stack Sullivan, Karen Horney, and Erik Erikson. Writing from the 1940's through the 1980's, all contributed independently, with their own particular genius, to a perspective that grants to the ego a status much more significant than its role in Freudian psychoanalysis. For them, it is people's relations with the world (and not their subterranean biological energy) that is the most important aspect of their psychological life. For this reason, these psychologists have also sometimes been known as the "social" or "interpersonal" analysts. While all four have unquestionably earned their enduring international reputations, Erik Erikson became the most well known, on account of his formulation of a powerful and comprehensive developmental theory to account for the growth of the ego throughout life. Freud had asserted that the ego was a weak aspect of the personality, whereas Hartmann posited a strong ego. However, there are wide individual differences in ego strength. Erikson demonstrated how ego strength emerges across stages of a person's development, and showed that its particular growth depends on the quality, at each stage, of a person's relations with the world and with other people.

ERIKSON'S SHIFT TO THE PSYCHOSOCIAL LEVEL

Freud had also sketched a developmental theory for psychoanalysis. Built upon his view of the primacy of the intrapsychic id and its bodily source of energy, this theory focused on psychosexual develop-

ment. For Freud, "sexual" means more than the usual notion of genital sexuality; it is a more general dynamic expression of bodily energy that manifests itself in different forms at different developmental stages. The adult (genital) stage of sexuality, reached at puberty, is the culmination and completion of one's psychosexual development. Preceding that development, Freud saw four pregenital stages of psychosexual development: the oral stage, the anal stage, the phallic stage, and the latency stage. Hence, for this theory of psychosexual development, each stage is centralized as a stage by a particular expression of sexual or erogenous energy. In each stage there is a particular mode of the bodying forth of this energy as desire, manifested by the unique bodily zone that becomes the erogenous zone of that specific stage. It is seen as erogenous because of that bodily zone's capacity to be especially susceptible to stimulation or arousal, such that it becomes the prime source of bodily satisfaction and pleasure at that stage.

Erikson concluded that this psychosexual level was a valid but incomplete portrait of development. More than other proponents of ego psychology, he sought to work with Freud's emphasis on the bodily zones while striving to include that vision within a larger, more encompassing framework. Erikson theorized that each bodily mode correlated with a psychological modality, one that implicated the person's developing ego relations with the world. In particular, he emphasized one's relations with other people as the most important "profile" of the world. He saw the psychosexual meaning of the various bodily zones grounded by changes in the person's social existence at each stage. For that reason, Erikson named his approach a theory of psychosocial development and argued that the growth of the ego could not be reduced to changes in bodily energies. He demonstrated how the psychosexual dimension always implied a key human relation at the heart of each stage, and so the interpersonal could not be reduced to some intrapsychic cause, but was itself the basis for the actual development of that stage.

The significance of this shift from the psychosexual level of development to the psychosocial one was enormous, but it can best be appreciated in the context of its depiction of each of the particular stages. One other impact was also strikingly noteworthy. Whereas Freud's theory of psychosexual development saw the process as coming to an end with the person's arrival at the genital stage (with puberty), Erikson realized that the growth of the ego in psychosocial development does not end there, but continues in subsequent stages throughout the person's life. In that way, he also transformed developmental psychology from its origins as merely a child psychology into a truly life-span psychology, a revision now widely accepted.

STAGES OF DEVELOPMENT

Erikson specified eight stages of psychosocial development over the course of the life cycle. He saw these unfolding not in a linear sense, but epigenetically, that is, in such a way that each stage builds upon those that came before. The first four of these stages are those of childhood, and here Erikson accepts Freud's delineation, but adds a psychosocial dimension to each.

The first stage of development (roughly the first year of life) Freud termed the oral stage, naming it (as he did with each) after that region of the body seen to be the erogenous zone of that stage. For Freud, the baby's psychosexuality expresses itself primarily through the erogenous power of the mouth and lips. Certainly babies' tendency to mouth almost anything they can get hold of would indicate a certain erotic appeal of orality at this time.

However, for Erikson, this bodily expression is not the foundational one. Rather, orality is a wider theme. The essence of this oral pleasure is the satisfaction of "taking in" the world. Such taking in is not restricted to the mouth. Babies take in with their eyes, their ears, their fingers—in every way possible. Orality, as taking in, is not merely a bodily zone, but a psychological modality of relating to the world. This world-relation also implicates another person. For a quite helpless baby to be able to get or take in, there must be another there giving (typically a parent). This psychological modality, in other words, is already essentially and profoundly interpersonal. As a result, it is the quality of this interpersonal relationship with the "mothering ones" that will provide the basis of the baby's growth at this stage. If the parents (as the face of the world) are dependably there for the baby, the baby will come to be able to count on their omnipresent beneficence.

With such experience, the baby develops a sense of "basic trust"—Erikson's term for the ego growth of this first stage. Basic trust implies a certain relation with the world: specifically, one in which the person can relax and take his or her own ongoingness for granted. Once trust is gained, such a person can face the uncertainties to come with the secure confidence that, whatever may happen, he or she will be fine. In contrast, if the baby does not encounter a trustworthy world at this stage, he or she will be unable to develop this core sense of basic trust. The baby will, instead, be overwhelmed by the experience of "basic mistrust"—the anxiety that accompanies the lurking, ever-present possibility of threat, that edge of anonymous malevolence. Then, full openness to the world is always constricted by the need for the self-preservation of the ego.

Freud identified the second psychosexual stage (roughly the period from age one to three) as the anal stage, on account of the pleasure available by the new ability of the child to control eliminative functioning—what is colloquially called toilet training. Here again, Erikson reexamined this bodily mode and discovered, at the heart of it, a psychosocial dynamic. The issue of control in mastering the processes of elimination involves two kinds of action: retention (of feces or urine) until one gets to the toilet, and then elimination (once one is at the toilet).

Erikson recognized that this interplay between retention and elimination is more than merely the organ mode of sphincter control. Rather, it manifests a more basic psychological modality: the interplay between holding on and letting go. It is not only with regard to the eliminative functions that this dynamic gets played out in this stage. Most important, it is in the social arena, with one's parents, that toddlers grow this new capacity to exercise control. Even toilet training itself is an exquisitely interpersonal interaction of the child with the parental "trainers."

It is not only toilet training that distinguishes children's quest for control at this stage. In many ways the child is now striving for a new encounter with others. Securely grounded now by the sense of basic trust gained in the previous stage, children are ready to move from a relationship of dependence to one of independence. Even being able to stand up on their own two feet evinces this new relationship. From a newfound delight in the power of speaking the word "no!" to the appearance of strong preferences in everything from clothes to food, and most evidently in their emotional reactions to the denial of these preferences, toddlers are asserting a declaration of independence. Though the consequent contest of wills with the parents can be difficult, ultimately the child learns both to have autonomy and to recognize its social limits. This growth of autonomy is the key gain of this second stage, as the ego grasps its radical independence from the minds or control of others. If the child does not have the opportunity to develop this experience, the consequence would be to develop a crippling sense of shame and self-doubt instead.

The third stage of psychosexual development (ages three through six) is Freud's phallic stage, because the child's sexual organs become the erogenous zone at this time. Freud did not mean to imply that children experience their sexuality in the sense of adult, genital sexuality; there is no experience of orgasms and no interest in intercourse at this time. Rather, for Freud, the sex organs become erogenous on account of their power to differentiate gender. Hence, the classic psychoanalytic themes of penis envy and castration anxiety are rooted in this stage, as well as the Oedipal conflict—children's imaginal working out of their now gender-based relations with their parents.

For Erikson, it is not the genitals as bodily organs that are the source of such anxiety or envy. Rather, they symbolize social roles. As a result, in a sexist culture, it would be no wonder that a girl may envy the greater psychosocial status enjoyed by the boy. Correlatively, the boy would experience the anxiety of losing his newfound gender-based potency. Here again, Erikson finds a profound interpersonal dynamic at work. This new positing of oneself is not done only in the child's fantasy life. The ego at this stage is growing new capacities to engage the world: the ability to use language, more fine locomotor activity, and the power of the imagination. Through these developing capacities, children can thrust themselves forth with a new sense of purpose. On the secure basis of trust and autonomy, they can now include initiative in their world relations, supported by their parents as encouraging prototypes. On the other hand, the parents can so stigmatize such projects of initiative that children may instead become convinced that they manifest their badness. In such cases, feelings of guilt can overwhelm their sense of initiative, as they become crippled by guilt not only for what they have done but also for who they are as initiating beings.

Freud identified the fourth psychosexual stage as the latency stage (ages seven to twelve) because psychosexuality was not manifest at that time. It had become latent, or driven underground, by the conclusion of the Oedipal conflict. For Freud, psychosexual development is arrested at this stage and must await the eruption of puberty to get it started again. Erikson sees in this stage a positive growth in the child's ego. Once more, changes in psychosocial relations lead the way. The child goes off to school, and to a wider world beyond the immediate family circle, to encounter the world beyond the imaginal realm: a place in which actual accomplishments await the application of actual skills. Rather than being satisfied with imagining hitting a home run, the child now strives to actually hit the ball. It is, in other words, a time for the development of skills, techniques, and competencies that will enable one to succeed at real-world events. Sports, games, school, bicycling, camping, collecting things, taking care of pets, art, music, even doing chores now offer children arenas to test their growing capacity to learn the ways of the world.

At the heart of this learning process are teachers, not only professionals, but learned others of many kinds. The child becomes a student to many experts, from coaches to cub scout leaders to the older boy next door who already knows about computers. Even sports heroes or characters in books, with whom the child has no personal contact, can emerge as profoundly valuable teachers, opening the world and showing the way to mastery of it. This is what Erikson means by a sense of industry, which is for him the key egoic gain of this stage. If children's efforts are not encouraged and cultivated, however, they can instead find their industrious tendency overwhelmed by a sense of inferiority and inadequacy.

PSYCHOSOCIAL STAGES OF LATER CHILDHOOD

It is when the child arrives at Freud's fifth stage that the psychosexual and psychosocial theories must part from their previous chronological company. Freud's fifth stage is the genital stage: the completion of psychosexual development. With puberty, the person attains the same capacities and erogenous orientation as an adult, and thus becomes as mature, psychosexually speaking, as any adult. For Erikson's theory, however, the onset of puberty does not mark the completion of psychosocial development, which continues throughout life, but only its next stage:

adolescence (ages twelve to twenty-one). Once more, the changing bodily zone implicates a changing social existence, for puberty is more than a merely chemical or hormonal change. More than the body, it is the whole person who is transformed by this flood of new issues and possibilities. This eruption provokes questions that had been taken for granted before. "Who am I becoming? Who am I to be?" appear, in small and large ways. The new adolescent must confront such new questions when on a date, at a party, or even when deciding what to wear to school that day. In other words, the adolescent ego has now developed a self-reflective loop, in which its own identity is now taken as an issue to be formed, a task that it must resolve for itself.

The formation of ego-identity can be an especially acute challenge in contemporary culture, where the traditional embeddedness in extended families and communities is too often no longer available to provide the network of identifications with which to resolve these questions. Instead, adolescent peer groups become the key psychosocial relationship for this stage. These reference groups offer the adolescent the prospect of trying on a new identity by embracing certain subgroup values, norms, and perspectives. This experimental phase is an acting "as if"—as if the person were who they are trying out to be.

Optimally, adolescents will have the latitude to assume and discard prospective identities within the fluidity of what Erikson called a psychosocial moratorium—a time out from having to bear the same weight of consequences for their choices that an adult would. For example, pledging a lifetime commitment to a boyfriend at thirteen does not in fact entail the same level of commitment that a marriage would; nor does deciding to major in accounting upon arriving at college actually bind one to follow through with a lifetime career as an accountant. With sufficient opportunity to explore and try out various tentative choices, adolescents will, optimally, conclude this stage by arriving at a more clarified sense of their own values and sense of direction. If this is not achieved, adolescents will either be left with a feeling of identity diffusion or have prematurely foreclosed on a possible identity that does not fit.

PSYCHOSOCIAL STAGES OF ADULTHOOD

Beyond adolescence, Erikson also identified three psychosocial stages of adulthood: early adulthood,

middle age, and old age. The first, roughly the period of one's twenties and thirties, begins with the person's moving out from under the insulating protection of the adolescent psychosocial moratorium. One's choices (of marriage, career, family) cease to be "as if"; they are now profoundly real commitments with long-term impact. Making such commitments is not only a momentary event (such as saying "I do"), but requires devoting oneself to living an ongoing and open-ended history. This new situation inaugurates the next psychosocial development, which Erikson names the crisis of intimacy versus isolation. Intimacy here has a broader range than its typical connotation of sexual relations: It encompasses the capacity to relate to another with fullness and mutuality. To be fully open with and to another person entails obvious risks—of being misunderstood or rejected—but with it comes the enormous gain of true love. To experience the closeness, sharing, and valuing of the other without boundaries is the hallmark of an infinite relationship (infinite, that is, not necessarily in duration, but in depth). The relationship with a loved other is the evident psychosocial context of this growth. If it does not occur, then the early adult will come to experience instead a deep sense of isolation and loneliness. This consequence can accrue either through the failure to enter into a relationship or through the failure, within a relationship, to achieve intimacy. Some of the most terrible afflictions of isolation at this stage are within those marriages so lacking in intimacy that the couple are essentially isolated even though living together.

Beginning around age forty, a further stage of adult psychosocial development begins: middle age. The situation has once again changed. People are no longer merely starting out on their adulthood, but have by now achieved a place in the adult world. Typically, if they are going to have a family, they have got it by now; if a career, they are well launched by now. Indeed, middle age, the period from forty to sixty-five, marks the attainment of the height of a person's worldly powers and responsibilities. Whatever worldly mountain one is going to climb in this lifetime, it is during middle age that one gets as high up it as one will go. The arrival at this new position opens the door to the next stage of development. Now the psychosocial growth will involve one's social relations with the next generation, centered on the issue of generativity versus stagnation. The long plateau of middle age offers the opportunity to become helpful to those who follow along that upward climb. These are, most immediately, one's own children, but also include the next generation in the community, on the job, in the profession, in the whole human family. The middle-aged adult is in the position of being the teacher, the mentor, the instituter, the creator, the producer—the generator. Having arrived at the peak of one's own mountain one no longer need be so concerned about placating someone else, and so is able now to fully be oneself. To be an original, the middle-aged adult can also originate in the truest sense: to give of oneself to those who, following along behind, need that help. In this way, the person grows the specific ego-strength of care: an extending of oneself to others in an asymmetric way, giving without expectation of an equal return, precisely because one can. The failure to grow in this way results in stagnation—the disillusioned boredom of a life going nowhere. Some middle-aged adults, trying futilely to ward off this gnawing feeling of stagnation, hide behind desperate efforts of self-absorption, what Erikson called "treating oneself as one's one and only child."

By the late sixties, a variety of changes mark the onset of the final stage of psychosocial development: old age. Retirement, becoming a grandparent, declining health, and even the increasingly frequent death of one's own age-mates, all precipitate a new issue into the forefront: one's own mortality. While people at every age know they are mortal, this knowledge has no particular impact on one's life when one is younger because it is then so easily overlooked. In contrast, by old age, this knowledge of one's mortality is now woven into the very fabric of one's everyday life, in a way that it can no longer be evaded by imagining it postponed until some distant, abstract future.

Contemporary American society tends to avoid really confronting one's being-towards-death. Some psychologists have gone so far as to say that death has replaced sex as the primary cultural taboo, hidden in hospital rooms and code words ("passed on," "put to sleep," "expired"). Fearing death, people find it very hard to grow old. If one is not available to the growth opportunities of this stage, one is likely to sink instead into despair—a feeling of regret over a life not lived. Often even one's despair cannot be faced and is then hidden beneath feelings of disgust

and bitterness: a self-contempt turned outward against the world.

Erikson points out that this final stage of life offers the opportunity for the ultimate growth of the ego. To embrace one's mortality fully allows one to stand open-eyed at the edge of one's life, a perspective from which it becomes possible to really see one's life as a whole. One can then see, and own, one's life as one's own responsibility, admitting of no substitutes. It is this holistic vision of one's life that Erikson calls integrity: the full integration of the personality. It is in this vision that people can actually realize that their own lives are also integrated with life as a whole, in a seamless web of interconnections. Thus, the ego finally finds its ultimate, transpersonal home within the whole of being. It is this perspective that opens the door to wisdom, the final growth.

SOURCES FOR FURTHER STUDY

Coles, Robert. *Erik H. Erikson: The Growth of His Work*. Boston: Little, Brown, 1970. A fine blend of Erikson's biography with his major ideas.

_____, ed. *The Erik Erikson Reader*. New York: W. W. Norton, 2000. A collection of Erikson's most influential and accessible writings.

Erikson, Erik H. *Childhood and Society*. 2d ed. New York: W. W. Norton, 1963. A wide-ranging compilation of Erikson's studies of development, clinical practice, cross-cultural analyses, and psychohistory. His most accessible and popular book.

_____. *Gandhi's Truth*. New York: W. W. Norton, 1969. Erikson's application of his developmental theory to the life of Gandhi. This book won the Pulitzer Prize.

_____. *Identity and the Life Cycle*. New York: W. W. Norton, 1980. Erikson's view of human development with particular emphasis on ego identity and its formation in adolescence.

_____. *The Life Cycle Completed*. Extended version. New York: W. W. Norton, 1997. Erikson's final book, examining the life cycle from the viewpoint of the final stage.

Friedman, Lawrence. *Identity's Architect: A Biography of Erik H. Erikson*. New York: Simon & Schuster, 1999. A thorough and balanced biography of Erikson, written by an author who interviewed his subject extensively in the last years of his life.

Hartmann, Heinz. *Essays on Ego Psychology*. New York: International Universities Press, 1964. A collection of Hartmann's foundational essays on the autonomy of the ego.

Yankelovich, Daniel, and William Barrett. *Ego and Instinct*. New York: Vintage, 1970. An original contribution to the dialogue of Freudian psychoanalysis and ego psychology on the question of human nature.

Christopher M. Aanstoos

SEE ALSO: Ego defense mechanisms; Ego, superego, and id; Erikson, Erik; Oedipus complex; Penis envy; Personality theory; Psychoanalytic psychology; Psychoanalytic psychology and personality: Sigmund Freud; Psychosexual development.

Ego, superego, and id

TYPE OF PSYCHOLOGY: Personality

FIELDS OF STUDY: Classic analytic themes and issues; personality theory; psychodynamic therapies

The ego, superego, and id are the three components of personality structure, according to Sigmund Freud. These hypothetical, interacting structures are used to explain human behavior.

KEY CONCEPTS
- conscience
- instincts
- introjection
- pleasure principle
- primary process
- reality principle
- secondary process

INTRODUCTION

The ego, superego, and id are terms used by the father of psychoanalysis, Austrian Sigmund Freud (1856-1939), to describe the three components in the structural model of personality. He developed and wrote about this model in his classic work *Das Ich und das Es* (1923; *The Ego and the Id*, 1926).

Prior to the structural model, Freud's focus was on understanding and differentiating conscious and unconscious processes. He came to realize that an additional model was needed to further elucidate the working of the mind and to describe the special functions that parts of the mind utilize. The structural model is not a replacement for his topographical model (unconscious and conscious), but rather it complements his previous work.

Freud's structural model proposes that the personality has a definite structure, with three interacting components called the id, ego, and superego. The id is present from birth and is essentially a psychical representation of instincts or passions. The ego represents reason and thoughtful deliberation, while the superego represents the morals of society and ideal aspirations. These components are hypothetical and are not located in a specific region of the brain. Since Freud's initial background and work were biologically based, this represented a major shift toward a more psychological understanding of human behavior.

ID

The id is present at birth, is totally unconscious, and contains everything inherited at birth, especially the innate instincts or impulses. The purpose of the id is to satisfy one's innate urges. Freud theorized that the id operates according to the pleasure principle, seeking immediate gratification of wishes and a reduction of pain and tension. Since the id is infantile and primitive by nature, it attempts to satisfy its desires by what Freud termed primary process. This means that the id is illogical, asocial, impulsive, and demanding. Primary process means that there is action or discharge without thought or delay. There is no consideration of reality or the needs of others.

The id is instinctual and the source of all energy and passions. Freud proposed two classes of instincts: the sexual instincts, or eros, and the destructive instincts, or thanatos. Eros includes humans' drives for self-preservation and the preservation of the species through sexuality. These instincts are life affirming, seeking development and renewal. In direct contrast, thanatos opposes life and seeks to bring about death and destruction. Freud viewed the death instinct (thanatos) as a desire to return to an earlier, inorganic state with an absence of undesired stimulation. Both classes of instincts can be directed inward toward the self or outward, toward others. Eros and thanatos are typically fused (combined) together, thus modifying the potential destructiveness of thanatos.

Very young children, with their wants and lack of self-control, exemplify the concept of the id. (CLEO Photography)

EGO

The ego, according to Freud, is the component of the mind that is able to adapt to the demands of the external environment. The ego develops from the id and learns about the external world through the senses. As the child interacts with the world, the ego gains important perceptual and cognitive abilities.

Freud proposed that the ego operates according to the reality principle, replacing the id's uninhibited search for gratification with thoughts and behaviors that take into account the conditions of real life and the needs of others. The ego uses secondary process, a higher level of mental functioning, including intelligent reasoning and problem-solving skills, to mediate between the demands of the id, superego, and external reality. The ego therefore functions as the executive component of personality structure. The ego exercises delay and restraint in meeting the unrealistic demands of the id's im-

pulses. It considers how pleasure can be obtained without bringing harm to self or others.

The metaphor of a horse and rider was used by Freud to describe the relationship between the ego and the id. The horse represents the power and strength of the id, while the rider (ego) attempts to guide the horse in an appropriate direction.

After Freud's death, his daughter Anna Freud and others focused their study on ego functioning in the personality. Ego psychology is a term used to describe the study of the ego and its role in adaptation and development.

SUPEREGO

Freud used the term superego, commonly referred to as conscience, to describe the third component of personality structure. The conscience is formed by the moral influences of parents and society, including rules and standards of conduct. It serves as the judge of what is right and wrong, and can be quite harsh and perfectionistic.

The superego develops as children identify with parents and authority figures. Freud believed that the superego forms by an introjection (a process of taking inside or incorporating) of the values of the parents. It is interesting to note that this concept served as precursor to object relations theorists, who pay close attention to relationships between internal objects and external relationships. The superego, as an internal object, takes over the initial role of the parents by giving the ego orders, judging, and threatening it with punishments. Guilt feelings result when behavior does not live up to the expectations of the superego.

INTEGRATION OF ID, EGO, AND SUPEREGO

Freud theorized there would always be some conflict between the urges of the id, the morality of the superego, and the pressures of reality. The ego, as mediator, strives to fulfill the id impulses in a reasonable way while conforming to the superego's moral standards. Impulsive, reckless behavior results when the id is too dominant, whereas a dominant superego leads to a loss of normal pleasure as impulses are too restricted.

SOURCES FOR FURTHER STUDY

Brenner, Charles. *An Elementary Textbook of Psychoanalysis.* New York: Anchor Books, 1973. In-depth analysis of the structural model.

Freud, Sigmund. *The Ego and the Id.* New York: W. W. Norton, 1960. Freud's classic work introducing the ego and the id.

Greenberg, Jay R., and Stephen A. Mitchell. *Object Relations in Psychoanalytic Theory.* Cambridge, Mass.: Harvard University Press, 1983. Examines the internal workings of a psychic apparatus governed by instinctual drives. Reviews the work of other psychoanalytic theorists who revised and expanded Freud's structural model.

Joanne Hedgespeth

SEE ALSO: Denial; Ego defense mechanisms; Ego psychology: Erik Erikson; Emotions; Freud, Sigmund; Moral development; Oedipus complex; Penis envy; Personality theory; Psychoanalytic psychology and personality: Sigmund Freud; Psychosexual development; Self; Women's psychology: Sigmund Freud.

Ellis, Albert

BORN: September 27, 1913, in Pittsburgh, Pennsylvania
IDENTITY: American psychotherapist, theorist, and trainer of therapists
TYPE OF PSYCHOLOGY: Psychotherapy
FIELDS OF STUDY: Cognitive therapies

Ellis created, developed, and promoted rational emotive behavioral therapy (REBT). For this efficient, easy-to-learn method, which he began in 1955, he is widely recognized as the founder of cognitive behavioral therapy.

Albert Ellis received his master's degree in clinical psychology in 1943 and his doctorate in 1947, both from Columbia University. After six years of practicing psychoanalysis, which he found inefficient, he developed rational emotive behavior therapy (REBT). In 1959, he founded the nonprofit Albert Ellis Institute, from which he offers individual and group therapy, public presentations, and training for therapists. Since his important early books (*A Guide to Rational Living* in 1961 and *Reason and Emotion in Psychotherapy* in 1962), Ellis has written voluminously on REBT.

REBT holds that people have two opposing types of beliefs: rational (contributing to their happiness and achievement of goals) and irrational (leading to self-defeat and dysfunctional behavior). Irrational beliefs fall into three categories: demands about the self ("I must always perform well and be approved of by significant people"); demands about others ("You must always treat me considerately"); and demands about life and the world ("Life must always be the way I want it and not too difficult").

REBT's principal technique is its ABCs, a way of analyzing the client's difficulties. "A" is the adverse or activating event which is retarding the client's goals. "B" is the client's belief (often irrational) about the event. "C" is the consequence (perhaps discomfort, anxiety, or procrastination) of the client's belief. The therapist disputes, through questions and challenges, the client's rigid, irrational beliefs so that they may be changed to less disturbing and absolute preferences.

Ellis received awards for distinguished contributions from the American Psychological Association, the American Counseling Association, and the Association for the Advancement of Behavior Therapy. Joseph Yankura and Windy Dryden sum up his influence by stating, "Ellis has not merely invented a widely practiced system of psychotherapy, he has created a philosophy of living which has the potential to help many human beings to lead happier, healthier and more productive lives."

SOURCES FOR FURTHER STUDY

Albert Ellis Institute. http://www.rebt.org/. Provides information on the Institute and its range of therapy options and training programs; a monthly "Ask Dr. Ellis" column; and a REBT featured essay of the month.

Dryden, Windy, and Raymond DiGuiseppe. *A Primer on Rational-Emotive Therapy.* Champaign, Ill.: Research Press, 1990. In a brief, readable style, this book explains the theory of REBT; outlines thirteen steps in practicing it; and illustrates the steps in a case example.

Epstein, Robert. "The Prince of Reason: An Interview with Albert Ellis." *Psychology Today* 34, no. 1 (January/February, 2001): 66-76. This wide-ranging conversation covers Ellis's reasons for breaking with psychoanalysis, his early career and development of REBT, initial reactions of the profession to his ideas, effects of REBT on Ellis's own life, and evidence for the effectiveness of REBT.

Yankura, Joseph, and Windy Dryden. *Albert Ellis.* London: Sage Publications, 1994. This concise, well-documented study reviews Ellis's life and career, major contributions to theory and practice, criticisms of Ellis's theories and rebuttals to those criticisms, and his overall influence.

Glenn Ellen Starr Stilling

SEE ALSO: Cognitive therapy; Rational-emotive therapy.

Emotional expression

TYPE OF PSYCHOLOGY: Emotion
FIELDS OF STUDY: Interpersonal relations

Emotional expression includes both facial expressions and body movements that accompany the internal experience of emotion and that clearly serve to communicate that emotion to others. Influenced by the work of Charles Darwin, psychologists have long regarded the communication of emotion as an important function with survival value for the species.

KEY CONCEPTS
- decoding
- emotion
- encoding
- nonverbal communication

INTRODUCTION

The study of human emotion is a complex endeavor. It is complex in part because emotion is not a single event or process but is, instead, a collection of discrete events and processes. Humans experience a vast array of emotions, and each of those emotions actually consists of several components—the physiological changes that occur, the nonverbal communication of the emotion, and the subjective or felt experience. The topic of emotional communication or expression includes two related aspects: encoding (the expression of emotion) and decoding (the perception and reading of cues that signify an emotion).

Nonverbal forms of expression play an integral role in the complex human communication system.

Examples of emotional expression by nonverbal means are easy to find. For example, if irritated, people may tense their bodies, press their lips together, and gesture with their eyebrows. With an averted glance or a prolonged stare, a person can communicate intimacy, anger, submission, or dominance.

In his now-classic 1872 book *The Expression of the Emotions in Man and Animals*, Charles Darwin argued that many nonverbal communication patterns, specifically emotional expressions, are inherited and that they evolved because they had survival value. He focused primarily on the expression of emotion through specific changes in the appearance of the face and argued that the primary function of emotional expression is to inform others about one's internal state and, therefore, to inform them of how one is likely to behave. For example, when enraged, individuals commonly grimace and bare their teeth; the observer's perception of that anger suggests that the individual may behave aggressively. Frequently, such an expression (and the appropriate perception on the part of the target) results in the retreat of the target, thus avoiding an actual fight. For social animals who live in groups, such as humans, this rapid communication of internal states is highly adaptive.

THE UNIVERSAL AND THE SPECIFIC

If emotional expressions are a product of evolution and are, therefore, shared by all members of the species, their production and their interpretation should be universal. Cross-cultural research supports the universality of certain facial expressions. People in various cultures agree on how to convey a given emotion and how to convey it most intensely. The universal expression of anger, for example, involves a flushed face, brows lowered and drawn together, flared nostrils, a clenched jaw, and bared teeth. Several researchers have also shown that people from a variety of countries, including the United States, Japan, Brazil, and others, as well as people from several preliterate tribal groups who have had no previous contact with the Western world, have little difficulty identifying the emotions of happiness, anger, sadness, disgust, fear, and surprise, as exhibited in photographs and/or videotapes of members of their own cultures and of other cultures. Thus, both the encoding and decoding of certain emotional expressions are the same for people all over the world regardless of culture, language, or educational background.

This universality, however, does not preclude the possibility that certain aspects of emotional expression may be learned. In fact, strong cultural (learned) differences can be found in the intensity and frequency with which certain emotions are expressed and in the situations that elicit certain emotions. For example, in cultures that encourage individuality, as in Western Europe and North America, emotional displays are often intense and prolonged. People express their emotions openly. In Asian and other cultures that emphasize social connections and interdependence, emotions such as sympathy, respect, and shame are more common than in the West, and people in such cultures rarely, and then only briefly, display negative emotions that might disrupt a peaceful group environment. Additional evidence for the role of learning in emotional expression is provided by research suggesting that women express emotions more intensely than men, who tend to hide their expressions to some degree.

People of different cultures also vary in their use of certain other forms of nonverbal cues to express emotion. That is, individual cultures have developed additional signals of emotion that are shared only within those cultures. For example, the psychologist Otto Klineberg reported in 1938 that Chinese literature was filled with examples of emotional expression that would easily be misunderstood by members of the Western world. Such examples include clapping one's hands when worried or disappointed, sticking out one's tongue to express surprise, and scratching one's ears and cheeks to express happiness.

DECODING EXPRESSIONS

The human ability to decode or interpret emotional expressions is, like the expression itself, also partly learned. Evidence for this can be found in the reactions of infants to novel situations and novel toys. Under such circumstances, infants frequently check their mother's facial expressions before approaching or avoiding the novel toy. If she looks happy or relaxed, the infant generally will approach; if she looks frightened, the infant will try to avoid the new situation or will approach the mother. Additional support is found in research that suggests that women are generally better at detecting emotional undercurrents and at detecting emotion from

visual information only (such as facial expressions presented in pictures or in silent films) than men are. Such individual differences are probably the result of socialization, with girls socialized to be more sensitive to the feelings of others.

The term "facial expression" is commonly defined as a motor response resulting from an emotional state. That is, the facial expression is believed to be a consequence of the emotion. This is the position implied by most of the theory and research in the area. Yet with regard to the role of the expressive component in the experience of emotion, there is another possibility. Some researchers have suggested that facial expressions not only communicate but also regulate emotion. For example, Darwin, in 1872, wrote that "the free expression by outward signs of an emotion intensifies it. . . . On the other hand, the repression, as far as possible, of all outward signs, softens our emotions." This statement clearly suggests that the outward expression of emotion can either amplify or attenuate the intensity of the emotional experience. Support for this hypothesis is now readily available.

FINE-TUNING INTERPRETATION

As more is learned about the subtle changes in facial expression and body movements that are associated with specific emotions, the behavior of individuals in specific situations may be interpreted more accurately. For example, therapists can observe more closely the facial expression changes in their patients, thereby gaining access to emotional reactions that their patients may not discuss openly.

Several researchers have already reported that close scrutiny of changes in facial expression among patients during interviews supports the notion that many expression changes occur too quickly for easy detection. E. A. Haggard and F. S. Isaacs, for example, while searching for indications of nonverbal communication between therapist and patient, ran filmed interactions at slow motion and noticed that the expression of the patient's face sometimes changed dramatically within a few frames of the film. These changes were not observable when the film was run at regular speed. Furthermore, these subtle changes appeared to take place at key points during the interview. For example, although the patient's detectable expression included a smile when discussing a "friend," closer inspection of the film suggested that the patient actually exhibited the subtle facial changes associated with the expression of anger during the conversation. These "micro-momentary" expressions are believed to reveal actual emotional states that are condensed in time because of repression.

Advanced technology allows researchers to measure subtle facial changes in other ways as well. For example, when a person is given mild emotional stimuli, electrodes attached to facial muscles can detect hidden reactions. Thus, although a person's face might not look any different, voltage changes on the skin may reveal micromuscular smiles or frowns underneath; perhaps this procedure will even result in a new approach to lie detection.

In addition to the work being done to develop an understanding of the normal but subtle changes associated with various emotions under normal circumstances, several researchers have looked at how emotional expressions change under abnormal circumstances. For example, the weightlessness experienced by astronauts results in the movement of body fluids toward the upper body, causing their faces to become puffy. Under these circumstances, a reliance on facial expressions for emotional information might increase the risk of misunderstanding. Thus, a full understanding of such changes is necessary for individuals likely to find themselves in such situations.

Nonverbal forms of emotional communication also play an important role in the normal development of the human infant. For example, the facial expressions of both infants and caregivers are important in the development of the attachment relationship. That is, the facial expressions of infants indicate to caregivers the infants' emotional states. Infants' expressions tell much about how they are "feeling" and thus allow adults to respond appropriately. Furthermore, the early signs of emotional expression in infants are events that clearly contribute to the development of the relationship between infant and caregiver. For example, the infant's first smile is typically interpreted in a personal way by the caregiver and is responded to with a returned smile and increased interaction on the part of the caregiver, thus resulting in a positive interaction sequence. Evidence of the first smile also leads to increased attempts by the caregiver to elicit smiling at other times, thus giving the caregiver a new topic with which to engage the infant in social interaction.

BODY LANGUAGE THROUGH TIME

Throughout history, humankind has acknowledged the existence of discrete emotions and has exhibited acceptance and understanding of the public aspect of emotions—the expressive movements that characterize each individual emotion. For example, sad (tragic) and happy (comic) facial masks were worn by actors during ancient times to portray the emotional tone of their characters and were correctly perceived by audiences. Similarly, today, in the theater and in everyday life, people accept the notion that the face has a real and definite function in communicating feelings or emotions; people automatically search the face of the speaker, studying facial expressions, to understand more fully what is being communicated in any interpersonal interaction.

Several well-known scientists of the nineteenth century and early scientific psychologists of the twentieth century acknowledged the importance of emotion and emotional expression. It was during the late nineteenth century that Darwin paved the way for theory and research on the facial patterns in emotion. In the early twentieth century, Wilhelm Wundt, the father of psychology, assumed that the face was the chief means of emotional expression. Thus the topic of emotion was considered a topic worthy of scientific investigation during the early years of psychology.

When behaviorism took over as the dominant psychological theory of the twentieth century, however, emotion, as well as all other topics that included "subjective" components, was forced out of the laboratory and out of the range of scientific study. During psychology's period of strong behavioristic orientation (the 1930's through the 1950's), most general theories of behavior and most major personality theories ignored emotion altogether or dealt with it only as a vague, global entity or process of little importance. There was very little scientific investigation into the existence of separate emotions, and therefore there was very little attention paid to the existence of discrete facial patterns for the communication of emotion. This overall lack of interest in facial patterns by behavioral scientists had little influence on common wisdom; people in general have maintained the age-old position that the patterns exist and that they have specific emotional significance.

As theories of emotion began to appear in the scientific literature, and as the potential importance of emotional expressions was considered, the question of innate versus learned facial patterns of emotional expression was addressed. For a substantial period of time, the dominant view was that there were no invariable patterns of expression. It was not until publication of the work of Silvan Tomkins, Carroll Izard, Paul Ekman, and other investigators during the 1960's that conclusive evidence for the existence of universal facial patterns in emotional expression was provided, confirming for science what people have always known. Since then, significant advances have been made in understanding the facial musculature changes associated with the expression of individual emotions and in understanding the development of the ability to interpret those facial musculature changes. It is, moreover, likely that significant advances will continue to be made in the identification of subtle changes in emotional expression and in understanding the important role of such facial patterns in interpersonal communication.

SOURCES FOR FURTHER STUDY

Atkinson, R. L., R. C. Atkinson, E. E. Smith, and D. J. Bem. *Hilgard's Introduction to Psychology.* 13th ed. Pacific Grove, Calif.: International Thomson, 1999. An introductory psychology text, aimed at the college-level student; includes a very good discussion of the field of emotion, clear examples of critical issues, and interesting and stimulating discussions of some controversial areas.

Darwin, Charles. *The Expression of the Emotions in Man and Animals.* Edited by Paul Ekman. 3d ed. New York: Oxford University Press, 1998. The original theory and scientific evidence of Charles Darwin, first published in 1872; includes a discussion of the adaptive value of emotions and emotional expression as well as evidence for the evolution of specific emotional signals.

Ekman, Paul. *Darwin and Facial Expression.* New York: Academic Press, 1973. Includes an in-depth discussion of Darwin's theory of emotional expression and presents evidence to support his theory.

Izard, Carroll E. *The Face of Emotion.* New York: Appleton-Century-Crofts, 1971. An excellent presentation of the history of the field of emotion in psychology. Includes a detailed discussion of the evidence regarding the heritability and universality of emotional expression. Presents a general theoretical framework relating neural activity, fa-cial patterning, and subjective experience as the principal components of emotion.

_____. *Human Emotions.* New York: Plenum, 1977. A full presentation of Izard's differential emotions theory as well as a detailed discussion of the discrete emotions and their accompanying facial expressions.

_____. *Measuring Emotions in Infants and Children.* New York: Cambridge University Press, 1986. A presentation of the measurement procedures commonly used to assess emotional experiences in infants and children. Discusses several important topics regarding the development of emotions and the study of emotions in a developmental context.

Myers, D. G. *Psychology.* 6th ed. New York: Worth, 2000. A general introductory psychology textbook. Contains a good discussion of many aspects of emotion; provides many examples and discusses important issues.

Wortman, Camille B., and Elizabeth F. Loftus. *Psychology.* 5th ed. New York: McGraw-Hill, 1999. A college-level introductory text with a clear presentation of the field of emotion; makes effective use of examples.

Loretta A. Rieser-Danner

SEE ALSO: Anger; Denial; Emotions; Facial feedback; Guilt; Jealousy; Love; Nonverbal communication.

Emotions

TYPE OF PSYCHOLOGY: Emotion
FIELDS OF STUDY: Motivation theory

Emotion is a basic aspect of human functioning. Emotions are personal experiences that arise from a complex interplay among physiological, cognitive, and situational variables. Theories and measurement of emotion allow psychologists to understand diverse expressions of behavior, and they form the cornerstone of many approaches to the treatment of psychological problems.

KEY CONCEPTS
- cognitive appraisal
- emotional intensity
- primary emotions

- psychosomatic disorders
- secondary emotions
- state emotion
- trait emotion
- visceral responses

INTRODUCTION

An emotion is a valenced experience that is felt with some degree of intensity, involves a person's interpretation of the immediate situation, and is accompanied by learned and unlearned physical responses. Emotions are transitory states, and they have five characteristics. First, emotions are experiences, not specific behaviors or thoughts. Although thoughts can sometimes lead to emotions and behaviors can sometimes be caused by emotions, an emotion is a personal experience. Second, an emotional experience has "valence," meaning that the emotion has a positive or negative quality. Because emotions have valence, they often motivate people toward action. People tend to seek activities, situations, and people that enhance their experience of positive emotional states, and they tend to avoid situations that are connected with the experience of negative emotions.

Third, emotions involve cognitive appraisals. That is, one's interpretation of the immediate situation influences which emotion is experienced. For example, a child may experience either joy or fear when being chased, depending on whether the child interprets the chase as playful or dangerous. Fourth, emotions involve physical responses. Physical responses may be internal, such as changes in heart rate, blood pressure, or respiration (called visceral responses); physical responses can also be external, such as facial expressions. In addition, the bodily responses that characterize emotions are partly reflexive (unlearned) and partly learned. An increase in heart rate is a reflexive response that accompanies intense fear. That which a person fears, however, and his or her accompanying bodily response may be the product of learning; crying when afraid is an emotional expression that is subject to learning experiences. Fifth, emotions can vary in intensity: Anger can become rage, amusement can become joy, and fear can be heightened to a state of terror.

Psychologist Robert Plutchik contends that there are eight innate, primary emotions: joy, anticipation, anger, disgust, sadness, surprise, fear, and ac-

ceptance. Like the colors of a color wheel, primary emotions can combine to produce secondary emotions: surprise plus sadness can produce disappointment; anger plus disgust can produce contempt; and fear plus surprise can produce awe. Since each primary emotion can vary in intensity, and each level of intensity for one emotion can combine with some other level of intensity of another emotion, the total number of possible emotions runs to the hundreds. Although many psychologists agree that there exist primary emotions, there is no way that a person could distinguish such a large number of personal emotional experiences. Moreover, psychologists have not even attempted to measure such an unwieldy array of secondary emotions.

STATE AND TRAIT EMOTIONS

Nevertheless, psychologists have developed numerous assessment instruments to study common emotions. (An assessment instrument is a method used to measure some psychological quality.) Since there are so many different emotions, the study of emotion requires the development of specific methods that can accurately measure each of the common emotions. The most popular method of measuring an emotion is a self-report questionnaire in which a person answers questions relevant to a particular emotion. When measuring emotions, researchers make a distinction between "state" and "trait" emotion. An emotional state refers to what a person is experiencing at the moment. If one were interested in assessing how anxious someone currently is, one might use a questionnaire that asks the person to respond to several anxiety-related statements, using a scale from 1 ("not at all") to 5 ("very much"). Some examples of relevant statements are "I feel tense," "I feel nervous and shaky inside," "My heart is beating rapidly," and "I feel a sense of foreboding." The higher the total score on the questionnaire, the more anxiety the person is experiencing at the moment.

Trait emotion refers to how often an emotion is experienced. An "anxious person" is someone who frequently experiences the state of anxiety. Moreover, one would call someone a "hostile person" if one determined that he or she frequently exhibits states of anger. Examples of statements that assess trait anxiety are "I frequently become tense," "I often feel afraid for no apparent reason," "I am bothered by dizzy spells," and "I tend to worry a lot."

ASSESSMENT MEASURES

Psychologists have developed numerous questionnaires to assess emotions. There are self-report measures to assess anxiety, anger, guilt, happiness, and hopelessness, to name a few. In addition to measures of specific emotions, researchers have developed methods for assessing emotional intensity. Emotional intensity refers to the strength with which a person experiences both positive and negative emotions. It has been found that people who are emotionally intense report a feeling of well-being as "exuberance, animated joyfulness, and zestful enthusiasm." On the other hand, people who score low on a measure of emotional intensity experience a state of well-being as "serenity, contentment, tranquil calmness, and easygoing composure."

In addition to the use of self-report measures of emotion, psychologists often use physiological measures. Using sophisticated biological measuring instruments, psychologists are able to assess emotional arousal by measuring, for example, heart rate, skin sweating, respiration, blood pressure, and muscle tension. By examining the amount these measures change in response to a stimulus, researchers are able to infer emotional arousal. For example, it has been found that people who have the type of personality that puts them at risk for heart attacks show greater increases in blood pressure when trapped in a traffic jam in comparison to those people who have personality characteristics that do not predispose them to heart attacks. In this instance, the psychologist uses the measure of blood pressure to infer a negative emotion, such as anger or frustration.

One question that arises when using physiological measures to assess emotions is whether each emotion has a specific pattern of physiological responses. For example, blood pressure appears to be particularly responsive to anger-inducing situations. People's heart rates, however, increase during emotional states of excitement, anxiety, anger, and sexual arousal. For this reason, researchers may use multiple measures of emotion, assessing self-reports of emotion while physiological responses are being recorded. Another way of assessing emotions is by direct observation of overt behavior. Approach behavior can indicate acceptance, and avoidance behavior can reflect fear or disgust. In addition, facial expressions have been used to assess various emotional states.

POLYGRAPHS

When researchers developed means for measuring visceral responses and discovered that these responses are associated with emotions, it was not long before the possibility of detecting lies was raised. The use of a polygraph to detect lying is based on the assumption that people will feel anxious or guilty when asked a question that has personal, emotional significance to past deeds. The polygraph tester measures and compares physiological responses to both control questions and relevant questions to infer lying. For example, if a person is suspected of murdering John Smith on May 16, the tester may ask the control question: "Have you ever hurt someone?" Since everyone has hurt someone at one time or another, and probably feels guilty about it, some level of emotional response will be registered in changes in heart rate and respiration. The relevant question is "Did you kill John Smith on May 16?" Supposedly, the innocent person will show a greater emotional response to the control question than the relevant question. The perpetrator of the crime should show a greater emotional response to the relevant question because of its extreme emotional significance.

The use of polygraph testing is surrounded by controversy. Although some liars can be detected, if a perpetrator does not feel guilty about the crime—or does not believe that the polygraph can measure lying—he or she will not show the expected response to the critical questions about the crime. In addition, research has shown that some innocent people will become so anxious when asked "relevant" questions that they are mistakenly viewed as guilty. The American Psychological Association has expressed grave concern over the validity of polygraph testing. The U.S. Congress has outlawed the use of preemployment testing to predict who might, for example, steal inventory. Despite the reservations of the American Psychological Association, however, security agencies and defense industries are allowed to use polygraph testing.

CLINICAL APPLICATIONS AND THEORY

The development of theories of emotion and of methods for measuring emotions has wide application in the field of clinical psychology. Many psychological disorders are defined by emotional problems. People with phobias exhibit excessive anxiety in situations that offer little or no possibility of harm. Strong fears of water, heights, insects, closed spaces, flying, and social situations are common examples of phobias. Theories of emotion provide a framework within which clinicians can understand the development of phobias. Measures of anxiety can be used to help diagnose those people who suffer from phobias.

Depression is another example of a psychological disorder that has a strong emotional component. Twenty percent of females and 10 percent of males will experience a major depression at some time in their lives. This complex disorder is manifested by distorted thinking (such as self-critical thinking), physical difficulties (such as fatigue), and an array of emotions. Some of the emotional symptoms of depression include sadness, anxiety, and guilt. Thus, when psychologists assess the emotional aspects of depression, they use questionnaires that include items that address several different emotions.

Not only does the study of emotion help psychologists to understand psychological disorders, but methods of treatment have also been developed based on the understanding of emotion. For example, psychological research has shown that emotional responses, such as anxiety, can be learned. Consequently, treatment strategies have been developed to help people unlearn their anxiety reactions. As a result, many people who suffer from simple phobias can be treated effectively in a short period of time. Theories of emotion that examine the relation between thinking and emotion have led to therapies to alleviate depression. Aaron Beck has shown that the sadness, anxiety, and guilt that accompany depression can be treated by helping people change their styles of thinking.

Another area within clinical psychology that has benefited by the increasing understanding of emotion is psychosomatic disorders. A psychosomatic disorder (also called a psychophysiological disorder) is an abnormal physical condition brought about by chronic negative emotions. Ulcers, hypertension, headaches, and arthritis are examples of conditions that can be brought about or worsened by negative emotions. The emotions that are most often implicated in the development of psychosomatic disorders are anger and anxiety. For example, researchers have discovered that prolonged anxiety induced by internal conflict can cause ulcers in susceptible people. In addition, researchers now have evidence that chronic hostility is a risk factor for the development of heart disease.

Social psychologists study the influence of social factors on behavior. Theories of emotion have been a focus of social psychologists because one's experience of emotion is in part determined by the immediate situation, and the immediate situation often includes the behavior of others. Indeed, Stanley Schachter, a social psychologist, is responsible for the development of a theory of emotion that underscores the importance of one's cognitive appraisal of the social context in determining the emotion that one experiences. For example, when people experience physiological arousal, their own emotional experience will most likely be consistent with their interpretation of the social context. If they are with a happy person, they will experience happiness; if they are in the presence of an angry person, they will experience anger. Theories of emotion have also increased understanding of many social phenomena, such as aggression and interpersonal attraction.

EMOTION RESEARCH
For centuries, philosophers and psychologists have recognized the importance of understanding personality differences based on the type and degree of emotional expression. In the fifth century B.C.E., the Greek physician Hippocrates classified people on the basis of emotional temperament. The view that people differ in temperament remains today. Arnold Buss and Robert Plomin have hypothesized that newborns differ in their susceptibility to distress, fear, and anger. Everyday descriptions of people as "happy-go-lucky," "stoic," and "volatile" represent the tendency to group people according to characteristic styles of emotional expression. Clinical psychologists speak of the "hysterical personality" as exhibiting excessive emotional lability and the "schizoid personality" as showing emotional indifference toward others.

Theologians have traditionally approached emotion as representing the dark side of human nature. What elevates humans above other animals has been thought to be the capacity to overcome passion with reason. Even this seemingly archaic view of emotion has its counterpart in modern psychology. Psychoanalysts help people gain control of their feelings through understanding the unconscious roots of their emotions. Cognitive therapists attempt to alleviate emotional dysfunctions by teaching clients to "think more rationally."

The modern era of research on emotion can be traced to Charles Darwin's 1872 book *The Expression of the Emotions in Man and Animals.* Darwin believed that emotional displays evolved as a means of communication and had adaptive significance for the survival of the species. Indeed, there is some scientific support for the assertion that emotional expressions are basic biological responses: Newborn infants show expressions of emotion that closely match the expressions of adults; all infants, including those born deaf and blind, exhibit similar facial expressions in similar situations; very young babies can tell the difference between different emotional expressions; and there is considerable similarity in the expression of emotions across diverse cultures.

In the last half of the twentieth century, psychologists made important advances in formulating theories of emotions and devising assessment instruments to measure emotions. Scientists have arrived at the point where they recognize many of the fundamental aspects of emotion: the nervous system, thought, behavior, and the immediate situation. The challenge for the future is to map the intricate interplay among these variables and achieve a thorough understanding of this basic facet of human functioning.

SOURCES FOR FURTHER STUDY

Barlow, David H. *Anxiety and Its Disorders.* 2d ed. New York: Guilford, 2001. In the early part of the book, the author reviews basic aspects of emotion. The remainder is devoted to the emotion of anxiety, and how anxiety forms the basis of many clinical disorders. Some of the disorders addressed are panic disorder, obsessive-compulsive disorder, phobias, and post-traumatic stress disorder. A very comprehensive treatment of anxiety disorders. Barlow takes a strong research orientation and presents the material at a college level.

Bernstein, Douglas A., Stewart Alison Clarke, and Louis A. Penner. *Psychology.* 5th ed. New York: Houghton Mifflin, 1999. Presents an introduction to the topic of emotion. Covers a wide range of areas: definition of emotion, physiology of emotion, major theories, social aspects of emotion, and facial expressions. The authors do not assume that the reader has any background in psychology, and they write in a clear, concise manner, providing interesting examples and graphics.

Corcoran, Kevin J., and Joel Fischer. *Adults.* Vol. 2 in *Measures for Clinical Practice: A Sourcebook.* 3d ed. New York: Free Press, 2000. Reprints more than one hundred self-report assessment instruments. An excellent source for learning how researchers measure emotions, and can be used should one want to conduct a study. However, this book does not include some of the most commonly used questionnaires for measuring emotions.

Ekman, Paul, and Richard J. Davidson, eds. *The Nature of Emotion: Fundamental Questions.* New York: Oxford University Press, 1997. The editors asked twenty-four leading theorists in the field of the psychology of emotions to answer the same twelve questions on their subject. Areas of agreement and disagreement are highlighted, along with a summary chapter at the end.

Laurence Grimm

SEE ALSO: Anger; Assessment; Clinical depression; Emotional expression; Guilt; Jealousy; Love; Nonverbal communication; Personality: Psychophysiological measures; Personality rating scales; Phobias.

Encoding

TYPE OF PSYCHOLOGY: Memory
FIELDS OF STUDY: Cognitive processes

Encoding strategies include both intentional and unintentional processes that are used to improve memory performance. Encoding refers to the ways information gets put into memory. Encoding specificity is a theory of memory encoding that predicts that any cue that is present at the time of encoding will serve as an effective cue for retrieval of that memory event.

KEY CONCEPTS
- cue
- encoding
- retrieval
- storage
- target word

INTRODUCTION
Most people find it easy to remember certain events from their past, such as the best vacation they ever

had. They would remember their age and the most interesting things they saw or did at that time, even if the events occurred years before. If people could not remember events in their lives, they would have no personal history, skills, or talents. Fortunately, humans are able to take information from the world and store it in a mental representation that allows them to use that past information in a current situation. This ability is a function of the way the human memory system works.

The memory system records events as they occur; this process is called encoding. The information is stored in a memory trace until it is needed. A memory trace remains in storage until a cue (a specific clue that triggers a memory) for that memory occurs, at which time the memory will be retrieved from long-term storage and outputted for use.

SHORT-TERM AND LONG-TERM MEMORY

In the model that is often used to illustrate memory systems, information comes into the memory system and is then transported to short-term memory (STM), where it is held for both further encoding into, and interaction with, long-term memory (LTM). There are different encoding strategies for information, depending on whether it is to be used by STM or LTM. Some encoding strategies are unintentional, but others can be used purposefully to increase memory abilities.

One of the characteristics of STM is that it can only store five to nine items, and these items remain in STM for only about eighteen seconds. Thus, information processed in STM must either be encoded into LTM or be lost from the system. If, for example, one needs the information of a telephone number, one probably will repeat the number until one can dial. This is known as a rehearsal strategy, and it serves to make the information available until one uses it.

One way of overcoming the capacity limitations of STM is by an encoding strategy called chunking: A group of items are chunked into meaningful units, which allows STM to hold more information and to be aided by LTM. For example, if one were asked to remember the letters FCTIIIBWAABM by rehearsing the letters, one would not easily remember the sequence. If, however, one were asked to remember the same letters arranged as FBI CIA TWA IBM, one would have no trouble recalling the sequence. The letters became chunked into four meaningful units

which were small enough for STM and were encoded into LTM because of their meaningfulness.

Another encoding strategy is the use of imagery. In order to remember a list of items, one makes a visual image of the items. For example, if one is to remember the pair of words "dog" and "ribbon," one might make an image of the dog with a big red ribbon on its neck and tail. Imagery is similar to another encoding strategy called elaboration. This, like imagery, adds details to an event and gives it more meaning so that it is more easily remembered. For example, given directions to a concert, one might start thinking about the time one walked down Main Street and was going to the ice-cream parlor, and so on. By adding these details, one elaborates on the event and increases one's memory. Elaboration is something that people do automatically, because memory is organized so that one event triggers memories of other events. If one hears the word "dog," one automatically begins to retrieve things that one knows about dogs.

Another encoding strategy is called organization. This process groups items into larger categories of relatedness. For example, given a list of words to remember, such as "dog," "knife," "rose," "cat," "horse," "fork," "daisy," "spoon," "pansy," one would likely remember the words in three categories: flowers, utensils, and animals. This could be an intentional encoding strategy, and it aids memory because the retrieval (the process of getting information from the memory system) of the larger category also activates all the members of that category that are associated with it.

ASSOCIATED CUES

The theory proposed by Endel Tulving called encoding specificity contradicts organizational encoding. Tulving proposes that any cue present and specifically encoded at the time of study will serve as an effective cue for retrieval, even over cues that would seem to be more likely to trigger the memory. For example, Tulving and Thompson, in 1971, gave subjects a list of word pairs to remember. One group was given a list of word pairs that were strong associates of each other, such as "hot-cold." The other list had words that were weakly associated with each other, such as "blow-cold." Later, at a test session, the first word was given as a cue, and subjects were asked to fill in the second target word. Each group was given both strong and weak associated cues. It might seem likely that given the cue "hot-_____," one would think of the target word "cold" even if one had been given the weakly associated pair of "blow-cold" at the time of study; however, this was not what happened. Subjects given the cue word "blow" at study could not recall "cold" when given "hot" as a cue, but did very well when given their original cue word, "blow." In other words, whatever cue word was encoded at the time of study was the best cue for retrieval of the target word at test regardless of how weakly or strongly associated the cue and target words were. Therefore, Tulving predicted that whatever cues are specifically encoded at the time of the event are the best cues for memory at the time of testing. Thus, encoding specificity can be extended to any context cues specific to the memory event. This includes the subject's mood, surroundings, or cues.

IMPORTANCE OF CONTEXT

Sometimes the information that is encoded into the memory event is related to the context or surroundings of that event; instead of a word cue, the environment at the time of encoding can be a cue for retrieval. For example, in 1975, Duncan Godden and Alan Baddeley found that memory was better if subjects were asked to remember something in the same physical environment in which they previously had learned the material. They had subjects study a list of words on shore and a list of words underwater. If the list was learned underwater, memory was better if the recall test was also underwater rather than on shore, and vice versa. They concluded that the context provided additional cues for memory.

These context effects have also been demonstrated to include a person's mood at the time of encoding, known as state-dependent effects. For example, in 1978 Gordon Bower hypnotized subjects into either a positive or negative emotional state and tested their memory for material when they were in the same and different emotional states. Students who were in congruent states of mind at study and test sessions had greater memory than students in different states of mind at study and test. Again, the contextual cues that were associated with a particular state of mind were present at both encoding and retrieval and served to aid recall by being specifically encoded with the event.

Thus, if one wants to increase one's memory skills, the more types of encoding strategies one uses, the better one will be able to remember. In addition, it is important to remember that using the same cues for both study and test sessions will also result in better performance. Therefore, one might try to do some studying in the same room where one will be taking a test.

EVOLUTION OF RESEARCH

Cognitive psychology encompasses the study of all the functions of the human mind, including thinking, problem solving, reasoning, attention, consciousness, and processing information. It is considered a relatively new field of psychology, although its roots go back to the work of early psychologists in the late nineteenth and early twentieth centuries; in a sense they go back even further, to the philosophers of centuries past. In the late 1800's, both the renowned psychologist William James and Sigmund Freud, the founder of psychoanalysis, wrote about aspects of consciousness and attention. In the same time period, Hermann Ebbinghaus began studying verbal learning and memory, while Wilhelm Wundt attempted to research the structure of the mind with his method of introspection.

Another significant contribution to cognitive psychology began in 1904, when Ivan Pavlov proposed his principles of conditioned learning. This led the way for further study into the learning processes of humans and animals; learning became considered to be an overt action, not a process of the mind. Thus, John B. Watson proposed in 1913 that behavior was the only suitable topic for psychology to study, and the processes of the mind became a taboo subject for many years.

It was not until World War II that cognitive psychology again became a legitimate topic for research. This occurred because the topic of human error became an important question for the military: Pilots' lives could be saved if more could be known about perception and actions. Researchers were employed to determine how decisions were made and to study the importance of attentional processes on performance. From this an entire field of study emerged, and the study of encoding strategies developed as a by-product of studying other processes of the memory system, such as attention, forgetting, and effective retrieval cues.

In the same time frame, the computer emerged; these areas of psychology were formulated in terms of an information-processing model of human memory. In other words, in order to understand the way memory systems work, a theoretical model of the brain was based on the computer. In 1968, Richard Atkinson and Richard Shiffrin suggested a model of memory which consisted of three memory stores, each with its own characteristics and functions. This consisted of the sensory register, the short-term memory, and the long-term memory. This information-processing model made the concepts of codes, storage capacity, trace duration, and retrieval failures an area of research. In studying these concepts, researchers discovered new topics of interest.

Research into encoding strategies is concerned with which elements of the environment are selected for encoding and how people can use this information to improve memory performance. The cue environment that is encoded is a topic of great interest, as it can aid performance if it can be predicted. Such components of the cue environment as gestures and emotions that are all encoded below the level of awareness are only beginning to be studied, and they should lead to a much better understanding of how to improve memory.

SOURCES FOR FURTHER STUDY

Anderson, J. R. *Cognitive Psychology and Its Implications*. 5th ed. New York: Worth, 1999. Although this book generally has an information-processing framework, it is still a thorough reference book on any area concerned with cognitive psychology. It is written in simple enough terms that a beginning psychology student can easily follow the line of thought.

Ellis, H. C., and R. R. Hunt. *Fundamentals of Human Memory and Cognition*. Dubuque, Iowa: Wm. C. Brown, 1989. This excellent book explains every aspect of cognitive functioning in a clear and precise way. It includes all topics necessary to understand the workings of human processing and illustrates these issues with research findings. It can be easily read and understood by the layperson.

Schwartz, Barry, and Dan Reisberg. *Learning and Memory*. New York: W. W. Norton, 1991. This book is a comprehensive outline of all aspects of psychology that pertain to learning and memory. Includes research and historical review. An excellent reference book.

Smith, Frank. *Comprehension and Learning: A Conceptual Framework for Teachers*. New York: Holt, Rinehart and Winston, 1975. This book is a cognitive textbook on the principles of learning in children. It has both an information-processing format and a psycholinguistic perspective, for a comprehensive presentation of research. It is easily read by student and teacher, and it includes comprehension, language, and concept development.

Tulving, Endel. *Elements of Episodic Memory*. London: Oxford University Press, 1983. A comprehensive overview of the complete theories of Tulving. Contains explanations of both the episodic memory system (which is related to encoding specificity) and the semantic memory system (which is more knowledge-based). The book is not too technical to be read by the novice, but it serves better as a resource than a book to be read in its entirety.

Donna Frick-Horbury

SEE ALSO: Artificial intelligence; Brain structure; Forgetting and forgetfulness; Long-term memory; Memory; Memory: Animal research; Memory: Empirical studies; Memory: Physiology; Memory: Sensory; Memory storage; Short-term memory.

Endocrine system

TYPE OF PSYCHOLOGY: Biological bases of behavior
FIELDS OF STUDY: Endocrine system

Behavior, by definition, includes physiological events which are responses to internal and external stimuli; the endocrine system, through the action of hormones and in cooperation with the nervous system, plays a necessary role in bringing about these reactions in animals and humans.

KEY CONCEPTS
• adrenal glands
• biopsychology
• endocrine system
• ethology
• hormone
• hypothalamus
• pituitary gland

INTRODUCTION

Curiosity about behavior, both animal and human, is of long standing. The suspicion that substances in the body contribute to behavior also has a long history. During the fifth century B.C.E., Hippocrates suggested, in his humoral theory, that personality was determined by four body fluids: phlegm, black bile, yellow bile, and blood. The dominance of one or another of the fluids was associated with a behavior pattern. A proportionate distribution of the fluids resulted in a balanced personality. This theory has contributed terms such as phlegmatic, sanguine, bilious, and good- or bad-humored to describe personality types and states of mind.

Aristotle (384-322 B.C.E.) is reported to have performed castration experiments on both fowl and men in order to alter behavior. He believed that something produced by the testes caused typically male behavior. Several nineteenth century researchers continued the study of the connection between the testes and male reproductive behavior. In 1849, Arnold Adolphe Berthold initiated a series of experiments on cockerels. He removed the testes from six birds and noted their loss of "male" behavior. Testes were transplanted into the abdomens of half the castrated birds. Successful transplantation restored the typical male crowing and combativeness.

During the late nineteenth and early twentieth centuries, the sciences became more organized. Interest in behavior and its causes continued. The science of ethology, which focuses on animal behavior, came into existence. In the early 1900's, John B. Watson founded a branch of psychology that became known as behavior science. This area of psychology concentrated on human behavioral studies. Eventually, ethology and behavior science contributed to biopsychology, a new branch of psychology which incorporates and applies data from neuroscience, genetics, endocrinology, and physiology in the quest for biological explanations of behavior. Biopsychology embraces several subdivisions. Physiological psychology focuses on nervous system and endocrine system research. Psychopharmacology specializes in the effects of drugs on the nervous system and, ultimately, on behavior. The development of therapeutic drugs is a goal of this discipline. The neuropsychologist studies the effects of brain damage on behavior. Psychophysiology differs from physiological psychology in that the psychophysiologist uses only human subjects while the physiological psychologist experiments on laboratory animals, especially rats.

Early research in physiological psychology focused on the nervous system, but it soon became evident that the endocrine system also influenced behavior and that the effects of the two systems were interrelated contributors to behavior. The endocrine system essentially consists of ductless glands that produce chemical substances called hormones. The hormones elicit physiological reactions, either locally or at some distant target site. When acting at a distance, the hormones travel to the site by way of the circulatory system.

Hans Selye, a Canadian scientist, proposed a direct connection between the endocrine system and behavior. In 1946, he described physiological events that were triggered by stress. This set of bodily changes became known as the general adaptation syndrome. The syndrome involved the mobilization of the autonomic nervous system, the adrenal glands, and the anterior lobe of the pituitary.

As research continued, data on the role of the endocrine system in determining behavior began to accumulate. Researchers continue to look to the endocrine system to provide clues about the causes of psychiatric diseases and the efficacy of hormone therapy in treating the diseases, as well as in altering behavior patterns.

INVERTEBRATES

Among most invertebrates (animals without backbones), endocrine glands are not in evidence. Specialized cells known as neurosecretory cells serve as endocrine tissue. The cells, which resemble neurons (the functional cells of the nervous system) are hormone producers. In invertebrate animals such as the hydra and planaria, the secretions (hormones) of the neurosecretory cells seem to influence growth and may be the underlying cause of the tremendous powers of regeneration possessed by the animals. There are indications that the development of sexuality, the laying of eggs, and the release of sperm may be under hormonal control in these animals. Attempts to establish the link between hormones and invertebrate behavior when the hormones are produced by neurosecretory cells have inherent problems. A common method of studying hormone influence involves removal of the secreting organ, which causes a hormone deficit. Changes in physiology and/or behavior are observed. A hormone is then provided to the animal to see if the original condition can be restored. Utilization of this method is complicated by the difficulty in removing all the functioning neurosecretory cells. In addition, the cells regenerate rapidly. This prevents an accurate assessment of the effects of hormone deficit.

Hormone effects are observable and measurable in the more developed invertebrates such as the *Arthropoda*. Studies carried out on insects and crustaceans indicate the presence of both neurosecretory cells and endocrine glands. Among the behaviors and activities controlled by the hormones released from either the cells or the glands are molting, sexual differentiation, sexual behavior, water balance, and diapause. Since arthropods are encased in an outer skeletal structure, it is necessary for the animals to shed their outer structure in order to grow.

During the growth years, the animals go through cycles of shedding the outer skeleton or molting, growing, and reforming an outer coat. There is evidence that insects are under hormonal control when they enter a state of diapause, or arrested behavior in adverse times.

VERTEBRATES

All vertebrates (animals with backbones) have a well-developed and highly organized endocrine system. The system consists of the following glands: the pituitary, the pineal, the thyroid, the thymus, the pancreas, a pair of adrenals (each adrenal actually acts as two glands—the adrenal cortex produces unique hormones and functions independently of the adrenal medulla), a pair of parathyroids, and a pair of ovaries or testes. Endocrine tissue in the gastrointestinal tract readies the system for the digestive process. During a pregnancy, the placental tissue assumes an endocrine function. Although the kidneys do not produce a hormone directly, they release an enzyme which converts a blood protein into a hormone that stimulates red blood cell production.

All vertebrates have a pituitary. The pituitary is a small, round organ found at the base of the brain. This major endocrine gland interacts with the hypothalamus of the nervous system. Together they control behavior. The hypothalamus keeps aware of physiological events in the body by monitoring the composition of the blood. In turn, the hypothalamus signals the pituitary by either a nerve impulse or a chemical messenger. The pituitary responds by releasing or ceasing to release hormones that will have a direct effect on physiology or will stimulate other endocrines to release their hormones in order to alter the physiological event and influence behavior. The endocrine system exerts its effects on a biochemical level.

The human endocrine system is typical of vertebrate endocrine systems and their effect on behavior, although cer-

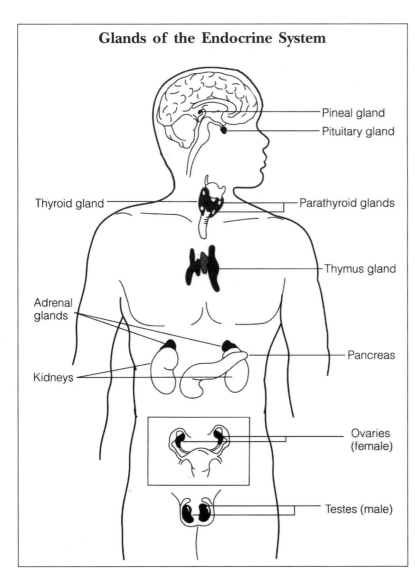

Glands of the Endocrine System

- Pineal gland
- Pituitary gland
- Thyroid gland
- Parathyroid glands
- Thymus gland
- Adrenal glands
- Pancreas
- Kidneys
- Ovaries (female)
- Testes (male)

(Hans & Cassidy, Inc.)

tain hormones may have a more pronounced and obvious effect in other vertebrates. For example, melanocyte-stimulating hormone, which is generated by the anterior lobe of the pituitary, greatly increases skin pigmentation in amphibians. This creates a protective coloration. In humans, the darkening effect is not achieved unless excessive hormone is administered. The protective function is not apparent. There are enough similarities among human and animal endocrine functions and effects, however, to warrant the use of data from both ethology and human behavioral studies in determining the biological bases for behavior.

INFLUENCE ON REPRODUCTIVE BEHAVIOR

The influence of the endocrine system on behavior has been studied on many levels. Much of the work has been done on animals; laboratory rats have been the most frequently used subjects. There is, however, a growing body of information on hormonal effects on a variety of human behaviors, including reproductive and developmental behavior, reaction to stress, learning, and memory. Studies carried out in reproductive and developmental biology on both animal and human subjects have substantiated the belief that hormones influence mating behavior, developmental events including sexual differentiation, and female and male sexuality.

Castration experiments have linked the testes with a male mating behavior pattern in animals. The sexually active adult male animal aggressively seeks and attempts to mount the female whether she is receptive or not. The castrated male retains the ability to mount a female but loses the aggressiveness and persistent pursuit of females. The male may assume the more submissive female behavior and even engage in homosexual encounters. Normally, the release of reproductive hormones in the male is noncyclic, whereas in the female it is cyclic. Castrated animals begin to exhibit the female, cyclic pattern of hormone release. The hormonal influence is confirmed by administering androgens (male hormones) to the castrated animals. Male mating behavior and the noncyclic release of hormones returns.

The presence of male hormones has an effect on the female cycle and sexual receptivity. Pheromones are substances secreted on the body of one individual which influence the behavior of another. These chemical messengers function during mate attraction, territoriality, and episodes of fear. Their exis-

tence and functions are well documented throughout the animal kingdom, especially among insects and mammals. In experiments using rats, it was shown that the pheromones act in conjunction with male hormones in bringing the female to a state of receptivity. The urine of noncastrated male rats contains androgens. When a male rat is introduced into a cage of sexually inactive females, the male sends off chemical signals by way of pheromones and the androgen-containing urine. The result is the accelerated onset of estrus, or sexual receptivity, on the part of the females. Castrated males produce pheromones but do not have androgens in the urine. When castrated males are introduced into a cage of inactive females, the estrous cycle is not affected.

Female mammals, with the exception of monkeys, apes, and humans, also experience estrus. Under hormonal control, the female is receptive to the male once or twice a year, when her eggs are available for fertilization. This period of receptivity is known as the estrous phase, or heat. Research shows that the particular female hormone which induces estrus is progesterone.

HORMONAL INFLUENCES

The work done by researchers in developing contraceptives clarified the role of hormones in the functioning of the human female reproductive system. The system operates in a monthly cycle during which ovarian and uterine changes occur under hormonal control. These hormones do not affect the human female's receptivity, which is not limited to fertile periods.

Testosterone derivatives known as anabolic steroids are illegally used by some athletes in an attempt to increase muscularity, strength, and performance. While both sexes do experience the desired effects, long-term, high-dosage usage has undesirable consequences. This is particularly true in the female, who begins to exhibit a deepening of the voice, a male body shape, and increased body and facial hair. Both males and females can become sterile. Psychotic behaviors and states such as depression and anger have been recorded.

Developmental biologists indicate that hormones exert their influence as early as six or seven weeks into embryonic development. At this point, undifferentiated tissue with the potential of developing into either a female or a male reproductive system will develop into a male system in the presence of testosterone, and into a female system in its absence. There is some evidence that the embryonic hormones have an effect on the developing brain, producing either a male or female brain. Functionally, this may account for the cyclic activity of female reproductive hormones and the noncyclic activity of the male. A few anatomical differences between male and female brains have been observed in both rats and humans. In the hypothalamus of the brain, there are cell bodies called nuclei. In rats and in humans, these nuclei are larger in males than in females.

Learning and memory can be experimentally affected by hormones. Experiments reveal that chemicals which resemble adrenocorticotropic hormone (ACTH) can extend the memory time of rats. Rats, stimulated by electric shock and provided with an avoidance possibility such as moving into another chamber of a cage or climbing a pole in the center of the cage, were administered ACTH-like molecules. The treated rats were able to remember the appropriate reaction to the stimulus for a longer period of time. In other experiments, rats in a maze were administered vasopressin, a posterior pituitary hormone, which increased their frequency in selecting the correct pathway through the maze.

The effect of vasopressin on human memory is not as clearly defined. There have been positive results with schizophrenic patients and patients with alcohol-induced amnesia. In these cases, memory has been enhanced to a limited degree. There is no solid evidence that learning and memory in humans will be greatly improved by the administration of vasopressin.

Areas such as eating disorders, psychotic behavior, hormone therapy, behavior modification, and biological clocks and rhythms challenge the physiological psychologist to further research to test hormonal influences.

SOURCES FOR FURTHER STUDY

Bioscience 33 (October, 1983). The entire issue is devoted to the effects of hormones on behavior. Includes an article on invertebrates in general, followed by articles on fish through primates. Written in nonesoteric language.

Brennan, James F. *History and Systems of Psychology.* 5th ed. Englewood Cliffs, N.J.: Prentice-Hall, 1997. Readable presentation of the history and development of psychology. Covers the highlights of the discipline from the time of ancient Greece. Good background material for those not well grounded in psychology, and interesting reading for those with a historical leaning.

Donovan, Bernard T. *Hormones and Human Behavior.* New York: Cambridge University Press, 1985. An excellent compilation of the information available on hormones and behavior up to 1985. Uses technical language, but one who reads on a high-school level and has had some exposure to science will find the book informative and interesting. Focuses on the pituitary, the gonads, and the adrenals, and their effect on human behavior.

Drickamer, Lee C., Stephen H. Vessey, and Elizabeth Jakob. *Animal Behavior.* 5th ed. New York: McGraw-Hill, 2001. Intended for undergraduate students who are interested in animal behavior. Of particular interest is chapter 10, which deals with hormones and behavior. Presents a clear explanation of the endocrine system and the mechanism of hormone action. Avoids highly technical language. The effect of hormones on behavior of invertebrates and vertebrates is well illustrated with many interesting examples from the animal world.

Highnam, Kenneth Charles, and Leonard Hill. *The Comparative Endocrinology of the Invertebrates.* New York: American Elsevier, 1969. The various types of invertebrate endocrine systems are described in this book. Although the book was published in 1969, it is a valuable source of information, especially on the insect and crustacean hormones. Technical language is used but is clearly explained in layperson's terms. Drawings and charts contribute to the understanding of the material.

Pinel, John P. J. *Biopsychology.* 4th ed. Boston: Allyn & Bacon, 1999. A textbook intended for use by the undergraduate college student. There are two chapters of particular interest. Chapter 1 defines the position of biopsychology within the larger field of psychology, delineates the subdivisions of biopsychology, and describes the type of research carried out in each area. An account of research involving the human reproductive hormones and their effects is found in chapter 10. Both chapters are interesting and well written. The author makes use of good examples, drawings, and charts.

Rosemary Scheirer

SEE ALSO: Adrenal gland; Emotions; General adaptation syndrome; Gonads; Hormones and behavior; Memory: Animal research; Pituitary gland; Sex hormones and motivation; Stress: Physiological responses; Thyroid gland.

Endorphins

TYPE OF PSYCHOLOGY: Biological bases of behavior
FIELDS OF STUDY: Nervous system

Endorphins have been identified as pain relievers that are produced by vertebrates. Although occurring only in low concentrations and for short periods of time, they play a significant role in the response to pain and may have other important effects.

KEY CONCEPTS
- endogenous substances
- exogenous substances
- neurotransmitters
- opiates
- receptors

INTRODUCTION

The endorphins are a class of chemicals, found in the nervous system, which resemble morphine. The name "endorphin" is derived from "endogenous" (naturally occurring) and "morphine," because the substances are morphinelike.

Morphine was one of the first painkillers known to humankind. It is the active component of opium, and its effects have been well known for several centuries. Morphine is still widely used clinically for the treatment of pain. Scientists found during the 1970's that there are naturally occurring chemicals in the bodies of vertebrates that are capable of controlling pain, and several of them have been identified. Since they are typically short chains of amino acids, they are often referred to as opiate peptides.

BETA ENDORPHINS AND ENKEPHALINS

Several endogenous opiates (a class of drugs that relieve pain) have been described: alpha, beta, gamma, and delta endorphins, as well as leucine enkephalin and methionine enkephalin. Of these, the beta endorphins and the enkephalins have been most widely studied. The endorphins are composed of about thirty amino acids, while the enkephalins are made up of about five amino acids. Beta endorphin is more potent and lasts longer in the body than the enkephalins.

Beta endorphin is found in varying concentrations in the neurons in the brain, spinal cord, and gastrointestinal tract. Beta endorphins in the brain are released in response to unpleasant stimuli that are entering the brain; in the spinal cord, they are released in response to impulses that are relayed from the brain to peripheral muscles. Enkephalins are neurotransmitters (substances released by neurons that cause another nerve, muscle, or gland to respond to a given stimulus) of the brain and spinal cord that are weaker than endorphins but still considerably stronger and longer lasting than morphine.

The most widely studied effect of the endorphins is their ability to block painful stimuli (the analgesic effect). They have also been associated with many other physiological activities, including thermoregulation, appetite, memory, lipolysis, reproduction, and pleasure experiences. On the surfaces of target cells are proteins that serve as binding sites for a variety of chemicals. These receptors are typically very specific and bind only those chemicals with compatible size, shape, and chemical charge. There are receptors on cells in the nervous system that are specific for the opiate peptides; they are the same receptors that bind morphine.

MECHANISM AND EFFECTS

It is believed that endorphins have their effect by binding to the receptors and thereby preventing the release of neurotransmitters from neurons. If no neurotransmitters are released, painful stimuli are prevented from being transmitted from the sensory receptors of the body to the cells of the spinal cord or the brain. This is the same mechanism of action that morphine possesses. In addition to the prevention of pain, the endorphins are said to produce a feeling of well-being in those persons with elevated endorphin levels.

It has been difficult to conduct studies on the effects of endorphins because of the low concentrations that have been found. Most research has been conducted in animals, in which cellular effects and injections into specific cells can be achieved. Animals, however, are unable to describe the feelings that are produced. In humans, endorphins have generally been studied through plasma levels in conditions in which changes in endorphin levels are expected.

Endorphins are released in humans in conditions of physical or psychological stress. The physical stress most closely associated with an increase in plasma endorphin levels is aerobic exercise, especially running. Although the endorphin levels return to normal within thirty minutes to an hour after cessation of the exercise, the endorphins are generally credited with decreased sensitivity to pain in athletes who suffer physical injury. Endorphins are also believed to be the reason that runners experience a feeling of well-being after prolonged strenuous exercise.

ADDICTION AND THE PLACEBO EFFECT

The explanation for morphine addiction may also lie with the endorphins. Since morphine and the endorphins bind to the same receptors in cell membranes, the theory suggests that morphine, when available, occupies some of the receptor molecules and the endorphins occupy the rest. Adequate quantities of exogenous or endogenous painkillers are available to prevent pain. Endogenous substances are naturally occurring whereas exogenous substances are those not normally occurring in the body and present only when administered; these can include substances such as drugs or synthetic test compounds mimicking endogenous substances.

In patients to whom morphine is supplied, however, the circulating levels of enkephalins appear to decrease. Once the enkephalin levels fall, the receptor sites to which they had bound are no longer occupied, and pain stimuli are able to reach the brain. This in turn signals a craving for more morphine to occupy the receptors which were previously occupied by the enkephalins.

Endorphins are also believed to be instrumental in the placebo effect. Patients who receive sugar in place of typical analgesics, and are told that they will feel better soon, often respond to the suggestion by experiencing an improvement in their condition. If the suggestion of pain relief could trigger the release of endorphins, it could explain the placebo effect.

ROLE OF STRESS AND EXERCISE

The control of pain has long been a problem for the medical profession. The most effective pain reliev-

ers that are available are often habit forming. The ability to relieve pain requires ever-increasing doses of the painkillers, and withdrawal of the pain reducers can lead to unpleasant side effects for the patient. The discovery of the endorphins and enkephalins has provided hope that scientists will one day be able to control pain without the fear of addiction or the production of withdrawal symptoms when the painkiller is removed. This would require that scientists learn how to stimulate the production of opiates endogenously or be able to synthesize synthetic forms of endogenous analgesics.

Studies have shown that animals under stress are better able to endure pain than those that are not under stress. Some of the ability to tolerate pain may be a result of the natural painkillers—the endogenously occurring opiates. This is also true in humans. Many instances have been described in which an individual has experienced severe stress and not felt the pain of an injury. For example, soldiers have described a feeling of detachment or curiosity when viewing their own serious injuries. Instances have been described in which they are not aware of the injury or, if they are aware, do not feel pain. Mood, too, may be a result of the endorphins and enkephalins. The soldiers describing their injuries without pain described a mood that is quite serene and accepting of the situation.

There are also correlates with more common experiences; one example is the athlete doing aerobic exercise. Continuous strenuous exercise leads to physiological changes very similar to stress reactions. It has been determined that intense exercise such as long-distance running can induce increases in the naturally occurring opiates. Runners tested after a long run have elevated levels of endorphins. The runners who exercise sufficiently to increase endorphin levels are less likely to experience pain than if they do not reach this intensity. Injuries are less bothersome and in some instances can be ignored.

Runners are also likely to experience a feeling of elation, the "runner's high," which some scientists attribute to elevated levels of endorphins. Although the levels of endorphins remain elevated for only thirty minutes, the mood remains positive for far longer. Dedicated runners and others who regularly do aerobic exercise describe a sense of loss when they are unable to run or exercise. Some have suggested that this need to exercise resembles a form of exercise addiction, which could be explained as the withdrawal of endorphins.

Research on endorphins has not yet revealed ways that they could be used clinically, and the only known way to increase endorphin levels is by strenuous exercise. This may not be satisfactory for those who experience pain as a result of serious illness, but exercise has proved successful in the treatment of mildly depressed individuals.

ANIMAL RESEARCH

Many known effects of endorphins and enkephalins appear to be related to their opiate properties. Scientists have sought other effects which would not involve analgesia. Although some of these effects have been observed in animals, correlations with humans have not yet been established. Hungry rats, for example, were more successful at running if they had received endorphins and enkephalins than if they had not. Rats also experienced increased grooming tendencies and increased sexual arousal after treatment with the opiate peptides.

Other animals also experienced changes in their behavior after administration of endogenous opiates. Young chicks that are isolated from their mother or from other young chicks would normally be expected to call for them extensively with loud vocalizations. After administration of endorphins, this behavior pattern was decreased. Goldfish tested with endorphins swam less and showed considerable immobility.

There is a good likelihood that other effects of the opiate peptides will be described in the future. There may be many types of behaviors that are effected by these substances in humans. Studies investigating this possibility await more information about the mechanisms involved in the release of endorphins and enkephalins, or the synthesis of similar compounds.

OPIATE STUDIES

During the early 1970's, the United States government declared a "war" on drugs. The federal government made money available to study the effects of drugs and the basis of drug addiction. The opiates, particularly heroin, were included in the target group.

It was theorized at that time that if the opiates were to have an effect on the brain, there must be opiate receptors. The opiate receptors were isolated

in 1973 at The Johns Hopkins University School of Medicine by Solomon H. Snyder and Candace Pert. The presence of opiate receptors in humans suggested the existence of endogenously occurring opiates. Many laboratories in the United States and Europe were already trying to explain the structure and function of some very interesting substances that had been isolated from nervous and endocrine tissue.

The endogenous opiates were isolated and identified in 1973. They were present in very low quantities in various areas of the brain, in the synaptic membranes, and in the pituitary gland. The fact that they were present in such small quantities complicated efforts to determine in which tissues they would be likely to be found. The importance of the opiates comes not only from the influence of the exogenously administered opiates but also from the endogenously produced opiates. The mechanism of addiction may be explained by the influence of both these substances on the opiate receptors.

The production of the endorphins and enkephalins is a major area of study. When scientists and physicians learn how to stimulate their production and release, they may be able to use this knowledge to control pain and stress. The ability to control pain would be a major advance for the medical community. By stimulating production of endorphins and enkephalins, physicians might be able to decrease the use of painkillers and thus reduce the risk of addiction. A treatment for those persons already addicted to opiates might also be a result of future research. Further, the fact that endorphins and enkephalins may be responsible for the placebo effect indicates that they may be involved in controlling how people feel. The ability to create a feeling of well-being using substances produced naturally within the body is certainly a goal worth pursuing.

SOURCES FOR FURTHER STUDY

Goldberg, Jeff. *Anatomy of a Scientific Discovery.* New York: Bantam Books, 1988. An examination of the scientific rivalry that occurred between the scientists who were trying to isolate the first endogenous opiates. Contains some scientific discussions, but focuses on the personal relationships of the scientists. Enlightening to anyone interested in the endorphins and enkephalins or the workings of the scientific community.

Hucho, Ferdinand. *Neurochemistry Fundamentals and Concepts*. Deerfield Beach, Fla.: VCH, 1986. A basic book of neurochemistry that can be understood by anyone who has had high school chemistry. The chemical formula of the opiate peptides and the role of receptors is described.

The Nervous System: Circuits of Communication. New York: Torstar Books, 1985. A well-written book which describes the nervous system in detail. Written for the student. Easy to understand and beautifully illustrated. Provides the background necessary for further research into the endorphins.

Restak, Richard. *The Brain*. New York: Bantam Books, 1984. Describes the brain and its functions. The experience of pain is described in some detail, and the role of the endorphins is included in this discussion. Written for the layperson.

Annette O'Connor

SEE ALSO: Biofeedback and relaxation; Meditation and relaxation; Nervous system; Neurons; Pain; Pain management; Stress: Physiological responses; Synaptic transmission.

Environmental psychology

TYPE OF PSYCHOLOGY: Stress
FIELDS OF STUDY: Coping; stress and illness

> *Traditionally, environmental psychology has examined the relations between the physical (natural or artificial) environment or, more generally, the context, and human behavior and experience; it has proved valuable for understanding individual, social, and societal processes.*

KEY CONCEPTS
- cognitive map
- context
- crowding
- environment
- environmental cognition
- environmental stressor
- personal space
- privacy
- proxemics
- territoriality

INTRODUCTION

Environmental psychology is concerned with the relationships between the physical environment—both natural and artificial—and human behavior and experiences; more specifically, it has traditionally dealt with contexts such as school and work settings. The term "environment" is best defined as the total set of circumstances by which one is surrounded, including physical, interpersonal, and sociocultural aspects.

In its early stages, the field proved valuable for understanding the relationships between the physical environment and individual processes (such as the interpretation of information from the environment), social processes (such as the sharing and division of space), and societal processes (usually identified with key settings in society, such as school, work, home, and urban environments). The field has expanded to include considerations of formal theories attempting to explain person-environment relationships and practical applications aimed at improving person-environment interactions—such as designing better environments and encouraging the management of natural resources through energy conservation and recycling.

THREE AREAS OF RESEARCH

Research examining the relations between the physical environment and individual processes has focused primarily on three areas. One encompasses environmental perception, or the ways people take in information from their environment, as well as environmental cognition—how people organize this information in their heads. Another area involves the ways people feel about and evaluate aspects of the physical environment. This includes both individual impressions, such as personal descriptions, preferences, and emotional responses (termed environmental appraisal), and collective impressions of places by expert groups (environmental assessment). A third area is the environmental aspects of personality, which looks at the ways characteristic patterns of behavior and experience influence people's transactions with the physical environment.

For example, studies have demonstrated that environmental perception is enhanced if the physical environment is novel, complex, surprising, or incongruous. Environmental cognition has been shown to be associated with life stage: In 1973, Roger A. Hart and Gary T. Moore demonstrated that, as children age, their mental organization of the physical environment (their cognitive map) becomes less egocentric, then more projective (thinking of settings from various physical vantage points), and finally more abstract (thinking of settings through the use of abstract concepts such as coordinates and directions). Research on person-oriented environmental appraisals and place- or policy-oriented environmental assessments has focused primarily on the scenic quality of natural settings such as river valleys but is expanding to include a variety of physical contexts—urban air quality and nursing homes, for example. Studies on environmental aspects of personality have indicated that traditional personality variables may explain some aspects of person-environment relationships. Compared with reserved individuals, outgoing individuals rated landscapes as more serene and beautiful. People with an internal sense of control over their lives have been shown to prefer buildings within the classical architectural style, while those believing their lives to be influenced by powerful others or by fate prefer the Romantic style.

PROXEMICS

Researchers in environmental psychology have extensively studied four areas in particular: personal space, territoriality, crowding, and privacy. These four areas make up what has come to be known as proxemics, a field concerned with the ways in which individuals and groups deal with space as a limited resource and structure their activities accordingly. Personal space is the area surrounding a person's body (as if there were invisible boundaries) into which intruders may not come without causing discomfort. This space has been shown to be larger for males, variable for disturbed individuals, smaller in situations of attraction or cooperation, and larger in situations involving stigma or unequal status. Studies of territoriality have typically shown that males are more territorial than females and that being within one's own territory is related to perceived control.

Research on crowding has distinguished between density (an objective measure of the number of individuals per unit area) and crowding, an individual's subjective perception of spatial restriction. Prolonged high indoor density acts as an environmental stressor, often impairing health (affecting blood pressure and other cardiac functions), performance of complex tasks, and social interaction (causing increased aggression, withdrawal, and lack of cooperation). Privacy refers to the selective control of access to one's self or one's group. Studies have shown that private preferences, expectations, values, and behaviors vary from person to person and from occasion to occasion.

CONTEXT-SPECIFIC SOCIETAL RESEARCH

Research on the relationship between the physical environment and societal processes has concentrated on living at home, learning in the classroom, and functioning in the workplace. Each of these environments involves many perceptions, activities, and attitudes. The home environment can include one's residence, neighborhood, and city; living there may include such varied activities as shopping, relaxing, waiting for the bus, deciding who really owns the bathroom, preparing for potential disasters, and moving.

Researchers have applied many of the individual and social processes described above in the specific contexts of the home, city, school, and workplace. For example, research has shown that neighborhood satisfaction is related to the absence of environmental stressors (such as noise, pollution, and ugliness), although some individuals seem able to adapt to at least some of these stressors. Climate has been shown, at the urban level, to influence prosocial and antisocial behavior slightly; high temperatures seem to increase aggression, while comfortable temperatures increase helping. Studies at schools have shown that classroom characteristics such as high noise and density levels may be associated with numerous difficulties, including decreased learning, participation, and classroom interaction, and may cause negative feelings about school.

PERSON-ENVIRONMENT THEORIES

Complementing the array of empirical studies are attempts at both theoretical and practical application. The theoretical applications have tried to provide integrative theories for the field—that is, for person-environment functioning more generally. A major theoretical point accepted by most investigators has been that the environment is composed not only of physical aspects but also of interpersonal (other people) and sociocultural (rules and customs) aspects.

To make sense of the field's varied theoretical applications, psychologists Irwin Altman and Barbara

Rogoff have utilized the philosopher Stephen C. Pepper's four worldviews (general beliefs about the nature of the world and how reality is constructed) to organize theories of person-environment functioning.

In formist, or trait, approaches to person-environment relations, the focus is on individuals or psychological processes as self-contained entities, with environments playing supplementary or secondary roles; for example, an investigator adhering to this type of approach might study how traditional personality characteristics (such as the locus of control) affect environmental appraisal. In mechanistic, or interactional, approaches, the focus is on person, group, and/or setting qualities as independently defined and operating entities influencing one another in causal fashions. Environmental factors, but sometimes person factors, are usually treated as causal influences on psychological functioning. For example, an investigator working from this type of approach might employ specific (operant) learning techniques to understand and then to decrease littering.

In organismic approaches, the emphasis is on dynamic and holistic systems, with complex reciprocal influences between person and environment components. For example, a researcher with this type of approach might study the development of individuals' cognitive maps across the life span. Finally, in contextual, or transactional, approaches, the focus is on the changing (temporal) relations among aspects of persons and of environments, which together compose holistic entities. An investigator might attempt to illustrate how descriptions of homes reflect inseparable confluences of psychological and environmental experiences.

DESIGNING OPTIMAL ENVIRONMENTS

Environmental psychology has also increasingly become concerned with practical applications such as optimizing person-environment relations. Such applications have included recommendations for the actual design of more fitting environments. For example, Barbara B. Brown and Irwin Altman have demonstrated that residential dwellings with real and symbolic barriers—communicating a strong sense of territoriality—are less likely to be burglarized than residences lacking such barriers. Harry Heft has reviewed the work on prolonged high indoor density on children and found it to be associated with diffi-

culties in visual and auditory discrimination, object permanence, and language development (verbal imitation and reading). M. Powell Lawton designed a nursing home (characterized by single and double bedrooms, lighting improvements, and better-located staff offices) that successfully enhanced patients' perceptual and social transactions with the environment.

INTERVENTION PROGRAMS

Further, research on environmental stress, at both the individual and societal levels, has generated intervention programs to decrease technological risk and to encourage the management and preservation of natural resources. For example, Jack Demick and his collaborators from Hiroshima University analyzed cultural differences in the impact of governmental legislation; whereas the Japanese value adherence to legislation for the group as a whole, Americans value individuality and personal expression. These differences were then employed in the design of differential programs to enhance the use of automobile safety belts. Appeals to national pride were used in Japan, whereas freedom of choice—with accompanying reductions in insurance rates—was emphasized in the United States. Related programs have been instituted aimed at decreasing such environmental problems as air pollution, litter, and homelessness as well as at increasing such processes as energy conservation and recycling. Robert Gifford's *Environmental Psychology: Principles and Practice* (1987) reviews many of the major applied programs in these and related areas.

CONTRIBUTIONS OF BRUNSWICK AND LEWIN

Historically, the first stirrings of environmental psychology occurred in the 1940's. This was followed by increased activity in the 1950's, which grew significantly throughout the 1960's and into the 1970's. The movement in each of these decades is perhaps summarized best through the work of its pioneering researchers.

In the 1930's, psychologist Egon Brunswik (1903-1955), born in Budapest and trained in Vienna, emigrated to the United States. Initially focusing on the process of perception, he expanded his ideas to make three contributions to the field that was to become environmental psychology: He was one of the first to call for a more detailed analysis of the ways in which (physical) environmental factors affect behavior; he advocated the use of more varied environmental stimuli in psychological research than was typically the case; and he coined the term "environmental psychology" in 1934.

Even more contributory than Brunswik was psychologist Kurt Lewin (1890-1947). Born in Prussia and trained in Germany, he also emigrated to the United States. He was extremely influential for several reasons. First, his work on field theory in the 1940's was the first to give significant attention to the molar physical environment; his original notion that behavior is a joint function of the interaction between person and environment became a basic premise of modern psychology. Second, he influenced many students, among them Roger Barker and Herbert Wright. In the 1950's, Barker and Wright developed "ecological psychology," in which they studied "behavior settings," small ecological units enclosing everyday human behavior (such as the restaurant or the pharmacy) with both physical-spatial and social aspects. Ecological psychology is often credited as being the forerunner of environmental psychology.

REAL-WORLD FOCUS

Environmental psychology in its own right emerged full force in the 1960's as a problem-focused field, responding to practical questions posed by architects and planners about real-world design decisions. The shift from basic laboratory research to work on real-world applications was perhaps also expedited by changing societal realities related to the United States' involvement in the Vietnam War. This real-world focus was subsequently reinforced by environmental events such as the 1979 nuclear accident at Three Mile Island in Pennsylvania.

Theoretically, this movement into the real world and its accompanying focus on the real-life functioning of individuals have highlighted, for the field of psychology as a whole, the need to take the environmental context into account in all theories and research on human behavior and experience. While various subfields of psychology (such as developmental psychology and personality) have acknowledged the importance of context, environmental psychology as a subfield has strongly reinforced this idea by providing a unique perspective—the person in the context of the environment—on all psychological processes. It will continue to be a driving force behind psychology's renewed commitment to understanding individuals' real-world functioning in all of its complexity.

SOURCES FOR FURTHER STUDY

Bechtel, Robert, and Arza Chruchman, eds. *Handbook of Environmental Psychology*. New York: John Wiley & Sons, 2002. Outlines models, methodological issues, implementation in numerous settings, the role of technology, and coming trends.

Downs, Roger M., and David Stea, eds. *Image and Environment: Cognitive Mapping and Spatial Behavior.* Chicago: Aldine, 1973. A landmark book in environmental psychology. Drawing on Kenneth Boulding's 1956 book *The Image: Knowledge in Life and Society* (the image refers to a person's known or believed universe), these researchers focus on that part of the image called a "cognitive map," defined as an internal representation of the spatial organization of the external world. Provides the reader with a valuable backdrop for the field's extensive work on cognitive maps.

Gifford, Robert. *Environmental Psychology: Principles and Practice*. 3d ed. Boston: Optimal, 2001. An excellent introductory textbook, slightly more sophisticated than its peers. A readable blend of theoretical and empirical work with an emphasis on practical application. An extensive bibliography is also provided. Can be understood by the high school or college student.

Hall, Edward Twitchell. *The Hidden Dimension*. 1969. Reprint. New York: Anchor, 1990. One of the best (relatively brief) introductions to the field of proxemics by one of its pioneers. Includes sections on crowding and social behavior, proxemics and culture, and proxemics and the future. Delightfully written and easily understood.

Holahan, Charles J. *Environmental Psychology*. New York: Random House, 1982. A beginning textbook by a leading researcher in the field. Particularly good coverage of topics such as environmental cognition, environmental stress, crowding, and privacy. The last chapter provides a unifying framework for the field; there is also an extensive bibliography. Can be understood by the high school or college student.

Proshansky, Harold M., William H. Ittelson, and Leanne G. Rivlin, eds. *Environmental Psychology: People and Their Physical Settings*. 2d ed. New York: Holt, Rinehart and Winston, 1976. An edited textbook with many outstanding selections from leaders in the field. The editors themselves established the first Ph.D. program in environmental psychology at the City University of New York in 1968; their introduction provides insights into the history and issues of the field.

Saegert, S., and G. H. Winkel. "Environmental Psychology." In *Annual Review of Psychology* 41. Stanford, Calif.: Annual Reviews, 1990. Reviews developments in the field, presenting major theories of person-environment relations. Evaluates research with an eye toward future synthesis. Although a good overview, it is slightly technical in spots.

Stokols, Daniel, and Irwin Altman, eds. *Handbook of Environmental Psychology.* 2 vols. New York: John Wiley & Sons, 1987. Presents a wide array of chapters on environmental psychology, including theories, history, cross-cultural approaches, the field's relationship to child development, and numerous individual approaches to environmental psychology. A very comprehensive source. A must for anyone in the field; can be understood by the college student.

Wapner, S., and J. Demick. "Development of Experience and Action: Levels of Integration in Human Functioning." In *Theories of the Evolution of Knowing*, edited by Gary Greenberg and Ethel Tobach. Hillsdale, N.J.: Lawrence Erlbaum, 1990. A summary of a holistic/systems, developmental approach to person-in-environment functioning across the life span. Attempts to integrate organismic and transactional worldviews. Illustrates the relations among problem, theory, and method in psychology generally and in environmental psychology specifically. Reviews relevant environmental psychological research on life transitions and provides an extensive bibliography.

Jack Demick

SEE ALSO: Cognitive maps; Coping: Strategies; Crowd behavior; Defense reactions: Species-specific; Field theory: Kurt Lewin; Health psychology; Stress.

Erikson, Erik

BORN: June 15, 1902, in Frankfurt, Germany
DIED: May 12, 1994, in Harwich, Massachusetts

IDENTITY: German-born American developmental psychoanalyst
TYPE OF PSYCHOLOGY: Developmental psychology
FIELDS OF STUDY: Aging; infancy and childhood; personality theory; social perception and cognition

Erikson was an innovator of the psychosocial theory of human development, who emphasized developmental change throughout the human life cycle through a series of eight developmental stages.

Erik Homburger Erikson was born in west-central Germany. His mother, a single parent, married Erik's pediatrician, Dr. Theodor Homburger, when Erik was three. Erikson took his stepfather's name and remained Erik Homburger throughout his childhood and into early adulthood. The details of his birth were kept secret, an aspect of Erikson's life that influenced his work.

The twenty-five-year-old Erikson acquired a position in Vienna as an art teacher at a private school which was founded by Anna Freud, daughter of Sigmund Freud, the father of psychoanalysis. With her encouragement, Erikson graduated from the Vienna Psychoanalytic Institute in 1933, where he studied under Sigmund Freud. That same year, Erikson moved to the United States, obtained a teaching position at the Harvard Medical School, and became the first child analyst in Boston, Massachusetts. He officially changed his name to Erik Erikson upon receiving his American citizenship. After leaving Harvard, he taught at Yale, and later at the University of California at Berkeley.

Erikson was interested in the influence of society and culture on child development. To help formulate his theories, he studied groups of Native American children in the United States. Through these studies he was able to correlate personality growth with parental and societal values. This research formed the basis for *Childhood and Society* (1950), which includes the "eight stages of psychosocial development," for which Erikson is best known.

Erikson emphasized developmental change throughout the human life cycle. He claimed that human beings develop through eight distinctive psychological stages spread over their entire life cycle. He further stated that each stage had a certain set of "crises" that must be resolved before moving on to the next stage. He believed that humans must complete each stage in successive order before entering the next, and that failure to successfully complete earlier stages could hinder their potential success in later stages.

Erikson's later studies centered on personal human development and social history. It was these psychohistorical studies that won him a Pulitzer Prize and National Book Award in 1969 for *Ghandi's Truth: On the Origin of Militant Nonviolence.*

After his formal retirement in 1970, Erikson continued to lecture and write essays and books. Following a brief illness, he died in 1994 in Harwich, Massachusetts at the age of ninety-one.

SOURCES FOR FURTHER STUDY

Friedman, Lawrence Jacob. *Identity's Architect: A Biography of Erik H. Erikson.* Cambridge, Mass.: Harvard University Press, 2000. A meticulous biography by historian Friedman, who worked with Erikson and his wife in the years immediately preceding Erikson's death in 1994.

Roazen, Paul. *Erik H. Erikson: The Power and Limits of a Vision.* Northvale, N.J.: Jason Aronson, 1997. A critical examination of Erikson's major contributions to psychoanalysis.

Welchman, Kit. *Erik Erikson: His Life, Work, and Significance.* Buckingham, England: Open University Press, 2000. An analysis of the connections between Erikson's life and his work, and the application of his theories to social and political issues.

Jack Carter

SEE ALSO: Ego psychology: Erik Erikson; Identity crises; Midlife crises; Personality theory.

Ethology

TYPE OF PSYCHOLOGY: Origin and definition of psychology

FIELDS OF STUDY: Biological influences on learning; motivation theory

Ethology, the study of animal behavior, is concerned with the adaptive significance of behavior and the physiological, genetic, and psychological basis of behavioral responses in the animal kingdom; ethology emphasizes the importance of heredity and evolutionary factors in the study of behavior.

KEY CONCEPTS
- adaptation
- conditioning
- imprinting
- innate
- instinct
- natural selection
- stimulus

INTRODUCTION

Ethology, from the Greek *ethos* ("behavior or manner"), is the study of animal behavior. It is concerned primarily with the accurate description and rigorous experimental evaluation of animals' behavior under natural conditions. Unlike the field of behaviorism, which traditionally emphasized the sole importance of the environment on behavior, ethology also recognizes the genetic and physiological mechanisms that regulate behavioral processes. Ethologists operate under the primary assumption that much of behavior is hereditary and thus strongly influenced by the forces of natural selection. Natural selection is the process of differential survival and reproduction which leads to heritable characteristics that are best suited for a particular environment.

In their search for a common, unifying explanation of behavioral processes, ethologists have sought to address three specific issues: the accurate, nonanthropomorphic description of behavior under natural conditions; the underlying mechanisms that regulate and control behavior; and the adaptive significance of various behavior patterns.

DESCRIPTIVE APPROACH

In its earliest stages, ethology was characterized by a highly descriptive approach. Early ethologists were concerned primarily with accurate and objective accounts of behavior. Behavior, however, unlike other aspects of an organism's biology (such as morphology or physiology), was a difficult and elusive thing to characterize, and thus required careful, unbiased approaches to understanding the ways in which animals responded to stimuli in their environment. Konrad Lorenz (1903-1989), one of the early founders of the field, insisted that the only way to study behavior was to make objective observations under completely natural field conditions. This approach, most evident in his classic studies on aggression and imprinting (the innate behavioral attachment that a young animal forms with another individual such as its mother, with food, or with an object during a brief critical period shortly after birth), greatly enhanced understanding of communication in the animal kingdom. In contrast to Lorenz's very subjective approach, the rigorous field experiments of Nikolaas Tinbergen (1907-1988) and Karl von Frisch (1886-1982) were similar to those that later would characterize modern ethology.

The classic work of all three of these early ethologists helped demonstrate how an animal's sensory limitations and capabilities can shape its behavior. For example, in a series of classic learning experiments, von Frisch convincingly documented the unusual visual capabilities of the honeybee. He first trained honeybees to forage at small glass dishes of sugar water and then, by attaching different visual cues to each dish, provided the animals with an opportunity to learn where to forage through the simple process of association. From these elegant but simple experiments, he found that bees locate and remember foraging sites by the use of specific colors, ultraviolet cues, and polarized light, a discovery that revolutionized the way in which humans view the sensory capabilities of animals.

MECHANISTIC BEHAVIOR

With the classic work of Lorenz, Tinbergen, and von Frisch came an increasing appreciation for the ways in which physiological limitations define behavioral differences between species. This awareness eventually gave way to a mechanistic approach to behavior, in which ethologists sought to determine how internal factors such as physiology, development, and genetics regulate and control behavior. The physiologically oriented ethologists, for example, focused on the influence of neuronal pathways and sensory organs on behavior. They were concerned with topics such as the control of feeding in insects, echolocation in bats, electric field detection in fish, and infrared detection in snakes. Similarly, neurobiologists attempted to show how behavioral changes are linked to modifications in the function of nerves and neuronal pathways. By observing the response of individual nerves, neurobiologists can observe changes that occur in the nerves when an animal modifies its behavior in response to some stimulus. In a similar way, they can show how learning and behavior are affected when specific nerve fibers are experimentally cut or removed.

The study of animal behavior, particularly primates, has taught researchers much about human beings as well. (Adobe)

ADAPTIVE BEHAVIOR

The third and perhaps most significant area in ethology is that which deals with the evolutionary (adaptive) significance of behavior. Since the seminal work of Charles Darwin (1809-1882), ethologists have maintained that a species' behavior is controlled largely by its genes. Darwin argued that an animal's behavior was no different from any other phenotypic characteristic (physical expression of the genes) in that it was heritable and therefore subject to the same kinds of selective processes that lead to evolutionary change among organisms. He considered instinctual (or innate) behavior a tremendous adaptation that frees some organisms from the risky and sometimes costly business of trial-and-error learning. At the same time, he recognized the adaptive plasticity that accompanies the more complex behaviors which involve various degrees of learning.

Both Lorenz and Tinbergen also recognized the importance of evolutionary questions in behavior, but Tinbergen was the first to put such hypotheses to rigorous experimental tests. In a classic experiment on the evolutionary significance of spines in sticklebacks, he tested predation rates by pike on several species of these fish. He found predation rates to be lowest on the three-spined stickleback (a conspicuous species with large horizontal spines), moderate on the more cryptic ten-spined stickleback (which possesses ten smaller vertical spines on its dorsal surface), and highest for unarmored minnows.

MECHANISMS OF HEREDITY

More recently, behavioral geneticists have shown that much of learning, and behavior in general, is intimately tied to mechanisms of heredity. The results of hybridization experiments and artificial breeding programs, as well as studies on human twins separated at birth, clearly demonstrate a strong genetic influence on behavior. In fact, it has been well documented that many animals (including both invertebrates and vertebrates) are genetically programmed (or have a genetic predisposition) to learn only specific kinds of behaviors. Such is the case for song learning in birds.

Thus, ethology places tremendous importance on the evolutionary history of an organism. It emphasizes the adaptive significance of the various types of behaviors, and it assumes that an animal's behavior is constrained largely by its genetic and evolutionary background.

LEARNING PROCESS RESEARCH

The field of ethology has contributed markedly to the understanding of several psychological and behavioral phenomena. One such area is the learning process. Learning is defined as any modification in behavior (other than that caused by maturation, fatigue, or injury) that is directed by previous experience.

The early experiments of the behaviorist psychologists on conditioning (the behavioral association that results from the reinforcement of a response with a stimulus) led to the notion that all behavior is learned. Traditionally, behaviorists maintained that all complex behaviors are learned by means of either classical or operant conditioning. Classical conditioning, first demonstrated by the Russian psychologist Ivan Pavlov, is a form of associative learning in which an animal responds to an unrelated, novel stimulus after it is repeatedly paired with a more relevant stimulus. Operant conditioning, also a form of associative learning, occurs when an animal learns by manipulating some part of its environment (for example, the animal might ring a bell to receive a reward). This form of learning usually improves with experience and is therefore referred to as trial-and-error learning.

The primary objective of the approaches employed by the early behaviorists was to eliminate or control as many variables as possible, and thereby remove any uncertainty about the factors that may influence the learning process. These approaches were especially successful at identifying the external mechanisms responsible for learning. Such techniques focused only on the input (stimulus) and output (response) of an experiment, however, and consequently deemphasized the importance of proximate mechanisms such as physiology and genetics. In addition, these approaches generally ignored the evolutionary considerations that ethologists considered so fundamental to the study of behavior.

INNATE BEHAVIOR

In contrast, studies by the early ethologists suggested that much of behavior was dominated by innate processes that were constrained by the physiological and genetic design of the organism. Lorenz and Tinbergen, for example, demonstrated that many behavioral responses in the animal kingdom are fixed or stereotyped (instinctive) and are often elicited by simple environmental stimuli. They referred to such responses as fixed action patterns and to the stimuli that triggered them as sign stimuli.

The egg-rolling behavior of the greylag goose is perhaps one of the most widely cited examples of this kind of innate behavior. When one of these ground-nesting birds notices an egg outside its nest, it stands, walks to the egg, extends its bill in a very characteristic manner, and proceeds to roll the egg back to the nest. Although at first glance this may seem to represent a simple learned response, Lorenz and Tinbergen found this to be a highly ritualized behavior that was initiated by a very specific environmental stimulus. Through a series of clever experiments, Tinbergen showed that this behavior could be elicited by an egglike object (a ball) or even any object with a convex surface (a bottle or can), and that objects larger than eggs caused a more vigorous (supernormal) response. He also found that once the behavior was initiated, it always ran to completion. In other words, even when the egg was removed, the goose would continue with the motions as if it were returning the egg to the nest.

This and countless other examples of very ritualized behaviors, such as the avoidance response of ducklings to hawk models, the imprinting of young vertebrates on their mothers, the aggressive displays of male stickleback fish to the red bellies of other males, and the various courtship displays of a wide range of species, led early ethologists to conclude that much of behavior is governed by instinct.

These opposing views of ethologists and behaviorist psychologists eventually led to the misconception that learned behavior is governed entirely by the animal's environment, whereas instinct is completely controlled by the genes. It is now widely accepted, however, that nearly all forms of behavior and learning involve certain degrees of both processes. Countless studies, for example, have demonstrated that numerous animals are genetically programmed to learn only certain behaviors. In contrast, it has been shown that instinct need not be completely fixed, but instead can be modified with experience.

SOCIOBIOLOGY

A second area of ethology that has received much attention from a variety of behavioral researchers and in some cases has sparked considerable controversy is sociobiology. In the early 1970's, Edward O. Wilson and Robert Trivers of Harvard University initiated a new area of behavioral research when they began their investigations of the evolutionary basis of social behavior in animals. Their attention focused on the evolutionary enigma presented by altruistic behaviors—acts that one organism performs (often at its own expense) to benefit another. Examples include alarm calls in the presence of a predator and nest-helping behavior. The most extreme cases of such behavior are found in those insect societies in which only a few individuals reproduce and others work to maintain the colony. Through careful experimentation and observation, it was soon determined that such unselfish behaviors are directed toward related individuals and that such behaviors probably evolve because they promote the survival of other individuals who also possess the genes for those same altruistic acts.

Although they initially sparked much debate, studies of the evolutionary basis for social behavior eventually strengthened the ethologists' long-held notion that much of behavior is coded in the genes.

RESEARCH DEBATES

Although ethology had its beginnings with the work of Charles Darwin and other early naturalists, it was Karl von Frisch, Konrad Lorenz, and Nikolaas Tinbergen who conducted the first formal ethological studies and who received a joint Nobel Prize for their pioneering work in 1973. Their approach represented a considerable departure from that of behaviorist psychologists, and the differences between the two fields sparked a heated debate during the 1950's and 1960's, often referred to as the nature-versus-nurture controversy. While this debate eventually led to the decline and virtual demise of behaviorism, it also helped shape modern ethology into a rigorous biological discipline that now holds a compatible niche within the realm of psychology.

While the early ethologists argued that behaviorists treated their study organisms as "black-boxes" and ignored the genetic, physiological, and evolutionary backgrounds of their subjects, the behaviorists leveled several criticisms in return. In addition to their disbelief in the genetic control of behavior, they were most critical of the methodological approaches employed by ethologists. In contrast with the rigorously controlled laboratory experiments of psychologists, in which blind observers (observers unaware of the experimenters' hypotheses or experimental design) were often used to collect data, behaviorists held that early ethologists conducted nearly all their studies under natural conditions without any regard for experimental control. In addition, their observations were often highly subjective and almost never quantified. Even when attempts were made to quantify the behavior, they never involved the rigorous statistical and analytical techniques of the behaviorists.

Furthermore, although the early ethologists argued that much of behavior is shaped by evolution and constrained by an organism's physiological hardware, little evidence was initially available to support these contentions. Behaviorists, for example, held that ethologists often observed a behavior and casually assigned some adaptive significance to it without testing such evolutionary hypotheses.

These criticisms forced early ethologists to improve their approaches to data collection, experimental design, and data analysis, and as their approaches to the study of behavior were strengthened, so were their original hypotheses about the underlying control of behavior. Thus, as ethologists gained ground, behaviorism began to fall out of favor with most of the scientific community.

The basic views of early ethologists are still well preserved in all prominent areas of ethological research. In fact, the work of nearly all modern ethologists can best be characterized by the two basic sets of questions they seek to answer: the "how questions," concerning underlying proximate causes, and the "why questions," concerning ultimate causes (or evolutionary bases). The first of these is pursued by traditional ethologists and neurobiologists, while the latter is primarily the realm of behavioral ecologists. The fields of ethology and comparative psychology have begun to complement each other, and, increasingly, researchers from the two areas are merging their efforts on a diversity of research topics.

SOURCES FOR FURTHER STUDY

Alcock, John. *Animal Behavior: An Evolutionary Approach*. 7th ed. Sunderland, Mass.: Sinauer Associates, 2001. A clearly written, well-illustrated volume covering both the proximate mechanisms and the evolutionary bases of behavior. Two chapters deal with the sociobiology controversy and the evolution of human reproductive behavior. Especially helpful as an introduction to behavioral ecology.

Fisher, Arthur. "Sociobiology: A New Synthesis Comes of Age." *Mosaic* 22 (Spring, 1991): 2-9. This review article provides a comprehensive overview of the biological basis of behavior and the sociobiology controversy. Includes a thorough historical perspective. A well-written summary of major research in the field between 1965 and 1990.

Gould, James L. *Ethology: The Mechanisms and Evolution of Behavior*. New York: W. W. Norton, 1982. A well-illustrated text offering a complete introduction to the basic concepts of ethology. Early chapters include a complete review of the history of ethology and the debate between ethologists and psychologists. Provides detailed descriptions of various ethological experiments; three chapters are devoted entirely to human ethology.

Grier, James W. *Biology of Animal Behavior*. 2d ed. New York: McGraw-Hill, 1992. A college-level text providing an excellent treatment of the study of animal behavior. Clearly written, well illustrated; a good introduction for the layperson. Integrates information from a variety of disciplines including ethology, behavioral ecology, psychology, and neurobiology.

Krebs, J. R., and N. B. Davies. *An Introduction to Behavioral Ecology*. 2d ed. Oxford, England: Blackwell Scientific Publications, 1991. Intended as a basic overview of behavioral ecology for individuals outside the profession. Covers many aspects of foraging ecology, social behavior, and predator avoidance from an evolutionary perspective. Well referenced; includes many diagrams and data figures.

McFarland, David, ed. *The Oxford Companion to Animal Behavior*. Rev. and enlarged ed. New York: Oxford University Press, 1987. Intended as a reference guide for both nonspecialists and people in the field. A comprehensive survey of behavior, written by a team of internationally known biologists, psychologists, and neurobiologists. Contains more than two hundred entries covering a variety of behavioral topics. A detailed index provides cross-references organized by both subject and species lists.

Manning, Aubrey, and Marian Stamp Dawkins. *An Introduction to Animal Behavior*. 5th ed. New York: Cambridge University Press, 1998. A concise introduction to many general aspects of animal behavior. Topics covered include learning, evolution and behavior, development of behavior, communication, conflict behavior, and social organization. Well researched, clearly written, and effectively illustrated.

Raven, Peter H, and George B, Johnson. *Biology*. 5th ed. New York: McGraw-Hill, 1999. Chapter 56 of this general text on the science of biology offers an excellent introduction to the general concepts of ethology and animal behavior, with a strong emphasis on many basic ethological concepts in addition to the learning-versus-instinct debate and the sociobiology controversy. A concise summary, suggestions for additional reading, and review questions appear at the end of the chapter.

Michael A. Steele

SEE ALSO: Animal experimentation; Behaviorism; Habituation and sensitization; Imprinting and learning; Learning; Reflexes.

Evolutionary psychology

DATE: The 1960's forward
TYPE OF PSYCHOLOGY: Biological bases of behavior
FIELDS OF STUDY: Aggression; biological influences on learning; cognitive development; cognitive processes; general constructs and issues; interpersonal relations; motivation theory; prosocial behavior; social motives; social perception and cognition

Evolutionary psychologists study the human brain and mind with the assumption that these are designed to produce behavior that was adaptive for human ancestors. Evolutionary psychologists believe that humans need to understand the origin of their mental processes in order to understand how they work, and therefore, how they might modify them to the advantage of their mental, psychological, and social health.

KEY CONCEPTS
- attachment
- emotion
- evolution
- language
- perception
- personality
- sensation
- sex differences
- stereotypes

INTRODUCTION

Humans share with other mammals basic behaviors, motivations, and emotions, but only humans can reflect upon and discuss their behaviors, motivations, and emotions, and only humans can influence the behaviors, motivations, and emotions of others through such abstract concepts as appeals to duty, religion, laws, blackmail, promises, and lies. Like other psychologists, evolutionary psychologists study the brain structures and mental functions that underlie these capacities. Unlike other psychologists, evolutionary psychologists start with the as-

sumption that human mental capacities evolved through natural selection the same way that human bodies did—that is, that the brain circuitry and processes underlying thought and behavior exist because they somehow helped human ancestors to survive and reproduce. It is this perspective, rather than research topics or methodology, that differentiates evolutionary psychology from other fields and approaches in psychology.

Arguing from this perspective, evolutionary psychologists have suggested that the aspects of brain and behavior that consistently conferred the greatest advantages on human ancestors are those that are most likely to now be automatic—that is, subconscious or instinctive. People do not need to be aware of how they avoid large moving objects, for example, as long as they can do it. The corollary line of reasoning is that those aspects of brain and behavior that are now the most automatic are likely to be those that had the greatest and most consistent advantages in the past. For this reason, it is the instinctive and automatic behaviors, as well as the subconscious bases of thoughts and feelings, that have received the most attention from evolutionary psychologists.

SENSATION, PERCEPTION, AND HEDONIC PREFERENCES

Certain important aspects of the behavior of the physical world seem to be innately wired into, or easily acquired by, the human brain. Babies experience anxiety about steep drop-offs as soon as they can see them—without having to learn by experiencing a fall. They also flinch or move away from objects that are getting larger on a projection screen and therefore appear to be coming toward them. Although babies cannot count or do math, they very quickly appreciate such fundamental concepts as length, mass, speed, and gravity, as well as the concepts of more and less, larger and smaller. All but the most profoundly retarded of individuals acquire easy grasp of one of the most abstract concepts of all: time.

Humans also exhibit innate preferences for things that were "good" for human ancestors and a dislike of things that were "bad." People naturally like sweet foods that provide them with the necessary glucose for their calorie-hungry brains and salty foods that provide them with the minerals to run their neuronal sodium-pump, yet they have to acquire (and may never acquire) a taste for bitter and foul-smelling foods, which signal their brains that the substance may contain toxins. The human brain also automatically causes people to develop intense aversions to foods that were ingested several hours before becoming ill. Even in cases when a person consciously knows that it was not the lime Jello (or the Thousand Island dressing or the broccoli au gratin) that actually caused the sickness, the very thought of that item may cause nausea ten years after an illness.

Humans are also wired for other kinds of "taste." Children around the world prefer parklike landscapes that provide plenty of water and trees and forms of play that provide exercise, strengthen muscles, and increase physical coordination. Adults admire the beautiful faces and shapely bodies of the young, healthy, and disease-free—those who are the safest friends and most profitable mates. In sum, experiences of pain or disgust signal that something is potentially dangerous and is to be avoided; experiences of pleasure or admiration signal safety or opportunity and encourage a person to approach.

EMOTION, MOTIVATION, AND ATTACHMENT

Important emotions, too, appear early in life, without having to be learned. These so-called primary emotions include fear, anger, happiness, sadness, surprise, and disgust. Like tastes, emotions serve as signals to alert the conscious awareness about important stimuli, but they also serve as signals to others. The facial expressions that accompany primary emotions are performed consistently across cultures, even in children blind from birth. People instinctively understand the facial expressions signifying emotion and pay special attention when they see them.

Perhaps the most important emotion for survival and reproduction is the attachment that develops between an infant and its mother. Human infants are completely dependent upon parental care and, even after weaning, require intensive investment and supervision. It is thus in the interest of both mother and child that a close bond form between them, to keep the child from wandering away and to keep the mother motivated to address the constant demands of her offspring. Infants can recognize their mother's voice and smell soon after birth, and, as soon as their eyes are able to focus, can recognize—and show preference for—her face. Once they are

old enough to crawl, babies develop an intense desire to be within sight of their mother and, when temporarily separated, experience and communicate great distress. Mothers, reciprocally, develop an intense attachment to their children, and they too experience distress upon separation.

Other social emotions also motivate people to repeat mutually beneficial interactions and to avoid people who might take advantage of them. Guilt and shame are cross-cultural universals that indicate disgust toward one's own behavior and signal to others that one is unlikely to repeat the "rotten" behavior; allegiance and sympathy signal a willingness to help allies when in need; vengeance and hatred warn those who have harmed someone that they endanger themselves if they approach again.

PERSONALITY, SEX DIFFERENCES, AND SOCIAL RELATIONS

Predicting other people's behavior is important, so any aspect of a person that is consistent and can help a person to predict accurately becomes worthy of attention. One source of predictability derives from consistent personality differences between the sexes. Boys and men around the world are, on average, more physically aggressive, more competitive, more impulsive, and more risk-prone than girls and women, who are, on average, more nurturant, more empathetic, more cooperative, and more harm-avoidant than boys and men. These differences have impacts on social behavior across the life span, influencing patterns of early childhood play, courtship, parenting, career choice, and participation in warfare, crime, and other high-risk activities.

In addition to sex differences, there are two major dimensions of personality which seem of particular importance: dominance/submissiveness and friendliness/hostility. As with tastes and emotions, one's assessment of another person's personality seems to highlight "good/safe" versus "bad/dangerous," and signals to approach or avoid, respectively. It seems that people attend to personality to determine who is likely to be a friend, to be trustworthy, and to be helpful, versus who is likely to hurt, to betray, and to take advantage.

In fact, it might have been the need to predict how other people might respond that led to human beings' great intelligence. Like other social species, humans constantly monitor who is who: who is fighting, who is having sex, who is popular, who is not.

Compared to other animals, however, humans have taken this kind of mental tracking to a level that is quite complex: A man can think about what a friend might think if his sister told him that she heard that he knew that his girlfriend had heard a rumor that he was seeing someone else but that he had not told him . . . and so on. Such multilevel cogitation requires a great deal of long-term and short-term memory, as well as an extensive ability to manipulate concepts and scenarios.

L<small>EARNING</small>, L<small>ANGUAGE</small>, <small>AND</small> T<small>HINKING</small>

Given humans' great intellectual capacity, evolutionary psychologists do not claim that all knowledge is inborn—it is obvious that humans acquire much information through learning. Nonetheless, evolutionary psychologists note that certain types of information are more easily learned than others.

Language, for example, is a kind of complex and abstract knowledge that comes as second nature to very young children. Across all cultures and languages, children progress through regular stages of language development, acquiring the ability to both understand and produce grammatical speech (or in the case of deaf children, visual signs). At their peak, children actually acquire several new words an hour. Most adults, on the other hand, have to work extremely hard to acquire a second or third language, and it is exceedingly difficult to teach even the smartest computers and robots how to understand elementary forms of speech. Language is an example of a highly specialized kind of learning that is prewired into the human brain; it is acquired quickly during a critical period of brain development and, once achieved, it is never forgotten.

Similarly, humans readily develop mental stereotypes which, once acquired, are difficult or impossible to disregard. Stereotypes are, basically, abstract generalizations that arise from the subconscious integration of personal and vicarious experience. Like tastes, emotions, and attention to personality, the automatic generation of stereotypes helps a person to respond quickly and appropriately to new stimuli without wasting precious time assessing each nuance of each situation encountered each new minute of every day.

A<small>PPLIED</small> E<small>VOLUTIONARY</small> P<small>SYCHOLOGY</small>

Evolutionary psychologists do not claim that behavior that was once adaptive is necessarily still adap-

tive, nor that behavior that has evolved is unchangeable. For example, while stereotypes were designed to work to a person's advantage, the experiences that now go into one's mental computations include not just real experiences but thousands upon thousands of images from movies, newspapers, and television. As a result, stereotypes do not necessarily reflect reality and true experience, but rather the biases of the society at large, often amplified in the make-believe world of Hollywood. Taking an evolutionary approach to psychology suggests that although people will continue to create stereotypes, by changing or monitoring media coverage, increasing exposure to positive images, or broadcasting the voices of the unheard, the content of stereotypes could be changed. Like other approaches to psychology, evolutionary psychology has practical implications that can help people to understand—and improve—the human condition.

S<small>OURCES FOR</small> F<small>URTHER</small> S<small>TUDY</small>

Baron-Cohen, S., ed. *The Maladapted Mind*. Hove, East Sussex, England: Psychology Press, 1997. For those interested in abnormal behavior, each chapter of this book discusses some form of psychopathology from an evolutionary perspective.

Crawford, C., and D. L. Krebs, eds. *Handbook of Evolutionary Psychology: Ideas, Issues, and Applications*. Mahwah, N.J.: Lawrence Erlbaum, 1998. Like many handbooks, this is actually a rather large, somewhat technical compilation. It is, however, exceptionally broad in the topics it covers, and each contributor is at the cutting edge of the field.

Damasio, A. R. *Descartes' Error: Emotion, Reason, and the Human Brain*. New York: Putnam, 1994. In this best-selling popular science book, a premier neuroscientist discusses his compelling work on emotion and cognition, arguing eloquently against René Descartes's conception of the mind as a "blank slate."

Frank, R. H. *Passions Within Reason: The Strategic Role of the Emotions*. New York: W. W. Norton, 1988. An evolutionary economist shows how and why humans are not simply rational beings, and how all aspects of people's lives are affected by their emotions and other inherent biases that affect their judgment.

Gaulin, S. J. C., and D. H. McBurney. *Psychology: An Evolutionary Approach*. Upper Saddle River, N.J.: Prentice Hall, 2001. This paperback textbook ad-

608 • Existential psychology

dresses the same topics covered by any introductory psychology book, but does so specifically from an evolutionary perspective. This book is very general as well as exceptionally reader-friendly.

MacDonald, K. B., ed. *Sociobiological Perspectives on Human Development*. New York: Springer-Verlag, 1988. An excellent introduction to developmental psychology from an evolutionary perspective, this book includes chapters on adolescence as a life stage, development of cognition, and family interactions.

Mealey, L. *Sex Differences: Developmental and Evolutionary Strategies*. San Diego, Calif.: Academic Press, 2000. This textbook compares sex differences in human behavior with those in other animals, highlighting common themes. There are also chapters on sexual politics and evolutionary theory in general.

Pinker, S. *The Language Instinct*. Cambridge, Mass.: MIT Press, 1994. Despite its level of difficulty, this book was a *New York Times* best-seller and is the best of a large number of books on the evolution of language.

Scheibel, A. B., and J. W. Schopf, eds. *The Origin and Evolution of Intelligence*. Boston: Jones & Bartlett, 1997. One of the best single books on this topic. Even though all chapters take an evolutionary approach, as an edited collection it does not restrict itself to one particular aspect or theory of intelligence.

Linda Mealey

SEE ALSO: Aggression; Attachment and bonding in infancy and childhood; Cognitive psychology; Emotions; Father-child relationship; Intelligence; Language; Learning; Mother-child relationship; Motivation; Social perception.

Existential psychology

TYPE OF PSYCHOLOGY: Personality
FIELDS OF STUDY: Humanistic-phenomenological models

Existential analysis, derived from the insights of existential philosophy, offers a powerful portrait of the fundamental dilemmas of human living. It stresses the individual's freedom to make choices responsi-

bly and to live life authentically according to those choices.

KEY CONCEPTS
- absurdity
- authenticity
- being-in-the-world
- existential analysis
- inauthenticity

INTRODUCTION

Existential psychology was inspired by the original insights of the philosophy of existentialism. By examining situations of great horror (such as the concentration camps of the Nazis) and of great beauty or joy (such as a father seeing his little girl happily skipping down the sidewalk), existentialism posited that human existence is without absolutes: There are no limits either to human cruelty or to human love. Existentialism removes all presuppositions, abstractions, and universal rules. It attacks the conformity and complacency caused by the illusion that a human is only a predetermined cog in a completely ordered, mechanical universe.

Contemporary culture can be extremely alienating, with its huge bureaucratic and technological structures that do not recognize one's concrete existence. In spite of the pervasiveness of this alienation, existentialism holds that the possibility of existing as an authentic individual is never lost. Existentialism depicts the "absurdity" (the sense that there is no inherent basis for conferring meaning to life) of the lack of preestablished systems of meaning, but it rejects the artificiality of schemes that try to account for meaning as somehow produced by systems "out there," beyond the individual. Instead, existentialism returns to concretely lived situations as the birthplace of whatever meaning may be found in life. In that sense, life is an adventure that unfolds as one lives it. As William Barrett has said, "Life is not handed to us on a platter, but involves our own act of self-determination."

Mainstream psychology has not, for the most part, addressed this existentialist outlook. Instead, it borrowed from natural science the viewpoint that human life is essentially mechanistic and causally determined—that personal life can be reduced to a bundle of drives, stimuli, or biochemical reactions. The problem with those approaches, notes existential psychologist Rollo May, is that "the man disappears; we can no longer find 'the one' to whom this or that experience has happened." Thus, the crucial innovation offered by existential psychology is its aim to understand the personal, experienced reality of one's free and meaningful involvement in one's world. This is accomplished by analyzing the experiential situations and concerns of persons as the most fundamental dimension of their existence. This approach has been especially evident in the areas of personality theory and psychotherapy. It is in those areas that psychologists are most directly confronted with real human problems and are therefore unable to settle for abstract laboratory experiments as a basis for knowledge.

Emergence of Study

Psychologists began to turn to existentialism in the 1940's. The pioneers of existential analysis were psychoanalysts originally influenced by the ideas of Sigmund Freud (who died in 1939). As analysts, they already stood outside mainstream experimental psychology, and so were not as influenced by its presumptions. Furthermore, as therapists, their overriding purpose was to assist actual people who were experiencing real distress, anxiety, and conflict. Abstract theories and dogmas about stimuli and responses were more easily recognized as insufficient in that context, and an approach that focused on patients' actual existence was welcome.

The first practitioners were the Swiss psychiatrists Ludwig Binswanger and Medard Boss, whose early writings date from the late 1940's. They were inspired by the existential philosophy of Martin Heidegger's key book *Sein und Zeit* (1927; *Being and Time*, 1962). They believed that analysis needed to be broadened beyond the limits that Freud had established. In place of Freud's psychoanalysis—the aim of which was to understand an interior mental apparatus—they developed existential analysis, with the aim of understanding the person's existence— that is, the person's "being-in-the-world." This term, developed by Heidegger, was meant by its hyphens to indicate that the relation of person and world is not merely one of the person being located "in" the world (as a pencil is located in a drawer). Rather, the person is always "worlded" in the sense that one's existence is a network of meaningful involvements—relationships that are specifically and uniquely one's own. Heidegger had called this the "care" structure, and he saw it as the very core of

what it means to be a human being: that people care, that the people, places, and things with which one is involved inevitably matter.

Being-in-the-world as involvement is revealed by the ways in which such basic dimensions of the world as time and space are actually experienced. Time is not lived as a clock would record it, in equal minutes and hours. Rather, some hours drag on and on, whereas others zip by, depending on one's involvements. Similarly, the space of a strange place looms differently when it has become familiar. Even one's own body reflects this understanding of existence as being-in-the-world. A great variety of symptoms, from cold feet to high blood pressure, disclose one's involvements, as do gestures, both habitual and spontaneous.

Other continental European psychiatrists who advanced the development of existential psychology include Karl Jaspers, Eugene Minkowski, Henri Ey, Erwin Straus, Frederik Jacobus Buytendijk, and Viktor Frankl. In England, R. D. Laing, a brilliant young psychiatrist originally influenced by the British "object relations" school of psychoanalysis, developed an existential account of schizophrenic persons, beginning around 1960. He sought to show "that it was far more possible than is generally supposed to understand people diagnosed as psychotic." He proceeded to do so by examining their "existential context." In books such as *The Divided Self: An Existential Study in Sanity and Madness* (1965), Laing attempted to unravel the mystery of schizophrenic speaking and symptoms by revealing how their apparently nonsensical quality does have a sense when seen in terms of the person's own experience of the totality of his or her relationships and existence.

Existential analysis came to the United States at the end of the 1950's mainly through the influence of Rollo May, who introduced the writings of the European analysts. May provided both a very scholarly background to the approach and an examination of its role in psychotherapy. His later books, such as *Man's Search for Himself* (1953), *Psychology and the Human Dilemma* (1967), and *Love and Will* (1969), did much to popularize existential psychology in the United States without trivializing its philosophical depth.

Appreciating Personhood

Existential therapists, such as May, have generally argued that they are not seeking to establish a new type of therapy with new techniques. Rather, they have developed a different approach, one that can be used with any specific therapeutic system. They developed a different way for the therapist to "be present" for the patient or client. This distinctive way of being present is well illustrated in R. D. Laing's therapeutic work; it hinges upon the type of relationship that exists between the therapist and the patient. Laing pointed out the difference between two ways of relating to a patient: as a biochemical organism (and a diseased organism at that) or as a person. He cited, as an example, the difference between listening to another's speaking as evidence of certain neurological processes and trying to understand what the person is talking about. When a therapist sees a patient as an "it," the therapist cannot really understand that patient's desire, fear, hope, or despair. Seeing the patient as a person, however, implies seeing the patient "as responsible, as capable of choice, in short, as a self-acting agent."

This undiluted respect for the personhood of the patient is well exhibited in Laing's work with schizophrenic persons. In place of the usual medical model, Laing offered them a "hospital" in the original sense of that word: a place of refuge, of shelter and rest for a traveler. Their experience was respected there, however different it appeared. They were allowed to complete their journey through madness, accompanied by another person (Laing) who was always respectful that it was real.

Rollo May similarly asserted that "the central task and responsibility of the therapist is to seek to understand the patient as a being and as being-in-his-world." That understanding does not deny the validity of any psychodynamic insights; rather, it holds that any such dynamics "can be understood only in the context of the structure of existence of the person." Indeed, the very aim of existential therapy is to help the patient experience his or her existence as real. What makes it possible for the patient to change, said May, is ultimately this experience of being treated, in the moment, as the real person that the person is. That is why existential therapy emphasizes a sense of reality and concreteness above a set of techniques.

BEING-IN-THE-WORLD DILEMMAS

While each person's reality is unique, there are certain basic dilemmas that arise by virtue of one's being-in-the-world. Because existence is fundamentally a relationship with a world, the givens of existing provide what Irvin Yalom has called the "ultimate concerns of life." He has identified four: death, freedom, existential isolation, and meaninglessness. Yalom notes that the confrontation with any of these existential issues can become a serious conflict for a person. Specifically, to the extent that a person begins to become aware of these conflicts without yet facing them fully, that person will experience anxiety, and so will seek to defend against the experience by turning away from the underlying concern. The task of the existential therapist is to use that experience of anxiety as a clue to help the patient find a way back to the ultimate concern and then, by fully facing it, discover the positive transformation it offers for authentic living. The first two of these ultimate concerns, death and freedom, can serve as illustrative examples.

The first of these conflicts is that one's life will end in death even though one wishes it could continue. Death therefore holds a terror that may leave one anxious. One may even try to evade any awareness of death, living as though one would live forever. For the existential therapist, however, this awareness of death can be used to propel the patient to live his or her life authentically. Because life's preciousness is most evident when one is aware that one will lose it, becoming authentically aware of one's mortality can give one a powerful commitment not to waste one's life. In that sense, the anxiety of trying to evade death can be turned around and transformed into a clue to help patients discover what it is that they would be most anxious about dying without having experienced.

The second of these conflicts has to do with freedom. Though it seems to be a positive value, realizing one's freedom fully can be terrifying, for it entails accepting responsibility for one's life. One is responsible for actualizing one's own true self. Experiences such as anxiety, guilt, and despair reveal the dilemma of trying to hide from oneself the fact that one was not willing to be true to oneself. They then provide the basic clue by which the patient can uncover the self.

ROOTS OF EXISTENTIALISM

Existentialism arose in the mid-nineteenth century with Søren Kierkegaard. He opposed the Hegelian philosophy dominant during his time with the criticism that its formalism and abstractness omitted the individual. He insisted that the existing person was the most basic starting point for philosophy, that the authentic acceptance of being an individual is the basic task of one's life, and that "the purpose of life is to be the self which one truly is." Through analyses of such experiences as passion and commitment, Kierkegaard showed the important truths of subjective life.

At the beginning of the twentieth century, Edmund Husserl established phenomenology as a philosophical method by which to investigate actual experience. This provided a powerful boost to existentialism, especially evident in Heidegger's subsequent analysis of the "care structure" as the meaning of being human. The next developments in existentialism arose in France, during and immediately after World War II. In a country occupied by the Nazis for five years, people who worked in the French resistance movement became intimately acquainted with their own mortality. Death awaited around every corner; one never could know that this day was not the last. Such direct experience had a powerful impact on the French existential philosophers who participated in the resistance movement, of whom Jean-Paul Sartre, Albert Camus, Simone de Beauvoir, and Maurice Merleau-Ponty are the best known.

While Merleau-Ponty wrote books of particular relevance for a psychology of perception and behavior, it was Sartre who most fully depicted the foibles of human life that are relevant to the psychotherapist. In philosophical books such as *L'Être et le néant* (1943; *Being and Nothingness*, 1956), as well as in plays and novels, Sartre lucidly revealed the ways people dodge rather than face their own freedom and their own responsibility to choose. For him, this living as if one were not really free (inauthentic living) was "bad faith." Sartre contrasted his "existential analysis" of phenomena such as bad faith with the Freudian psychoanalysis of the unconscious. In doing so, he replaced Freud's conceptions of a theoretical construct (the unconscious) with descriptions of experiences of living inauthentically.

These developments in France led to a burst of expanded interest in existentialism throughout the 1950's, in both Europe and the United States. By the 1960's, many new books, journals, and even graduate programs began to emphasize existential philosophy and psychology. Graduate programs that focused on existential psychology appeared at Du-

quesne University, West Georgia College, and Sonoma State University.

Existentialism became one of the primary sources of inspiration for an alternative to the dominant psychoanalytic and behavioristic psychologies that began to gather momentum in the 1960's under the name "humanistic psychology." By offering the perspective that people's experiences of their own situations are vitally important to an understanding of their behavior, this view posed a central challenge to mainstream experimental psychology. This existential insight did not sway most psychologists, however; instead, the rise of cognitive psychology in the 1970's and 1980's established a new paradigm. It, too, offered the key notion that a person's involvement was crucial to understanding behavior, but cognitive psychology defined that involvement in terms of a computational model: The person "takes in" the world by "processing information." That model preserved the mechanistic assumption so important to mainstream psychology—the very assumption that existential psychology most decisively disputed. As a result, existential psychology remains a lively critic on psychology's periphery rather than being an equal partner with more traditional approaches.

SOURCES FOR FURTHER STUDY

Boss, Medard. *Psychoanalysis and Daseinsanalysis.* New York: Da Capo Press, 1982. This book is Boss's clearest and most comprehensive presentation of his own approach to existential analysis. It offers a philosophically sophisticated critique of Freudian psychoanalysis with regard to neuroses and therapy and presents an alternative rooted in the existential insights of one's being-in-the-world.

Frankl, Viktor Emil. *Man's Search for Meaning.* Rev. and updated ed. New York: Washington Square, 1998. Includes Frankl's gripping account of his experience as a prisoner in a Nazi concentration camp during World War II and the insights he gained from it. Also presents Frankl's basic formulation of "logotherapy"—his original form of existential therapy, centered on the question of what it is that gives one's life meaning.

_____. *Man's Search for Ultimate Meaning.* Cambridge, Mass.: Perseus, 2000. A set of nine essays comprising a sequel to and extension of the existential psychology proposed in *Man's Search for Meaning.*

The Humanistic Psychologist 16, no. 1 (1988). This special issue, "Psychotherapy for Freedom," edited by Erik Craig, focuses on the existential approach to psychotherapy developed by Medard Boss known as Daseinsanalysis. It features original articles by Boss and his colleagues at the Daseinsanalytic Institute in Switzerland, as well as pieces by Erik Craig and Martin Heidegger and an annotated bibliography of relevant readings on Daseinsanalysis.

Laing, Ronald David. *The Divided Self: An Existential Study in Sanity and Madness.* 1965. Reprint. New York: Routledge, 1999. This brilliant study of schizophrenia from an existential approach was a breakthrough for a totally new way of understanding the experience of the psychotic person. Though difficult for a general reader, the profound value of Laing's vision is worth the effort.

May, Rollo. *The Discovery of Being.* 1983. Reprint. New York: W. W. Norton, 1994. This collection of May's essays offers a clear and easily grasped introduction to existential psychology. Though the emphasis is mostly on its relation to psychotherapy, the volume also covers some of the basic principles and background of the existential approach.

May, Rollo, Ernest Angel, and Henri F. Ellenberger, eds. *Existence.* 1958. Reprint. Northvale, N.J.: Jason Aronson, 1995. This famous volume was the first to introduce European existential psychology to American audiences. It includes the first English translations of articles by Binswanger, Minkowski, Straus, and others, as well as a now-classic introductory chapter by May that describes the significance of an existential approach to psychology and psychotherapy.

Review of Existential Psychology and Psychiatry 20, nos. 1-3 (1986-1987). These special issues of this journal, edited by Keith Hoeller and collectively entitled "Readings in Existential Psychology and Psychiatry," feature a collection of classic articles from the 1960's to the 1980's. Included are articles by Van Kaam, Frankl, Boss, Laing, Rogers, May, and others on such topics as existential psychotherapy, anxiety, guilt, freedom, imagination, myth, schizophrenia, suicide, the unconscious, and will.

Valle, Ronald S., and Steen Halling, eds. *Existential-Phenomenological Perspectives in Psychology.* New York: Plenum, 1989. Designed as an introduction to the field, this book examines, from an existential and phenomenological perspective, many of psychology's standard topics, such as learning, perception, psychotherapy, development, and research, as well as areas that traditional psychology overlooks, such as aesthetics, passion, forgiveness, and transpersonal experiences.

Yalom, Irvin D. *Existential Psychotherapy.* New York: Basic Books, 1980. A very well written presentation of an existential understanding of psychological problems and therapy. Yalom grasps the basic conflicts of psychological life as flowing from "the individual's confrontation with the givens of existence," and he identifies these givens as death, freedom, existential isolation, and meaninglessness. For each theme, he presents the conflict and the way that existential therapy addresses it.

Christopher M. Aanstoos

SEE ALSO: Gestalt therapy; Humanism; Person-centered therapy; Personality theory; Self-actualization; Social psychological models: Erich Fromm.

Experimental psychology

DATE: 1879 forward
TYPE OF PSYCHOLOGY: Psychological methodologies
FIELDS OF STUDY: Experimental methodologies

Experimental psychology is a broad term that covers research in the various areas within psychology. Research is classified as either applied or basic, depending on whether it is being conducted to solve problems directly or to further academic knowledge. There are certain qualifications for research based on the scientific method, and research designs are classified as either descriptive or experimental depending on the amount of control present, which will affect the types of conclusions that can be drawn. Within experimental research, variables are classified as independent, dependent, or extraneous.

KEY CONCEPTS
- basic and applied research
- dependent variable
- descriptive research
- extraneous variable
- functionalism
- independent variable
- operationism
- structuralism

INTRODUCTION

Wilhelm Wundt founded the field of psychology, which he termed "experimental psychology," upon establishing his lab at the University of Leipzig in Germany in 1879. Wundt was the first to identify psychology as a separate science, on par with the natural sciences such as biology, physics, and chemistry. Wundt himself was trained as a physiologist and philosopher, and the methods he used in both of those disciplines combined to give structure to the new field. The role of experimental psychology at its founding was to answer philosophical questions using scientific methods. Wundt defined consciousness as the appropriate subject matter for experimentation and devised methods such as introspection (reporting on inner experiences by the subjective observer) to study the activity and structures of the mind (the basis for the school of thought later termed structuralism). Wundt was responsible for removing psychology from the metaphysical realm, providing conclusive evidence that the mind could be studied scientifically. This profoundly affected the development of psychology in the years following, establishing an emphasis on the importance of scientific research methods.

Over the first century of its existence and beyond, psychology came to be defined as the scientific study of consciousness, emotions, and behavior, and experimental psychology is no longer the only type. There now are many other subfields in psychology, such as clinical psychology, social psychology, and developmental psychology, but experimental methods still underlie most of them because that is how knowledge is accumulated in each area. Experimental psychology itself has expanded to include both basic and applied research.

BASIC AND APPLIED RESEARCH

Basic research, the kind that Wundt himself conducted, is undertaken for the purpose of advancing scientific knowledge, even if the knowledge gained is not directly relevant to improving the lives of individuals. This type of research is more likely to take place in laboratory settings, often on university campuses, using undergraduate students or specially bred lab animals as experimental subjects. These settings do not approximate the natural environment, permitting factors that could interfere with interpretation of the results to be controlled or eliminated, making conclusions more accurate. Ex-

amples of basic research include studying animal behavior, examining the perceptual abilities of humans, or determining the factors contributing to aggressive behavior.

Basic research was the only type of research conducted in experimental psychology until the first decade of the twentieth century, when applied psychology was introduced through the American school of thought termed functionalism. It was at this time that psychologists began being interested not only in how the mind works but also in how the mind works to help individuals interact with their environment. Most of the newer research involved conducting research with humans in their natural environment. For example, school psychologists were trying to find effective tests so that students could be taught at the appropriate levels (the first intelligence tests) and to identify how behavioral problems in the school or home could be controlled. Researchers also were trying to determine the factors that would increase efficiency and satisfaction in the workplace. In addition to these scenarios, researchers now attempt to solve such problems as finding effective ways to teach children with developmental disabilities, identifying new therapy techniques for those with psychological disorders, and developing strategies to increase healthy behaviors such as exercise and decrease unhealthy behaviors such as drug abuse. Applied research results tend to be more generalizable to others, but the relative lack of control sometimes limits the conclusions that can be drawn based on the results, so caution must be taken when recommending procedures from experiments.

THE SCIENTIFIC METHOD

The methods used for conducting either basic or applied research in experimental psychology are essentially the same as for conducting research in any other science. The first step in the process is identifying a research problem, a question that can be answered by appealing to evidence. Next will be a search for a theory, a general statement that integrates many observations from various research studies and is testable. From the theory is formed a hypothesis, a more precise version of the theory that is a specific prediction about the relationship between the variables in the research being conducted. At this point the research is designed, which involves decisions about how many and what type of participants will be used, where the research will be conducted, the measurement procedures to be developed, and so on. After the relevant data are collected, they must be analyzed visually or statistically. This allows the drawing of conclusions about the findings, which are communicated to others in the form of presentation or publication. The research process is circular, in that the more questions that are answered the more new questions arise, and that is how science advances.

There are key characteristics that must be present for good scientific research. Objectivity means that research must be free from bias. Data are to be collected, analyzed, interpreted, and reported objectively so that others are free to draw their own conclusions, even if they are different from those of the researchers. Control of factors that may affect the results of the research is necessary if those factors are not the specific ones being studied. For example, control for the effects of gender can be accomplished by ensuring that research samples include approximately the same number of males and females, unless the researcher is interested in looking for potential gender differences in behavior. In that case, the researcher would still want to control for factors such as age, education, or other characteristics that might be relevant. Control allows researchers to be more confident about the accuracy of their conclusions.

Operationism involves defining the variables to be studied in terms of the way they are measured. Many different operational definitions are possible for a particular concept such as aggression or love, and the results of research studies that use different operational definitions when combined provide more complete knowledge than if only one operational definition were used. Finally, replication is a key part of the research process because the aim of science is to accept only knowledge that has been verified by others. This requirement that results be replicable helps prevent bias and furthers objectivity.

DESCRIPTIVE VERSUS EXPERIMENTAL RESEARCH

Descriptive research is conducted to describe and predict behavior. Often these results are useful on their own, or such studies provide information to be used in future, more controlled, experiments. It can include archival research, an analysis of existing records of behavior, case studies, in-depth analysis of one or a few individuals, naturalistic observation, monitoring the behavior of subjects in their natural environment, or survey research in which individuals report on their own behavior. Descriptive research also includes correlational research, which examines relationships between variables that cannot be manipulated (such as gender, family background, or other personal characteristics that are not changeable). Correlational studies make it possible to predict changes in one variable based on observing changes in another, but as in all descriptive research, it is impossible to know whether or not changes in one variable caused the observed changes in another, so the conclusions to be drawn are limited.

The only type of research that can explain the causes of behavior is true experimental research, because that is the only type of research in which variables can be manipulated to see the observed effects on behavior. The variable that is manipulated is called the independent variable, and the variable that is measured to see the effects of the manipulation is called the dependent variable. Independent variables can be manipulated by measuring the effects of their presence versus absence (for instance, how reaction times differ when alcohol is consumed), their degree (how reaction times change as more alcohol is consumed), or their type (reaction times when alcohol is consumed as compared to when caffeine is consumed). Dependent variables are measured in terms of their latency (how long it takes for a response to occur) or duration (how long a response lasts), force (how strong the response is), rate or frequency (how often a response occurs within a period of time), or accuracy (the correctness of the response). There can be one or more each of the independent and dependent variables in any experiment, although having more variables increases the complexity of the analysis of the results. Every other variable that is present that could have an effect on the dependent variable in addition to the independent variable is considered an extraneous variable. These must be controlled (kept constant) or eliminated so that the researcher can be sure that changes in the dependent variable are due only to changes in the independent variable.

SOURCES FOR FURTHER STUDY

Christensen, Larry B. *Experimental Methodology.* 8th ed. Boston: Allyn & Bacon, 2001. A detailed summary of experimental methods, appropriate for undergraduate behavioral sciences students.

Kantowitz, Barry H., Henry L. Roediger III, and David G. Elmes. *Experimental Psychology: Understanding Psychological Research.* 6th ed. Minneapolis-St. Paul, Minn.: West, 1997. This text is a good overview of the types of research conducted in the various subfields of psychology as well as a summary of basic experimental methods.

Lundin, Robert W. *Theories and Systems of Psychology.* 5th ed. Lexington, Mass.: D. C. Heath, 1996. An overview of theories and methods in the field of psychology from the ancient Greeks to modern times. Very in-depth, written for the undergraduate student in psychology.

Myers, David G. *Exploring Psychology.* 5th ed. New York: Worth, 2002. A good, readable text that covers all of the subfields of psychology broadly and leaves the reader with a competent general understanding of the field.

Smith, Randolph A., and Stephen F. Davis. *The Psychologist as Detective: An Introduction to Conducting Research in Psychology.* 2d ed. Upper Saddle River, N.J.: Prentice Hall, 2001. This is an overview of basic methods in psychology research, appropriate for those with a general knowledge of psychology and research statistics.

April Michele Williams

SEE ALSO: Animal experimentation; Archival data; Behaviorism; Case-study methodologies; Complex experimental designs; Data description; Experimental psychology; Experimentation: Ethics and participant rights; Experimentation: Independent, dependent, and control variables; Field experimentation; Hypothesis development and testing; Observational methods; Quasi-experimental designs; Sampling; Scientific methods; Statistical significance tests; Survey research: Questionnaires and interviews; Within-subject experimental designs.

Experimentation

Ethics and participant rights

DATE: The 1960's forward
TYPE OF PSYCHOLOGY: Psychological methodologies
FIELDS OF STUDY: Evaluating psychology; experimental methodologies; methodological issues

One of the tasks of government is to protect people from exploitation and abuse, including potential abuse by unethical researchers. American society has instituted several levels of control over research, thus ensuring that experimental ethics reflect the ethics of society at large. Still, few ethical decisions are easy, and many remain controversial.

KEY CONCEPTS
- anonymity
- clinical trials
- informed consent
- macroallocation issues
- participant debriefing
- placebo condition
- professional ethics
- right to privacy

INTRODUCTION

A primary task of government is to protect people from exploitation. Since scientists are sometimes in a position to take advantage of others and, unfortunately, have occasionally done so, there is a role for government to regulate research in order to prevent exploitation of research participants. On the other hand, excessive regulation can stifle innovation; if scientists are not allowed to try new (and perhaps risky) experimental techniques, science will not progress, and neither will human understanding. This puts government in a bind: Since research topics, scientific methodology, and public attitudes are continuously changing, it would be impossible to write a single law or set of laws defining which research topics and methods are acceptable and which are not. As soon as such a law were written, it would be out of date or incomplete.

INSTITUTIONAL REVIEW BOARDS

The United States Congress has decided to deal with this dilemma by letting local communities determine what research with human participants is and is not appropriate according to contemporary local standards. Today, each institution conducting research must have a committee called an institutional review board (IRB) consisting of a minimum of five members, all of whom belong to the local community. In order to ensure that the committee is kept up to date on current human research methodologies, the IRB membership must include at least one person who does, or has done, research using human participants. The committee must also include at least one person who does research without using human participants (for example, who specializes in animal research, theoretical modeling, or statistical analysis), who would be capable of suggesting alternative research methodologies if deemed necessary. A third member must be trained in ethics, such as a member of the local clergy, and at least one member must represent the general public and have no official or unofficial relationship with the institution where the research is taking place. (These latter two roles can be fulfilled by the same person.)

Each IRB is required to review written proposals for all local research on human participants before that research can begin. At most large institutions, the IRB has enough staffing to break into subcommittees to review proposals from different areas. It is the job of the IRB to ensure that unethical research is screened out before it starts. Government agencies which fund research projects will not consider a proposal until it has been approved by the local IRB, and, if research is conducted at an institution without IRB approval, the government can withhold all funds to that institution, even funds unrelated to the research.

INFORMED CONSENT

In order to evaluate all aspects of a proposed research project, the IRB must have sufficient information about the recruitment of participants, the methods of the study, the procedures that will be followed, and the qualifications of the researchers. The IRB also requires that proposals include a copy of the informed consent contract that each potential participant will receive. This contract allows potential participants to see, in writing, a list of all possible physical or psychological risks that might occur as a result of participation in the project. People cannot be coerced or threatened into signing the form, and the form must also tell participants that, even if they agree to begin the research study, they may quit at any time for any reason. Informed consent contracts must be written in nontechnical prose that can be understood by any potential participant; it is generally recommended that contracts use vocabulary consistent with an eighth-grade education.

Except for the file holding the signed contracts between the researcher and the participants, names of participants generally do not appear anywhere in the database or in the final written documents describing the study results. Data are coded without using names, and in the informed consent contract, participants are assured of the complete anonymity of their responses or test results unless there are special circumstances which require otherwise. If researchers intend to use information in any way that may threaten participants' privacy, this issue needs to be presented clearly in the informed consent contract before the study begins.

Sex Research and Conflicts of Macroallocation

One controversy surrounding psychological research has to do with what economists call macroallocation decisions. Researchers must decide which topics are most worthy of study. Society, too, must decide what kinds of topics its taxpayers want to support. Traditionally, psychology and other behavioral sciences have not received as much financial support from the government as have "harder" sciences such as molecular biology and physics. In addition, there are more sociopolitical and moral questions raised about the value of psychological research than about the research of other sciences.

An example of the impact of ethics and morals on macroallocation decisions regarding psychological research is the debate over government support for surveys of sexual behavior. Researchers argue that information about peoples' sexual behavior and attitudes is needed in order to address problems such as teenage pregnancy, sexual harassment, and the spread of acquired immunodeficiency syndrome (AIDS). Many people believe, however, that asking questions about sexual behavior is an invasion of privacy; there is particular concern that adolescents would be asked to participate in such surveys without parental consent. Some people believe that government sponsorship of research on sexual behavior is a tacit stamp of approval of the behaviors addressed in the survey; they consider such studies to be propaganda which influences people's values and behavior as well as assessing it.

Ethical decisions about psychological research are made at all levels, from government to individual researchers and participants. There may be no obvious right or wrong answers, but, at each level, the decisions that are made tend to reflect the ethical judgment of society; that is perhaps the best that can be hoped.

DECEPTION

Occasionally in psychology researchers use a form of deception by telling the participants that the study is about one thing when it really is about something else. Although it usually is considered unethical to lie to participants, deception is sometimes necessary, because participants may behave differently when they know what aspect of their behavior is being watched. (This is called a demand characteristic of the experimental setting.) More people will probably act helpful, for example, when they know that a study is about helpfulness. A researcher studying helpfulness thus might tell participants that they are going to be involved in a study of, say, reading. Participants are then asked to wait in a room until they are each called into the test room. When the first name is called, a person may get up and trip on his or her way out of the room. In actuality, the person who was called was really the experimenter's assistant (although none of the participants knows that), and the real point of the research is to see how many of the participants get up to help the person who fell down. In situations such as this, where demand characteristics would be likely, IRBs will allow deception to be used as long as the deception is not severe and the researchers debrief participants at the end by explaining what was really occurring. After deception is used, experimenters must be careful to make sure that participants do not leave the study feeling angry at having been "tricked"; ideally, they should leave feeling satisfaction for having contributed to science.

Even when participants have not been deceived, researchers are required to give an oral or written debriefing at the end of the study. Researchers are also obliged to ensure that participants can get help if they do experience any negative effects from their participation in the research. Ultimately, if a participant feels that he or she was somehow harmed or abused by the researcher or the research project, a civil suit can be filed in an attempt to claim compensation. Since participants are explicitly told that they can drop out of a study at any time for any reason, however, such long-term negative feelings should be extremely rare.

SPECIAL ISSUES IN CLINICAL TRIALS

Clinical psychology is perhaps the most difficult area in which to make ethical research decisions. One potential problem in clinical research that is usually not relevant for other research settings is that of getting truly informed consent from the participants. The participants of clinical research are selected specifically because they meet the criteria for some mental disorder. By making sure that participants meet the relevant criteria, researchers ensure that their study results will be relevant to the population who suffers from the disorder; on the other hand, depending on the disorder being studied, it may be that the participants are not capable of giving informed consent. A person who suffers from disordered thinking (as with schizophrenics) or dementia (as with Alzheimer's disease patients) or is otherwise mentally handicapped cannot be truly "informed." In the cases of individuals who have been declared incompetent by the courts, a designated guardian can give informed consent for participation in a research study. There are also cases, however, of participants being legally competent yet not capable of truly understanding the consequences of what they read. Authority figures, including doctors and psychologists, can have a dramatic power over people; that power is likely to be even stronger for someone who is not in full control of his or her life, who has specifically sought help from others, and who is trusting that others have his or her best interests in mind.

Another concern about clinical research is the susceptibility of participants to potential psychological damage. The typical response of research participants is positive: They feel they are getting special attention and respond with healthy increases in self-esteem and well-being. A few, however, may end up feeling worse; for example, if they feel no immediate gain from the treatment, they may label themselves as "incurable" and give up, leading to a self-fulfilling prophecy.

A third concern in clinical research regards the use of control or placebo treatments. Good research designs always include both a treatment group and a control group. When there is no control group, changes in the treatment group may be attributed to the treatment when in fact they may have been caused by the passage of time or by the fact that participants were getting special attention while in the study. Although control groups are necessary to ensure that research results are interpreted correctly, the dilemma that arises in clinical research is that it may be unethical to assign people to a control group if they need some kind of intervention. One way of dealing with this dilemma is to give all participants some form of treatment and to compare the different treatment outcomes to one another rather than to a no-treatment group. This works well when there is already a known treatment with positive effects. Not only are there no participants who are denied treatment; the new treatment can be tested to see if it is better than the old one, not only if it is better than nothing. Sometimes, if there is no standard treatment for comparison, participants assigned to the control group are put on a "waiting list" for the treatment; their progress without treatment is then compared with that of participants who are getting treatment right away. To some extent, this mimics what happens in nonresearch settings, as people sometimes must wait for therapy, drug abuse counseling, and so on. On the other hand, in nonresearch settings, those who get assigned to waiting lists are likely to be those in less critical need, whereas in research, assignment to treatment and nontreatment groups must be random. Assigning the most critical cases to the treatment group would bias the study's outcome, yet assigning participants randomly may be perceived as putting research needs ahead of clients' needs.

THE MILGRAM STUDIES

Concern about potential abuse of research participants arose in the 1960's, in response to publicity following a series of studies by Stanley Milgram at Yale University. Milgram was interested in finding out how physicians who had devoted their lives to helping people were so easily able to hurt and even kill others (in the name of science) in experiments in Nazi concentration camps.

In Milgram's now-famous experiment, each participant was paired with one of Milgram's colleagues but was told that this partner was another volunteer. Then each participant, both real and pretend, drew a slip of paper assigning him or her to the role of either "teacher" or "learner." Actually, both slips always said "teacher," but the assistants pretended that theirs said "learner"; this way, the real participants were always assigned the role of teachers. Milgram then showed participants an apparatus which supposedly delivered shocks; teachers, on one side of a partition, were instructed to deliver a shock to the learner on the other side whenever a mistake was made on a word-pairing task. The apparatus actually did not deliver shocks, but the learners pretended that it did; as the experiment continued and the teachers were instructed to give larger and larger shocks, the learners gave more and more extreme responses. At a certain point, the learners started pounding on the partition, demanding to be released; eventually, they feigned a heart attack.

When Milgram designed this study, he asked psychiatrists and psychologists what percentage of people they thought would continue as teachers in this experiment; the typical response was about 0.1 percent. What Milgram found, however, was that two-thirds of the participants continued to deliver shocks to the learner even after the learner had apparently collapsed. The participants were clearly upset; they repeatedly expressed concern that someone should check on the learner. Milgram would simply reply that although the shocks were painful, they would not cause permanent damage, and the teacher should continue. In spite of their concern and distress, most participants obeyed.

Milgram's results revealed much about the power of authority; participants obeyed the authority figure (Milgram) even against their own moral judgment. These results help explain the abominable behavior of Nazi physicians, as well as other acts of violence committed by normal people who were simply doing what they were told. Ironically, although Milgram's study was so valuable, he was accused of abusing his own participants by "forcing" them to continue the experiment even when they were clearly upset. Critics also claimed that Milgram's study might have permanently damaged his participants' self-esteem. Although interviews with the participants showed that this was not true—they generally reported learning much about themselves and about human nature—media discussions and reenactments of the study led the public to believe that many of Milgram's participants had been permanently harmed. Thus began the discussion of experimental ethics which ultimately led to the system of regulation in force today.

SOURCES FOR FURTHER STUDY

American Psychological Association. "Ethical Principles of Psychologists and Code of Conduct." http://www.apa.org/ethics/code.html. This online document details the ethical guidelines of the largest psychological association in the world. Most of the guidelines refer to clinical practice, but section 6 (of eight) covers ethical issues in teaching, training, research and publication. Plenty of links.

Boyce, Nell. "Knowing Their Own Minds." *New Scientist* (June 20, 1998): 20-21. This short article in an excellent popular science magazine addresses the question of use/abuse of psychiatric patients as participants in clinical research trials.

Penslar, Robin L. *Research Ethics: Cases and Materials.* Bloomington: Indiana University Press, 1995. This volume was designed to help teach research ethics. It is organized as a series of real and hypothetical cases chosen to stimulate discussion. "Thought questions" are offered at various places throughout, and there are no "right answers" provided for any of the scenarios. Of the four parts, one is devoted specifically to research ethics in psychology.

Rothman, K. J., and K. B. Michels. "The Continuing Unethical Use of Placebo Controls." *The New England Journal of Medicine* 331, no. 6 (August 11, 1994): 394-398. This article appeared in one of the world's leading medical journals, where it subsequently triggered a heated debate (some of which appeared in the January 5, 1995, issue of the same journal). Although not specifically directed at psychology or psychiatry, this exchange highlights the many issues related to ethics of using placebo conditions as control groups in clinical trials.

Sales, Bruce D., and Susan Folkman, eds. *Ethics in Research with Human Participants.* Washington, D.C.: American Psychological Association, 2000. This book is aimed at researchers themselves, and so gives an insider's look at practical aspects of ethical problems and some potential solutions.

Sieber, Joan E. *Planning Ethically Responsible Research: A Guide for Students and Internal Review Boards.* Newbury Park, Calif.: Sage Publications, 1992. This practical 160-page volume from the Applied Social Research Methods Series gives straightforward answers to the many frequently asked questions about the operation of institutional review boards, their mission, and their policies. Extensive discussion of privacy, confidentiality, deception, cost-benefit analysis, and special risk populations. Includes plenty of case histories and examples, all in the social sciences.

Slife, Brent, ed. *Taking Sides: Clashing Views on Controversial Psychological Issues.* 11th ed. Guilford, Conn.: Dushkin/McGraw-Hill, 2000. Volumes of the Taking Sides series each present a series of contemporary debates on controversial issues in various fields. The psychology volumes have always included a debate on the classic obedience study of Stanley Milgram; this edition has a contribution from Milgram himself. New editions of the Taking Sides volumes come out every two years; if this particular edition is unavailable, it is likely that another edition that will include a similar debate.

Linda Mealey

SEE ALSO: Animal experimentation; Experimentation: Independent, dependent, and control variables; Field experimentation; Observational methods; Research ethics; Survey research: Questionnaires and interviews.

Experimentation

Independent, dependent, and control variables

TYPE OF PSYCHOLOGY: Psychological methodologies
FIELDS OF STUDY: Experimental methodologies; methodological issues

The scientific method involves the testing of hypotheses through the objective collection of data. The experiment is an important method of data collection in which the researcher systematically controls multiple factors in order to determine the extent to which changes in one variable cause changes in another variable. Only the experimental method can reveal cause-effect relationships between the variables of interest.

KEY CONCEPTS
• control group
• control variables
• dependent variable
• ecological validity
• experiment
• field experiment
• hypothesis
• independent variable
• random assignment

INTRODUCTION

Psychology is typically defined as the science of behavior and cognition and is considered a research-oriented discipline, not unlike biology, chemistry, and physics. To appreciate the role of experimentation in psychology, it is useful to view it in the context of the general scientific method employed by psychologists in conducting their research. This scientific method may be described as a four-step sequence starting with identifying a problem and forming a hypothesis. The problem must be one suitable for scientific inquiry—that is, questions concerning values, such as whether rural life is "better" than city life, are more appropriate for philosophical debate than scientific investigation. Questions better suited to the scientific method are those that can be answered through the objective collection of facts—for example, "Are children who are neglected by their parents more likely to do poorly in school than children who are well treated?" The hypothesis is the tentative guess, or the prediction regarding the question's answer, and is based upon other relevant research and existing theory. The second step, and the one with which this article is primarily concerned, is the collection of data (facts) in order to test the accuracy of the hypothesis. Any one of a number of methods might be employed, including simple observation, survey, or experimentation. The third step is to make sense of the facts that have been accumulated by subjecting them to careful analysis; the fourth step is to share any significant findings with the scientific community.

RESEARCH APPROACHES

In considering step two, the collection of data, it seems that people often mistakenly use the words "research" and "experiment" interchangeably. A student might ask whether an experiment has been done on a particular topic when, in fact, the student really wants to know if *any* kind of research has been conducted in that area. All experiments are examples of research, but not all research is experimental. Research that is nonexperimental in nature might be either descriptive or correlational.

Descriptive research is nearly self-explanatory; it occurs when the researcher wants merely to characterize the behaviors of an individual or, more likely, a group. For example, one might want to survey the students of a high school to ascertain the level of alcohol use (alcohol use might be described in terms of average ounces consumed per student per week). One might also spend considerable time observing individuals suffering from, for example, infantile autism. A thorough description of their typical behaviors could be useful for someone investigating the cause of this disorder. Descriptive research can be extremely valuable, but it is not useful when researchers want to investigate the relationship between two or more variables (things that vary, or quantities that may have different values).

In a correlational study, the researcher measures how strongly the variables are related, or the degree to which one variable predicts another variable. A researcher who is interested in the relationship between exposure to violence on television (variable one) and aggressive behavior (variable two) in a group of elementary school children could administer a survey asking the children how much violent television they view and then rank the subjects from high to low levels of this variable. The researcher could similarly interview the school staff and rank the children according to their aggressive behavior. A statistic called a correlation coefficient might then be computed, revealing how the two variables are related and the strength of that relationship.

CAUSE AND EFFECT

Correlational studies are not uncommon in psychological research. Often, however, a researcher wants even more specific information about the relationships among variables—in particular, about whether one variable causes a change in another variable. In such a situation, experimental research is warranted. This drawback of the correlational approach—its inability to establish causal relationships—is worth considering for a moment. In the hypothetical study described above, the researcher may find that viewing considerable television violence predicts high levels of aggressive behavior, yet she cannot conclude that these viewing habits cause the aggressiveness. After all, it is entirely possible that aggressiveness, caused by some unknown factor, prompts a preference for violent television. That is, the causal direction is unknown; viewing television violence may cause aggressiveness, but the inverse (that aggressiveness causes the watching of violent television programs) is also feasible.

As this is a crucial point, one final illustration is warranted. What if, at a certain Rocky Mountain university, a correlational study has established that high levels of snowfall predict low examination scores? One should not conclude that something about the chemical composition of snow impairs the learning process. The correlation may be real and highly predictive, but the causal culprit may be some other factor. Perhaps, as snowfall increases, so does the incidence of illness, and it is this variable that is causally related to exam scores. Maybe, as snowfall increases, the likelihood of students using their study time for skiing also increases.

Experimentation is a powerful research method because it alone can reveal cause-effect relationships. In an experiment, the researcher does not merely measure the naturally occurring relationships between variables for the purpose of predicting one from the other; rather, he or she systematically manipulates the values of one variable and measures the effect, if any, that is produced in a second variable. The variable that is manipulated is known as the independent variable; the other variable, the behavior in question, is called the dependent variable (any change in it depends upon the manipulation of the independent variable). Experimental research is characterized by a desire for control on the part of the researcher. Control of the independent variable and control over extraneous variables are both wanted. That is, there is a desire to eliminate or hold constant the factors (control variables) other than the independent variable that might influence the dependent variable. If adequate control is achieved, the researcher may be confident that it was, in fact, the manipulation of the independent variable that produced the change in the dependent variable.

CONTROL GROUPS

Returning to the relationship between television viewing habits and aggressive behavior in children, suppose that correlational evidence indicates that high levels of the former variable predict high levels of the latter. Now the researcher wants to test the hypothesis that there is a cause-effect relationship between the two variables. She decides to manipulate exposure to television violence (the independent variable) to see what effect might be produced in the aggressiveness of her subjects (the dependent variable). She might choose two levels of the independent variable and have twenty children watch fifteen minutes of a violent detective show while another

twenty children are subjected to thirty minutes of the same show.

If an objective rating of playground aggressiveness later reveals more hostility in the thirty-minute group than in the fifteen-minute group, she still cannot be confident that higher levels of television violence cause higher levels of aggressive behavior. More information is needed, especially with regard to issues of control. To begin with, how does the researcher know that it is the violent content of the program that is promoting aggressiveness? Perhaps it is the case that the more time they spend watching television, regardless of subject matter, the more aggressive children become.

This study needs a control group: a group of subjects identical to the experimental subjects with the exception that they do not experience the independent variable. In fact, two control groups might be employed, one that watches fifteen minutes and another that watches thirty minutes of nonviolent programming. The control groups serve as a basis against which the behavior of the experimental groups can be compared. If it is found that the two control groups aggress to the same extent, and to a lesser extent than the experimental groups, the researcher can be more confident that violent programming promotes relatively higher levels of aggressiveness.

The experimenter also needs to be sure that the children in the thirty-minute experimental group were not naturally more aggressive to begin with. One need not be too concerned with this possibility if one randomly assigns subjects to the experimental and control groups. There are certainly individual differences among subjects in factors such as personality and intelligence, but with random assignment (a technique for creating groups of subjects across which individual differences will be evenly dispersed) one can be reasonably sure that those individual differences are evenly dispersed among the experimental and control groups.

SUBJECT VARIABLES

The experimenter might want to control or hold constant other variables. Perhaps she suspects that age, social class, ethnicity, and gender could also influence the children's aggressiveness. She might want to make sure that these subject variables are eliminated by either choosing subjects who are alike in these ways or by making sure that the groups are balanced for these factors (for example, equal numbers of boys and girls in each group). There are numerous other extraneous variables that might concern the researcher, including the time of day when the children participate, the length of time between television viewing and the assessment of aggressiveness, the children's diets, the children's family structures (single versus dual parent, siblings versus only child), and the disciplinary styles used in the homes. Resource limitations prevent every extraneous variable from being controlled, yet the more control, the more confident the experimenter can be of the cause-effect relationship between the independent and dependent variables.

INFLUENCE OF REWARDS

One more example of experimental research, this one nonhypothetical, will further illustrate the application of this methodology. In 1973, Mark Lepper, David Greene, and Richard Nisbett tested the hypothesis that when people are offered external rewards for performing activities that are naturally enjoyable, their interest in these activities declines. The participants in the study were nursery school children who had already demonstrated a fondness for coloring with marking pens; this was their preferred activity when given an opportunity for free play. The children were randomly assigned to one of three groups. The first group was told previously that they would receive a "good player award" if they would play with the pens when later given the opportunity. Group two received the same reward but without advance notice; they were surprised by the reward. The last group of children was the control group; they were neither rewarded nor told to expect a reward.

The researchers reasoned that the first group of children, having played with the pens in order to receive a reward, would now perceive their natural interest in this activity as lower than before the study. Indeed, when all groups were later allowed a free play opportunity, it was observed that the "expected reward" group spent significantly less time than the other groups in this previously enjoyable activity. Lepper and his colleagues, then, experimentally supported their hypothesis and reported evidence that reward causes interest in a previously pleasurable behavior to decline. This research has implications for instructors; they should carefully consider the kinds of behavior they reward (with gold stars, lavish

praise, high grades, and so on) as they may, ironically, be producing less of the desired behavior. An academic activity that is enjoyable play for a child may become tedious work when a reward system is attached to it.

CRITICISMS

While most would agree that the birth of psychology as a science took place in Leipzig, Germany, in 1879, when Wilhelm Wundt established the first laboratory for studying psychological phenomena, there is no clear record of the first use of experimentation. Regardless, there is no disputing the attraction that this method of research has had for many psychologists in the twentieth century. Psychologists clearly recognize the usefulness of the experiment in investigating potential causal relationships between variables. Hence, experimentation is employed widely across the subfields of psychology, including developmental, cognitive, physiological, clinical, industrial, and social psychology.

This is not to say that all psychologists are completely satisfied with experimental research. It has been argued that an insidious catch-22 exists in some experimental research that limits its usefulness. The argument goes like this: Experimenters are motivated to control rigorously the conditions of their studies and the relevant extraneous variables. To gain such control, they often conduct experiments in a laboratory setting. Therefore, subjects are often observed in an artificial environment, engaged in behaviors that are so controlled as to be unnatural, and they clearly know they are being observed— which may further alter their behavior. Such research is said to be lacking in ecological validity or applicability to "real-life" behavior. It may show how subjects behave in a unique laboratory procedure, but it tells little about psychological phenomena as displayed in everyday life. The catch-22, then, is that experimenters desire control in order to establish that the independent variable is producing a change in the dependent variable, and the more such control, the better; however, the more control, the more risk that the research may be ecologically invalid.

FIELD EXPERIMENTS

Most psychologists are sensitive to issues of ecological validity and take pains to make their laboratory procedures as naturalistic as possible. Additionally, much research is conducted outside the laboratory in what are known as field experiments. In such studies, the subjects are unobtrusively observed (perhaps by a confederate of the researcher who would not attract their notice) in natural settings such as classroom, playground, or workplace. Field experiments, then, represent a compromise in that there is bound to be less control than is obtainable in a laboratory, yet the behaviors observed are likely to be natural. Such naturalistic experimentation is likely to continue to increase in the future.

Although experimentation is only one of many methods available to psychologists, it fills a particular need, and that need is not likely to decline in the foreseeable future. In trying to understand the complex relationships among the many variables that affect the way people think and act, experimentation makes a valuable contribution: It is the one methodology available that can reveal unambiguous cause-effect relationships.

Sources for Further Study

Barber, Theodore Xenophon. *Pitfalls in Human Research.* New York: Pergamon Press, 1976. It is useful to learn from the mistakes of others, and Barber provides the opportunity by describing ten categories of likely errors in designing and conducting research. This is not a long book (117 pages), and it is enjoyable reading, especially the specific accounts of flawed research.

Carlson, Neil R. *Psychology: The Science of Behavior.* 5th ed. Upper Saddle River, N.J.: Prentice Hall, 1999. The second chapter of this introductory psychology text may be the most reader-friendly reference in this bibliography. Entitled "The Ways and Means of Psychology," it provides a brief introductory overview of the scientific method, experimental and correlational research, and basic statistics; it is well suited for the novice. Colorful graphics, a concluding summary, and a list of key terms are all helpful.

Hearst, Eliot, ed. *The First Century of Experimental Psychology.* Hillsdale, N.J.: Lawrence Erlbaum, 1979. Primarily for the student interested in the history of experimental psychology. This is a 693-page book; while most of the fourteen chapters are devoted to specific topics in psychology such as emotion, development, and psychopathology, the final chapter by William Estes provides an excellent overview of experimental psychology and considers some broad, profound issues.

Shaughnessy, John J., and Eugene B. Zechmeister. *Research Methods in Psychology.* 6th ed. New York: McGraw-Hill, 2002. This is one of a number of textbooks that discusses psychological research in the light of the scientific method. It is fairly accessible, has a thorough and competent description of experimentation, and, as a bonus, considers some ethical issues. Glossary, index, and references are all provided.

Stern, Paul C., and Linda Kalof. *Evaluating Social Science Research.* 2d ed. New York: Oxford University Press, 1996. This is a clearly written, nonthreatening book for the early to middle-level college student. The focus of the author is on encouraging the critical analysis of research; to this end, case-research examples are presented for examination. End-of-chapter exercises are included to aid the student in integrating information.

Mark B. Alcorn

See also: Animal experimentation; Complex experimental designs; Data description; Hypothesis development and testing; Quasi-experimental designs; Sampling; Scientific methods; Statistical significance tests; Within-subject experimental designs.

Eyewitness testimony

Type of psychology: Memory
Fields of study: Social perception and cognition

In the study of memory and eyewitness testimony, knowledge of the factors that affect memory is applied to evaluate the ability of a witness to an event to recall details of the event and to recognize participants in the event. This knowledge is often applied to witnesses of a crime in regard to identifying the perpetrator.

Key concepts
- encoding
- perception
- recall
- recognition
- retrieval
- storage

INTRODUCTION

Knowledge of how the memory process operates has been applied to the analysis of eyewitness testimony in order to assess the likelihood that a witness is correct in making an identification. The task of eyewitness identification depends upon the three stages of the memory process: encoding, storage, and retrieval. The last stage, retrieval, can be divided into two parts: recall and recognition. Each of these stages is subject to the influence of several factors that may contribute to error in the process.

Encoding is the stage of acquiring information. In the case of eyewitness identification, it is the sighting of a person during an event. The circumstances of the event will affect the ability of a person to encode information, including the facial appearance of another person. A short period of viewing time, poor lighting, greater distance, and an obtuse angle of view will reduce the observer's ability to acquire information about appearance. Any distractions present will reduce the attention paid to the face of the person and reduce the facial information encoded. If there are other people present, they serve as distractions. If a weapon is present, it attracts the attention of the observer and reduces the attention to faces. This phenomenon is called the "weapons effect." If the weapon is used in a threatening manner, it will be likely to attract even more attention and further reduce the encoding of facial detail. Highly salient features of the face may dominate the encoding of the face. For example, a prominent scar may attract attention and reduce the attention to other facial details. When this happens, the witness may easily mistake another person with a similar scar for the original person, even though other features are different. Only information that is encoded can be retained and retrieved later, so the encoding stage sets the limits for later identification.

Once information is encoded, it must be stored until it is retrieved for use. One is not constantly aware of the information one has; such information is held in storage until one retrieves it. The brain holds information by some electrochemical process. It is not known exactly how it works, but it is clear that the storage stage of memory is not passive and inert like a videotape. Memories can change while they are stored. The memory may change in two ways: It may fade, or it may be distorted. Information fades away over time. This effect of time on memory is one of the oldest findings in the field of psychology, documented by Hermann Ebbinghaus in 1885. His findings indicate that memory fades rapidly at first and continues to fade over time at a reducing rate. This fading could be evidenced by loss of details or a less accurate recall of details. Sometimes witnesses may still believe that they recall a face, but the memory has really changed so that their identification is inaccurate.

The other major factor affecting memory during the storage period is interference. Events that occur during the storage period may change the memory without the awareness of the witness. A witness may be exposed to information after an event and, without knowing it, incorporate that information into the memory of the event. One example of this type of effect is called "unconscious transference." This occurs when a person seen in one setting is remembered as having been in another. Sometimes a witness will mistakenly identify someone seen in another setting as the one who committed a crime. The witness has, without knowing it, transferred the memory of the face of the innocent person into the crime memory.

The third stage of memory is retrieval. Witnesses may be asked to retrieve information by either recall or recognition. Giving a description of a person is an example of free recall. There are no external stimuli from which to select; witnesses simply retrieve whatever information they can. In the case of recognition, the witness is asked to identify someone from a photograph, in person, or from a group of photographs (a photo lineup) or a group of people (a live lineup). Sometimes lineups are videotaped. Recall may be distorted by suggestive questions or nonverbal cues. Elizabeth Loftus reported in her 1979 book *Eyewitness Testimony* that when people were asked, "How tall was the basketball player?" their descriptions averaged seventy-nine inches. When they were asked, "How short was the basketball player?" they estimated sixty-nine inches. This ten-inch difference was caused simply by the change in the wording of the question.

The accuracy of a witness's recognition in lineup situations can be greatly affected by the nature of the lineup. If a witness is asked to identify a person from a single photograph or a one-person lineup, there is a possibility of error attributable to the witness's expectation that this must be the person or the police would not produce the person. In multiple-choice lineups, the similarity of the alternative choices to the suspect is the major determinant of error. If only one or two people in the lineup are similar to the original description of a suspect, a witness really has few choices, and the result is similar to the single-choice lineup. Witnesses may sometimes select a person in a lineup who is similar to the one seen or who looks familiar for some other reason.

EYEWITNESSES AND THE JUSTICE SYSTEM

In some cases, the only evidence against a person accused of a crime is an identification by an eyewitness. In their 1973 book *Wrongful Imprisonment: Mistaken Convictions and Their Consequences*, Ruth Brandon and Christie Davies describe seventy cases in which an incorrect identification by an eyewitness led to a conviction. In 1973, after conducting his own study of the subject, New York surrogate court judge Nathan Sobel concluded that incorrect eyewitness identification led to more miscarriages of justice than all other factors combined. Because of the serious consequences of an incorrect identification and the possibility that misidentifications frequently occur, psychologists have applied their expertise in memory to the study of the factors that would affect the accuracy of eyewitness identification.

Elizabeth Loftus has reported a case of eyewitness testimony that illustrates one of the most important applications of the field, a criminal trial. The background to the trial began on October 12, 1977, at approximately 8:30 in the evening. Two men entered a liquor store in Watsonville, California. The first man stood directly across from a young male clerk and pointed a gun at him, demanding all the money. The second man stood four or five feet away, pointing a gun at an older clerk, who stood behind the first clerk. The first robber demanded the money from the cash register and the clerks' wallets. As the young clerk turned to replace his wallet, he heard a shot and dove to the floor. When he looked up, the first robber was almost out the door, and the second robber stood in the doorway smiling; the older clerk lay dead on the floor. As soon as the robbers left, the young clerk hit the alarm. A security guard responded immediately, and the clerk, in a state of shock, could only say, "Two men, one with a mustache, two men, one with a mustache."

The clerk was interviewed by police the next day, and he described one robber as a male Mexican,

thirty-two to thirty-seven years old, about five feet, ten inches tall, 175-180 pounds, with black, collar-length, unkempt hair. A composite drawing was made. During the next week, the clerk viewed two live lineups and a large set of black-and-white photographs. Two of the photographs were of a man named José Garcia. The clerk said that one of them looked similar to the robber. About a week later, the clerk viewed the set of photographs again, and again said one of them was similar to the robber. Another week went by, and the clerk was shown a different set of color photographs. He picked out Garcia as "the guy; I wouldn't forget the face." Three days later, the clerk picked a man from a live lineup whose voice sounded like the robber. This man was an innocent policeman, so the clerk went back to the color photographs and said that Garcia was definitely the murderer.

José Garcia was arrested and charged with murder and robbery. He was thirty-nine years old; he was five feet, ten inches tall, and he weighed 242 pounds. He spoke with a heavy Spanish accent and had tattoos lining both arms; his left hand was deformed from a sawblade accident.

Loftus was hired by the defense to testify about the factors that might cause the eyewitness to be inaccurate. After being sworn in, her qualifications as an expert in eyewitness memory were presented to the court. The prosecution argued that the data from experiments only allowed general conclusions and not conclusions about the eyewitness in this case, and that experiments were not performed on real-life crimes. The judge ruled that the testimony would be heard by the jury. Through a long series of questions, the defense attorney attempted to bring before the jury the factors from the psychological research that are known to affect the ability of an eyewitness to make a correct identification. Some of the factors Loftus mentioned were the storage interval (there were several weeks between the crime and an identification); the high stress level of the witness during encoding; the possibility that the weapon used in the crime may have created a "weapons focus"; and the possibility that the viewing of pictures of the suspect several times before making an identification could have allowed for unconscious transference to occur.

The jury, after hearing Loftus's expert testimony, was unable to reach a verdict. The defendant was tried again a few weeks later; the process was repeated, and again the jury could not reach a verdict, so the defendant was set free. Interviews with the jury indicated that they valued the expert testimony of Loftus in their deliberations; nine were for acquittal and three were for conviction.

THE SCIENCE OF TESTIMONY

In 1900, French psychologist Alfred Binet (later famous for the development of intelligence testing) argued for the creation of a practical science of testimony. German psychologist Louis William Stern was publishing studies of eyewitness testimony as early as 1902. In 1903, Stern testified in German courts of law as an expert on eyewitness testimony. Beginning in 1909, American psychologist Guy Montrose Whipple began a four-year series of articles in *Psychological Bulletin* in which he translated and interpreted European work on the subject as well as presenting his own.

Although it appeared that the field was ready to develop rapidly, it did not. Probably because most psychologists of the time focused more on theoretical issues than on applied problems and because the early psychologists working on eyewitness testimony were criticized for overgeneralization, the explosion of research on eyewitness testimony did not occur until the 1970's. Ulric Neisser, in his book *Cognition and Reality: Principles and Implications of Cognitive Psychology* (1976) and later in *Memory Observed: Remembering in Natural Contexts* (1982), presented the view that the advances in understanding human memory and social perception called for a new emphasis on observations made in a natural context. Probably 90 percent of the research on memory applied to eyewitness testimony has been carried out since then.

Modern research has developed a large database on variables that affect the accuracy of an eyewitness, as well as on such issues as the best way to interrogate a witness, how to construct fair lineups, and how to help witnesses remember more accurately. A major topic of the 1980's and 1990's was the usefulness and appropriateness of the testimony of psychological experts in court proceedings. Some judges do not allow psychologists to testify about eyewitness reliability; however, other judges do allow such testimony. Psychologists themselves disagree on whether this testimony serves a good purpose. It is clear that, if testimony is given, the psychologist cannot say whether a given witness is correct or not.

The psychologist may provide the jury with information that can help them to evaluate the eyewitness testimony better. There may be scientific data about the circumstances of the case being tried that jurors do not know. Telling the jurors about the data can give them a better basis for evaluating the credibility of a witness. This can lead to improvement of the judicial process by more often convicting the guilty, as well as saving the innocent.

SOURCES FOR FURTHER STUDY

Ainsworth, Peter B. *Psychology, Law, and Eyewitness Testimony.* New York: John Wiley & Sons, 1999. Covers the psychology of memory, techniques of improving eyewitness memory such as hypnosis, the use of children as eyewitnesses, and the role of the psychologist as an expert witness.

Loftus, Elizabeth F. *Eyewitness Testimony.* 1979. Reprint. Cambridge, Mass.: Harvard University Press, 1996. One of the foremost experts on eyewitness testimony presents a comprehensive overview of the empirical work on such testimony. Also examines the role that eyewitness testimony has played in the American legal system.

McCloskey, Michael, Howard Egeth, and Judith McKenna. "The Experimental Psychologist in Court: The Ethics of Expert Testimony." *Law and Human Behavior* 10, nos. 1-2 (1986): 1-13. This special journal issue contains thirteen articles on issues relating to a psychologist giving expert testimony in court—not highly technical, but written for the reader with a background in the subject.

Wells, Gary L., and Elizabeth F. Loftus, eds. *Eyewitness Testimony: Psychological Perspectives.* New York: Cambridge University Press, 1984. Fifteen chapters by various authors on topics related to eyewitness testimony. Good source for in-depth coverage on subtopics such as lineups and witness confidence.

Wrightsman, Lawrence S. "Crime Investigation: Eyewitnesses." In *Psychology and the Legal System.* 5th ed. Belmont, Calif.: Wadsworth, 2001. Chapter focuses on the application of memory and eyewitness research on the criminal investigation. Uses interesting examples and mentions basics in brief form.

Yarmey, A. Daniel. *The Psychology of Eyewitness Testimony.* New York: Free Press, 1979. An introductory-level book that describes the knowledge of psychological and legal aspects of eyewitness identification and testimony. It is interesting and easily understood.

Gary T. Long

SEE ALSO: Encoding; Forgetting and forgetfulness; Law and psychology; Long-term memory; Memory; Memory: Empirical studies; Memory storage; Short-term memory; Social schemata; Social perception.

Eysenck, Hans

BORN: March 4, 1916, in Berlin, Germany
DIED: September 4, 1997, in London, England
IDENTITY: German-born British research psychologist
TYPE OF PSYCHOLOGY: Personality; psychological methodologies; social psychology
FIELDS OF STUDY: Behavioral therapies; intelligence assessment; personality assessment; personality theory; social motives

Eysenck was best known for his theory of human personality.

Hans Jürgen Eysenck was born in Berlin during World War I. His parents divorced when he was only two. As a result, his mother's mother reared him. When the Nazis came to power, Eysenck, a Jewish sympathizer, left Germany at the age of eighteen, seeking exile in France and then England.

Studying at the University of London, Eysenck earned a bachelor's degree in psychology in 1938. With Sir Cyril Burt as his graduate adviser, Eysenck earned a doctorate in psychology in 1940. During World War II, he served as a psychologist at the Mill Hill Emergency Hospital, doing research on the reliability of psychiatric diagnoses. His findings made him antagonistic toward mainstream clinical psychology for the rest of his life.

After the war, Eysenck taught at the University of London and founded the psychological department at the newly formed Institute of Psychiatry. He was promoted to a professor of psychology in 1955. His research ranged from personality and intelligence to behavioral genetics and from social attitudes to behavior therapy.

In 1964, he published *Crime and Punishment,* in which he suggested that criminals had failed to develop conditioned moral and social responses. He published *Smoking, Health, and Personality* in 1965 and suggested that lung cancer was due to an underlying emotional disorder rather than to smoking. His very controversial book *Race, Intelligence, and Education* was released in 1971. Based on data he had accumulated, it stated that intelligence quotient (IQ) scores were persistently lower among African Americans in comparison to white Americans. During a lecture in London, Eysenck was kicked and punched by students because of the content of this book. In 1981, he and Leon Kamin wrote *The Intelligence Controversy.*

Eysenck tried to reduce the list of human personality traits to the smallest number of trait clusters. Common to the majority of trait systems are variables related to emotional stability, energy level, dominance, and sociability. Eysenck reduced the trait names to three higher-order factors: introversion-extroversion, neuroticism, and psychoticism.

Hans Eysenck. (Hulton Archive)

He attempted to explore the biological roots of each factor. He also founded and edited the journal *Personality and Individual Differences.*

Eysenck was a prolific writer, publishing 75 books and 1,050 articles. He was awarded the American Psychological Association's Distinguished Scientific Award in 1988, a United States Presidential Citation for Scientific Contribution in 1993, and the American Psychological Association's William James Fellow Award in 1994 and its Centennial Award for Distinguished Contributions to Clinical Psychology in 1996.

SOURCES FOR FURTHER STUDY

Dana, Richard Henry, ed. *Handbook of Cross-Cultural and Multicultural Personality Assessment.* Hillsdale, N.J.: Lawrence Erlbaum, 2000. Addresses Eysenck's personality theory and assessment as applied to different ethnic groups and cultures.

Inman, Sally, Martin Buck, and Helena Burke, eds. *Assessing Personal and Social Development: Measuring the Unmeasurable.* London: Falmer, 1999. Ideas of Eysenck on personality theory and assessment as applied to children.

Shrout, Patrick E., and Susan T. Fiske, eds. *Personality Research, Methods, and Theory.* Hillsdale, N.J.: Lawrence Erlbaum, 1995. Discusses personality theory, traits, and assessment proposed by Eysenck.

Alvin K. Benson

SEE ALSO: Intelligence quotient (IQ); Introverts and Extroverts; Personality theory; Race and intelligence.

F

Facial feedback

TYPE OF PSYCHOLOGY: Emotion
FIELDS OF STUDY: Social perception and cognition

The facial feedback theory of emotion concerns the relationship between emotional experience and facial expression. The theory argues that emotional experience (feelings) can be managed by producing different or opposite facial expressions. It also suggests that people do not experience emotions directly; instead, they infer or "read" their emotions from the expressions that appear on their faces.

KEY CONCEPTS
- emotional experience
- expressive behavior
- self-perception processes
- self-regulatory mechanisms

INTRODUCTION
The purpose of facial expressions has been a topic of interest to writers, poets, philosophers, and social scientists for centuries. Some scientists have suggested that facial expressions are simply the external manifestations of internal emotional states (sometimes referred to as "affective" states). Others claim that facial expressions are designed to communicate information about how people are feeling to other people. Still others have argued that facial expressions are the "data" on which people base decisions about the emotions they themselves may be experiencing. This latter idea is the foundation of the facial feedback theories of emotion.

FACIAL FEEDBACK THEORIES
In the early 1970's, psychologists first confirmed Charles Darwin's speculations, advanced in the 1870's, that a set of basic human facial expressions is innate and constant across cultures. Since then, researchers have sought to understand the function and significance of facial expressions in the production and experience of emotion. This search has led to the formulation of theories about the role of facial expressions in emotional experience, of which the facial feedback theories are one subset. Although there are several variants of the central theme, all facial feedback theories share three defining characteristics. First, all hold that the experience of naturally occurring emotions (such as anger or fear) can be managed by producing different or opposite facial expressions. In other words, if a person feels sad and "puts on a happy face," the experience of sadness will be reduced. Second, all these theories argue that, in the absence of a naturally occurring emotion, self-generated facial expressions can produce their corresponding internal emotional states. In other words, even though a person may not feel sad, smiling will make that person feel happy. Finally, all the theories share a belief that internal emotional states are not experienced directly but are instead mediated by some sort of mechanism involving feedback from the skin or the muscles of the face (hence the term "feedback" in the name). Put simply, this means that the specific configuration of people's facial muscles tells them that they are experiencing a particular emotion. If people's faces display smiles, the particular arrangement of the muscles involved in smiling "tells" them that they are happy.

An example that was first offered by nineteenth century psychologist William James may help clarify how facial (and other bodily) feedback is thought to lead to emotional experience. A woman encounters a growling bear in the woods. Upon noticing the bear, her heartbeat increases, her body secretes adrenaline (epinephrine), her face tenses in fear, and she runs away. Does she first notice she is afraid and then respond by fleeing from the bear, or does she flee first and then decide that she must have been afraid because she made a terrified facial expression? The latter idea explains the woman's behavior in terms of a feedback theory of emotional experience.

THEORETICAL VARIATIONS

Because they seem to suggest a process that is at odds with most people's intuitions, facial feedback theories have had a long and controversial history in social psychology. Their origins can be traced at least as far back as Charles Darwin and William James, and some social scientists have noted that the ideas embodied in facial feedback theories can be found in the writings of Homer and William Shakespeare. In *The Expression of the Emotions in Man and Animals* (1872), Darwin claimed that freely expressing an emotion would intensify its experience, whereas repressing or dampening the expression of an emotion would tend to reduce its effects. James echoed a similar idea in the second volume of *The Principles of Psychology* (1890). James's ideas, coupled with similar ideas offered independently by Danish physician Carl Lange, led to one of the earliest feedback theories, the James-Lange theory. More recently, psychologist Silvan Tomkins and social psychologists Carroll Izard, James Laird, John Lanzetta, and their colleagues have each proposed similar theories implicating facial expressions in the experience of emotions. Although they all differ in regard to the exact mechanism through which facial expressions produce or manage emotional experiences, all are collectively referred to as facial feedback theories. For example, the idea that facial expressions are emotions (or that being aware of one's facial expression is essentially the same as being aware of an emotion) is attributable to Tomkins. He argued that sensory receptors in the skin of the face provide information on the status of facial expressions that trigger emotional experiences from memory. The somewhat different idea that facial expressions are used (through self-perception processes) to infer an emotional state is based on the work of Laird. Laird argued that when people are unsure of what emotion they may be experiencing, they use attributional and self-perception processes to work backward, deciding that "if I am smiling, I must be happy."

EXPERIMENTS

Numerous social psychological experiments have supported the role of facial expressions in the production and regulation of emotions as predicted by the facial feedback theories. One of the proposi-

tions of facial feedback theories is that in the presence of naturally occurring emotions such as disgust or delight, generating an opposite facial expression should have the effect of reducing the intensity of the original emotional experience. In contrast, exaggerating a spontaneous facial expression should have the effect of enhancing the intensity of the original emotional experience. Psychologist Robert Kraut examined this proposition in an experiment in which subjects sniffed a set of substances with characteristically unpleasant, neutral, and pleasant odors. Subjects then rated how pleasant each odor was. The substances Kraut used ranged from pyridine and butyric acid (both of which have a disgusting odor) through water (a neutral odor) to vanilla, wintergreen, and tangerine (all of which are very pleasant smelling to most people). In addition to smelling and rating the odors spontaneously, the subjects were sometimes instructed to pose a facial expression of delight or disgust when sniffing the odors, irrespective of the odor's actual pleasantness. Kraut found a strong effect for posing the different facial expressions. Consistent with the first proposition of facial feedback theories, when subjects posed a delighted expression, they rated all the odors as more pleasant smelling than when they rated the odors after reacting to them spontaneously. In contrast, and consistent with the facial feedback hypothesis, when subjects posed a disgusted expression, they rated all the odors as less pleasant smelling than when they rated the odors after reacting to them spontaneously. The results of Kraut's experiment suggest that the proverbial wisdom of "putting on a happy face" when a person feels sad may contain more than a little truth.

A second proposition of the facial feedback theories is that in the absence of naturally occurring emotions, generating a facial expression should have the effect of producing the corresponding emotional experience. In an early experiment, James Laird examined just this proposition. He covertly manipulated college students' facial muscles to produce a frown while attaching electrodes to their faces. In other words, as part of an experiment in which brain-wave recordings were supposedly being made, Laird told subjects to contract or relax various facial muscles. These instructions had the net effect of producing a frown without the subjects knowing that they were frowning. These subjects subsequently reported that they felt angry. Other students' facial muscles were arranged into smiles. These subjects reported feeling happy and rated cartoons to be funnier than did control subjects. These studies have been criticized, however, because subjects might have been aware that their faces were being arranged into frowns and smiles and may have been responding to experimental demand characteristics.

In a different study, social psychologists Fritz Strack, Lenny Martin, and Sabina Stepper had subjects rate cartoons while holding pens in their mouths. Some of these subjects clenched the end of a pen in their teeth, which models the facial muscle actions of smiling. Other subjects pursed the end of a pen in their lips, which models the facial muscle actions of frowning. According to these psychologists, these tasks model smiling and frowning more subtly than did Laird's manipulations. Consistent with facial feedback theory predictions, Strack and his colleagues found that the induced smilers rated the cartoons as being funnier than did the induced frowners.

RELATIONSHIP TO BIOFEEDBACK

Although facial feedback theories are concerned primarily with the effects of facial expressions on emotional experience, many of them acknowledge that facial expressions are not the only bodily cues that can produce or manage emotional experiences. For example, psychologists have found that people's physical posture (slumping versus sitting erect) affected their performance on a task. Similarly, a number of studies have shown that biofeedback techniques can be used to reduce anxiety and stress. When using biofeedback, a person concentrates his or her attention on some internal event, such as breathing rate, pulse rate, or heartbeat, and consciously tries to manage the event. With practice, biofeedback techniques have produced some surprising results.

Perhaps one of the most exciting potential applications for facial feedback theories is in clinical therapy settings. Carroll Izard has suggested that manipulation of facial expression can be used in a manner similar to biofeedback to help people cope with and overcome adverse emotional responses to situations and events. Although this application has not yet been put to the test, it could well become an important technique for use with such psychological problems as phobias, anxiety disorders, panic disorders, and depression.

CONTROVERSIES

Facial feedback theories of emotion are, as they have been since they were first suggested, surrounded by controversy. Facial feedback theories have received considerable attention from psychologists and psychophysiologists. They have attracted staunch supporters as well as vehement critics. Part of the controversy may be attributable to the theories' counterintuitive nature; they seem to fly in the face of common sense. On the other hand, proverbial wisdom suggests that at least some aspects of facial feedback theories make intuitive sense. Another part of the controversy has resulted from the difficulty of demonstrating the phenomenon in the laboratory. Although numerous studies have supported the facial feedback hypothesis, many have also failed to support it. In fact, two summaries of research related to facial feedback theories reached opposite conclusions concerning how well the available research has actually supported the theories.

As facial feedback research approaches its fourth decade, a number of questions about the role of facial expressions (and other bodily movements) in the production and regulation of emotional experience remain unanswered. For example, what is the exact mechanism through which facial (and bodily) expressions produce and regulate emotion? Is it sensory feedback from the facial muscles and skin, unmediated by thinking, that affects emotional experience, as William James, Charles Darwin, Silvan Tomkins, and Carroll Izard have suggested? Is it sensory feedback mediated by self-perception processes, as James Laird has proposed? Is it caused by some other, as yet unspecified, mechanism? These questions will be important focuses of future research on the facial feedback theories.

In addition, a number of newer approaches to and formulations of facial feedback theories have been offered. One of the most intriguing is psychologist Robert Zajonc and colleagues' vascular theory of facial efference. According to this formulation, facial expressions produce their effects on emotion not through sensory feedback from the muscles and skin but through changes in the volume of blood that reaches the brain. Expanding on a model originally proposed by Israel Waynbaum at the beginning of the twentieth century, Zajonc proposes that the facial muscles regulate the amount of blood that reaches and helps cool the brain. He and his colleagues have shown, for example, that changes in brain temperature are related to changes in emotional experience and that changes in facial expressions affect brain temperature. This seemingly improbable theory has received some experimental support and promises to maintain interest in facial feedback theories. Along more practical lines, Carroll Izard's suggestions for using facial feedback as a therapeutic tool may provide an alternative technique for managing specific psychological problems. Because of the interest in human self-regulatory mechanisms within social psychology, facial feedback theories and their successors will undoubtedly receive additional theoretical and empirical attention. The future holds considerable promise for advances in understanding the true relationship between facial expressions and the emotions they represent.

SOURCES FOR FURTHER STUDY

Buck, Ross. *The Communication of Emotion.* New York: Guilford, 1984. Presents the views of a critic of facial feedback theories and argues that facial expression is simply the automatic and unavoidable output of emotional experience. Intended for advanced college students, graduate students, and professionals.

Darwin, Charles. *The Expression of the Emotions in Man and Animals.* Chicago: University of Chicago Press, 1965. This classic text, first published in 1872, presents Darwin's evolutionary approach to emotional expression, including ideas that led to later formulations of facial feedback theories.

Ekman, Paul, ed. *Darwin and Facial Expression: A Century of Research in Review.* New York: Academic Press, 1972. This book, edited by a leading researcher on facial expression, surveys the research that has been generated as a result of Darwin's 1872 treatise. Includes a review of Ekman's work on the universality of emotional expression. Most suitable for college students and graduate students.

Fiske, Susan T., and Shelley E. Taylor. *Social Cognition.* 2d ed. New York: McGraw-Hill, 1991. A comprehensive textbook on social cognition that contains a brief but excellent summary of research and theory related to the facial feedback hypothesis. Reviews a number of the formulations of theories related to emotion and facial expression, including Robert Zajonc and his colleagues' vascular theory of facial efference.

Izard, Carroll E. *The Face of Emotion.* 1971. Reprint. New York: Irvington, 1993.

_____. "Facial Expressions and the Regulation of Emotions." *Journal of Personality and Social Psychology* 58, no. 3 (1990): 487-498. The book and journal article above present Izard's approach to the facial feedback hypothesis and his application of facial feedback principles to clinical therapy. Offering detailed and broad overviews and reviews of topics related to emotion and to facial feedback theories, these works describe major theories and research in detail and provide a useful context with which to understand the importance of emotion and facial expression in everyday life.

Tomkins, Silvan Solomon. *The Positive Affects.* Vol. 1 in *Affect, Imagery, Consciousness.* New York: Springer, 1962. This book presents possibly the most radical variant of the facial feedback theories. Tomkins argues that facial expression itself is emotional experience. Suitable for advanced college students and graduate students.

John H. Fleming

SEE ALSO: Biofeedback and relaxation; Emotional expression; Emotions; Nervous system; Neuropsychology; Nonverbal communication; Self-perception theory.

Family life
Adult issues

TYPE OF PSYCHOLOGY: Developmental psychology
FIELDS OF STUDY: Adulthood; aging

Family life provides one of the most important venues for adult psychological growth. Families provide a context, opportunities, and support for rich development of the adult stages of intimacy, generativity, and personality integration. When families are psychologically healthy, these stages lead to the development of the capacity for love, caring, and wisdom.

KEY CONCEPTS
- generativity
- intimacy
- life structure
- personality integration
- psychosocial development

INTRODUCTION

People develop psychologically throughout the life cycle, including the three stages of adulthood identified by Erik Erikson: early adulthood, middle adulthood, and later adulthood. Each stage is initiated by situationally new challenges and results in the growth of a new psychological capacity. Family life can provide the love and support needed to adapt to the changing demands of each phase in the life cycle.

Adults, unlike children, have membership in two families: the family of origin and the family they form as adults. While both are influential, for healthy adults it is the family they create that will exert the most significant impact on their adult psychological development.

THE FAMILY IN EARLY ADULTHOOD

A new family begins when a couple agrees to support each other's physical, social, emotional, and spiritual well-being. In contrast to the experimental nature of adolescent relationships, an adult partnership requires a deep sense of commitment, an open-ended investment of oneself to a shared history. This committed relationship provides the context for the development of intimacy, the key requisite for psychosocial development in early adulthood. Intimacy is being authentically available for reciprocal, boundless connecting with an other in mutuality.

Intimacy means being in one's own space while also in a shared space. It is not a loss of oneself, but a sharing that transforms one's own self. The two members of an intimate couple do not merge into each other. Such submergence is a sign of a dependent relationship and the loss of oneself. In contrast, healthy intimacy affords a quality of emergence, as the members become more fully themselves. One can be as unconstrained in the presence of the other as when one is by oneself. When intimacy is successfully achieved, the result is the development of a new psychological strength. The unique new strength of this stage is what Erikson calls simply "love."

Such openness and commitment entail many risks, not only of committing oneself inappropriately but also of being misunderstood or rejected. However, if adults do not develop intimacy they will, over time, feel an increasing sense of isolation: cut off from deep human connection, lonely, without anyone with whom to share their deepest selves,

even if married. They will retreat psychologically to a regressive reliving of earlier conflicts and to using others in self-centered ways.

The birth of a child marks the second milestone in the family life cycle, as the couple adds the role of parent into their lives. Parents must set aside many of their own needs to take care of a very dependent baby. Certain aspects of self will be neglected as this new role becomes central for the development of the parental self. New parents sacrifice sleep, free time, and time alone as a couple. They may also experience increased financial pressure. Moreover, caring for a baby is a significant responsibility and new parents are often insecure about their parenting skills. If the couple, or one spouse, have difficulty adapting to their role as parents, their relationship as a couple may become strained. On the other hand, sharing in the care of children offers a profound context for deepening the sense of mutuality between the couple.

Children's early years are characterized by intense caregiving by the parents, who play a very formative role as ideal prototypes internalized by the child's emerging sense of itself as an independent ego. When children reach the latency stage (around age six) and start school, yet another milestone in the parent-child relation emerges. Children now spend much of their time away from home, and the parents must adapt to this change. Their children will now be taught by others—teachers, coaches, friends—beyond the family circle. Increasingly, parents have the opportunity to become the joyful "witnesses" of their children becoming their own persons with their own networks of world relations and burgeoning interests and competencies.

The beginning of school can also prompt a change in the parents' schedule. If one parent had stayed at home to raise the child, that parent now typically enters or reenters the workforce beyond the home or attends college. While such a change brings added income, it also decreases homemaking time and can introduce new stresses on family life, especially if these changes are not anticipated and agreed upon by both parents.

THE FAMILY IN MIDDLE ADULTHOOD

The family undergoes another major reorganization when the child reaches adolescence, the transition between dependent child and independent adult. Parents need to allow their adolescent gradually increasing independence and responsibility, so the child can increasingly rely on his or her own internal resources for emotional support and authority. What the adolescent seeks now is a different form of the parental relation: what psychologist Terri Apter characterizes as validation rather than interference.

This step is not usually smooth; parents and adolescents often experience confusing power struggles as they negotiate their new roles. Adolescents may behave angrily and rebelliously or withdraw into their world of friends. This behavior can be stressful for the whole family, but it serves a function. Emotional and physical distance from their parents allows adolescents an opportunity to begin to see themselves for who they are apart from their family, and allows them to develop their own support system independent of the family. That all this takes place while adolescents are still under the care of their parents makes it psychologically difficult but provides a valuable buffering for adolescents' forays beyond the family.

A particularly exemplary context for this change is adolescents' sexual maturation. Adolescents attain adult sexual capacity before attaining the social status of adults, introducing a disjuncture between these two dimensions of their development. On the one hand, they are already adults (sexually speaking), but on the other hand they are not yet adults (societally speaking). Adolescents need to understand their sexuality and learn to socialize with the other gender while postponing fully adult enactment of their sexual capacities.

A successful resolution of this phase results in a mutual liking and respect between parents and their adolescent children, and the readiness of both for the adolescent to leave home, on internal and external levels. For parents, the experience of their adolescents' leaving home must be integrated and a changed relationship with them established. Next, without children at home, the parents must reconfigure who they are for each other, now that their long-standing role as mutual caretakers of children will no longer define their lives together. Issues that had been embedded within the parenting roles may make this adjustment extremely difficult. For those, male or female, who derived their identity from parenting, the ending of this role can result in a disorienting loss of self. For those parents who have been extremely involved in their children's lives as a way of avoiding marital problems, these issues will now become more obtrusive and may lead to divorce.

Rediscovering themselves as a couple apart from children can be distressing or joyful, but it will be a time for major modifications, not only of the couple's relation with each other but also of their entire life structure. New interests, jointly and individually, can now emerge as their creativity is no longer tied to procreation. Previously neglected aspects of self now need to be balanced within a larger self-understanding. A more encompassing form of generativity becomes available as adult caring now transcends taking care of one's children and can extend to one's community, to one's profession, and to the next generation. Otherwise, adults risk becoming self-absorbed, treating themselves as their "one and only baby." With that comes stagnation, as life appears to be ever more disillusioning and boring.

THE FAMILY IN LATER ADULTHOOD

Another milestone for both husband and wife is retirement. Retirees may experience a loss of their sense of purpose, self-esteem, and contact with a broader group of adults. Those who worked primarily taking care of the home may experience an intrusion on their responsibilities and sense of privacy when the now-retired spouse has no particular place to go each morning. A successful adjustment to retirement is marked by taking pleasure in the increased company of the other, a discovery of mutually pleasing activities, and sufficient time alone in order to pursue individual interests and friendships.

Becoming a grandparent is another major development of older adulthood. When their children have children, parents usually experience a sense of pride and completion. First, their own child has grown into a responsible adult and become a parent, and another generation of their family has begun. Second, spending time with grandchildren may be a renewing experience for grandparents, especially if they primarily spend their time with older people. Third, grandparenting evokes memories of ones' own parenting that can lead to making peace with one's own children regarding residual resentments and regrets from their parent-child relationship.

An aging adult's relationship with his or her child also changes in other ways at this time. It often becomes a relationship between equals, rather than between parent and child. A new dimension of friendship develops in their relationship, as one's adult children now become sources of authority and support.

A major concern of older adults is the loss of physical or cognitive functioning, requiring greater dependency. When one spouse can no longer do some of the things her or she used to, a healthy adjustment would include the ill spouse coming to accept this new dependency and the partner accommodating to these new responsibilities. Such optimal development will result in a heightened sense of intimacy, trust, and commitment. Disability in older adulthood may also transform parent-child relationships, with the children assuming the now-reversed role of caretaker.

The next phase of family life, widowhood (or, less commonly, widowerhood) is characterized by completing the mourning process, assuming roles formerly assumed by the other, and a renewed interest in people and activities. This process entails absorbing the shock of the other no longer being present, and the accompanying feelings, which typically include anger, sadness, fear, relief, or guilt. When one's partner dies, it is a time to review the marriage and to acknowledge what was and what was not. Husbands or wives may find themselves unable to accept the other's death. If so, they may become embittered or depressed. This happens especially if there was some major unresolved conflict in the marriage or if there was a personal dysfunction which interferes with functioning emotionally, physically, or financially on one's own.

Old age is not only about loss. A life well lived now nearing its end affords a momentous positive growth opportunity as well: a uniquely insightful perspective from which to see one's life as one's own. As author Betty Friedan has pointed out, to "own" one's own life, and so take full responsibility for it, enables the person to embrace it as a whole, in which every thread fits perfectly within an unbroken tapestry that admits of no substitutes. This vantage point opens a profound gratitude for one's family, and for one's place in the family of life itself. This final growth is what Erikson meant by the term "integrity" and what is now more often referred to as "personality integration." With this sense of completion comes true wisdom and deep spiritual joy.

SOURCES FOR FURTHER STUDY

Apter, Terri. *Altered Loves: Mothers and Daughters During Adolescence.* New York: St. Martin's Press, 1990. A study of the ways the mother-daughter relation changes during adolescence, especially with respect to aspects unique to it.

Erikson, Erik. *The Life Cycle Completed: A Review.* New York: W. W. Norton, 1982. Erikson's final outline of his theory of lifelong psychosocial development.

Friedan, Betty. *The Fountain of Age.* New York: Simon & Schuster, 1993. A thoughtful reflection on the "mystique" of old age.

Levinson, Daniel J. *The Seasons of a Man's Life.* New York: Ballantine, 1978. A detailed and influential research study of men's early adulthood and midlife.

_____. *The Seasons of a Woman's Life.* New York: Alfred A. Knopf, 1996. Levinson's companion research on women's adult development.

Malone, Thomas, and Patrick Malone. *The Art of Intimacy.* New York: Prentice-Hall, 1987. A careful analysis of the meaning of intimacy and its connection with the growth of the self.

Scarf, Maggie. *Intimate Partners: Patterns in Love and Marriage.* New York: Random House, 1987. A thoughtful analysis of problems in intimate relationships.

Washbourn, Penelope. *Becoming Woman: The Quest for Wholeness in Female Experience.* New York: Harper & Row, 1977. A descriptive analysis of the significant milestones in women's adult development.

Yablonsky, Lewis. *Fathers and Sons.* New York: Simon & Schuster, 1982. Descriptions of the types and stages of the father-son relationship.

Christopher M. Aanstoos and Judi Garland

SEE ALSO: Behavioral family therapy; Couples therapy; Family life: Children's issues; Father-child relationship; Mother-child relationship; Parental alienation syndrome; Parenting styles; Retirement; Separation and divorce: Adult issues; Separation and divorce: Children's issues; Stepfamilies; Strategic family therapy.

Family life
Children's issues

TYPE OF PSYCHOLOGY: Developmental psychology
FIELDS OF STUDY: Infancy and childhood

Children's issues in family life are a function of the cognitive, emotional, physical, linguistic, and social aspects of the child's development. Issues facing children in the family change as the child grows. Most families go through stages of development dependent on the issues with which the child is dealing. These stages contain common characteristics.

KEY CONCEPTS
- authority stage
- departure stage
- family development stage theory
- image making stage
- interdependent stage
- interpretive stage
- nurturing stage

INTRODUCTION

Childhood is a time of rapid development and change. The family adjusts to these changes daily as the child develops physically, cognitively, socially, and emotionally. Families pass through several separate developmental stages as children are growing up. Perhaps the best known is the eight-stage model outlined in 1948 in the *Report of the Committee on the Dynamics of Family Interaction* written by Evelyn Millis Duvall, secretary of the National Conference on Family Relations, and Reuben Hill, a sociologist at Iowa State College. This theory of family development focuses on group processes that resemble the aging and maturation of individuals. Briefly, those eight stages are the following: married couples (no children); childbearing families (oldest child aged birth to thirty months); families with preschool children (oldest child aged two and a half to six years); families with schoolchildren (oldest child aged six to thirteen years); families with teenagers (oldest child aged thirteen to twenty years); families launching young adults (beginning when the oldest child leaves home and ending when the youngest child leaves home); middle-aged parents (beginning with the "empty nest" and ending at the start of retirement); and aging family members (beginning with the spouses' retirements and ending at their deaths).

This eight-stage model was published in many textbooks for decades. It provided the base for many more stage models, some of which were created to correct what scholars called flaws in the original model. Although the number of stages varies widely, from two to twenty-four, these theories nevertheless present structures that must be dealt with. Early stage theories had structures that effectively issued rules about what constituted a family task in a particular stage and how it could be deemed accomplished. Complaints about such structures promoted new stage theories that had more flexible definitions and offered transition periods between stages. The most modern of the stage theories also provide for families going through stages out of order or repeating stages due to remarriage. Modern versions also combine family development stage theory with concepts from systems theory to better reflect how change is processed in families. In surveying the diverse family forms in American society, it is hard to defend the use of traditional stage theories. After all, if a stage theory outlines normative stages, then a family that does not follow it might be labeled nonnormative or abnormal. Family development stage theories do give a common-sense lexicon for describing families. For example, protection, safety, and health are the typical concerns of the people living in the family with infants and toddlers. Using these terms quickly identifies what is on the family's mind.

CONTEMPORARY STAGES OF PARENTHOOD

In the early 1980's, Ellen Galinsky, the president and cofounder of Families and Work Institute, a Manhattan-based nonprofit organization that conducts research on the changing family, took a creative approach to stage theory. She looked at family life from the parent's perspective and developed a six-stage model that described parent development. The image-making stage occurs during pregnancy, when parents form and reform images of the upcoming birth and the changes they anticipate. This is a period of preparation. In the nurturing stage, parents compare image and actual experience during the time from the baby's birth to the toddler's first use of the word "no" (about age eighteen to twenty-four months). This is a period of attachment and also of questioning. Parents may question their priorities and also how they spend their time. The authority stage occurs when the child is between two years and four to five years, when parents decide what kind of authority to be. This is a period of developing and setting rules, as well as enforcing them. The interpretive stage stretches from the child's preschool years to the approach to adolescence; this stage has the task of interpretation. In this period, parents interpret their own self-concepts as well as their children's. Parents also are concerned with interpreting the world to their children. The interdependent stage occurs during the child's teen years, when families revisit some of the issues of the authority stage but find new solutions to them as parents form a new relationship with their almost-adult child. The final stage, the departure stage, is when children leave home and parents evaluate not just their offspring's leavetaking but also the whole of their parenting experience. During each of these stages of parenthood the child is developing emotionally, cognitively, socially, and physically.

CHILD DEVELOPMENT WITHIN FAMILY STAGES
Child development during the image-making stage of parenthood involves the development of the fetus in utero. This translates into the importance of good prenatal care for the mother.

During the nurturing stage of parenthood, from the child's birth to eighteen to twenty-four months, families go through numerous transitions. Much of the infant's day involves activities such as feeding, diapering, and holding. This is the time for parents or caregivers to provide opportunities for the infant to interact naturally with the environment. Parents need to respond to the infant's interests and abilities and create a healthy and challenging environment that will promote physical, mental, social, and emotional growth.

New research on infant brain development confirms the importance of loving and protecting children. An infant's experiences during the first three years of life shape both learning and behavior. Everyday moments, such as feeding a child while lovingly gazing into his or her eyes, provide nourishment for the child's brain as well as for the body. During the nurturing stage of family life, the interaction between parent and child stimulates brain growth and development.

In traditional family development theory, the preschool level is stage 3 or the authority stage of parenthood. Determined by the age of the oldest child, preschool refers to children two and a half to six years of age. A preschooler's main developmental task is self-mastery. It is with high awareness that the preschooler experiments with expanding language and abilities. During this stage, parents' growing awareness of power issues and their control of

children result in the family working through developing and setting rules. Important parental tasks for this age include providing attention and security for the child, encouraging his or her development in all areas, meeting the preschooler's needs, maintaining active involvement in all areas of the preschooler's life, setting definite behavior boundaries for the child, and providing him or her with consistent responses and discipline. As a time of great change, the preschooler stage presents many new challenges for the family.

Parental attachment continues to build during these years, although secure children will explore on their own and utilize their parents as a safety net. Children will move away from their parents to explore for extended periods of time but will still watch the parent for encouragement and security. Passive experiences such as watching videos and television are not as stimulating for preschoolers as interactions with parents, caretakers, and positive age-appropriate peers. Interactive experiences that stimulate (without overwhelming) the brain will build neural connections. The growing preschooler needs exposure to new and novel experiences that are not frightening or overwhelming. Noises such as loud music, bass drum beats, or gunfire are negative experiences for the developing brain. Fear and lack of security create changes in brain chemistry that can affect the child's temperament, behavior, and ability to learn social skills and to interpret social cues.

The interpretive stage stretches from children's preschool years to their approach to adolescence. In this period, parents interpret their own self-concepts as well as those of their children. Parents also are concerned with interpreting the world to their children. The school-aged child's life becomes group centered during this stage. Group influence is inevitable in modern society. Few families are so isolated that their children do not have contact with other youth. Group influence is usually positive. Although parents often worry about peer pressure having a negative affect on their children (mistakenly thinking that it is something that only occurs during adolescence), the positive side of the issue is peer support. As children develop friendships and form social groups, they learn lessons of loyalty, kindness, fairness, and cooperation.

The fifth stage of parenthood is the stage during the child's teen years, when families revisit some of the issues of the authority stage but find new solutions as parents form a new relationship with their almost-adult child. The parent role shifts from leader to partner. Partnership does not imply increased time together, however. During the junior high and high school years, parents and teens spend less time together. For some parents, the drop in shared activity feels like rejection. For others, it is a relief. Still others report that they spend just as much time in family activity, but at arm's length from their children. As teens seek to form an identity, they almost always look for ways to be separate from their families. Autonomy can be achieved by making decisions on their own. Privacy may entail what looks like secrecy to the family.

The teen is an individual who is in a transitional stage. This may mean that the parent's role can become more that of a consultant or adviser. As direct caretaking is reduced, the parent also must make adjustment. Confusion may develop, however, when the teen occasionally demands a return to direct care.

When children leave home during the departure stage, parents evaluate not just their offspring's leavetaking but also the whole of their parenting experience. For most families in this stage, the launch is of primary importance. It is the time when younger family members take on adult responsibilities, typically by moving, taking employment, or marrying. Going away to college may be a launching, either full or partial, and as a result some families consider the age of eighteen or nineteen to be the start of adulthood. By most standards, Americans consider a launch to be appropriate before young adults reach their mid-twenties.

SOURCES FOR FURTHER STUDY

Arnold, Catharine. *Child Development and Learning, Two to Five Years: Georgia's Story.* Newbury Park, Calif.: Sage Publications, 1999. Documents the study of one child's social, emotional, and cognitive development. Provides insight about child development on a personal level.

Galinsky, Ellen. *The Six Stages of Parenthood.* Cambridge, Mass.: Perseus Press, 1987. While there are many books on child development, this is the first book to describe parents' growth comprehensively. Based on a nationwide study of a diverse group of 228 parents, this book is a valuable aid to parenting.

Keenan, Thomas. *An Introduction to Child Development.* Newbury Park, Calif.: Sage Publications,

2001. Provides a comprehensive introduction to developmental psychology. Covers methods and theories and offers a grounding in the principles of developmental psychology.

Sutherland, Peter, A. *Cognitive Development Today: Piaget and his Critics.* Newbury Park, Calif.: Sage Publications, 1992. This book provides a general outline of the dominant schools of thought on cognitive development, with a focus on Piaget. Application of theories to preschool, primary, and secondary children.

White, James A. *Dynamics of Family Development: A Theoretical Perspective.* New York: Guilford, 1991. This book extends the theory of family development and reformulates some of its fundamental concepts.

Shelley A. Jackson

SEE ALSO: Behavioral family therapy; Family life: Adult issues; Father-child relationship; Mother-child relationship; Parental alienation syndrome; Parenting styles; Separation and divorce: Adult issues; Separation and divorce: Children's issues; Sibling relationships; Stepfamilies; Strategic family therapy.

Father-child relationship

TYPE OF PSYCHOLOGY: Developmental psychology
FIELDS OF STUDY: Adolescence; childhood and adolescent disorders; infancy and childhood

The father-child relationship has been studied less than the mother-child relationship. There has, however, been enough research to help clarify the father-child relationship. In general, there are more similarities than differences between fathers and mothers with regard to what constitutes good parenting. Fathers (as well as mothers) who show warmth and age-appropriate structure tend to have children who are well adjusted.

KEY CONCEPTS
- authority
- family
- fathers
- mothers
- risk factors

INTRODUCTION

When many people think about fathers, they immediately think of absent fathers rather than fathers who are involved extensively with raising their children. However, in the first years of the twenty-first century within the United States, approximately 61 percent of children under the age of eighteen live with both their biological father and mother. An additional 11 percent live within a stepfamily with their biological mother and a stepfather. For children who do not live with their biological father, approximately 61 percent have some type of regular contact with him. Thus, although not all children live with their father in a two-parent family, the great majority have a father or father figure in their lives.

Given the potential importance of fathers in children's lives, it is surprising to find that there has been very little research completed on the father-child relationship (especially in comparison to the amount of research available on the mother-child relationship). When research has been completed with fathers, it has focused more on normal developmental processes than on abnormal developmental processes.

FATHERS AND NORMAL CHILD DEVELOPMENT

More similarities than differences arise when comparing fathers and mothers in relation to their children. Some of the most salient differences deal with the ways in which fathers and mothers interact with their children. For example, throughout childhood (from infancy to young adulthood), fathers are more playful with their children than are mothers. Even when conducting caretaking activities (such as changing diapers or helping with homework), fathers tend to play with their offspring more than do mothers. This difference is neither good nor bad—it is just different.

Another difference that is found consistently between fathers and mothers is the amount of time spent with children. No matter the age of the child (infancy, toddlerhood, childhood, adolescence, or young adulthood) and no matter the way that involvement is defined (such as direct time spent in interactions, accessibility to the parent, or responsibility for the child's behavior), mothers spend more time with their children than do fathers, and they have more responsibility for their children than do fathers. This pattern is found consistently in study

Fathers spend more time, and more quality time, with their young children than did fathers of previous generations. (CLEO Photography)

after study and in country after country, even when both parents are employed full time.

Interestingly, the amount of time spent with children does not appear to be as important as the quality of the time that is spent with children. That is, if a father or mother spends large amounts of time with the child but is not sufficiently engaged with the child (for instance, they are on the phone or responding to e-mail during much of the time), then the child is likely not to behave as well as a child who experiences slightly less time with parents but who experiences higher quality time (as with parents who sit and play with their children, with no other agenda to focus on their children at that point in time). Thus, it is important for both fathers and mothers to reflect on the quality of time they spend with their children rather than just the quantity of time.

Regarding similarities, one similarity between fathers and mothers that surprises many people is that both fathers and mothers spend more time with their infants, less time with their older children, and even less time with their adolescents. Many people may think that fathers get more involved when children are old enough to be involved in sports, for example, but a number of research studies have shown that fathers tend to show the most time involvement with their infants. These patterns reflect the amount of direct caretaking that is required for infants in comparison to adolescents. It appears that both fathers and mothers spend the most time involved with caring for their infants, and then spend progressively less time with their children as they grow to be more independent and self-sufficient.

One of the most important similarities between fathers and mothers is that good parenting looks the same regardless of the parent's gender. Specifically, authoritative parenting in both fathers and mothers is associated with healthy outcomes for children. Authoritative parenting is characterized by parents who give their children firm and appropriate behavior limitations, while also being warm and supportive. Authoritative parents most often set age-appropriate limits on their child's behavior but explain those limits in a way that the child can understand. They exude warmth and caring for the child but also try to ensure that their children are learning appropriate guidelines for their behavior. Whether the authoritative parenting is exhibited by a father or a mother (or a custodial grandparent or a foster parent, for that matter), children tend to show the best emotional and behavioral functioning in the context of this parenting style.

FATHERS AND ABNORMAL CHILD DEVELOPMENT

While little research has been done on the father-child relationship regarding normal development (when there are no major psychological problems), even less research has been completed on the father-child relationship when either the father or the child has psychological problems. When research has been completed, there are two primary designs—one that explores the children of troubled fathers and another that explores the fathers of troubled children.

There are relatively consistent findings from research exploring the children of troubled fathers. Regardless of the type of psychological disturbance the father is experiencing (such as depression, alcohol dependence, or schizophrenia), children of psy-chologically distressed fathers tend to have poorer outcomes than do children of psychologically healthy fathers. These findings parallel those found with children of psychologically distressed mothers. The outcome for these children varies: Sometimes the children show the same problems as the father (the child of a depressed father also shows depression) and sometimes the children show different problems from those of the father (the child of an alcoholic father shows severe conduct problems). Overall, children of psychologically distressed fathers are at greater risk for maladjustment than are children of psychological healthy fathers. This risk is magnified if there are other risk factors in the child's life, such as interparental conflict, poverty, or abuse.

When fathers of psychologically distressed children are compared with fathers of psychologically healthy children, less clear patterns emerge depending on the specific disorder that the child is experiencing. For example, there are few meaningful differences between fathers of children with attention-deficit hyperactivity disorder (ADHD) and fathers of psychologically healthy children. In contrast, fathers of children with severe conduct problems tend to show significantly higher rates of psychopathology than fathers of well-functioning children. There are mixed findings when fathers of children with anxiety problems and depressed children are compared with fathers of children who are psychologically healthy. These results follow a similar pattern to research on mothers of maladjusted children in comparison to mothers of well-functioning children.

Overall, there are clear linkages between troubled fathers and troubled children for some psychological problems but not for others. These linkages are made even stronger when children are also exposed to other risk factors, such as abuse, neglect, interparental conflict, and poor parental supervision.

HELPING TROUBLED FATHERS AND FAMILIES

Because both professionals and nonprofessionals tend to blame mothers rather than fathers for children's emotional and behavioral problems, it is not surprising to learn that mothers are included in therapy for children's maladjustment much more often than are fathers. This pattern is less salient for therapists and counselors who have received extensive family therapy training and those who value equality within the family. In many cases, however, mothers are the only parents who are invited to therapy and are the only ones who are involved in helping their troubled children.

The effectiveness of including fathers in child-oriented therapy depends on the type of presenting problem and the type of therapy. For example, behavioral parent training is effective in helping decrease oppositional behavior in young children regardless of whether it is the father or the mother who is involved in treatment. When fathers are involved in behavioral parent training, however, there are also noticeable increases in the healthy communication patterns between the parents. In addition, including fathers in child-oriented therapy tends to help decrease interparental conflict (such as arguing and fighting) that might be exacerbating the child's problems. Thus, there is some evidence that including fathers in therapy is more helpful than not including them.

Overall, the same qualities make a well-functioning father as make a well-functioning mother. Although it is important to continue to explore differences between fathers and mothers, it is striking to find the level of similarity in fathers and mothers in relation to the well-being of infants, toddlers, children, and adolescents.

Sources for Further Study

Biller, H. B., and R. J. Trotter. *The Father Factor: What You Need to Know to Make a Difference.* New York: Pocket Books, 1994. This book was written specifically for fathers who are interested in becoming more involved in their children's lives.

Booth, A., and A. C. Crouter, eds. *Men in Families: When Do They Get Involved? What Difference Does It Make?* Mahwah, N.J.: Lawrence Erlbaum, 1998. Provides a series of chapters of the father-child relationship and fathers within the context of marriage.

Dreman, S., ed. *The Family on the Threshold of the Twenty-first Century: Trends and Implications.* Mahwah, N.J.: Lawrence Erlbaum, 1997. Written for sophisticated readers. Provides discussions of the family in relation to psychology, sociological, and political perspectives.

Griswold, R. L. *Fatherhood in America: A History.* New York: Basic Books, 1993. Written by a historian, this fascinating book provides an overview of fatherhood from 1800 to the present day.

Lamb, M. E., ed. *The Role of the Father in Child Development.* 3d ed. New York: John Wiley & Sons, 1997. Offers a comprehensive review of father-child relationships.

Marsiglio, W., ed. *Fatherhood: Contemporary Theory, Research, and Social Policy.* Thousand Oaks, Calif.: Sage Publications, 1995. Written from a sociological perspective, this book provides readings on single-fatherhood, divorced fathers, and issues of race and poverty in relation to fatherhood.

Phares, V. *Fathers and Developmental Psychopathology.* New York: John Wiley & Sons, 1996. Written for professionals. Reviews research of the father-child relationship when either fathers or children are psychologically distressed.

_____. *Poppa Psychology: The Role of Fathers in Children's Mental Well Being.* Westport, Conn.: Greenwood Press, 1999. Written for a general audience. Reviews the father-child relationship in well-functioning families and families with troubled family members.

Ryan, J. A., ed. *Lessons from Dad: A Tribute to Fatherhood.* Deerfield Beach, Fla.: Health Communications, 1997. This collection of personal essays and poetry includes writings by Bill Cosby, Gilda Radner, and Elizabeth Barrett Browning about fatherhood.

Shapiro, J. L., M. J. Diamond, and M. Greenberg, eds. *Becoming a Father.* New York: Springer, 1995. Focuses on the early stages of fathering. Provides professional articles as well as poetry about becoming a father.

Vicky Phares

SEE ALSO: Mother-child relationship; Parental alienation syndrome; Parenting styles; Separation and divorce: Adult issues; Separation and divorce: Children's issues.

Feminist psychotherapy

TYPE OF PSYCHOLOGY: Psychotherapy
FIELDS OF STUDY: Evaluating psychotherapy; models of abnormality; psychodynamic therapies

Feminist psychotherapy integrates feminist philosophy with principles of counseling and therapy. It promotes consciousness raising and awareness, fosters egalitarian therapist-client relationships, focuses on the ways in which personal problems are influenced by social forces and sexism, encourages individuals to acknowledge and act on their strengths, and emphasizes the importance of both personal change and social change.

KEY CONCEPTS
- consciousness raising
- equality
- feminist analysis
- gender bias
- gender-role analysis
- informed choice
- the personal as political

INTRODUCTION

Feminists are people who advocate political, social, and economic equality between women and men. Feminist therapy is much more difficult to define, because interpretations of feminist therapy depend upon the particular feminist philosophy and therapeutic orientation that a therapist adopts. At the most basic level, feminist psychotherapy involves the integration of feminist principles with psychotherapeutic practices, but the nature of this combination takes many forms. A wide range of psychotherapies may be employed or combined in feminist psychotherapy, excluding those that are gender biased.

An assumption underlying feminist psychotherapy is that personal behavior and social expectations are interwoven in an intricate, complex manner. Problems are shaped by social and cultural environments that limit choices or encourage individuals to see themselves in restricted ways. Psychological conflicts are not viewed as personal deficits; they often arise from efforts to cope with or survive unjust or oppressive environmental conditions. When problems are viewed solely as internal conflicts or symptoms that need to be removed, women learn to feel responsible for and guilty about pain that is promoted or reinforced by inequality or gender-role expectations. The personal is considered political in the sense that personal change should be connected to social change that allows all people to meet their goals effectively.

ROOTS AND INFLUENCES

Feminist psychotherapy emerged during the women's movement of the 1970's in response to traditional mental health practices that contributed to an unequal, oppressive environment for women. Phyllis Chesler, in *Women and Madness* (1972), charged that women were diagnosed for both underconforming and overconforming to gender-role stereotypes and that the higher treatment and hospitalization rates of women were related to sexist mental health practices. Feminists within the mental health field noted that the goals, psychological theories, and practices of psychotherapists were based on masculine criteria of psychological health, encouraged hierarchical relationships between therapists and clients, and promoted adjustment to traditional, stereotyped roles for women. Feminist psychotherapy became a method for counteracting these negative influences.

The consciousness-raising groups associated with the feminist movement also influenced feminist psychotherapy. These groups provided women with an increasing awareness of sexism and its impact on personal lives and choices. Women reported therapeutic benefits of consciousness raising, including increased feelings of self-esteem and autonomy, awareness of commonalities between women, an expanded ability to express strong feelings such as anger, and an awareness of the ways in which sociopolitical forces influence the female experience. Feminist psychotherapists incorporated many elements of consciousness-raising groups into their work, and the group practice of feminist therapy has remained important.

ROLE OF THERAPY

Feminist psychotherapy began as a strong reaction against traditional therapy rather than as a particular form of therapy; however, feminist therapists have also transformed mainstream therapies by applying feminist perspectives. Feminist therapists have also developed personality theories that value women on their own terms rather than viewing them as diverging from the male norm. During the early 1970's, the feminist movement and feminist therapy did not adequately consider the needs of women of color and the combined impact of racism and sexism. Subsequent efforts have focused on acknowledging the diversity of women's lives and increasing the sensitivity of feminist practices to these complexities. Feminist therapy has also extended to counseling men and emphasizes the importance of integrating relationship and achievement needs, increasing the capacity for intimacy, creating mutual, collaborative relationships, and learning noncoercive problem-solving methods.

Feminist psychotherapists are often critical of the standard diagnostic criteria adopted by psychiatry and psychology, and outlined in the American Psychiatric Association's *Diagnostic and Statistical Manual of Mental Disorders: DSM-IV-TR* (rev. 4th ed., 2000). They believe that these categories have highly judgmental qualities and are based on a medical model which implies that psychological problems are lodged primarily within the person; such categorization may lead to blaming victims rather than solving the social problems that contribute to these personal problems.

The therapist-client relationship in feminist psychotherapy is based on egalitarian values. Therapists inform clients about their orientation and goals and attempt to demystify the counseling experience. Clients are encouraged to take on the attitude of a consumer and to ask questions of the therapist to ensure that they receive what they need from the therapy. Although feminist therapists work toward equalizing the balance of power, they also recognize that, because of their professional skills and the special status given to helping professionals, the relationship will not be fully equal. Clients are seen as their own best experts, as competent and powerful, and as capable of making productive choices.

THERAPEUTIC GOALS AND TECHNIQUES

The goals of feminist psychotherapy emphasize the importance of healthy, self-chosen change, rather than adjustment to status-quo definitions of mental health. Consciousness raising about sexism in society is a central feature of feminist therapy, and clients are encouraged to understand the role of socialization and culture in shaping their lives. Because women are frequently socialized to define themselves according to expectations of significant others, feminist therapy emphasizes the importance of self-nurturing behaviors and defining one's own identity. In addition, since women are frequently taught to use covert, indirect forms of influence and communication in relationships, special emphasis is placed on learning direct, constructive, assertive forms of expression. Finally, it is hoped that as clients meet personal goals, they will become interested in working toward social change that will benefit all women and thus, indirectly, all people.

Although many forms of therapy can be integrated with feminist therapy, certain techniques are associated with feminist psychotherapy. Through gender-role analysis, clients are encouraged to examine their own gender-role behaviors and attitudes and choose alternatives to behaviors that are not productive for them. Gender-role analysis helps people identify how they learned from their culture the behaviors and emotions that are expected of them as "normal" women or men and to consider other ways of fulfilling their potential as competent persons. In addition, feminist analysis, or social analysis, is used to convey information about the sociocultural barriers that limit the development of women. This analysis may focus on the ways in which job discrimination, sexual harassment, stereotypes, or poverty may contribute to personal problems, and it helps clients understand the ways in which the environment limits their potential. Insight into these power structures decreases their damaging effects because clients recognize that they are not to blame for many of the problems they experience. In feminist analysis, clients are encouraged to separate internal causes of problems from external ones. When clients are able to distinguish between these factors, they feel greater freedom and commitment to make active, constructive changes within their own lives and within their environments.

Two additional techniques are the expression of anger and therapist self-disclosure. The recognition of sexism and oppression in society may lead to intense anger, and the healthy expression of emotion within a safe, mutual relationship is considered essential. Because women are frequently socialized to express only "soft" emotions, they may not have a vocabulary with which to express anger or may fear its destructive qualities. Techniques that help individuals express strong emotion in healthy, constructive ways contribute to their confidence. Finally, appropriate self-disclosure on the part of the therapist is an important tool because it decreases a client's feelings of aloneness and models the healthy expression of issues and feelings. The human qualities of the therapist help motivate and empower the client.

ROLE IN ANALYZING DEPRESSION

Feminist psychotherapy provides an alternative to traditional psychotherapy. The differences between a feminist approach and a traditional approach to problems can be illustrated by the discussion of depression in women. From a traditional perspective, depression is often viewed as resulting from biological vulnerabilities, faulty thinking patterns, skills deficits, or a depressive personality style. Psychotherapy focuses on removing the symptom and alleviating suffering so that the client can readjust to her living environment. A feminist perspective does not ignore personal factors and vulnerabilities, but it goes beyond them to examine the ways in which depression is associated with women's limited access to power and with other environmental factors.

The American Psychological Association National Task Force on Women and Depression reported in 1990 that women are twice as likely as men to experience depression and that the interpersonal violence, poverty, and discrimination that women face contribute to these higher rates. Multiple roles, inequities in division of labor at home, the presence of young children in the home, and expectations that women will define themselves in terms of others contribute to suppressed anger and frustration and may lead to depression. In feminist therapy, the therapist and client identify and understand these factors, practice healthy ways of expressing suppressed emotion, focus on ways the client can define herself on her own terms, and establish ways of altering the environment so that the client can reach her potential.

ROLE IN MEDIATING VIOLENCE

Therapy for survivors of violence, such as rape, battering, or incest, is an important application of feminist psychotherapy. Gender-biased attitudes that were based on Sigmund Freud's view of women have promoted psychological myths and encouraged blaming the victim by suggesting that women are inherently masochistic and gain pleasure through experiencing pain. Other cultural attitudes contribute to notions that women's personal flaws lead to abuse, that sexual violence is caused by women's seductiveness, that women precipitate battering incidents through verbal provocation, and that women tend to remain in violent relationships. Many survivors of violence, having absorbed these negative cultural myths, struggle with low self-esteem and suffer in secrecy. Feminist therapists help clients talk about and deal with the intense feelings of shame and guilt that are fostered by myths about sexual and interpersonal violence. They validate women's experiences and acknowledge the painful circumstances, such as poverty or limited resources, that contribute to their pain. Feminist psychotherapists help women place blame outside themselves and deal with the

anger that must be expressed toward perpetrators and a social system that condones violence against women. Providing support and a safe physical environment are also crucial components of feminist intervention. Finally, many survivors of violence experience further healing and empowerment by helping other women. They may become advocates on behalf of other women, engage in political efforts to establish new programs, or become involved in peer-counseling activities in a crisis center.

GROUP WORK

Group work is another component of feminist therapy. Groups enable individuals to decrease their isolation from other women, construct mutual support systems, and validate one another's strengths. When group members share experiences, the similarities of their concerns are often striking and they become aware that broader social issues are often mistakenly identified as individual problems. Groups help counter the negative aspects of socialization that encourage women to adopt passive roles; they provide a safe environment in which members can practice new skills, develop confidence, and make new choices. The original feminist therapy groups were modeled after the consciousness-raising groups of the 1970's. Specialized feminist therapy groups deal with many issues, such as eating disorders, self-esteem concerns, or incest and abuse issues.

CONTRIBUTIONS TO PSYCHOLOGY

Feminist therapy not only is a distinct entity but also seeks to transform mainstream psychological practice. For example, because of the efforts of feminist psychologists, the American Psychological Association adopted the "Principles Concerning the Counseling and Therapy of Women." This document recommends that counselors and therapists become knowledgeable about and seek training in women's issues, utilize skills that will facilitate women's development, and work toward eliminating gender bias within institutions and individuals. Feminist therapists continue to work toward heightening the sensitivity of all therapists to women's concerns.

SOURCES FOR FURTHER STUDY

Brodsky, Annette M., and Rachel T. Hare-Mustin. *Women and Psychotherapy*. New York: Guilford, 1980. Chapters summarize research issues on gender and gender-role stereotyping, describe disorders of high prevalence in women's lives, and propose a variety of therapeutic approaches for intervening in women's lives.

Brown, Laura S. *Subversive Dialogues: Theory in Feminist Therapy*. New York: Basic Books, 1994. Examines the power of the therapist; assessment and diagnosis; the nature of change; the ethics of practice; and differences in race, class, and sexual identity from a feminist perspective.

Chesler, Phyllis. *Women and Madness*. Garden City, N.Y.: Doubleday, 1972. One of the original, classic documentations of the way in which sexism has operated within mental health systems and contributed to unequal treatment of women.

Dutton-Douglas, Mary Ann, and Lenore E. A. Walker. *Feminist Psychotherapies*. Norwood, N.J.: Ablex, 1988. Includes chapters on the integration of feminist philosophy and mainstream therapy systems, feminist psychotherapy with special populations, feminist therapy with men, and future directions.

Enns, Carolyn Zerbe. *Feminist Theories and Feminist Psychotherapies: Origins, Themes, Variations*. New York: Haworth Press, 1997. Explores the ways in which feminist theory influences a therapist's personal practice.

Franks, Violet, and Esther D. Rothblum, eds. *The Stereotyping of Women: Its Effects on Mental Health*. New York: Springer, 1983. Describes ways in which gender-role stereotypes contribute to disorders such as depression, agoraphobia, weight and communication problems, sexual dysfunction, and violence against women.

Greenspan, Miriam. *A New Approach to Women and Therapy*. 2d ed. New York: McGraw-Hill, 1993. A highly readable account of the ways in which mental health systems and mainstream therapies discriminate against women. Describes feminist therapy, compares it to humanistic therapy, and provides case studies.

Johnson, Karen, and Tom Ferguson. *Trusting Ourselves: The Complete Guide of Emotional Well-Being for Women*. New York: Atlantic Monthly Press, 1991. Discusses common psychological concerns of women, such as self-esteem, depression, anxiety, sexuality, alcohol, body image, and violence. Highly readable, written for a lay audience. Includes a consumer guide to seeking psychological help.

McGrath, Ellen, ed. *Women and Depression: Risk Factors and Treatment Issues*. Washington, D.C.: American Psychological Association, 1990. Report of the APA Task Force on Women and Depression. Includes discussions of gender differences, women's status, the influence of victimization and poverty, and treatment considerations.

Rosewater, Lynne Bravo, and Lenore E. A. Walker, eds. *Handbook of Feminist Therapy: Women's Issues in Psychotherapy*. New York: Springer, 1985. Includes brief chapters dealing with feminist philosophy, techniques, special populations, and ethics. Includes the American Psychological Association's "Principles Concerning the Counseling and Therapy of Women."

Carolyn Zerbe Enns

SEE ALSO: Abnormality: Psychological models; Cognitive ability: Gender differences; Depression; Psychotherapy: Effectiveness; Psychotherapy: Historical approaches; Women's psychology: Carol Gilligan; Women's psychology: Karen Horney; Women's psychology: Sigmund Freud.

Field experimentation

TYPE OF PSYCHOLOGY: Psychological methodologies
FIELDS OF STUDY: Descriptive methodologies; experimental methodologies

Field experimentation comprises a variety of techniques to study people or other organisms within their natural environments; typically it involves observing, recording, tracking, and interviewing subjects to produce an in-depth study written as a narrative.

KEY CONCEPTS
- covert research
- field notes
- Hawthorne effect
- inductive research
- laboratory research
- naturalistic observation
- nonparticipant observer
- participant observer

INTRODUCTION

As an alternative to studying behavior in the sometimes restricted and sterile confines of the laboratory, scientists can turn to field experimentation as a method of finding out how people or other organisms interact with their natural environment. As the term "field experimentation" implies, genuine science is being conducted; however, the research takes place in the context of the places where the subjects normally live, work, and play. Instead of removing subjects from their normal surroundings and placing them in artificial situations, a field researcher attempts to study behaviors as they occur spontaneously in the real world.

EVOLUTION OF PRACTICE

Royce Singleton, Jr., Bruce Straits, Margaret Straits, and Ronald McAllister, in their book *Approaches to Social Research* (1988), make the point that field experimentation procedures were used long before the techniques were recognized by the scientific community. The authors also state there is a consensus that anthropologists—followed shortly thereafter by sociologists—first developed and then legitimized this approach to research. Antrhopologist Franz Boas and sociologist Robert Park were among the early pioneers of field research during the late nineteenth century and the beginning of the twentieth century. Boas was noted for his research in cultural anthropology. He emphasized the importance of circumventing one's Western cultural biases by living in other cultures for an extended time and acquiring that culture's perspective. On the other hand, Park, who taught for a number of years at the University of Chicago, was influential in encouraging students to use the city as an alternative laboratory—studying people where they lived.

Field experimentation grew out of a need to seek answers to questions that could not be brought into a laboratory setting. Foreign cultures, complex social relationships, and secretive sects are examples of the phenomena that lend themselves to this method. Laboratory research—research in which phenomena are studied in an artificial setting with rigorous procedures in place to control for outside influences—might be seen as a hindrance to understanding dynamic human behavior. An alternative method needed to be found, and field research filled this vacuum.

Early in its development, field experimentation used data-collection procedures that almost entirely consisted of informal notes. A long narrative describing a sequence of behaviors would not have been uncommon. There has been a gradual move toward the use of more "objective" techniques such as standardized rating scales, behavioral checklists, and structured surveys. These methods were created in order to quantify better the observations being made. Once the behaviors could be quantified (that is, once specific behaviors could be assigned numbers), they could be subjected to the same statistical analyses used by laboratory experimenters. This improved approach to data collection helped field experimentation methods play a significant role in the social and behavioral sciences.

ADVANTAGES

Studying people in their natural environments can yield a number of advantages over more traditional laboratory research methods. For example, it has been found that when subjects are aware that they are being studied, their actions sometimes differ from their actions when they are unaware that they are being observed. This phenomenon is known as the Hawthorne effect. A field study can avoid the Hawthorne effect by enabling the researcher to go "undercover" and study the subjects without their being aware that a study is going on. A field study helps ensure that genuine, rather than contrived, behaviors will emerge.

Another advantage of the field experimentation method is that it lends itself to the study of complex behaviors, such as relationships among family members, that would be too difficult to simulate in a laboratory setting. Another important strength is that the researcher can maintain the interaction between the subject and the setting in which the subject lives or works. Under this set of circumstances, the field study is the method most preferred. In addition, there are some instances in which time does not allow the researcher to bring the phenomena under study into the laboratory. Such instances include those associated with natural disasters or national calamities. For example, a researcher might want to study the psychological reactions of people who have lost their homes in a hurricane. Since it would be imperative to begin collecting data immediately, taking the time to develop a comprehensive survey or to identify and eventually test the important variables in a more controlled setting would jeopardize the data collection of this dynamic, rapidly changing situation.

DISADVANTAGES

Conducting a field experiment does not come without its share of disadvantages. First, there are many topics worthy of study that are too difficult to stage outside the well-controlled confines of a laboratory. Studying memory loss or the processes involved in solving a complex algebra problem are examples of these kinds of topics. Second, some researchers argue that because so many uncontrolled outside influences are present in a field study, it is difficult, if not impossible, to understand causal relationships among the behaviors being studied. Third, field research is particularly susceptible to the biases of the researcher while the data are being collected. Since data collection is typically less standardized and formal than in other methodologies, it is possible that the researcher may be unaware that observations that support the researcher's hypothesis may be recorded and given more attention than behaviors that go contrary to the researcher's beliefs. Some of the research published by anthropologist Margaret Mead during the 1920's, for example, has been called into question for this reason by other researchers who have reached different conclusions.

TECHNIQUES

Field experimentation usually entails going into a naturalistic setting to collect data that can be used to generate research questions. The researcher will take such information, begin to organize it, and try to draw some general conclusions from it. This process, referred to as "inductive research," occurs when data are first collected and then used to formulate general principles. Thus, field research differs from many other kinds of research methodologies. Field research begins with a broad theory, then sets out to test specific aspects of the theory to see if the data support it.

Field experimentation represents a variety of strategies for studying behavior. One specific technique involves a researcher who goes into the field and chooses to identify herself or himself to the subjects; the researcher also becomes actively involved in the group's activities. The researcher has become a "participant observer." An example of this method would be a person who wanted to study a violent inner-city gang. The researcher might approach the gang's leadership, then identify himself and give reasons for studying the group. The researcher would also participate in the gang's meetings and

other activities. Perhaps a better approach, in this situation, would be to do everything described except participating in the group's activities, especially if the gang's activities were illegal or harmful to others. In that case, the researcher, who revealed his or her true identity to the group yet chose to play a passive, inactive role from a distance, would be considered a "nonparticipant observer."

An equally important field study technique involves concealing the identity of the researcher from the group that is being studied. In a classic study by John Howard Griffin described in the book *Black Like Me* (1962), Griffin colored his skin to take on the appearance of a black man. He then traveled throughout the American South, documenting his experiences, especially those involving race discrimination. This kind of activity is called covert research.

Conducting research in the field does not prevent the researcher from manipulating or altering the environment. In fact, it is a rather common occurrence for the "field" to be contrived. For example, a study on altruism might be designed for field experimentation. A scenario would be designed to discover what kind of person would come to the assistance of someone in need. The "need" could be helping to fix a flat tire or helping a lost child find his or her mother. In either case, since both scenarios occur infrequently in the real world and would be difficult to study, the setting would need to be staged. The ability to stage events opens the possibility of studying a variety of phenomena in a convenient context.

FIVE STEPS OF FIELD EXPERIMENTATION

Five steps need to be completed in field experimentation. First, an appropriate field must be selected. This is a crucial decision, because the quality of the research hinges on the vitality of the data collected. Second, specific methods and techniques (for example, nonparticipant observation) must be developed to ensure that the behaviors the experimenter wants to observe can occur. In addition, an attempt must be made to eliminate outside influences that might bias the research. Third, the data must be collected. Fourth, the data must be organized, analyzed, and interpreted. The fifth and final step is to report the study within an appropriate format—which might be either a journal article or a book. In order to show how these steps are implemented and how field experimentation can contribute to scientific knowledge, two examples will be explored in detail.

CULTURAL PERCEPTIONS OF TIME

In his article "The Pace of Life," published in *American Scientist* (1990), Robert Levine attempted to understand how different cultures perceived time. In his opinion, attitudes toward time could affect a society's pace of life and ultimately might lead to detrimental health problems for its members. Levine chose to collect data from the largest city in six different countries: Japan, Taiwan, Indonesia, Italy, England, and the United States. To gauge the general pace of life, he chose to study three unique indicators: the accuracy of outdoor bank clocks, the average time it took pedestrians to walk a distance of 100 feet (about 30.5 meters), and the time needed for a postal clerk to complete a transaction that entailed selling stamps and returning some change. None of these measures relies on subjective evaluations of the pace of life by the person collecting the data. Levine preferred these particular "objective" measures over a survey approach, which might have required subjects to respond to how they "feel" about the pace of life. He was more interested in direct measures of behavior as indicators of pace.

Standardized techniques were employed while collecting the data to ensure that the pace-of-life indicators would be measured fairly. For example, walking speed would not be measured if it were raining outside. Levine chose a covert approach, since he did not want subjects to be aware that they were in a study, thus eliminating any Hawthorne effect. In addition, both participant and nonparticipant observations were made. Measuring walking speed some distance away from a subject would be an example of nonparticipant observation. On the other hand, the purchasing of stamps on the part of the experimenter was an example of the participant observer technique.

The data were collected primarily by Levine's students, who visited the countries. The data were then analyzed via basic statistical procedures. The study revealed that Japan had the fastest pace of life of the six countries, scoring the highest on all three measures. The United States came in with the second-fastest pace, followed by England; Indonesia was last, having the slowest walkers and the most inaccurate clocks.

Levine extended this research by looking at associations between the pace of life and both psychological and physical health. He found that the tempo of a society is significantly related to the prevalence of heart disease. In fact, the time-related variables often turned out to be better predictors of heart disease than psychological measures which identify high-energy behaviors in individuals. He concluded that a person who chooses to live in a fast-paced city should take necessary precautions to keep from becoming a time-urgent person. Living in a busy and stressful city can lead to unhealthy behaviors such as smoking and poor eating habits.

PSYCHOLOGICAL LABELS

In another field study, David Rosenhan studied mental health professionals' ability to distinguish the "sane" from the "insane." Rosenhan later published the research in the article "On Being Sane in Insane Places" in *Science* (1973). He sent eight psychologically stable individuals to twelve different mental institutions to find out if they would be admitted as patients. Each "pseudopatient" went to an institution with an assumed name and a false occupation; this was necessary because three of the pseudopatients were psychologists and one was a psychiatrist, and they might be treated differently from other patients. The pseudopatients told the admitting staff that they had been hearing voices that appeared to say the words "hollow," "empty," and "thud." All pseudopatients were admitted and diagnosed as schizophrenic or manic-depressive. From the moment the pseudopatients gained entrance into the institutions, they began to act in a completely normal manner.

Rosenhan's study used both covert and participant observation techniques to collect the data. Field notes (the recorded behaviors and observations which make up the data of the field study) concerning the behavior of staff members were taken on a daily basis. Although Rosenhan was shocked that all of his assistants (as well as himself) were admitted, he was even more dismayed that the pseudopatients' "insanity" was never questioned by the staff. When the pseudopatients were observed writing their field notes, the behavior was interpreted by many of the staff members as paranoid and secretive.

The pseudopatients were released from the hospital between seven and fifty-two days later. Field studies, as this example indicates, can be filled with risks. None of the pseudopatients truly expected being admitted, let alone having to stay an average of nineteen days in the hospital before the mental health professionals declared them well enough to be released. Rosenhan's study was significant because it underscored the problem of distinguishing the normal from the abnormal with conventional diagnostic procedures. Rosenhan applied the results of this study to the broader issue of psychological labels. He pointed out that categorizing an individual with a particular mental illness can be misleading, and in many instances harmful. Rosenhan's pseudopatients were discharged with the label "schizophrenia in remission"—that is, according to the mental health workers, they had been relieved of their insanity, although perhaps only temporarily.

SOURCES FOR FURTHER STUDY

Baker, Therese L. *Doing Social Research.* 3d ed. New York: McGraw-Hill, 1998. Gives the reader a general introduction to field research, observational studies, data collection methods, survey research, sampling techniques, and other topics that will help the reader distinguish good field experiments from those that are poorly constructed.

Berg, Bruce Lawrence. *Qualitative Research Methods for the Social Sciences.* 4th ed. Boston: Allyn & Bacon, 2000. Discusses a field strategy used by anthropologists and sociologists to study groups of people. In addition, discusses the ethical issues that arise while conducting such research. The dangers of covert research are discussed; the book also provides the guidelines established by the National Research Act.

Griffin, John Howard. *Black Like Me.* 35th ed. New York: Signet, 1996. This excellent book, first published in 1962, is a narrative of the author's experiences traveling around the United States and observing how people react to him after he has taken on the appearance of a black man. This monumental field study, which contributed to the understanding of social prejudice, provides the reader with an excellent example of the significance of and need for conducting field research.

Levine, Robert V. "The Pace of Life." *American Scientist* 78 (September/October, 1990): 450-459. Levine describes his research on cross-cultural perspectives of time. Also describes research done within different regions of the United States.

Reason, Peter, and Hilary Bradbury. *Handbook of Action Research: Participative Inquiry and Practice.* Thousand Oaks, Calif.: Sage Publications, 2001. A handbook for carrying out participant-observation research.

Rosenhan, David Leonard. "On Being Sane in Insane Places." *Science* 179 (January 19, 1973): 250-258. Rosenhan describes his research on psychiatric facilities after he and his associates assumed the identity of psychiatric patients. An interesting and provocative example of field research, this paper also raises the question of the dangers of conducting covert research and the dangers inherent in psychological labels.

Singleton, Royce, Jr., Bruce C. Straits, M. M. Straits, and Ronald J. McAllister. *Approaches to Social Research.* 3d ed. New York: Oxford University Press, 1999. This well-written text discusses various aspects of field experimentation such as selecting a research setting, gathering information, how to get into the field, and when a field study should be adopted. The chapter "Experimentation" can be used to contrast "true" experiments with field studies.

Bryan C. Auday

SEE ALSO: Case-study methodologies; Data description; Experimentation: Ethics and participant rights; Hypothesis development and testing; Observational methods; Research ethics; Survey research: Questionnaires and interviews.

Field theory
Kurt Lewin

TYPE OF PSYCHOLOGY: Personality
FIELDS OF STUDY: Motivation theory; personality theory; social perception and cognition

Kurt Lewin's field theory maintains that behavior is a function of the life space, or psychological reality, of the individual. Individuals are motivated to reduce tensions that arise in this life space. Lewin's theory can be used to understand a wide range of everyday behavior and to suggest strategies for addressing social problems such as the reduction of prejudice and the resolution of social conflicts.

KEY CONCEPTS
- life space
- locomotion
- quasi-stationary equilibrium
- region of life space
- tension

INTRODUCTION

Kurt Lewin was a theorist of everyday life. His field theory attempts to explain people's everyday behavior, such as how a waiter remembers an order, what determines the morale and productivity of a work group, what causes intergroup prejudice, how a child encounters a new environment, or why people eat the foods that they do.

For Lewin, what determines everyday behavior is the "life space" of the individual. The life space represents the psychological reality of the individual; it is the totality of all psychological facts and social forces that influence an individual at a given time and place. For example, the life space of a child entering a novel domain is, for the most part, undifferentiated, and thus results in exploration on the part of the child. On the other hand, the life space of an employee at work may be well differentiated and populated with demands from the employer to produce more goods, from coworkers to follow a production norm, and from home for more income. There might, additionally, be physical needs to slow down.

EVOLUTION OF LEWIN'S THEORY

Field theory was born on the battlefields of World War I. Kurt Lewin served as a soldier in the German army. His first published article was titled "The War Landscape," and it described the battlefield in terms of life space. The soldier's needs determined how the landscape was to be perceived. When the soldier was miles from the front, the peaceful landscape seemed to stretch endlessly on all sides without direction. As the war front approached, the landscape took on direction and peaceful objects such as rocks and trees became elements of battle, such as weapons and places to hide.

After the war, Lewin took an academic appointment at the Psychological Institute of Berlin, where he served on the faculty with Gestalt psychologists Wolfgang Köhler and Max Wertheimer. While at the institute, Lewin further developed his field theory and conducted the first program of experimental social psychological research exploring topics such as memory for interrupted tasks, level of aspiration, and anger. His work derived as much from field theory as it did from his curiosity about the social world. For example, research on memory for interrupted tasks began when he and his students wondered why a waiter could remember their rather lengthy order but would forget it immediately after the food was served. In field theory terms, noncompleted tasks (such as the waiter's recall before delivering the order) were recalled better because they maintained a tension for completion compared to completed tasks, for which this tension is resolved.

As the Nazi Party rose to power in Germany, Lewin correctly perceived that his own Jewish life space and that of his family were becoming progressively more threatened and intolerable. Like many Jewish intellectuals of the time, Lewin emigrated to the United States; he obtained a number of visiting appointments until he established the Center for Group Dynamics at the Massachusetts Institute of Technology in 1944. Lewin's American research was much more applied than his work in Europe, and it concentrated particularly on social problems such as prejudice and intergroup conflict—perhaps as a result of his own experience of prejudice as a Jew in Germany.

Before his early death in 1947, Lewin helped train the first generation of American students interested in experimental social psychology, including such notables as Leon Festinger, Harold Kelley, Stanley Schachter, and Morton Deutsch. As a result, Lewin's intellectual legacy pervades the field of experimental social psychology. Today, first-, second-, third-, and even fourth-generation Lewinian social psychologists continue to carry on his research legacy by investigating topics of long-standing interest to Lewin such as prejudice, achievement, organizational behavior, social cognition, and the reduction of cognitive tensions or dissonance, and by attempting to explain how individuals construe their environments and how those environments affect behavior.

LIFE SPACE REGIONS

The concept of life space is usually divided into two parts: person and environment. These two parts can be differentiated further into regions. A region is any major part of the life space that can be distinguished from other parts and is separated by more or less permeable boundaries. For example, regions differentiated within the person might consist of needs, goals, hopes, and aspirations of the individual, whereas the differentiation of the environment might consist of profession, family, friendships, social norms, and taboos.

Locomotion, or behavior and change in the life space, is determined by the differentiation of regions in the life space and by the forces for change emanating from each region. Often, in any given life space, there are opposing or conflicting forces. For example, the boss may want to increase productivity as much as possible, whereas coworkers may seek to limit production to levels obtainable by all workers. According to Lewin, these tensions, or opposing social forces, provide the motivation for behavior and change in the life space. Tension can be resolved by any number of activities, including reconfiguring the life space either physically (for example, getting a new job) or mentally (for example, devaluing either the boss's or coworkers' opinions); performing a substitute task that symbolically reduces tension (for example, performing different tasks of value to the boss); or finding the "quasi-stationary equilibrium," or position where all opposing forces are equal in strength (for example, performing at a level between boss's and coworkers' recommendations).

COMPARISON WITH BEHAVIORISM AND PSYCHOANALYSIS

It is useful to compare Lewin's field theory with the two other major theories of the time: behaviorism and psychoanalysis. Lewin's field theory can be summarized by the equation $B = f(P,E)$, or, "Behavior is a function of person and environment." In other words, behavior is function of the life space of a total environment as perceived by the individual. In psychoanalytic thought, behavior is a function of the history of the individual. For example, past childhood experience is supposed to have a direct impact on current psychological processes. In contrast, Lewin's theory is ahistorical. Although the individual's past may influence that person's approach and construal of the psychological field, its influence is only indirect, as behavior is a function of the current and immediate life space.

Lewin's field theory differs from behaviorism on at least two key dimensions. First, Lewin emphasized the subjectivity of the psychological field. To predict and understand behavior successfully, a therapist needs to describe the situation from the viewpoint of the individual whose behavior is under consideration, not from the viewpoint of an observer. Second, Lewin's theory emphasizes that behavior must be understood as a function of the life space or situation as a whole. In other words, behavior is motivated by the multitude of often interdependent forces affecting an individual, as opposed to one or two salient rewards or reinforcers that may be present.

ROLE IN SOCIAL CHANGE

Kurt Lewin's field theory has had many applications, particularly in the area of social change. Lewin's approach to solving social problems was first to specify in as much detail as possible, the life space of the individual involved. Next, he would identify the social forces affecting the individual. Finally, Lewin would experiment with changing these social forces or adding new ones to enact social change. Two applications of field theory performed by Lewin and his associates serve as good examples. One deals with changing food preferences, and the other with the reduction of intergroup conflicts and prejudice.

During World War II, there was a shortage of meat, an important protein source, in the United States. As part of the war effort, Lewin was assigned the task of convincing Americans to eat sweetbreads—certain organ meats, which many Americans find unappetizing—to maintain protein levels. Lewin began by first describing the consumption channel, or how food reaches a family's table. At the time, housewives obtained food from either a garden or a grocery store and then moved it to the table by purchasing it, transporting it home, storing it in an icebox or pantry, and then preparing it. At each step, Lewin identified forces that prevented the gatekeeper—in this case, the housewife—from serving sweetbreads. Such forces might have included the belief that family members would not eat sweetbreads, inexperience with the selection and preparation of sweetbreads, or inherently distasteful aspects of the food.

In attempting to remove and redirect these forces, Lewin experimented with two approaches, one successful and the other not. In the unsuccessful case, Lewin presented housewives with a lecture detailing the problems of nutrition during the war and stating ways of overcoming obstacles in serving sweetbreads; he discussed ways to prepare sweetbreads, provided recipes, and indicated that other women had successfully served sweetbreads for their families with little complaint. Only 3 percent of the housewives hearing this lecture served sweetbreads. From Lewin's perspective, such a lecture was ineffective because it did not involve the audience and arouse the level of tension needed to produce change. Lewin's second method was a group discussion. The housewives were asked to discuss how they could persuade "housewives like themselves" to serve sweetbreads. This led to a discussion of the obstacles that the housewife might encounter, along with ways of overcoming these obstacles (just as in the lecture). Such a discussion was effective because it created tension for the housewife: "I just told everyone why they should and how they could eat sweetbreads, and I am not currently serving them myself." After this group discussion, 32 percent (an almost elevenfold increase) of the housewives involved served sweetbreads.

CONFLICT AND PREJUDICE

Lewin approached the problem of intergroup conflict and racial prejudice by describing the life spaces of the members of the conflicting parties. For example, Lewin saw the life space of many minority group members (such as religious and racial minorities) as full of obstacles and barriers which restrict movement in the life space. The life space of the majority member often consigned the minority member to a small and rigidly bounded region (for example, a ghetto). By isolating minority group members, majority group members can develop unrealistic perceptions or stereotypes of the out-group. Such life spaces are very likely to result in intergroup conflict.

The field theory analysis of racial prejudice suggests that one way to reduce intergroup conflict is to remove obstacles and increase the permeability of intergroup barriers. In the later part of his career, Lewin established the Commission on Community Interrelations as a vehicle for discovering ways of removing intergroup barriers. Lewin and his colleagues discovered some of the following successful techniques for promoting intergroup harmony: enacting laws that immediately removed barriers, such as racial quotas limiting the number of Jews who could attend certain universities; immediate hiring of blacks as sales personnel, thereby increasing the permeability of intergroup boundaries by making contact between group members more likely; responding directly to racial slurs with a calm appeal based on American traditions and democracy to provide a countervailing force to the slur; promoting meetings of warring groups in a friendly atmosphere as a means of breaking down group boundaries; and immediately integrating housing as a successful way of promoting racial harmony.

SOURCES FOR FURTHER STUDY

De Rivera, Joseph, comp. *Field Theory as Human-Science: Contributions of Lewin's Berlin Group.* New York: Gardner Press, 1976. An English translation of research conducted by Lewin and his students when Lewin was at the University of Berlin.

Lewin, Kurt. *A Dynamic Theory of Personality.* New York: McGraw-Hill, 1935. Lewin's first major English work, consisting of a translation of many of his first papers published in Germany.

_____. "Group Decision and Social Change." In *Readings in Social Psychology*, edited by Theodore M. Newcomb and Eugene L. Hartley. New York: Henry Holt, 1947. Describes how Lewin changed food preferences during World War II, providing an excellent example of how to apply field theory to practical problems.

_____. *Resolving Social Conflicts; and, Field Theory in Social Science.* Washington, D.C.: American Psychological Association, 1997. A reprint of two of Lewin's most influential works, collecting his major papers discussing practical problems of modern society such as prejudice and group conflict. Provides excellent examples of how to apply field theory to social problems.

Marrow, Alfred Jay. *The Practical Theorist: The Life and Work of Kurt Lewin.* New York: Basic Books, 1969. This definitive biography of Lewin, written by one of his students, describes the life of Lewin and provides a glimpse of the personality behind field theory.

Wheelan, Susan A., Emmy A. Pepitone, and Vicki Abt, eds. *Advances in Field Theory.* Thousand Oaks, Calif.: Sage Publications, 1991. A collection of essays addressing issues in field theory such as managing social conflict, self-help groups, field theory and the construction of social problems, and academic sex discrimination.

Anthony R. Pratkanis and Marlene E. Turner

SEE ALSO: Achievement motivation; Cognitive dissonance; Cooperation, competition, and negotiation; Group decision making; Groups; Motivation; Prejudice reduction; Thought: Inferential.

Fight-or-flight response

TYPE OF PSYCHOLOGY: Biological bases of behavior; emotion; stress

FIELDS OF STUDY: Biology of stress; critical issues in stress; general constructs and issues

The fight-or-flight response describes a physiological reaction that occurs when one is confronted with a stimulus which is perceived as threatening. It may be considered the alarm phase of the body's reaction to a stressor. It is an adaptive response and becomes pathological only if it occurs when there is no obvious threatening stimulus or when it continues over a long period of time.

KEY CONCEPTS
- adrenal glands
- autonomic nervous system
- homeostasis
- hypothalamus
- parasympathetic nervous system
- stress
- sympathetic nervous system

INTRODUCTION

In his classic book *The Wisdom of the Body* (1932), American physiologist Walter B. Cannon introduced the term "fight-or-flight" to describe the physiological (or bodily) reaction that occurs when humans or animals are confronted with something that they see as threatening. He was also the first person to use the word "stress," a term borrowed from engineering, to describe situations or responses to situations perceived as threatening.

Perhaps the best way to illustrate the fight-or-flight response is to look at common animals. It can be seen in cats or dogs: The hair on the back of their necks stands up and they may take a position which indicates they are ready to fight. This is the "Halloween cat" stance, with the back arched, hair standing on end, spitting and hissing and in general trying to look threatening; it is the dog growling,

head lowered, eyes narrowed, feet planted wide, ready to take on the enemy. Alternatively, the animal simply runs: it is the puppy or kitten racing away from something frightening, leaving a trail of urine behind it. This is fight-or-flight at its most obvious.

In humans, the fight-or-flight response is usually less obvious, but it contains most, if not all, of the same physiological reactions. The heart pounds, the blood rushes to the muscles to prepare to fight or run, sweating begins, and the bowels may actual loosen. Maxims referring to persons being so frightened that they wet themselves actually describe part of the physiological reaction that occurs during the fight-or-flight response. Further, one may feel a strange feeling on the back of one's neck. This is piloerection, which is the scientific name for the hair on the back of the neck standing up. If one is unaware of what is causing the sensation, it can make what is already stressful even more so.

BASIC BIOLOGY

In order to understand the fight-or-flight response, it is necessary to review some of the basic biology of the nervous system. In the nineteenth century, French physiologist Claude Bernard first proposed the idea that there was a need for a stable internal environment even as external conditions change. Cannon further developed this idea in his book *The Wisdom of the Body*, and proposed the concept of negative feedback as the mechanism for maintaining homeostasis (which means "same-staying, or physiological equilibrium") in the body.

The nervous system of all vertebrates is composed of two major divisions, the central nervous system (CNS) and the peripheral nervous system (PNS). The CNS consists of the brain and spinal cord, everything encased in bone. The PNS is everything else, all the motor and sensory nerves in the body outside of the brain and spinal cord. The PNS is further divided into two parts, the skeletal (also called somatic) system, which controls voluntary muscle movement for the most part, and the autonomic nervous system, which for the most part mediates involuntary activity in the body. The autonomic nervous system is divided further into the parasympathetic division, which is what maintains homeostasis, operating to keep the body, including internal organs, in a mode that allows it to "rest and digest," terms introduced by Cannon at the same time as he introduced "fight-or-flight." The parasympathetic nervous system maintains the basal heart rate, respiration, and metabolism under normal conditions. This is the opposite of the sympathetic nervous system, which reacts to anything perceived as stressful or threatening and is responsible for getting the body ready to stand or run, fight or flee.

The body needs to be able to react to changes in either the internal or external environment. These may be anything from blood loss from an accident or injury, running a marathon, changes in temperature, emotional stress, or an earthquake, or hearing an unexplained noise in the night. In fact, although people sometimes say that they wish they did not react to stress, it has been demonstrated experimentally that animals that lack stress responses require special care to stay alive. The fight-or-flight response is, therefore, a very adaptive reaction, and becomes pathological only when it goes on for long periods of time or when it happens when there is nothing to precipitate it.

Cannon first recognized that the sympathetic and parasympathetic nervous divisions had different functions, although the two divisions actually work together most of the time. It may seem as if they are pulling in opposite directions, but there is a balance between the two systems resulting from an interaction between what is going on inside the body and what is going on in the environment. The body needs a certain amount of tension between the two systems to maintain the correct balance of arousal and relaxation (homeostasis) under normal circumstances.

A good example of how the two systems work together, and how one can be more active than the other at any given time, is the situation of a person sitting quietly in the living room, reading a book after eating dinner. During this time, the parasympathetic nerves have slowed the heart rate and the digestive system has become active. The nerves mediating the sympathetic nervous system are not inactive, but the parasympathetic is "in control." If the motion-sensor-controlled light outside the house were suddenly to come on and the person in the living room were to see a figure standing outside the window, the sympathetic nervous system would react, within one or two seconds. The digestion would slow down, the heart rate increase, the blood diverted from the skin and digestive organs and rush

to the muscles and brain. The person would begin to breathe harder in order to make more oxygen available, the mouth would get dry, the pupils of the eyes dilate (letting more light in for better sight), and the sweat glands become more active, getting ready to cool the body during its coming activity—either fighting or running. When the figure turns and the person realizes it is a neighbor retrieving a wayward cat, the parasympathetic system resumes control. Heart rate slows and pupils return to normal.

BRAIN ACTIVITY

The fight-or-flight response is mediated by the hypothalamus, which is very small (about only 4 grams of the approximately 1,400 grams a normal adult brain weighs), but a very important group of nuclei (groups of nerve cells, or neurons, which are functionally related) deep in the brain. The hypothalamus integrates the functions of the autonomic nervous system, both the parasympathetic and the sympathetic divisions, via the pituitary gland and ascending and descending fibers which pass through it, connecting the brain with the rest of the body, including the internal organs.

When the brain perceives a threatening stimulus, whether it is something that one assesses cognitively (such as realizing that one is being attacked verbally) or something that suddenly appears and to which one reacts reflexively (such as being confronted by a bear or a snake in the wild), a cascade of events begins. It may be that by the time the actual physiological reaction takes place, one would have already started to respond, protecting oneself from the bear, for instance, or confronting the person who is attacking. There are hierarchical neural pathways from the sensory receptors that send messages to the brain. Some messages travel through the thalamus—an important area deep within the brain for sending and receiving messages between the brain and the environment—and up to the cortex so appropriate action can be taken. Simultaneously, messages are also sent via the thalamus to the hypothalamus (which contains many nuclei that actually control the autonomic nervous system) and the frontal cortex, passing through the amygdala (a part of the brain important in remembering emotional responses to previous occurrences) and the hippocampus (a part of the brain known to be important in forming memories).

If these brain systems concur that there is a threatening stimulus, the hypothalamus initiates a cascade of events that activates the sympathetic portion of the autonomic nervous system, and the fight-or-flight response begins within one or two seconds. Thus, the hypothalamus sends a chemical signal to the pituitary gland causing it to release adrenocorticotropic hormone (ACTH) and also activates the adrenal glands (a set of glands, one of which sits on top of each kidney). Before a person can even begin cognitively processing what has happened, the adrenal medulla, the center of the adrenal gland, has begun to secrete epinephrine (also known as adrenaline), norepinephrine, and steroid stress hormones called glucocorticoids. The substances secreted by the pituitary and adrenal medulla are distributed systemically, which means they are blood-borne. They take longer to reach their destinations than messages traveling along neural pathways, which explains why people can slam on their brakes at the sight of an oncoming car within seconds, and then notice that they are shaking and their heart is pounding minutes later.

Pathological Manifestations

Although the fight-or-flight response is an appropriate reaction to many threatening stimuli, there are times when people report all the symptoms of the fight-or-flight response when there are no threatening stimuli. People who describe panic attacks will often describe all the physiological signs of fight-or-flight, including racing heart, dry mouth, disturbed bowel function, and increased breathing (sometimes even hyperventilation). Panic attacks can be very unnerving. People who experience them are usually unaware of what is causing the feelings they are experiencing and may think they are having a heart attack. Evidence suggests that panic attacks have a genetic component, with family history suggesting it is carried on a single dominant gene.

The fight-or-flight response may be considered to correspond to the first, or alarm, phase of the general adaptation syndrome described by Hans Selye in 1956. When the fight-or-flight response (or alarm phase) is not quickly resolved so that the body is returned to homeostasis, with the parasympathetic division of the autonomic nervous system regaining control, the body then progresses into the second, or resistance phase, and then on to exhaustion. The long-term release of corticosteroids can be harmful to the body because every cell in the body has receptors for them. This is good in the short run, during the fight-or-flight or alarm phase, because these hormones help the body to use glucose for energy more efficiently, among other effects. However, continued production of corticosteroids has been associated with disruption of the immune system, high blood pressure, and other cardiovascular illnesses.

Sources for Further Study

Bloom, Floyd E., and Arlyn Lazerson. *Brain, Mind, and Behavior.* New York: W. H. Freeman, 1988. This is a textbook of physiological psychology, which describes fight-or-flight, and many other facets of brain-mind interaction. This is a very easy-to-understand book which the average reader would find accessible even without background knowledge of anatomy.

Carlson, Neil R. *Physiology of Behavior.* Boston: Allyn & Bacon, 1998. An advanced textbook of physiological psychology that describes in greater depth how the anatomy of the brain and how it mediates behavior in many situations. Suitable for someone with a background in psychology or biology.

Kandel, Eric R., James H. Schwartz, and Thomas M. Jessell, eds. *Principles of Neural Science.* New York: McGraw-Hill, 2000. This book, coedited by Nobel Prize winner Eric Kandel, is considered to be the bible of neuroscience and is used by many graduate schools and some undergraduate. This text contains the most in-depth discussion of the complete anatomy of the stress response, from fight-or-flight through pathological results of long-term stress.

Kolb, Bryan, and Ian Whishaw. *An Introduction to Brain and Behavior.* New York: Worth, 2001. The authors of this textbook previously wrote one of the most popular texts for the study of clinical psychology. In this introductory text, easy and enjoyable to read, they have incorporated clinical examples of nearly every concept they cover, making it much more interesting to beginning students of the physiology of behavior.

Gayle L. Brosnan-Watters

See also: Adrenal gland; Aggression; Behaviorism; Brain structure; Cannon, Walter B.; General adaptation syndrome; Selye, Hans; Stress: Physiological responses.

Forensic psychology

TYPE OF PSYCHOLOGY: Motivation; personality; psychological methodologies

FIELDS OF STUDY: Behavioral and cognitive models; interpersonal relations; models of abnormality; motivation theory; personality assessment

Forensic psychology is the study of psychology pertaining to the law. It specifically examines issues of competency, deviant and criminal behavior, courtroom practices, prediction of future criminal behavior, psychological profiling of criminal offenders, and correctional practices of rehabilitation.

KEY CONCEPTS
- competency
- correctional practices of rehabilitation
- courtroom practices
- criminal behavior
- prediction of future criminal behavior
- profiling of criminal offenders

INTRODUCTION

Forensic psychology is the practice of psychology as it pertains to aspects of the law. The specific functions of forensic psychology are multifaceted; however, they are dominated by participation in the criminal justice system. The legislative process of the proposal and passage of laws acknowledges and identifies behavior that society has determined to be inappropriate. Persons who choose to perform behavior that falls outside societally determined parameters are considered deviant and commonly criminal. It is this set of behaviors and the persons who commit the behaviors that are the subject of the study of forensic psychology. Specific activities and concerns of this field of study include competency, the prediction of future behavior of convicted criminals and the profiling of the unknown criminal offender.

COMPETENCY

Prior to the recognition of forensic psychology as a specific discipline of psychology, the determination of competency was a criminal justice activity of psychologists and psychiatrists. Historically, psychologists and psychiatrists have been utilized by the courts to issue professional opinions pertaining to the competency of persons brought before the court. The earliest determinations of competency were associated with persons whose mental capacities to make rational decisions were impaired by age, disability, and/or injury. To determine the validity of claims that a person was incompetent to make rational decisions for himself or herself and was in need of assistance and guardianship in decision making, the courts referred these individuals for examination and determination to psychologists and psychiatrists. Upon a determination of incompetence, the court would appoint a relative to serve as a guardian of the incompetent person. This guardian would assume legal responsibility for the estate and person of the individual deemed incompetent. Forensic psychologists and psychiatrists continue to perform these types of competency determinations today and are critical to the activities of juvenile and probate courts.

Forensic psychologists and psychiatrists also perform critical competency functions for the criminal courts. Since the M'Naghten decision in the 1800's in England, the courts have struggled with determining whether individuals afflicted with mental health disorders and intelligence deficiencies should be held accountable for their criminal behavior. Defense attorneys argue that their clients afflicted with deficiencies in mental health and intelligence should not be held accountable for their alleged criminal conduct. Persons afflicted with certain mental illnesses do not have a reality perspective that allows them the ability to discriminate between lawful and unlawful behavior. Individuals who have reduced intellectual capacity do not possess the ability to understand right from wrong and cannot appreciate the consequences of their actions. Attorneys also argue (and the law recognizes) that children cannot be compared with adults and consequently cannot completely appreciate the consequences of their behavior and should not be held accountable in the same ways that adults are held accountable for their behaviors.

The Sixth Amendment to the United States Constitution guarantees the rights of due process, which include the right to assist in one's own defense. Persons who, because of age, mental illness, or diminished intellectual capacity, are not capable of assisting in their own defense, and consequently, their defense counsels argue that they should not be prosecuted. Numerous challenges to this amendment have resulted in appellate decisions that have influenced judicial procedure. The judicial system is administrated by attorneys who are not clinically trained or qualified to make determinations regarding whether or not a defendant was competent at the time of the offense or at the time of the trial. Courts appoint forensic psychologists and psychiatrists to determine whether the defendant was competent at the time of the offense and whether the defendant is competent to stand trial.

If an individual is determined to have been competent at the time of the offense, an insanity defense is not acceptable to the court. If an individual is determined to be competent at the time of the trial, then the court will proceed with the trial. If the individual is determined to be incompetent at the time of the trial and incapable of assisting in his or her own defense, then the defendant is remanded to a psychiatric facility until it is determined that he or she is sufficiently competent to assist in the defense, at which time the trial will commence.

John W. Hinckley, Jr., was found to be incompetent at the time of his attempted assassination of President Ronald Reagan in 1981, and consequently was acquitted of the charge and remanded to a psychiatric facility until the point in time that he was found to be sane. The Hinckley determination of incompetence initiated a national legislative movement to modify the state statutes pertaining to findings of "not guilty by reason of insanity." As of 2002, most states had modified their laws pertaining to competency and at least two states have completely abolished the insanity defense.

Appellate courts are inundated with appeals of convictions and sentences by defendants who have been found to be too young, too old, or too intellectually deficient to understand the consequences of their acts. Several states have determined that persons determined to be clinically retarded cannot be executed because of their inability to understand the relationship between their criminal behavior and the consequence of execution, a position affirmed by the U.S. Supreme Court in 2002. Competency is a contemporary criminal justice issue that requires the involvement of forensic psychology.

PREDICTION OF FUTURE CRIMINAL BEHAVIOR
Following the initial utilization of forensic psychology in determinations of competency, the next step was the prediction of future criminal behavior. Forensic psychologists and psychiatrists have been uti-

lized in the process of making parole decisions as long as parole boards have been determining the early release of inmates.

The length of incarceration for a crime, established in states' criminal codes, is commonly a range of years with a minimum and a maximum. Judges and prosecutors utilize this range of years in plea bargaining and in consideration of mitigating circumstances. Prior to sentencing to a term of incarceration, a pre-sentence investigation is conducted on the convicted defendant. Pre-sentence investigations commonly include psychological evaluations performed by forensic psychologists and psychiatrists. These evaluations contain recommendations for therapeutic interventions and predictions of future criminal behavior.

Similarly, forensic psychologists and psychiatrists conduct evaluations on incarcerated inmates who have met their minimum lengths of sentence. These evaluations are intended to ascertain the effectiveness of the period of incarceration and whether it is safe to release the inmate back to the community. If the evaluator recommends early release, then a list of parole conditions intended to assist in success on parole is commonly attached to the recommendation.

Forensic psychologists have conducted empirical research that has successfully precipitated the development of statistically reliable recidivism prediction instruments that are utilized in sentencing and diversion.

PROFILING UNKNOWN CRIMINAL OFFENDERS
The Federal Bureau of Investigation (FBI) initiated the Violent Criminal Apprehension Program (ViCAP) in the mid-1980's with the objective of collecting demographic, personal, and behavioral data on violent offenses and offenders. Prior to the ViCAP initiative, there was no central depository of data on violent offenses committed in the United States; consequently, it was impossible for law enforcement agencies to share information. Persons committing violent crimes in different jurisdictions and particularly in different states had the advantage over law enforcement agencies because of the lack of a central depository. Shortly after the FBI began to serve as the central depository, law enforcement agencies began to contact ViCAP personnel, asking them to search the database for crimes committed in other jurisdictions that were similar to ones committed in their jurisdictions.

In response to these inquiries, the FBI special agents in charge of ViCAP began to consult with law enforcement agencies with unsolved violent crimes. These consulting activities resulted in the formal formation of the Behavioral Sciences Unit of the FBI as a consulting agency on unsolved violent crimes. The Behavioral Sciences Unit of the FBI achieved national notoriety with the release of the movie *Silence of the Lambs* (1991), which depicts the FBI's involvement in the identification and apprehension of a serial killer. The psychological aspects of criminal investigation were clearly exposed in this movie, which was the single most significant contribution to society's infatuation with the forensic sciences and particularly forensic psychology.

There is a significant relationship between criminal investigation and psychology. This relationship is easy to understand because criminal behavior is behavior first and criminal second. If one considers that behavior is learned, or precipitated by a stimulus or a motive, then crime can be evaluated like any other behavior. It has been empirically demonstrated that no one variable is directly correlated with criminal behavior, but rather criminal behavior is caused by many variables, and that individuals commit crime because of their unique relationship to the precipitating variables. Consequently, the physical evidence procured at a crime scene provides criminal investigators not only with fingerprints, deoxyribonucleic acid (DNA), and modus operandi but also with clues to the psychological profile of the offender. Individuals afflicted with clinically different personality disorders and mental illnesses may commit the same legally classified crime, but the manner in which they perform the crime will differ and the physical evidence will demonstrate these differences. Persons who commit sexual assaults do so in a fashion that meets their own dysfunctional needs. The characteristics of the victim as well as the manner in which the assault was inflicted are indicative of the perpetrator's psychological disturbances. Analysis of the physical evidence for psychological clues assists criminal investigators in delineating the suspect group.

OTHER FORENSIC PSYCHOLOGY FUNCTIONS

Forensic psychology is utilized in a variety of other functions pertaining to the law. Forensic psychologists conduct interviews and evaluations pertaining to the abuse and neglect of dependent children, adoptions, and domestic violence. Forensic psychologists are also retained by lawyers to assist in the selection of jurors for jury trials, preparation of witnesses, and proper and influential courtroom decorum.

SOURCES FOR FURTHER STUDY

American Psychiatric Association. *Diagnostic and Statistical Manual of Mental Disorders: DSM-IV-TR.* Rev. 4th ed. Washington, D.C.: Author, 2000. The DSM-IV-TR is the most comprehensive and authoritative description of mental health and personality disorders.

Bartol, Curt. *Criminal Behavior: A Psychosocial Approach.* Upper Saddle River, N.J.: Prentice Hall, 2002. The author summarizes the theories, concepts, and practices of forensic psychology.

Dobbert, Duane, ed. *Forensic Psychology.* Columbus, Ohio: McGraw-Hill Primus, 1996. The editor compiles significant contributions from distinguished authors on a variety of topics pertaining to forensic psychology.

Goode, Erich. *Deviant Behavior.* Upper Saddle River, N.J.: Prentice Hall, 1997. The author provides an excellent description of deviant behavior.

Wrightsman, Lawrence. *Forensic Psychology.* Belmont, Calif.: Wadsworth, 2001. This undergraduate/ graduate level textbook is a comprehensive discussion of the practice of forensic psychology.

Duane L. Dobbert

SEE ALSO: Abnormality: Legal models; Confidentiality; Cultural competence; Eyewitness testimony; Incompetency; Insanity defense; Law and psychology; Psychology: Fields of specialization.

Forgetting and forgetfulness

TYPE OF PSYCHOLOGY: Memory
FIELDS OF STUDY: Cognitive processes

Forgetting is one of the many puzzling aspects of memory, and various theories have tried to explain it in different ways; among the proposed theories are the concepts of memory decay, interference, and purposeful forgetting. One approach describes different types of forgetting as by-products of otherwise desirable, adaptive features of memory.

Key concepts
- absentmindedness
- bias
- blocking
- decay
- encoding
- interference
- misattribution
- persistence
- purposeful, or intentional, forgetting
- retrieval
- suggestibility
- tip-of-the-tongue phenomenon
- transience

Introduction

The mysteries of remembering and forgetting have fascinated humankind for hundreds, even thousands, of years. In the late nineteenth century, memory was one of the areas of interest to early psychologists such as Hermann Ebbinghaus and William James. Ebbinghaus conducted an experiment in 1885 in which he tested his own memory; he graphed a "forgetting curve," illustrating how much information on a particular list he forgot over time. William James wrote about the "tip-of-the-tongue" phenomenon in 1890, evocatively describing the gap that exists in the place of a name one is trying to recall as "intensely active" and containing the "wraith of the name" beckoning within it.

Though often reliable—and, at times, astoundingly accurate—human memory is fallible. Daniel Schacter, a prominent cognitive psychologist, has referred to this duality as "memory's fragile power." Memory's power is evident in what it makes possible in one's everyday life: a sense of personal history, knowledge of countless facts and subtle concepts, and learning and mastery of complex skills. The fragile side of memory is also quite apparent, in both mundane and dramatic ways. Most people struggle to remember the names of others they have just met or of those they have not seen for some time. People forget events rapidly or gradually; even wonderful memories seem to fade in time. The past is distorted with sometimes surprising results that belie strongly held beliefs or deep-seated feelings.

Physical Causes of Forgetting

Research on the causes of memory failure has examined normal forgetting and the more malignant memory loss seen, for example, in Alzheimer's disease. Head injuries, for example, can cause difficulties remembering certain information after an accident. In cases of brain tumor, when certain parts of the brain are removed, aspects of memory may be irreparably lost. Alcoholics who drink heavily for many years frequently encounter difficulties remembering; this condition is sometimes termed Korsakoff's syndrome. Those who use drugs may also experience memory impairment; actual brain damage may occur in such cases. Older people with Alzheimer's disease or other types of dementia have trouble remembering. Strokes or internal injuries can also cause memory loss, as can epilepsy; during an epileptic seizure, oxygen is not getting to the brain, a condition that may result in brain damage and memory loss. Aging itself seems to affect memory retrieval, but the reasons are not completely understood; changes in brain physiology and diminished care, concern, or motivation are all possible factors.

It is not known exactly how people learn or why they remember or forget. Some psychologists posit that the brain's chemical makeup and activity (particularly involving those substances known as neurotransmitters) are central to learning and remembering; others contend that the brain's electrical activity is crucial in determining one's memory. If there is either a chemical or an electrical abnormality in the brain, people may have difficulties in learning or in recalling information and events that have been learned. With newer methodologies for brain scanning, including such noninvasive procedures as nuclear magnetic resonance (NMR) imaging, positron emission tomography (PET) scanning, and computer tomography (CT) scanning, researchers may be better able to probe various physiological reasons for forgetting. With functional magnetic resonance imaging (fMRI) it is possible to track changes in brain activity as someone, for example, attempts to remember a past event.

Theories of Normal Forgetting

One theory of forgetting holds that "forgotten" material was never learned in the first place. In other words, the information was never encoded. Another possibility is that such little importance was attached to the material that it was poorly learned—or encoded—and was subsequently forgotten. Sometimes people are overwhelmed by the sheer amount of information they must learn and are simply incapable of remembering the massive amount of material.

Another theory about forgetting suggests that material is never really forgotten; rather, one cannot find the key to retrieve the information from the brain's filing system—its long-term memory. Nearly everyone has experienced the tip-of-the-tongue phenomenon (one sees someone at a party, for example, and cannot quite remember the person's name). Sometimes concentration aids memory retrieval; often association helps the process. Psychologists have also noted primacy and recency effects regarding memory; that is, one remembers what is learned first and what is learned last most efficiently. Material that is presented in the middle tends to be more easily forgotten.

In William James's "booming, buzzing confusion," one frequently is unable to process adequately all the information encountered; forgetting of some information is necessary. Moreover, one must often replace existing information with new information, as when a friend or family member relocates and acquires a new address and telephone number. Research on directed forgetting has shown that one is able to deal more effectively with large amounts of information by following instructions to treat some of the information as "to be forgotten." In this way, interference is reduced and one is able to devote all of one's resources to the remaining to-be-remembered information.

Other theories of normal forgetting attempt to explain the ways in which various types of interference affect one's ability to remember material. If one is taking classes at nine, ten, and eleven in the morning, for example, one may have difficulty remembering material because the information from each of the three classes interferes with that of the other classes; this will be especially true if the subject matter is similar. This same process can affect memories of everything from motion pictures to events in one's own life. The greater the number of similar films or events (such as dinners in the same type of restaurant) there have been, the more interference there may be. There are two types of interference, retroactive and proactive interference. In proactive interference, occurrences that come before an event or learning situation interfere with one's ability to learn or remember; in retroactive interference, the occurrence that interferes with remembering comes after the event or learning situation.

One's mental state, according to many psychologists, has much to do with one's ability to learn, retain, and recall information. If one is suffering from grief or loss, one's ability to remember will be severely impaired. Children who are abused often have difficulties learning and remembering since they are preoccupied with the worries and concerns caused by their traumatic home situation. People suffering from depression also may have problems remembering. Counseling or therapy will sometimes alleviate a person's emotional concerns and therefore result in better recall. Emotional problems that may be helped in this way include depression, anxiety, and fear of failure.

There has been debate among psychologists as to whether information stored in long-term memory is stored there permanently. Some memory theorists believe that a decay or fading factor is at work when one forgets information. That is, memory traces naturally fade away and are lost simply because of the passage of time. If one is a freshman in college, one may remember many members of one's senior class in high school very well. In another ten years, however, one may be less able to remember one's classmates and may have forgotten some of those with whom one had only superficial friendships. In twenty years, more information will fade unless one actively tries to rehearse or review the people who were in the class. For example, if one takes out one's high school yearbook every June for twenty years and reminisces about the people in it, one will better be able to recall the names at a twenty-fifth high school reunion.

Some theorists believe that if one can link or associate people, places, or events with other things, one may be able to recall past people or events more effectively. This theory holds that people's minds normally tend to associate one thing with another. These "associationistic" theories are based on the idea that bonds are formed in the brain between places or bits of information. If the bonds are inadequately or poorly formed, then forgetting may occur; bonds must periodically be reformed to guard against forgetting.

The psychoanalytic (or Freudian) perspective on forgetting emphasizes the idea that people "forget" events that are emotionally traumatic. This is motivated, or purposeful, forgetting; the Freudian term for it is "repression." An example would be a woman who, as a six-year-old girl, had been sexually molested by her father or another relative and who has since forgotten the incident. Interestingly, repression has been known to occur in both victims and perpetrators of violent crimes.

FORGETTING AS A BY-PRODUCT OF AN ADAPTIVE SYSTEM

In *The Seven Sins of Memory: How the Mind Forgets and Remembers* (2001), Daniel Schacter presents a framework for classifying the various ways memory fails. He reviews decades of research evidence from social, cognitive, and clinical psychology, as well as more recent work using imaging methods that make it possible, for example, to observe changes in brain activity as someone retrieves previously learned information. Schacter suggests that like the biblical seven deadly sins—pride, anger, envy, greed, gluttony, lust, and sloth—the seven sins of memory occur frequently in everyday life.

Memory's seven sins are transience, absentmindedness, blocking, misattribution, suggestibility, bias, and persistence. The first three are different types of forgetting. Transience involves decreasing accessibility of information, with recent evidence indicating that forgetting over time is best described mathematically as a power function; that is, the rate of forgetting slows down with the passage of time. Absentmindedness results from inattentive or shallow processing of information that in turn causes weak memories of ongoing events, such as forgetting where one recently placed an object. When absentminded lapses involve forgetting to carry out a planned action at some time in the future, such as picking up the dry cleaning on the way home from work, they are referred to as failures of prospective memory. Blocking refers to the temporary inaccessibility of information that is stored in memory. The tip-of-tongue phenomenon is a commonly experienced example of blocking; the incidence of this type of blocking appears to increase with aging.

The next three sins involve distortion or inaccuracy of memory. Misattribution occurs when one attributes a recollection or idea to the wrong source, such as recalling having read something in the newspaper when, in fact, one heard it on the radio. Another type of misattribution occurs when people falsely recall or recognize items or events that never happened. Suggestibility refers to memories that are implanted, for example, as a result of leading questions during attempts to elicit recall of past events.

This phenomenon is closely related to the controversy concerning false and recovered memories of childhood sexual abuse. Bias occurs when memories of previous experiences are influenced or distorted by current knowledge, beliefs, or expectations or by present mood and emotional states. A number of studies have identified a consistency bias in retrospection: People's recollections tend to exaggerate the degree of similarity between their past and present feelings, attitudes, or beliefs.

The final sin, persistence, refers to intrusive recollections of traumatic events or obsessional thinking about negative symptoms and events or chronic fears. In other words, these are memories that people wish they could forget but cannot. Just as current feelings can distort recollections of past events or emotions, they can also increase the likelihood of persistence; for instance, memories whose affective tone matches one's current mood are more accessible.

Schacter asserts that it is wrong to view the seven sins as flaws in the design of the human memory system. Rather, they should be thought of as by-products of what he calls "otherwise adaptive features of memory." Consider, for example, what would happen without blocking, the sin whereby information is temporarily inaccessible due to some inhibitory process. In a system without blocking, all information that is potentially relevant to what is sought would invariably and rapidly come to mind. The likely result would be massive confusion.

WAYS TO MINIMIZE FORGETTING

Two different types of tests are used to assess memory and learning; one type tests recognition, while the other tests recall. A multiple-choice test assesses the first type of memory, because in this type of test one needs to recognize the correct answer when one sees it. An essay examination tests recall—all the responsibility is on the learner to recall as much relevant information as possible.

Research on memory and forgetting can be applied in both academic and nonacademic settings. There are a number of things one can do to aid learning and protect against forgetting. Overlearning is one tactic that ensures that one has learned material and will remember it later. In this technique, a student repeats the material by rehearsing it in his or her head to ensure later recall. If one needs to learn a formula, one may repeat it over and over—perhaps writing it a hundred times. This can be tedious, which undoubtedly spurred the search for other options to learn and remember more effectively. Constant review is another strategy. In spaced practice, students study materials to be learned for one hour each night before the test. These students seem to remember the material better than those who spend eight hours studying the material the night before the test. (That type of study—"cramming"—is called massed practice.) For some students, cramming does work, but the material is easily forgotten following its use immediately after the cramming session. Cramming also creates anxiety and fatigue, which may interfere with optimal performance. It is important to eat and sleep well the night before a test.

Some students with poor organizational skills need to expend extra effort to organize the material they have learned. They may employ index cards, for example, to help group and link relevant materials. Mnemonics are memory tricks or devices that help one recall information. The rhyme that begins "Thirty days have September, April, June, and November," for example, helps one remember the number of days in each month. The word "homes" is frequently used as an acronym for the names of the Great Lakes: Huron, Ontario, Michigan, Erie, and Superior.

Note taking is one way to minimize forgetting; reviewing notes can help one prepare for an examination. For this to be most effective, however, one must be able to discriminate between useful and unimportant information at the time of writing the material down. The same holds true for underlining or highlighting material in books or notes. Taping lectures for later review is particularly useful in cases where a lecturer speaks very rapidly, making effective note taking difficult. Tapes are also effective and important aids in learning a foreign language. One advantage is that material can be reviewed in the car or while using a portable cassette player.

Concentration is an important part of learning and remembering, and people do not often spend enough time concentrating intensely. It has been said that thirty minutes of concentrated, uninterrupted study is better than two hours of haphazard study. The minimizing of outside stimuli is also important; one should study in a quiet place with few distractions. Studying in the same place (and at the same time) every night is also thought to be impor-

tant for optimal results. Learning should be active in order to minimize forgetting. Making decisions regarding material to be learned is a useful tool for facilitating learning; one may ask oneself questions about topics or subjects in order to learn or review. Students should be prompted to think about their own learning styles and to allot the necessary time to learn a given amount of material. Many people have their own preferred learning style. Some people learn better by seeing data and information; others assimilate information better by hearing it. Ideally, one should find and maximize one's preferred mode. There are tests designed to determine one's preferred mode of learning.

If one is trying to assimilate too much information in too short a time, one may experience "information overload." Students taking summer classes in which a semester's worth of information is compressed into a few weeks experience this overload, as may those taking eighteen or more hours of classes in a semester. Overload may also affect someone beginning a new job that involves mastering a large amount of information or technical material. Material that is meaningful to the learner has been found to be easier to remember and recall.

With more and more information available to be learned, research on memory and forgetting will continue to be imperative. Teachers must teach students how to learn and remember, and students must participate actively in the learning process as well as employ many of the available tactics for aiding recall.

SOURCES FOR FURTHER STUDY
Bjork, Elizabeth Ligon, and Robert A. Bjork, eds. *Memory*. 2d ed. San Diego, Calif.: Academic Press, 1998. A volume in the series Handbook of Perception and Cognition, *Memory* links important historical work with current findings, concepts, and methods. Foremost researchers in cognitive psychology discuss storage and access of information in both short-term and long-term memory; how memory is controlled, monitored, and enhanced; individual differences in mnemonic ability; and the processes of retrieval and retention, including eyewitness testimony, and training and instruction.
Golding, Jonathan M., and Colin M. MacLeod, eds. *Intentional Forgetting*. Mahwah, N.J.: Lawrence Erlbaum, 1997. This book reviews thirty years of re-

search, as well as new studies, that have examined one phenomenon of memory—directed forgetting or memory. Investigating memory's updating ability has been the main thrust of research on intentional forgetting.

Schacter, Daniel L. *The Seven Sins of Memory: How the Mind Forgets and Remembers.* Boston: Houghton Mifflin, 2001. Schacter, a leading expert on memory, has developed the first framework that describes the basic memory failures everyone encounters. The book offers vivid examples of the memory sins and presents recent research—such as imaging that shows memories being formed in the brain that led to the development of the framework. Schacter also discusses various memory-enhancing techniques that exist.

Thompson, Charles P., Douglas Herrmann, Darryl Bruce, J. Don Read, David Payne, and Mike Toglia, eds. *Autobiographical Memory: Theoretical and Applied Perspectives.* Mahwah, N.J.: Lawrence Erlbaum, 1997. Includes a chapter entitled "Loss and Distortion of Autobiographical Memory Content."

_____. *Eyewitness Memory: Theoretical and Applied Perspectives.* Mahwah, N.J.: Lawrence Erlbaum, 1997. Proceedings of the first Society for Applied Research in Memory and Cognition (SARMAC) conference, centered on autobiographical memory and eyewitness memory.

Michael F. Shaughnessy;
updated by Allyson Washburn

SEE ALSO: Alzheimer's disease; Aphasias; Brain damage; Brain structure; Encoding; Long-term memory; Memory; Memory: Animal research; Memory: Empirical studies; Memory: Physiology; Memory: Sensory; Memory storage; Short-term memory.

Freud, Anna

BORN: December 3, 1895, in Vienna
DIED: October 9, 1982, in London
IDENTITY: Jewish Austrian psychoanalyst and child psychologist
TYPE OF PSYCHOLOGY: Developmental psychology; psychological methodologies
FIELDS OF STUDY: Childhood and adolescent disorders; classic analytic themes and issues; infancy and childhood

Anna Freud was the founder of child psychoanalysis and a contributor to the development of ego psychology.

Anna Freud was born in Vienna, Austria, daughter of Sigmund Freud, the founder of psychoanalysis, and the only one of his six children to follow in his footsteps. She learned psychoanalysis from her father and in turn helped him to develop many of his theories, including those on repression and other defense mechanisms. Anna Freud was a gifted teacher, a skill she later put to use to further the interests of psychoanalysis.

Despite being plagued with ill health, Anna Freud maintained a rigorous work schedule and a lively interest in many topics. Her teaching work and volunteer work with Jewish children orphaned or homeless due to World War I nurtured her interest in child psychology and development. Around this same period, 1918-1922, her father psychoanalyzed her and in 1922 she became a member of the International Psychoanalytic Congress. In 1925, she became a member of the executive board of the Vienna Psychoanalytic Institute. In the same year, She began a career as a training analyst and assumed control of the psychoanalytic publication *Verlag.*

In her first book, *Einführung in die Technik der Kinderanalyse* (1927; *Introduction to the Technique of Child Analysis*, 1928), she brought together her ideas on the new field of child psychoanalysis, later applying these ideas in her teaching. Her techniques with children differed from those of her father with adults, and Sigmund Freud delighted in her initiative even when she refuted his findings in the case of "Little Hans." Her book *Einführung in die Psychoanalyse für Pädagogen* (1929; *Psychoanalysis for Teachers and Parents*, 1935) demonstrated her continued desire to move psychoanalysis to the forefront in the care of working-class people and away from its elite concerns. She became increasingly involved in the upheaval of Europe's financial decline and the rise of dictator Adolf Hitler, running the Vienna Psychoanalytic Association and aiding those seeking refuge from Hitler's Germany. She found time to write *Ich und die Abwehrmechanismen* (1936; *The Ego and Mechanisms of Defense*, 1946), moving her child psychology into the study of adolescence and arguing that the id, ego, and superego each deserve equal attention in the study of human development. In 1939, she accompanied her father to England, fleeing Nazis.

Psychiatrists Anna Freud and Sigmund Freud. (Library of Congress)

After Sigmund Freud's death in 1939, Anna Freud's own contribution to psychoanalysis became clearer. In 1947, for example, she and a friend, Kate Fridländer, established the Hampstead Child Therapy Courses. In 1952, they added a children's clinic. Additionally, Anna published a number of books in which she contributed to the study of child and ego psychology.

Anna became a British subject; she received the Order of the British Empire in 1967, adding it to her long list of honors, including an honorary doctorate from Clark University. She often visited the United States, teaching in various places, including Yale Law School, where she collaborated with Joseph Goldstein and Albert Solnit on *Beyond the Best Interests of the Child* (1973). Her collected works were published between 1968 and 1983. She died in 1982 in London, and in 1986 her home became the Freud Museum.

SOURCES FOR FURTHER STUDY

Dreher, Anna Ursula. *Foundations for Conceptual Research in Psychoanalysis.* Reprint. New York: W. W. Norton, 1994. Anna Freud's contributions to psychoanalysis are placed in the context of the field's overall development.

Peters, Uwe Henrik. *Anna Freud: A Life Dedicated to Children.* New York: Schocken Books, 1984. A biography that focuses on what Anna Freud considered the essence of her life's work.

Young-Bruehl, Elisabeth. *Anna Freud: A Biography.* Reprint. New York: W. W. Norton, 1994. An overall view of a remarkable life.

Frank A. Salamone

SEE ALSO: Ego defense mechanisms; Ego, superego, and id; Freud, Sigmund; Play therapy; Psychotherapy: Children.

Freud, Sigmund

BORN: May 6, 1856, in Freiberg, Moravia
DIED: September 23, 1939, in London, England
IDENTITY: Jewish Austrian psychoanalyst

TYPE OF PSYCHOLOGY: Personality; psychotherapy
FIELDS OF STUDY: Classic analytic themes and issues; personality theory; psychodynamic therapy

Sigmund Freud was a pioneer in psychoanalytic theory and therapy.

Sigmund Freud was born in Freiberg, a small town in Moravia, which is now part of the Czech Republic. His family moved to Vienna when he was four years old, and he lived there for most of his life. When he entered the University of Vienna at the age of seventeen, his initial interest was the study of law. After deciding to become a medical student, he earned his degree as a doctor of medicine in 1881. During his medical studies, Freud was most influenced by Ernest Brucke, a noted physiologist who viewed humans as being controlled by dynamic physiological forces.

Freud's initial work was in theory and research in the field of neurology. For financial reasons, he soon left the physiological laboratory and began a private practice. In 1886, he married Martha Bernays and had six children within a period of nine years. Just prior to his marriage, Freud spent about six months with Jean-Martin Charcot, a famous French neurologist, who was treating neurotic patients with hypnosis, and began his specialization in nervous disorders and therapeutic treatment.

In the 1890's, Freud tried several techniques for the treatment of nervous disorders, including hypnosis, concentration techniques, catharsis (releasing emotions by talking), and free association (saying whatever comes to mind without censorship). He coined the term "psychoanalysis" in 1896. Although Freud had been rooted thoroughly in physiological interpretations of mental events, he began exploring psychological explanations of human behavior. Freud's work in the late nineteenth century culminated in the completion of one of his key books, *Die Traumdeutung* (1900; *The Interpretation of Dreams*, 1913), explaining his theory of the mind and dream analysis.

During the next twenty years, Freud published extensively, writing about such varied subjects as sexuality, jokes, religion, creativity, and psychoanalytic techniques. His increasing fame led to an invitation in 1909, from G. Stanley Hall, to give a series of lectures at Clark University. His increased recognition also brought ridicule and forceful criticism.

World War I served to darken his view of human nature. He expressed his changing views by writing of the significance of aggression and the death instinct (a wish to die) in *Jenseits des Lustprinzips* (1920; *Beyond the Pleasure Principle*, 1922). Freud continued to write and revise his ideas throughout the 1920's and 1930's. He was persecuted as a Jew by the Nazis and in 1938 was persuaded to leave Vienna for England. Freud had been quite ill from cancer of the jaw and mouth, enduring much pain from his illness, which required thirty-three operations. Freud died in London on September 23, 1939, at the age of eighty-three.

SOURCES FOR FURTHER STUDY

Bettelheim, Bruno. *Freud and Man's Soul.* New York: Vintage Books, 1982. Succinctly outlines Freud's key concepts and carefully examines translation issues influencing a proper understanding of Freud's ideas.

Freud, Sigmund. *An Autobiographical Study.* New York: W. W. Norton, 1952. Freud writes about his life and psychoanalytic concepts.

Gay, Peter. *Freud: A Life for Our Time.* New York: W. W. Norton, 1988. Comprehensive study of Freud's life. Includes a bibliographical essay.

Jones, Ernest. *The Life and Work of Sigmund Freud.* New York: Basic Books, 1963. Biographical analysis detailing Freud's life experiences and their relevance to his ideas.

Joanne Hedgespeth

SEE ALSO: Breuer, Josef; Dreams; Ego, superego, and id; Freud, Anna; Hypnosis; Hypochondriasis, conversion, somatization disorder, and somatoform pain; Hysteria; Oedipus complex; Penis envy; Personality theory; Psychoanalysis; Psychoanalytic psychology; Psychoanalytic psychology and personality: Sigmund Freud; Psychosexual development; Psychosomatic disorders; Women's psychology: Sigmund Freud.

Fromm, Erich

BORN: March 23, 1900, in Frankfurt am Main, Germany
DIED: March 18, 1980, in Muralto, Switzerland
IDENTITY: German American psychoanalyst

TYPE OF PSYCHOLOGY: Personality; psychotherapy
FIELDS OF STUDY: Humanistic-phenomenological
   models; models of abnormality; personality theory; psychodynamic and neoanalytic models

*Erich Fromm practiced and taught a social psycho-
analysis and a socialist humanistic philosophy.*

Erich Fromm was born in 1900, the only child of a
middle-class, German, orthodox Jewish family in
Frankfurt, Germany. Influenced by the rabbinical
tradition of study and by his readings in the Old
Testament and in Karl Marx, coauthor with
Friedrich Engels of the *Manifest der Kommunistischen
Partei* (1848; *The Communist Manifesto*, 1850),
Fromm became a committed socialist humanist. He
received a Ph.D. from Heidelberg in 1922, joining
the Frankfurt School for Social Research, which
sought to integrate history with the ideas of Marx
and with Freudian psychoanalysis under the rubric
of critical theory. After training in psychology and
psychiatry at Munich, he became a psychoanalyst,
graduating from the Berlin Psychoanalytic Institute
in 1931. In 1934, Fromm emigrated to America,
where he, Karen Horney, Harry Stack Sullivan, and
Clara Thompson collaborated in creating a psychoanalytic theory and practice that was oriented to social and cultural factors, arousing the ire of the traditional Freudian psychoanalytical associations.

In 1941, Fromm published his most important
work, *Escape From Freedom*, which presented a historical explanation of social character development,
the idea that the needs and pressures of a particular
society require a particular adaptation by the members of a society. Because of the historical changes
that have occurred since the medieval period, which
include the Protestant revolution and capitalism,
the Western person has been freed from the shack-
les and also the security of that preindividualistic
period. The contemporary person who does not
find productive love and work defends the self from
this freedom by creating character traits that favor

authoritarianism or submissiveness, leading to the
political choice of fascism. *The Sane Society* (1955)
continued this argument and suggested socialistic
humanism as a solution to psychological alienation
and destructive political options.

Fromm was a prolific and popular writer. Other
examples are *The Art of Loving* (1956), which defined love as active caring for the life and growth of
the other, and *The Anatomy of Human Destructiveness*
(1973), which offers Fromm's humanistic psychoanalysis as a preferred mode of explanation to purely
instinctual or environmental approaches.

Through his adult life, Fromm studied and practiced a form of Zen Buddhism and worked for the
international peace movement, cofounding the National Committee for a Sane Nuclear Policy (SANE)
in 1957. He taught at many institutions in the United
States and Mexico, influencing other academics in
the arts and sciences with his philosophy. In 1974 he
and his third wife made their home in Switzerland,
where he died in 1980.

SOURCES FOR FURTHER STUDY

Evans, Richard I. *Dialogue with Erich Fromm*. New
   York: Harper, 1966. A personal interview reveals
   Fromm's important ideas.
Funk, Rainer. *Erich Fromm: The Courage to Be Human*.
   New York: Continuum, 1982. A thorough presen-
   tation of Fromm's ideas and their early develop-
   ment. Includes a detailed bibliography of
   Fromm's work and of those written about him.
Landis, Bernard, and Edward S. Tauber, eds. *In the
   Name of Life: Essays in Honor of Erich Fromm*. New
   York: Holt, Rinehart and Winston, 1971. A
   festschrift written by younger and distinguished
   scholars attesting to Fromm's significance.

Everett J. Delahanty, Jr.

SEE ALSO: Horney, Karen; Humanism; Personality
theory; Social psychological models: Erich Fromm;
Sullivan, Harry Stack.

G

Gender-identity formation

TYPE OF PSYCHOLOGY: Developmental psychology
FIELDS OF STUDY: Cognitive development; infancy and childhood

Gender-identity formation refers to the complex processes through which young children come to incorporate their gender into their behavior, attitudes, and self-understanding. This includes the development of an inner sense of one's femaleness or maleness; the acquisition of knowledge about cultural expectations for females and males; and the development of attitudes, interests, and behavior that reflect these expectations.

KEY CONCEPTS
- gender constancy
- gender identity
- gender schema
- sex role
- sex-role socialization
- sex typing

INTRODUCTION

The first question that is usually asked about a newborn baby is whether it is a boy or a girl. The single fact of the child's gender has enormous implications for the course of his or her entire life. Gender-identity formation refers to the complex processes through which children incorporate the biological and social fact of their gender into their behavior, attitudes, and self-understanding.

This area includes ideas about two major interrelated processes: gender-identity development and sex typing. The term "gender-identity development," used in its narrower sense, refers to the process through which children come to label themselves cognitively as boys or girls and to have an inner sense of themselves as male or female. "Sex typing," also called gender-role acquisition, refers to the pro-

cesses through which children learn what is expected of members of their gender and come to exhibit primarily those personality traits, behaviors, interests, and attitudes.

CULTURAL CONTEXTS

Social-learning theorists such as Walter Mischel have described mechanisms of learning through which children come to exhibit sex-typed behavior. Boys and girls often behave differently because they are rewarded and punished for different behaviors. In other words, they receive different conditioning. In addition, children's behavior becomes sex typed because children observe other males and females regularly behaving differently according to their gender, and they imitate or model this behavior.

Parents are especially important in the process of learning one's gender role, both as models for gender-appropriate behavior and as sources of rewards or reinforcement. Because parents become associated with positive experiences (such as being fed and comforted) early in life, children learn to look to them and other adults for rewards. Parents and other adults such as teachers often react differentially to gender-typed behaviors, rewarding gender-appropriate behavior (for example, giving praise or attention) and punishing gender-inappropriate behavior (for example, frowning, ignoring, or reprimanding).

As children become more involved with their peers (children their own age), they begin to influence one another's behavior, often strongly reinforcing traditional gender roles. The fact that children are usually given different toys and different areas in which to play based on their gender is also important. Girls are given opportunities to learn different behaviors from those of boys (for example, girls learn nurturing behavior through playing with dolls) because they are exposed to different experiences.

Using what is called a cognitive developmental perspective, Lawrence Kohlberg described devel-

DSM-IV-TR Criteria for Gender-Identity Disorder

Strong and persistent cross-gender identification, not merely a desire for any perceived cultural advantages of being the other sex

In children, disturbance manifested by four or more of the following:
- repeatedly stated desire to be, or insistence that he or she is, the other sex
- in boys, preference for cross-dressing or simulating female attire; in girls, insistence on wearing only stereotypically masculine clothing
- strong and persistent preferences for cross-sex roles in make-believe play or persistent fantasies of being the other sex
- intense desire to participate in the stereotypical games and pastimes of the other sex
- strong preference for playmates of the other sex; in adolescents and adults, symptoms such as stated desire to be the other sex, frequent passing as the other sex, desire to live or be treated as the other sex, conviction that he or she has the typical feelings and reactions of the other sex

Persistent discomfort with his or her sex or sense of inappropriateness in the gender role of that sex

In children, disturbance manifested by any of the following:
- in boys, assertion that his penis or testes are disgusting or will disappear or assertion that it would

be better not to have a penis, or aversion toward rough-and-tumble play and rejection of male stereotypical toys, games, and activities
- in girls, rejection of urinating in a sitting position, assertion that she has or will grow a penis, or assertion that she does not want to grow breasts or menstruate, or marked aversion toward normative feminine clothing

In adolescents and adults, disturbance manifested by symptoms such as preoccupation with getting rid of primary and secondary sex characteristics (request for hormones, surgery, or other procedures to physically alter sexual characteristics to simulate the other sex) or belief that he or she was born the wrong sex

Disturbance not concurrent with a physical intersex condition

Disturbance causes clinically significant distress or impairment in social, occupational, or other important areas of functioning

DSM code based on current age:
- Gender Identity Disorder in Children (DSM code 302.6)
- Gender Identity Disorder in Adolescents or Adults (DSM code 302.85)

For sexually mature individuals, specify if Sexually Attracted to Males, Sexually Attracted to Females, Sexually Attracted to Both, or Sexually Attracted to Neither

---

opmental changes in children's understanding of gender concepts. These changes parallel the broad developmental changes in the way children's thinking is organized, first described by Jean Piaget and Barbel Inhelder. Children mature naturally through stages increasingly complex cognitive organization. In the area of understanding gender, the first stage is the acquisition of a rudimentary gender identity, the ability to categorize oneself correctly as a boy or a girl.

Children are able to apply correct gender labels to themselves by about age three. At this stage, young children base gender labeling on differences in easily observable characteristics such as hairstyle and clothing, and they do not grasp the importance of genital differences in determining gender. As children's thinking about the physical world becomes more complex, so does their understanding of gen-

der. Gradually, by about age seven, children enter a second stage and acquire the concept known as gender constancy.

GENDER CONSTANCY

Gender constancy refers to the understanding that gender is a stable characteristic that cannot change over time and that is not altered by superficial physical transformations such as wearing a dress or cutting one's hair. As children come to see gender as a stable, important characteristic of themselves and other people, they begin to use the concept consistently to organize social information. They learn societal expectations for members of each gender by watching the actions of the people around them.

Kohlberg proposed that children use their developing knowledge of cultural gender expectations to teach themselves to adopt culturally defined gender roles (self-socialization). He argued that children acquire a strong motive to conform to gender roles because of their need for self-consistency and self-esteem. A young boy says to himself, "I am a boy, not a girl; I want to do boy things, play with boy toys, and wear boy clothes."

Children hold more rigid gender stereotypes before they acquire gender constancy (ages two through seven); once gender constancy is achieved, they become more flexible in their adherence to gender roles. As children enter adolescence, their thinking about the world again enters a new stage of development, becoming even more complex and less rigid. As a result, they may be able to achieve what Joseph Pleck has called "sex-role transcendence" and to choose their interests and behaviors somewhat independent of cultural gender-role expectations.

Gender Schema

Gender-schema theory is a way of explaining gender-identity formation, which is closely related to the cognitive developmental approach. The concept of a schema or a general knowledge framework comes from the field of cognitive psychology. Sandra Bem proposed that each person develops a set of gender-linked associations, or a gender schema, as part of a personal knowledge structure. This gender schema filters and interprets new information, and as a result, people have a basic predisposition to process information on the basis of gender. People tend to dichotomize objects and attributes on the basis of gender, even including qualitites such as color, which has no relevance to biological sex.

Bem proposed that sex typing develops as children learn the content of society's gender schema and as they begin to link that schema to their self-concept or view of themselves. Individuals vary in the degree to which the gender schema is central to their self-concept; it is most central to the self-concept of highly sex-typed individuals (traditionally masculine males or traditionally feminine females).

Gender Identity Disorder

Ideas about gender-identity formation have important implications for child rearing and education. Most parents want to help their child identify with and feel positive about his or her own gender. Those few children who fail to develop a clear inner sense of themselves as male or female consistent with their biological sex may have significant social adjustment

difficulties; they are sometimes given psychological treatment for a condition called gender-identity disorder.

According to the American Psychiatric Association's *Diagnostic and Statistical Manual of Mental Disorders: DSM-IV-TR* (rev. 4th ed., 2000), gender-identity disorder is defined by a strong and persistent cross-gender identification. In a child, it is manifested by such features as repeated statements of the desire to be, or insistence that he or she is, the other gender; preference for or insistence on wearing stereotypical clothing of the opposite sex; strong and persistent preference for cross-sex roles in make-believe play or fantasies of being the other gender; an intense desire to participate in the stereotypical games of the opposite sex; and a strong preference for playmates of the other sex. A boy with this disorder may assert that his penis is disgusting or will disappear, or that it would be better not to have one. He may show an aversion toward rough-and-tumble play and reject male stereotypical toys, games, and activities. A girl with this disorder may reject urinating in a sitting position, assert that she has or will grow a penis, claim that she does not want to grow breasts or to menstruate, or show a marked aversion toward feminine clothing.

Adults who continue to have a gender identity that is inconsistent with their biological sex may desire surgery and hormonal treatments to change their sex. This rare condition, called transsexualism, is more common among biological males than females. Although many people have interests, personality characteristics, or sexual preferences commonly associated with the other gender, they are not transsexuals; their inner sense of their gender is consistent with their biological sex.

Gender Equality

Often, parents and educators want to help children avoid becoming strongly sex typed. They do not want children's options for activities, interests, and aspirations to be limited to those traditionally associated with their gender. Adopting strongly sex-typed interests may be especially problematic for girls because the traditional female role and the qualities associated with it (that is, emotionality, nurturance, and dependence) tend to be devalued in American culture. Traditionally masculine interests and behaviors are usually tolerated in girls before puberty; it is all right to be a "tomboy." Traditionally feminine interests and behaviors, however, tend to be vigorously discouraged in boys; it is not acceptable to be a "sissy."

Considerable research has focused on whether and how socializing agents, including parents, teachers, peers, and media such as children's books and television, reinforce gender stereotypes and teach children to exhibit sex-typed behaviors. Researchers have been concerned both with how gender roles are modeled for children and with how sex-typed behavior is rewarded. A study by Lisa Serbin and her colleagues carried out in the 1970's is an example. These researchers observed teachers' interactions with children in a preschool setting and recorded their observations in a standardized way. They found that teachers gave more attention to girls when they were physically close to them than when they were farther away; however, teachers' attention to boys did not vary with the child's proximity. This finding suggests that teachers reinforce girls more than boys for "dependent" behavior without necessarily meaning to do so.

Parents often report that they try to treat their children the same regardless of their gender. Many of the most powerful influences parents exert result from behaviors of which they are probably unaware. Research studies have shown that parents consistently interact differently with male and female children in areas such as engaging in gross motor play (for example, running, jumping, throwing), encouraging children's sex-typed play (particularly discouraging doll play among boys), demanding effort and giving help with problem-solving tasks, and allowing children to have independence and freedom from supervision.

Children's peers have been shown to play an important role in sex-role socialization. Particularly in early childhood, when children's gender concepts tend to be far more rigid than those of adults, peers may be the source of misinformation (for example, "girls can't be doctors; girls have to be nurses") and of strong sanctions against behavior that is inconsistent with one's gender role.

Laboratory studies have shown that exposure to gender stereotypes in books and on television tends to have a measurable effect on children's sex-typed behavior. For example, children are more likely to play with a "gender-inappropriate" toy after reading a story in which a child of their gender played with that toy. In addition, these media may be important in the development of a child's gender schema because they provide a rich network of information and associations related to gender. Extensive studies of the gender-related content of children's books and children's television were conducted in the 1970's, and this led to reform efforts by some textbook publishers and television producers.

One influential study by a group called Women on Words and Images published in 1975 analyzed the contents of 134 grade-school readers and found gender-stereotypic portrayals of male and female characters, gender-stereotypic themes, and male dominance to be the rule. Boys outnumbered girls as major characters by five to two; in 2,760 stories examined, only three mothers were shown working outside the home. Systematic studies of children's television have produced similar results.

FREUDIAN THEORY

Psychologists have been interested in gender-identity formation since the work of Sigmund Freud and other early psychoanalytic theorists in the beginning of the twentieth century. Since the early 1970's, however, there has been a major shift in thinking about this topic, largely as a result of the women's movement. Early work in this area considered sex typing to be a healthy and desirable goal for children. Since the 1970's, much research has been based on the assumption that rigid adherence to traditional gender roles is restrictive and undesirable.

Freud's theory of psychosexual development was the first to attempt to explain gender-identity formation. Freud believed that sex-typed behavior results primarily from girls identifying with (wanting to be like) their mothers and boys identifying with their fathers; however, he believed that during infancy both boys and girls form strong sexual feelings for their mothers and identify with them. Thus, Freud tried to explain how boys come to identify with their fathers and how girls transfer their sexual feelings to their fathers.

Freud believed that the discovery that girls and women do not have penises leads the three- to five-year-old boy to develop great fear that he will lose his own penis (castration anxiety). As a result, the boy begins to identify with his father out of fear that the father will take away his penis. He gives up his identification with his mother and suppresses his sexual feelings toward her. For a little girl, the same discovery leads to penis envy and to blaming her mother for her lack of this desired organ. Because of her disappointment, she transfers her sexual feelings from her mother to her father, and she fantasizes that her father will give her a penis substitute—a baby.

Freud's theory was an important inspiration for much of the work done on gender identity prior to the late 1960's. Since that time, however, developmental psychologists have not often used Freud's theory because most of its concepts rely on the idea of unconscious forces that cannot be evaluated scientifically.

Freud's idea that "anatomy is destiny"—that profound psychological differences between the sexes are inevitable—has met with strong criticism with the rise of the women's movement. The issue of the relative importance of biological, genetic factors (or "nature") compared with experiential, social factors (or "nurture") in gender-identity formation has been a major source of controversy in psychology. Most psychologists acknowledge a role for both nature and nurture in forming differences in the behavior of boys and girls. Psychologists are interested in understanding the ways in which inborn capacities (such as cognitive organization) interact with environmental experiences in forming a person's identity as a male or a female.

The twentieth century experienced a great upheaval in thinking about gender roles, and this has been mirrored by changes in psychological research and theory about gender. The growing scientific understanding of gender identity may help to form future societal attitudes as well as being formed by them.

Sources for Further Study

Abbott, Tina. *Social and Personality Development*. New York: Routledge, 2002. An introductory psychology textbook. Part 2 covers gender and gender identity development.

Bem, Sandra Lipsitz. *The Lenses of Gender: Transforming the Debate on Sexual Inequality*. New Haven, Conn.: Yale University Press, 1994. Discusses contemporary theories about gender relations through the lenses of androcentrism (taking male experience for the norm), gender polarization (placing male and female experience at opposite ends of a cultural spectrum, with nothing in between), and biologic essentialism (using biological differences to account for cultural realities).

Butler, Judith. *Gender Trouble*. Reprint. New York: Routledge, 1999. The tenth anniversary reprint of this classic work on gender formation and transgression in American society.

Fast, Irene. *Gender Identity: A Differentiation Model*. Hillsdale, N.J.: Lawrence Erlbaum, 1984. Reviews current theories in the light of Freudian psychoanalytic theory.

Kimmel, Michael. *The Gendered Society*. New York: Oxford University Press, 2001. Examines gender from the positions of difference (placing "male" and "female" on a spectrum rather than opposite ends of a pole) and dominance (arguing that gender inequality causes the perception of gender difference, which in turn is used to justify inequality).

Unger, Rhoda K., ed. *Handbook of the Psychology of Women and Gender*. New York: John Wiley & Sons, 2001. A clinical and research handbook covering major contemporary theories, trends, and advances in the psychology of women and gender. Emphasizes multicultural issues and the impact of gender on physical and mental health.

Lesley A. Slavin

SEE ALSO: Cognitive ability: Gender differences; Development; Hormones and behavior; Personality theory; Psychoanalytic psychology and personality: Sigmund Freud; Sexism; Women's psychology: Karen Horney; Women's psychology: Sigmund Freud.

General adaptation syndrome

TYPE OF PSYCHOLOGY: Stress
FIELDS OF STUDY: Critical issues in stress

General adaptation syndrome (GAS) is the name given to the manifestations of the state of stress in a body. Stress is the most active specific conditioning factor in the human organism. Psychosomatic medicine had its beginnings with the discovery of the GAS.

KEY CONCEPTS
- adaptation
- adrenal glands
- alarm reaction
- conditioning factors

- glucocorticoids
- lymphatic tissue
- mineralocorticoids
- stage of exhaustion
- stage of resistance
- thymus gland

INTRODUCTION

Stress is the rate of wear and tear, in particular the strain on the nervous system, in an organism. It is the sum of all adaptive reactions in the body, and it manifests itself by a specific syndrome which consists of all the nonspecifically induced changes within the individual.

Adaptive reactions, or adaptation, are the processes by which the organism adjusts itself to changed circumstances. A syndrome is a group of symptoms usually appearing together in a disease. Nonspecific changes are those that involve many organs of the body and can be induced by a variety of causal factors. Nevertheless, the form in which these changes appear is quite specific: It is the general adaptation syndrome (GAS), first described by Hans Selye in the 1950's. The explanation of this seeming contradiction lies in the fact that stress produces two kinds of change: one that is nonspecifically caused and appears in a nonspecific form, called the primary change; and one that, although nonspecifically caused, is specific in form, the secondary change called GAS.

STAGES OF THE GAS

The GAS is composed of three stages. The first is the alarm reaction, in which the body arms itself for defense against an aggression (such as a bacterial or viral infection, physical damage, or a strong nervous stimulus) but has had no time to adjust itself to the new condition. The second is the stage of resistance, in which the body succeeds in adapting itself to the condition. The third is the stage of exhaustion, in which the body's resistance breaks down with the loss of its adaptive response, a development that can lead to death.

There are three main signs of the first (alarm reaction) stage: an enlargement of the cortex (outer layer) of the adrenal glands; a degeneration of the thymus gland (located in the front of the chest, playing an important role in defense against infections) and the lymphatic system (the vessels that carry the lymph, or white blood, and the lymph nodes, including the spleen and tonsils); and the appearance of gastrointestinal (stomach and gut) ulcers.

In the second (resistance) stage, the body is at its highest level of adaptation, above the normal range, and the body organs return to their normal state. The adrenals, which in the first stage completely discharged their hormones, now again accumulate large amounts of them. In the last (exhaustion) stage, the adrenals again loose their secretions and the other organs degenerate even more; the body's resistance drops to below-normal levels. Although the third stage can lead to death, this is not necessarily the outcome. Often a person undergoes all three stages only to recuperate at the end. A marathon runner goes through all stages of the GAS and, although completely exhausted at the end of the race, regains strength after only a few hours of rest.

The adrenal glands have an important role in the GAS. These are two little glands, each sitting on top of one of the kidneys. The gland is composed of an outer part, or cortex, and a core, or medulla. The cortex is subdivided into layers, one of which manufactures the so-called mineralocorticoids, aldosterone and desoxycorticosterone (DOCA), which have a role in electrolyte (salt) metabolism and have a proinflammatory effect in the body; the second layer secretes the glucocorticoids, cortisol and cortisone, which play a role in sugar metabolism and have an anti-inflammatory effect. Inflammation is a local defense mechanism of the body; the anti-inflammatory hormones suppress this defensive weapon. They also promote the spread of infections and the formation of gastrointestinal ulcers. In spite of this apparent antagonism between the two types of cortical hormones, their effects are absolutely necessary for the body to resist aggression. If the adrenal glands are damaged to a degree that they can no longer produce these hormones, then, without treatment, death is inevitable. In contrast, the hormones secreted by the medullary part of the adrenal gland, epinephrine (also known as adrenaline) and norepinephrine, are not absolutely necessary for survival because they are also produced by nerve endings in other parts of the body.

AGENTS AND EFFECTS

Any agent that attacks the body will induce both specific and nonspecific effects. These are direct effects, such as a burn wound, and indirect effects, which are of two kinds: one that triggers the pro-inflammatory mechanism, inducing it to fight the damage, and one that triggers the anti-inflammatory mechanism, which limits the extent of the damage. The system is actually a bit more complex than this; another component, the so-called conditioning factors, must be taken into account.

Conditioning factors are agents or situations which themselves have no independent effects; however, they can modify the response to a particular stimulus. There are external and internal conditioning factors. The external ones comprise, for example, geographical, social, and nutritional factors, whereas the internal conditioning factors are those determined by genetics and previous experiences.

Based on this information, the sequence of events that occurs when a stressor (a stress inducer) acts on an individual may be summarized as follows: The brain senses the stimulus and sends messages to the adrenal medulla, inducing it to release epinephrine, and to the pituitary gland, inducing it to release adrenocorticotropic hormone (ACTH). Epinephrine has two effects: It acts on the pituitary gland, increasing the secretion of ACTH, and it acts on most of the body tissues, increasing their rate of activity. The heart rate, breathing rate, and blood pressure are increased, as well as the blood sugar level. All these changes prepare the organism for "fight or flight." ACTH, in the meantime, reaches the adrenal cortex and induces the secretion of anti-inflammatory hormones. Simultaneously, pro-inflammatory hormones are released. Both types act on the tissues affected directly by the stressor, and also have a systemic effect on the whole body, inducing the GAS. The particular type and degree of response are modulated by the conditioning factors.

STRESS AND DISEASE

Disease could be defined as an alteration, as a result of a changed environment, of the structure and function of tissues that interferes with their ability to survive. To produce a disease, two types of factors are necessary: environmental, that is, external factors; and the response of the organism, that is, internal factors. The discovery that stress elicits a specific response, the general adaptation syndrome, made it possible to apply exact measurements to the state of stress and its consequences (stress-induced dis-

eases). Although the GAS has a defensive purpose in the body because it promotes adaptation to new conditions, an excess of adaptive hormones can induce untoward symptoms, that is, cause disease. This aspect of stress, that adaptive reactions can themselves become harmful, is one of the most important characteristics of the phenomenon. It made physicians realize that there are many diseases which are not caused by specific agents such as microorganisms, toxic chemicals, or injuries, but rather by the response of tissues to these aggressors (stressors). One type of such diseases is an allergy such as hay fever or hives. It was found that the inflammation of the nasal passages, eyes, or skin is caused by the tissues reacting against chemicals contained in pollen or in some foods. The body fights these reactions with glucocorticoids (anti-inflammatory hormones) secreted by the adrenal cortex. This discovery, that adrenal glucocorticoids have anti-inflammatory and antiallergic effects, was immediately applied in clinical medicine to treat very grave diseases such as arthritis and asthma. The glucocorticoids proved to be lifesaving in these cases.

As the phenomenon of stress is primarily produced by a strain on the nervous system, it seemed reasonable to look into the role of the GAS in nervous and mental diseases. It became clear that what is called maladaptation can be the cause of a nervous breakdown or even outright mental disease. This realization led physicians to search for the connection between psychological maladjustments and bodily diseases. The result was the foundation of the medical specialty called psychosomatic medicine. It is now known that what is called "executive disease"—that is, gastrointestinal ulcers and high blood pressure, sometimes accompanied by a nervous breakdown—is induced by the inability to adjust to a new situation, or by an exceptionally heavy workload, or by fear of responsibility and an inability to make decisions. Psychosomatic medicine attempts to elucidate the way in which maladaptation causes disease as well as the way in which it influences aging and the degenerative diseases of old age, in particular, coronary heart disease and cancer. It is known that chronological age is not the same as physiological age. That is, a fifty-year-old person, from the point of view of tissue integrity and function, may be much older than a seventy-year-old person whose tissues are still in good functioning order. The underlying causes of these individual differences are based in an individual's differential response to stressful situations.

As an outgrowth of the study of stress and the GAS, two subfields of research opened up: the psychology of stress and psychophysiology. The study of stress psychology implies that human behavior is affected by biological mechanisms which appear to be a common heritage of all mammals. The aim of the study would be to enable people to control their emotions and, thus, their behavior. This would be of obvious benefit in the rehabilitation of persons who come in conflict with the law because of their violent behavior and, possibly, would allow society to reduce violent crimes. Psychophysiology, which was founded as a separate branch of psychology in 1960, studies psychological or behavioral variables with their respective physiological responses. For example, one of the major preoccupations of psychophysiology is the study of biofeedback, or the control by a subject of his or her own heart rate or brain function. There is great interest in biofeedback studies, because it is hoped that psychosomatic disturbances could be treated successfully by this technique. In 1949, researchers studied two groups of patients: one group which had recurring head and neck pains, and another which complained of cardiovascular (heart) symptoms. When the researchers administered painful stimuli to the two groups, the members of each group reported an increased intensity in its particular symptoms, although they had been well before the test. The researchers concluded that psychosomatic disorders are caused by the exaggerated response of a particular physiological system, characteristic for the individual. This phenomenon has been named "symptom specificity."

HISTORY OF STRESS RESEARCH

In ancient Greece, the father of medicine, Hippocrates, taught that in every diseased body there is a natural force that fights the disease from within. Later, in eighteenth century England, John Hunter stated that every injury has the tendency to produce the means for a cure. That is, the concept of being sick includes a battle between the aggressor and the defense mechanisms of the body. Rufus of Ephesus, a Greek physician, around the year 100 C.E. discovered that high fever had a beneficial effect upon the progression of many illnesses. This fact was rediscovered by a nineteenth century Viennese psychiatrist,

Julius Wagner von Jauregg, who tried to alleviate the mental disease of patients in the last stage of syphilis. In 1883, he observed that the symptoms improved markedly when the patients contracted typhoid fever. Subsequently, he introduced the treatment with malaria and achieved spectacular results, but without knowing the reason for the cure.

The great French physiologist Claude Bernard, in the nineteenth century, taught that a characteristic of living organisms is their ability to maintain a constant internal environment in spite of significant fluctuations in the external conditions in which they live. Walter B. Cannon, at Harvard University, gave this phenomenon the name "homeostasis." He also coined the term "emergency reaction" to describe the immediate functional changes occurring in the body as a consequence of stressful stimuli. When the homeostatic mechanisms of the body fail to maintain the constancy of the internal medium, disease and eventually death ensue. Although all these findings converged in the treatment of disease by nonspecific means, it was a Viennese physician, Hans Selye, who formulated a scientific theory of the "syndrome of being sick," or, in other words, the concept of stress and of the general adaptation syndrome.

Selye, who was born in Vienna but immigrated to Canada, discovered in 1936 that the physical response to stress could cause disease and even death. He detected the effects of stress when he injected ovarian extracts into laboratory rats. He found that the extract induced enlargement of the adrenal cortex, shrinkage of the thymus gland, and gastric ulcers. Selye realized that it was the stress caused by the impurities in the extract that induced the characteristic changes. He extrapolated his findings to humans and stated that stress could initiate disease and cause death. In 1950, he published *The Physiology and Pathology of Exposure to Stress*, in which he gave a detailed description of the GAS concept.

In the beginning, the medical establishment was reluctant to accept the idea that hormones could have a role in the causation of nonspecific aspects of disease; until that time, hormones were only known to act on specific target tissues. They caused disease either by too little or too much of a particular hormone. For example, a lack of growth hormone resulted in dwarfism, whereas too much of the same created a giant. Selye, however, postulated general hormonal effects that transcended their known immediate action on target tissues. Another, unjustified, criticism of his theory was that he attributed too great a role to the hormonal system, neglecting the part played by the nervous system. These criticisms did not hold up in the long run, and Selye's teachings on stress and the GAS were in the end accepted by medical and physiological researchers.

SOURCES FOR FURTHER STUDY

Allen, Roger J. *Human Stress: Its Nature and Control.* Minneapolis: Burgess, 1983. A well-written account of the broad concept of stress, with good chapters on the general adaptation syndrome and on the psychophysiology on the stress response (that is, the mind-body link). The work is divided into three parts: the nature of stress; the causes and effects of stress; and stress control, which includes the psychophysiological subjects of meditation, relaxation, and biofeedback.

Kerner, Fred. *Stress and Your Heart.* 1961. Reprint. Lincoln, Nebr.: iUniverse.com, 2001. Gives a good overview of the effects of stress on the heart; succeeds in outlining, for the layperson, the essentials of the relationship between stress and heart disease. Augmented by an appendix containing an appreciation and a curriculum vitae of Hans Selye, the discoverer of the general adaptation syndrome. Includes an index and a glossary, but no illustrations.

Sapolsky, Robert. *Why Zebras Don't Get Ulcers: An Updated Guide to Stress, Stress-Related Diseases, and Coping.* New York: W. H. Freeman, 1998. An entertaining comparison of the physiology of stress in humans and other mammals, written by a neuroscientist. Argues that the human nervous system evolved to cope with short-term stressors, and that contemporary stress-related diseases, such as heart disease and diabetes, are the result of living in an environment that instead produces long-term stress.

Selye, Hans. *The Stress of Life.* Rev. ed. New York: McGraw-Hill, 1978. The discoverer of the general adaptation syndrome provides in this work a lucid, comprehensible, nontechnical description of the stress concept and the stress response (GAS).

Straus, Marshall E. *The Biology of the General Adaptation Syndrome in Health and Disease: Index of New Information.* Washington, D.C.: ABBE Publishers Association, 1996. A guide to current information on the GAS.

René R. Roth

SEE ALSO: Adrenal gland; Cannon, Walter B.; Endocrine system; Fight-or-flight response; Hormones and behavior; Nervous system; Selye, Hans; Stress; Stress: Behavioral and psychological responses; Stress: Physiological responses; Stress-related diseases; Stress: Theories.

General Aptitude Test Battery (GATB)

DATE: 1947 forward
TYPE OF PSYCHOLOGY: Intelligence and intelligence testing; personality; social psychology
FIELDS OF STUDY: Ability tests; intelligence assessment

The General Aptitude Test Battery is a vocational aptitude test that takes about three hours to complete, and includes both physical tests, such as manipulating objects, and paper-and-pencil questions.

KEY CONCEPTS
- aptitude tests
- job satisfaction
- race norming

INTRODUCTION

Developed by the United States Employment Service, the General Aptitude Test Battery (GATB, often pronounced "gat-bee") can identify aptitudes for different occupations. It is used by state employment services as well as other agencies and organizations, such as the U.S. Employment Service and the Employment Security Commission.

The GATB is comprised of twelve timed subtests: vocabulary, arithmetic, computation, mark making, assembling, disassembling, turning, placing, name comparison, tool matching, form matching, and three-dimensional space. These twelve subtests correspond to nine aptitudes: intelligence, verbal, numerical, spatial, form perception, clerical perception, motor coordination, finger dexterity, and manual dexterity. These nine aptitudes in turn can be divided into three composite aptitudes: cognitive, perceptual, and psychomotor.

The entire test takes about three hours to complete. About one-half of the test deals with psychomotor tasks, such as manipulating small objects with the fingers; the other half consists of paper-and-pencil questions. In some cases, an examiner might administer only selected tests of the battery as a measure of aptitude for a specific line of work. Scores for each test are based on the total number of correct answers. Raw scores are converted to norm-referenced aptitude scores. Its average is 100; its standard deviation is 20. Anyone of working age can take the GATB. Most people complete less than half of the items, but people who are familiar with timed tests may be able to increase their scores by quickly completing all the items.

USES AND LIMITATIONS

The GATB can be used to help job seekers or employers. Typically, job seekers who take the GATB receive counseling on their scores for each of the nine aptitudes. Their pattern of scores can be compared with the patterns deemed necessary for different occupations. Employers might use the GATB in their efforts to hire qualified employees. Also, the GATB has been used in research, such as exploring the differences in abilities of different groups, or assessing the impact of various training programs or work experience.

The GATB has been translated into several languages and has been used in many different countries, including Australia, Brazil, Canada, China, Colombia, France, India, Italy, Portugal, and Switzerland, as well as in the United States. There is also a completely computerized version.

As is true of other tests, the GATB has limitations. In the late 1980's, the GATB became a center of controversy when people discovered that it had been race normed. Subsequently, the National Academy of Science studied the situation and concluded that race norming was reasonable, because it corrected for the bias of the test. In a controversial move, the National Academy of Sciences recommended to continue the practice of race norming. In July, 1990, the Department of Labor proposed a two-year suspension of the GATB to study whether it worked well enough to continue to be used. The question became moot in 1991, however, when Congress passed the Civil Rights Act of 1991, a law that made the practice of race norming illegal.

Today, the GATB is still being used by the U.S. Employment Service. However, reports are no longer race normed. Instead, raw scores of people from all racial and ethnic groups are converted to standard scores using the same norms. The GATB can be useful in predicting who will be the most successful person on the job, but it is not strong enough to be the sole determinant in selection.

SOURCES FOR FURTHER STUDY

Baydoun, Ramzi B., and George A. Neuman. "The Future of the General Aptitude Test Battery (GATB) for Use in Public and Private Testing." *Journal of Business and Psychology* 7 (Fall, 1992): 81-91. Provides a good description of the GATB and discusses its limitations and issues of concern.

Gottfredson, L. S. "The Science and Politics of Race-Norming." *American Psychologist* 49 (November, 1994): 955-963. Discusses race norming from the perspective of personnel psychology.

Leahy, Michael J. "Assessment of Vocational Interests and Aptitudes in Rehabilitation Settings." In *Psychological Assessment in Medical Rehabilitation. Measurement and Instrumentation in Psychology*, edited by Laura A. Cushman and Marcia J. Scherer. Washington, D.C.: American Psychological Association, 1995. Reviews interest and aptitude testing within the overall assessment process for individuals following disability.

Savickas, Mark L., and Arnold R. Spokane, eds. *Vocational Interests: Meaning, Measurement, and Counseling Use.* Palo Alto, Calif.: Consulting Psychologists Press, 1999. Provides an overview of vocational interests, including genetic and personality influences. Summarizes research on measuring vocational interests, including the technical problems involved in measurement.

Schmidt, Frank L., and John E. Hunter. "The Validity and Utility of Selection Methods in Personnel Psychology: Practical and Theoretical Implications of Eighty-five Years of Research Findings." *Psychological Bulletin* 124 (September, 1998): 262-274. Summarizes the practical and theoretical implications of eighty-five years of research in personnel selection.

Wigdor, Alexandra K., and Paul R. Sackett. "Employment Testing and Public Policy: The Case of the General Aptitude Test Battery." In *Personnel Selection and Assessment: Individual and Organizational Perspectives*, edited by Heinz Schuler, James L. Farr, and Mike Smith. Hillsdale, N.J.: Lawrence Erlbaum, 1993. Describes the social and political context in which controversy over the GATB arose.

Lillian M. Range

SEE ALSO: Ability tests; Assessment; Career and personnel testing; Career Occupational Preference System (COPS); College entrance examinations; Creativity: Assessment; Human resource training and development; Intelligence tests; Interest inventories; Kuder Occupational Interest Survey (KOIS); Peabody Individual Achievement Test (PIAT); Race and intelligence; Scientific methods; Stanford-Binet test; Strong Interest Inventory (SII); Testing: Historical perspectives; Wechsler Intelligence Scale for Children-Third Edition (WISC-III).

Gesell, Arnold

BORN: June 21, 1880, in Alma, Wisconsin
DIED: May 29, 1961, in New Haven, Connecticut
IDENTITY: American pediatrician and
   developmental psychologist
TYPE OF PSYCHOLOGY: Developmental psychology
FIELDS OF STUDY: Infancy and childhood

Gesell was a pioneer in the study of the physical and mental development of children.

Arnold Lucius Gesell was born in a small village on the Mississippi. He received a scholarship to Clark University in Worcester, Massachusetts, where he studied under scholars such as psychologist G. Stanley Hall; Gesell earned his Ph.D. in 1906. Lewis M. Terman, an innovator in intelligence testing, invited him to teach at Los Angeles State College, where Gesell met and married colleague Beatrice Chandler in 1909. Gesell returned to Wisconsin and studied medicine and anatomy. He was appointed assistant professor of education at Yale University, where he earned his M.D. in 1915.

Gesell helped organize the Yale Clinic of Child Development, providing laboratories and playrooms where mothers brought their infants for observation and testing. In 1930, a grant from the Laura Spelman Rockefeller Memorial allowed Gesell to build a homelike studio to film babies' daily activities: sleeping, walking, feeding, and playing. The Yale Clinic added a nursery school, allowing the staff to follow children from infancy through adolescence to adulthood.

These studies were the basis of Gesell's most important work: *Infant Behavior: Its Genesis and Growth* (1934), with Helen Thompson and Catherine Amatrude. The three joined Burton Castner in writing the two-volume *Biographies of Child Development: The Mental Growth Careers of Eighty-four Infants and Children* (1939), which discussed the differences in physical and mental development among normal, superior, atypical, and premature infants.

Gesell stressed that the growth characteristics of children are determined primarily by hereditary factors but that these factors do not operate independently of environmental influences. Every individual has a distinctive complex of growth, but each infant goes through the same fundamental sequences. Developmental norms are useful for comparison and diagnosis but not as a unit of absolute measurement.

Gesell wrote books reassuring parents and challenging them to stimulate their children's development. *Infant and Child in the Culture of Today*, written with Frances Ilg, went through seventeen editions in the United States between 1943 and 1974. Gesell and Ilg also published *The Child from Five to Ten* (1946), providing further norms for growing children and recommending books, records, and games. He, Ilg, and Louise Ames concluded their child development studies with *Youth: The Years from Ten to Sixteen* (1956).

In 1948, Gesell retired from Yale but continued to work in his field. He died in 1961, leaving a legacy of studies showing the importance of prenatal and infant care.

SOURCES FOR FURTHER STUDY

Ames, Louise Bates. *Arnold Gesell: Themes of His Work.* New York: Human Sciences Press, 1989. An expert in adolescent and child psychology, Ames has also coauthored a book with Gesell. Includes an index and extensive bibliography.

Cravens, Hamilton. "Child-Saving in the Age of Professionalism, 1915-1930." In *American Childhood: A Research Guide and Historical Handbook*, edited by Joseph M. Hawes and N. Ray Hiner. Westport, Conn.: Greenwood Press, 1985. An evaluation of Gesell and such contemporaries as Henry Herbert Goddard, Lawrence K. Frank, and John Dewey.

Bernard Mergen

SEE ALSO: Adolescence: Cognitive skills; Attachment and bonding in infancy and childhood; Birth: Effects on physical development; Development; Developmental disabilities; Learning; Reflexes in newborns.

Gestalt therapy

TYPE OF PSYCHOLOGY: Psychotherapy
FIELDS OF STUDY: Humanistic therapies

Gestalt therapy, founded by Fritz Perls, is an outgrowth of the existential-humanistic approach to psychotherapy. It focuses on nonverbal behaviors, dreams, and current thoughts and emotions; as clients become more aware of denied feelings, their innate healing powers are activated.

KEY CONCEPTS
- dreamwork
- empty-chair technique
- existential-humanistic psychotherapy
- here and now
- hot seat

INTRODUCTION

Gestalt therapy emerged during the 1960's as a powerful alternative to the two main available therapeutic techniques, psychoanalysis and behavioral therapy. This approach to therapy, founded by Frederick (Fritz) Perls, attempts to integrate clients' thoughts, feelings, and actions into a unified whole; *Gestalt*, in fact, is the German word for "whole." Gestalt therapists believe that emotional problems as well as some of the dissatisfactions experienced by ordinary individuals are attributable to a lack of recognizing and understanding one's feelings. The fast pace of technological society and the general loss of purpose in individuals' lives has led to a numbing of emotions. Gestaltists believe that many people deny or lose parts of themselves when they are faced with the overwhelming task of coping in society; for example, a person may deny anger toward a loved one.

The role for the Gestalt therapist is to help the client become more aware of the split-off emotions. The therapist takes an active role by requiring the patient to talk about current experiences and feelings. The patient is neither allowed to look for ex-planations or problems from the past nor expected to talk about future plans. Gestaltists believe that anxiety is the result of an excessive focus on the future. The client is expected to attend to current feelings and experiences—to stay in the "here and now."

Gestalt therapy arose from the existential-humanistic school of psychology. Prior schools had portrayed individuals rather pessimistically, believing that human beings are relatively evil creatures whose actions are determined by forces outside their control (such as instincts or the environment). People were seen as adaptive hedonists trying to receive the greatest amount of pleasure for the least amount of effort. The existential-humanistic school of psychology portrays individuals more optimistically, believing people innately strive to achieve their fullest human potential. Failure to do so is not the result of an evil nature but rather the fault of obstacles on this path to perfection. Gestalt therapists agree with the existential-humanistic focus on individual responsibility. One freely chooses one's actions and therefore is responsible for them. There is no provision for blaming a past situation or one's current environment. Gestalt therapists encourage independence and uniqueness in their clients. They push them to be themselves rather than adopting the "shoulds" and "oughts" recommended by society. Perls emphasized this focus on independence and responsibility by stating that the process of maturation is moving from environmental support to self-support.

Probably the greatest contribution of the Gestalt style of therapy has been the techniques it developed to increase individual self-awareness. These techniques are consistent with the belief that emotional problems stem from avoidance of or failure to recognize one's feelings. The Gestalt therapist is very active and confrontational during the therapy session (in fact, in a group setting, talking to the therapist is called "taking the hot seat") and frequently interprets and questions the client's statements. The goal is a genuine relationship between two individuals, free of normal social conventions, in which a free exchange of thoughts and feelings can take place.

THERAPEUTIC TECHNIQUES

In one technique of Gestalt therapy, called the "dreamwork," the client reports a recent dream. The

Gestalt school believes that the events in a dream represent fragmented and denied parts of the personality. Rather than search for explanations in one's childhood, as in the technique of dream analysis originated by Sigmund Freud, clients are encouraged to bring the dream into the present by acting out different parts of the dream. Rather than saying "There was a train in my dream," they are required to act out the part of the train. They might say, "I am a train. I am very powerful and useful as long as I stay on track." This moves the focus of the dream into the here and now.

Another therapeutic technique used by Gestalt therapists involves a focus on and exaggeration of nonverbal behaviors. Gestaltists believe that much denied information is accessible through body language. For example, a client may state that she is happy and content in a relationship, while she is scowling and keeping her arms and legs crossed in a tight and tense fashion. Gestalt therapists help their clients become aware of these feelings by getting them to exaggerate their actions. A man who is talking about his wife while clenching his hand in a fist and tapping it on the table may be told to clench his fist tighter and bang it hard on the table. This exaggeration of nonverbal behavior would be to make him acutely aware of his anger toward his wife.

Another well-known procedure developed by the Gestalt school of psychotherapy is the "empty-chair technique." This strategy is employed to bring past conflicts into the here and now, where feelings can be reexperienced. The client often will relate to the therapist a disagreement with some significant other. Rather than ask for details of the encounter (a procedure that keeps the focus in the past), the therapist will encourage the client to address an empty chair in the office as though that person were sitting in it. The client must role-play the relevant situation. The therapist may also get the client to play the part of the significant other in the empty chair. This switching back and forth of chairs and roles is a powerful technique to foster empathy, understanding, and a clarification of feelings. This technique can be used not only for conflicts between individuals but also for discrepant feelings within one person.

GESTALT IN PRACTICE

The Gestalt approach to psychotherapy is best explained by examples. A student once reported a dream in which she remembered a gum wrapper being dropped outside a nearby church. Rather than search for a meaning of the dream's symbols in her childhood, her friend, a clinical psychologist, asked her to become the elements in the dream. She initially chose the gum wrapper. She stated that as a gum wrapper she concealed something very good and appealing and that most people took the good part from inside her and then threw her away. She stated that she felt like trash littered on a beautiful lawn and that eventually some caring person would come and throw her away.

The student then began to play the role of the church in the dream. She stated that as a church she was a beautiful building constructed by caring hands. She indicated that good things happened inside her but that she was used too infrequently. Many people were afraid of or disliked coming to her, she said, and most of the time she was empty inside. The student was surprised as she completed this description of the dream. She talked about the similarity of her explanations of the two elements in the dream. When asked if she felt this way, she stated that this idea at first surprised her somewhat; however, as she continued to elaborate, she became more aware of her feelings of emptiness and loneliness. She had become aware of denied aspects of her emotions.

Gestalt therapy's active focus on nonverbal behavior and denied portions of the personality often can be quite dramatic. The judicious use of these techniques may allow insights into dynamics that are not available through ordinary interpersonal interactions. In one case, a family was being seen by cotherapists in family therapy. The family consisted of a mother, father, son, and daughter. The son was identified as the troublemaker in the family, and he demonstrated a wide range of symptoms that caused the family much pain and suffering. During the course of therapy, it became apparent that the mother was an unwitting conspirator in these troubles. She often would rescue her son from his precarious and often dangerous situation and restore matters to normal. This served the function of ensuring her role as a "good mother," while providing the son with the reassurance that he was loved by her. Whenever she threatened not to rescue him, he accused her of not caring for him. She inevitably crumbled and provided for his needs. The father and daughter had their own alliance in the family and, although they complained, they did not interfere in this dysfunctional family pattern that frequently ended in severe problems.

The two therapists hypothesized the pathological nature of this interaction and periodically attempted to present it to the family; however, the pattern was so important and so entrenched in the family's style of interaction that any mention of it led to vehement protests and denials that it was an issue of importance. During a therapy session, one of the therapists noticed the pattern in which the family members usually seated themselves. The mother and son sat close to each other on one side of the therapy room, while the father and daughter sat near each other across from them. The two therapists sat across from each other on the other sides of the room. One therapist, taking a cue from the Gestalt emphasis on the importance of nonverbal behaviors, moved his chair and sat in the small space between the mother and son. A stunned silence ensued. The mother and son began to show agitation, while the father and daughter, from across the room, became increasingly amused at the nature of this interaction.

The therapists elicited the reactions and analyses of the family to this new seating arrangement. The mother and son continued to display uncertainty and bewilderment, while the father and daughter immediately recognized that someone had dared to come between "Mom and her boy." This led to a more open discussion of the pathological nature of the family interactions. The father and daughter could see that they had allowed this damaging pattern to continue. The mother and son, while not quite as open to this discovery because of the threatening nature of the disclosure, could not deny the emotions that were aroused by someone physically invading their territory. The insights that resulted from this simple Gestalt technique moved therapy along much more quickly than had previous verbal interactions. It demonstrates the Gestalt tenet that a focus on nonverbal patterns of communication may allow clients to become aware of previously denied aspects of their personalities.

EXISTENTIAL-HUMANISTIC PSYCHOLOGY

Gestalt therapy emerged during a period of increased popularity for the existential-humanistic position in psychology. This approach, sometimes known as the "third force" in psychology, came from opposition to the earlier forces of psychoanalysis and behaviorism. Existential-humanistic proponents objected to the pessimistic psychoanalytic view of humans as vile creatures held captive by primitive, unconscious desires. They also differed from the environmental determinism, set forth by the behavioral school, that people are simply products of past punishments and rewards. The existential-humanistic therapists focused on the human freedom to choose one's actions (regardless of unconscious desires and past consequences), the relative goodness of the human species, and people's innate desire to reach their fullest potential. This approach fit well with the period of great social upheaval and change following World War II.

The Gestalt approach often is compared to the client-centered (or person-centered) therapy of Carl Rogers. Both types of psychotherapy endorse the basic assumptions of the existential-humanistic school; however, they differ considerably in their approach and techniques. In client-centered therapy, the client is encouraged to express his or her thoughts and feelings about a situation. The therapist remains relatively passive, giving minimal verbal prompts or paraphrasing the client's statements. The client is responsible for the direction and content of the therapy session; the therapist provides only a clarification of unclear statements or feelings. The idea behind this approach is that the therapist is providing an atmosphere of unconditional acceptance in which the client can explore his or her emotional issues. Eventually, the client's innate curative ability will take over. The Gestalt therapist, in contrast, is much more confrontational in interpreting statements and asking questions. The Gestalt approach places a greater emphasis on the interpretation of nonverbal behaviors and the usefulness of dreams. Although different in technique, both approaches point to the freedom to choose, the innate goodness of the client, and the strength of the therapeutic relationship as curative factors.

The influence of the Gestalt approach to psychotherapy diminished with the death of Fritz Perls in 1970. He was the emotional and spiritual leader of the group, and his charisma was not replaced easily. Gestalt therapy is not considered a mainstream psychotherapy; however, it does have numerous enthusiastic followers. The greatest contribution of the

Gestalt orientation has been the techniques developed to assist clients in becoming more aware of hidden thoughts and emotions. Therapists with a wide variety of orientations have adapted and applied these procedures within their own theoretical framework. The impact of dreamwork, the hot seat, nonverbal interpretations, and the empty-chair techniques seems to have outlasted the theory from which they came.

SOURCES FOR FURTHER STUDY

Clarkson, Petruska. *Gestalt Therapy in Action.* 2d ed. Thousand Oaks, Calif.: Sage Publications, 2000. A popular introductory guide to the theory and practice of Gestalt therapy.

Davison, G. C., and J. M. Neale. *Abnormal Psychology.* 8th ed. New York: John Wiley & Sons, 2001. A frequently used textbook in the field of abnormal psychology. It gives an interesting overview of Gestalt therapy practice as well as an explanation of how these techniques may be applied to abnormal behaviors. The authors present a balanced critique of Gestalt therapy and of how it fits with the existential-humanistic approach to abnormality.

Ivey, Allen E., Michael D'Andrea, Mary Bradford Ivey, and Lynn Simek-Morgan. *Theories of Counseling and Psychotherapy: A Multicultural Perspective.* 5th ed. Boston: Allyn & Bacon, 2001. This popular textbook on psychotherapy gives a brief overview of Gestalt therapy. It includes examples of Gestalt therapists working with clients and analyzes each statement in terms of type of approach (confrontation, question, or empathy).

Perls, Frederick S. *The Gestalt Approach and Eye Witness to Therapy.* Ben Lomond, Calif.: Science & Behavior Books, 1973. Two short works printed in one volume. *The Gestalt Approach* was Perls's last attempt to rework Gestalt therapy and is one of his most complete attempts to do so. *Eye Witness to Therapy* is a collection of verbatim therapy transcripts. They are easily readable and present excellent examples of practical applications of Gestalt theories.

Brett L. Beck

SEE ALSO: Abnormality: Psychological models; Dreams; Existential psychology; Group therapy; Humanism; Person-centered therapy; Self-actualization.

Giftedness

TYPE OF PSYCHOLOGY: Developmental psychology; intelligence and intelligence testing
FIELDS OF STUDY: Ability tests; cognitive development; general issues in intelligence; intelligence assessment

Giftedness refers to a capability for high performance in one or more areas of accomplishment. The focus on giftedness as a human capability has led to efforts to identify giftedness early in life, to develop special programs of instruction for gifted children and adolescents, and to design counseling interventions to help gifted learners realize their potentials.

KEY CONCEPTS
• asynchronous development
• child prodigies
• gifted education program
• intelligence test scores
• Marland definition
• precociousness
• prodigious savants
• standardized test scores
• talent

INTRODUCTION

Modern studies of giftedness have their origin in the work of Lewis Terman at Stanford University, who in the 1920's used intelligence test scores to identify intellectually gifted children. His minimal standard for giftedness was an intelligence quotient (IQ) of 140 on the Stanford-Binet Intelligence Test, a number at or above which only 1 percent of children are expected to score. (The average IQ score is 100.) Terman and his associates identified more than fifteen hundred children in California as gifted, and follow-up studies on "the Terman gifted group" were conducted throughout their adult lives. Although individuals in the gifted group tended to achieve highly in school and in their careers, they were not greatly different from average scorers in other ways. Terman's research dispelled the myths that high scorers on IQ tests were, as a group, socially maladjusted or "burned out" in adulthood. They were high achievers and yet normal in the sense that their social relationships were similar to those of the general population.

By the time the Terman gifted group reached retirement age, it was clear that the study had not realized the hope of identifying eminence. None of the children selected had, as adults, won the Nobel prize, although two children who were rejected for the study later did so (physicist Luis Alvarez and engineer William Shockley). Nor did high IQ scores seem to be characteristic of artistic ability. Apparently, an IQ score of 140 or above as a criterion for giftedness in children was not able to predict creative accomplishments in later life.

Studies conducted in the 1950's under the direction of Donald MacKinnon at the University of California, Berkeley, tended to confirm this conclusion. Panels of experts submitted the names of whomever they believed to be the most creative architects, mathematicians, and research scientists in the United States; then these individuals were invited to take part in assessments, including measurement of their intelligence through the Wechsler Adult Intelligence Scale. The IQ scores of these highly creative individuals ranged from 114 to 145, averaging around 130, significantly below Terman's criterion for giftedness. No one knows how these adults would have scored on the Stanford-Binet as children, or how creative adults in other domains would have scored, but the results confirmed that a score of 140 on an intelligence test is not a prerequisite for outstanding creative accomplishment.

More recent studies have cast light on the importance of nurture in the development of a broader range of talent. A team of researchers at the University of Chicago headed by Benjamin Bloom investigated the lives of 120 talented adults in six fields: concert piano, sculpture, swimming, tennis, mathematics, and research neurology. They found that in most cases, accomplishments on a national or international level by the age of forty had their origin not in a prodigious gift, but in child-centered homes. The child's early experiences of the field were playful, rewarding, and supported by parents. Rapid progress was due to a work ethic instilled by parents ("always do your best") and by increasingly expert and selective teachers, whom parents sought out. Bloom's findings did not exactly contradict those of Terman (no testing was done), but they suggested to the researchers that nurture and motivation play the lead and supporting roles in the development of a wide range of talent.

Just what general ability IQ tests measure remains uncertain, but increasingly, psychologists and educators have conceptualized giftedness as a function of specialized capabilities and potential for performance in specific fields such as mathematics, biology, dance, or visual arts. A definition of giftedness first offered in a 1971 report to the Congress of the United States by Sidney Marland, then Commissioner of Education, indicates a much broader concept of giftedness than high IQ scores have been found to measure. "Gifted and talented children are those identified by professionally qualified persons who, by virtue of outstanding abilities, are capable of high performance." He continued,

> Children capable of high performance include those with demonstrated achievement and/or potential ability in any of the following areas, singly or in combination:
>
>   1. general intellectual ability
>
>   2. specific academic aptitude
>
>   3. creative or productive thinking
>
>   4. leadership ability
>
>   5. visual or performing arts
>
>   6. psychomotor ability.

This definition of giftedness, known after its author as the Marland definition, does not distinguish giftedness from talent and includes performance capabilities that are sometimes related only distantly to performance on an IQ test. Nevertheless, the legacy of the Terman study of giftedness is that high IQ test scores remain one among several ways for psychologists and educators to identify intellectual giftedness among children in the general population. Giftedness in academic, creative, leadership, artistic, and psychomotor domains, however, is generally identified in other ways.

IDENTIFICATION OF GIFTEDNESS
Different percentages of the general population have been identified as gifted, depending on the definition of giftedness. Terman's use of IQ scores of 140 or above identified 1 percent of scorers as gifted. The common, contemporary indicator of intellectual giftedness is a score of 130 or above on a standardized, individually administered intelligence test, which is achieved by the top 2.5 percent of scorers. By the broader Marland definition, some form of

which has been enacted through legislation by most states that have mandated gifted education programs, a minimum of 3 to 5 percent of school children are estimated to be gifted. Other definitions would identify as many as 10 to 15 percent of schoolchildren as gifted, or as many as 15 to 25 percent in a talent pool. Gifted and talented students receiving services in schools in the United States constitute about 6 percent of all children who are enrolled.

By almost any definition, giftedness is very difficult to identify during infancy. Most researchers would agree that giftedness has a biological foundation, but whether this foundation exists as a general or a specific capability is unknown. One of the earliest indicators of many forms of giftedness is precociousness, or unusually early development or maturity. During preschool years, precociousness can generalize across several domains, such as the use of logic with an extensive vocabulary, or it can be more

Children who display advanced cognitive skills at an early age may need additional educational opportunities to maximize their potential. (CLEO Photography)

specialized, such as drawing realistic pictures of animals or objects, or picking out a tune by ear on a musical instrument. Development does not seem to proceed in all areas at the same pace, however, so a young child may develop early in one or two areas but still behave in many ways like other children of the same age. Because of such asynchronous development, parents should not assume that a child who can master the moves of checkers at four years old, for example, will accept losing a game any better than the average four-year-old.

A surprising number of gifted children are their parents' only children or first-borns, but this fact only reveals that their precocious development is due, at least in part, to learning from the models in their early environment, who are adults rather than age-mates. As Bloom's study suggested, parents or other adult caretakers provide opportunities, resources, and encouragement to learn. Whatever reading ability a child may have, for example, can be nurtured by adults who read both to her and around her, who provide appropriate materials to read, and who show interest in the child's spontaneous efforts to read.

A child who is developing a talent early often will tend to rehearse it spontaneously, or call for repeated performance or for explanation by the parent (or other model) to review or understand what the child wants to learn. An eight-year-old, for example, might draw a whimsical but easily recognizable portrait of a parent's face while watching cartoons. A nine-year-old might play a competent if not yet masterful game of chess with the school principal, who then asks the child to explain certain moves, and so on. The products and performances of gifted children in elementary school are often similar to the products and performances of skilled but less gifted adolescents. For this reason, gifted children are often bored when instruction is designed for their age level rather than for an advanced level and rapid pace of learning.

By the school years, children's giftedness can be assessed reliably in ways other than observation of precociousness. Assessment usually begins with nomination by a teacher, parent, group of peers, or possibly the child himself or herself to identify who is gifted. Some psychologists have argued that nominations by those who know children well can be sufficient for placement in a gifted education program, or a set of services beyond those normally provided by the regular school program, in order to help gifted children realize their potentials.

Teacher nominations cannot be the sole indicator of who is gifted, however, because studies have shown them to miss about half of all gifted children. Nominations by teachers and others are often supported by academic marks during the previous year, and these evidences of achievement are often supplemented by standardized test scores. These scores can result from individual or group assessments of intelligence, school ability, cognitive abilities, academic aptitudes or achievements, and creative or productive thinking abilities. Since tests themselves have been found to identify only half of all gifted children, test scores are sometimes supplemented by scores from other types of instruments (such as checklists), ratings of portfolios or performances, or interviews to complete the assessment process. No single assessment technique or instrument has been found to identify satisfactorily all types of giftedness in the Marland definition. Underrepresentation of African American, Hispanic, and Native American children in gifted education programs in the United States remains largely a problem of identification.

INSTRUCTION OF GIFTED CHILDREN AND ADOLESCENTS

Eligibility for a gifted education program may be decided as a result of the process of identification, but the design of a program of instruction for each child is often a separate set of decisions, sometimes requiring further assessments. It must be decided whether a child who is nearing the end of first grade but who has performed at the seventh-grade level on a standardized achievement test should be promoted to a much higher grade next year. An adolescent who is writing commercial music, and who is successfully performing it on weekends, might be allowed to leave school during the day to make a recording. The programming decisions to be made are as diverse as the talents of the children themselves.

It is not surprising, then, that no single strategy for teaching gifted children has been found best. Rather, broad strategies of intervention can be classified as modifications in curriculum content or skills and modifications in school environment. Either of these strategies might be formalized by means of a written plan or contract, which is an agreement between individuals, such as the learner, the teacher, and (when relevant) others, including the gifted education teacher or the parent(s). Parents have the right to refuse special services for their children, but few do.

Modifications in curriculum content for gifted students might include content acceleration (such as early admission, grade skipping or "telescoping" two years into one); content enrichment (materials to elaborate on basic concepts in standard program); content sophistication (more abstract or fundamental considerations of basic concepts); and content novelty (such as units on highly specialized topics). Modifications in skills include training in component skills of problem solving; various forms of problem solving (such as creative, cooperative, or competitive); and development of creativity. A program for the first-grader who is performing on achievement tests at the seventh-grade level, for example, might call for placement in a higher grade level (grade skipping), although which grade level to place the child in would have to be determined using teacher observations, interview results, and diagnostic tests.

Possible modifications in the school environment include provisions for enrichment in the regular classroom (such as access to special equipment); a consultant teacher (who helps the classroom teacher develop lessons); a resource room (or "pullout" program); mentoring (often by a professional in the community); independent study (often a special project); special-interest classes (such as creative writing); special classes (such as advanced placement biology); and special schools (such as a statewide math and science school). A program for the musically creative adolescent might incorporate mentoring by a music professional, who would report to the school on a regular basis about work completed by the adolescent at a recording studio or while otherwise away from school during school hours.

Of all of these modifications, teachers and parents seem to be most concerned about content acceleration, particularly if it involves grade skipping. As long as children are not socially and emotionally "hurried" by adults to achieve early, research suggests that the impact of content acceleration is positive. Most children who spend all or part of the school day with older children have ample opportunities to socialize with age-mates (if they wish) after school, on weekends, or in their neighborhoods. Being gifted can imply a preference for working alone or with older children, but it does not imply being lonely, particularly for those who are moderately gifted.

Individualized education programs (IEPs) are especially important for highly gifted children, such as child prodigies, who have either an extremely high IQ (180 or above) or expertise in a domain-specific skill by age ten; prodigious savants, formerly known as *idiots savants*, who have an IQ below 70 but expertise in a domain-specific skill (such as calendar calculating); and gifted children with disabilities. Children with disabilities (some of them multiple disabilities) may represent several percent of those who are gifted. In the United States, an IEP for these children is mandated by law. The importance of an individual program is evidenced by the case of Helen Keller, whose home tutoring not only resulted in the development of her intellectual abilities but also enabled her later accomplishments as an advocate for the blind throughout the world.

COUNSELING GIFTED LEARNERS

Beginning in the 1920's, Leta Hollingworth at Columbia University investigated characteristics of children who scored over 180 on the Stanford-Binet test. Her study of twelve children (eight boys and four girls) suggested that despite their overall adjustment, children who were highly intellectually gifted tended to encounter three challenges not encountered by most other children. The first was a failure to develop work habits at school because of a curriculum paced for much less capable learners. The second was difficulty in finding satisfying companionship because of their advanced interests and abilities in relation to their age-mates. The third was vulnerability to frustration and depression because of a capacity to understand information on an adult level without sufficient experience to know how to respond to it.

Hollingworth suggested that the problem of work habits could be addressed by a combination of acceleration and enrichment. The problem of loneliness could be solved by training gifted children in social games—such as checkers or chess—that could be played by people of any age, and the problems of frustration and depression by careful adult supervision and patience. Research has tended to confirm that the problems Hollingworth identified often

need to be addressed, not only in cases of extreme precociousness but, to a lesser extent, in the lives of many people identified as gifted.

If underachievement by a gifted child has its source in an unchallenging or otherwise inappropriate educational program, the recommended action is to assess strengths and weaknesses (a learning disability may be the problem), then design a more appropriate program or place the child in one that already exists. If the source of underachievement is low self-esteem, the home environment may be unlike that found by Bloom to nurture talent. In this case, family counseling can often reverse underachievement.

To help a gifted child with peer relations, group counseling with other gifted children can be particularly beneficial. Not only can group members share their experiences of being gifted, but they can establish and maintain friendships with those who have similar (or sometimes quite different) exceptionalities. Group sessions can be both therapeutic and developmental.

At least some of the emotional challenges facing gifted children develop from their emotional sensitivity and excitability. Since parents and siblings often share these characteristics, the stage is set for conflict. What is surprising is that conflict does not create unhappiness more often. In the main, gifted people report satisfaction with their home lives. If tensions in the home arise more often than average, the parents of gifted children and the children themselves may need to develop more effective conflict resolution strategies and higher levels of self-understanding. Developmental counseling can assist parents and children in making these changes.

SOURCES FOR FURTHER STUDY

Bloom, Benjamin S., ed. *Developing Talent in Young People.* New York: Ballantine, 1985. A landmark study of the environmental influences which shape talent.

Colangelo, Nicholas, and Gary A. Davis, eds. *Handbook of Gifted Education.* 2d ed. Boston: Allyn & Bacon, 1997. A valuable collection of chapters for readers with some background knowledge of gifted education.

Gallagher, James, and Shelagh Gallagher. *Teaching the Gifted Child.* 4th ed. Boston: Allyn & Bacon, 1994. A general overview of strategies for teaching gifted learners.

MacKinnon, Donald W. *In Search of Human Effectiveness.* Buffalo, N.Y.: Creative Education Foundation, 1978. A technical but readable account of an intensive effort to assess adult creativity.

Marland, Sidney P. *Education of the Gifted and Talented.* Washington, D.C.: Government Printing Office, 1971. Many contemporary definitions of giftedness have their origin in this report, which is accessible in the Educational Resource Information Center (ERIC) collection as document Nos. ED056243 (Volume 1, *Report to the Congress of the United States*) and ED056244 (Volume 2, *Background Papers*).

Shurkin, Joel N. *Terman's Kids: The Groundbreaking Study of How the Gifted Grow Up.* Boston: Little, Brown, 1992. A highly readable summary of Terman's findings, set in a contemporary perspective by a journalist.

Silverman, Linda K. *Counseling the Gifted and Talented.* Denver, Colo.: Love, 1993. Describes the personal and emotional characteristics of gifted children, their home lives, and the challenges of raising them. Recommended reading for parents as well as professionals.

Winner, Ellen. *Gifted Children: Myths and Realities.* New York: Basic Books, 1996. Responds to nine myths about gifted children with a balance of case studies and research evidence. Recommended especially for those interested in the nature and nurture of unusually gifted children.

John F. Wakefield

SEE ALSO: Ability tests; Creativity: Assessment; Creativity and intelligence; Intelligence; Intelligence quotient (IQ); Intelligence tests; Learning; Teaching methods.

Gilligan, Carol

BORN: November 28, 1936, in New York City
IDENTITY: American psychologist
TYPE OF PSYCHOLOGY: Developmental psychology
FIELDS OF STUDY: Adolescence; interpersonal relations

Gilligan theorized that there are differences between men and women in values and views when confronted with ethical dilemmas.

Carol Gilligan grew up in the 1940's in the Upper West Side of Manhattan. After completing a highest honors degree in English at Swarthmore College and earning a doctorate in clinical psychology at Harvard University, she began teaching at Harvard during the early 1970's.

While researching moral and personality development, Gilligan became convinced that the study of psychology was based primarily on studies of men and lacked women's voices. Although a collaborator of developmental psychologist Lawrence Kohlberg (1927-1987), she argued that his theory of moral development explained the "moral voice" of only boys and young men.

Gilligan is best known for her book *In a Different Voice* (1982), which presents a conceptual framework for two different "themes" or "voices." Her theory of moral development contrasts the masculine ethic of justice, as presented by Kohlberg, with the feminine ethic of care. She explains these gender differences in moral perspective as caused by contrasting images of self. The ethic of care stresses the connectedness or relatedness of persons. The ethic of justice or ethic of rights is based on separateness or distinctiveness of the self. Individuals stand alone and independently make moral decisions. Gilligan does not argue for the superiority of either the interpersonal theme of women or the formal rule-bound morality of men. Instead, she insists that male and female moral orientations should be considered apart from each other and that development within each should be studied according to the unique facets of each. Her own studies have also included boys and their development into manhood.

Critics note a lack of empirical research to support Gilligan's argument that women score lower than men on Kohlberg's scale. Nevertheless, Gilligan's work is accepted as having created an appreciation of women's voices, resulting in a new interest in female developmental psychology and an abundance of literature on feminist ethics.

Gilligan was selected by *Time* magazine as one of the twenty-five "most influential people in 1996." In 1997, she became the first holder of a chair on gender studies at Harvard's graduate school of education. Collaborative publications include *Between Voice and Silence* (1997), *Meeting at the Crossroads* (1993), *Making Connections* (1990), and *Mapping the Moral Domain* (1990).

Sources for Further Study

Berube, Maurice R. *Eminent Educators, Studies in Intellectual Influence.* Westport, Conn.: Greenwood Press, 2000. Gilligan was selected as one of four intellectual giants of the twentieth century for her theory on the moral development of girls and women. Includes biographical information and an analysis of Gilligan's intellectual contribution.

Hekman, Susan J. *Moral Voices, Moral Selves: Carol Gilligan and Feminist Moral Theory.* University Park: Pennsylvania State University Press, 1995. Discusses Gilligan's theory in terms of postmodernism and the challenge to provide more localized moral voices.

Puka, Bill. *Caring Voices and Women's Frames: Gilligan's View.* Vol. 6 in *Moral Development: A Compendium.* New York: Garland, 1994. This seven-volume series includes a volume devoted to Gilligan's work. Volume 4, on the justice debate, is also helpful in understanding Kohlberg-Gilligan differences.

Lillian J. Breckenridge

See also: Development; Feminist psychotherapy; Moral development; Women's psychology: Carol Gilligan.

Gonads

Type of psychology: Biological bases of behavior
Fields of study: Endocrine system

The gonads are the mammalian male testes and female ovaries, which secrete sex hormones. These hormones determine sex differences in reproductive structures and functions and have been strongly implicated in the expression of sexual, aggressive, and maternal behaviors.

Key concepts
- activational effects
- adrenogenital syndrome
- androgen insensitivity syndrome
- androgenization
- androgens
- estradiol
- H-Y antigen
- organizational effects
- ovaries
- progesterone
- testes
- Turner's syndrome

Introduction

The gonads are endocrine glands that secrete sex hormones in all mammalian species. In males, the gonads are the testes, which secrete sex hormones called androgens; in the female, the gonads are the ovaries, which secrete estradiol and progesterone. These sex hormones, which are released into the bloodstream, have effects on the formation of both internal and external reproductive organs during prenatal development; later, they have important behavioral effects, particularly in the expression of sexual behaviors. They are also implicated in maternal and aggressive behaviors.

Prenatal Development

In the prenatal period, as the embryo is developing, the gonads are the first sex organs to differentiate into male and female organs. Prior to the seventh week of human gestation, the gonads are identical for the two sexes. If the embryo is genetically male, the gonads differentiate into male testes at the seventh or eighth week of development. If the embryo is female, the gonads differentiate into ovaries at the same point in development. This differentiation is controlled by a protein called the H-Y antigen, which is present only if the embryo has a Y chromosome and is therefore a genetic male. When the H-Y antigen is present, it will stimulate receptors on the surface of the gonads to become testes. If it is absent, ovaries will automatically develop.

Once the sexual differentiation of the gonads has occurred, a sequence of events takes place which will determine the sexual dimorphism of both the internal and the external reproductive organs, and therefore the gender of the individual. This is known as the organizational effect of the gonads. If the gonads have differentiated into testes, the testes will begin to secrete androgens, primarily testosterone, which have a masculinizing effect and cause the development of the internal male structures such as the prostate, the vas deferens, and the epididymis. If there is an absence of androgens, the female uterus, Fallopian tubes, and the inner two-thirds of the vagina will develop instead. A genetic disorder called

The Male Reproductive System

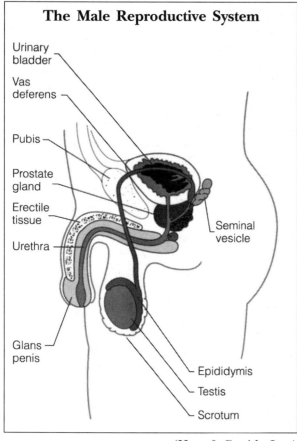

Urinary bladder

Vas deferens

Pubis

Prostate gland

Erectile tissue

Urethra

Glans penis

Seminal vesicle

Epididymis

Testis

Scrotum

(Hans & Cassidy, Inc.)

Turner's syndrome illustrates how the absence of androgens results in the development of female structures. In this disorder, the individual has only one X chromosome, which prevents the development of ovaries, and no Y chromosome to create H-Y antigen; therefore, there are no testes to secrete androgens. This individual's other internal sexual organs are normal female structures.

The external or visible genitalia develop in much the same way, governed by the presence or absence of androgens. The embryos of both sexes begin with undifferentiated genitals that are capable of becoming characteristically male or female, depending on androgen exposure. If there is androgen exposure, the primordial phallus will differentiate into the glans or head of the penis, the genital swelling will become the scrotum (into which the testes will eventually descend from the abdominal cavity), and the genital tubercle will differentiate into the shaft or main body of the penis. If there is no androgen ex-

posure, then the primordial phallus will become the clitoris, the genital swelling will become the labia majora, and the genital tubercle will become the labia minora and the outer one-third of the vagina. Again, regardless of the genetic sex of the embryo, the absence of stimulation of primordial genital tissue by androgens will result in female structures. The presence of androgens is required for masculine development. In the example of Turner's syndrome, the external genitalia are those of a normal female even though she lacks ovaries.

PUBERTY

At birth, the infant has his or her primary sex characteristics: testes or ovaries and both internal and external sexual organs characteristic of males or females. It is not until puberty that an individual's gonadal hormones begin to determine further development. Puberty begins with the secretion of hormones by the hypothalamus and the pituitary located in the brain; the hormones travel via the bloodstream to the testes or ovaries, causing the production of the gonadal hormones that will direct the development of sexual maturation. These hormones will direct the emergence of secondary sexual characteristics. The ovaries begin to produce estradiol, while the testes secrete testosterone. Estradiol causes enlargement of the breasts, growth in the lining of the uterus, widening of the hips, changes in the deposition of fat, and maturation of the female genitalia. Testosterone is responsible for growth of facial hair, deepening of the voice, masculine muscular development, and growth of the male genitalia.

Estradiol secretion in the female is also responsible for the onset of the first menstrual cycle. The cycle begins when an ovarian follicle is stimulated by hormones from the pituitary and thereby matures. It then secretes estradiol, which causes growth in the lining of the uterus in preparation for implantation of a fertilized ovum. It also causes ovulation, in which the follicle ruptures, releasing an ovum. During the second half of the cycle, the follicle itself becomes the corpus luteum, which produces both estradiol and progesterone. The latter hormone is responsible for maintaining the lining of the uterus during pregnancy. If the ovum is not fertilized, both estradiol and progesterone production decrease and the uterine lining is sloughed off in menstruation.

ROLE IN SEXUAL BEHAVIOR

The influence of gonadal hormones has been studied in relation to the activation of sexual, maternal, and aggressive behaviors. The effects of gonadal hormones on behavior can be subdivided into organizational and activational influences, with the former occurring during prenatal development and the latter occurring after puberty.

Psychologists have studied the ways in which prenatal exposure or insensitivity to androgens organizes sexual behavior. In the adrenogenital syndrome, the adrenal glands secrete unusually high levels of androgens, to which the developing embryo is exposed. If the embryo is male, normal development will occur. If the embryo is female, masculinization will occur, with enlargement of the clitoris and possibly fused labia. Researchers at The Johns Hopkins University studied thirty young women with adrenogenital syndrome to determine whether androgenization (exposure of the developing embryo to male sex hormones) affected their sexual orientation— that is, the gender of their preferred sexual partners. The women described themselves as homosexual or bisexual at approximately four times the rate that occurs naturally in random populations of women. This hints that exposure of the developing female fetus to androgens may affect sexual orientation, possibly by altering the organization of the brain in ways that are not yet understood. A similar finding has occurred in primate research. When androgens were injected into monkeys pregnant with female fetuses, these androgenized infants became significantly different from their nonandrogenized peers in displaying more malelike behaviors, such as engaging in attempted mountings of other females.

The failure of male fetuses to be androgenized properly occurs in the androgen insensitivity syndrome. These genetically male individuals will develop female genitalia and, if reared as females, will easily assume female sexual identities and overwhelmingly prefer male sexual partners. There is some possibility, then, that prenatal androgenization encourages a preference for female sexual partners, while lack of such exposure results in a preference for male sexual partners, regardless of genetic sex. It should be remembered, however, that this remains quite speculative and conclusive research has not yet been conducted.

The activational effects of gonadal hormones on adult sexual behavior have also been of interest to psychologists. While estradiol and progesterone strongly influence the sexual behaviors of lower animals, these hormones do not seem to influence human female sexual behavior. For example, while both estrogen and progesterone levels fluctuate considerably over the menstrual cycle, women can become aroused at any time in the cycle and are not more easily aroused when these hormones are especially high or low. Further, when a woman's ovaries are surgically removed or cease to produce hormones after menopause, sexual activity and interest are not affected.

There is some evidence that androgens, either present in small amounts secreted by the adrenal glands or ingested in the form of synthetic male hormones, will cause greater sexual desire in females and more frequent instigation of sexual activity but will have no effect on an already-established sexual orientation. The influence of androgens on male animals is direct: All male mammals respond to the presence of testosterone with increased sexual desire. Without testosterone, sperm production and copulatory ability cease.

ROLE IN AGGRESSIVE BEHAVIOR

Much aggressive behavior among animals takes place within the context of reproductive behavior. It comes as no surprise, then, that aggressive behaviors in both sexes are also strongly influenced by gonadal hormones, particularly androgens. Male of-

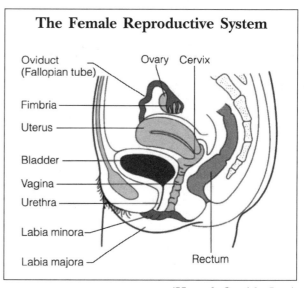

The Female Reproductive System

Oviduct (Fallopian tube)
Ovary   Cervix
Fimbria
Uterus
Bladder
Vagina
Urethra
Labia minora
Labia majora
Rectum

(Hans & Cassidy, Inc.)

fensive attacks and competitive behaviors, as well as interfemale aggressiveness and maternal aggression, are increased by exposure to androgens in most mammals.

One of the most stable behavioral differences between males and females is aggression; males display higher levels of aggression at all ages and in all forms. Because this sex difference has been observed in toddlers, before strong socialization influences have had their impact, it is speculated that prenatal exposure to androgens is partly responsible for these behavioral differences. This same relationship holds for all other mammalian species: the greater the prenatal androgenization, the more aggressive the subsequent behavior.

The relationship between aggressive behavior and testosterone levels has been studied in a variety of ways. One avenue of research has been to examine the testosterone levels of males who display different levels of aggressive behavior. For example, the testosterone levels of male prisoners with histories of violent crime have been compared with the frequency of their violent behavior while incarcerated. No relationship between the androgen levels and current aggressive expression has been found; however, androgen levels have been positively correlated with the frequency of these prisoners' aggressive behaviors in adolescence. Perhaps by adulthood, learning had intervened to modulate this relationship, with some high-testosterone males able to exert control over their aggressive impulses while some men with lower testosterone levels learn to vent their aggressiveness.

MATERNAL BEHAVIOR AND GENDER IDENTITY

With regard to the effects of gonadal hormones on maternal behavior, the findings are clear in most lower animals. In laboratory rats, for example, sequences of progesterone followed by estradiol will facilitate nest-building behaviors. No such relationship, however, seems to hold for humans. It seems that maternal behavior is determined largely by learning and by an early bonding between mother and infant and that caretaking behaviors are not influenced by hormonal activation.

Research concerning the effects of gonadal hormones on behavior is one of the many avenues of investigation into the development of gender identity, an individual's sense of being a man or a woman. There are many determinants of such identity: one's genetic makeup, prenatal sex hormone exposure, one's internal and external genitalia, the gender to which one is assigned at birth, and socialization—learning about culturally appropriate gender behaviors through interaction with parents and peers. Most often, all these determinants are consistent with one another, and the individual develops a clear, stable sense of gender identity.

RESEARCH DIRECTIONS

Future research concerning gonadal hormones will continue in two major directions: the effects of gonadal hormones on the sexual differentiation of the brain and the interaction between sex hormones and adult sexual behaviors. Most research on sexual differentiation of the brain has been conducted with nonhuman species. For example, it has been found that testosterone "masculinizes" the brains of birds to produce typical male birdsong and produces male or female sexual behaviors in laboratory animals. The way in which this masculinization occurs is somewhat paradoxical: Inside the brain of the male embryo, testosterone is converted to estrogen, the hormone that actually produces the masculinization. In females, on the other hand, a protein exists in the neurons of the brain that prevents estrogen from effecting such masculinization.

In humans, it is known that the absence of prenatal androgen exposure sets the brain in a female pattern, which causes the pituitary to function in a cyclical manner, thus creating the menstrual cycle. Some interesting initial research with humans suggests that, as a result of prenatal hormone exposure, there is greater lateralization of male brains than of female brains. Therefore, there is more specialization of the two cerebral hemispheres in males and more crossover of functions across the two hemispheres in females. This notice remains speculative and will be subject to considerable scrutiny.

Research interest will continue to be directed toward discovering the role of gonadal hormones in adult sexual behavior. More recent areas of study concern the question of prenatal hormonal determinants of sexual orientation (homosexual or heterosexual partner preferences). Studies will also continue to be focused on the age-old question of sexual motivation in general to determine the levels and kinds of sex hormones that either enhance or depress sexual interest.

SOURCES FOR FURTHER STUDY

Beyer, Carlos, ed. *Endocrine Control of Sexual Behavior.* New York: Raven Press, 1979. A superb collection of review articles concerning hormonal influences on the sexual behavior of mammals. Particularly helpful in describing the methodology of such analysis.

Drickamer, Lee C., Stephen H. Vessey, and Elizabeth Jakobson. *Animal Behavior.* 5th ed. New York: McGraw-Hill, 2001. An excellent, detailed text that describes the various physiological determinants of animal behavior. Includes chapters on sexual, reproductive, and aggressive behaviors.

Graham, Robert B. *Physiological Psychology.* Belmont, Calif.: Wadsworth, 1990. A comprehensive presentation of the major aspects of the physiological determination of behavior in all mammalian species. The chapter devoted to sexuality and reproduction covers most of the effects of gonadal hormones in detail.

Money, John, and Anke A. Ehrhardt. *Man and Woman, Boy and Girl.* 1972. Reprint. Northvale, N.J.: Jason Aronson, 1996. This is an accessible text that describes genetic and hormonal anomalies in fetal development and the consequences of these conditions on gender-identity development.

Unger, Rhoda Kesler. *Female and Male: Psychological Perspectives.* New York: Harper & Row, 1979. This classic text concerning the psychology of sex differences has two chapters that focus on the interaction between sex hormones and the development of gender identity, both prenatally and at puberty.

Barbara E. Brackney

SEE ALSO: Adolescence: Sexuality; Endocrine system; Gender-identity formation; Hormones and behavior; Pituitary gland; Prenatal physical development; Sex hormones and motivation; Sexual behavior patterns.

Grammar and speech

TYPE OF PSYCHOLOGY: Language
FIELDS OF STUDY: Descriptive methodologies

Grammar and speech are the building blocks of the human communication systems known as lan- *guages. The study of language structure has enhanced growth in a number of areas in psychology, including language acquisition, the biological basis for language, and the relationship between language and thought.*

KEY CONCEPTS
- critical period
- generative grammar
- morpheme
- morphology
- phonology
- suffix
- syntax

INTRODUCTION

Human beings everywhere, despite differences in geography, culture, and ethnicity, have a capacity for language, a system of communication primarily involving a patterned, rule-governed sequence of oral sounds. The rules that human beings implicitly use to produce and understand such communication are collectively known as grammar, and the vocalizations that serve as the vehicle of the communication are called speech.

When people think of grammar, they usually think of a set of arbitrary rules learned in school about correct and incorrect ways of speaking or writing. Indeed, such rules do constitute a grammar of sorts, one that prescribes standards of appropriate style. Grammar, however, has a wider and more important meaning, because without a grammar no language is possible. In fact, every speaker of a language knows the rules of the grammar of that language without being explicitly taught them. Grammar, in its most important sense, is the set of rules that each language has and that each native speaker of that language knows even before going to school; it determines what the basic building blocks of the language are (the words, morphemes, and sounds) and specifies the rules for combining those basic elements into meaningful utterances. Grammar is simply the structure of that unique human behavior called language.

LANGUAGE SUBSYSTEMS

Language scientists generally subdivide language into a set of structural subsystems, each of which has its own set of rules, or regular patterns. When discovered, these rules can be seen to operate in every utterance of that language. Each of these subsystems—syntax, morphology, and phonology—therefore is a grammar, although the term "grammar" itself in its everyday use is usually associated only with syntax.

The syntax of a language is the set of rules which govern how meaningful elements, the words, are combined into the permissible sequences known as sentences. Syntax also dictates how sentences can be combined with other sentences to form more complex utterances and how elements within sentences can be rearranged to change the focus of a sentence without changing its meaning. For example, speakers of English know that the sequence of words "the dog chased the cat" means that an instigator of an action, a dog, behaved in such a way to affect the second participant mentioned in the string of words, the cat. Moreover, they know that the word "the" must precede and never follow words such as "cat" and "dog." Finally, they know that the sequence "the cat was chased by the dog" is merely a paraphrase, a restatement, of the original string and not a contradiction of it.

The morphology of a language, the second subsystem, defines the basic set of elements which operate in the formation of words. Each of these basic elements is called a morpheme. Many morphemes may be words in a language, but some morphemes are less than an entire word. For example, the English suffix -s attached to a word such as "cup" states that there is more than one cup; it is apparent to any speaker of English that this suffix (ending) is considerably less than a word. Nevertheless, the -s is a meaningful element in the English language and constitutes a morpheme, or minimal meaningful unit, of the language. The way words are constructed is rule-governed and is therefore a kind of grammar; for example, the -s that signals "more than one" is always attached to the end of the word, not to the beginning of it, and it cannot be inserted in the middle. This fact about English is predictable. If English speakers encounter a new word which designates some object, they know that talking about more than one of these objects usually requires the addition of the -s suffix to the new word. This implicit knowledge is a kind of grammar known as morphology.

The third important structural subsystem of language is phonology, or the sound system of a language. Each of the world's languages uses only some of the vocal sounds that human beings are capable of producing, and this limited set is further constrained regarding what sounds may follow one another at the beginnings, middles, and ends of words. For example, the English language has both /t/ and /l/ as sounds that may be used in words, and though /l/ may follow /t/ in the middle of words such as "antler" and "butler," there are no English words beginning with this sequence of sounds, nor are there likely to be any. The sequence *tl* simply does not occur at the beginning of English words, although there is no physiological reason that it cannot. Human beings are perfectly capable of producing such a sound combination and it does exist at the beginning of words in other languages. It is the grammar of the sound system of English—its phonology—that prohibits such a possibility.

UNIQUE GRAMMAR OF LANGUAGES

These subsystems of language are found in every one of the world's languages, even though each subsystem's particulars and importance are unique for each language. As an example, languages such as Modern English can be compared to classical Latin, the ancestor language of French, Italian, and Spanish. In English, the ordering of words is of paramount importance. A sentence such as "The boy loved the girl" has only one meaning, and changing the sequencing of words would drastically change that meaning. That is, if the words "boy" and "girl" were interchanged, the resulting sentence, "The girl loved the boy," would mean something entirely different. The initiator of the state of love is now the girl, not the boy. Thus, in English, the critical information of who is doing what to whom is given in the syntax, in the ordering of words. In Latin, on the other hand, although there is surely word sequencing, since words can only be expressed one at a time, the word order—the syntax—does not indicate relationships as it does in English. Instead, the matter of who is doing what to whom is given by morphology, by suffixes attached to the ends of words. The sentence "The boy loved the girl" could be expressed by any of the following: *puer puellam amabat, puellam puer amabat, amabat puer puellam, puellam amabat puer,* and so on. That is, the arrangement of words has little effect on meaning; the endings on the words tell speakers of Latin who does what. The *-m* at the end of the word for "girl" signals that the girl is affected by the action and is not the initiator of it. These facts about the two languages show that word order is more important to English than it is to Latin and that endings on words are more important to Latin, even though English continues to make use of endings to some degree (the -ed on "love" indicates, for example, that an action or state occurred at some past time).

The fact that all languages have a grammar, a predictable pattern underlying every utterance, allows human languages to be unique among all the communication systems found in nature. Most important, grammar allows people to talk about new things, about events that occurred in the past, about events that might possibly occur in the future, and even about things that can never be. A grammar allows people to produce an infinite number of possible sentences because words can be combined and recombined in many ways to generate many different meanings. This possibility makes language qualitatively different from the songs and calls of birds, which are rigidly structured to allow only a limited number of meanings; from the dances of bees, which have the single function of indicating the location of nectar; and even from the gestures of the apes, which can indicate only a limited set of communications.

LANGUAGE ACQUISITION

The complexity and variation in systems of grammar have led to a number of speculations about the nature of the human mind in particular, about the relationship between language and thought, and about how such complex systems could be achieved by human children before they are capable of logical thought. The first of these two areas is also known as linguistic relativity. The second, the possibility that at base all languages are essentially the same because they are constructed by human beings who have an innate capacity for language, has been proposed by linguist Noam Chomsky, the founder of the field of syntactic inquiry known as generative grammar. Generative grammar can be defined as a grammar that projects the structure of a potentially infinite number of sentences, including both those already produced and those yet to be uttered.

Examining the complexity of the syntax of English, Chomsky suggested that the capacity for language must be innate, that human beings have an inborn language acquisition device which enables them to determine the grammar of the language spoken by the people who rear them. Chomsky ex-plained that much of what young children hear must be full of errors and false starts, and yet before age five, most children speak their native language with a high degree of accuracy. He suggested that the language acquisition device must act as a kind of analyzer that assigns a structure to the incoming stream of speech. The resulting analysis then becomes the foundation of the grammar that permits children to produce new, original sentences in the language they hear all around them.

This speculation fueled much research during the 1960's and 1970's, and the result is that most language scientists—linguists and psychologists alike—agree that indeed the capacity for language acquisition is innate; the actual nature of the innate capacity, however, remains uncertain. Research has generally found that parents and other caregivers tend to be extremely careful in the kinds of speech they address to children; that is, they tend to speak without the errors and the false starts Chomsky had supposed. Moreover, they tend to pause and change the pitch of their voices at precisely those places in an utterance where the grammar would assign an important boundary. In many ways, then, the speech addressed to children seems an ideal teaching device, and so Chomsky's hypothesis that children formulate a grammar on the basis of fragmentary and poorly structured input has been disconfirmed. It also has been found that even very young infants tend to prefer the sound of human voices to other sounds and are capable of telling the difference between very similar but distinct speech sounds. Thus, it is clear that human beings are predisposed to acquire language.

CRITICAL PERIOD HYPOTHESIS

Other evidence supports the notion that there is a biological predisposition to language. In his book *Biological Foundations of Language* (1967), Eric Lenneberg proposed that there is a critical period for language acquisition, an age beyond which the acquisition of a first language would not be possible. That is, Lenneberg contended that a child deprived of the opportunity to acquire a language—any language at all—would never be able to do so if the deprivation continued past the onset of puberty. Supporting evidence for this hypothesis suggested a discontinuity in language abilities at adolescence. Children who suffer trauma to the parts of the brain where language is processed, for example, tend to recover if the injury occurs before puberty but typically do not recover their language abilities if the injury occurs in their mid-teen years. In addition, children who are exposed to a second language during childhood apparently acquire that language with little difficulty when compared with adults facing the same task. This too seems to support the hypothesis of a critical period for language acquisition. Moreover, case studies of feral children raised without language by nurturing animals such as wolves have indicated that these children failed to acquire language when introduced into civilization.

These kinds of evidence provide only partial (and debatable) support for the critical period hypothesis. For example, no two injuries are exactly alike, so the successful recovery of one patient from a brain injury compared to the failure of another may stem from a number of causes. The facility of children compared to the difficulty for adults with respect to second-language acquisition may result from children's lack of self-consciousness. Finally, children raised by wolves during the last several centuries may have been abandoned by their parents because they had some apparent disability; perhaps the children lacked the cognitive or speech skills necessary to acquire language.

THE "GENIE" CASE STUDY

In 1970, however, a thirteen-year-old girl suffering from severe neglect was found. The child of a psychotic father and an abused and half-blind mother, "Genie," as she came to be called, had been locked in a darkened room since infancy and deprived of all genuine human contact. She was absolutely devoid of any language skills, although her hearing was found to be normal. Since medical records indicated normal development during infancy, save for a hip defect, and since she was clearly past puberty, Genie provided a test case for the critical-period hypothesis.

Removed from her abusive environment and given the attention of caring adults, Genie made remarkable progress. At first, she seemed able to acquire language after all, and reports of her linguistic achievements were thought to herald the demise of the critical-period hypothesis. It soon became evident, however, that although Genie was making excellent progress with social and cognitive skills, her development of syntax and morphology lagged far behind. She was able to acquire a vocabulary of

some size—a word list—but she failed to put words together in the ways that were typical of children acquiring language during the usual developmental period. She also had difficulty with those English morphemes that show relationship among elements in a sentence. In short, although Genie could understand words and word meanings, she was having considerable difficulty mastering grammar. Genie's case provides partial support for the critical-period hypothesis; after puberty, parts of language may still be acquired, but a full elaboration of the grammatical patterns that underlie a language will not be achieved. The importance of the early childhood years to the acquisition of language skills is clearly demonstrated by this case.

Genie's progress with language acquisition—or lack of it—could not be mapped without a knowledge of the parts of language, an understanding of syntax and morphology. Similarly, the accomplishments of young children with respect to language acquisition could not be appreciated without a knowledge of the structures underlying grammar and speech. The field of language acquisition is an entire area of study that crucially depends on knowledge of the structure of language. To study acquisition requires a knowledge of what is being acquired.

EVOLUTION OF LANGUAGE RESEARCH

Although interest in language is as old as language itself, prior to the nineteenth century investigations were philosophical and speculative. Questions about language were likely to concern the origins of language or the identity of the oldest language. During the early part of the nineteenth century, newly discovered relationships between languages fueled interest in a field of study now called comparative and historical linguistics, which attempted to ascertain which languages derived from the same prehistoric ancestor language. Late in that century, however, interest began to turn away from the comparison of languages and toward an investigation of languages on their own terms. In the early part of the twentieth century, the scientific study of language was encouraged by the great American linguists Edward Sapir and Leonard Bloomfield.

Both Sapir and Bloomfield were spurred by the study of the indigenous languages of America, the languages spoken by the peoples often called American Indians. These languages were unwritten, so recording them involved a detailed investigation of their phonology, morphology, and syntax. The languages of Europe were also subjected to this new, rigorous scientific study, now called linguistics.

At first, scientific linguistics dealt mainly with phonology and morphology and studied syntax only as an afterthought. The publication of Noam Chomsky's *Syntactic Structures* (1957), however, revolutionized the field. This small book redistributed the rankings among the various subfields of language by showing the formal relationships among apparently diverse structures in syntax; what had previously been backgrounded in the study of language, the syntax, was now seen as the central focus of linguistic inquiry. In fact, syntax became so important within linguistics that Chomsky and his colleagues argued for an autonomous syntax, a system of structural relations that has an existence apart from sound and meaning. In the last decades of the twentieth century, many linguists abandoned this notion and opted instead for a pragmatic analysis of language, a description based on how particular words, syntactic structures, phonological features, and other patterns of discourse such as overlaps and interruptions among participants in a conversation are used to achieve certain effects in the real world. This approach has the effect of integrating the subsystems of language so that the focus is on the basic circumstance of communication: people talking.

S<small>OURCES FOR</small> F<small>URTHER</small> S<small>TUDY</small>

Baker, Mark C. *The Atoms of Language: The Mind's Hidden Rules of Grammar.* New York: Basic Books, 2001. Attempts to uncover the universal similarities in the grammars of human languages.

Chomsky, Noam. *Aspects of a Theory of Syntax.* Cambridge, Mass.: MIT Press, 1969. Chomsky's classic statement of his linguistic theories.

Harley, Trevor A. *The Psychology of Language: From Data to Theory.* 2d ed. Washington, D.C.: Psychology Press, 2001. This undergraduate textbook offers a lucid introduction to the field of psycholinguistics.

Jackendorff, Ray. *Foundations of Language: Brain, Meaning, Grammar, Evolution.* New York: Oxford University Press, 2002. A survey of late twentieth century linguistic theory from a post-Chomskeyian perspective. Requires a knowledge of linguistics.

Karmiloff, Kyra, and Annette Karmiloff-Smith. *Pathways to Language: From Fetus to Adolescent.* Cambridge, Mass.: Harvard University Press, 2002. An

overview of the myriad processes of and theories about language development.

Loritz, Donald. *How the Brain Evolved Language.* New York: Oxford University Press, 2002. Traces the development of what Loritz calls "adaptive grammar" through the evolution of the human brain, contradicting the theories of "innateness" proposed by Noam Chomsky and Steven Pinker.

Sapir, Edward. *Language: An Introduction to the Study of Speech.* 1921. Reprint. New York: Harvest Books, 1955. The classic introduction to language. Sapir demonstrates how all languages share some common features and yet differ markedly in their structures. Much of the foundation for theories of linguistic relativity can be found in this slim volume, along with much of the justification for the universality of language structures. Required reading for all those interested in language study.

Marilyn N. Silva

S<small>EE ALSO</small>: Analytic psychology: Jacques Lacan; Artificial intelligence; Bilingualism; Communication; Concept formation; Lacan, Jacques; Language; Linguistics.

Grieving

T<small>YPE OF PSYCHOLOGY</small>: Emotion; psychopathology; stress

F<small>IELDS OF STUDY</small>: Coping; depression; stress and illness

Grieving is the usual, expectable reaction to loss. There is a normal process that occurs in grieving that follows realization of a loss. This process involves feelings such as anger and sadness, which induce a reassessment and reorganization of oneself and one's perspective. If this normal process is hindered, psychologists and physicians look for problems such as depression, which is associated with other physical ailments and a heightened mortality rate.

K<small>EY CONCEPTS</small>
- anger
- denial
- depression
- loss
- mourning

- realization
- reassessment
- sadness
- stress

INTRODUCTION

A good deal of life has to do with adaptation to change. When that change is experienced as a loss, the emotional and cognitive reactions are properly referred to as grief. When the specific loss is acknowledged by one's culture, the loss is often met with particular rituals, behaviors that follow a certain pattern, sanctioned and choreographed within the culture. It is common, when the loss is that of a significant person (such as a spouse, parent, child, or close relative or friend) to apply the term "bereavement." In this case the grief and the sanctioned rituals are referred to as mourning, although some writers have used the terms "mourning" and "grieving" as synonymous.

Several phenomena are central in the experience of loss. Depending on whether the loss is experienced as central as opposed to peripheral in relation to the self, it will have a greater or lesser impact on the person's ability to function. Certain kinds of thinking and evaluation may take place: obsessive thoughts about who or what was lost; a sense of unreality; a conviction that one was personally responsible for the loss; a sense that there is no help or hope; a conviction that one is a bad person; and a sense that one is not able to concentrate and remember.

One's emotional response may at first be more engrossing. Shock, anger, sadness, guilt, anxiety, or even loss of feeling are all possible and likely. One may display crying, fatigue, agitation, or even withdrawal from social contact. All are possible in the grief reaction. There is also the possibility of denial. Depending on cultural, family, and individual patterns of learning, some individuals will suppress, repress, and deny part of their awareness and/or grief reaction.

Finally, the centrality of loss within the self is also related to the circumstances of the loss. If one is prepared for the loss, one has made oneself less vulnerable to the loss of that person, place, or object. For instance, if the person has lived a long and satisfying life or has been ill and suffering for a protracted time, then one may be more ready to let the person go when death finally occurs.

THE HISTORY OF GRIEF STUDIES

The study of grief as a scholarly concern was started by an essay, "Mourning and Melancholia," written in 1917 by the Austrian founder of psychoanalysis, Sigmund Freud (1856-1939). In it, Freud proposed that hysteria (a disorder of emotional instability and dissociation) and melancholia are symptoms of pathological grief. He indicated that painful dejection, loss of the ability to love, inhibition of activity, and decrease in self-esteem that continues beyond the normal time are what distinguish melancholia from mourning (the pathological from the normal). In melancholia it is the ego (or self) that becomes poor and impoverished. In the pathological case, the damage to self is becoming permanent instead of being a temporary and reversible deprivation.

The study of grief as a normal process of loss evolved over two and a half decades. It was not until 1944 that a German physician who became an American psychiatrist, Erich Lindemann (1900-1974), published a study based mostly on interviews with relatives of victims of the Cocoanut Grove nightclub fire in Boston in 1942. He characterized five different aspects of the grief reaction. Each of the five was believed by Lindemann to be normal. Each would give way as the individual readjusted to the environment without the deceased, formed new relationships, and released the ties of connection with the deceased. Morbid or pathological grief reactions were seen as distortions of the normal patterns. A common distortion had to do with delay in reacting to the death. In these cases, the person would either deny the death or continue to maintain composure and show little or no reaction to the death's occurrence. Other forms of distorted reactions were overactivity, acquisition of symptoms associated with the deceased, social isolation, repression of emotions, and activities that were detrimental to one's social status and economic well-being. Examples of such detrimental activities might be getting drunk, being promiscuous, giving away all one's money, and quitting one's job.

In the early 1950's, the British psychoanalyst and physician John Bowlby (1907-1990) began to study loss in childhood, usually with children who were separated from their mothers. His early generalization summarized the child's response in a threefold way: protest, despair, and detachment. From his later work, which included adult mourning, he came to

The loss of a life partner, particularly after a lengthy relationship, is a source of intense grief and may trigger guilt in the survivor. (PhotoDisc)

the conclusion that mourning follows a similar pattern whether it takes place in childhood, adolescence, or adulthood. While specifying wide time frames for the first and second phases in this latter work, he has also expanded his threefold description of the process to identify four phases of mourning. All of the four phases overlap and the person may go back for a while to a previous phase. These phases were numbing, which may last from a few hours to a week and may be interrupted by episodes of intense distress and/or anger; yearning and searching for the lost figure, which may last for months and even for years; disorganization and despair; and reorganization to a greater or lesser degree.

What was new and interesting about the fourth phase is Bowlby's introduction of a positive ending to the grieving process. This is the idea of reorganization, a positive restructuring of oneself and one's perceptual field. This is a striking advance beyond Lindemann's notion that for the healthy person, the negative aspects of grieving would be dissipated in time.

Meanwhile, in the mid-1960's, quite independently of Bowlby, a Swiss physician who became an American psychiatrist, Elisabeth Kübler-Ross, was interviewing terminally ill patients in Chicago. She observed closely, listened sensitively, and reported on their experiences in an important book, *On Death and Dying* (1969). Her work was written from a perspective of wanting to aid the dying patient.

Kübler-Ross was there as patients first refused to believe the prognosis, as they got angry at themselves and at others around them, as they attempted to argue their way out (to make a deal with God or whoever might have the power to change the reality), as they faced their own sadness and depression, and finally as they came to a sense of acceptance about their fate. (Her idea of acceptance is similar to Bowlby's concept of reorganization.) From her interviews, she abstracted a five-stage process in which terminally ill patients came to deal with the loss of their own lives: denial and isolation; anger; bargaining (prayer is an example); depression; and acceptance.

A REVIEW OF THE GRIEF PROCESS

It is possible to summarize the process of the grief reaction. The reaction only follows when there is a realization that a loss has occurred. Denial stops the reaction for as long as the person can sustain the denial. This refusal to be aware of a loss depends upon the intensity of the person's defenses against facing reality in this particular circumstance. Once realization has taken place, it is often followed by numbing (a reduction in feeling), anger, searching, and bargaining. This stage is likely to be followed by disorganization in thinking, despair, guilt, and depression. When this stage is worked through, the individual arrives at acceptance and reassessment, a new outlook on self and the world.

Grieving is the psychological, biological, and behavioral way of dealing with the stress created when a significant part of the self or prop for the self is taken away. Austrian endocrinologist Hans Selye (1907-1982) made a vigorous career in defining stress and considering the positive and negative effects that it may have on a person. He defined stress as "the nonspecific response of the body to any demand made upon it." It is obvious that any significant change in the life of a person calls for adjustment and thus involves stress. Selye indicated that what counts is the severity of the demand, and this depends on the perception of the person involved. Perhaps the term "grief" might be retained only for cases of extreme loss, but it seems that, from minor loss to extreme loss, the process is the same and only differs in degree. Extreme loss is correlated with a higher degree of stress, a greater sense of hopelessness, and a higher rate of mortality.

CULTURAL AND SOCIAL INFLUENCES ON GRIEF

Since loss is such a regular part of life, one's reaction to it is likely to be regulated by family and cultural influences. Thus it should not be surprising that religious and cultural practices have developed to govern the expected and acceptable ways of responding to it. Many of these religious and cultural practices provide both permission for and boundaries to the expression of grief. They provide both an opportunity to express feelings and a limit to the time when their expression may be seemly. Often a religion or culture will stipulate the rituals that must be observed, how soon they must be concluded, how long they must be extended, what kind of clothing is appropriate, and what kinds of expressions are permissible and fitting. They also provide a cognitive framework in which the loss may be understood and, perhaps, better accepted; for instance, if it can be seen as God's will, then it may seem more part of a divine plan and less capricious.

Since not every culture has been examined for practices and reactions following loss, including death, there have been objections claiming that the grief reaction may not be universal. However it is certainly a regular phenomenon in most societies.

Some social influences may be limiting, to the extent that the grief reaction is short-circuited and the individual may suffer as a result. Some social influences may be deliberately designed to profit from the regularity of loss and grief. The funeral home industry in the United States has been very successful in institutionalizing the process of grieving and profiting thereby. At the same time, there are a large number of individuals professionally trained to counsel and help others through the process of grieving.

SOURCES FOR FURTHER STUDY

Bowlby, John. *Loss: Sadness and Depression.* London: Tavistock Institute, 1980. A classic study that makes the argument that grieving in infancy is the same process as grieving at any other time in life.

Freud, Sigmund. "Mourning and Melancholia." In *Collected Papers.* Vol. 4. London: Hogarth, 1956. Freud's classic 1917 paper that introduced the modern study of grief and loss.

Harvey, John H., ed. *Perspectives on Loss: A Sourcebook.* Philadelphia: Taylor & Francis, 1998. Articles by leading investigators in the field of loss and grieving show the wide variety of perspectives that have developed in this field. Many different examples of loss are presented and described together with the personal consequences.

Lindemann, Erich. "Symptomatology and Management of Acute Grief." *American Journal of Psychiatry* 101 (1944): 141-148. Another classic article that shows how Lindemann examined the survivors' responses to the famous Coconut Grove fire. The fire, in Boston on November 28, 1942, claimed 491 lives. Lindemann summarized his work in this area in *Beyond Grief: Studies in Crisis Intervention* (Northvale, N.J.: Jason Aronson, 1979).

Marrone, Robert. *Death, Mourning, and Caring.* Pacific Grove, Calif.: Brooks/Cole, 1997. A useful general text that demonstrates the growing professional interest in the area of grief and loss. It contains cross-cultural examples of grief rituals, a developmental examination of what grief means at stages from childhood to old age, and a list of resources for those who need to grieve.

Mitford, Jessica. *The American Way of Death.* London: Hutchinson, 1963. An examination of the American funeral industry by an investigative reporter.

Parkes, Colin Murray. *Bereavement: Studies of Grief in Adult Life.* 2d ed. Madison, Conn.: International Universities Press, 1987. In a very readable style, Parkes, a collaborator of Bowlby, traces the development of psychoanalysis to a case of grieving (Anna O's loss of her father), makes the case that grief is a "diagnosable condition," and examines the stages of grief.

Everett J. Delahanty, Jr.

SEE ALSO: Coping: Social support; Coping: Terminal illness; Death and dying; Denial; Depression; Emotions; Post-traumatic stress disorder; Support groups.

Group decision making

TYPE OF PSYCHOLOGY: Social psychology
FIELDS OF STUDY: Group processes

Group decision making is one of the oldest areas of inquiry in social psychology. Research has shown that groups have profound effects on the behavior of their individual members; the decisions that people make in groups can be quite different from those that they make on their own.

KEY CONCEPTS
- choice shift
- group confidence
- heterogeneity
- informational influence
- normative influence
- process loss
- social decision scheme

INTRODUCTION

Important societal, business, medical, legal, and personal decisions are often made by more than one person. Psychologists in the field of group decision making have attempted to describe the processes through which such decisions are made. The process by which a set of individual group members' decisions becomes transformed into a single group decision can be described by a "social decision scheme." Research by James H. Davis and his colleagues at the University of Illinois has shown the conditions under which groups use various decision-making rules, such as adopting the preference of the majority or that of the member who has the best answer.

VARIABLES IN GROUP TASKS

The nature of the decision problem facing a group must be considered in an evaluation of the group's decision process. Psychologist Ivan Steiner pioneered the analysis of the group's task in his book *Group Process and Productivity* (1972). Steiner identified three characteristics of group tasks that should be considered in analyzing group decision making. The first is the ability to subdivide the task into subtasks that members can perform individually. For example, a group can plan a meal by making one member responsible for selecting a meat dish, another for choosing a vegetarian entrée, another

for choosing desserts, and so forth. Other tasks, in which division of labor is not feasible, are said to be "unitary." In general, the more important the decision, the more difficult it is to divide it among group members. Yet it is often precisely because a decision task is important that it is given to a group rather than an individual. Therefore, even if some aspect of the task (such as gathering information) can be done individually, final responsibility for the decision rests with a set of people.

Another variable in group tasks is the nature of the goal. In many cases, there is no "best" or "right" decision; the process is simply a matter of determining the group preference. Other decision tasks were called "optimizing" by Steiner because it was assumed that some optimal decision exists. The group's task is to find it. Most important group decision tasks are not only unitary but also optimizing. Finally, Steiner noted that the rules governing the group's decision-making activities were a critical feature of the task. If the group members are not constrained to particular procedures, the task is "discretionary."

CHOICE SHIFT

Important insights about decision process and quality in unitary, optimizing, and discretionary tasks have been gained by comparing the decision-making behavior of individuals acting alone to that of persons in groups. It is apparent that the way people behave in groups is different from the way they behave alone. As a consequence, decisions made in groups can differ radically from those made by the same persons acting alone. It is not uncommon for group decisions to be more extreme than an average of members' individual decisions.

Such a "choice shift" (the difference between the decision of a group and the average decision of group members as individuals) can lead to group decisions that are better than—or not as good as—the average member's decision. The average group member's judgment or choice provides one standard against which group decision quality can be compared. Another is the quality of the best decision from an individual member. Steiner called any decrease in quality from the decision of the best member, acting alone, to the group decision "process loss." Reviews of group decision research typically conclude that an average group performs above the level of its average member but below that of its best member. It is possible, however, for groups to reach better decisions than can any of their members alone.

NORMATIVE AND INFORMATIONAL INFLUENCES

Social psychologists recognize two types of influence that can cause group decisions to differ from those of individual group members: normative and informational. Normative influence comes merely from knowledge of the positions of others. One may come to doubt the quality of the alternative that one has selected simply by learning that everyone else believes that another alternative is superior. Confidence in a belief is difficult to maintain in the face of others who are in consensus about a contrary belief. The second type of influence, informational influence, results from logic or argument concerning the relative merits of various choice alternatives. Both types of influence usually operate in group decision making. Through normative or informational influence, individual group members can shift their positions.

Since groups usually make decisions under conditions of uncertainty, it can be difficult to evaluate the actual quality of a group decision. For this reason, the study of "group confidence" has become increasingly important. In general, groups exhibit greater confidence about the quality of their decisions than do individuals. This can be a desirable outcome if commitment to the group decision is necessary. As Irving Janis has shown in his analyses of political and managerial decision making, however, groups can be highly confident even while making disastrous decisions. Proper evaluation of group decision quality and confidence requires an ability to evaluate objectively the decision outcome. This has been done in a number of laboratory studies.

TASK ACCURACY AND CONFIDENCE

Experiments on group judgment by Janet A. Sniezek and her colleagues show how different group and individual decision making can be. These studies examine two aspects of group performance in judgment tasks. The first, accuracy, refers to the proximity of the consensus group judgment of some unknown value to the actual value. The other performance measure is one of confidence. Results show that consensus group judgments are typically far more accurate, and somewhat more confident,

than the independent judgments of two or more comparable individuals.

Two factors appear to be related to an increase in judgment accuracy in groups. One is the tendency of some groups to develop group judgments that are quite different from the members' individual judgments. A representative study asked students to judge various risks by estimating the annual frequency of deaths in the United States from each of several causes. A minority of group judgments were either higher or lower than all the members' individual estimates. For example, individual members' estimates for a given cause of death were 300, 500, and 650, but the consensus of these persons as a group was 200. This phenomenon is often associated with great gains in group judgment accuracy, but unfortunately, such radical shifts in judgment as a result of grouping can also lead to extreme process loss. Some groups become far more inaccurate than their average members by going out of the range of individual estimates.

The second factor that is related to improvements in the accuracy of group judgment is heterogeneity (variety in a group) within the group. On the whole, groups that begin with a wide variety of judgments improve more in comparison to their average members than groups that begin with more homogeneity. This supports the creation of groups with members from different ethnic, racial, religious, or educational backgrounds. Such differences are likely to promote heterogeneity, because the members of the group will have different sources of information and varying perspectives. Groups that lack sufficient heterogeneity face the danger of merely averaging their individual contributions. The result of averaging is to fail to improve appreciably in comparison to the level of quality of the average member.

TECHNIQUES

There have been many efforts to identify procedures that are better than discretionary procedures in improving the quality of group decisions for optimizing tasks. Many group techniques have been developed in an attempt to eliminate factors that are thought to contribute to process loss. The most popular techniques are designed to alter group discussion. Some inhibit normative influence by restricting the extent to which group members can reveal their preferences. Instead, group discussion is limited—at least initially—to a through evaluation of all options.

Other techniques for enhancing group decision making are designed to suppress the extent to which members are influenced by irrelevant factors. For example, status effects can operate in groups, causing the person with the highest status to exert a greater influence on the group decision than other members. This is undesirable if the high-status person's judgments are no more accurate—or even less accurate—than those of other group members. Other factors that have been shown to be irrelevant include the amount of participation in group discussion and self-confidence. Perhaps the most well-known technique developed to maximize informational influence and minimize irrelevant influences is the Delphi technique. This procedure prevents any potential problems of noninformational influence by not allowing face-to-face interaction. Instead, group members are given periodic anonymous feedback about the current positions of other group members. Often, group members provide information and logic to support their positions. More advanced technology, such as that available with computerized group decision support systems, has greatly expanded the ability to control group decision-making processes.

In addition to the goal of improving the quality of group decision making, some theorists have stressed the importance of increasing group members' satisfaction with their decisions. This objective remains somewhat controversial, since it is not always the case that people are more satisfied with better decisions and less satisfied with inferior ones. Ironically, people appear to be most satisfied when given the opportunity for group discussion—though this is precisely what is often eliminated in the hope of improving group decision quality.

Nevertheless, high group confidence can be an important end in itself. Presumably, groups with more confidence in their decisions are more committed to implementing them successfully. The increasing use of groups for decision making in organizations is based in part on this principle. Confidence in decision making can be increased by encouraging the participation of employees from various segments and levels of the organization. With such participative decision making, not only is confidence increased, but the number of organizational members who support the decision is increased as well.

SOCIAL IMPLICATIONS

Historically, scientific interest in group phenomena in general has been linked to social movements. Group research seems to thrive in the "we" decades, compared with the "me" decades. Interest specifically in group decision making, however, has tended to be stimulated by political and economic events.

Irving Janis carefully analyzed decision making by groups in President John F. Kennedy's administration. He diagnosed numerous problems regarding the way in which the Bay of Pigs crisis of 1961 was handled during group meetings. Collectively, the symptoms represent "groupthink," a narrow-minded approach to decision making that is caused primarily by a strong attachment of the group to its prevailing viewpoints. Janis shows how Kennedy altered the group decision process to accommodate and stimulate diverse perspectives during meetings about the Cuban Missile Crisis one and a half years later.

For many reasons, the study of decision making by groups is likely to become increasingly important to psychologists. As a result of the collectivist nature of most cultures, the dicipline of psychology will need to become less individualistic as it grows in non-Western societies and as social psychology expands to encompass more cultures. In addition, the growing interdependence of nations means that more and more global decisions will be made by groups of leaders, not by individual leaders.

Events within the United States can also be expected to create further demand for scientific investigation of group decision making. American organizations are using groups to a larger extent than ever before. For example, the group meeting is the most common approach to forecasting within organizations. The movement toward group decision making has been influenced in part by the apparent success of groups in Japanese firms. The desire to provide greater representation of workers in decisions should result in the increased use of groups for decision making.

While group decision-making research and applications are encouraged by national and global changes, these are not sufficient to bring about a genuine revolution in the making of decisions. There must also be an increase in the capacity to use groups. Here, too, it is reasonable to expect developments that support the use of groups in decision making. Major advances in communications allow more people to participate in the decision process in a timely fashion. These advances also have the potential for creating techniques that lead to higher-quality decision making than can be provided by traditional meetings.

SOURCES FOR FURTHER STUDY

Cannon-Bowers, Janis, and Eduardo Sales, eds. *Making Decisions Under Stress: Implications for Individual and Team Training.* Washington, D.C.: American Psychological Society, 1998. Report of a seven-year study conducted at the Office of Naval Research on mitigating the stress of decision making.

Davis, James H. "Social Interaction as a Combinatorial Process in Group Decision." In *Group Decision Making*, edited by H. Brandstatter, James H. Davis, and Gisela Stocker-Kreichgauer. London: Academic Press, 1982. Emphasizes models of group process. Good presentation of the social decision scheme approach, particularly as it has been applied in research on jury decision making.

Guzzo, Richard A., ed. *Improving Group Decision Making in Organizations.* New York: Academic Press, 1982. A collection of articles by group decision researchers. Despite its title, it is not a how-to book but rather an exploration of research paradigms that have potential applications to the improvement of decision making by groups. Topics include coalition formation, group remembering, and social judgment analysis.

Hastie, Reid. "Experimental Evidence on Group Accuracy." In *Decision Research*, edited by B. Grofman and G. Owen. Vol. 2. Greenwich, Conn.: JAI Press, 1986. A review of research on the quality of decisions made by groups. Strong emphasis on literature pertaining to decision making by juries. Also includes discussion of data on confidence.

Janis, Irving Lester. *Victims of Groupthink.* Boston: Houghton Mifflin, 1972. An illustration of the factors that can lead groups to make poor decisions with great confidence; includes dramatic examples based on historical incidents. Appropriate for a general audience.

McGrath, Joseph Edward. *Groups: Interaction and Performance.* Englewood Cliffs, N.J.: Prentice-Hall, 1984. Thorough and thoughtful integration of research on group performance. Includes numerous figures and research reports, as well as balanced discussions of ongoing and past debates. Appropriate as a text or reference book.

Parks, Craig D., and Lawrence J. Sanna. *Group Performance and Interaction.* Boulder, Colo.: Westview Press, 1999. A social psychology textbook on group dynamics and decision making.

Sniezek, Janet A., and Rebecca A. Henry. "Accuracy and Confidence in Group Judgment." *Organizational Behavior and Human Decision Processes* 43 (February 1, 1989): 1-28. A research article showing how group and individual judgment accuracy and confidence can be compared. Technical, but the figures and main results can be appreciated by the student.

Steiner, Ivan Dale. *Group Process and Productivity.* New York: Academic Press, 1972. A classic work that will remain important in the group decision-making literature. Analyzes the components of successful group performance and the processes required to get there. Scholarly rather than entertaining.

Janet A. Sniezek

SEE ALSO: Consumer psychology; Cooperation, competition, and negotiation; Crowd behavior; Decision making; Groups; Intergroup relations; Leadership.

Group therapy

TYPE OF PSYCHOLOGY: Psychotherapy
FIELDS OF STUDY: Group and family therapies

Group therapy allows individuals to enter into the therapeutic process with others who have the same or similar problems. This gives an individual much more freedom of expression as well as the support of others from within the group.

KEY CONCEPTS
• disclosure
• group dynamic
• group leader
• session
• therapeutic process

INTRODUCTION
Society to a greater or lesser degree always forms itself into some kinds of groupings, whether they are

for economic stability, religious expression, educational endeavor, or simply a sense of belonging. Within the field of psychotherapy, many theories and practices have been developed that deal with specific problems facing individuals as they try to relate to their environment as a whole and to become valuable members of society. Available approaches range from psychoanalysis to transpersonal therapy. Taking advantage of the natural tendency for people to form groups, therapists, since the years following World War II, have developed various forms of group therapy. Therapy groups, although they do not form "naturally," are most frequently composed of people with similar problems.

Immediately after World War II, the demand for therapeutic help was so great that the only way to cope with the need was to create therapeutic groups. Group therapy did not boast any one particular founder at that time, although among the first counseling theorists to embrace group therapy actively were Joseph Pratt, Alfred Adler, Jacob Moreno, Trigant Burrow, and Cody Marsh. Psychoanalysis, so firmly placed within the schools for individual psychotherapy, nevertheless became one of the first therapeutic approaches to be applied to group therapy. Gestalt therapy and transactional analysis have proved extremely successful when applied to the group dynamic. Fritz Perls was quick to apply his Gestalt theories to group therapy work, although he usually worked with one member of the group at a time. Gestalt group therapists aim as part of their treatment to try to break down the numerous denial systems which, once overcome, will bring the individual to a new and more unified understanding of life. Eric Berne, the founder of transactional analysis, postulated that the group setting is the ideal therapeutic setting.

TYPES AND ADVANTAGES OF GROUP COUNSELING
Among the different types of group counseling available are those that focus on preventative and developmental aspects of living. Preventative group counseling deals with enhancing the individual's understanding of a specific aspect of life. These aspects range from simple job-seeking skills to more complex studies of career changes in midlife. Developmental groups are composed of well-adjusted people who seek to enhance their social and emotional skills through personal growth and transformation. Conversely, group therapy is concerned

with remedial help. The majority of people entering group therapy are aware that they have dysfunctional components in their life; they are seeking group work as a possible way of resolving those problems. The size of most groups ranges from four to twelve participants. Sometimes all the members in the group belong to one family and the group becomes a specialized one with the emphasis on family therapy. Treating the problems of one family member in the larger context of the whole family has proved successful.

There are as many approaches to therapy as there are therapists; thus, the direction that any given group takes will be dependent on the group leader. Group leadership is probably the one factor that is vital in enabling a group to succeed in reaching both individual and group goals. A leader is typically a qualified and trained therapist whose work is to lead the group through the therapeutic process. Often there will be two therapists involved with the one group, the second therapist sometimes being an intern or trainee.

There are definite advantages, both economic and therapeutic, to group therapy. The economic burden of paying for therapy does not fall solely on one person's shoulders; moreover, the therapist can use his or her time economically, helping a larger number of people. More important, group work may be much more beneficial than individual therapy for certain people. Often the group setting will produce conditions similar to those the member faces in real life and can thus offer an opportunity to face and correct the problem.

STAGES OF GROUP SESSIONS
In group therapy, a "session" consists of a number of meetings; the number is specific and is usually determined at the beginning by the group leader. Flexibility is a key concept in counseling, however, and if a group requires more time and all the participants agree, then the number of sessions can usually be extended. Therapists have generally come to accept five stages as being necessary for a group to complete a therapy session. These five stages do not have definite boundaries; indeed, if a group experiences problems at any stage, it may return to earlier stages.

Orientation is a necessary first step in establishing a sense of well-being and trust among the group's members. A therapy group does not choose its own members; it is a random and arbitrary gathering of different people. Each member will assess the group critically as to whether this group will benefit him or her. One way for participants to discover the sincerity of the membership of the group is to reveal something of the problem that brought them to the group in the first place, without going into a full disclosure (the point at which a member of a group will share private feelings and concerns). An individual can then assess from the responses of the other members of the group whether they are going to be empathetic or critical. After the orientation stage comes the transitional stage, in which more self-revelation is required on the part of the individual members. This is usually an anxious time for members of the therapy group. Yet despite this anxiety, each member must make a commitment to the group and must further define the problem that has brought him or her to the group in the first place.

When the transitional stage has proved successful, the group will be able to begin the third stage, which involves a greater sense of cohesiveness and openness. This sense of belonging is a necessary and important aspect of group therapy. Without this feeling, the subsequent work of resolving problems cannot be fully addressed. By this time, each member of the group will have disclosed some very personal and troubling part of their lives. Once a group cohesiveness has been achieved, the fourth stage—actually wanting to work on certain behavior-modifying skills—becomes dominant. At this point in the therapeutic continuum, the group leader will play a less significant role in what is said or the direction taken. This seeming withdrawal on the part of the leader allows the group participants to take the primary role in creating changes that will affect them on a permanent basis.

As with all therapeutic methods and procedures, regardless of school or persuasion, a completion or summation stage is vital. The personal commitment to the group must be seen in the larger context of life and one's need to become a part of the greater fabric of living. By consciously creating a finale to the therapy sessions, members avoid being limited in their personal growth through dependence on the group. This symbolic act of stepping away from the group reaffirms all that the group work achieved during the third and fourth stages of the therapeutic process.

GROUP DYNAMICS

Group work offers participants an opportunity to express their feelings and fears in the hope that behavioral change will take place. Group therapy only takes on significance and meaning when the individual members of the group want to change their old behavioral patterns and learn a new behavioral repertoire. Most individuals come from a background in which they have experienced difficulties with members of their immediate family. Whether the problem has been a spousal difficulty or a parental problem, those who enter into therapy are desperately looking for answers. The very fact that there is more than one person within the group who can understand and sympathize with another's problem begins the process of acceptance and change. Group dynamic is thus defined as the commonality of purpose that unites a group of people and their desire to succeed.

A group will very quickly become close, intimate, and in some ways self-guarding and self-preserving. Through continually meeting with one another in an intense emotional environment, members begin to look upon the group as a very important part of their lives. When one member does not come to a meeting, it can create anxiety in others, for the group works as a whole; for one person not to be present undermines the confidence of those who already lack self-esteem. There are also those who come to group meetings and express very little of what is actually bothering them. While even coming into the therapeutic process is one large step, to disclose anything about themselves is too painful. For those who remain aloof and detached, believing that they are the best judge of their own problems, the group experience will be a superficial one.

EMOTIONAL INVOLVEMENT AND COHESIVENESS

According to Irvin D. Yalom, therapy is "an emotional and a corrective experience." The corrective aspect of therapy takes on a new meaning when placed in a group setting. There is general agreement that a person who seeks help from a therapist will eventually reveal what is truly troubling him or her. This may take weeks or even months of talking—generally talking around the problem. This is equally true of group participants. Since many difficulties experienced by the participants will be of an interpersonal nature, the group acts as a perfect setting for creating the conditions in which those behavioral problems will manifest. One major advantage that the group therapist has over a therapist involved in individual therapy is that the conditions that trigger the response can also be observed.

For those people who believe that their particular problem inhibits them from caring or even thinking about others, particularly those with a narcissistic or schizoid personality, seeing the distress of others in the group often evokes strong sympathy and caring. The ability to be able to offer some kind of help to another person often acts as a catalyst for a person to see that there is an opportunity to become a whole and useful member of the greater community. For all of its limitations, the group reflects, to some degree, the actual real-life situations that each of its members experiences each day.

The acknowledgment of another member's life predicament creates a cohesiveness among the members of the group, as each participant grapples with his or her own problems and with those of the others in the group. As each member becomes supportive of all other members, a climate of trust and understanding comes into being. This is a prerequisite for all group discovery, and it eventually leads to the defining of problems and thus to seeking help for particular problems shared by members. When the individual members of a group begin to care and respond to the needs of the other members, a meaningful relationship exists that allows healing to take place. Compassion, tempered by understanding and acceptance, will eventually prove the ingredients of success for participating members.

ASSESSING EFFECTIVENESS

Group therapy has not been fully accepted in all quarters of the therapeutic professions. Advocates of group therapy have attempted to show, through research and studies, that group therapy is equally effective as individual therapy, but this claim has not settled all arguments. In fact, what has been shown is that if the group leader shows the necessary warmth, understanding, and empathy with the members, then success is generally assured. If the group leader is more on the offensive, however— even taking on an attacking position—then the effects are anything but positive.

Group therapy continues to play an important role within the field of professional care. Perhaps

what has been lacking and will need to be reassessed is not so much whether the theories work but whether the participants gain as much as they can from group work. There has been a general lack of systematized study and research into the effectiveness of group therapy, especially as far as feedback from the participants of the group therapy experience is concerned. This reluctance on the part of psychologists and counselors to assess more closely the type of therapy that is being offered will change as participants of group work expect a greater degree of accountability from the professionals who serve them.

SOURCES FOR FURTHER STUDY

Corey, Gerald, and Marianne Schneider Corey. *Groups: Process and Practice.* 6th ed. Belmont, Calif.: Wadsworth, 2001. This book is primarily concerned with identifying the main therapeutic stages and assessing the important role that the group leader plays in the process.

Donigian, Jeremiah, and Richard Malnati, *Critical Incidents in Group Therapy.* Monterey, Calif.: Brooks/Cole, 1987. Six incidents are presented to therapists from six different therapeutic approaches. Client-centered therapy, Gestalt therapy, individual psychology, reality therapy, rational-emotive therapy, and transactional analysis approaches are then applied to the same incidents.

Peterson, Vincent, and Bernard Nisenholz. "Group Work." In *Orientation to Counseling.* 3d ed. Needham Heights, Mass.: Allyn & Bacon, 1995. This chapter gives a very concise yet broad survey of group work as it relates to the general field of counseling and counseling theory. Acts as a good introduction to the field.

Rogers, Carl Ransom. *On Becoming a Person.* 1961. Reprint. Boston: Houghton Mifflin, 1995. Carl Rogers's influence on group work is acknowledged by all in the field. Rogers was mostly involved with encounter groups, but the theories and approaches spoken about in his book from the basis of much of group therapy practice today.

Yalom, Irvin D. *The Theory and Practice of Group Psychotherapy.* 4th ed. New York: Basic Books, 1995. Yalom's book is a comprehensive work on group therapy. The entire subject of group therapy, from method to application, is covered both from a theoretical viewpoint and from the experiential perspective. Actual cases are used as examples of what happens during a group therapy session, making this work indispensable.

Richard G. Cormack

SEE ALSO: Behavioral family therapy; Community psychology; Couples therapy; Group decision making; Groups; Person-centered therapy; Psychotherapy: Goals and techniques; Self-actualization; Strategic family therapy.

Groups

TYPE OF PSYCHOLOGY: Social psychology
FIELDS OF STUDY: Group processes

The structure and function of groups have stimulated a large quantity of research over the years. What groups are, how groups form, and the positive and negative effects of groups on individuals are the primary areas of research that have provided insights into social behavior.

KEY CONCEPTS
- deindividuation
- density
- group formation
- identity
- self-attention
- social support

INTRODUCTION

In any newspaper, one is likely to find several captivating stories that highlight the powerful negative influence that groups can exert on individuals. For example, one may recall the tragic violence exhibited by British sports fans at the international soccer matches in Belgium in the spring of 1985. One may also consider the one-man crime wave of Fred Postlewaite. For twenty years, Postlewaite engaged in a cross-country vandalism spree against the Sigma Alpha Epsilon college fraternity, which had rejected him in his youth.

There are equally dramatic instances of the powerful positive influences of groups. When the Spy Run Creek in Fort Wayne, Indiana, began to flood its banks in 1982, a group of the community's youths voluntarily participated in efforts to hold back its rising waters. There was also the rescue of four-year-old Michelle de Jesus, who had fallen from a subway platform into the path of an onrushing train. Everett Sanderson, a bystander, leapt down onto the tracks and flung the child into the crowd above. After he failed in his attempt to jump back to the platform, he was pulled up to safety at the last instant by bystanders.

These real-life events are noteworthy because they illustrate the universality of groups and the various ways that groups influence individual behavior. Although everyone can attest the prevalence of groups and the power that they can wield over individuals, several characteristics of groups are not as well defined. Several questions remain as to what groups are, how groups form, what groups look like, and the disadvantages and advantages of group membership. In spite of these questions, psychologists have come to understand many aspects of groups and the ways in which they influence individual behavior.

DEFINITION AND FORMATION OF GROUPS

The members of Congress who compose the House of Representatives of the United States are a group. The urban committee deciding how to allocate budgetary resources for unwed mothers in a particular city is a group. The members of a carpool sharing a ride to the train station every day are a group. The family seated around the dinner table at home in the evening is a group. The acting troupe performing *Hamlet* is a group. There are other examples of groups, however, that may be a little less obvious. All the unwed mothers in an urban area might be considered a group. A line of people waiting to buy tickets to a Broadway show might be thought of as a group. People eating dinner at the same time in a diner might even be considered a group. The people in the audience who are watching an acting troupe perform could behave as a group.

There are several ways in which people come to join the groups to which they belong. People are born into some groups. Several types of groupings are influenced in large part by birth: family, socioeconomic status, class, race, and religion. Other groups are formed largely by happenstance: for example, a line of the same people waiting for the 8:05 ferry every day. Some groups, however, are determined more clearly by intentional, goal-oriented factors. For example, a group of people at work who share a common concern for well-being, health, and fitness may decide to form an exercise and nutrition group. Students interested in putting on a concert might decide to form a committee to organize bake sales, car washes, and fund drives in order to raise the money needed to achieve this goal. Finally, group memberships are sometimes created or changed as an effort toward self-definition or self-validation. For example, one can try to change one's religion, political orientation, professional associations, friendships, or family in an effort to enhance how one feels about oneself—or how others feel about one. An individual searching for a positive self-definition may join a country club, for example, to benefit from the social status acquired from such group membership.

STAGES OF GROUP DEVELOPMENT

Although there are countless underlying reasons for someone's membership in a given group, the work of Bruce Tuckman suggests that groups progress through a relatively consistent series of stages or phases in their development. Forming refers to a phase of coming together and orientation. Group members become acquainted with one another and define the requirements of group membership as well as the tasks to be performed. Storming refers to a phase of polarization and conflict. During this phase, group members deal with disagreements, compete for attractive positions within the group, and may become dissatisfied with other group members or the group as a whole. Norming refers to a phase when conflicts are solved and group members arrive at agreements regarding definitions of tasks and the requirements of group membership. Performing refers to the phase when group members concentrate on achieving their major task and strive toward shared goals. Finally, for some groups, adjourning refers to the disbanding or dissolution of the group after task completion.

For example, consider a special task force created to search for a missing child. During the forming stage, the members of this group will volunteer for, or be appointed to the group. Although the general goals and definition of the group may have

Studying group dynamics, such as the reactions of an audience, can yield important psychological information.
(CLEO Photography)

been established with the decision to implement such a task force, a storming phase would occur that would lead the group members into the sometimes difficult task of defining specific procedures of operation, responsibilities of particular task force members, a functional hierarchy, and so on. The norming phase would represent the resolution of the polarizations that emerged during the storming phase, as the committee proceeded to establish an agenda, a decision structure, and a means of implementing decisions. During the performing phase, the task force would actually perform the tasks agreed upon during the norming phase. Having finished its task, the group would then be adjourned.

GROUP TOPOGRAPHY

The topography of a group refers to its physical features. This includes such elements as the size of the group, the composition of the group, and the relationships between the various members of the groups. These topographical features of groups have been the focus of countless studies.

One obvious physical feature that could vary from one group to another is size. Some scholars have categorized group types in terms of size. For example, some researchers have found it useful to distinguish between small primary groups (from two to twenty group members), small nonprimary groups (from three to a hundred members), large groups (one thousand to ten thousand members), and largest groups (ten thousand-plus members). While such classifications may be interesting, the realities of everyday groups are typically more modest than such grand schemes would suggest. In a large number of settings, naturally occurring, free-forming groups typically range in size from two to seven persons, with a mean of about three. There are certainly exceptions to this rule of thumb; for example, most audiences watching theater troupes are considerably larger than three people. Nevertheless, most of the groups in which people interact on a day-to-day basis are relatively small. The size of a group tends to set the stage for many other topographical features of group life.

VARIATIONS IN GROUP COMPOSITION

The number of relationships possible in a group, according to James H. S. Bosard, is a direct consequence of the size of the group: the larger the group, the larger the number of possible relation-

ships the individual might find within the group. It is possible to express the precise mathematical function relating the number of possible relationships between individuals in a group and group size (N): This function is represented by the formula $(N^2-N)/2$. For example, if the group is made of Tom and Dick, there is only one possible relationship between members of the group (Tom-Dick). If the group is made up of the three people Tom, Dick, and Harry, there are three possible relationships (Tom-Dick, Tom-Harry, and Dick-Harry). If the group is made up of seven people, there are twenty-one possible relationships between individuals; if there are ten people in the group, there are forty-five possible relationships between individuals.

Thus, groups have the potential to become increasingly complex as the number of people in the group increases. There are many possible consequences of this increasing complexity. For one thing, it becomes increasingly harder to pay an equal amount of attention to everyone in the group as it increases in size. Brian Mullen and colleagues state that the person in the group who talks the most is paid the most attention, and in turn is most likely to emerge as the leader of the group; this effect (sometimes referred to as the "blabbermouth" theory of leadership) increases as the size of the group increases. It also becomes increasingly difficult to get to know everyone in the group and to spend equal amounts of time with everyone in the group as the group increases in size.

SIMPLIFYING GROUP COMPLEXITY

People in groups may tend toward a convenient simplification of this inevitable complexity. Scholars have long recognized the tendency for group members to divide other group members into groups of "us" and "them" rather than to perceive each person as a distinct entity. Groups can often be divided into perceptually distinct, smaller groups. For example, a committee might be composed predominantly of elderly members, with only one or a few young members. The general tendency is for people to focus their attention on the smaller group. The reason for this is that the smaller group seems to "stand out" as a perceptual figure against the background of the larger group. Thus, the youthful member of an otherwise elderly committee is likely to attract a disproportionate amount of attention from the committee members.

Not only will the members of the larger group pay more attention to the smaller group, but the members of the smaller group will do so as well. Thus, the members of the smaller group will become more self-attentive, more aware of themselves and their behavior. On the other hand, the members of the larger group become less self-attentive, or, as Ed Diener contends, more deindividuated—less aware of themselves and their behavior. For example, the single female in a group of mechanical engineers that is otherwise male will quickly stand out. The male mechanical engineers may tend to think of that one distinct individual in terms of her status as a female. Moreover, the lone female may become more sensitive than usual about her behavioral transgressions of the norms guiding sexual roles in an all-male working environment.

IMPLICATIONS FOR SOCIAL BEHAVIOR

Thus, group composition has been demonstrated to predict the extent to which people pay attention to, and are aware of, themselves and specific facets of themselves, and to predict a variety of social behaviors including participation in religious groups, bystander intervention in emergencies, worker productivity, stuttering in front of an audience, and conformity.

For example, an analysis of the participation of congregation members in their religious groups documented the powerful effect of group composition on behavior of group members. As the size of the congregation increased relative to the number of ministers, the congregation members were less likely to participate in the group (in terms of activities such as attending worship services, becoming lay ministers, or "inquiring for Christ"). In this instance, becoming "lost in the crowd" impaired the normal self-regulation behaviors necessary for participation. Alternatively, analysis of the behavior of stutterers in front of an audience also documented the powerful effects of group composition on the behavior of group members. As the size of the audience increased relative to the number of stutterers speaking, the verbal disfluencies (stuttering and stammering) of the speakers increased. In this instance, becoming the center of attention exaggerated the normal self-regulation behaviors necessary for speech, to the point of interfering with those behaviors. Group composition's effects of making the individual lost in the crowd or the center of atten-

tion are not inherently good or bad; positive or negative effects depend on the context.

GROUP DENSITY

Another facet of the topography of the group that is related to group size is density. Density refers to the amount of space per person in the group (the less space per person, the higher the density). Doubling the number of people in the group meeting in a room of a given size will decrease by one-half the amount of space available for each member of the group. Alternatively, halving the number of people in the group will double the amount of space available per person. Thus, in a room of a given size, density is directly linked to the size of the group. This particular approach to density is called social density, because it involves a change in density by manipulation of the social dimension (group size). One could also manipulate the physical dimension (room size), rendering a change in what is called spatial density. Thus, halving the size of the room will halve the amount of space available to each group member.

Density has been demonstrated to influence a variety of social behaviors. People have been found to report feeling more anxious, more aggressive, more unpleasant, and, understandably, more crowded as a function of density. An analysis of the effects of "tripling" in college dormitories illustrates these types of effects. As a cost-cutting measure, colleges and universities will often house three students in a dormitory room that was initially constructed for two (hence, tripling). Tripling has been demonstrated to lead to an increase in arguments among the roommates, increased visits to the student health center, decreased grades, and increased overall dissatisfaction.

ROLE IN BEHAVIOR AND IDENTITY

Groups exert sometimes dramatic, sometimes subtle influences on behavior. These influences are sometimes beneficial and sometimes detrimental. An understanding of the effect of groups on the individual sets the stage for a deeper understanding of many facets of social life. One of the reasons for the formation or joining of groups is the definition of the self. On a commonly used questionnaire that requires a person to respond twenty times to the question "Who am I?," people tend to respond with references to some sort of group membership, be it family, occupation, hobby, school, ethnic, religious, or neighborhood. Groups help establish one's identity, both for one's own benefit and for the benefit of others with whom one interacts.

COSTS OF GROUP MEMBERSHIP

Belonging to groups has its price, however; as discussed at length by Christian Buys, one's very membership in a group may carry with it hidden costs, risks, or sacrifices. A more complete understanding of groups requires a consideration of this aspect of membership in a group. Attaining certain types of rewards may be incompatible with belonging to a group. For example, the goal of completing a difficult and complicated task may be facilitated by belonging to a group of coworkers who bring the varied skills and knowledge required for successful task completion. Yet one group member's goal of always being the center of attention, or of needing to feel special and unique, may have to be subverted if the group is to perform the task for which it formed. What the individual wants or needs may sometimes be displaced by what the group needs.

Moreover, the deindividuation (an individual's loss of self-awareness, resulting in a breakdown in the capacity to self-regulate) fostered by groups breaks down the individual's ability to self-regulate. Research has demonstrated the state of deindividuation to increase the (simulated) electric shocks people will deliver to other people in experiments, to increase the use of profanity, and to increase stealing among Halloween trick-or-treaters. The paradigmatic illustration of the negative effects of deindividuation is the lynch mob. An analysis of newspaper accounts, conducted by Brian Mullen, of lynch mob atrocities committed in the United States over a sixty-year period showed that the savagery and atrocity of the mob toward its victim(s) increased as the size of the mob increased relative to the number of its victims.

GROUP MEMBERSHIP BENEFITS

Yet, as discussed by Lynn Anderson, just as there are costs involved in belonging to a group, there are also benefits that accrue from group membership. Although the negative aspects of group membership may capture one's attention more forcefully, the positive aspects are no less common or important. A complete understanding of the purpose of groups requires a consideration of the positive side

of belonging to a group. A considerable amount of evidence has documented the physiological, attitudinal, and health effects of social support systems. For example, people who belong to a varied and tight social support network have been found to be in better physical health and to be better able to resist stress than those lacking such support. As examples, one might consider the effects of such popular support groups as Alcoholics Anonymous and Mothers Against Drunk Driving as well as less popular support groups that deal with specific issues such as loss and bereavement. These groups provide the imperative psychological function of allowing their members a new avenue for coping with their problems.

Perhaps the most notable effects of the group on self-definition and identity are observed when these taken-for-granted benefits are taken away. The woman who has defined herself in terms of her marital status can find her identity cast adrift after a divorce. Similarly, foreign-exchange students often report dislocation or disorientation of identity immediately upon their return home. After months or years of trying to establish a new identity based on new friends, new social contexts, or new groups, that new identity is now inappropriate and out of place in their old social context.

SOURCES FOR FURTHER STUDY

Brown, Rupert, ed. *Group Processes: Dynamics Within and Between Groups.* 2d rev. ed. New York: Basil Blackwell, 2000. This is a very readable treatment of theories and research on group processes, with a particular emphasis on British and European contributions. A variety of compelling and relevant social issues are covered, such as social conformity, crowd behavior, group productivity, and ethnic prejudice.

Canetti, Elias. *Crowds and Power.* Translated by Carol Stewart. 1962. Reprint. New York: Noonday Press, 1998. This is a classic historical discussion of the effects of crowds on individuals and societies. Such avenues of group behavior are described as open and closed crowds, invisible crowds, baiting crowds, and feast crowds.

Forsyth, Donalson R. *Group Dynamics.* 3d ed. Belmont, Calif.: Wadsworth, 2000. This thorough volume provides access to a wide-ranging review of evidence regarding all aspects of group processes.

Mullen, Brian, and George R. Goethals, eds. *Theories of Group Behavior.* New York: Springer-Verlag, 1987. This comprehensive edited volume considers several theories of group behavior in order to expand fully on this phenomenon. Classic as well as contemporary and controversial theories are described by several of the social psychologists who originally formulated the accounts.

Turner, John C., Michael A. Hogg, et al. *Rediscovering the Social Group: A Self-Categorization Theory.* Oxford, England: Basil Blackwell, 1987. A sophisticated in-depth treatment of a new theory of behavior in groups. This theoretical approach integrates a vast amount of data and sets the stage for further research in group behavior.

Tara Anthony and Brian Mullen

SEE ALSO: Affiliation and friendship; Affiliation motive; Bystander intervention; Cooperation, competition, and negotiation; Crowd behavior; Group decision making; Group therapy; Intergroup relations; Leadership; Prejudice; Prejudice reduction; Social identity theory; Social networks; Support groups.

Guilt

TYPE OF PSYCHOLOGY: Emotion

FIELDS OF STUDY: Attitudes and behavior; classic analytic themes and issues

The psychoanalytic and psychological concept of guilt has received extensive attention. Guilt, the feeling of tension when violating a moral code, is one of the significant ideas in psychoanalytic theory. Its psychological understanding has changed over time and continues to evolve.

KEY CONCEPTS
- ambivalent feelings
- conscience
- neurotic guilt
- Oedipus complex
- superego
- unconscious guilt

INTRODUCTION

The concept of guilt has played an important role in the development of human behavior and culture since the early days of civilization. More recently, there has been a focus on the psychological understanding of guilt. One of the first people to write extensively about the psychological meaning of guilt was the Austrian founder of psychoanalysis, Sigmund Freud (1856-1939). His writings from the 1890's to the 1930's provide the basic foundation of the contemporary understanding of guilt. Guilt is the feeling of tension when one feels that one has violated a moral code by thought, action, or nonaction. Guilt is considered to be a type of anxiety. The unpleasant feeling of guilt usually prompts the guilty person to take some type of action to relieve the tension.

Freud believed that guilt started in early childhood as a result of the child's fear of being punished or of losing the love of the parent through misbehavior. Freud stressed that the most significant event in establishing guilt is the Oedipus complex. At the age of four or five, Freud hypothesized, the male child wants to kill his father and have sex with his mother. In a similar vein, sometimes called the Electra complex, the female child wants to kill her mother and have sex with her father. The child becomes anxious with these thoughts and attempts to put them out of consciousness. As a result of the Oedipus complex, the child develops a conscience. The conscience represents inner control and morality. There is the ability to recognize right from wrong and to act upon the right and refrain from doing wrong. Freud would later use the concept of the superego to explain conscience. The superego represents the parental thoughts and wishes that have been internalized in the child. Now the internal supergeo can monitor the morality of the child and guilt can be generated when the superego is displeased.

An important distinction is to be made between normal guilt and neurotic guilt. Normal guilt is experienced when one has acted in such a way as to violate one's moral code. A person then usually takes some action to relieve the guilt. Neurotic guilt relates to thoughts or wishes that are unacceptable and cause anxiety. These thoughts are pushed out of consciousness. The person feels guilt-ridden but is not aware of the source of the guilt. There is no relief from the guilt. In neurotic guilt, the thought is equated with the deed.

ORIGIN

The origin of guilt can be traced back to childhood. In human development there is a long period in which the baby is dependent on the parent. The young baby cannot survive without someone providing for its care. As the baby begins to individuate and separate from the parent, ambivalent feelings are generated. These are opposing feelings, typically love and hate, felt for the same person. The child begins to worry that these hateful feelings can cause the parents to punish it or remove their love. With this fear of parental retaliation, the child becomes guilty when thinking about or acting in a way that might displease the parent.

The Oedipus complex dramatically changes this situation. The dynamics of this complex are based on the play by the Greek playwright Sophocles (c. 496-406 B.C.E.). Without knowing that they are his parents, Oedipus murders his father and takes his mother as his wife. When Oedipus finds out the truth, he blinds himself and goes into exile. Freud believed the Oedipal situation to be a common theme in literature. He also discussed the play *Hamlet* by the English playwright William Shakespeare (1564-1616). Hamlet's uncle had killed Hamlet's father and married Hamlet's mother. There is the question as to why Hamlet hesitates in killing his uncle, and Freud attributed this indecision to Hamlet's Oedipus complex. Freud considered that Hamlet had thoughts of killing his father and having sex with his mother, and Hamlet's uncle only put into action what Hamlet had thought. Hamlet's guilty desires prevent him from taking any action.

Freud believed that the Oedipus complex can exist throughout one's life. People can feel guilty about separating from their parents or achieving more than their parents, as this can unconsciously represent killing them off.

Freud's examination of neurotic guilt led him to the concept of unconscious guilt. Neurotics experience guilt but they are not sure what they are guilty about. Freud first noticed this attitude in obsessive patients. These patients tended to be perfectionistic and overly conscientious, and yet they were wracked by guilt. Freud believed them to be guilty of thoughts and wishes they had pushed out of consciousness, that is, Oedipal wishes. Freud observed the paradox that the more virtuous a person, the more there are self-reproaches and guilt as temptations increase.

Freud's final writings on guilt highlighted its importance for civilization. He wrote that guilt enabled people to get along with others and form groups, institutions, and nations. Without the ability to curb impulses, particularly aggression, society would suffer. Freud did feel that humans pay a price for this advance in civilization, in that there is a loss of personal happiness due to the heightening of the sense of guilt.

HISTORY

Writing in the 1930's, child psychoanalyst Melanie Klein (1882-1960) believed that the Oedipus complex started much earlier in the child's development than Freud had suggested. She considered that it started toward the end of the first year of life and centered primarily on the mother. The baby hates the mother for withdrawing the breast during feeding. The baby then feels guilty and worries that the mother will no longer breast-feed. Klein felt that the baby will want to relieve its guilt by making amends to the mother. The baby will show concern and care for the mother. Klein felt that this was the most crucial step in human development, the capacity to show concern for someone else. Guilt is thus seen as a critical ingredient in the ability to love.

The psychoanalyst Franz Alexander (1891-1964) further advanced understanding of guilt. He wrote that feeling guilty can interfere with healthy assertiveness. The guilty person may need excessive reassurance from other people. When the guilty person is assertive, he or she fears retaliation from others. Alexander also wrote about the concept of guilt projection. This term refers to situations in which people who tend to be overly critical induce guilt in other people.

The psychoanalyst Erik Erikson (1902-1994) also wrote on the theme of guilt interfering with assertiveness. He formulated a theory of eight stages of human development, focusing primarily on early development. The fourth stage of development, around the age of four to five, is called guilt/initiative. The child must successfully repress Oedipal wishes in order not to feel excessive guilt. The child can then proceed with normal initiative.

Another perspective on guilt is the concept of existential guilt, discussed by American psychiatrist James Knight. Existential guilt is the failure to live up to one's expectations and potentialities. It can lead to questioning one's existence and to states of despair until personal meaning can be established.

Erich Fromm (1900-1980) expanded the concept of guilt the better to understand group psychology. He wrote that there are essentially two types of conscience, authoritarian and humanistic. Authoritarian conscience is the voice of internalized external authority. It is based on fear and danger. It is afraid of displeasing authority and actively seeks to please authority. Authoritarian conscience can lead to immoral acts committed as the individual conscience is given over to this higher authority. Humanistic conscience is one's own voice expressing one's own true self. It is the essence of one's moral experience in life. It includes integrity and self-awareness.

CURRENT STATUS

Since 1960, there has been a significant change in the views of psychoanalytic theory on guilt. The psychoanalyst Hans Loewald (1906-1993) wrote extensively about guilt. He considered that guilt does not necessarily lead to punishment; sometimes punishment is sought to evade guilt. Bearing the burden of guilt makes it possible to master guilt by achieving a reconciliation of conflicting feelings. Guilt is thus seen not as a troublesome feeling but one of the driving forces in the organization of the self. Guilt plays a critical part in developing self-responsibility and integrity.

The American psychoanalyst Stephen Mitchell, writing in 2000, expanded on Loewald's ideas. Mitchell concerned himself with the concept of genuine guilt. He believes it is important to tolerate, accept, and utilize this feeling. People need to take responsibility for the suffering they have caused others and themselves. People particularly hurt those they love, but by taking personal responsibility for their behavior, they can repair and deepen their love.

GUILT AND SHAME

Throughout the 1990's, there were a number of writings about the concept of shame and its comparison to guilt. Shame is experienced as a feeling of inadequacy in the self. There can be physical, psychological, or emotional shame.

The American psychoanalyst Helen Lewis (1913-1987) wrote extensively about this topic. She believed that shame includes dishonor, ridicule, humiliation, and embarrassment, while guilt includes duty, obligation, responsibility, and culpability. A person can feel both guilt and shame

SOURCES FOR FURTHER STUDY

Freeman, Lucy, and Herbert S. Strean. *Understanding and Letting Go of Guilt*. Northvale, N.J.: Jason Aronson, 1986. This book provides a good overall understanding of guilt written for the layperson. It highlights the differences in guilt between men and women and the sexual and aggressive roots of guilt. The book focuses primarily on contemporary American culture. There are useful ideas on overcoming excessive guilt.

Joseph, Fernando. "The Borrowed Sense of Guilt." *International Journal of Psychoanalysis* 81, no. 3 (2000): 499-512. The author gives three case examples of the borrowed sense of guilt. In this concept, a parent (due to his or her own needs) will unconsciously induce his or her child to feel guilty. The author demonstrates how he helped his guilt-ridden patients by making the source of their guilt conscious.

Piers, Gerhart, and Milton B. Singer. *Shame and Guilt: A Psychoanalytic and a Cultural Study*. New York: W. W. Norton, 1971. This book compares and contrasts the psychological concepts of guilt and shame. The first half of the book, regarding the psychoanalytic views, is particularly rewarding. The author provides the definition, origin, and meaning of these two terms.

Reilly, Patrick. *The Literature of Guilt: From Gulliver to Golding*. Iowa City: University of Iowa Press, 1988. This book examines several short stories and novels emphasizing the part that guilt plays in fictional characters. The book brings to life a number of different types of guilt such as neurotic, authoritarian, and lack of guilt. The stories provide clear examples of the impact of guilt on individuals, groups, and society.

Tournier, Paul. *Guilt and Grace: A Psychological Study*. New York: Harper & Row, 1958. This book examines the relationship between guilt, psychology, and religion. The author is both a psychologist and a theologian. The author uses personal examples from everyday life to illustrate his points. Nontechnical, easy to read.

Daniel Heimowitz

SEE ALSO: Anger; Ego, superego, and id; Emotional expression; Emotions; Freud, Sigmund; Grieving; Hysteria; Jealousy; Love; Moral development; Neurotic disorders; Oedipus complex; Post-traumatic stress disorder; Psychoanalytic psychology; Psychoanalytic psychology and personality: Sigmund Freud; Self-esteem.

H

Habituation and sensitization

TYPE OF PSYCHOLOGY: Learning
FIELDS OF STUDY: Biological influences on learning

Habituation is a decrease in behavioral response that results from repeated presentation of a stimulus, whereas sensitization is a heightened behavioral response that results from a stronger stimulus. These two processes differ physiologically and are the most fundamental and widespread forms of learning in the animal kingdom.

KEY CONCEPTS
- adaptation
- innate
- learning
- neuron
- neurotransmitter
- opponent process theory
- stimulus
- synapse

INTRODUCTION

Habituation and sensitization are the two most fundamental and widespread forms of learning in the animal kingdom. According to ethologists, learning is any modification in behavior that results from previous experience, in some way involves the nervous system, and is not caused by development, fatigue, or injury. More advanced forms of learning include association, perceptual or programmed learning, and insight; the two simplest (nonassociative) forms are habituation and sensitization. These two processes can be characterized as behavioral modifications that result from repeated presentation of simple environmental stimuli.

Habituation is a decrease in response to repeated presentation of a stimulus—an environmental cue that can potentially modify an animal's behavior via its nervous system. One of the most widely cited examples of this kind of learning involves the startle response exhibited by nestling birds in response to potential predators such as hawks. A young duck, for example, will exhibit an innate startle response whenever a hawk-shaped model or silhouette is passed overhead. With repeated presentation of the model, however, the intensity of the bird's response will decline as the animal becomes habituated, or learns that the stimulus bears no immediate significance.

Common throughout the animal kingdom and even among some groups of protozoans, habituation is important for preventing repeated responses to irrelevant environmental stimuli that could otherwise overwhelm an organism's senses and interfere with other critical tasks. In the case of a nestling bird, there is a clear advantage to an alarm response in the presence of a potential predator; however, a continued fixed response would result in an unnecessary expenditure of energy and distraction from other important activities such as feeding.

In identifying a habituation response, it is necessary to distinguish between true habituation and sensory adaptation and fatigue. These latter two phenomena involve a waning in responsiveness that is caused by temporary insensitivity of sense organs or by muscle fatigue, and thus are not considered forms of learning. In contrast, habituation results in a drop in responsiveness even though the nervous system is fully capable of detecting a signal and eliciting a muscle response.

In contrast to habituation, sensitization is the heightened sensitivity (or hypersensitivity) that results from initial or repeated exposure to a strong stimulus. Examples of sensitization include the increased sensitivity of humans to soft sounds following exposure to a loud, startling noise such as a gunshot, or the increased responsiveness and sensitivity of a laboratory animal to mild (usually irrelevant) tactile stimulation after an electric shock. Sensitization increases an organism's awareness and responsiveness to a variety of environmental stimuli, thereby preparing it for potentially dangerous situations.

COMPARISON OF RESPONSES

At first glance, habituation and sensitization seem to be opposite behavioral responses—one a decrease in responsiveness and the other an increase—but, in fact, they are physiologically different processes, each with its own set of unique characteristics.

At the physiological level, the two responses are determined by contrasting neurological processes that take place in different parts of the nervous system. Habituation is thought to take place primarily in the reflex arc (or SR) system, which consists of short neuronal circuits between sense organs and muscles. In contrast, sensitization is assumed to occur in the state system, or that part of the nervous system that regulates an organism's state of responsiveness. The SR system controls specific responses, whereas the state system determines an organism's general level of readiness to respond. The interaction between habituation and sensitization and these systems determines the exact outcome of a response. At the cellular level, habituated sensory neurons produce fewer neurotransmitters on the postsynaptic membrane, while sensitized neurons are stimulated by other neurons to increase neurotransmitter production and hence responsiveness of the nerves. Thus, while their ultimate neurological effects are somewhat opposite, the mechanisms by which such effects are achieved are quite different.

Other important differences between habituation and sensitization include contrasting recovery times, opposite patterns of stimulus specificity, and differences in responsiveness to stimulus intensity. Sensitization is generally characterized by a short-term or spontaneous recovery, as are some cases of habituation. In certain situations, however, recovery from habituation may take several days, and even then it may result in incomplete or less intense responses.

In comparison to sensitization, habituation is usually elicited by very specific sign stimuli such as certain colors, shapes, or sounds. Thus, even after complete habituation to one stimulus, the organism will still respond fully to a second stimulus. Sensitization, on the other hand, can be characterized as a more generalized response, one in which a single stimulus will result in complete sensitization to a variety of stimuli. Such fundamental differences between these two learning processes reflect differences in their function and survival value. It is a clear advantage to an organism to increase its general awareness to a variety of stimuli (such as occurs in sensitization) once it is alarmed. A similar generalized pattern of habituation, however, would shut down the organism's sensitivity to many important stimuli and possibly put the organism in danger.

A final important difference between habituation and sensitization is the manner in which the two processes are affected by stimulus strength. Habituation is more likely to occur if the repeated stimulus is weak, and sensitization will occur when the stimulus is strong.

These various characteristics have important survival implications, especially for species that rely on stereotypic responses to avoid predation and other life-threatening situations. They ensure that the response is elicited in a timely fashion, that the animal is returned to a normal state in a relatively short period of time, and that the animal is not overwhelmed with sensory input.

APLYSIA RESEARCH

Habituation and sensitization have been studied in a variety of contexts and in a number of organisms, from simple protozoans (such as *Stentor*) to human subjects. Such studies have focused on the adaptive significance of these simple learning processes, their neurological control, and the range of behavioral responses that result from interaction between these two forms of learning.

One particular organism in which the neurological basis of habituation and sensitization has been extensively studied is the marine slug *Aplysia*. Eric Kandel and his associates at Columbia University showed that when the mantle of this organism is prodded, the slug quickly withdraws its gills into a central cavity; but after repeated prodding, it learns to ignore the stimulus (that is, it becomes habituated). Conversely, when the slug is stimulated with an electric shock, its sensitivity to prodding increases greatly, and it withdraws its gills in response to even the slightest tactile stimulation (that is, it becomes sensitized).

Because *Aplysia* possesses only a few, large neurons, it is an excellent organism in which to study the physiological basis of learning. Capitalizing on this unique system, Kandel and his colleagues have been able to establish the neurological changes that accompany simple forms of learning. In the case of habituation, they have shown that repeated stimulation interferes with calcium ion channels in the nerve which, under normal circumstances, causes synaptic vesicles to release neurotransmitters, which in turn relay a nervous impulse between two neurons. Thus, habituation results in a blocking of the chemical signals between nerves and thereby prevents gill withdrawal.

When *Aplysia* is stimulated (or sensitized) by an electric shock, an interneuron (a closed nerve circuit contained within one part of the nervous system) stimulates the sensory neuron by opening calcium ion channels, increasing neurotransmitter production and promoting gill withdrawal. Thus, the proximate neurological changes that take place during sensitization and habituation are nearly opposite, but they are achieved by very different neurological circuits.

STUDIES OF THE SUCKING REFLEX

A second area in which habituation and sensitization responses have been the subject of extensive investigation is the sucking reflex exhibited by human infants. When the cheeks or lips of a young child are touched with a nipple or finger, the infant will automatically begin sucking. In a study designed to explore how various stimuli affect this reflex, it was shown that babies respond much more vigorously to a bottle nipple than to the end of a piece of rubber tubing. In addition, repeated presentation of a bottle nipple causes an increase in sucking response, whereas repeated stimulation with rubber tubing causes a decrease in sucking. The sensitized or elevated response to a rubber nipple is a result of activation of the state system, which increases the baby's awareness and readiness to respond. Sensitization, however, does not occur when the baby is stimulated with rubber tubing, and instead the child habituates to this stimulus.

ROLE IN EMOTIONAL REACTIONS

In addition to influencing simple innate behaviors such as sucking reflexes and withdrawal responses, habituation is believed to be responsible for a number of more complex emotional reactions in humans. Explanations for the effects of habituation on emotions are derived primarily from the opponent process theory of motivation.

The opponent process theory holds that each emotional stimulation (or primary process) initi-

ated by an environmental stimulus is opposed by an internal process in the organism. The emotional changes that actually occur in the organism are predicted to result from the net effect of these two processes. The opponent process detracts from the primary process, and summation of the two yields a particular emotional response. It is hypothesized that when the organism is repeatedly stimulated, the primary process is unaffected but the opponent process is strengthened, which results in a net reduction in the overall emotional response. In other words, repeated presentation of an emotion-arousing stimulus results in habituation in the emotional response, primarily as a result of the elevated opponent response.

An increase in drug tolerance, which results from repeated usage of a drug, is best explained by this kind of habituation. Habitual users of alcohol, caffeine, nicotine, and various opiate derivatives must consume greater quantities of such drugs each time they are ingested in order to achieve the same emotional stimulation. Thus, with repeated usage, there is a decline in the overall emotional response. This decline in the euphoric effects of a drug is primarily the result of an increase in the opponent process, which can be characterized as the negative effects of the drug. This is presumably why habitual users experience more severe physiological problems (for example, headaches or delirium tremens) upon termination of a drug.

Similar patterns of habituation have also been suggested to explain the human emotional responses associated with love and attachment, and the extreme feelings of euphoria derived from various thrill-seeking activities such as skydiving. Thus, while habituation and sensitization are simple forms of learning, they may be involved in a variety of more complex behaviors and emotions as well.

INTERACTION OF LEARNING AND INSTINCT

Studies of habituation and sensitization have been especially helpful in clarifying the physiological and genetic mechanisms that control various forms of learning. Such investigations have also shown that habituation and sensitization are widespread phenomena with tremendous adaptive significance throughout the animal kingdom.

Ethologists, in marked contrast with psychologists (especially behaviorist psychologists), historically have emphasized the importance of underlying physiological mechanisms in the regulation of various behavioral phenomena. Traditionally, they argued that many forms of behavior are not only genetically determined, or innate, but further constrained by the physiological hardware of the organism. They held that psychologists completely ignored these factors by focusing on only the input and output of experiments. Psychologists, on the other hand, have maintained that nearly all forms of behavior are influenced in some way by learning. These contrasting views, which developed largely as a result of different experimental approaches, eventually gave way to a more modern and unified picture of behavior.

One area of research that greatly facilitated this unification was the study of habituation and sensitization. By discovering the chemical and neurological changes that take place during these simple forms of learning, neurobiologists succeeded in demonstrating how the physiological environment is modified during the learning process and that such modifications are remarkably similar throughout the animal kingdom. Thus, it became quite clear that an understanding of proximate physiological mechanisms was central to the study of behavior and learning.

In addition, other studies on sensitization and habituation helped establish the generality of these processes among various groups of animals. They showed that simple forms of learning can occur in nearly all major animal phyla, and that these learning processes often result in modification of simple innate behaviors as well as a variety of more complex responses. From these and other studies, it was soon evident that learning and instinct are not mutually exclusive events, but two processes that work together to provide animals with maximum adaptability to their environment. The kind of learning that occurs during habituation and sensitization allows animals to modify simple, fixed behaviors in response to repeated exposure to environmental stimuli. Habituation allows an organism to filter irrelevant background stimuli and prevent sensory overload and interference of normal activities critical to its survival. Sensitization helps increase an organism's awareness of stimuli in the face of potentially dangerous situations.

These two forms of learning represent important behavioral adaptations with tremendous generality in the animal kingdom. Even in humans, a variety of

seemingly complex behaviors can be attributed to interactions between sensitization and habituation and the simple neurological changes that accompany them.

SOURCES FOR FURTHER STUDY

Domjan, Michael, and Barbara Burkhard. *Principles of Learning and Behavior.* Belmont, Calif.: Wadsworth, 1997. Provides a complete treatment of the psychological basis and mechanisms of learning. Chapter 3 is devoted entirely to habituation and sensitization, and it provides several specific examples of these processes in both human and animal subjects. Includes many original data tables and graphs and a thorough review of the literature.

Grier, James W. *Biology of Animal Behavior.* 2d ed. New York: McGraw-Hill, 1992. This college-level text provides comprehensive treatment of the study of animal behavior. Clearly written and well illustrated; should provide a good introduction for the layperson. Integrates information from a variety of disciplines, including ethology, behavioral ecology, psychology, and neurobiology. Six chapters are devoted to the physiological control of behavior, and one chapter deals entirely with learning and memory.

McFarland, David, ed. *The Oxford Companion to Animal Behavior.* Rev. and enlarged ed. New York: Oxford University Press, 1987. Intended as a reference guide, this comprehensive survey of behavior was written by a team of internationally known biologists, psychologists, and neurobiologists, and it contains more than two hundred entries covering a variety of topics. Provides a detailed summary of various forms of learning, including habituation and sensitization. The index provides cross-references organized by both subject and species lists.

Manning, Aubrey, and Marian Stamp Dawkins. *An Introduction to Animal Behavior.* 5th ed. New York: Cambridge University Press, 1998. A concise handbook offering a light introduction to many general aspects of animal behavior and learning. Provides a discussion on stimulus filtering, an entire chapter on the physiological basis of behavior and motivation, and a complete summary of various forms of learning. Well researched, clearly written, and effectively illustrated.

Raven, Peter H., and George B. Johnson. *Biology.* 5th ed. New York: McGraw-Hill, 1999. Chapter 56 of this general text on the science of biology offers an excellent first introduction to the general concepts of ethology and animal behavior. Includes a brief summary of learning and detailed coverage of habituation, sensitization, and conditioning in *Aplysia*. A concise summary, suggestions for additional reading, and review questions appear at the end of each chapter.

Shepherd, Gordon Murray. *Neurobiology*. 3d ed. New York: Oxford University Press, 1997. This somewhat advanced college-level volume on neurobiology offers an in-depth account of the physiological basis of learning and memory. A portion of chapter 30 is devoted specifically to the neurological changes associated with habituation and sensitization. Detailed diagrams, data summaries, and complete literature reviews are provided.

Michael A. Steele

SEE ALSO: Aversion, implosion, and systematic desensitization; Conditioning; Ethology; Learning; Motivation; Operant conditioning therapies; Neurotransmitters; Pavlovian conditioning; Reflexes.

Hallucinations

TYPE OF PSYCHOLOGY: Consciousness; psychopathology
FIELDS OF STUDY: Cognitive processes

Hallucinations are unusual perceptual phenomena that cause a person to experience imaginary perceptions as reality. There are several different types of hallucinations, and they can result from several different causes.

KEY CONCEPTS
- atypical antipsychotic medications
- delusions
- hallucinogens
- phenothiazines
- schizophrenia

INTRODUCTION

Hallucinations are defined as sensory experiences that occur in the absence of sensory stimulation. Hallucinations, therefore, are false perceptions. There are five major types of hallucinations, which correspond with the five senses. Visual hallucinations occur when a person sees something that is not there, such as a person whom others do not see. Visual hallucinations usually involve the false perception that one sees God, the devil, or a meaningful person in one's life. Visual hallucinations are usually reported to appear in black and white. They can be very frightening for the individual experiencing them. An individual initially may be reluctant to tell others about these visual phenomena. Auditory hallucinations are more common than visual hallucinations and refer to the phenomenon of hearing things that others do not hear, such as voices which seem to be coming from the person's own mind. Tactile hallucinations correlate with the sense of touch and involve the perception of feeling things which are actually not present. The mistaken perception that bugs are crawling down one's arm is an example of a tactile hallucination. The insistence that one feels two strands of hair in one's eye is another example of a tactile hallucination. Gustatory hallucinations involve the false perception of tasting things that are not present, such as experiencing an imaginary metallic taste in one's mouth. Olfactory hallucinations involve smelling things in the absence of stimuli to create such smells, such as the smell of burning flesh.

A hallucination is a perceptual experience that differs from the occasional mistaken perception, such as the belief that one's name has been called. It is different from the infrequent mistaken belief that one has seen a friend or acquaintance across the street. Instead, a hallucination is believed by the person to be real, in spite of repeated evidence to the contrary. Individuals experiencing hallucinations will insist vehemently on the existence of such stimuli and will reject explanations that suggest they are mistakenly perceiving something. Hallucinatory behavior is often recurrent.

Hallucinations are altered states of consciousness or awareness and can result from several different causes. They may be caused by changes in neurological stimulation, such as a high fever, delirium, or epileptic fever. Different somatic, or bodily, states may foster the development of hallucinations. For example, the effects of starvation, oxygen deprivation, sleep deprivation, or a heightened state of awareness can increase the likelihood of hallucinating. Hallucinations also may be a symptom of a psychological disorder such as schizophrenia or major depression. Hallucinations may be induced with psychoactive substances, such as hallucinogenic drugs.

SCHIZOPHRENIC HALLUCINATIONS

Schizophrenia is a mental disorder characterized by a loss of contact with reality and the presence of psychotic behaviors, including hallucinations and delusions. Symptoms of schizophrenia are classified as positive or negative; positive symptoms of schizophrenia refer to behavioral excesses whereas negative symptoms refer to behavioral deficits. Examples of positive symptoms of schizophrenia include hallucinations, delusions, and disorganized speech. Negative symptoms include the neglect of one's hygiene, social withdrawal, and a flattening of one's emotions.

The most commonly experienced hallucinations among schizophrenic patients are auditory hallucinations. Schizophrenic patients will report that they hear voices commenting on their behavior. Others will report hearing voices that are arguing with each other. Some with schizophrenia state that the voices they hear are insulting and antagonistic toward them. The voices may be of either gender. Command hallucinations are hallucinations which involve voices that order one to do something, such as cause harm to oneself or others. Research has suggested that individuals with command hallucinations are more likely to obey a command hallucination if they recognize the "voice" issuing the command. These perceptual experiences can be very distressing to the person experiencing them. A person suffering from schizophrenia may feel plagued by the voices that are heard. An individual experiencing chronic auditory hallucinations may wear headphones in a desperate attempt to stop the perceived voices. It is common for the individual experiencing auditory hallucinations to experience depression.

Schizophrenia is also characterized by the presence of delusions. Delusions are false beliefs which persist in spite of contrary evidence. Delusions might involve the false and persistent belief that one is being followed or poisoned, or that one's thoughts are being broadcast for others to hear. Delusions often develop in an effort by the individual to explain their hallucinations. Individuals who experience frequent auditory hallucinations may develop the delusion that others are plotting against them and are lying when they say that they do not hear the voices that the delusioned person claims to hear.

The auditory areas in the temporal lobes of the brain are associated with hearing ability. Stimulation of these parts can create the false perception of sound. Magnetic resonance imaging (MRI) scans of the brains of schizophrenics who experience auditory hallucinations reveal activity in the auditory centers of the brain even when no external sound has stimulated that brain region. Research has suggested that patients who claim to be hearing voices may actually be unable to distinguish their internal thoughts from external stimuli. Therefore, an individual experiencing auditory hallucinations may be attributing internally generated thought processes to an external source. This research, however, fails to offer plausible explanations for the occurrence of visual, tactile, olfactory, or gustatory hallucinations.

Schizophrenic patients are often treated with antipsychotic medications to alleviate the psychotic symptoms they experience. In the 1930's and 1940's French chemists developed a group of medications called phenothiazines. The phenothiazines were found to be effective in decreasing the positive symptoms, such as hallucinations and delusions, among schizophrenic patients. While effective with these symptoms, the phenothiazines were associated with the risk of serious side effects. In the 1980's, new antipsychotic drugs, referred to as atypical antipsychotics, were found to be effective in treating both the positive and negative symptoms of schizophrenia with fewer side effects than the phenothiazines. Clozapine, risperidone, and olanzapine are some of the atypical antipsychotics that became increasingly popular in the 1990's. These drugs have been especially successful in treating some of the symptoms of schizophrenia, including hallucinatory experiences. Research studies have suggested that cognitive-behavioral therapy is effective in treating schizophrenic patients who experience hallucinations and delusions.

DRUG-INDUCED HALLUCINATIONS AND DELIRIUM

Certain psychoactive drugs (substances which affect the brain's functioning) can induce hallucinatory experiences. Hallucinogens are the class of psychoactive substances which include lysergic acid diethylamide (LSD), psilocybin, ecstasy, and mescaline. All these drugs are powerful and potentially dangerous substances that unfortunately have proved harmful to many who have ingested them in a recreational context.

LSD gained notoriety during the 1960's. Harvard University professor Timothy Leary was an influential advocate for the use of LSD, touting its ability to induce a greater self-awareness. LSD is a powerful hallucinogen that is odorless and tasteless. After using the drug, the individual will experience about eight hours of altered perception, accompanied by mood changes and other symptoms. Psilocybin is another hallucinogen which is found in certain types of mushrooms. Psilocybin is a less potent hallucinogen than LSD and has for centuries been considered sacred by the Aztecs in Mexico and Central America. Methylenedioxymethamphetamine (MDMA), more commonly known as ecstasy, stimulates the central nervous system, resulting in hallucinogenic experiences. Mescaline is a hallucinogen derived from a cactus plant called the peyote. For hundreds of years, Native Americans have used peyote during religious ceremonies to facilitate and intensify spiritual experiences.

Much of what is known about the hallucinatory experiences of people who use hallucinogens is derived from their self reports. Hallucinogens usually induce colorful, vivid images in the initial stages of use. These hallucinations may include images of places, scenes, people or animals. Some hallucinatory experiences among those who have used hallucinogens are reported to be pleasant, and sometimes inspiring, perceptual experiences. Individuals who use hallucinogens are frequently searching for a spiritual transcendence. Others who have used these substances report a "bad trip," or a hallucinatory experience that was unpleasant or frightening and which could lead to panic attacks and heightened anxiety. Heavy use of stimulant drugs, such as cocaine and amphetamines, can cause frightening hallucinations and delusions. Marijuana may produce mild hallucinatory effects, as sensory experiences are enhanced by the effects of the substance. Hallucinations can also be a part of the withdrawal symptoms from alcohol dependence.

Delirium is a mental state characterized by a clouding of consciousness in which a person may seem confused and disorganized. The symptoms of delirium have a rapid onset and include a difficulty in maintaining or shifting attention, disorientation, and at times, the presence of visual and tactile hallucinations. There are many possible causes of delirium (including metabolic disease, infection, endocrine disease, and side effects of certain medications) and treatment involves identifying and then treating the source of the delirium.

Sleep deprivation seems to alter people's perceptions of their surroundings and can also produce mild hallucinations. Research suggests that hallucinations have been reported among subjects who were deprived of sleep for sixty hours.

SOURCES FOR FURTHER STUDY

American Psychiatric Association. *Diagnostic and Statistical Manual of Mental Disorders: DSM-IV-TR.* Rev. 4th ed. Washington, D.C.: Author, 2000. This official diagnostic manual provides a wealth of information about symptoms, prevalence, and other issues related to the psychological disorders. An excellent resource for professionals and nonprofessionals.

Caballo, Vincent E. *International Handbook of Cognitive and Behavioral Treatments for Psychological Disorders.* New York: Pergamon Science, 1998. An excellent resource for professionals, this book offers specific cognitive-behavioral programs for treatment of several different psychological disorders, including anxiety disorders, somatoform disorders, and psychosis.

Heinrichs, R. Walter. *In Search of Madness: Schizophrenia and Neuroscience.* New York: Oxford University Press, 2001. The author provides a thorough collation of twenty years of neuroscience information regarding schizophrenia. A very informative resource.

Jung, John. *Psychology of Alcohol and Other Drugs.* Thousand Oaks, Calif.: Sage Publications, 2001. An educational book that describes physical and psychological issues related to different psychoactive substances.

Leudar, Ivan, and Anthony David. "Is Hearing Voices a Sign of Mental Illness?" *Psychologist* 14, no. 5 (2001): 256-259. This article presents a debate about whether hallucinations are always indicative of a mental disorder. Diagnostic and treatment issues are also explored.

Tarrier, Nicholas, Caroline Kinney, Ellis McCarthy, Anja Wittkowski, Lawrence Yusupoff, Ann Gledhill, Julie Morris, and Lloyd Humphreys. "Are Some Types of Psychotic Symptoms More Responsive to Cognitive-Behavior Therapy?" *Behavioral and Cognitive Psychotherapy* 20, no. 1 (2001): 45-55. Explores the results of a study of the efficacy of cognitive-behavioral therapy com-

pared to supportive therapy in treating hallucinating schizophrenics.

Janine T. Ogden

SEE ALSO: Consciousness; Consciousness: Altered
states; Hearing; Schizophrenia: Background, types,
and symptoms; Schizophrenia: Theoretical explanations; Sensation and perception; Smell and taste;
Touch and pressure; Visual system.

Health psychology

DATE: The late 1970's forward
TYPE OF PSYCHOLOGY: Stress
FIELDS OF STUDY: Coping; critical issues in stress;
  stress and illness

*Health psychology studies the biological, psychologi-
cal, and social interactions of health, illness, recovery from illness, and the impact of health care systems on these interactions. It encompasses the
maintenance and promotion of health, the treatment
and prevention of illness, the growth of health care
services, and the development of health policy.*

KEY CONCEPTS
- behavioral components of chronic disease
- biomedical model
- biopsychosocial model
- cost of health care
- dispositional optimism
- perceptions of control
- positive psychology
- psychoneuroimmunology
- salutogenic focus

INTRODUCTION

Health psychology is concerned with the psychological components of promoting and maintaining
health, treating and preventing illnesses, improving
health care services, and developing health care
policy. Health psychology seeks to generate new
knowledge about people's health beliefs and practices and to apply existing knowledge to improve
health and well-being. Psychologists interested in
health psychology generally adhere to the belief
that health cannot be understood exclusively by focusing on the physical condition of the body. The
psychological side—the state of the mind—must be
considered as well.

THE BIOPSYCHOSOCIAL MODEL

The relationship between mind and body, and its
impact on health, is best understood by utilizing
what has been labeled the biopsychosocial model.
This model assumes that one's health state is based
on the often complicated interactions of three sets
of factors: biological factors, psychological factors,
and social factors. Biological factors include genetic
or inherited influences that may predispose some
individuals to be more susceptible than average to
certain maladies such as heart disease. Examples of
psychological factors could include the amount of
stress perceived in a work place, a personality trait
such as optimism, or the degree of belief in control
over one's own health. Support and empathy one
receives from family, friends, or colleagues constitute social factors. Such social support can come in
the form of emotional, informational, or even tangible resources. Other social factors that play roles in
health and illness are cultural, ethnic, and gender
differences.

Thus, the biopsychosocial model assumes that
health is based on more than the absence of illness;
it is also based on attaining physical, social, and
mental well-being. Indeed, this model highlights
the role of psychosocial variables. Psychosocial variables can be internal mental states, such as depression, or external situational factors, such as the quality of social support one receives. The important
point is that psychosocial factors should be examined in combination with, not independent of, biological influences.

While this model's biological aspects are readily
accepted as important to understanding health, the
psychosocial components are controversial in some
areas in which the biomedical model is heavily re-
lied upon. This more traditional model assumes
that disease or illness is exclusively biological in nature, so that diagnosis and subsequent treatment
are focused on the state of the body as distinct from
the mind. The controversy concerning the biopsychosocial model is relatively minor, however, because there is a recognition among many researchers and health professionals that psychosocial
variables often add more to knowledge concerning
health, illness, and disease than do biological factors alone.

THE RISE OF LIFESTYLE DISEASES

The rise in interest concerning psychosocial variables specifically, and health psychology generally, can be attributed in part to the changing conditions of health problems. Because of the relatively high standard of living in the United States, most of the primary health problems are no longer major infectious diseases, such as polio, smallpox, or rubella. (Acquired immunodeficiency syndrome, AIDS, is one major exception.) The threat of these acute diseases has been successfully eliminated through vaccination programs, which resulted in a doubled life expectancy within the twentieth century. This increased life span, however, coupled with American affluence, has a price. A collection of more chronic diseases, including cancer, heart disease, and stroke, now are the major health problems faced in the United States. Unlike infectious diseases, these threats cannot be treated through vaccination because they are largely caused by people's lifestyles or aging.

The intriguing aspect of these modern lifestyle diseases is that they are largely preventable. Ironically, most people are probably aware of ways they could reduce their susceptibility to these diseases, yet they choose not to change their lifestyles. In order to decrease the risk of lung cancer, for example, people should simply not smoke. Heart disease can be controlled by a sensible diet and a reasonable amount of exercise. Alcohol consumption should be moderate, and nonmedicinal drugs should be avoided altogether. Making people aware of the origins of these lifestyle diseases is no longer the key problem. It has been replaced by the problem of how to alter negative behaviors affecting health. Many of these negative behaviors, such as binge drinking, have rewarding short-term consequences that increase these negative behaviors more effectively than delayed punishment, such as a hangover, can decrease them.

Some advances in dealing with the problems of lifestyle and behavior have been made. There has been a downward trend in smoking; more people are aware that exercise and eating healthier food improves the quality and quantity of life. However, people in industrialized countries are showing alarming increases in obesity and decreases in physical activity. The advent of technological solutions to problems that earlier required physical exertion and the ready access to high-fat fast food no doubt contribute to these trends. Finding ways to alter health behaviors is one of the major contributions health psychologists can provide, one which relies on an understanding of biological as well as psychosocial factors in health.

The changing nature of illness, related in complex ways to biology and behavior, must be understood in relation to broader issues in health psychology, such as the expansion and development of adequate health care services. It has been estimated that more than $1 trillion per year is spent by Americans on health-related expenses. According to C. Everett Koop, the former U.S. surgeon general, and his colleagues writing in *The New England Journal of Medicine* in 1993, preventable illnesses make up about 70 percent of the burden of illness and associated costs, and they account for eight of the nine leading categories of death—980,000 deaths a year. On the average, individuals pay about $225,000 for health care in a lifetime. This money supports escalating health expenses such as health care, health care workers' jobs, and health-related research. The health care industry, then, is a major economic force that comes in contact with practically every citizen. Health psychology can address the effects that this industry has on people both within and outside it, as well as make recommendations concerning future directions for health care.

OPTIMISM AND HEART SURGERY

Because health psychology encompasses both basic and applied elements, researchers work in both laboratory and field settings. Given the variety of research efforts that potentially fall within the bounds of health psychology, only a brief review of representative pieces of research is possible. This review will be highly selective, focusing on two studies that explicitly link psychosocial variables to health-related issues: recovery following coronary artery bypass surgery and adjustment to a nursing care facility.

Heart disease is an important topic within health psychology because it accounts for more deaths annually in the United States than all other diseases combined. Each year, many persons require lifesaving cardiac surgery to increase blood flow to the heart, thereby decreasing the risk of subsequent heart attack. The surgery itself, however, can be a stressful experience. It is useful for medical professionals to be able to predict which patients will cope better with the coronary artery bypass operation and show more rapid rates of recovery.

Michael F. Scheier and Charles S. Carver have argued that a personality trait they call "dispositional optimism" can lead to more effective coping with a threatening event such as heart surgery. Dispositional optimism refers to a person's general belief that positive outcomes will occur in the future. If individuals can envision good things happening in the future, then these expectations might allow them both to cope effectively with and to recover more quickly from the surgery. Pessimists, those who anticipate relatively negative outcomes, might show a slower rate of recovery and poorer adjustment to the surgery.

In an article published in the *Journal of Personality and Social Psychology* in 1989, Scheier, Carver, and their colleagues assessed the optimism of a group of middle-aged men one day prior to their coronary artery bypass surgeries. As expected, following surgery the optimists showed earlier signs of physical recovery, such as walking around their hospital rooms, than did the pessimists. They were also judged by the medical staff to have demonstrated faster recovery rates. After six months, optimists were more likely to have resumed their normal routines of work, exercise, and social activity, and to have done so more quickly than the pessimists. Furthermore, there is accumulating evidence that even mild depression, which is related to pessimism, increases the chances of death from a future heart attack.

Clearly, a more optimistic orientation can lead some people to deal effectively with adverse health problems. It may be that dispositional optimism promotes a reliance on useful coping strategies, such as making future plans or setting goals. In turn, these strategies affect one's adjustment to the physical illness. Further research has shown that optimism leads people to seek social support and to focus on the positive aspects of stressful events. As a psychosocial variable, then, dispositional optimism has important implications for adjusting to physical problems related to disease.

CONTROL IN THE NURSING HOME

Other psychosocial variables are relevant to adequate adjustment to health problems posed by particular environments. While the majority of older adults are not institutionalized in nursing homes, many are forced to live out their lives in nursing care facilities because of health or economic difficulties. Such facilities provide adequate shelter and

health care, but they frequently operate under fixed financial resources which limit the individualized activities and freedoms enjoyed by their residents.

Writing in the *Journal of Personality and Social Psychology* in 1976, Ellen J. Langer and Judith Rodin argued that such institutional environments unwittingly reduce morale and health by gradually taking away the patients' perceptions of control over daily events. As a psychosocial variable, the perception of control is the belief that one can influence outcomes. Nursing home residents may lack such perceptions of control, because almost no aspect of their environment is their responsibility. Practically all decisions, from hygiene to entertainment, are made for them by staff members.

Langer and Rodin reasoned that by creating opportunities for institutionalized patients to perceive even relatively small amounts of control, their health and well-being might improve. To test this idea, these researchers gave one floor of patients in a nursing home plants to care for and then asked them to make some decisions regarding participation in recreational activities in the facility. Patients on a comparison floor also received plants but were told that the nursing staff would be responsible for their care. This group also participated in the same recreational activities but made no decisions about them. Several weeks later, staff observations and comments made by the patients showed that those individuals who perceived control were more physically active and had a stronger sense of well-being. One year later, those patients who were made to feel responsible for events in their environment were still physically and psychologically healthier, even exhibiting a lower mortality rate than those who did not perceive control.

Perceived control is only one psychosocial variable that can be linked to environmental effects on health and well-being, just as the elderly represent only one group who may benefit from interventions of this sort. Based on these results, however, a few conclusions can be drawn. Perceived control can be engendered in fairly simple ways with profound effects on people's physical and mental states. The adverse effects of some environments, such as institutions that care for patients with chronic health problems, can be reduced. Finally, some health interventions can be implemented in a cost-effective manner. Many applications of the biopsychosocial model are clearly possible.

EVOLUTION OF THE FIELD

The belief that a sound mind leads to a sound body is by no means novel. The medical and psychological communities have long operated under the assumption that mental and physical states affect one another, though active cooperation between professionals in these two groups was limited. Psychiatry, for example, served as one of the bridges for communication between these groups. Within psychology itself, there have always been scholars whose research focused on health and medical issues, although they tended to identify themselves with areas such as clinical, social, or physiological psychology.

In the late 1970's, there was growing recognition that a distinct subdiscipline of psychology relating to health matters was coalescing. Various names for this subdiscipline, such as behavioral medicine, medical psychology, and behavioral health, became more common, as did specialized journals, texts, symposia, and organizations. A division of health psychology became an official part of the American Psychological Association in 1978. Health psychology has since become more formalized, articulating its goals, defining its scientific and professional orientations, and evaluating the training needs of students drawn to it. One prominent health psychologist, Shelley E. Taylor, has described the field as a "maturing discipline."

Because philosophers have always speculated about the association between mind and body, the philosophical roots of health psychology can be located in antiquity and traced forward to modern times. Psychology's interest and experimental approaches are a more recent development. From the 1930's to the 1950's, researchers such as Flanders Dunbar and Harold Wolff attempted to link personality variables and psychosocial stressors to specific diseases. In the early 1960's, Stanley Schachter and Jerome E. Singer examined the role of cognitive and physiological processes in the perception of emotional states. In related work during the same period, Richard S. Lazarus pioneered the study of stress and coping. The 1970's and 1980's led to the study of topics such as the Type A, or coronary-prone, personality; of commonsense ideas about illness; and of the perception of physical symptoms. In the 1990's, AIDS grew as a serious worldwide threat to personal health, and continues to threaten the very survival of some developing economies. Research into vaccines and other treatments must be not only effective but also affordable to subsistence economies. In some cases, cultural beliefs may have to be changed. At present, the best treatment is behavioral: the effective use of sexual protection, sexual abstinence, and avoidance of contaminated drug paraphernalia.

In the twenty-first century, diseases with strong behavioral components such as diabetes, heart disease, and various types of cancer will continue to be major concerns. The human genome will provide new insights into on interplay of genes and behavior in the development of health and illness. The developing field of psychoneuroimmunology, which is the study of the complex interplay of behavior, the nervous system, the endocrine system, and the immune system, will take on more significance in this century. For example, psychoneuroimmunological research is progressing rapidly on the effects of social stress on upper respiratory infections and speed of wound healing. Finally, the new discipline of positive psychology will become infused into health psychology. Martin Seligman and Mihaly Csikszentmihalyi wrote in the *American Psychologist* in 2000 that scientific study of the development and fostering of positive traits in humans and their institutions will eliminate many of the mental and physical maladies that affect the human condition. Scientific research in this millennium will help to develop and foster traits such as hope, wisdom, creativity, courage, and perseverance and will determine how these traits can positively influence health and allow individuals and social groups to thrive.

Because of this growing interest in health threats, health psychology may increasingly adopt a salutogenic rather than a pathogenic focus. A salutogenic focus seeks to understand the origins of health by attending to those factors which promote people's health and psychological well-being. Healthy people behave in ways that keep them healthy, and researchers attempt to uncover the aspects of healthy lifestyles that may aid individuals suffering from illness or disease. In contrast, a pathogenic focus highlights the causes of illness and disease, and is less prevention-oriented. This is not to say that the cause of illness is a secondary concern. Rather, the onset of illness should be understood in relation to behaviors and psychological factors that maintain good health.

Health psychology promises to continue as an important arena for interdisciplinary research on health. Basic and applied approaches to understanding health will develop by examining the interplay of biological, psychological, and social factors. As a growing subdiscipline of the field of psychology, health psychology will yield intriguing insights regarding the relationship between mind and body.

SOURCES FOR FURTHER STUDY

Antonovsky, Aaron. *Unraveling the Mystery of Health: How People Manage Stress and Stay Well.* San Francisco: Jossey-Bass, 1987. This work, which advocates the salutogenic view of health and illness, is written by a medical sociologist. Following up on ideas begun in an earlier book, Antonovsky elaborates on the implications of the "sense of coherence concept," an enduring confidence that events, both within and outside the individual, are predictable and will work out well.

Jones, Fiona, and Jim Bright. *Stress: Myth, Theory and Research.* Upper Saddle River, N.J.: Prentice Hall, 2001. This book provides a comprehensive overview of the research on stress. It discusses some of the misconceptions and myths about stress and the difficulties in defining and describing it. It looks at laboratory and real world stress research and points out the shortcomings of both approaches. Finally, it suggests stress may become an outmoded concept in the future as psychosocial variables in illness, health, and well-being are more clearly defined.

Peterson, Christopher, and Lisa M. Bossio. *Health and Optimism.* New York: Free Press, 1991. A very readable and enjoyable introduction to early research on positive thinking and physical health. Optimism is contrasted with pessimism and explored in biological, emotional, behavioral, and interpersonal contexts. Notes at the book's end provide rich detail and further reading. For readers at all levels.

Rodin, Judith, and P. Salovey. "Health Psychology." In *Annual Review of Psychology.* Vol. 40. Stanford, Calif.: Annual Reviews, 1989. Summarizes early work in health psychology, with a strong emphasis on health models, and discusses the often complex interactions among relevant variables. The latter include personality traits, cognitive factors, and environmental and cultural influences. Specific behaviors, both health-promoting and damaging, are also discussed.

Seligman, Martin E. P., and Mihaly Csikszentmihalyi. "Positive Psychology: An Introduction." *American Psychologist* 55 (January, 2000): 5-14. This definitive journal article spells out the new field of positive psychology. It encourages research on the positive human qualities such as hope and perseverance that have been neglected in the psychological research literature. It advocates research on human strengths and positive qualities as ways to stem mental and physical illness and to foster life-enhancing approaches in human groups and institutions.

Taylor, Shelley E. *Health Psychology.* 4th ed. New York: McGraw-Hill, 1999. Written by an active researcher in the field, this engaging text provides substantive coverage of health psychology. A novel quality is its separate chapters on health-enhancing and health-compromising behaviors. Includes detailed sections on stress and coping, patients in treatment settings, and the management of chronic and terminal illnesses.

Dana S. Dunn;
updated by William M. Miley

SEE ALSO: Biofeedback and relaxation; Coping: Chronic illness; Coping: Social support; Coping: Strategies; Coping: Terminal illness; Emotions; Environmental psychology; Meditation and relaxation; Positive psychology; Stress: Behavioral and psychological responses; Stress: Physiological responses; Stress-related diseases; Stress: Theories.

Hearing

TYPE OF PSYCHOLOGY: Sensation and perception
FIELDS OF STUDY: Auditory, chemical, cutaneous, and body senses

Hearing, like vision, transmits information about things and events in the distance. Like smell, it can transmit information about things that cannot be seen. It impels people to take action that their lives may depend on, triggers emotional states, and makes spoken language possible. Hearing depends on sound waves made by the motion of objects.

KEY CONCEPTS
• amplitude
• complex waves
• frequency

- fundamental
- harmonics
- loudness
- pitch
- sound pressure level
- timbre
- wavelength

INTRODUCTION

Most things produce sound waves by vibrating or by moving quickly. All vibrations are similar in that they result from the basic physical properties of elasticity and inertia. For example, if one takes a rubberband and stretches it between thumb and forefinger and plucks one strand, the band, stretched into elastic tension and then released, accelerates as the elastic force stored in it by the pluck is changed to kinetic energy (movement). The elastic tension of the strand is fully spent and its velocity highest when it is at its midpoint of flight, where it was before it was plucked. The strand's inertia (tendency to keep moving) then carries it almost as far as did the pluck, but in the opposite direction, until this kinetic energy is stored again as potential energy in the elastic tension of the restretched strand. The process repeats itself rapidly, many times, until all the energy imparted to the strand has been lost in friction in the rubber and air molecules and, more important, by transferring kinetic energy to air molecules. It is this movement of air molecules that is the physical stimulus for sound. Thus, objects' elasticity and mass allow them to produce sound waves when energized. This is how musical instruments and the vocal apparatus of animals, including humans, work.

Sound waves move over distances through an elastic medium such as air as air. A violin string, like the rubber band, moves back and forth—but virtually continuously as it is being continually "replucked" by the bow. The vibrating string moves in air. Although originally distributed evenly, these gas molecules are compressed when the string moves one way against them and then are placed in a partial vacuum (a region of lower density of molecules) by the motion of the string in the opposite direction. The compressed particles push against the molecules just down the line, compressing them. Then, with their elastic energy transferred, they return to fill the space created initially by the opposite movement of the string. The just-compressed molecules

now push against their neighbors before returning to fill the space created by their predecessors' reverse motion. Thus, there are two kinds of particle motion involved in a sound wave: a back-and-forth oscillation of compressed and rarefied air that remains essentially in place, and a linear, continuous, outward movement of successive waves. The acoustic waves move outward from the vibrating object like waves in the ocean.

AMPLITUDE AND VIBRATION

Pressure wavefronts traveling in air like waves in the ocean provide the clearest example of what is meant by the amplitude of the wave. When a water wave reaches a barrier, it exerts a pressure against that obstruction proportional to its amplitude (like the force of waves against a jetty). The height (or depth) of a wave measured from the zero-reference of the average water level is the wave's amplitude. In air, an acoustic wave's amplitude is the maximum amount of compression (or rarefaction) of air molecules compared to the ambient atmospheric pressure. When this pressure wave reaches an object, it also exerts a force, although vastly weaker. Since the amplitude of a wave may be equated with the pressure created against an object in its path, such as an eardrum, the strength of a sound wave is referred to as its sound pressure level, or SPL. Sound pressure level is measured by the number of physical units of force, called dynes, that are exerted per square centimeter.

The amplitude of a wave determines how fast air molecules move back and forth in a very small space. A large wave will require that the particles move at a higher average velocity to complete a large back-and-forth displacement compared to a smaller one. However, the waves themselves move at the same speed for all sounds. This is called the speed of sound, and in air at room temperature it is approximately 335 meters per second (1,100 feet per second). Knowing this allows the determination of a sound wave's wavelength: the distance a wave travels in the time taken to complete one cycle (or the distance between any two corresponding points representing one full cycle of the wave).

The mass and elasticity of a vibrating object also determine how fast it vibrates. This rate of vibration determines the frequency of the sound wave, or how many times per second the air molecules move through one back-and-forth cycle. This value of cy-

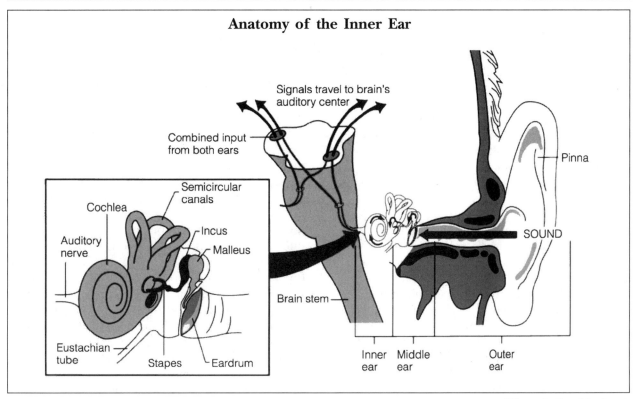

Anatomy of the Inner Ear

(Hans & Cassidy, Inc.)

cles per second is expressed in units called Hertz (Hz). The range of sound wave frequencies audible to humans is roughly 20 to 20,000 Hertz.

When objects vibrate, their rate of movement back and forth is not linear. It is fastest at the vibration's midpoint and slows down to where the motion actually reverses and then accelerates again to maximum velocity at the midpoint. The movement is like that of a seat on a Ferris wheel, which rises and falls most quickly when it is at the "nine o'clock" and "three o'clock" positions, while its motion relative to the ground is greatest at "twelve o'clock" and "six o'clock." The mathematical function that describes these changes, and thus the changes in pressure or displacement over time that comprise the sound wave, is the sine function of an angle rotated through 360 degrees. The simplest sound wave (one that has only a single frequency) is a pure tone or sine wave. The instantaneous amplitude (the point in its 360 degree cycle) of such a wave is described by the phase angle of the wave. Thus, the peak of a wave is at 90 degrees and its trough occurs at 270 degrees. When sound waves reach the ear, they are funneled by the outer ear to

the eardrum. The eardrum is elastic and is pushed by the sound wave's compression and pulled by its rarefaction. It then transfers, by a specialized lever and hydraulic system, the energy derived from the sound wave to a complex receptor mechanism located in the inner ear. This receptor system sends signals to the brain which tell it about the sound wave, and that are heard as sound.

HEARING SOUNDS

In everyday life, however, pure sine waves are seldom heard, because vibrating objects rarely move only as a single piece. They normally have several integer subdivisions of themselves simultaneously vibrating at integer multiples, called harmonics, of their lowest frequency of vibration, called the fundamental. Each harmonic is produced at its own amplitude, determined by the physical characteristics of the sound source. In addition to the vibrating material, which includes the elastic column of air in a wind instrument or organ pipe, the overall size and shape of the source also selectively serve to increase, reduce, or even eliminate specific harmonics by the effect of resonance. Thus normal sounds, even from a single source, are complex waves made up of several simultaneously occurring sine waves of different frequencies, amplitudes, and phase relationships. Sounds from several sources interact still further. Images of sound on an oscilloscope screen, or on the oscilloscope visualization of a computer sound player application, show that such pictures of sound waves are highly irregular, quite unlike the smooth and symmetrical undulations of a sine wave. Nonetheless, all vibrating objects emit sine waves; it is simply that they emit many of them at the same time.

The complexity of a sound wave, how many harmonics it contains and which ones, determines its timbre or quality. Typically, it is the fundamental (lowest) frequency that gives the sound its characteristic pitch. A low-frequency fundamental provides a low bass pitch; higher-frequency fundamentals produce higher midrange or, still higher, treble pitches. Thus, many different types of musical instruments, or many different singers, can produce the same note pitch, but sounds can be distinguished from one from another by their characteristic timbre. For example, timbre can range from the very "smooth" sound of the flute, which has few harmonics and is close to a pure sine wave, through the "full" sound of a consonant piano chord, which has moderate, mostly even, harmonics, to the "rough" and "sharp" sound of a distorted, loud, metal-rock guitar, which has many, mainly odd, harmonics.

How the auditory system allows people to hear timbre is one of the astonishing properties of hearing. Although frequencies below a few hundred Hertz are relayed directly to the brain by a corresponding number of impulses in the auditory nerve, the processing of the full range of frequencies that form the more typical complex sound wave are processed is much more complex. For example, it is easy to hear three individual notes struck separately on a keyboard. If one note is struck, then that note and another simultaneously, it is possible to keep track of the different sounds of the two notes even though they form a single harmony. Even when the three or four component notes of a chord are struck simultaneously, the complex sum of the underlying tones is not the only thing heard. Instead, the auditory system is able to extract each fundamental tone from the complex wave. This ability is based on the ability of the ear to analyze complex waves into their sine wave components, the possibility of which was for-

mally established by the nineteenth century French mathematician and physicist Jean Fourier and applied to hearing by his German contemporary, the physicist Georg Ohm.

Indeed, this principle is applied to a common piece of modern sound reproduction electronics: the real-time spectrum analyzer. Many home and automotive sound systems, as well as computer sound player visualizations, have versions of this device. It displays the relative amplitude of several bands of frequencies, often at octave separation, as a constantly changing set of graphically presented columns, each column representing a range of frequencies and the height of each illuminated column indicating the amplitude of the frequencies displayed by that column. The ear performs the same function but on a vastly finer scale, using thousands of very finely tuned frequency detectors that are placed along the sound-sensitive membrane of the inner ear. Unlike the dedicated detectors displayed by stereos or computers, the ear can tell the difference between sounds that differ by only a few Hertz. Much of what humans hear, then, corresponds and is limited to the output of these individual detectors.

LOCALIZING A SOUND'S SOURCE

Not only is the ear a remarkable sound wave analyzer, but because the two ears are separated by a solid skull-width, a sound wave originating off to one side arrives at each ear at a very slightly different time (phase) and at a slightly different amplitude (weaker in the ear away from the sound source). The brain's computations are extremely sensitive to arrival time and phase differences that exist between the ears. The auditory system uses this information, along with small head movements, to let the listener perceive where the sounds seem to come from in the surrounding space, both in the natural environment and in multichannel sound reproduction environments, and to let attention be directed appropriately. The ability of the auditory system to use extremely small differences in the timing and amplitude of sound waves reaching the ear is the basis of the multichannel surround-sound reproduction used in movie theaters and home theater sound systems. By surrounding the listener with multiple sound sources, the system creates a realistic or even spectacular sense of ambience. The brain computes perceived locations completely surrounding the listener from the differing arrival times, phase relationships, and amplitudes provided by the surround-sound sources, just as it does in nature.

The ability to analyze and locate sounds is more than equaled by the ear's incredible sensitivity and dynamic (amplitude) range. Sound waves whose pressure moves the eardrum only slightly more than the width of a hydrogen atom (the proverbial pin dropping) can be heard. The sound of a rock band, or loud sounds played through earphones, can be more than a million times greater. Because of the need to respond to such a large dynamic range the ear responds in a roughly logarithmic way, with the perceived loudness of a sound increasing linearly as the sound wave's amplitude leaps ahead exponentially (by ratios). Values along this large linear range are thus expressed by a logarithmic unit, the decibel (dB). The auditory system can also become fatigued or can actively reduce its sensitivity when exposed to extremely loud sounds (as when exposed to sound through headphones), making it easy to think that those sounds are less intense than they really are. Sustained exposure to high-amplitude sound waves can permanently damage the delicate receptor cells of the inner ear. This is another reminder that the sound wave is a physical pressure, and can produce tissue damage just like any sufficient impact.

THE HISTORY OF UNDERSTANDING HEARING

Plato (c. 428-348 B.C.E.) was one of the first thinkers to be struck by the fact that humans live in a subjective world of sensations, perceptions, and ideas, not the "real" world of objective physical phenomena. Psychology's preoccupation with "knowing one's self" is really an outgrowth of philosophy's attempt to understand this strikingly problematic gap between the subjective view from inside the self and the objective view from, as much as is ever possible, outside the self and in the world as it is.

It was not until the seventeenth century that scientists realized that sounds correspond to physical vibrations, and not until late in the nineteenth century that the brilliant German physicist Hermann von Helmholtz (1821-1894) developed a theory of how complex waves are analyzed into individual signals. Research into the relationship between physical states and their psychological counterparts was an important part of nineteenth century German science and became known as psychophysics. Psy-

chophysics then became a major part of the research program of the first experimental psychology laboratory, established in 1879 by the father of modern psychology, Wilhelm Wundt (1832-1920). Along with the psychophysicists Ernst Weber (1795-1878) and Gustav Fechner (1801-1887), Wundt argued that lawful relationships between physical stimulation and subjective sensation showed that the scientific study of the mind was feasible.

People are often struck by the complexity of psychophysical research, but it is important to remember its roots. While the subjective beauty of great instrumental music and song can never be reduced to "nothing but vibrations," recognizing how such subjective sensory experience fits into the larger objective scheme of things provides a valuable self-awareness. This same rationale applies to all sensory modalities, but it even goes beyond the senses. Somewhat metaphorically, personality, values, interests, and psychological adjustment all can be understood as the way in which humans uniquely tune in, select, and respond to external stimuli. Understanding the way hearing is related to sound waves provides a valuable model for psychology's concern for making the subjective more objective.

SOURCES FOR FURTHER STUDY

Coren, Stanley. *Sensation and Perception.* 5th ed. San Diego, Calif.: Harcourt Brace Jovanovich, 1999. This book is a particularly comprehensive and well-written survey of sensory processes. The section on audition contains many felicitous examples that make a complex topic accessible. Other chapters place the study of sound waves and hearing into a valuable general perspective.

Deutsch, Diana. *Ear and Brain: How We Make Sense of Sounds.* New York: Copernicus Books, 2002. This volume shows the nonspecialist how ear and brain interact to process sounds into forms we can hear and understand. A CD of sounds and samples that will help the reader understand the complex relationship between ear and brain is included.

Gulick, W. Lawrence. *Hearing: Physiology and Psychophysics.* New York: Oxford University Press, 1971. A classic. Beautifully written so as to present difficult topics comprehensively but accessibly. All topics basic to the sense of hearing are included.

Van Bergeijk, W. A., J. R. Pierce, and E. E. David, Jr. *Waves and the Ear.* New York: Doubleday, 1960. Specifically written for the general reader and high school student, this is a very good introduction to wave theory and hearing. Key research is simply and clearly presented with excellent figures and examples. Physiology and applications are also covered.

John Santelli

SEE ALSO: Brain structure; Hallucinations; Sensation and perception; Smell and taste; Touch and pressure; Visual system.

Help-seeking

TYPE OF PSYCHOLOGY: Social psychology
FIELDS OF STUDY: Attitudes and behaviors; coping; problem solving

Few people who experience significant psychological distress seek professional help. Research has identified a number of factors that contribute to help-seeking behavior. These include demographic factors, patients' attitudes toward a service system that often neglects the special needs of racial and ethnic minorities, financial factors, and organizational factors. People most likely to be in need of help are least willing to seek it, and if they do seek help, they are least likely to benefit from it.

KEY CONCEPTS
- acculturation
- cultural heritage
- demographics
- mental illness
- stigma
- stigmatization

INTRODUCTION

According to the first Surgeon General's Report on Mental Health in 1999, a total of about 15 percent of the U.S. adult population uses mental health services in any given year; however, 28 percent of the U.S. adult population has a diagnosable mental or substance abuse disorder. In short, this means that the majority of those with a diagnosable mental disorder do not receive treatment.

Help-seeking provides a critical step between the onset of mental health problems and the provision of help. Help-seeking is viewed as the contact between individuals and health care providers prompted by the distressed person's efforts and his or her significant others. Help-seeking has been defined as behavior that is designed to elicit assistance from others in response to a physical or emotional problem. There are three dimensions to help-seeking behavior, which include whether a person decides to seek help, at what time the person seeks help (delayed or prematurely), and the appropriateness of the help-seeking behavior. Attitudes and belief systems prevalent in society have a major impact on help-seeking behavior. Understanding patterns of when and why people seek help is fundamental to devising effective responses.

Evolving attitudes concerning mental illness have been monitored by nationally representative surveys since the 1950's to study how people cope with, and seek treatment for, mental illness if they become symptomatic. The 1996 survey report indicated that people were likelier than in the past to approach mental illness by coping with, rather than avoiding, the problem. They also were likelier than in the past to want informal social supports (such as self-help groups). Stigmatization of mental illness is often an excuse for inaction. Although stigma associated with mental health services was expected to dissipate from 1950 to 1996 with the public's increased knowledge of mental illness, just the opposite occurred: Stigma in some ways has intensified, even though the public's understanding of mental illnesses has improved. The public attitude that mental disorders are the result of moral failings or limited willpower is responsible for the negative stereotyping that has occurred and is one of the reasons for the underutilization of mental health services. Stigma interferes with the willingness of many people, even those who have a serious mental illness, to seek help.

BARRIERS TO SEEKING HELP

Most people with mental disorders do not seek treatment. The barriers to treatment include demographic factors, people's attitudes toward a service system that often neglects the special needs of racial and ethnic minorities, financial factors, and organizational factors.

Demographic factors also affect help-seeking behavior. African Americans, Hispanics, and poor women are less inclined than non-Hispanic white females to seek treatment. L. K. Sussman, L. N. Robins, and F. Earls, in a 1987 study of differences in help-seeking behavior between African American and white Americans, found that common patient attitudes deter people from seeking treatment. These attitudes include not having enough time, fear of being hospitalized, thinking that they can handle it alone, thinking that no one can help, cost of treatment, and stigma. Cost is a major factor that predisposes people against seeking treatment, even people with health insurance, because of the inferior coverage of mental health as compared with health care in general. Finally, organizational barriers to help-seeking include the fragmentation of services and unavailability of services. Racial and ethnic minority groups often perceive that services offered by the existing system will not meet their needs because helpers will not taking into account their cultural and linguistic practices.

Seeking treatment is a complex process that begins with the individual or parent recognizing that thinking, mood, or behaviors are unusual and severe enough to require treatment; interpreting these symptoms as a medical or mental health problem; deciding whether or not to seek help and from whom; receiving care; and evaluating whether continuation of treatment is warranted.

A number of barriers deter racial and ethnic minority groups from seeking treatment. Many members of minority groups fear or feel ill at ease with the mental health system. Minority groups also may experience the system as a product of white, European culture. Clinicians often represent a white, middle-class orientation, with biases, misconceptions, and stereotypes of other cultures.

Cultural heritages may also impart patterns of beliefs and practices that impact the willingness to seek help. Mental health issues may be viewed as spiritual concerns, and a number of ethnic groups, when faced with personal problems, therefore seek guidance from religious figures.

Asian Americans are less likely than whites, African Americans, and Hispanic Americans to seek help. Amy Okamura, a professor at the School of Social Work at San Diego State University, concludes that for many Asians and Pacific Islanders, it is more culturally appropriate to go to a doctor with physical symptoms that are a manifestation of mental and emotional problems. Furthermore, Asians

and Pacific Islanders may first try to change their diet, use herbal medicine, try acupuncture, or use a healer.

Julia Mayo, chief of the Clinical Studies Department of Psychiatry at St. Vincent's Hospital and Medical Center in New York, has found that often African Americans wait until they are in crisis and then go to emergency rooms for treatment rather than approach a white therapist. The practice of using the emergency room for routine care is generally attributed to lack of insurance. Cost and lack of insurance have been found to be barriers to treatment. Minority persons are less likely than whites to have private health insurance.

In addition, level of acculturation, as measured by language preference, has been identified as an obstacle to seeking help; that is, people who do not speak English are less able to access formal help sources. For example, Asian international students were found to indicate a significant relationship between levels of acculturation and attitudes toward seeking professional psychological help. The most acculturated students were most likely to have positive attitudes toward seeking professional help. Several hypotheses, most of which assume a conflict between the psychotherapy process and the values of traditional East Asian culture, are offered to explain this pattern of underutilization of mental health services. For example, attitudes and beliefs about mental illness among Asians have been identified as influencing Asians' underuse of psychotherapy. Examples of these attitudes and beliefs include the belief that seeking outside help for psychological problems will bring shame upon one's family, that psychological problems are the result of bad thoughts and a lack of willpower, and that one must resolve problems of this type on one's own.

HELP-SEEKING PATTERNS AND MODELS

A number of factors seem to contribute to a person's willingness to seek help, including age, gender, availability of social support, expectations about help-seeking outcome, self-concealment tendencies, fear of psychological treatment, and type of psychological problem. Adults ask for help less often for intimate problems, for problems that are perceived as stigmatizing, and for problems that reflect personal inadequacy. Help is sought more often for problems that are regarded as serious and when the cause of the problem is attributed to external causes. Help-seeking increases with age, and women have been found to seek help more often than men. Understanding patterns of help-seeking aids professionals in devising effective interventions for people in need.

Generally, people seek help based on the problem factors, such as the perceived normality of the problem, the perceived preventability of the problem, and the perceived cause of the problem. The level of pain or disability associated with the problem, the seriousness of the problem, and past positive history with help-seeking all contribute to one's decision to seek help.

Help-seeking behavior can be characterized by the following principles: The need for help arises from the help-seeker's situation; the decision to seek help or not to seek help is affected by many factors; people tend to seek help that is most accessible; people tend first to seek help or information from interpersonal sources, especially from people like themselves; help-seekers expect emotional support; and people follow habitual patterns in seeking help. Furthermore, people will go to anonymous sources of help if the personal cost of revealing a need is too much to go to an interpersonal source.

SOURCES FOR FURTHER STUDY

Bergin, A. E., and S. L. Garfield. *Handbook of Psychotherapy and Behavior Change*. 4th ed. New York: John Wiley & Sons, 1994. This standard reference is an impartial, eclectic, and scholarly review of research concerned with psychotherapy. Features implications for both research and practice. Incorporates the latest developments and data, reflecting important changes in the field. Includes a major new spectrum of research on culturally diverse populations.

Harris, Roma M., and Patricia Dewdney. *Barriers to Information: How Formal Help Systems Fail Battered Women*. Westport, Conn.: Greenwood Press, 1994. Explores the relationship between the information needs of battered women and the information response provided through social networks in six communities of varying size. Demonstrates that the response of information delivery systems does not adequately meet the needs and expectations of those women who would seek such services. The final chapters of the volume focus on the implications of this study for the design of social service systems.

Leung, Kwok, Uichol Kim, Susumu Yamaguchi, and Yoshihisa Kashima. *Progress in Asian Social Psychology*. Vol. 1. New York: John Wiley & Sons, 1997. This book is based on research presented at the Inaugural Conference of the Asian Association of Social Psychology. It includes both basic and applied topics that involve social processes to help researchers and professionals acquire a better understanding of the mental, social, and psychological perspectives of countries in Asia.

Torrey, E. Fuller. *Out of the Shadows: Confronting America's Mental Illness Crisis*. New York: John Wiley & Sons, 1996. A fact-filled, compellingly argued, and compassionate assessment of mental illness in America. It is essential reading for healers, policymakers, and the millions of families whose lives have been touched by serious mental illness.

U.S. Department of Health and Human Services. *Mental Health: A Report of the Surgeon General-Executive Summary*. Rockville, Md.: Author, 1999. The first Surgeon General's Report on Mental Health asserts that mental illness is a critical public health problem that must be addressed by the Nation. The Surgeon General urges people to seek help if they or their family members have symptoms of mental health problems.

_____. *Mental Health: Culture, Race, and Ethnicity—A Supplement to Mental Health: A Report of the Surgeon General*. Rockville, Md.: Author, 2001. A supplement to the Report on Mental Health focuses on the specific issues relevant to help-seeking by nonwhite Americans.

Zeidner, Moshe, and Norman S. Endler, eds. *Handbook of Coping: Theory, Research, Applications*. New York: John Wiley & Sons, 1996. Provides a study of social support and its relationship to personality, health, and adjustment. This book contains integrative surveys of clinical and field studies, experimental investigations, and life-span explorations. It approaches social support as an important facet of interpersonal relationships and shows its undesirable, as well as its positive, features.

Shelley A. Jackson

SEE ALSO: Addictive personality and behaviors; Clinical interviewing, testing and observation; Confidentiality; Helping; Law and psychology; Mental health practitioners; Social networks; Substance use disorders; Support groups.

Helping

Type of psychology: Developmental psychology, motivation, personality, social psychology
Fields of study: Prosocial behavior

Theories of helping behavior have attempted to explain why people offer physical and psychological assistance to others in both emergency and non-emergency situations. These theories have considered the roles of physiological arousal, judgments of costs and rewards, mood states, and attributions of responsibility in influencing helping behavior.

Key concepts
- arousal cost-reward model
- attributions about responsibility
- mood and helping
- norm of reciprocity
- prosocial behavior
- self-help groups
- spirituality

Introduction

Helping involves assisting, in some way, another person or animal in need. Helping behaviors can take a variety of forms. Some, such as carrying a book for a friend, require little effort. Others, such as jumping into a frozen lake to rescue a drowning stranger, are life-threatening. To explain helping behavior, researchers have studied many variables and have developed theories to organize them and account for their interrelationships.

Arousal Cost-Reward Model

In 1981, Jane Allyn Piliavin, John Dovidio, Samuel Gaertner, and Russell Clark introduced the "arousal cost-reward" model. This model assumes that witnessing the need or distress of another person is physiologically arousing. When one attributes the source of one's arousal to another person's distress, the arousal is sometimes experienced as emotionally unpleasant, and one becomes motivated to reduce it.

According to the arousal cost-reward model, a person will choose to engage in the arousal-decreasing response associated with the fewest net costs. Net costs are based on two types of rewards and costs associated with the helping situation: costs for

not helping and rewards and costs for helping. Costs for not helping occur when no assistance is given and may include experiences such as feeling troubled because someone in need is continuing to suffer or receiving criticism from others for being callous. Costs for helping are direct negative outcomes that the potential helper might experience after offering help, such as loss of time, embarrassment, or injury. Helping, however, can also be associated with positive outcomes such as praise, gratitude, and feelings of self-worth.

Piliavin and her colleagues suggest that both types of costs influence the decision to help. When net costs are low, as the costs for not helping increase, helping in the form of direct intervention becomes more likely. If net costs for helping are high, however, direct intervention is unlikely regardless of potential costs for not helping. In this latter situation, a person may give indirect assistance (for example, call someone else to help). Alternatively, the person may deny responsibility for helping, reinterpret the situation as one in which help is not needed, or try to leave the scene altogether.

Attributions of Responsibility

Philip Brickman and his colleagues argue that when one sees a person in need, one makes attributions about how responsible that person is for the problem he or she faces and also about how much responsibility that person should take for its solution. These attributions in turn influence one's judgment about who one thinks is best suited to deliver help, and, if one decides to offer help oneself, they influence its form. One may be most likely to offer direct assistance if one attributes little responsibility to that person for solving the problem—as when a child is lost in a shopping mall. In contrast, if one judges a person as responsible for solving his or her problem, as when a friend has a nasty boss, one may offer encouragement and moral support but not directly intervene. Thus, who one thinks should provide the remedy—oneself, experts, or the person who needs the help—depends on attributions that one makes about responsibility.

Mood

One's mood may also influence one's decision to help someone who is in need. In general, people experiencing a positive mood, such as happiness, are more likely to offer help than are those in neutral

Helping, Sacrificial Care, and Spirituality

According to R. D. Foss, only a small proportion of studies of helping prior to 1980 involved situations demanding long-term sacrificial care, such as caring for the terminally ill or helping at natural disaster sites. Since then, some social scientists have concerned themselves with the meaning of help given or received in settings requiring long-term commitments, and the motives for helping. For example, Pearl and Samuel Oliner studied the characteristics of non-Jewish rescuers of Jews during the Holocaust; the rescuers represented a very small percentage (less than 1 percent) of Germans during World War II. Clearly, an important question was: Why did the rescuers give aid when most other empathic people did not? In their book *The Altruistic Personality: Rescuers of Jews in Nazi Europe* (1988), the Oliners describe the personality and situations of people who risked their lives and the lives of their family members to aid and give shelter to Jews, often for many months. In a follow-up book, *Toward a Caring Society* (1995), they define care as the assumption of personal responsibility for others' welfare by acting responsively. Given what is known about helping or caring in a variety of domains (for example, psychology, history, and philosophy), they offer pragmatic guidelines for improving the private and public lives of people in social settings.

In a similar vein, the Jewish theologian David R. Blumenthal offers ideas on how to promote prosocial behavior to avert future savagery. His ideas are based on Jewish theology, ethics, social psychology, and child development (especially moral development). He presents a theory that considers both goodness and evil as ordinary. Hence, according to the Oliners and Blumenthal, prosocial behavior in the service of goodness may be taught and practiced.

Other social scientists and clinicians have studied the impact of religious orientation or affiliation on helping. While spirituality, or the experience of the sacred, is at the core of all religions, the body of empirical research has not borne out a positive relationship between religion and helping—even though all major religions teach some form of moral, social responsibility as exemplified in the "golden rule" of doing unto others as you would have others do unto you. Psychologists point to the difficulty of measuring religiosity and spirituality as separable constructs. Nevertheless, the anecdotal evidence stands. For example, Peter C. Hill comments that committed Christians who emulate Christ (a moral exemplar of self-sacrifice for Christians) are called to help those in need as a way to salvation (Matthew 25:31-46).

In a chapter in the *Handbook of Religion and Mental Health* (1998), Stephen G. Post writes of spirituality in terms of connectedness with humanity, nature, and the transcendent. The experience of connectedness or union with humanity implies a change in the way one sees other people. In response to spiritual insight or to religious behaviors such as prayer, meditation, or attendance at church, mosque, or synagogue services, the caregiver "reframes" the situation in such a way as to enable long-term sacrificial care.

Harold G. Koenig, a psychiatrist at the Duke University Center for the Study of Religion/Spirituality and Health, writes in *The Healing Power of Faith* (1999) of friends, spouses, and members of faith communities who tend to the despondent, the grieving, the gravely ill. In tending to others, they report a deepening relationship with God and a stronger sense of community. Often, this sense of caring generalizes to other people in other kinds of distress. Furthermore, those cared for also may experience an enhanced spirituality.

A very successful program that incorporates spiritual language and recognizes the link between spirituality and mental health is Alcoholics Anonymous (AA). The twelve steps to recovery are dedicated to guiding an alcoholic through a process that culminates in a "spiritual awakening." Alcoholics in recovery are enjoined to help themselves by helping other alcoholics. The success of AA has influenced the growth of a variety of self-help groups such as Narcotics Anonymous, Overeaters Anonymous, and Incest Survivors Anonymous. Counselors, psychologists, and psychiatrists have generalized the AA approach to professional, clinical settings. However, there is considerable theoretical debate regarding the reasons for the efficacy of AA. In particular, some see the integration of the spiritual aspects of AA into therapy as problematic. Others see the fit as natural and appropriate. At the beginning of the twenty-first century, some of the best professional programs based on AA principles are in the field of chemical dependency.

The spiritual needs of clients or patients are increasingly important to professional caregivers of various kinds. These concerns are a clear divergence from the scientific empiricism of the twentieth century and are characteristic of the postmodern response to an overly rational and materialistic worldview. As a result, some holistic therapeutic approaches encourage professional caregivers to help patients move away from the self-centeredness associated with spiritual distress along a continuum toward God and health.

Tanja Bekhuis

moods. Using quantitative procedures for summarizing the results of thirty-four experimental studies, Michael Carlson, Ventura Charlin, and Norman Miller concluded that the best general explanation for why positive moods increase helpfulness is that they heighten sensitivity to positive reinforcement or good outcomes. This sensitivity includes both thinking more about good outcomes for oneself and increased thought about the goodness of behaving prosocially. This general summary incorporates many explanations that have been proposed for the relation between positive moods and helping, among them the mood maintenance and social outlook explanations.

Mood maintenance argues that one behaves more helpfully when happy because doing so prolongs one's good mood. The social outlook explanation points instead to the fact that positive moods are often the consequences of another person's behavior (for example, being given a compliment). Such actions by others trigger thoughts about human kindness, cooperativeness, and goodness. These thoughts, if still present when someone asks for help, make a person more likely to respond positively.

The effects of bad moods on helpfulness are more complex. Carlson and Miller also quantitatively summarized the effects found in forty-four studies concerned with the impact of various mood-lowering events on helpfulness. These studies included such diverse procedures for inducing negative moods as having subjects repeat depressing phrases, view unpleasant slides, imagine sad experiences, and fail at a task. Two factors can apparently account for most of the findings on negative moods and helping. The first is whether the target of the mood-lowering event is the self or someone else; the second is whether the self or an outside force is responsible for the mood-lowering event. When one is responsible for imposing a mood-lowering event on another person and therefore feels guilty, helping is very likely. When one is responsible for an event that lowers one's own mood (as when one engages in self-harm) or when one witnesses another person impose a mood-lowering event on someone else (that is, when one experiences empathy), a positive response to a subsequent request for help is more likely, but not as much so as in the first case. In contrast, when someone else is responsible for one's own negative mood—when one has been victimized—one's helpfulness tends to be inhibited.

Theoretical Explanations

These explanations can be applied to a wide range of helping situations—reactions to both physical and psychological distress, situations in which helping appears to be determined by a rational consideration of costs and rewards, and situations in which the help offered seemingly is irrational and very costly.

One study on which the arousal cost-reward model was based suggests how consideration of costs and rewards might affect the decision to offer direct physical assistance. In this study, a man feigned collapse on the floor of a New York subway a few minutes after boarding the train and remained there until help was given. In some cases, the man smelled of alcohol and carried an alcohol bottle wrapped in a paper bag, giving the impression that drunkenness had caused his fall. In other instances, the man carried a cane, suggesting that he had fallen because of a physical impairment. Although many people offered assistance in both conditions, more people helped the man with the cane than the man who appeared to be drunk.

The different amounts of assistance in the two conditions may result from differences in perceived net costs. Potential helpers may have expected greater costs when the man looked drunk than when he appeared to be disabled. Helping a drunk may require more effort and be more unpleasant than helping someone with a physical impairment. It may also be less intrinsically and extrinsically rewarding than helping someone with a physical impairment. Finally, costs for not helping may be lower in the case of the drunk than for the man with the cane. The drunk may be perceived as "only drunk" and therefore not really needy. Thus, the finding that more people helped the man with the cane is consistent with the hypothesis that helping increases as the net costs associated with the helping response decrease.

Although considerations of costs and rewards are important, it would be unrealistic to think that helping only occurs when net costs are low. People may engage in very costly helping behaviors when physiological arousal is especially high, such as in clear, unambiguous emergencies. The actions of an unknown passenger aboard an airplane that crashed into a frozen river illustrate this point. As a helicopter attempted to pull people out of the water to safety, this passenger repeatedly handed the lowered life ring to other, more seriously injured passengers, even though these acts of heroism eventually cost him his life.

Much research on helpfulness has asked, When do people help? It is also important, however, to look at what type of help is given and how the person in need is expected to react to offers of assistance. The Brickman model, involving attributions of responsibility for the problem and its solution, does this. It also looks at more everyday forms of helping. According to Brickman, if one attributes responsibility for both the problem and its solution to the person in need, one is applying the moral model of helping. With this orientation, one may have the tendency to view the person in need as lazy and undeserving of help. In the subway example, people may not have helped the fallen drunk because they made such attributions. Although people who apply the moral model may not give direct assistance, they may sometimes support and encourage the person's own effort to overcome the problem.

If one sees people as responsible for their problem but not for its solution, then one is applying the enlightenment model. Criminals are held responsible for violating the law but are jailed because they are judged incapable of reforming themselves, and jail is believed to be rehabilitating as well as punishing. Discipline from those in authority is seen as the appropriate helping response, and submission to it is expected from the person receiving the "assistance."

The medical model applies when the person is seen as responsible for neither the problem nor its solution. This orientation is often taken toward the ill. Such situations call for an expert whose recommendations are to be accepted and fulfilled.

In the final combination of attributions of responsibility for a problem and its solution, the compensatory model, the person is not held responsible for having caused the problem. The problem may be judged to be caused by factors beyond the person's control, such as when an earthquake occurs. In this model, however, the person is held responsible for solving the problem. Helpers may provide useful resources but are not expected to take the initiative for a solution. In the case of an earthquake, the government may offer low-interest loans for rebuilding, but victims must decide whether to apply for one and rebuild their homes.

HISTORICAL BACKGROUND
Concern with helping behavior has its roots in early philosophy. Thinkers such as Aristotle, Socrates, Niccolò Machiavelli, and Thomas Hobbes debated whether humans are by nature good or bad, selfish or selfless. Most empirical psychological research on the topic, however, was only initiated after the 1950's. This was probably not coincidental. Many people were concerned with the atrocities of World War II and, in the United States, with rising crime rates. In response, psychologists not only began to investigate human cruelty but also gave increased attention to what could be done to offset it. Similarly, the emergence of the Civil Rights movement, with its emphasis on cooperation and harmony, probably further propelled the study of prosocial behavior. The term "prosocial behavior," or behavior intended to benefit other people, is sometimes used synonymously with "helping" and is sometimes meant to be a larger category that includes helping.

Early studies of helping behavior examined situational variables that influence the decision to help someone who is in physical distress. The arousal cost-reward model and the subway experiment characterize this type of work. Also important during this period were Alvin Gouldner's theorizing on the norm of reciprocity and subsequent empirical investigation of the norms governing helping behavior, such as Leonard Berkowitz's work in the 1960's. As social psychologists explored situational variables that influence helping, developmental psychologists examined the emergence of positive social behavior in children. Some, such as Jean Piaget and Lawrence Kohlberg, postulated distinct stages of moral development. Others focused on how people who model helping behavior influence children's subsequent behavior.

EXTENSIONS OF THE EARLIER RESEARCH
While research continues in all these areas, other questions also attract interest. Studies of people's responses to others' physical distress have been extended by research on how people respond to someone in psychological distress. Similarly, researchers have extended their interests in the potential helper to examine how the person in need of help is affected by seeking and receiving it.

Also important in understanding helping behavior has been the study of personality and how individuals differ in their tendency to help. Some of this work is related to research on norms, in that it looks at whether people develop a personal set of rules or standards which govern their helping behavior. Another approach, adopted by Margaret Clark and Judson Mills, has looked at how the relationship between the help requester and the help giver influences helpfulness. Research on helping now incorporates many different influences on the helping process, from individual to social to developmental factors. In the process, the applicability of the research findings has grown and has given rise to a broader understanding of the types of helping behavior that may occur, when they may occur, who might engage in them, and why.

SOURCES FOR FURTHER STUDY

Batson, Charles Daniel. *The Altruism Question: Toward a Social-Psychological Answer.* Hillsdale, N.J.: Lawrence Erlbaum, 1991. Discusses altruism and empathy from a social psychological perspective and addresses the debate about whether or not altruism is merely self-serving egoism. Also discusses altruistic motivation and personality. Batson is highly regarded for his many experimental studies of helping behavior.

Blumenthal, David R. *The Banality of Good and Evil: Moral Lessons from the Shoah and Jewish Tradition.* Washington, D.C.: Georgetown University Press, 1999. The author is a theologian who reviews social psychological, child developmental, and personality research in the presentation of his ideas regarding the ordinariness of good and evil. The book is a study of the behavior, character, and motivation of people who rescued or protected Jews in Nazi Europe. The commentary on what it means to be a moral human is often moving. This book is especially important in light of the Christian bias in much of the helping and prosocial research literature. Very highly recommended.

Clark, Margaret S., ed. *Prosocial Behavior.* Newbury Park, Calif.: Sage Publications, 1991. Focuses on the broader area of positive social behaviors and therefore includes discussions of altruism as well as chapters on helping. Two chapters deal with the development of prosocial behavior. Also noteworthy is a chapter that covers aspects of help-seeking behavior. A chapter on moods and one on the arousal cost-reward model are included as well.

Derlega, Valerian J., and Janusz Grzelak, eds. *Cooperation and Helping Behavior: Theories and Research.* New York: Academic Press, 1982. The first chapter provides a nontechnical discussion of the similarities and differences between the related issues of helping and cooperation, while also serving as an introduction to later chapters. Chapters on helping discuss the arousal cost-reward model and extend the model to show how help seekers may be influenced by cost/reward considerations.

Oliner, Pearl M., and Samuel P. Oliner. *Toward a Caring Society: Ideas into Action.* Westport, Conn.: Praeger, 1995. The Oliners are social scientists affiliated with the Altruistic Personality and Prosocial Behavior Institute. They offer guidelines for promoting caring behavior in families, in schools, at work, and in religious organizations based on careful consideration of a variety of sources, including the literature on altruism, helping, and prosocial behavior. They present caring, or the assumption of responsibility for the welfare of others, as a way to redress an overly individualistic and materialistic culture. Many poignant and inspiring narrative excerpts are included.

Rushton, J. Philippe, and Richard M. Sorrentino, eds. *Altruism and Helping Behavior: Social, Personality, and Developmental Perspectives.* Hillsdale, N.J.: Lawrence Erlbaum, 1981. Covers, as the title implies, three main areas. Under developmental issues, varied topics such as the influence of television and the role of genetics (sociobiology) are covered. Also includes a discussion of moods and a model of how norms may influence helping.

Schroeder, David A., Louis A. Penner, John F. Dovidio, and Jane A. Piliavin. *The Psychology of Helping and Altruism: Problems and Puzzles.* New York: McGraw-Hill, 1995. Good review of the research literature. Includes discussions of the relationships among biology, personality, and social learning as they relate to prosocial behavior. Also, the reciprocity involved in seeking and giving help is discussed. The book is intended for upper-level undergraduate and graduate students.

Staub, Ervin, Daniel Bar-Tal, Jerzy Karylowski, and Janusz Reykowski, eds. *Development and Maintenance of Prosocial Behavior: International Perspectives on Positive Morality.* New York: Plenum, 1984. This set of twenty-four chapters from various researchers focuses not only on helping but also on other positive behaviors such as cooperation, generosity, and kindness. Covers a range of topics, from developmental aspects of prosocial behavior to the effects of help seeking and help receiving to applications of knowledge about helping behavior. A unique aspect of this book is its consideration of research done in many different countries.

Tiffany A. Ito and Norman Miller;
updated by Tanja Bekhuis

SEE ALSO: Aggression; Aggression: Reduction and control; Altruism, cooperation, and empathy; Bystander intervention; Crowd behavior; Moral development; Social perception.

Histrionic personality

TYPE OF PSYCHOLOGY: Psychopathology
FIELDS OF STUDY: Personality disorders

Histrionic personality is a personality disorder characterized by excessive emotionality and attention-seeking. Although researchers have found that it overlaps extensively with many other disorders, its causes and treatment remain controversial.

KEY CONCEPTS
- antisocial personality disorder
- borderline personality disorder
- conversion symptoms
- hysteria
- personality disorders
- somatization disorder

INTRODUCTION

Of all psychiatric conditions, personality disorders are perhaps the most controversial. Nevertheless, virtually all researchers agree that they are disorders in which maladaptive and inflexible personality traits cause impairment. Although some personality disorders are distinguished by the suffering they produce in affected individuals, others are distinguished by the suffering they inflict on others. Histrionic personality disorder (HPD) falls into the latter category.

HISTORY

HPD traces its roots to hysteria, from Greek *hysterikos* ("wandering womb"), a concept with origins in ancient Egypt and Greece. Hysteria was thought to be a state of excessive emotionality and irrational behavior in women caused by a migration of the uterus to the brain. Derogatory views of hysterical women continued throughout the Middle Ages, but in the centuries that followed, writers proposed that hysteria was not limited to women, and was a condition of the brain rather than the uterus. In the late 1800's, French neurologist Jean Charcot used hypnosis to relieve conversion symptoms (deficits in sensory or motor function brought about by psychological factors) in hysterics. In doing so, Charcot approached hysteria as psychological rather than physiological in etiology. One doctor intrigued by the seeming efficacy of the new technique was the young Austrian neurologist Sigmund Freud. This early work with hysterical patients laid the groundwork for his theories of the unconscious.

Following World War II, a classification manual was developed by the American Psychiatric Association in an attempt to unify the array of diagnostic systems that were being used. This manual, the *Diagnostic and Statistical Manual of Mental Disorders* (DSM), has seen many versions and has remained standard in the mental health field. Hysterical personality was not included in the first DSM (1952, DSM-I) but is similar to the DSM-I description of "emotionally unstable personality."

DESCRIPTION

In 1958, two American psychiatrists, Paul Chodoff and Henry Lyons, delineated the primary characteristics of hysterical personality. Among these core features were vanity, theatrical behavior, and coy flirtatiousness. DSM-II (1968) introduced the primary diagnosis of hysterical personality, with "histrionic personality" in parenthesis. The DSM-III (1980) marked an official shift in the nomenclature to "histrionic personality," and "hysterical personality" was dropped completely.

DSM-IV (1994) and its revised text edition DSM-IV-TR (2000) describe the contemporary stance on the features of HPD. The essential feature is "pervasive and excessive emotionality and attention-seeking behavior." Individuals with HPD feel uncomfortable being paid attention. Their vivacious and energetic manner initially may charm new acquaintances. However, such characteristics often grow tiresome as it becomes apparent that these individuals' energy is directed primarily at gaining attention at any cost. They frequently use flamboyant displays of emotion, self-dramatization, and sexual suggestiveness to get attention. Their speech is often vague and tends toward global impressions without supporting details (for instance, they may declare enthusiastically that the film they just saw was wonderful, but be unable to say why). Distorted interpersonal functioning is also characteristic of persons with HPD; they may accord relationships an unrealistic level of intimacy (such as introducing a casual acquaintance as "my dear friend"), and are also easily influenced by others.

Many associated features of HPD (those that are not formally included in the diagnostic criteria) reflect the poor relationships experienced by these individuals; true emotional intimacy, whether with romantic partners or same-sex friends, is often absent. Though dependent in their romantic relationships, they tend not to trust their partners and often manipulate them. Friends may become alienated by these individuals' constant demands for attention and sexually provocative behavior.

PREVALENCE AND DEMOGRAPHIC CORRELATES

Data from the general population indicate a prevalence rate of HPD of 2-3 percent. Higher rates, from 10-15 percent, are reported in clinical settings, with much of this variation probably attributable to differences in diagnostic measures used across studies. Although HPD has traditionally been viewed as a disorder of females, researchers in clinical settings have typically reported only a slight female predominance or, in some cases, approximately equal rates in men and women.

Although research examining cultural differences in HPD is scant, some researchers hypothesize that different social norms may produce disparate rates of this condition across cultures. For example, the impropriety of overt sexuality in Asian society could result in lower rates of HPD, whereas the spontaneous emotionality valued in Hispanic and Latin American society could lead to higher rates. Nevertheless, there are few systematic data addressing this possibility.

RELATIONS TO OTHER DISORDERS

Other personality disorders can be difficult to distinguish from HPD. Borderline personality disorder is classified by the same attention-seeking and manipulative behavior as HPD, but differentiated from HPD by self-destructiveness, angry interpersonal relations, and persistent feelings of emptiness. Antisocial personality disorder and HPD both include reckless, seductive, and manipulative tendencies, but the former condition is distinguished by antisocial and often criminal acts. Persons with narcissistic personality disorder similarly strive for attention, but usually as a means of validating their superiority rather than satisfying interpersonal and sexual needs. Dependent personality disorder is characterized by the same reliance on others for approval and guidance, but tends to lack the theatrical behaviors of HPD.

Further complicating the diagnosis of HPD are its high rates of co-occurrence with other conditions. Among the conditions that overlap the most frequently with HPD are somatization disorder (characterized by multiple bodily complaints for which there is no discernible medical cause), dissociative disorders (characterized by disruptions in identity,

---

DSM-IV-TR Criteria for Histrionic Personality Disorder (DSM code 301.50)

Pervasive pattern of excessive emotionality and attention seeking, beginning by early adulthood and present in a variety of contexts

Indicated by five or more of the following:
- discomfort in situations when not the center of attention
- interaction with others often characterized by inappropriate sexually seductive or provocative behavior
- rapidly shifting and shallow expression of emotions
- consistent use of physical appearance to draw attention to self
- style of speech that is excessively impressionistic and lacking in detail
- self-dramatization, theatricality, and exaggerated expression of emotion
- suggestibility (easily influenced by others or circumstances)
- belief that relationships are more intimate than they actually are

memory, or consciousness), and dysthymic disorder (a chronic form of relatively mild depression).

CAUSES AND TREATMENT

Finally, little is known about either the causes or treatment of HPD. Although some authors, such as American psychiatrist C. Robert Cloninger, have argued that this condition is an alternative manifestation of antisocial personality disorder that is more common in women than in men, the evidence for this hypothesis is equivocal. Some psychodynamic theorists have conjectured that HPD stems from cold and unloving interactions with parents. Nevertheless, there is little research support for this hypothesis. Cognitive explanations of HPD typically focus on the underlying assumptions (such as, "Without other people, I am helpless") characteristic of this condition. It is not clear, however, whether these explanations provide much more than descriptions of the thinking patterns of individuals with HPD.

A variety of treatments for HPD have been developed. These treatments include behavioral techniques, which focus on extinguishing inappropriate (such as dependent, attention-seeking) behaviors and rewarding appropriate (that is, independent) behaviors, and cognitive techniques, which focus on altering irrational assumptions (such as the belief that one is worthless unless constantly showered with attention). Nevertheless, because no controlled studies have examined the efficacy of these or other techniques, it is not known whether HPD is treatable.

SOURCES FOR FURTHER STUDY

Bornstein, Robert F. "Dependent and Histrionic Personality Disorders." In *Oxford Textbook of Psychopathology*, edited by Theodore Millon, Paul H. Blaney, and Roger D. Davis. New York: Oxford University Press, 1999. A comprehensive and well-written account of the primary features of HPD, along with historical background and theoretical perspectives concerning this condition.

Chodoff, Paul, and Henry Lyons. "Hysteria, the Hysterical Personality, and 'Hysterical' Conversion." *American Journal of Psychiatry* 114 (1958): 734-740. A classic exposition of the primary features of various conditions previously subsumed under the rubric of "hysteria." Includes a good description of the characteristics of the older diagnosis of "hysterical personality," which bears a close resemblance to the modern concept of HPD.

Pfohl, Bruce. "Histrionic Personality Disorder." In *The DSM-IV Personality Disorders*, edited by W. John Livesley. New York: Guilford, 1995. An in-depth review of recent diagnostic issues concerning HPD. Includes a helpful and detailed list of questions for further research.

Shapiro, David. "Hysterical Style." *Neurotic Styles*. New York: Basic Books, 1965. An old but classic explication of the cognitive and emotional dysfunction of individuals with histrionic personality traits. Engaging clinical anecdotes help to illustrate the main concepts.

Veith, Ilza. *Hysteria: The History of a Disease*. Chicago: University of Chicago Press, 1965. A landmark work of its time, in which the author provides an exhaustive history of hysteria, from ancient through psychoanalytic times. It is a useful illumination of the social, historical and religious climate in which hysteria emerged and evolved.

Katherine A. Fowler and Scott O. Lilienfeld

SEE ALSO: Antisocial personality; Borderline personality; Hypochondriasis, conversion, somatization disorder, and somatoform pain; Hysteria; Narcissistic personality.

Homosexuality

TYPE OF PSYCHOLOGY: Motivation
FIELDS OF STUDY: Attitudes and behavior; interpersonal relations; physical motives

Sexuality is one of the most complex and individual attributes of the human psyche. There are four types of theories with regard to the development of sexual orientation, but none seems sufficient to explain the huge diversity to be found in sexual expression across ages and cultures.

KEY CONCEPTS
- androgyny
- gay
- homophobia
- homosexual
- lesbian

- pedophile
- transsexual
- transvestite

INTRODUCTION

Theories on the origin and development of homosexual orientation can be categorized into four groups: psychoanalytic, biological, social learning, and sociobiological theories. Psychoanalytic theories are based on the Freudian model of psychosexual stages of development, developed by Austrian psychiatrist Sigmund Freud. According to this model, every child goes through several stages, including the "phallic stage," during which he or she learns to identify with his or her same-sex parent. For boys, this is supposed to be particularly difficult, since it requires redefining the strong bond that they have had with their mother since birth. According to Freudian theorists, homosexuality is an outcome of the failure to resolve this developmental crisis: If a boy's father is absent or "weak" and his mother is domineering or overprotective, the boy may never come to identify with his father; for a girl, having a "cold" or rejecting mother could prevent her from identifying with the female role.

THEORETICAL MODELS

Research has found that homosexuals are, in fact, more likely to feel an inability to relate to their same-sex parent than are heterosexuals and to report that the same-sex parent was "cold" or "distant" during their childhood. Some studies have suggested, however, that this psychological distance between parent and offspring is found mostly in families with children who show cross-gender behaviors when very young and that the distancing is more likely to be a result of preexisting differences in the child than a cause of later differences.

Biological theories have suggested that homosexuality is genetic, a result of unusual hormone levels, or is a result of prenatal maternal effects on the developing fetus. Although there may be genes that predispose a person to become homosexual under certain circumstances, there are no specific genes for homosexuality. Similarly, there are no consistent differences between levels of hormones in homosexual and heterosexual adults. The possibility remains that subtle fluctuations of hormones during critical periods of fetal development may influence brain structures which regulate sexual arousal and attraction.

Social-learning models suggest that homosexual orientation develops as a response to pleasurable homosexual experiences during childhood and adolescence, perhaps coupled with unpleasant heterosexual experiences. Many boys have homosexual experiences as part of their normal sexual experimentation while growing up. According to the model, some boys will find these experiences more pleasurable or successful than their experiments with heterosexuality and will continue to seek homosexual interactions. Why only certain boys find their homosexual experiences more pleasurable than their heterosexual experiences could be related to a variety of factors, including the child's age, family dynamics, social skills, and personality. Young girls are less likely to have early homosexual experiences but may be "turned off" from heterosexuality by experiences such as rape, abuse, or assault.

Sociobiological models are all based on the assumption that common behaviors must have evolved because they were somehow beneficial, or related to something beneficial, which helped the individuals who performed them to pass their genes to the next generation. From this perspective, homosexuality seems incongruous, but since it is so common, researchers have tried to find out how homosexual behavior might in fact increase a person's ability to pass on genes to subsequent generations. Theorists have come up with three possible explanations—the parental manipulation model, the kin selection model, and the by-product model.

The parental manipulation model suggests that homosexuals do not directly pass on more of their genes than heterosexuals, but that their parents do. According to this model, parents subconsciously manipulate their child's development to make him or her less likely to start a family; in this way, the adult child is able to contribute time, energy, and income to brothers, sisters, nieces, and nephews. In the end, the parents have "sacrificed" one child's reproduction in exchange for more grandchildren—or, at least, for more indulged, more evolutionarily competitive grandchildren.

The kin selection model is similar, but in it, the homosexual individual is not manipulated but sacrifices his or her own reproduction willingly (although subconsciously) in exchange for more nieces and nephews (that is, more relatives' genes in subsequent generations). According to this model, individuals who are willing to make this sacrifice (no matter how subconscious) are either those who are not likely to be very successful in heterosexual interactions (and are thus not actually making much of a sacrifice) or those who have a particular attribute that makes them especially good at helping their families. As an analogy, theorists point out how, through much of human history, reproductive sacrifice in the form of joining a religious order often provided income, protection, or status for other family members.

The by-product model suggests that homosexuality is an inevitable outcome of evolved sex differences. According to this model, the facts that, overall, men have a higher sex drive than women and that, historically, most societies have allowed polygyny (where one man has more than one wife) will result in many unmated males who still have an urge to satisfy their high sex drive. Thus, men will become (or will at least act) homosexual when male partners are easier to find than females. This model is the one most likely to explain "facultative homosexuality," that is, homosexual behavior by people who consider themselves basically heterosexual.

SOCIAL CONTEXTS

Prior to the gay liberation movement of the 1970's, homosexuality was classified as a mental disorder. In the 1970's, however, when psychiatrists were revising the American Psychiatric Association's *Diagnostic and Statistical Manual of Mental Disorders* (DSM), they removed homosexuality from the list of illnesses. The third edition of the manual (DSM-III), published in 1980, reflected this change. Homosexuality is not associated with disordered thinking or impaired abilities in any way. Therefore, counseling or therapy for the purpose of changing sexual orientation is not recommended. Even when sought, such therapy is rarely successful. On the other hand, many gays, especially adolescents, find benefit from counseling in order to find information, support, and ways to cope with their sexuality.

For men, sexual orientation seems to be fixed at an early age; most gay men feel as though they were always homosexual, just as most heterosexual men feel they were always heterosexual. In women, however, sexual orientation is less likely to be fixed early; some women change from a heterosexual to homosexual orientation (or vice versa) in adulthood. In

such cases, sexual orientation is better seen as a choice than as an acting out of something preexisting in the psyche, and often such changes are made after a woman has left an unhealthy or abusive relationship or has experienced some other sort of emotional or psychological awakening that changes her outlook on life. In these cases, counseling for the sake of changing sexual orientation per se is not recommended, but it may be appropriate for the woman to seek help dealing with the other changes or events in her life. Most women in this circumstance find that a same-sex, even lesbian, therapist is most helpful, since she will be more likely to empathize with her client.

Many women who change sexual orientation in midlife already have children, and many who are lesbian from adolescence choose to have children by artificial insemination or by having intercourse with a male friend. Often, such women have found a lack of support for their parenting and sometimes experience legal problems retaining custody rights of their children. Gay men, too, have had difficulty retaining parental rights or becoming foster or adoptive parents.

Psychological research shows, however, that homosexuals are as good at parenting as heterosexuals and that they are as effective at providing role models. Homosexuals are more likely than heterosexuals to model androgyny—the expression of both traditionally masculine and traditionally feminine attributes—for their children. Some research has shown that an androgynous approach is healthier and more successful in American society than sticking to traditionally defined roles. For example, sometimes women need to be assertive on the job or in relationships, whereas traditionally men were assertive and women were passive. Similarly, men are less likely to experience stress-related mental and physical health problems if they learn to express their emotions, something only women were traditionally supposed to do.

Neither modeling androgyny nor modeling homosexuality is likely to cause a child to become homosexual, and children reared by homosexual parents are no more likely to become homosexual than children reared by heterosexual parents. Similarly, modeling of androgyny or homosexuality by teachers does not influence the development of homosexuality in children and adolescents. Having an openly homosexual teacher may be a stimulus for a gay child to discover and explore his or her sexuality, but it does not create that sexuality.

Other variations in adult sexual expression, sometimes associated with, or confused with, homosexuality, are transvestism and transsexuality. Transvestism occurs when a person enjoys, or is sexually excited by, dressing as a member of the opposite sex. Some gay men enjoy cross-dressing, and others enjoy acting feminine. The majority of homosexuals, however, do not do either; most transvestites are heterosexual. Transsexuality is different from both homosexuality and transvestism; it is categorized by a feeling that one is trapped in a body of the wrong sex. Transsexuality, unlike homosexuality or transvestism, is considered a mental disorder; it is officially a form of gender dysphoria—gender confusion. Transsexuals may feel as though they are engaging in homosexual activity if they have sexual relations with a member of the opposite sex. Some transsexuals decide to cross-dress and live as a member of the opposite sex. They may have hormone treatments and surgery to change legally into a member of the opposite sex. Transsexuality, unlike homosexuality or transvestism, is very rare.

The Homosexual Spectrum

The word "homosexual" is usually used in everyday language as a noun, referring to someone who is sexually attracted to, and has sexual relations with, members of the same sex. As a noun, however, the word is misleading, since few people who call themselves homosexual have never engaged in heterosexual activity; similarly, many people who call themselves heterosexual have at some time engaged in some sort of homosexual activity. Therefore, many sex researchers (sexologists) use a seven-point scale first devised for the Alfred Kinsey surveys in the 1940's, ranging from 0 (exclusively heterosexual) to 6 (exclusively homosexual). Others prefer to use the words "heterosexual" and "homosexual" as adjectives describing behaviors rather than as nouns.

Homosexual behavior has been documented in every society that sexologists have studied; in many societies it has been institutionalized. For example, the ancient Greeks believed that women were spiritually beneath men and that male-male love was the highest form of the emotion. In Melanesian societies, homosexual activity was thought to be necessary in order for young boys to mature into virile, heterosexual adults. Homosexuality as an overall preference or orientation is harder to study, but it is thought that between 5 and 10 percent of adult males, and between 2 and 4 percent of females, have a predominantly homosexual orientation.

Negative Cultural Stereotypes

In Western, Judeo-Christian culture, homosexual behavior has long been considered taboo or sinful. Thus, in the United States and other predominantly Christian cultures, homosexuality has been frowned upon and homosexuals have been ostracized, being seen as perverted, unnatural, or sick. In 1974, however, the American Psychiatric Association determined that homosexuality was not indicative of mental illness. In contrast to early twentieth century studies of homosexuals who were either psychiatric patients or prison inmates, later studies of a representative cross-section of people showed that individuals with a homosexual orientation are no more likely to suffer from mental illness than those with a heterosexual orientation.

In spite of these scientific data, many heterosexuals (especially males) still harbor negative feelings about homosexuality. This phenomenon is called homophobia. Some of this fear, disgust, and hatred is attributable to the incorrect belief that many homosexuals are child molesters. In fact, more than 90 percent of pedophiles are heterosexual. Another source of homophobia is the fear of acquired immunodeficiency syndrome (AIDS). This deadly, sexually transmitted disease is more easily transmitted through anal intercourse than through vaginal intercourse and thus has spread more rapidly among homosexuals than heterosexuals. Education about safe sex practices, however, has dramatically reduced transmission rates in homosexual communities.

Sexologists have not been able to avoid the political controversies surrounding their field, making the study of a difficult subject even harder. Research will continue, but no one should expect fast and simple explanations. Sexuality, perhaps more than any other attribute of the human psyche, is personal and individual. Questions about sexual orientation, sexual development, and sexual behavior are all complex; it will take a long time to unravel the answers.

Sources for Further Study

Baird, Vanessa. *The No-Nonsense Guide to Sexual Diversity*. New York: Verso, 2001. A wide-ranging survey of cultural attitudes toward homosexuality throughout the world and over time. Provides a country-by-country survey of laws concerning homosexuality, and addresses the rise in opposition to sexual nonconformism among religious fundamentalists of all stripes.

Bell, Alan P., and Martin Weinberg. *Homosexualities: A Study of Diversity Among Men and Women.* New York: Simon & Schuster, 1978. This official Kinsey Institute publication presents the methods and results of the most extensive sex survey to focus specifically on homosexual behavior. Presents descriptions of homosexual feelings, partnerships, and lifestyles, based on intensive interviews with more than fifteen hundred men and women.

Brookey, Robert Alan. *Reinventing the Male Homosexual: The Rhetoric and Power of the Gay Gene.* Bloomington: Indiana University Press, 2002. Discusses recent attempts to identify a genetic component to sexual orientation and the cultural effect of such research on gay identity.

Dean, Tim, and Christopher Lane, eds. *Homosexuality and Psychoanalysis.* Chicago: University of Chicago Press, 2001. Reviews the often conflicted relationship between psychoanalytic theory and homosexuality. Covers the attitudes toward homosexuality found in the writings of Sigmund Freud, Melanie Klein, Wilhelm Reich, Jacques Lacan, and Michel Foucault, among others.

Garnets, Linda, and Douglas C. Kimmel, eds. *Psychological Perspectives on Lesbian and Gay Male Experiences.* New York: Columbia University Press, 1993. A collection of essays focusing on gay identity development, gender differences, ethnic and racial variation, long-term relationships, adult development, and aging.

Koertge, Noretta, ed. *Nature and Causes of Homosexuality: A Philosophic and Scientific Inquiry.* New York: Haworth Press, 1981. This volume is the third in an ongoing monograph series entitled "Research on Homosexuality," each volume of which was originally published as an issue of the *Journal of Homosexuality*. All volumes are valuable, although somewhat technical. This one is a good place to start; others cover law, psychotherapy, literature, alcoholism, anthropology, historical perspectives, social sex roles, bisexuality, and homophobia.

Tripp, C. A. *The Homosexual Matrix.* 2d ed. New York: McGraw-Hill, 1987. For those who want to read

for pleasure as well as for information. Tripp covers fact, culture, and mythology, both historical and modern. A good representative of the "gay liberation" era books on homosexuality, most of the text is as valid as when it was written (though it clearly does not cover post-AIDS changes in homosexual culture and behavior).

Whitham, Frederick L. "Culturally Invariable Properties of Male Homosexuality: Tentative Conclusions from Cross-Cultural Research." *Archives of Sexual Behavior* 12 (1983): 40. Unlike much of the cross-cultural literature on homosexuality, this article focuses specifically on cross-cultural prevalence and attributes of those with a homosexual orientation, rather than on the institutionalized and ritual forms of homosexual behavior found in many non-Western cultures.

Linda Mealey

SEE ALSO: Adolescence: Sexuality; Attraction theories; Gender-identity formation; Love; Physical development: Environment versus genetics; Psychosexual development; Sex hormones and motivation; Sexual behavior patterns; Sexual variants and paraphilias.

Hormones and behavior

TYPE OF PSYCHOLOGY: Biological bases of behavior
FIELDS OF STUDY: Auditory, chemical, cutaneous, and body senses; endocrine system

Hormones are chemical messengers, usually of protein or steroid content, that are produced in certain body tissues and that target specific genes in the cells of other body tissues, thereby affecting the development and function of these tissues and the entire organism. By exerting their influences on various parts of the body, hormones can affect behavior.

KEY CONCEPTS
- endocrine gland
- hormone
- human growth hormone (HGH)
- hypothalamus
- melatonin
- oxytocin
- pheromone

- pituitary
- steroid
- vasopressin

INTRODUCTION

Cell-to-cell communication among the trillions of cells that make up multicellular animals relies primarily upon the specialized tissues of the nervous and endocrine systems. These two systems are intricately connected, with the former having evolved from the latter during the past five hundred million years of animal life. The endocrine system consists of specialized ductless glands located throughout the animal body that produce and secrete hormones directly into the bloodstream. Hormones are chemical messengers that usually are composed of protein or steroid subunits. The bloodstream transports the hormones to various target body tissues, where the hormones contact cell membranes and trigger a sequence of enzyme reactions which ultimately result in the activation or inactivation of genes located on chromosomes in the cell nucleus.

A gene is a segment of a chromosome that is composed of deoxyribonucleic acid (DNA). The DNA nucleotide sequence of the gene encodes a molecule of messenger ribonucleic acid (mRNA) which, in turn, encodes a specific protein for the given gene. If the control sequence of a gene is activated, then ribonucleic acid (RNA) and protein will be produced. If the control sequence of a gene is inactivated, then RNA and protein will not be produced. Hormones target the genes in specific cells to start or stop the manufacture of certain proteins. Within cells and the entire organism, proteins perform important functions. Therefore, hormones control the production of proteins by genes and, as a result, control many activities of the entire animal.

The nervous system, which in vertebrate animals has evolved to become more elaborate than the endocrine system, consists of billions of neurons (nerve cells) that conduct electrical impulses throughout the body. Neurons transmit information, contract and relax muscles, and detect pressures, temperature, and pain. Neuron networks are most dense in the brain (where there are one hundred billion neurons) and spinal cord, where much of the electrical information is centralized, relayed, and analyzed. Neurons must communicate electrical information across the gaps, or synapses, which separate them. To accomplish this goal, the trans-mitting neuron releases hormones called neurotransmitters, which diffuse across the synapse to the receiving neuron, thereby instructing the receiving neuron to continue or stop the conduction of the electrical message. There are many different types of neurotransmitters, just as there are many different types of regular hormones.

NERVOUS SYSTEM-ENDOCRINE SYSTEM INTERACTIONS

The link between the nervous and endocrine systems lies in two glands located between the cerebrum and the brain stem, the hypothalamus and the hypophysis (the pituitary gland). Electrical impulses from neurons in the cerebral cortex may activate the hypothalamus to release hormones that activate the hypophysis to release its hormones, which in turn activate or inactivate other endocrine glands throughout the body. These glands include the thyroid, parathyroids, thymus, pancreas, adrenals, and reproductive organs. This entire system operates by negative feedback homeostasis so that, once information is transferred and specific bodily functions are achieved, nervous or hormonal signals travel back to the hypothalamus to terminate any further action.

Animal behavior occurs as a result of the actions of the nervous and endocrine systems. There is a complex interplay among these two body systems, the environment, and an individual's genetic makeup in terms of the cause-and-effect, stimulus-response events that constitute behavior. An animal receives external information via its special senses (eyes, ears, nose, mouth) and somatic sense organs (touch, pain, temperature, pressure). This external information travels along sensory neurons toward the brain and spinal cord, where the information is analyzed and a motor response to the external stimulus is initiated. Some of these motor responses will be directed toward the sense organs, locomotory muscles, and organs such as the heart and intestines. Other impulses will be directed toward the hypothalamus, which controls body cycles such as all endocrine system hormones, heart rate, sleep-wake cycles, and hunger.

When the hypothalamus releases the hormone corticoliberin, the pituitary gland (the hypophysis) releases the hormones thyrotropin (which activates the thyroid gland), prolactin (which stimulates milk production in the female breast), and growth hormone (which triggers growth in children and metabolic changes in adults). When the thyroid gland is activated, hormones such as thyroxine and triiodothyronine are released to accelerate cellular metabolism, an event which may occur in certain situations such as stress or fight-or-flight encounters.

If the pituitary gland releases adrenocorticotropic hormone (ACTH), the adrenal glands will be activated to release their hormones. The adrenal cortex produces and secretes a variety of hormones, such as aldosterone, which regulates the blood-salt balance directly and blood pressure indirectly; cortisol, which accelerates body metabolism; and androgens, or sex hormones. All of these are steroid hormones, which are involved in rapidly preparing the body for strenuous performance. Even more pronounced are the effects of the adrenal medulla, which produces and secretes the hormone neurotransmitters epinephrine and norepinephrine; these two hormones accelerate heart, muscle, and nerve action as well as stimulate the release of fat and sugar into the bloodstream for quick energy, all of which are extremely important for spontaneous activity such as fighting with or fleeing from enemies. The control of sugar storage and release from the liver by the pancreatic hormones insulin and glucagon also are important in this process.

THE EFFECTS OF HORMONES ON BEHAVIOR

The study of hormones and their effects upon individual and group behaviors is of immense interest to psychologists. Hormones represent the biochemical control signals for much of animal and human behaviors. Understanding precisely how hormones affect individuals, both psychologically and physiologically, could be of great value in comprehending many different human behaviors, in treating abnormal behaviors, and in helping individuals to cope psychologically with disease and stress. The hormonal control of behavior in humans and in many other animal species has been extensively studied, although much research remains to be performed. Hormones have been clearly linked to reproductive behavior, sex-specific behavioral characteristics, territoriality and mating behaviors, physiological responses to certain external stimuli, and stress.

The pineal gland, located in the posterior cerebrum, releases the hormone melatonin, which regulates the body's circadian rhythms and possibly its sexual cycles as well. Melatonin is normally synthesized and secreted beginning shortly after dusk throughout the night and ending around dawn. It thus corresponds with the individual's normal sleep-wake cycle. Melatonin may play an important role in humans adapting to shift work. It is promoted as a nutritional supplement to help people get a good night's sleep.

HORMONES AND REPRODUCTION

The most extensive research involving hormonal effects on behavior has been conducted on reproductive behavior. Among the most powerful behavior-influencing hormones are the pituitary gonadotropins luteinizing hormone (LH) and follicle-stimulating hormone (FSH). These two hormones target the reproductive organs of both males and females and stimulate these organs to initiate sexual development and the production of sexual steroid hormones—estrogen and progesterone in females, testosterone in males. These sex hormones are responsible not only for the maturation of the reproductive organs but also for secondary sexual characteristics such as male aggression and female nesting behavior.

Reproductive patterns vary from species to species in occurrence, repetition of occurrence, and behaviors associated with courtship, mating, and caring for young. The achievement of reproductive maturity and reproductive readiness in a given species is subject to that species' circadian rhythm, a phenomenon regulated by hormones released from the hypothalamus, hypophysis, and pineal gland. These three endocrine glands are influenced primarily by the earth's twenty-four-hour rotation period and the twenty-eight-day lunar cycle. Furthermore, genetically programmed hormonal changes at specific times during one's life cycle also play a major role in the occurrence of reproductive behaviors.

In female vertebratesm, LH, FSH, and estrogen are responsible for the maturation of the ovaries, the completion of meiosis (chromosome halving) and the release of eggs for fertilization, and secondary sexual characteristics. The secondary sexual characteristics involve physiological and closely related behavioral changes. In bird species, these changes include the construction of a nest and receptivity to dominant males during courtship rituals. In mammals, these same hormones are involved in female receptivity to dominant males during courtship. Physiological changes in mammals include the deposition of fat in various body regions, such as the breasts and buttocks, and increased vascularization (more blood vessel growth) in the skin. Females of most mammal and bird species go into heat, or estrus, one or several times per year, based on hormonally regulated changes in reproductive organs. Human females follow a lunar menstrual cycle in which LH, FSH, estrogen, and progesterone oscillate in production rates. These hormonal variations influence female body temperature and behavior accordingly.

Male sexual behavior is controlled predominantly by testosterone produced in the testicles and male androgens produced in the adrenal cortex. These steroid hormones cause muscle buildup, increased hair, and aggressive behavior. As a consequence, such steroids are often used (illegally) by athletes to improve their performance. In a number of mammal and bird species, elevation of sex steroids causes increased coloration, which serves both as an attractant for females and as an antagonistic signal to competitor males. The aggressive behavior that is stimulated by the male sex steroid hormones thus plays a dual role in courtship and mating rituals and in territorial behavior, phenomena which are tightly linked in determining the biological success of the individual.

Pheromones are hormones released from the reproductive organs and skin glands. These hormones target the sense organs of other individuals and affect the behavior of these individuals. Sex pheromones, for example, attract males to females and vice versa. Other pheromones enable a male to mark his territory and to detect the intrusion of competitor males into his territory. Others enable an infant to imprint upon its mother. Such hormones number in the hundreds, but only a few dozen have been studied in detail. Pheromones released by males serve as territorial markers, as is evidenced by most mammalian males spraying urine on objects in their own territory. Exchanges of pheromones between males and females are important stimulants for courtship and mating. In some species, the release of pheromones—or even the sight of a potential mate—will trigger hormonally controlled ovulation in the female. Furthermore, in several species, such as elephant seals and lions, the takeover of a harem by a new dominant male, a process that usually involves the murder of the previous male's offspring, stimulates the harem females to

ovulate. The diversity of reproductive behaviors that is regulated by hormones seems to be almost as great as the number of species.

Hormones and Stress
The fight-or-flight response is a hormonally controlled situation in which the body must pool all of its available resources within a relatively short time span. The detection of danger by any of the special senses (sight, smell, hearing) triggers the hypothalamus to activate the pituitary gland to release adrenocorticotropic hormone, which causes the adrenal gland to release its highly motivating hormones and neurotransmitters. Many body systems are subsequently affected, especially the heart and circulatory system, the central nervous system, the digestive system, and even the immune system. One reason the fight-or-flight response is of major interest to psychologists is its link to stress.

Stress is overexcitation of the nervous and endocrine systems. It is caused by the body's repeated exposure to danger, excessive physical exertion, or environmental pressures that affect the individual psychologically. Stress is a major problem for humans in a fast-paced technological society. The physiological and behavioral manifestations of stress are very evident. There is considerable evidence that stress is associated with heart disease, cancer, weakened immune systems, asthma, allergies, accelerated aging, susceptibility to infections, learning disorders, behavioral abnormalities, insanity, and violent crime. The demands that are placed upon individuals in fast-paced, overpopulated societies are so great that many people exhibit a near-continuous fight-or-flight response. This response, in which the body prepares for maximum physical exertion in a short time span, is the physiological basis of stress. It is not intended to be maintained for long periods of time; if it is not relieved, irreparable effects begin to accumulate throughout the body, particularly within the nervous system. Medical psychologists seek to understand the hormonal basis of physiological stress in order to treat stress-prone individuals.

Hormones and Aging
Another hormone that greatly influences human behavior/development is human growth hormone (HGH). This hormone is produced by the anterior pituitary (adenohypophysis) gland under the control of the hypothalamus. HGH production peaks

during adolescence, corresponding to the growth spurt. While it is produced throughout life, it declines with age in all species studied to date. In humans, HGH production tends to drop quickly beginning in the thirties so that by age sixty, HGH production is only about 25 percent of what it was earlier in life, and it continues to decline until death. The decrease in HGH production with age has been tied to thinning of skin and wrinkle formation, muscle wasting, sleep problems, cognitive and mood changes, decreased cardiac and kidney function, lessening of sexual performance, and weakening of bones, contributing to osteoporosis. Nutritional supplements including the amino acids arginine, lysine, and glutamine are being investigated as growth hormone releasers, which may then decrease signs of aging.

HORMONE TREATMENT OF HEALTH PROBLEMS

The ultimate goals of hormone studies are to arrive at an understanding of the physiological basis of behavior and to develop treatments for behavioral abnormalities. Synthetic hormones can be manufactured in the laboratory. Their mass production could provide solutions to many psychological problems such as stress, deviant behavior, and sexual dysfunction. Synthetic hormones already are being used as birth control mechanisms aimed at fooling the female body's own reproductive hormonal systems.

Ongoing research focuses on the importance of many hormones, especially on understanding their functions and how they might be used in the treatment of common disorders. Two hormones produced by the hypothalamus and released by the posterior pituitary (neurohypophysis) gland are vasopressin (antidiuretic hormone) and oxytocin. Vasopressin keeps the kidneys from losing too much water and helps maintain the body's fluid balance. Variants of vasopressin which decrease blood pressure, identified by Maurice Manning, may lead to a new class of drugs to control high blood pressure. Oxytocin induces labor by causing uterine contractions and also promotes the production of milk for breastfeeding. Manning and Walter Chan are working to develop oxytocin receptor antagonists that may be used to prevent premature births.

THE PAST, PRESENT, AND FUTURE OF HORMONES

The activities of all living organisms are functionally dependent upon the biochemical reactions that make up life itself. Since the evolution of the first eukaryotic cells more than one billion years ago, hormones have been utilized in cell-to-cell communication. In vertebrate animals (fish, amphibians, reptiles, birds, and mammals), endocrine systems have evolved into highly complicated nervous systems. These nervous systems are even evident in the invertebrate arthropods (crustaceans, spiders, and so on), especially among the social insects, such as ants. The endocrine and nervous systems are intricately interconnected in the control of animal physiology and behavior.

Psychologists are interested in the chemical basis of human behavior and therefore are interested in human and mammalian hormones. Such hormones control a variety of behaviors, such as maternal imprinting (in which an infant and mother bond to each other), courtship and mating, territoriality, and physiological responses to stress and danger. Animal behaviorists and psychologists study the connection between hormones and behavior in humans, primates, and other closely related mammalian species. They identify similarities in behaviors and hormones among a variety of species. They also recognize the occurrence of abnormal behaviors, such as antisocial behavior and sexual deviance, and possible hormonal imbalances that contribute to these behavioral anomalies.

While the biochemistry of hormones and their effects upon various behaviors have been established in considerable detail, numerous behaviors that are probably under hormonal influence have yet to be critically analyzed. Among them are many subtle pheromones that affect a person's interactions with other people, imprinting pheromones that trigger attraction and bonding between individuals, and hormones that link together a variety of bodily functions. These hormones may number in the hundreds, and they represent a challenging avenue for further research. Unraveling the relationships between hormones and behavior can enable researchers to gain a greater understanding of the human mind and its link to the rest of the body and to other individuals. These studies offer potential treatments for behavioral abnormalities and for mental disturbances created by the physiologically disruptive effects of drug use, a major problem in American society. They also offer great promise in the alleviation of stress, another major social and medical problem.

SOURCES FOR FURTHER STUDY

Campbell, Neil A., Jane B. Reece, and Laurence G. Mitchell. *Biology.* 5th ed. Menlo Park, Calif.: Benjamin-Cummings, 1999. This introductory biology text presents an exhaustive overview of biology. Unit 7, dealing with animal form and function, gives an overview of the endocrine system, along with a discussion of its effects on reproduction, development, and behavior.

James, Vivian, ed. "Hormones and Sport Symposium." *Journal of Endocrinology* 170 (2001). This special issue is devoted entirely to the effects of hormones on sporting activity. The coverage within the issue focuses on the role of hormones in sports, as well as the problems in attempting to eliminate potentially problematic drug abuse by athletes.

Manning, Aubrey. *An Introduction to Animal Behavior.* 3d ed. Reading, Mass.: Addison-Wesley, 1979. Manning's concise, thorough survey of animal behavior theory and research employs hundreds of experimental studies to describe major aspects of the subject. Chapter 2, "The Development of Behavior," discusses the roles of hormones in animal development and social behavior. Chapter 4, "Motivation," is an extensive study of animal drives and motivations as influenced by hormones, pheromones, and environmental stimuli.

Martini, Frederic H., E. F. Bartholomew, and K. Welch. *The Human Body in Health and Disease.* Upper Saddle River, N.J.: Prentice Hall, 2000. This college-level text outlines the structure and function of the endocrine system and demonstrates its interrelationship with the nervous system and its effects on behavior. Well-written and illustrated.

Nelson, Randy J. *An Introduction to Behavioral Endocrinology.* 2d ed. Sunderland, Mass.: Sinauer Associates, 1999. This text covers hormones and behavior in historical perspective, knowledge in cell and molecular biology and behavior, present and contemporary and future research in the field.

Raven, Peter H., and George B. Johnson. *Biology.* 5th ed. Boston: McGraw-Hill, 1999. Raven and Johnson's book is an introductory survey of biology for the beginning student. It contains beautiful illustrations and photographs. Describes the endocrine systems of human and mammals, the major hormones produced by each endocrine gland, and the effects of these hormones upon the body.

Sherwood, Lauralee. *Human Physiology: From Cells to Systems.* 4th ed. Pacific Grove, Calif.: Brooks-Cole, 2001. This college physiology text outlines the functioning of the endocrine glands and the hormones that they produce. Chapters 18 and 19 focus on endocrinology, highlighting the effects of hormones on behavior.

Wallace, Robert A., Gerald P. Sanders, and Robert J. Ferl. *Biology: The Science of Life.* 4th ed. New York: HarperCollins, 1999. Wallace, Sanders, and Ferl's introduction to biology for the beginning student exhausts the subject, but it does so by providing a wealth of information, constructive diagrams, and beautiful photographs dealing with human hormones and their effects upon the body.

David Wason Hollar, Jr.;
updated by Robin Kamienny Montvilo

SEE ALSO: Adrenal gland; Emotions; Endocrine system; Gonads; Nervous system; Pituitary gland; Sex hormones and motivation; Smell and taste; Stress; Synaptic transmission; Thyroid gland.

Horney, Karen

BORN: September 15, 1885, near Hamburg, Germany

DIED: December 4, 1952, in New York City

IDENTITY: German-born American psychoanalyst

TYPE OF PSYCHOLOGY: Psychotherapy; personality; social psychology

FIELDS OF STUDY: Adolescence; adulthood; anxiety disorders; childhood and adolescent disorders; classic analytic themes and issues; evaluating psychotherapy; interpersonal relations; personality disorders; personality theory; prejudice and discrimination; social motives

Rebelling against traditional psychiatric theories of female motivation and behavior, Horney formulated theories dependent on social and environmental influences rather than sexual trauma.

Karen Clementina Theodora Danielsen was born in Eilbek, a village near Hamburg, Germany. Determined to study medicine, she was among the first to be admitted to Hamburg's new, highly controversial, girls' Gymnasium, a preparatory program to train women for admission to German universities. From 1906 to 1908, she studied medicine at Freiburg and Göttingen universities, completing her work in Berlin. There she studied psychoanalysis with Karl Abraham, a follower of Sigmund Freud, and began to practice and teach. She married fellow student Oscar Horney in 1909. They had three daughters before separating in 1926. Alarmed by the rise of Adolf Hitler and the Nazi Party, she moved to the United States in 1932, becoming a citizen in 1938. She settled in New York, where she became a member of the New York Psychoanalytic Institute and a teacher at the New School for Social Research.

Although at first a disciple of Freud, Horney perceived the antifeminism of Freudian theory by the time of the 1937 publication of her book *The Neurotic Personality in Our Time*. She attacked that theory in *New Ways in Psychoanalysis* (1939), emphasizing the importance of environmental and social factors upon personality development, as opposed to Freud's insistence that sexual conflicts were at the basis of psychological problems. Increasingly, she stressed the importance of the parent-child relationship. Not only must biological needs be met, she believed, but children must experience warmth and affection as well. The child who is not lovingly nurtured will develop hostility and distrust. This hostility may be projected onto the world in general or may be repressed to reappear as neurotic compliance or withdrawal.

Her theories brought her into conflict with the Freudian-dominated New York Psychoanalytic Institute, from which she was forced to resign in 1941. She then helped form the Association for the Advancement of Psychoanalysis and its *American Journal of Psychoanalysis*. Her later publications include *Self-Analysis* (1942), *Our Inner Conflicts* (1945), and *Neurosis and Human Growth* (1950), the posthumously published *Feminine Psychology* (1967), and many articles. *The Adolescent Diaries of Karen Horney* appeared in 1980.

In her last years, her interest turned to questions of faith. Shortly after a trip to Japan, where she studied Zen Buddhism, she was diagnosed with cancer, of which she died in 1952.

SOURCES FOR FURTHER STUDY

Paris, Bernard J. *Karen Horney: A Psychoanalyst's Search for Self-Understanding*. New Haven, Conn.: Yale University Press, 1996. Traces the relationship between Horney's personal life and development of her thought; includes extensive bibliography.

Quinn, Susan. *A Mind of Her Own: The Life of Karen Horney*. Reading, Mass.: Addison-Wesley, 1987. Comprehensive general biography in the Radcliffe Biography Series.

Sayers, Janet. *Mothers of Psychoanalysis: Helene Deutsch, Karen Horney, Anna Freud, Melanie Klein*. New York: W. W. Norton, 1991. Traces the revolution in psychoanalysis through the work of four key women.

Betty Richardson

SEE ALSO: Ego, superego, and id; Freud, Sigmund; Personality theory; Psychoanalytic psychology; Psychoanalytic psychology and personality: Sigmund Freud; Women's psychology: Karen Horney.

Human resource training and development

TYPE OF PSYCHOLOGY: Motivation
FIELDS OF STUDY: Cognitive learning; social motives

Human resource training and development programs provide employees with the knowledge and skills they need to perform their jobs successfully. In an increasingly technical and complex world, training and development programs are vital for organizational survival.

KEY CONCEPTS
- apprenticeships
- computer-aided instruction (CAI)
- job analysis
- modeling
- programmed instruction
- role playing
- transfer of training

INTRODUCTION

The term "human resources" implies that human abilities and potential, such as aptitudes, knowledge, and skills, are as important to a company's survival as are monetary and natural resources. In order to help employees perform their jobs as well as they can, companies develop training and development programs.

Most employees must go through some form of training program. Some programs are designed for newly hired or recently promoted employees who need training to perform their jobs. Other programs are designed to help employees improve their performance in their existing jobs. Although the terms are used interchangeably in this discussion, the former type of program is often referred to as a "training program" and the latter as a "development program."

There are three phases to a training or development program. During the first phase, managers determine training needs. One of the best ways to determine these needs is with job analysis. Job analysis is a process that details the exact nature and sequencing of the tasks which make up a job. Job analysis also determines performance standards for each task and specifies the corresponding knowledge, skills, and aptitudes (potential) required to meet these standards. Ideally, job analysis is used as the basis for recruiting and selecting employees. Managers like to hire employees who already have the ability to perform the job; however, most employees enter an organization with strong aptitudes but only general knowledge and skills. Consequently, during the second phase of training, a method of training is designed that will turn aptitudes into specific forms of task-related knowledge and skills.

A long history of training and educational research suggests a number of guidelines for designing effective training programs. First, training is most effective if employees have strong intellectual potential and are highly motivated to learn. Second, trainees should be given active participation in training, including the opportunity to practice the skills learned in training. Practice will usually be most effective if workers are given frequent, short practice sessions (a method called distributed practice) rather than infrequent, long practice sessions (called massed practice). Third, trainees should be given continuous feedback concerning their performance. Feedback allows the trainee to monitor and adjust performance to meet training and personal standards.

One of the greatest concerns for trainers is to make certain that skills developed in training will transfer to the job. Problems with transfer vary greatly with the type of training program. In general, transfer of training will be facilitated if the content of the training program is concrete and behavioral, rather than abstract and theoretical. In addition, transfer is improved if the training environment is similar to the job environment. For example, a manager listening to a lecture on leadership at a local community college will have more difficulty transferring the skills learned in the classroom than will a mechanic receiving individual instruction and on-the-job training.

Once training needs have been analyzed and a training program has been implemented, the effectiveness of the training program must be measured. During the third phase of training, managers attempt to determine the degree to which employees have acquired the knowledge and skills presented in the training program. Some form of testing usually serves this goal. In addition, managers attempt to measure the degree to which training has influenced productivity. In order to do this, managers must have a performance evaluation program in place. Like the selection system and the training program, the performance evaluation system should be based on job analysis. Ideally, a third goal of the evaluation phase of training should be to examine whether the benefits of training, in terms of productivity and job satisfaction, warrant the cost of training. A common problem with training programs is that managers do not check the effectiveness of programs.

Training and development is an integral part of a larger human resource system which includes selection, performance evaluation, and promotion. Because employee retention and promotion can be considerably influenced by training, training and development programs in the United States are subject to equal employment opportunity (EEO) legislation. This legislation ensures that the criteria used to select employees for training programs, as well as the criteria used to evaluate employees once in training programs, are related to performance on the job. When managers fail to examine the effectiveness of their training programs, they cannot tell whether they are complying with EEO legislation. EEO legislation also ensures that if minority group members do not perform as well as majority group members in training, minorities must be given the opportunity for additional training or a longer training period. Minorities are given the additional time based on the assumption that their life experiences may not have provided them with the opportunity to develop the basic skills that would, in turn, allow them to acquire the training material as fast as majority group members.

ON-THE-JOB TRAINING

The most common form of training is on-the-job training, in which newly hired employees are put to work immediately and are given instruction from an experienced worker or a supervisor. On-the-job training is popular because it is inexpensive and the transfer of training is excellent. This type of training program is most successful for simple jobs not requiring high levels of knowledge and skill. On-the-job training is often used for food service, clerical, janitorial, assembly, and retail sales jobs. Problems with on-the-job training arise when formal training programs are not established and the individuals chosen to act as trainers are either uninterested in training or are unskilled in training techniques. A potential drawback of on-the-job training is that untrained workers are slow and tend to make mistakes.

An apprenticeship is a form of long-term training in which an employee often receives both on-the-job training and classroom instruction. Apprenticeships are one of the oldest forms of training and are typically used in unionized skilled trades such as masonry, painting, and plumbing. Apprenticeships last between two and five years, depending on the trade. During this time, the apprentice works under the supervision of a skilled worker, or "journeyman." Once a worker completes the training, he or she may join a trade union and thereby secure a position in the company. Apprenticeships are excellent programs for training employees to perform highly complex jobs. Apprenticeships offer all the benefits of on-the-job training and reduce the likelihood that training will be carried out in a haphazard fashion. Critics of apprenticeship programs, however, claim that some apprenticeships are artificially long and are used to keep employee wages low.

SIMULATION TRAINING

While on-the-job training and apprenticeship programs allow employers to utilize trainees immediately, some jobs require employees to obtain considerable skill before they can perform the job. For example, it would be unwise to allow an airline pilot to begin training by piloting an airplane filled with passengers. Where employees are required to per-

form tasks requiring high levels of skill, and the costs of mistakes are very high, simulator training is often used.

In simulator training, a working model or reproduction of the work environment is created. Trainees are allowed to learn and practice skills on the simulator before they start their actual jobs. Simulators have been created for jobs as varied as pilots, mechanics, police officers, nuclear power plant controllers, and nurses. The advantage of simulator training is that trainees can learn at a comfortable pace. Further, training on simulators is less expensive than training in the actual work environment. For example, flight simulator training can be done for a fraction of the cost of operating a plane. An additional benefit of simulator training is that simulators can be used to train employees to respond to unusual or emergency situations with virtually no cost to the company for employee errors. A potential disadvantage of simulator training is the high cost of developing and maintaining a simulator.

These simulator training programs are used for technically oriented jobs held by nonmanagerial employees. Simulator training can also be used for managers. Two popular managerial simulations are in-basket exercises and business games. Here, managers are put in a hypothetical business setting and asked to respond as they would on the job. The simulation may last a number of days and involve letter and memo writing, telephone calls, scheduling, budgeting, purchases, and meetings.

Interpersonal skills training programs teach employees how to be effective leaders and productive group members. These programs are based on the assumption that an employee can learn how to be a good group participant or a good leader by learning specific behaviors. Many of the interpersonal skills programs involve modeling and role playing. For example, videotapes of managerial scenarios are used to demonstrate techniques a manager might use to encourage an employee. After the manager has seen the model, he or she might play the role of the encouraging manager and thus be given an opportunity to practice leader behaviors. An advantage of role playing is that people get the opportunity to see the world from the perspective of the individual who normally fills the role. Consequently, role playing is a useful tool in helping members of a group in conflict. Role playing allows group members to see the world from the perspective of the adversary.

PROGRAMMED INSTRUCTION

Programmed instruction is a self-instructed and self-paced training method. Training material is printed in a workbook and presented in small units or chapters. A self-administered test follows each unit and provides the trainee with feedback concerning how well the material has been learned. If the trainee fails the test, he or she rereads the material. If the trainee passes the test, he or she moves on to the next unit. Each successive unit is more difficult.

Programmed instruction has been used for such topics as safety training, blueprint reading, organizational policies, and sales skills. The advantage of programmed instruction is that trainees proceed at their own pace. Further, because training and tests are self-administered, employees do not feel much evaluation pressure. In addition, when units are short and tests are frequent, learners get immediate feedback concerning their performance.

Computers have increasingly replaced the function of the workbook. Computer-assisted instruction is useful because the computer can monitor the trainee's performance and provide more information in areas where the trainee is having trouble. A potential drawback of programmed instruction is that employees may react to the impersonal nature of training. Further, if the employees are not committed to the program, they may find it easier to cheat.

THE NEED FOR ONGOING TRAINING

Over the last two hundred years, there have been dramatic changes in both the nature of jobs and the composition of the workforce. Consequently, there have also been dramatic changes in the scope and importance of training. The history of formal employment training dates back thousands of years. Training programs were essential for jobs in the military, church, and skilled trades. Prior to the Industrial Revolution, however, only a small percentage of the population had jobs that required formal training. Training for the masses is a relatively new concept. At the beginning of the Industrial Revolution, the vast majority of workers lived in rural areas and worked on small farms. Training was simple and took place within the family. During the Industrial Revolution, the population started to migrate to the cities, seeking jobs in factories. Employers became responsible for training. While early factory work was often grueling, the jobs themselves were rela-

tively easy to learn. In fact, jobs required so little training that children were often employed as factory workers.

Since the Industrial Revolution, manufacturing processes have become increasingly technical and complex. Now, many jobs in manufacturing require not only lengthy on-the-job training but also a college degree. In addition, technology is changing at an ever-increasing pace. This means that employees must spend considerable time updating their knowledge and skills.

Just as manufacturing has become more complex, so has the process of managing an organization. Alfred Chandler, a business historian, suggests that one of the most important changes since the Industrial Revolution has been the rise of the professional manager. Chandler suggests that management used to be performed by company owners, and managerial skills were specific to each company. Today, managers work for company owners and are trained in universities. Because management functions are so similar across organizations, managers can take their skills to a wide variety of companies and industries.

In contrast to the increasingly technical nature of jobs, there has been an alarming increase in the number of illiterate and poorly trained entrants into the workforce. There has also been an increase in the number of job applicants in the United States who do not speak English. In response to these problems, many companies have begun to provide remedial training in reading, writing, and mathematics. Companies are thus taking the role of public schools by providing basic education. Training and development programs will continue to be essential to organizational survival. As the managerial and technological worlds become more complex, and as the number of highly skilled entrants into the workforce declines, companies will need to focus on both remedial training for new employees and updating the knowledge and skills of older employees. The use of the Internet for distance-learning training programs is expected to increase, offering opportunities for people in remote locations who traditionally have not had access to local training resources.

SOURCES FOR FURTHER STUDY

Bandura, Albert. *Social Learning Theory.* Englewood Cliffs, N.J.: Prentice-Hall, 1977. Describes the ways people learn by observing others' behavior, thus describing the conditions under which modeling is an effective training technique. Social learning theory is one of the most widely studied theories in psychology.

Craig, Robert L., ed. *The ASTD Training and Development Handbook: A Guide to Human Resource Development.* 4th ed. New York: McGraw-Hill, 1996. Well-respected authors in training and development contribute chapters. This book is useful for both academics and practitioners.

Landy, Frank J., and Don A. Trumbo. "Personnel Training and Development: Concepts, Models, and Techniques." In *Psychology of Work Behavior.* Pacific Grove, Calif.: Brooks/Cole, 1989. This chapter provides a good overview of training and development programs. Similar textbooks on either industrial/organizational psychology or human resource management will also have chapters on training and development.

Latham, Gray P. "Human Resource Training and Development." In *Annual Review of Psychology.* Vol. 39. Stanford, Calif.: Annual Reviews, 1988. A review of academic research on training and development. Topics include training history, identifying training needs, evaluating training programs, training programs in other cultures, and leadership training. New updates are published every few years.

Wexley, K. N., and Gary P. Latham. *Developing and Training Human Resources in Organizations.* 3d ed. Upper Saddle River, N.J.: Prentice Hall, 2002. Provides an overview of training methods. The book is well written and includes many examples of actual training programs. A useful tool for students, educators, and trainers.

Daniel Sachau

SEE ALSO: Ability tests; Assessment; Career and personnel testing; Career Occupational Preference System (COPS); Career selection, development, and change; College entrance examinations; Educational psychology; General Aptitude Test Battery (GATB); Industrial and organizational psychology; Intelligence tests; Interest inventories; Kuder Occupational Interest Survey (KOIS); Peabody Individual Achievement Test (PIAT): Race and intelligence; Scientific methods; Social learning: Albert Bandura; Stanford-Binet test; Strong Interest Inventory (SII); Survey research: Questionnaires and interviews; Testing: Historical perspectives; Wechsler Intelligence Scale for Children-Third Edition (WISC-III); Work motivation.

Humanism

TYPE OF PSYCHOLOGY: Origin and definition of psychology

FIELDS OF STUDY: Humanistic therapies; humanistic-phenomenological models

Humanistic psychology attempts to understand a person's experience precisely as it is lived. By respecting the reality of a person's own experiential viewpoint, humanistic psychologists can examine the actual meanings a situation has for the person; in doing so, humanistic psychology develops a comprehensive understanding of human nature and of psychological life in general.

KEY CONCEPTS
- existence
- existentialism
- human science
- intentionality
- person-centered therapy
- phenomenology
- self-actualization

INTRODUCTION

Humanism became influential in psychology through a loosely knit movement that began in the 1950's and became a significant force in the 1960's. Known as humanistic psychology, it is not a single branch of psychology, focused on a particular content area, but a unique approach to all of psychology's content areas. Because humanistic psychology was not created around the work of one founder, it has avoided becoming dogmatic, but it suffers the corresponding disadvantage of having no unanimously inclusive doctrines. Nevertheless, humanistic psychology does offer a distinctive approach to psychological life, based on respect for the specifically "human" quality of human existence. In humanistic psychology, an existence is one's irreducible being in a world that is carved out by one's personal involvements. Fidelity to the full meaning of being human requires understanding human psychological life on its own terms, as it actually presents itself, rather than on models borrowed from other fields of inquiry. In contrast, traditional psychology assembled its foundational concept about human existence during the nineteenth century from such disciplines as physiology, biology, chemistry, and physics. These natural sciences share a common assumption about their subject matter—namely, that it is "matter," objective things that are completely determined by the causal impacts of other things in mechanical and lawful ways that can be explained, measured, predicted, and controlled.

CENTRAL TENETS

Humanistic psychology arose to counter the prevailing scientifically oriented beliefs within the field of psychology during the mid-twentieth century. It argues that the natural science model distorts, trivializes, and mostly neglects the real subject matter: human existence. When love is reduced to a biological drive and insight to a conditioned response, humanistic psychologists protest, psychology has lost contact with the real humanness of its subject matter. Their alternative approach includes four essential features.

First, integral to humanistic psychology is its appreciation of the person as a whole. Such a holistic emphasis holds that people cannot be reduced to parts (labeled processes, instincts, drives, conditioned responses), since the meaning of any part can only be understood in relation to the whole person. For example, a humanistic psychology of thinking also takes into account the thinker's feelings and motives, since it is the person as a whole who thinks, not only the brain or an information-processing system. Even the most seemingly isolated physiological events cannot be fully comprehended apart from the person's total existence. A study of women recently widowed, for example, showed that their bodies' immune systems weakened in the year after their husbands' deaths. This subtle yet profound way of embodying grief is best understood when the human body is grasped as a "bodying forth" of a whole existence and personal history.

A second essential feature of humanistic psychology concerns its notion of consciousness, which is informed by the phenomenological concept of intentionality. Consciousness is seen as "intending" an object, meaning not the everyday sense of intending as a deliberate choice but rather that consciousness is always consciousness of something. Whereas traditional psychologies conceive of consciousness as a machine, a brain, or a container, or dismiss it altogether, the concept of intentionality means that consciousness is fundamentally relational: It is an encountering and dwelling in one's world. For example, to be conscious of the room means to be intertwined with it. To be immersed in a memory means to be there, in that remembered scene. This communion is reciprocal in the sense that the objects of consciousness are also implicated in this relation. It is neither objective stimulation nor variables that ordinary consciousness intends, but a meaningful world, intended through one's own way of being with it. For example, a student driver is conscious of other cars as looming too close, whereas the consciousness of the race car driver intends the spaces through which he or she could drive the car.

Third, this notion of consciousness leads to humanistic psychology's recognition of the irreducible reality of the person's own experience as the core of his or her psychological life. Rather than preconceiving a person's behavior from an outside point of view, humanistic psychology seeks to clarify its significance by understanding the behaving person's own viewpoint. In other words, behavior is seen as an expression of a person's involvement in a situation. For example, a man walking across a snow-covered frozen lake could not be said to be brave (or foolhardy) if he experienced it as a field instead.

A fourth essential constituent is a vision of human freedom. For humanistic psychology, a person unfolds his or her existence over time by responsibly owning and becoming who he or she is. This does not mean that the self is whatever a person wants to be. On the contrary, one's own choice is to be the self that one authentically is. This choice, because one is free to make it or not, is also the source of anxiety, as people confront their own ultimate responsibility for what they will make of their lives. Terms such as "self-actualization" and "self-realization" depict this most crucial obligation of being human. Selfhood, in other words, is not simply what one has been given by environmental or genetic sources. It is, rather, a possibility to be owned and lived by transcending the given. Instead of determining the course of psychological life, the givens of one's existence must be freely engaged in the process of one's own authentic self-becoming.

CONTRIBUTIONS TO PSYCHOLOGY

Within psychology, the humanistic approach's most important applications have been in the areas of psychotherapy, personality theory, and research methods. Rollo May aptly described the humanistic idea of psychotherapy as helping patients experience their existence as real. Carl Rogers's person-centered therapy depicts the humanistic purpose: to assist clients in unblocking and experiencing their own self-actualizing tendencies. This is accomplished by nonjudgmentally clarifying and mirroring back to clients their own spontaneous expressions of self with genuine empathy and unconditional positive regard.

A second area of major application has been personality theory. Among the many who have contributed in this regard are Gordon Allport, Henry Murray, Charlotte Buhler, and James Bugental. The three most famous are Rogers, May, and Abraham Maslow. They see personality as a tendency of self-actualizing: of "becoming" (May), of realizing one's possibilities for "full humanness" (Maslow), of being "fully functioning" (Rogers). They emphasize that the personality is oriented toward growth, thus dynamic rather than static, yet recognize that this process is unfinished and far from automatic. Rogers noted that "incongruence" between one's self-concept and one's actual self blocks actualizing tendencies. If a person experiences positive regard from significant others, such as parents, as being conditional (for example, "I love you because you never get angry" or "I'll love you if you always agree with me"), the effort to meet these conditions results in an "incongruence" between one's self-concept and the self one actually is being.

May stressed that to become self-actualized, one must be aware of oneself. Facing one's own being requires risk and commitment, based on one's capacities for love and will, courage and care. This "central distinguishing characteristic," the human capacity for self-awareness, can be blocked. People may evade the insecurity of this risk by not facing themselves, but the resulting deadening leads to boredom and a trivialization of life.

Maslow specified his conception of self-actualization in the context of his theory of motivation. He described a hierarchy of motives, extending from "deficiency needs" (physiological needs and safety) to "being needs" (belonging, love, self-esteem, and self-actualization). He considered "growth motiva-tion" an inherent tendency of people to fulfill ever higher motives on this hierarchy.

A third application of the humanistic approach has been innovative methods for psychological research. These methods, known as human science, can be used to study human experience as it is actually lived in the world. Human science research is phenomenologically based, and it utilizes data gathered by interviews and written descriptions, which are then analyzed qualitatively. The aim is not to reduce experience to the traditional operationally defined variables, but to understand the essential structure of the person's actually lived experience. A leading figure in these innovations has been Amedeo Giorgi at Duquesne University.

CONTRIBUTIONS TO OTHER FIELDS

Humanistic innovations have been widely applied beyond psychology, in such areas as medicine, politics, feminism, law, religion, social action, international relations, and ecology. For example, former United States president Jimmy Carter used Rogers's techniques (in consultation with Rogers) during the successful Camp David peace talks he facilitated between Anwar Sadat of Egypt and Menachem Begin of Israel. The three areas in which humanistic psychology has had the widest impact are business management, education, and personal growth. In each, humanistic innovations derive from the basic point that the fully functioning person is one whose striving for self-actualization is unblocked.

Within management, humanistic psychology was an early contributor to the emerging field of organizational development. Rogers's person-centered approach was a key influence on the development of the human-relations training for business managers conducted by the National Training Laboratory. In *Eupsychian Management: A Journal* (1965), Maslow provided a humanistic theory of management. He proposed that employees could be most productive if, through more democratic boss-worker relationships, they were given the opportunity to grow in terms of self-actualization and reach their highest human potential. (This book was translated into Japanese and was influential in the development of the managerial style that became characteristic of Japanese business.) Maslow's motivation hierarchy also was the basis for Douglas McGregor's well-known contrast between "theory X" (a traditional authoritarian managerial approach) and "theory Y" (a humanistic one proposing a more participative managerial style).

As humanistic psychology became more prevalent, it also had an impact on the adjoining field of education. Both Rogers and Maslow were severe critics of the prevailing system of education, in which education had been reduced to the acquisition of skills, as if it were merely technical training. Disgusted by the extrinsic focus of education, they promoted the view that educators needed to foster students' intrinsic or natural sense of wonder, creativity, capacity for self-understanding, and growth toward their own self-actualization. Rogers's *Freedom to Learn: A View of What Education Might Become* (1969) became an influential summary of those views.

Beyond the professional fields of business and education, humanistic psychology affected the larger society most directly through spawning the human potential movement. In many "growth centers" (Esalen, in California, being the most prominent), a wide assortment of services are offered. They include such techniques as sensitivity training, encounter groups, sensory awareness, and meditation. The length of time involved varies but is usually of a short duration, such as a weekend or a week. The aim is not treatment for psychologically disturbed persons, but a means of facilitating personal growth.

ROOTS AND EVOLUTION

Humanistic psychology's roots include European psychology and philosophy. Among its psychological predecessors are Kurt Goldstein's organismic theory, Karen Horney's self theory, and Erich Fromm's social analyses. Its philosophical heritage includes existentialism and phenomenology. Fearing the eclipse of the human in a world dominated by science, existentialism began with the recognition that "[i]t is important . . . to hold fast to what it means to be a human being," as originally stated by Søren Kierkegaard in 1846. Beginning in the early twentieth century, Edmund Husserl, phenomenology's founder, articulated the key notion of the intentionality of consciousness. Husserl also fashioned a distinction between the natural sciences and the human sciences (made earlier by Wilhelm Dilthey) into a powerful critique of psychology's traditional scientific foundations. Later philosophers, particularly Martin Heidegger, Jean-Paul Sartre, and Maurice Merleau-Ponty, joined existentialism and phenomenology into a compelling philosophy of existence.

Existential phenomenology first affected the work of European psychologists, especially R. D. Laing, Jan Hendrik van den Berg, Viktor Frankl, Erwin Straus, Ludwig Binswanger, and Medard Boss. In the United States, May was influential in importing these European currents through his edited book of translated readings, *Existence: A New Dimension in Psychiatry and Psychology* (1958). In 1959, Duquesne University established a pioneering graduate program devoted to existential phenomenological psychology. In the 1960's, graduate programs in humanistic psychology were established at Sonoma State University, Saybrook Institute, and West Georgia College.

Much of the movement's early organizational work was done by Maslow, who, with Tony Sutich, launched the *Journal of Humanistic Psychology* in 1961. In 1963, Maslow, Sutich, and Bugental inaugurated the Association for Humanistic Psychology. Within psychology's main organization, the American Psychological Association, the Division of Humanistic Psychology was established in 1971 in response to a petition by its members. It began a journal, *The Humanistic Psychologist.*

EMERGENCE OF COGNITIVE PSYCHOLOGY

With the rapid pace of such developments, by the end of the 1960's humanistic psychologists saw themselves as a "third force": an alternative to behaviorism and psychoanalysis, the two dominant traditions in American psychology at that time. A naïve optimism characterized their sense of the future; humanistic psychology has not succeeded in supplanting those traditions. What happened instead was the rise of cognitive psychology as the main challenger for dominance. Like humanistic psychology, the cognitive approach was formed during the 1950's to dispute traditional psychology's narrow focus on behavior as an objective, observable event, but it offered a more conventional alternative. While returning to the mind as a topic of psychology, it did so while retaining the traditional mechanistic view of mental life. In comparison, humanistic psychology's more fundamental proposal that psychology set aside its mechanistic assumption's altogether continues to cast it in the role of a less palatable alternative for most psychologists.

In other ways, however, the humanistic approach has been a victim of its own successes beyond psychology. Its applications to psychotherapy, management, and education are now so commonly known that they are scarcely recognized anymore as "humanistic." It appears that, for now at least, humanistic psychology has found greater integration beyond psychology than within it.

SOURCES FOR FURTHER STUDY

Bugental, James F. T. *Intimate Journeys: Stories from Life-Changing Therapy.* San Francisco: Jossey-Bass, 1990. A memoir of the struggles, defeats, and triumphs of a humanistic psychotherapist.

Maslow, Abraham H. *Toward a Psychology of Being.* 3d ed. New York: John Wiley & Sons, 1998. Maslow's study of human nature and the conditions and blocks to self-actualization. Topics include growth, motivation, cognition, creativeness, and values.

May, Rollo. *Psychology and the Human Dilemma.* 1967. Reprint. New York: W. W. Norton, 1996. May's accessible yet probing analysis of humans' paradoxical capacity to experience themselves as both subject and object. Topics include meaning, anxiety, freedom, responsibility, values, psychotherapy, science, and the social responsibilities of psychologists.

Pollio, Howard R. *Behavior and Existence: An Introduction to Empirical Humanistic Psychology.* Monterey, Calif.: Brooks/Cole, 1982. A coherent introductory textbook on general psychology from a humanistic standpoint. It covers the usual survey of psychology topics (such as learning, thinking, perceiving, and remembering) from a humanistic approach.

Rogers, Carl. *On Becoming a Person.* 1961. Reprint. Boston: Mariner, 1995. Rogers's most widely read book, providing his views of person-centered psychotherapy, including its key characteristics and how to research its effectiveness. Also includes Rogers's philosophy of persons and analyses of education, families, personal growth, creativity, relationships, and the fully functioning person.

Rowan, John, ed. *Ordinary Ecstacy: The Dialectics of Humanistic Psychology.* New York: Routledge, 2001. Revises classic humanistic psychology in the light of postmodern theories and approaches of the late twentieth century.

Valle, Ronald S., and Steen Halling, eds. *Existential-Phenomenological Perspectives in Psychology: Exploring the Breadth of Human Experience.* New York: Ple-

num, 1989. A widely ranging collection of topics, many centrally important to psychology, each approached phenomenologically in original and creative ways. Topics include social psychology, assessment, perception, learning, child development, emotion, and many others, including transpersonal psychology.

Christopher M. Aanstoos

SEE ALSO: Abnormality: Psychological models; Allport, Gordon; Existential psychology; Gestalt therapy; Humanistic trait models: Gordon Allport; Motivation; Murray, Henry A.; Person-centered therapy; Personology: Henry A. Murray; Play therapy; Rogers, Carl R.; Self-actualization.

Humanistic trait models
Gordon Allport

TYPE OF PSYCHOLOGY: Personality
FIELDS OF STUDY: Humanistic-phenomenological models; personality theory

The humanistic trait model of Gordon Allport explains how a person's unique personal characteristics provide a pattern and direction to personality. It reveals the limitations of psychological theories that focus only on general rules of human behavior and provides insight into how to conduct in-depth study of individual dispositions.

KEY CONCEPTS
- cardinal disposition
- central dispositions
- common traits
- functional autonomy
- idiographic or morphogenic study
- nomothetic study
- personal dispositions
- proprium
- secondary dispositions

INTRODUCTION

The humanistic trait model of Gordon Allport (1897-1967) was based on his profound belief in the uniqueness of every personality, as well as his conviction that individuality is displayed through dominant personal characteristics that provide continuity and direction to a person's life. He saw personality as dynamic, growing, changing, and based on one's personal perception of the world. Like other humanists, Allport believed that people are essentially proactive, or forward moving; they are motivated by the future and seek tension and change rather than sameness. In addition, each individual possesses a set of personal dispositions that define the person and provide a pattern to behavior.

Allport's approach is different from those of other trait theorists, who have typically sought to categorize personalities according to a basic set of universal, essential characteristics. Allport referred to such characteristics as common traits. Instead of focusing on common traits that allow for comparisons between many people, Allport believed that each person is defined by a different set of characteristics. Based on his research, he estimated that there are four thousand to five thousand traits and eighteen thousand trait names.

Functional Autonomy and Personal Dispositions

Most personality theorists view adulthood as an extension of the basic motives present in childhood. Consistent with his belief that personality is always evolving, Allport believed that the motivations of adulthood are often independent of the motivations of childhood, and he referred to this concept as functional autonomy. For example, a person who plays a musical instrument during childhood years because of parental pressure may play the same instrument for relaxation or enjoyment as an adult. Although not all motives are functionally autonomous, many adult activities represent a break from childhood and are based on varied and self-sustaining motives.

According to this perspective, personality is based on concrete human motives that are represented by personal traits or dispositions. Human traits are seen as guiding human behavior, but they must also account for wide variability within a person's conduct from situation to situation. As a result, Allport distinguished between different types and levels of traits or dispositions. Common traits represent those elements of personality that are useful for comparing most people within a specific culture, but they cannot provide a complete profile of any individual person. In contrast, personal disposi-

tions represent the true personality, are unique to the person, and represent subtle differences among persons.

Three kinds of personal dispositions exist: cardinal dispositions, central dispositions, and secondary dispositions. When a person's life is dominated by a single, fundamental, outstanding characteristic, the quality is referred to as a cardinal disposition. For example, Adolf Hitler's cruelty and Mahatma Ghandhi's pacifism are examples of cardinal dispositions. Central dispositions represent the five to ten important qualities of a person that would typically be discussed and described in a thorough letter of recommendation. Finally, secondary dispositions are characteristics that are more numerous, less consistently displayed, and less important than central dispositions.

Three Aspects of the Proprium

Allport referred to the unifying core of personality, or those aspects of the self that a person considers central to self-identity, as the proprium. During the first three to four years of life, three aspects of the proprium emerge. The sense of a bodily self involves awareness of body sensations. Self-identity represents the child's knowledge of an inner sameness or continuity over time, and self-esteem reflects personal efforts to maintain pride and avoid embarrassment. Self-extension emerges between the fourth and sixth year of life; this refers to the child's concept of that which is "mine," and it forms the foundation for later self-extensions such as career and love of country. The self-image, which also emerges between ages four and six, represents an awareness of personal goals and abilities, as well as the "good" and "bad" parts of the self. The ability to see the self as a rational, coping being emerges between ages six and twelve and represents the ability to place one's inner needs within the context of outer reality. Propriate striving often begins in adolescence and focuses on the person's ability to form long-term goals and purposes. Finally, the self as knower represents the subjective self and one's ability to reflect on aspects of the proprium.

Idiographic Research

From this humanistic trait framework, human personality can only be fully understood through the examination of personal characteristics within a single individual. The emphasis on individuality has significant implications for the measurement of personality and for research methods in psychology. Most psychological research deals with standardized measurements and large numbers of people, and it attempts to make generalizations about characteristics that people hold in common. Allport referred to this approach as nomothetic. He contrasted the study of groups and general laws with idiographic research, or approaches for studying the single person. Idiographic research, which is sometimes referred to as morphogenic research, includes methods such as autobiographies, interviews, dreams, and verbatim recordings.

One of Allport's famous studies of the individual appears in *Letters from Jenny* (1965), a description of an older woman's personality that is based on the analysis of approximately three hundred letters that she wrote to her son and his wife. Through the use of personal structure analysis, statistical analysis, and the reactions of various trained judges, Allport and his colleagues identified eight clusters of characteristics, including the following: artistic, self-centered, aggressive, and sentimental. Through revealing the central dispositions of a single individual, this study provided increased insight about all people. It also demonstrated that objective, scientific practices can be applied to the study of one person at a time.

PERSONAL ORIENTATIONS

Gordon Allport preferred personality measures designed to examine the pattern of characteristics that are important to a person and that allow for comparison of the strengths of specific characteristics within the person rather than with other persons. The *Study of Values* (3d ed., 1960), which was developed by Allport, Philip Vernon, and Gardner Lindzey, measures a person's preference for the six value systems of theoretical, economic, social, political, aesthetic, and religious orientations. After rank ordering forty-five items, the individual receives feedback about the relative importance of the six orientations within himself or herself. Consistent with the emphasis on uniqueness, the scale does not facilitate comparisons between people. Although the language of this scale is somewhat outdated, it is still used for value clarification and the exploration of career and lifestyle goals.

Allport's research also focused on attitudes that are influenced by group participation, such as religious values and prejudice. Through the study of churchgoers' attitudes, he distinguished between extrinsic religion, or a conventional, self-serving approach, and intrinsic religion, which is based on internalized beliefs and efforts to act upon religious beliefs. Allport and his colleagues found that extrinsic churchgoers were more prejudiced than intrinsic religious churchgoers; however, churchgoers who strongly endorsed both extrinsic and intrinsic religion were even more prejudiced than either extrinsic or intrinsic religious church attenders. Allport also examined cultural, family, historical, and situational factors that influence prejudice.

AMALGAMATION OF APPROACHES

Gordon Allport provided theoretical and research alternatives at a time when a variety of competing approaches, including humanistic, psychoanalytic, and behavioral perspectives, were seeking preeminence in psychology. Allport found many existing theories to be limiting, overly narrow, and inadequate for describing the wide variations in human personality. As a result, he proposed an eclectic approach to theory that combined the strengths of various other perspectives. Instead of emphasizing a single approach, Allport thought that personality can be both growth-oriented and proactive, as well as reactive and based on instinctual processes. Through an eclectic approach, he hoped that the understanding of personality would become more complete.

Allport was also concerned that many of the existing theories of his time, especially psychoanalytic theories, virtually ignored the healthy personality. In contrast to Sigmund Freud, Allport strongly emphasized conscious aspects of personality and believed that healthy adults are generally aware of their motivations. Unlike Freud's notion that people are motivated to reduce the tension of instinctual drives, he believed that people seek the kind of tension that allows them to grow, develop goals, and act in innovative ways.

TRAIT APPROACHES

Like humanistic theorists Carl Rogers and Abraham Maslow, Allport identified vital characteristics of mature persons. His list of the characteristics of mature persons overlaps substantially with Maslow's enumeration of the qualities of self-actualizing persons and Rogers's definition of the "person of tomorrow." Allport's list includes extension of the sense of self (identifying with events and persons outside oneself), emotional security, realistic perception, insight and humor, and a unifying philosophy of life.

Allport developed his theory at a time when other trait approaches that were based on nomothetic study were gaining prominence. Whereas Allport emphasized individual uniqueness, Raymond Cattell identified twenty-three source traits, or building blocks of personality, and Hans Eysenck identified three primary dimensions of extroversion, neuroticism, and psychoticism. Within the nomothetic tradition, more recent researchers have reexamined earlier nomothetic trait theories and have identified five primary common dimensions of personality: surgency (active/dominant persons versus passive/submissive persons), agreeableness (one's warmth or coldness), conscientiousness (one's level of responsibility or undependability), emotional stability (unpredictability versus stability), and culture (one's intellectual understanding of the world). Allport would have found these efforts to identify basic dimensions of personality to have limited usefulness for defining and understanding individual personality styles.

Recent criticisms of trait approaches that emphasize universal characteristics of people indicate that these approaches underestimate the role of situations and human variability and change across different contexts. Furthermore, those approaches that focus on general traits provide summaries and demonstrate trends about behavior but do not provide explanations for behavior.

The awareness that general trait approaches are inadequate for predicting behavior across situations has led to a resurgence of interest in the types of idiographic research methods proposed by Allport. Approaches to personality have increasingly acknowledged the complexity of human beings and the reality that individuals are influenced by a wide array of features that are often contradictory and inconsistent. Allport's emphasis on the scientific study of unique aspects of personality provided both the inspiration and a general method for examining the singular, diverse variables that define human beings.

SOURCES FOR FURTHER STUDY

Allport, Gordon W. "An Autobiography." In *A History of Psychology in Autobiography*, edited by Edwin Garrigues Boring and Gardner Lindzey. Vol. 5. New York: Appleton-Century-Crofts, 1967. Allport provides an interesting account of his life, including an encounter with Sigmund Freud.

_____. *Becoming: Basic Considerations for a Psychology of Personality*. New Haven, Conn.: Yale University Press, 1955. A short, straightforward, clear statement of Allport's basic assumptions about personality. Allport attempts to provide the basic foundation for a complete personality theory and emphasizes the importance of both open-mindedness and eclecticism in the study of personality.

_____. *The Nature of Prejudice*. 1954. Reprint. Cambridge, Mass.: Perseus, 1988. An extensive review of Allport's theoretical perspective on prejudice. Includes definitions of prejudice and discussions of how individuals perceive and think about group differences, sociocultural influences on prejudice, how prejudice is acquired and maintained, the personality of the prejudiced person, and methods for reducing prejudice.

_____. *Pattern and Growth in Personality*. New York: Holt, Rinehart and Winston, 1961. This textbook is the most complete account of Gordon Allport's personality theory. It includes extensive descriptions of Allport's approach to personality and individuality, personality development, the structure of the personality, the characteristics of the mature personality, and methods of personality assessment.

_____. *Personality and Social Encounter*. Boston: Beacon Press, 1960. A collection of Allport's essays that are scholarly but not overly technical. It is organized into five parts that focus on basic assumptions about personality, personality structure and motivation, personality problems, group tensions associated with prejudice and religion, and social issues and personality.

Allport, Gordon W., Philip E. Vernon, and Gardner Lindzey. *Study of Values*. 3d ed. Boston: Houghton Mifflin, 1960. A scale that measures a person's preference for six value orientations: religious, theoretical, economic, aesthetic, social, or political values. The personal ordering of these values provides a framework for reflecting upon and understanding the values that make up one's philosophy of life. The language is outdated and gender-biased, but the book represents one application of Allport's work.

Evans, Richard I. *Gordon Allport: The Man and His Ideas*. New York: E. P. Dutton, 1971. This book is based on a series of dialogues with Allport that focus on his unique contributions and his vision of the future of personality psychology. Also includes a discussion and evaluation of Allport's ideas by three distinguished psychologists who studied under his direction.

Maddi, Salvatore R., and Paul T. Costa. *Humanism in Personology: Allport, Maslow, and Murray.* Chicago: Aldine-Atherton, 1972. This volume compares the work of Allport with the contributions of two other humanistic personality theorists. Although the theories of these three differ substantially, they share an emphasis on human uniqueness, a faith in human capabilities, and a view of people as proactive, complex, and oriented toward the future.

Masterson, Jenny (Gove) [pseud.]. *Letters from Jenny.* Edited and interpreted by Gordon W. Allport. New York: Harcourt, Brace & World, 1965. An example of idiographic or morphogenic study of the personality. After studying 301 letters from an older woman to her son and his wife, Allport grouped her characteristics into eight clusters that correspond to the number of central dispositions that he proposed make important elements of personality.

Peterson, Christopher. *Personality.* 2d ed. San Diego, Calif.: International Thomson, 1992. This text on personality contains three chapters that summarize, compare, and evaluate various trait approaches along the following dimensions: theory, research, and applications. Describes major criticisms of trait approaches and discusses the practical implications of trait theories.

Carolyn Zerbe Enns

SEE ALSO: Allport, Gordon; Existential psychology; Gestalt therapy; Humanism; Personality interviewing; Psychoanalytic psychology and personality: Sigmund Freud; Religion and psychology; Self-actualization.

Hunger

TYPE OF PSYCHOLOGY: Motivation
FIELDS OF STUDY: Physical motives

The psychological bases of hunger play an important role in the external and internal mediating forces that can affect and modify the physiological aspects of hunger.

KEY CONCEPTS
- appetite
- bingeing
- deprivation
- eating disorders
- external cues
- homeostasis
- hypothalamus
- primary motives
- satiety
- set point

INTRODUCTION

Primary motives are generated by innate biological needs that must be met for survival. These motives include hunger, thirst, and sleep. Hunger has been studied extensively, yet there is still uncertainty as to exactly how this drive works. A large body of research about the physiological analysis of hunger has led to the identification of important differences between physical hunger and psychological hunger.

Physical hunger theories assume that the body's physiological mechanisms and systems produce hunger as a need and that when this need is satisfied, the hunger drive is, for the time being, reduced. Psychologists have developed models and theories of hunger by analyzing its boundaries and restraint or regulation. The early findings on hunger regulation mechanisms emphasized the biological state of the individual and the control of an individual over the hunger drive. If a person experiences hunger, consumption of food will continue until it is terminated by internal cues. This is referred to as regulation.

The individual learns to avoid hunger by reacting to the internal cues of satiety or fullness. The satiety boundary is characterized by feelings of fullness ranging from satisfaction to uncomfortable bloating. The normal eater learns to avoid transgression far or often into this latter zone. Beyond the reaction to internal cues is a zone of indifference, in which the body is not subject to biological cues. Instead, hunger is influenced by social, cognitive, and psychological cues. These cues may be external and/or internalized but do not rely on satiety cues for restraint.

Eating past the point of satiety is referred to as counterregulation or, more commonly, as binge eating or compulsive eating. Because the inhibitors of hunger restraint are not physiological in this zone, the restraint and dietary boundaries are cognitively determined. The physical hunger mechanisms may send signals, but quite ordinary ideas such as "being hungry" and "not being hungry" must be interpreted or received by the individual. The person must learn to distinguish between bodily sensations that indicate the need for food and the feelings that accompany this need, such as anxiety, boredom, loneliness, or depression.

Thus, there are both internal cues and external cues that define hunger and lead an individual to know when to eat and how much to eat. External cues as a motive for eating have been studied extensively, particularly in research on obesity and eating disorders such as binge behavior and compulsive overeating. External cues include enticing smells, locations such as restaurants or other kinds of social settings, and the social environment—what other people are doing. When external cues prevail, a person does not have to be hungry in order to feel hungry.

CHILDREN'S HUNGER

The awareness of hunger begins very early in life. Those infants who are fed on demand, whose cries of hunger determine the times at which they are fed, are taught soon after they can feed themselves that their eating must conform to family rules about when, what, and how much to eat in order to satisfy their hunger. Infants fed on a schedule learn even earlier to conform to external constraints and regulations regarding hunger. Throughout life, responding to hunger by feeding oneself is nourishing both physiologically and psychologically. Beginning in infancy, the sequences of getting hungry and being fed establish the foundations of the relationship between the physiological need or drive and the psychological components of feelings such as affiliation, interaction, calm, and security when hunger is satisfied.

In preschool and early school years, when children are integrating themselves into their social world, food acceptance and cultural practices are learned. Prior to the peer group and school environment, the family and media are usually the main vehicles of cultural socialization of the hunger drive. According to social learning theory, these agents will play an important role in the child's learning to interpret his or her level of hunger and

Hunger is a physiological response, but eating is a learned behavior. (CLEO Photography)

in subsequent eating patterns, both directly and indirectly. The modeling behavior of children is also related to hunger learning.

Experiences of hunger and satiety play a central role in a person's relationship to hunger awareness, eating, and food. Some dispositions that influence hunger and eating behavior are long-term (fairly stable and enduring), while other habits and attitudes may fluctuate. There are numerous theories about the relation between the hunger drive and other factors such as genetic inheritance and activity level.

HUNGER AND THE BRAIN

A strictly physiological analysis claims that an individual's responses to hunger are caused by the brain's regulation of body weight. If the body goes below its predetermined "set point," internal hunger cues are initiated to signal the need for food consumption. External restraints, such as attempts to live up to ideal cultural thinness standards, also affect behavior and may result in restrained eating in order to maintain a body weight below the body's defined set point.

The idea of a body set point is rooted in the work of physiologist Claude Bernard (1813-1878), a pioneer in research based on the concept of homeostasis, or system balance in the body. Homeostasis has played a fundamental role in many subsequent investigations regarding the physiology of hunger and the regulatory systems involved in hunger satisfaction. Inherent in the set-point theory is the concept of motivation, meaning that an organism is driven physiologically and behaviorally toward maintenance of homeostasis and the body's set point and will adapt to accommodate the systems involved in maintenance.

In addition, there appear to be two anatomically and behaviorally distinct centers located in the hypothalamus, one regulating hunger and the other regulating satiety. The area of the hypothalamus responsible for stimulating eating behavior is the lateral hypothalamus. The ventromedial hypothalamus is the area responsible for signaling the organism to stop eating. The lateral hypothalamus is responsible for establishing a set point for body weight.

In comparing hunger and satiety sensation differences, increased hunger and disturbed satiety appear to be two different and quite separate mechanisms. Imbalance or dysfunction of either the hunger mechanism or the satiety sensation can lead to obesity, overeating, binge eating, and other eating disorders. It appears that the way hunger is experienced accounts, in part, for its recognition. Whether hunger is experienced in context with other drives or becomes a compulsive force that dominates all other drives in life is a complex issue. The prevalence of eating disorders and the multitude of variables associated with hunger drives and regulation have provided psychologists with an opportunity to examine the ways in which hunger might take on different meanings. To a person who is anorexic, for example, hunger may be a positive feeling—a state of being "high" and thus a goal to seek. To others, hunger may produce feelings of anxiety, insecurity, or anger. In this case, a person might eat before feeling hunger to prevent the feelings from arising. People's ability to experience hunger in different ways provides psychologists with two types of hunger, which are commonly referred to as hunger and appetite.

Hunger and appetite are not the same. Actual physical need is the basis of true hunger, while appetite can be triggered by thought, feeling, or sensation. Physical need can be separate from psychological need, although they may feel the same to the person who is not conscious of the difference. Compulsive eaters are often unable to recognize the difference between "real" hunger and psychological hunger, or appetite. While psychological hunger can be equally as motivating a need as stomach hunger, and appetite (or mouth hunger) is emotionally, cognitively, and psychologically based thus cannot be fed in the same way. Stomach hunger can be satisfied by eating, whereas "feeding" mouth hunger must involve other activities and behaviors, since food does not ultimately seem to satisfy the mouth type of hunger.

THE CULTURAL CONTEXT OF HUNGER

One approach to increasing understanding of hunger and its psychological components is to examine hunger in its cultural context. In American culture, the experience of hunger is inextricably tied to weight, eating, body image, self-concept, social definitions of fatness and thinness, and other factors which take the issue of hunger far beyond the physiological facts. Historian Hillel Schwartz has traced the American cultural preoccupation with hunger, eating, and diet by examining the cultural fit between shared fictions about the body and their psychological, social, and cultural consequences. Hunger becomes a broader social issue when viewed in the context of the culture's history of obsession with diet, weight control, and body image. The personal experience of hunger is affected by the social and historical context.

Eating disorders such as anorexia, bulimia, and compulsive overeating provide evidence of the complex relationship between the physiological and psychological components of hunger. Obesity has also been examined using medical and psychological models. The etiology of hunger's relationship to eating disorders has provided insight, if not consensus, by investigating the roles of hereditary factors, social learning, family systems, and multigenerational transmission in hunger as well as the socially learned eating patterns, food preferences, and cultural ideals that can mediate the hunger drive. Body image, eating restraint, and eating attitudes have been assessed by various methods. The focus of much of the research on hunger beyond the early animal experiments has been eating disorders. The findings confirm that hunger is more than a physiological need and is affected by a multitude of variables.

HUNGER REGULATION

The desire to regulate hunger has resulted in a wide variety of approaches and techniques, including professional diet centers, programs, and clinics; self-help books and magazines; diet clubs and support groups; self-help classes; and "diet doctors." Many people have benefitted from psychotherapy in an effort to understand and control their hunger regulation mechanisms. Group therapy is one of the most successful forms of psychotherapy for food abusers. Types of group therapy vary greatly and include leaderless support groups, nonprofessional self-help groups such as Overeaters Anonymous, and groups led by professional therapists.

Advantages of group support for hunger regulation include the realization that one is not alone. An often-heard expression in group therapy is "I always thought I was the only person who ever felt this way." Other advantages include group support for risk taking, feedback from different perspectives, and a group laboratory for experimenting with new social behaviors. Witnessing others struggling to resolve life issues can provide powerful motivation to change. Self-help and therapy groups also offer friendship and acceptance. Creative arts therapies are other forms of psychotherapy used by persons seeking to understand and control their hunger regulation mechanisms. Creative therapy may involve art, music, dance, poetry, dreams, and other creative processes. These are experiential activities, and the process is sometimes nonverbal.

A more common experience for those who have faced the issue of hunger regulation is dieting. Despite the high failure rate of diets and weight-loss programs, the "diet mentality" is often associated with hunger regulation. Robert Schwartz studied the elements of the diet mentality, which is based on the assumption that being fat is bad and being thin is good. Dieting often sets up a vicious cycle of failure, which deflates self-esteem, thus contributing to shame and guilt, and to another diet. The diet mentality is self-defeating. Another key element to the diet mentality is the mechanism of self-deprivation that comes from not being allowed to indulge in certain foods and the accompanying social restrictions and isolation that dieting creates. Dieting treats the symptom rather than the cause of overeating.

Numerous approaches to hunger regulation share a condemnation of the diet mentality. Overcoming overeating; understanding, controlling, and recovering from addictive eating; and being "thin-within" are approaches based on addressing hunger regulation from a psychological perspective rather than a physiological one. These approaches share an emphasis on the emotional and feeling components of hunger regulation. They encourage the development of skills to differentiate between stomach hunger and mind hunger—that is, between hunger and appetite—and thereby to learn to recognize satiety as well as the reasons for hunger.

Behavior modification consists of a variety of techniques that attempt to apply the findings and methods of experimental psychology to human behavior. Interest in applying behavioral modification to hunger regulation developed as a result of the research on external cues and environmental factors that control the food intake of individuals. By emphasizing specific training in "stimulus control," behavior modification helps the individual to manage the environmental determinants of eating.

The first step in most behavior modification programs is to help the patient identify and monitor activities that are contributing to the specific behavior. In the case of an individual who overeats, this could involve identifying such behaviors as frequent eating of sweets, late evening snacking, eating huge meals, or eating in response to social demands. Because most people have more than one stimulus for eating behavior, the individual then observes situational stimuli: those that arise from the environment in which eating usually takes place. Once the stimuli are identified, new behaviors can be substituted—in effect, behavior can be modified.

MODELS OF HUNGER

Early scientific interest in hunger research was dominated by medical models, which identified the physiological mechanisms and systems involved. One of the earliest attempts to understand the sensation of hunger was an experiment conducted in 1912, in which a subject swallowed a balloon and then inflated it in his stomach. His stomach contractions and subjective reports of hunger feelings could then be simultaneously recorded. When the recordings were compared to the voluntary key presses that the subject made each time he experienced the feeling of hunger, the researchers concluded that it was the stomach movements that caused the sensation of hunger. It was later found, however, that an empty stomach is relatively inactive and that the stomach contractions experienced by the subject were an experimental artifact caused by the mere presence of the balloon in the stomach.

Further evidence for the lack of connection between stomach stimuli and feelings of hunger was provided in animal experiments which resulted in differentiating two areas of the hypothalamus responsible for stimulating eating behavior and signaling satiety—the "start eating" and "stop eating" centers.

Psychologist Stanley Schachter and his colleagues began to explore the psychological issues involved in hunger by emphasizing the external, nonphysiological factors involved. In a series of experiments in which normal-weight and overweight individuals were provided with a variety of external eating cues, Schachter found that overweight subjects were more attentive to the passage of time in determining when to eat and were more excited by the taste and sight of food than were normal-weight persons. More recently, the growth of the field of social psychology has provided yet a different perspective on hunger, one that accounts for the situational and environment factors which influence the physiological and psychological states. For example, psychologists have examined extreme hunger and deprivation in case studies from historical episodes such as war, concentration camps, and famine in the light of the more recent interest in the identification and treatment of eating disorders.

There does not appear to be a consistent or ongoing effort to develop an interdisciplinary approach to the study of hunger. Because hunger is such a complex drive, isolating the factors associated with it poses a challenge to the standard research methodologies of psychology such as the case study, experiment, observation, and survey. Each methodology has its shortcomings, but together the methodologies have produced findings which clearly demonstrate that hunger is a physiological drive embedded in a psychological, social, and cultural context.

Viewing hunger as a multidimensional behavior has led to an awareness of hunger and its implications in a broader context. Changing dysfunctional attitudes, feelings, thoughts, and behaviors concerning hunger has not always been seen as a choice. Through continued psychological research into the topic of hunger—and increasing individual and group participation in efforts to understand, control, and change behaviors associated with hunger—new insights continue to emerge that will no doubt cast new light on this important and not yet completely understood topic.

SOURCES FOR FURTHER STUDY

Arenson, Gloria. *A Substance Called Food.* 2d ed. Boston: McGraw-Hill, 1989. Presents a variety of perspectives on eating: the physiological, the physiological, and the transpersonal. Particularly useful in providing self-help advice and treatment modalities. Examines the compulsiveness of food addiction and sees behavior modification as a means of addressing the addictive behavior.

Battegay, Raymond. *The Hunger Diseases.* Northvale, N.J.: Jason Aronson, 1997. Addresses the emotional hunger that, the author contends, underlies all eating disorders, from anorexia to obesity.

Hirschmann, Jane R., and Carol H. Munter. *When Women Stop Hating Their Bodies: Freeing Yourself from Food and Weight Obsessions.* New York: Fawcett, 1997. A follow-up to the authors' *Overcoming Overeating* (1988). Reviews the psychological bases for compulsive eating and provides alternative strategies to persons who have an addictive relationship with food. Presents convincing arguments against dieting and proposes that self-acceptance, physical activity, and health are more appropriate long-term solutions to the problem of overeating.

Nisbett, Richard E. "Hunger, Obesity, and the Ventromedial Hypothalamus." *Psychological Review* 79, no. 6 (1972): 433-453. Based on research which differentiated the two areas of the hypothalamus that involve hunger: the "start eating" and "stop eating" mechanisms. Explains the idea of "set point," or the body mechanism which regulates homeostasis. This article is a classic in the field of hunger because it explains the physiological location of hunger and the important role of the hypothalamus.

Schachter, Stanley, and Larry P. Gross. "Manipulated Time and Eating Behavior." *Journal of Personality and Social Psychology* 10, no. 2 (1968): 98-

106. Schachter's experiments provide the basis for attention to, and recognition of the importance of, external, nonphysiological factors affecting hunger. This article was one of the first to address the psychological components of hunger by examining the external triggers to eating.

Schwartz, Hillel. *Never Satisfied: A Cultural History of Diets, Fantasies, and Fat.* New York: Free Press, 1986. Schwartz, a historian, looks at diets and eating from the perspective of American social and cultural history. Begins with the first weight watchers, in the early nineteenth century; examines how "shared fictions" about the body fit with various reducing methods and fads in different eras.

Schwartz, Robert. *Diets Don't Work.* 3d ed. Oakland, Calif.: Breakthru, 1996. Practical "how-to" guide to dismantling the diet mentality. This book is a good, basic, and sensible guide for taking stock of the self-defeating weight-loss attitudes and behaviors prevalent in temporary diets versus long-term attitudinal and behavior strategies for permanent weight control.

Tribole, Evelyn, and Elyse Resch. *Intuitive Eating: A Recovery Book for the Chronic Dieter.* 5th ed. New York: St. Martin's Press, 1996. Advocates, and advises how to, listen to authentic hunger cues and avoid emotion-based overeating.

Robin Franck

SEE ALSO: Addictive personality and behaviors; Anorexia nervosa and bulimia nervosa; Drives; Eating disorders; Obesity; Thirst.

Hypnosis

TYPE OF PSYCHOLOGY: Consciousness
FIELDS OF STUDY: Cognitive processes

Hypnosis is a trancelike altered state of consciousness in which the hypnotizable subject is typically more responsive to suggestions than is a waking subject. Hypnosis research has provided psychology with a number of useful theoretical insights into human cognition, as well as practical benefits in controlling pain and treating behavior disorders such as obesity, smoking, and sexual dysfunction.

KEY CONCEPTS
- hypnotic analgesia
- hypnotic anesthesia
- hypnotic dissociation
- hypnotic hypermnesia
- hypnotic susceptibility
- somnambulism

INTRODUCTION

Hypnosis derives its name from the Greek term *hypnos*, which translates into English as "sleep." Hypnosis was so named by the Scottish physician James Braid (1795-1860), who noted the sleeplike features of the somnambulistic trance. Though hypnosis may appear to be a sleeplike state, several differences exist between hypnosis and sleep. First, hypnotic subjects will respond to suggestions from the hypnotist. Second, hypnotizable subjects exhibit a phenomenon known as waking hypnosis, in which they will open their eyes and behave as if awake yet continue to be under hypnosis. Last, brain-wave recordings in hypnosis reveal primarily an alpha pattern characteristic of a relaxed state, while those in sleep reveal theta and delta activity.

THEORETICAL PERSPECTIVES

If hypnosis is not a sleeplike state, how can it be characterized? Since two major theoretical views exist on hypnosis, the answer to that question is quite complex. From one perspective, hypnosis is an altered state of consciousness involving a trance state that is usually accompanied by heightened suggestibility. The primary feature of the hypnotic trance is the loss or suspension of a normal reality-testing orientation. Subjects become so absorbed in the hypnotist's words that they subjectively create the reality of those suggestions and limit their awareness of the environment to a very narrow range of external stimuli. Other qualitative dimensions of the hypnotic trance include a loss of volition, a sense of unreality, a diminished sense of identity, and physical relaxation.

A view of hypnosis as a trance state or an altered state of consciousness is represented by the neodissociation theory, which was developed by Ernest Hilgard in 1973. He was conducting studies on the anesthetic properties of hypnosis. Hilgard produced cold pressor pain in his subjects by placing one of their arms into a circulating pool of ice water, which resulted in reports of intolerable pain in approximately one minute. In contrast, when hypnotic subjects were given suggestions for limb anesthesia, they reported low levels of pain or the complete absence of pain. Yet if subjects were told to write down their experience, they reported the presence of pain. These results suggested a discrepancy between the subjects' oral and written reports of pain. Hilgard dubbed this phenomenon the "hidden observer" effect, because it was as though a hidden observer, who saw and felt everything, were present in the brain. According to Hilgard, the hidden observer effect suggests that the perceiver experiences pain at two levels. One level is experienced in immediate awareness and is subject to the effects of hypnotic analgesia (the use of hypnotic procedures to reduce or eliminate present pain) and anesthesia (the use of hypnotic procedures for preventing the occurrence of future pain). Subjects report a diminution in pain when this level of awareness is blocked by suggestions for pain relief. The second level of pain is dissociated from immediate awareness and maintains constant vigilance to detect the presence of pain. It is at the second level that the hidden observer operates in the brain. Since Hilgard's theory implies cognitive control of a stimulus event, it suggests that a trance or altered state of consciousness is operating during hypnosis.

The second major theoretical perspective emphasizes the importance of the social context in which hypnosis occurs, and it has been referred to as the social psychological theory. From this viewpoint, hypnotized subjects are not in a trance or an altered state of consciousness. Rather, they meet the implicit and explicit demand characteristics of hypnosis by enacting the role of a hypnotic subject. In other words, subjects simulate hypnotic behavior in response to their own preconceived notions and motivations, as well as those expectations conveyed by the hypnotist. T. R. Sarbin and W. C. Coe, in 1972, proposed several variables that influence hypnotic role enactment. They include the location of individual participants in their proper roles, perceived congruence between self and role, accuracy of role expectations, possession of role-relevant skills, and the influence of the audience. If these factors are positive for the subject, hypnotic role enactment may be convincingly demonstrated to the audience and the subject.

While both theories may explain hypnotic behavior, it is clear that not all subjects are simulating hyp-

nosis to enact the role of a hypnotized subject. Measurements of hypnotic responsiveness indicate that hypnosis significantly increases suggestibility beyond that found in a waking state. If subjects were merely simulating hypnosis, hypnotic suggestibility would not exceed waking suggestibility. Clearly, hypnosis involves more than motivation to enact the role of a hypnotized subject.

HYPNOTIC RESPONSIVENESS AND SUSCEPTIBILITY

Measurements of hypnotic responsiveness are typically undertaken with two scales: the Harvard Group Scale of Hypnotic Susceptibility, Form A (HGSHS:A), and the Stanford Hypnotic Susceptibility Scale, Form C (SHSS:C). The HGSHS:A is used primarily as a screening device for large groups. Most of its suggestions are motor in nature, although some cognitive ones are included. The SHSS:C is usually administered to individuals and includes both cognitive and

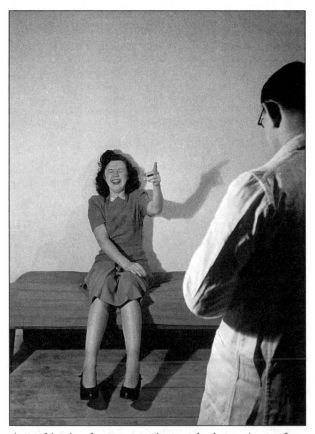

A psychiatrist observes a patient under hypnosis at a London clinic in 1947. She has been told that the doctor is wearing a funny hat. (Hulton Archive)

motor suggestions. Generally, the SHSS:C is considered to be a better measure of hypnotic susceptibility. Both scales include a sample of twelve total suggestions, with high hypnotizables defined as 9 to 12 on each scale, mediums as 4 to 8, and lows as 0 to 3.

Exactly what makes some people more hypnotizable than others is not entirely clear. Surprisingly, personality traits are not reliably correlated with hypnotic susceptibility. Instead, the following three cognitive variables seem to be more strongly related to hypnotic susceptibility: imaginative involvement, concentrated attention, and suspension of reality testing. In general, the higher a person scores on these three variables, the more hypnotizable that person tends to be. One thing is certain: There is no correlation between hypnotic susceptibility and strength of will. Although hypnosis reduces inhibitions and increases compliance to suggestions the subject considers to be acceptable, hypnotized subjects cannot be forced to perform acts that they would find morally reprehensible.

USE IN PAIN CONTROL

Among forms of altered consciousness, hypnosis may have the greatest practical utility. Hypnosis has been used to control pain, to treat behavior disorders, and to recover lost memories or enhance existing memories of eyewitnesses.

The use of hypnotic anesthesia has a long history, beginning with surgical amputation allegedly performed by the British physician W. S. Ward in 1842. Ward's report was strongly criticized at the time, but evidence suggests that it was legitimate. Another early report of hypnotic anesthesia use was provided by the nineteenth century Scottish physician James Esdaile, who was practicing in India at the time. Esdaile performed more than thirteen hundred operations on hypnotized subjects in the 1840's. Many of those surgeries involved the removal of scrotal tumors, which resulted in a recovery rate of only 50 percent for unanesthetized patients. With the use of hypnotic anesthesia, however, the mortality rate dropped to 5 percent. Esdaile's findings were also criticized by the British scientific community on the rather dubious and racist grounds that "native" assistants hypnotized the patients and that the patients actually liked to undergo operations.

The effectiveness of hypnotic anesthesia and analgesia has been examined in a number of well-controlled laboratory studies. Using cold pressor pain,

Ernest and Josephine Hilgard demonstrated that hypnotic analgesia significantly reduces verbal reports of pain and increases pain tolerance levels as compared with a normal waking state. Reports of pain relief were correlated with hypnotic susceptibility levels; high hypnotizables tended to benefit more from hypnotic analgesia than did low hypnotizables.

Based on laboratory findings, three clinical procedures have been developed for using hypnosis to control pain. The first procedure involves giving the patient a direct suggestion that the painful body part is getting numb and can no longer feel any pain. If the patient requires a more concrete suggestion, the hypnotist may suggest that a local anesthetic is being injected into the shoulder. A second procedure is to alter the experience of pain by giving suggestions for its displacement to a less sensitive region of the body and/or by converting the pain into a less aversive experience. With diffuse pain, the patient may be told that the pain is diminishing in size to a small spot; then a transfer of the pain to a less sensitive body region, where it can be converted into a tingling sensation, is suggested. Finally, therapists use hypnotic anesthesia to direct attention away from the pain and its source. For example, the patient may be told that the painful body part no longer exists. Alternatively, age regression to an earlier and happier experience may be employed, or the therapist may engage the patient in hypnotic fantasies. The latter two approaches presumably distract the patient's attention away from the pain.

BEHAVIOR DISORDERS TREATMENT

A second major field of application for hypnosis has been in the treatment of behavior disorders. Hypnotherapy has been used to treat a variety of behavior disorders, including smoking and obesity, both of which involve poor habit control. The use of hypnotherapy to alter bad habits may be successful because the strength of the habit is not in full force in an altered state of consciousness. In a normal waking state, the habit exerts its dominance over the patient's behavior and may be difficult to reshape or modify. In addition, the highly concentrated state of attention in hypnosis may allow patients to direct all of their resources to the task of altering the negative habit.

Hypnotherapy in the treatment of smoking and obesity seems to be more effective with several treatment sessions or with procedures for reinforcing the hypnotic suggestions on a daily basis. For example, in 1975 H. E. Stanton combined the following hypnotic procedures to treat overweight patients: direct suggestions to reduce food intake, ego-enhancing suggestions to improve self-esteem, self-hypnosis to reinforce the therapist's suggestions, and hypnosis audiotapes to provide additional support following the completion of formal treatment. The combined use of these hypnotic procedures resulted in marked weight loss among patients who completed the therapeutic process.

Although repeated hypnotherapy sessions appear to be most effective for treating behavior disorders, even one session may be useful. In 1970, Harold Spiegel used a competing-response hypnotic technique for the treatment of smoking. Subjects were told that cigarette smoke is a toxin to the body, that life is not possible without the body, and that life is possible only if one protects and treats the body well. The adverse effects of smoking were then placed in competition with the life process. The subjects could choose smoking, thereby threatening their lives, or they could choose to enhance life by abandoning the smoking habit. Although subjects were only exposed to one hypnotic session, 20 percent quit smoking. In 1970, using a total of five hypnotic sessions, Harold Crasilneck and James Hall reported a success rate of 75 percent. Many subjects do subsequently begin smoking again, but with a greater number of therapy sessions, the rate of recidivism declines.

Finally, hypnosis has been used to enhance recall of past events, which is termed hypnotic hypermnesia. A sensational example of hypnotic hypermnesia was reported in Chowchilla, California, in 1976. This incident involved the kidnaping of a group of children who were on a field trip. The bus, with all occupants aboard, was buried underground and kept there until a ransom was paid. The case was cracked by law enforcement officials when the bus driver was able to recall under hypnosis the license plate of the car driven by the kidnappers. He was not able to do so in a normal waking state.

EVOLUTION OF PRACTICE

Franz Anton Mesmer (1734-1815), an Austrian physician, is generally credited with the discovery of hypnosis. In his medical practice, Mesmer was sometimes confronted with patients who reported symptoms of physical illness but did not manifest any underlying physical pathology. To treat these seemingly incurable patients, Mesmer would pass magnets over the patients' bodies. In many cases, the patient would go into what Mesmer described as a "crisis," with trembling, twitching, intense pain at body regions associated with symptoms, and sometimes convulsions. After completion of the magnetic therapy, most patients would report a relief of symptoms. Eventually, Mesmer discovered that a cure could be wrought by simply passing his hands over the patient, usually accompanied by soft, soothing words.

One of Mesmer's students, Armand-Marie Jacques de Chastenet, the marquis de Puységur, disliked the rather violent and painful magnetic "crises" elicited in patients. While treating a young male patient, Puységur discovered that a peaceful, sleeplike state, resembling sleepwalking and talking in sleep, could be spontaneously induced. Because of its resemblance to these phenomena, he coined the term "artificial somnambulism" ("somnambulism' is now used as the scientific term for sleepwalking). Puységur later reproduced this trance state by suggesting it overtly.

It was left to the nineteenth century Scottish physician James Braid to incorporate artificial somnambulism into the mainstream of science. Braid made three important contributions. First, he scientifically demonstrated the existence of many somnambulistic phenomena and published his results. Second, Braid convinced the scientific establishment that the main effects of hypnosis were a function of the subject's hypnotic susceptibility level, and not attributable to the power of the magnetizer. Finally, Braid provided magnetic and somnambulistic phenomena with a new, more scientific sounding name. He coined the term "neuro-hypnology," which was shortened first to "hypnology" and later to the modern term "hypnosis."

In the twentieth century, Ernest Hilgard and his colleagues were instrumental in obtaining psychological recognition for hypnosis, especially as an altered state and as a method for controlling pain. Since the 1960's, hypnosis has been integrated into mainstream psychology, enjoying greater acceptance than ever before in areas such as cognitive and clinical psychology. The dissociative processes in hypnosis and the mechanisms by which hypnosis enhances cognitive functioning are especially important in cognitive psychology. In clinical psychology, hypnosis offers a host of practical applications for treating clients. Clinicians are also interested in the parallels between hypnotic dissociation (a hypnotic state in which thoughts, feelings, and perceptions are separated or dissociated from conscious awareness) and dissociative disorders, such as multiple personalities.

FUTURE RESEARCH

Future research will continue to examine the controversy that surrounds the fundamental nature of hypnosis—whether it induces a trance state or is simply role modeling, an instance of simulation. This controversy continues to fester, with no apparent end in sight to the heated debate. Additional research will also be needed to understand why some people are hypnotizable and others are not. Some cognitive and physiological correlates of hypnotizability have been discovered, but such correlations are only moderate in magnitude. Research into potential clinical applications of hypnosis will continue to be a central focus. Hypnotherapy is only in its infancy and will require much research to provide it with a solid scientific foundation. Finally, exploring the range of hypnotic effects on psychological and behavioral processes will continue to be a central concern among researchers. Only tightly controlled laboratory investigations will yield answers to questions such as what perceptual and cognitive processes are affected by hypnosis, how, and why.

SOURCES FOR FURTHER STUDY

Hilgard, Ernest Ropiequet, and Josephine Rohrs Hilgard. *Hypnosis in the Relief of Pain.* Rev. ed. New York: Brunner/Mazel, 1994. Provides a comprehensive review of the Hilgards' own research on hypnotic anesthesia and analgesia, as well as the research of others. Examines the physiological and psychological bases of pain, and explores laboratory and clinical methods of controlling pain with hypnosis. Highly recommended for college students and advanced high school students.

Kirsch, Irving, Antonio Capafons, Etzel Cardena, and Salvador Amigo, eds. *Clinical Hypnosis and Self-Regulation: Cognitive-Behavioral Perspectives.* Washington, D.C.: American Psychological Association, 1999. A collection of papers, written for professionals. Argues that hypnosis is underused in clinical settings and attempts to show its benefits.

Sheehan, Peter W., and Kevin M. McConkey. *Hypnosis and Experience: The Exploration of Phenomena and Process.* New York: Brunner/Mazel, 1996. An advanced treatise on hypnosis, focusing on the experiential analysis of hypnotic phenomena, such as ideomotor responses, age regression, hypnotic dreams and hallucinations, and posthypnotic amnesia. Because of its technical nature, recommended only for serious, advanced students.

Wallace, Benjamin, and Leslie E. Fisher. *Consciousness and Behavior.* 3d ed. Boston: Allyn & Bacon, 1991. A general textbook on consciousness containing an excellent, updated chapter on hypnosis. The chapter reviews theories and the history of hypnosis, describes ways of assessing hypnotic susceptibility, reviews research on basic hypnotic phenomena, and discusses practical applications of hypnosis. Highly recommended for high school and college students, as well as interested adults.

Yapko, Michael D. *Treating Depression with Hypnosis: Integrating Cognitive-Behavioral and Strategic Approaches.* New York: Brunner/Mazel, 2001. Practical guidance to alleviating depression with hypnosis, written by a practicing psychotherapist.

Richard P. Atkinson

SEE ALSO: Amnesia and fugue; Attention; Automaticity; Consciousness; Consciousness: Altered states; Meditation and relaxation; Multiple personality; Observational learning; Pain management.

Hypochondriasis, conversion, somatization disorder, and somatoform pain

TYPE OF PSYCHOLOGY: Psychopathology
FIELDS OF STUDY: Anxiety disorders; models of abnormality

Conversion, hypochondriasis, somatization, and somatoform pain are a group of mental disorders that are typically referred to as the somatoform disorders. The primary feature of these disorders, as their name suggests, is that psychological conflicts take on a somatic, or physical, form.

KEY CONCEPTS

- cathartic method
- conversion disorder
- hypochondriasis
- somatization disorder
- somatoform disorders
- somatoform pain

INTRODUCTION

Conversion, hypochondriasis, somatization, and somatoform pain are thought by most mental health professionals, such as psychiatrists and clinical psychologists, to be the four major types of somatoform disorders. These disorders are typically studied together because they have an important similarity. With each of these disorders, a psychological conflict is expressed through a somatic, or physical, complaint.

CONVERSION DISORDER

The manifestation of a psychological conflict through a physical complaint is perhaps most apparent with conversion disorder. When an individual suffers from conversion disorder, the psychological conflict results in some type of disability. Symptoms vary widely; some of the most common involve blindness, deafness, paralysis, and anesthesia (loss of sensation). In all these cases, medical examinations reveal that there is nothing wrong physiologically with the individual. The handicap stems from a psychological or emotional problem.

In many instances, the handicap is thought to develop because it gives the person an unconscious way of resolving a conflict. For example, an adult who is feeling powerful yet morally unacceptable feelings of anger and rage may wish to strike his or her young child. Rather than carry out this dreadful action, this person will suddenly develop a paralyzed arm. The unacceptable emotional impulse is then "converted" (thus the term "conversion") into a physical symptom. When this happens, individuals will sometimes seem strangely unconcerned about their new physical disabilities. They will have what is

known by the French term *la belle indifférence* (beautiful indifference). While most people would be quite upset if they suddenly became blind or paralyzed, conversion patients will often be rather calm or nonchalant about their disability, because their symptom unconsciously protects them from their desire to act on an unacceptable impulse.

HYPOCHONDRIASIS

The situation is somewhat different for individuals with hypochondriasis or somatization disorder, since individuals with these syndromes generally do not experience a dramatic physical disability. Individuals with hypochondriasis or somatization disorder are troubled instead either by fear of illness or by complaints about being sick.

With hypochondriasis, the afflicted individual, who is typically referred to as a hypochondriac, often misinterprets ordinary physical symptoms as a sign of some extremely serious illness. For example, the hypochondriac with mild indigestion may think that he or she is having a heart attack. In a similar fashion, a mild headache may be interpreted as a brain tumor. Hypochondriacs are usually quite interested in medical information and will keep a wide array of medical specialists at their disposal.

DSM-IV-TR Criteria for Conversion Disorder (DSM code 300.11)

One or more symptoms or deficits affecting voluntary motor or sensory function suggest neurological or other general medical condition

Psychological factors judged to be associated with the symptom or deficit because initiation or exacerbation of symptom or deficit preceded by conflicts or other stressors

Symptom or deficit not intentionally produced or feigned (as in Factitious Disorder or Malingering)

Symptom or deficit cannot, after appropriate investigation, be fully explained by general medical condition, by direct effects of a substance, or as culturally sanctioned behavior or experience

Symptom or deficit causes clinically significant distress or impairment in social, occupational, or other important areas of functioning or warrants medical evaluation

Symptom or deficit not limited to pain or sexual dysfunction, not occurring exclusively during the course of Somatization Disorder, and not better accounted for by another mental disorder

Types: with Motor Symptom or Deficit; with Sensory Symptom or Deficit; with Seizures or Convulsions; with Mixed Presentation

Even after physician visits reveal that the hypochondriac does not suffer from some dreaded disease, the individual persists in this preoccupation.

SOMATIZATION DISORDERS AND SOMATOFORM PAIN

While the hypochondriac is typically afraid of having one particular disease, the individual with somatization disorder will often have numerous medical complaints with no apparent physical cause. Somatization disorder is also sometimes known as Briquet syndrome, after the physician of that name who described it in detail in 1859. The individual who develops a somatization disorder is known as a somatizer. This person is not bothered by the fear of disease but rather by the actual symptoms that he or she reports. This individual will generally describe numerous aches and pains in a vague and exaggerated manner. According to the definition of somatization disorder in the American Psychiatric Association's *Diagnostic and Statistical Manual of Mental Disorders: DSM-IV-TR* (rev. 4th ed., 2000), the patient must have a history of pain related to at least four different sites or functions as well as at least two gastrointestinal symptoms, at least one sexual or reproductive symptom, and at least one symptom or deficit suggesting a neurological condition.

Like the hypochondriac, the somatizer will often seek out frequent, unnecessary medical treatment. The somatizer, however, will be a particularly difficult patient for the physician to handle. The somatizer will often present the physician with a long, vague, and confusing list of complaints. At times, it may seem as if the somatizer is actually developing new symptoms while talking to the physician. The dramatic and disorganized manner in which these patients describe their problems and their tendency to switch from one doctor to the next with great frequency make somatizers some of the most frustrating patients that medical professionals are likely to encounter.

It will also be difficult for even the most capable of medical professionals to work effectively with an individual who is suffering from somatoform pain. Pain disorder is a relatively new diagnostic category,

> ### DSM-IV-TR Criteria for Hypochondriasis (DSM code 300.7)
>
> Preoccupation with fears of having, or the idea that one has, serious disease based on one's misinterpretation of bodily symptoms
>
> Preoccupation persists despite appropriate medical evaluation and reassurance
>
> Belief not of delusional intensity (as in Delusional Disorder, Somatic Type) and not restricted to circumscribed concern about appearance (as in Body Dysmorphic Disorder)
>
> Preoccupation causes clinically significant distress or impairment in social, occupational, or other important areas of functioning
>
> Duration of at least six months
>
> Preoccupation not better accounted for by Generalized Anxiety Disorder, Obsessive-Compulsive Disorder, Panic Disorder, Major Depressive Episode, Separation Anxiety, or another Somatoform Disorder
>
> Specify if with Poor Insight (most of the time during current episode, concern not recognized as excessive or unreasonable)

in which the individual experiences physical pain for which psychological factors are judged to have an important role in the onset, severity, exacerbation, or maintenance. Somatoform pain is similar to conversion disorder, except that the individual experiences only pain rather than other types of disability or anesthesia. Since pain is a subjective sensory experience rather than an observable symptom, it is often quite difficult for physicians to determine whether pain is caused by psychological or physical factors. It is therefore very hard to diagnose somatoform pain with any certainty.

THE CASE OF "ANNA O."

The somatoform disorders, like all psychiatric diagnoses, are worth studying only when they can contribute to an understanding of the experience of a troubled individual. In particular, the somatoform disorders are useful when they help show that while an individual may genuinely feel sick, or believe he or she has some physical illness, this is not always the case. There are times when a psychological conflict can manifest itself in a somatic form.

A classic example of this situation is a famous case of conversion disorder that was reported by Josef Breuer and Sigmund Freud in 1895. This case involved "Anna O.," a well-educated and extremely intelligent young Viennese woman who had rapidly become bedridden with a number of mysterious physical symptoms. By the time that Anna O. sought the assistance of Breuer, a prominent Austrian physician, her medical condition was quite serious. Both Anna O.'s right arm and her right leg were paralyzed, her sight and hearing were impaired, and she often had difficulty speaking. She also sometimes went into a rather dreamlike state, which she referred to as an "absence." During these periods of absence, Anna O. would mumble to herself and appear quite preoccupied with disturbing thoughts.

Anna O.'s symptoms were quite troubling to Breuer, since she did not appear to suffer from any particular physical ailment. To understand this young woman's condition, Breuer encouraged her to discuss her symptoms at length, and he used hypnosis to explore the history of her illness. Over time, Breuer began to get Anna O. to talk more freely, until she eventually discussed some troubling past events. Breuer noticed that as she started to recall and discuss more details from her emotionally disturbing history, her physical symptoms began to go away.

Eventually, under hypnosis, Anna O. described what Breuer thought was the original trauma that had precipitated her conversion reaction. She indicated that she had been spending a considerable amount of time caring for her seriously ill father. After many days of patiently waiting at her father's bedside, Anna naturally grew somewhat resentful of the great burden that his illness had placed upon her. These feelings of resentment were morally unacceptable to Anna O., who also experienced genuine feelings of love and concern for her father. One day, she was feeling particularly tired as she sat at her father's bedside. She dropped off into what Breuer describes as a waking dream, with her right arm over the back of a chair. After she fell into this trancelike state, Anna O. saw a large black snake emerge from the wall and slither toward her sick father to bite him. She tried to push the snake away, but her right arm had gone to sleep. When Anna O. looked at her right hand, she found that her fingers had turned into little snakes with death's heads.

The next day, when Anna O. was walking outside, she saw a bent branch. This branch reminded her of her hallucination of the snake, and at once her right arm became rigidly extended. Over time, the paralysis in Anna O.'s right arm extended to her entire right side; other symptoms began to develop as

well. Recalling her hallucination of the snake and the emotions that accompanied it seemed to produce a great improvement in her condition. Breuer hypothesized that Anna O. had converted her original trauma into a physical symptom and was unable to recover until this traumatic memory was properly expressed and discussed. The way in which Breuer treated Anna O. eventually became known as the cathartic method.

MIND AND BODY

Anna O.'s case and the development of the cathartic method eventually led to widespread interest in conversion disorders, as well as in the other types of somatoform disorders. Many mental health professionals began to suspect that all the somatoform disorders involved patients who were unconsciously converting unpleasant or unacceptable emotions into somatic complaints. The manner in which somatoform patients could misinterpret or misperceive their bodily sensations, however, remained rather mysterious. For example, how can an individual who has normal vision truly believe that he or she is blind? Research conducted by the team of Harold Sackheim, Johanna Nordlie, and Ruben Gur suggested a possible answer to this question.

Sackheim and his colleagues studied conversion patients who believed they were blind. This form of blindness, known as hysterical blindness, can be quite debilitating. Patients who develop hysterical blindness are generally unable to perform their usual functions and often report total loss of vision. When the vision of these patients was tested in an empirical fashion, an interesting pattern of results emerged. On each trial of a special visual test there were two time intervals, each of which was bounded by the sounding of a buzzer. During each trial, a bright visual target was illuminated during one of the intervals. Hysterically blind subjects were asked to report whether the visual target was illuminated during the first or the second interval. If truly blind subjects were to attempt this task, they should be correct by chance approximately 50 percent of the time. Most hysterically blind subjects were correct only 20 to 30 percent of the time, as if they were deliberately trying to demonstrate poor vision. A smaller number of hysterically blind subjects were correct on almost every trial, suggesting that they were actually able to see the visual stimuli before them.

Sackheim and his colleagues suggested that a two-state defensive reaction can explain these conflicting findings. First, the perceptual representations of visual stimuli are blocked from conscious awareness, so that subjects report that they are blind. Then, in the second part of the process, subjects continue to gain information from the perceptual representations of what they have seen. The performance of subjects on a visual task will then depend on whether the subjects feel they must deny access to the information that was gained during the second part of the visual process. If subjects believe that they must deny access to visual information, they

will perform more poorly on a visual task than would be expected by chance. If subjects believe that they do not need to deny access to visual information, they will perform like a normal subject on a visual task. In other words, according to Sackheim and his colleagues, hysterically blind patients base their responses on the consequences of their behavior.

The way in which hysterically blind patients can manipulate their ability to see has led many scholars to question whether these patients are being truthful. Sackheim, Nordlie, and Gur, however, report that there are patients with lesions in the visual cor-

DSM-IV-TR Criteria for Somatization and Pain Disorders

SOMATIZATION DISORDER (DSM CODE 300.81)

History of many physical complaints (beginning before age thirty) occurring over a period of several years and resulting in treatment being sought or significant impairment in social, occupational, or other important areas of functioning

Each of the following criteria must have been met, with individual symptoms occurring at any time during the course of the disturbance:
- history of pain related to at least four different sites or functions (head, abdomen, back, joints, extremities, chest, rectum, during menstruation, during sexual intercourse, during urination)
- history of at least two gastrointestinal symptoms other than pain (nausea, bloating, vomiting other than during pregnancy, diarrhea, intolerance of several different foods)
- history of at least one sexual or reproductive symptom other than pain (sexual indifference, erectile or ejaculatory dysfunction, irregular menses, excessive menstrual bleeding, vomiting throughout pregnancy)
- history of at least one symptom or deficit suggesting a neurological condition not limited to pain (conversion symptoms, dissociative symptoms, loss of consciousness other than fainting)

Either of the following:
- after appropriate investigation, symptoms cannot be fully explained by known general medical condition or direct effects of a substance
- when related general medical condition exists, physical complaints or resulting social or occupational impairment exceed what would be expected

from history, physical examination, or laboratory findings

Symptoms not intentionally feigned or produced (as in Factitious Disorder or Malingering)

PAIN DISORDER

Pain in one or more anatomical sites as predominant focus of clinical presentation and of sufficient severity to warrant clinical attention

Pain causes clinically significant distress or impairment in social, occupational, or other important areas of functioning

Psychological factors judged to have an important role in the onset, severity, exacerbation, or maintenance of the pain

Symptom or deficit not intentionally produced or feigned (as in Factitious Disorder or Malingering)

Pain not better accounted for by Mood, Anxiety, or Psychotic Disorder and does not meet criteria for Dyspareunia

DSM code based as follows, specifying if Acute (duration of less than six months) or Chronic (duration of six months or longer):
- Associated with Psychological Factors (DSM code 307.80): Psychological factors judged to have major role in onset, severity, exacerbation, or maintenance of pain; this type of Pain Disorder not diagnosed if criteria are also met for Somatization Disorder
- Associated with Both Psychological Factors and General Medical Condition (DSM code 307.89): Both psychological factors and general medical condition judged to have important roles in the onset, severity, exacerbation, or maintenance of pain

tex (a part of the brain which processes visual information) who report that they are blind. These patients believe that they cannot see, even though they have normal eyes and can respond accurately to visual stimuli. They believe they are blind because they have trouble processing visual information. It is thus possible that an individual can have normal eyesight and still believe that he or she is blind. It may thus be the case that many somatoform patients truly and honestly believe that they have a physical symptom, even though they are actually quite healthy.

METAPHORICAL AND REAL ILLNESSES

The study of somatoform disorders is an important area of concern for both medical professionals and social scientists. The somatoform disorders are relatively common, and their great prevalence poses a serious problem for the medical establishment. A tremendous amount of professional energy and financial resources is expended in the needless medical treatment of somatoform patients, who really suffer from emotional rather than physical difficulties. For example, when Robert Woodruff, Donald Goodwin, and Samuel Guze compared fifty somatization patients with fifty normal control subjects in 1974, they found that the somatization patients had undergone major surgical procedures three times more frequently than had the normal controls. Since an effort was made to match the somatizing and control patients on the basis of their actual medical condition, one can assume that much of the surgery performed on the somatization patients was unnecessary.

On the other hand, there is also considerable evidence to indicate that many people who are genuinely ill are misdiagnosed with somatoform disorders. Charles Watson and Cheryl Buranen published a follow-up study of somatization patients in 1979 which found that 25 percent of the patients actually suffered from real physical disorders. It seems physicians who are unable to explain a patient's puzzling medical problems may be tempted to label the patient prematurely with a somatoform disorder. The diagnosis of a somatoform disorder needs to be made with great caution, to ensure that a genuine medical condition will not be overlooked. There is also a need for further research into the causes and nature of the somatoform disorders, so that they can be diagnosed in a more definitive fashion.

One hopes that further research will also shed light on the ways in which somatoform disorders can be treated. Most somatoform patients are truly in need of assistance, for while their physical illness may be imaginary, their pain and suffering are real. Unfortunately, at this time, it is often difficult for mental health professionals to treat somatoform patients effectively since these individuals tend to focus on their physical complaints rather than on their emotional problems. More research is needed on the treatment of somatoform patients so that they can overcome the psychological difficulties that plague them.

SOURCES FOR FURTHER STUDY

Alloy, Lauren, Neil S. Jacobson, and Joan Acocella. *Abnormal Psychology: Current Perspectives.* 8th ed. New York: McGraw-Hill, 1998. This textbook contains an excellent chapter on the somatoform disorders which describes relevant case studies and explains how different psychological theorists view the somatoform diagnoses. Discussion of hypochondriasis and conversion disorder is particularly informative. Clear, easy to read, and comprehensible to the high school or college student.

Breuer, Josef, and Sigmund Freud. *Studies in Hysteria.* Translated and edited by James Strachey, with the collaboration of Anna Freud. New York: Basic Books, 1982. In many ways, this landmark book, first published in 1895, was the genesis of contemporary psychotherapy. Describes the famous case of Anna O., as well as the histories of a number of other conversion patients. A challenging book, useful to the college student who has a serious interest in either conversion disorders or the history of psychology.

Kirmeyer, L., and S. Taillefer. "Somatoform Disorders." In *Adult Psychopathology and Diagnosis,* edited by Samuel M. Turner and Michel Hersen. 3d ed. New York: John Wiley & Sons, 1997. Provides the reader with a scholarly overview of somatoform disorders. Relevant diagnostic issues are discussed, in conjunction with a thorough review of the major research studies that have been conducted on somatization disorder, hypochondriasis, and conversion disorder. This chapter is recommended for the college student who seeks a detailed and challenging discussion of somatoform disorders.

Sackheim, Harold A., Johanna W. Nordlie, and Ruben C. Gur. "A Model of Hysterical and Hypnotic Blindness: Cognition, Motivation, and Awareness." *Journal of Abnormal Psychology* 88 (October, 1979): 474-489. Recommended for the college student or serious adult reader who is interested in learning about contemporary research on conversion disorders. In particular, research on hysterical blindness is described in a complete and detailed fashion. The authors attempt to explain why hysterically blind patients believe they have lost their vision, when in reality they are able to see.

Sarason, Irwin G., and Barbara R. Sarason. *Abnormal Psychology: The Problem of Maladaptive Behavior.* 9th ed. Englewood Cliffs, N.J.: Prentice-Hall, 1998. Includes a very readable chapter on the psychological factors which can produce physical symptoms. A well-organized overview of somatization disorders is enhanced with a number of lively examples. Recommended for the high school student, college student, or casual reader.

Waldinger, Robert J. *Psychiatry for Medical Students.* 3d ed. Washington, D.C.: American Psychiatric Press, 1997. An introductory clinical textbook designed for individuals (such as medical students) who are having their first encounters with emotionally disturbed patients. Contains a concise and informative section on the somatoform disorders which explains how to look for and recognize these syndromes.

Steven C. Abell

SEE ALSO: Abnormality: Psychological models; Anxiety disorders; Breuer, Josef; Health psychology; Pain; Pain management; Psychoanalytic psychology and personality: Sigmund Freud; Psychosomatic disorders; Stress-related diseases.

Hypothesis development and testing

TYPE OF PSYCHOLOGY: Psychological methodologies
FIELDS OF STUDY: Methodological issues

A useful strategy for answering questions about behavior is to propose several possible answers (hypotheses), generate predictions based on these hypotheses, and collect information (data) to determine which hypothesis appears to have produced a correct prediction.

KEY CONCEPTS
- experiment
- falsifiability
- hypothesis
- prediction
- specificity
- testability

INTRODUCTION

All psychological research begins with observations of behavior, either informal, everyday observations or formal observations based on prior psychological research. Such observations frequently lead to questions. For example, many people drink beverages containing caffeine throughout the day. When asked why, these people often say that it helps them stay alert. Does caffeine really help people stay alert?

For every question one can ask, there are many possible answers. Caffeine might affect alertness at all dosages. It might only affect alertness at certain dosages, or only in some situations. On the other hand, caffeine might decrease, not increase, alertness. Finally, one should not discount the possibility that caffeine has no effect on alertness and that the reported effects are "placebo effects"—that is, they might be caused by expectations about caffeine and not by caffeine itself.

In the language of science, the possible answers to questions are called hypotheses, and the procedure scientists employ to choose among these hypotheses is called hypothesis testing. Hypothesis testing, when used correctly, is a powerful tool for advancing knowledge because it provides a procedure for retaining hypotheses that are probably true and rejecting those that are probably false.

Scientists test hypotheses by making predictions and collecting information. A prediction is a statement of the evidence that would lead the scientist to accept a particular hypothesis. The hypothesis that caffeine maintains alertness leads to the prediction that people who ingest a measured dose of caffeine a given time before engaging in a task that requires alertness will perform better than people who do not ingest caffeine. An experiment could be conducted to test this hypothesis. An experiment is a set of controlled conditions used to test hypotheses. It contains at least one experimental group and one or more comparison, or control, groups.

ROLE OF PREDICTIONS

Hypothesis tests are only as good as the predictions generated. Good predictions tell the researcher what evidence to collect. To be a good test of the hypothesis, predictions must have three characteristics. The predictions must follow as a logical consequence from the hypothesis and the assumptions the researcher makes about the test situation. The hypothesis and its corresponding prediction must be testable, in the sense that the researcher could decide from the data whether a given prediction has been confirmed. Finally, it should be unlikely that a given prediction is confirmed unless the hypothesis upon which it is based is correct.

If the prediction was not logically related to the hypothesis, a confirmation by the data would reveal nothing about the truth of the hypothesis. This logical relationship is complicated by the fact that rarely is it the case that a prediction can be generated solely from the hypothesis. In order to generate a prediction, a number of additional assumptions are usually required. It takes a certain amount of time for caffeine to enter the system and affect behavior; any behavioral effects will not be evident until the dosage reaches a certain level. The time it takes to detect the occurrence of a new object on a computer screen is a valid measure of alertness.

Although the prediction may logically follow from the hypothesis, it will not be confirmed if any of the assumptions are incorrect. Unfortunately, there is no foolproof way to avoid this problem. Researchers must carefully consider all assumptions they make.

The condition of testability means that it must be possible to decide on the basis of evidence whether the prediction has been confirmed. Testable predictions are falsifiable; that is, certain experimental outcomes would lead the researcher to conclude that the prediction and the hypothesis are incorrect. A prediction that is not potentially falsifiable is worthless. If researchers cannot conceive of data that would lead them to disconfirm a prediction, the prediction cannot be tested; all data would lead to confirmation.

The third condition, that it should be unlikely for a given prediction to be confirmed unless the hypothesis upon which it is based is correct, is met when the hypothesis leads to a very specific prediction. Specificity is a characteristic of the hypothesis; if the hypothesis is specific, it should lead to a specific prediction. Hypotheses that meet the criterion of specificity tend to require fewer additional assumptions. Unfortunately, such hypotheses are rare in psychological research. Because of this lack of specificity, a single experiment rarely provides a definitive test of a hypothesis. As knowledge about behavior increases, the ability of psychologists to generate and test such hypotheses will no doubt improve.

TESTING STRATEGIES

Hypotheses are tested by comparing predictions to data. If the data confirm the prediction, then the researcher can continue to consider the hypothesis as a reasonable explanation for the phenomenon under investigation and a possible answer to the research question. If subjects react faster to new objects after ingesting caffeine, the investigator would conclude that caffeine affects alertness in this situation. If the data do not confirm the prediction, however, then the investigator would conclude that the hypothesis does not provide a correct explanation of the phenomenon and is not a correct answer to the research question. If subjects given caffeine perform similarly to those not given caffeine, then the researcher would conclude that caffeine does not have much, if any, effect on alertness in this experimental situation.

A useful strategy for testing hypotheses is to generate two hypotheses and attempt to show that if one is false, the other must be true. This can be accomplished if the hypotheses selected are mutually exclusive (they cannot both be true) and exhaustive (they are the only logical possibilities). When two hypotheses satisfy these conditions, demonstrating the truth or falseness of one of these hypotheses determines the status of the other: If one is probably true, the other must be probably false, and vice versa.

The conclusion drawn from a hypothesis test is that the hypothesis is either probably true or probably false—"probably" because it is possible that the wrong conclusion has been reached. The success of any hypothesis test depends on the logical connections among the hypothesis, assumptions, and prediction. Even when these connections are sound, however, different results might occur if the experiment were repeated again. Repeating the experiment and obtaining similar results increases the researcher's confidence in the data.

It is typically the case that a given experiment will not answer the research question unambiguously. By performing additional experiments with a variety of dosages, times, and tasks, researchers should discover the range of conditions under which caffeine affects alertness. Testing one hypothesis typically leads to more questions, and the cycle of asking questions, generating hypotheses, making predictions, collecting data, and drawing conclusions is repeated. Each round of hypothesis tests increases knowledge about the phenomenon in question.

GROUP BEHAVIOR RESEARCH

An excellent example of hypothesis testing was described by Bibb Latan and John M. Darley in their 1970 book *The Unresponsive Bystander: Why Doesn't He Help?* Latan and Darley became interested in this topic from reading newspaper accounts of people assaulted in the presence of bystanders who did little to assist the victims. The most famous of these was the murder of Kitty Genovese in the presence of thirty-eight neighbors who witnessed this event from their apartment windows; none of them intervened or even called the police. Latan and Darley asked the question, What determines in a particular situation whether one person will help another?

One of their hypotheses was that the number of people present is an important factor affecting how likely it is that someone will react to a dangerous situation. They also hypothesized that what a person does also depends on the behavior of other people at the scene. Latan and Darley predicted that people would be more likely to respond to an emergency when alone than when in the presence of others. They also predicted that what others who are present do affects a person's behavior.

To test this hypothesis, Latan and Darley solicited the participation of male college students to complete a questionnaire. Students went to a room in a university building where they worked on the task alone, along with two confederates of the experimenters, or with two other people who were also naïve subjects. After several minutes, smoke was introduced into the room through a small vent in the wall. The response measures were whether subjects would seek assistance, and, if they did, how long it

took them to do so. If subjects did not respond after six minutes of sitting in a room that was filling with smoke, someone came in to get them.

The predictions and the experiments to test them were based on the above hypotheses and on assumptions about how subjects would view the test situation. Darley and Latan assumed that subjects would believe the emergency in the experiment was real and not contrived, and that subjects would perceive the situation as potentially dangerous.

Their predictions were confirmed by the data. Subjects were most likely to report the smoke when alone. When there were two passive confederates who acted in a nonchalant manner in the presence of the smoke, subjects were least likely to respond. Being in a group of three naïve subjects also inhibited responding, but not as much as when the other two people ignored the apparent danger.

The results of this experiment appear to provide rather convincing evidence for the correctness of Latan and Darley's hypotheses; however, the assumption that subjects would view the smoke as potentially dangerous is suspect. Postexperimental interviews revealed that some subjects did not perceive the smoke as potentially dangerous. Furthermore, the results of this experiment suggested additional questions to Latan and Darley: "Does the inhibitory effect of other people depend on the fact that in a three-person group, the subject is in a minority? What would happen if only one other person were present? Does the effect depend on the fact that the other people were strangers to the subject? What would happen if the subject were tested with a close friend?"

These questions were addressed in subsequent experiments. In each case, hypotheses were generated and predictions were derived and tested. Care was taken to make the dangerous situation as unambiguous as possible and not to give away the fact that it was contrived. The general results confirmed Latan and Darley's predictions and validated their hypotheses about bystander apathy.

EYEWITNESS TESTIMONY RESEARCH

For more than eighty years, psychologists have studied people's accuracy at describing events they have witnessed (eyewitness testimony). The history of this work is recounted by Gary Wells and Elizabeth Loftus in their edited volume *Eyewitness Testimony: Psychological Perspectives* (1984). Considerable evidence, collected in a wide variety of settings, demonstrates that people's recollections of an event can be influenced by postevent experiences such as interviews by the police and attorneys or the viewing of mug shots. This raises an interesting question: When people's recollection of an event is changed by postevent information, is the underlying memory changed, or is the original memory still intact but rendered temporarily inaccessible? In other words, does reporting of the event change following postevent experiences because the memory has changed, or because the new information blocks the ability to recall the event as originally experienced?

This is an example of an interesting question to which no satisfactory answer has yet been obtained—but not for lack of trying. The question suggests two mutually exclusive and exhaustive hypotheses: The underlying memory is changed by the postevent experience, so that what the person reports is not what he or she originally saw or heard, or the postevent experience has created a new memory that is in competition with the existing, original memory, and the new memory simply overwhelms the old memory. Both hypotheses lead to the prediction that postevent experiences will affect what a subject reports, but the second hypothesis leads to the additional prediction that the original memory can be teased out into the open under the right circumstances. The problem is how to do this in a convincing manner.

David Hall, Elizabeth Loftus, and James Tousignant reviewed the research on this question. They note that it is difficult, if not impossible, to disprove the hypothesis that both memories coexist. In some studies, what appear to be original memories seem to have been recovered, but not always. The question as asked assumes an either-or situation (either the original unaltered memory still exists or it does not). Unfortunately, this question cannot be answered unambiguously with present knowledge and technology. On the other hand, the question of under what conditions recollections (as opposed to memories) are changed can be answered, because it leads to a number of testable predictions based on hypotheses about these conditions.

Clearly, not all questions lead to testable hypotheses and falsifiable predictions. When data support more than one hypothesis, or if the data are likely to occur even if the hypotheses are false, hypotheses have not been adequately tested. The hypotheses about the status of the original memory are an excellent illustration of this. Knowledge of the effects of postevent experiences was advanced by asking the more limited question which led to testable hypotheses. Scientific understanding advances when people ask the right question.

LABORATORY VERSUS FIELD EXPERIMENTATION

Laboratory experimentation, with its tight control over the variables that affect behavior, is the best way to test hypotheses. By randomly assigning subjects to conditions and isolating the variables of interest through various control procedures, researchers are afforded the opportunity to arrange situations in which one hypothesis will be confirmed to the exclusion of all other hypotheses. Unfortunately, laboratory experimentation is not always an appropriate way to test hypotheses.

When laboratory experimentation is neither possible nor appropriate, researchers can use field experiments, in which experimental methods are used in a natural setting. The inability to control the field setting, however, makes it more difficult to exclude some explanations for the data. Thus, the advantages and disadvantages of field experimentation must be weighed against those of the laboratory. The earliest research of Latan and Darley on bystander apathy involved field experimentation; however, they found it inadequate for rigorous hypothesis testing and moved their research to the laboratory.

ALTERNATE FORMS OF INQUIRY

Surveys and questionnaires can provide answers to some kinds of questions that experiments cannot: Do certain characteristics distinguish people with different attitudes or opinions on an issue? How many people have a given attitude or opinion? Do certain attitudes or opinions tend to occur together? Predictions can be made and tested with carefully designed surveys and questionnaires.

Archival data and case studies can be extremely useful sources for generating questions and hypotheses, but they are poor techniques for testing hypotheses. Both archival research and case studies can indicate relationships among various factors or events. Whether these relationships are causal or accidental cannot be determined by these methodologies; therefore, the only question that can be answered from archival data and case studies is whether certain relationships have been observed.

An experiment is necessary in order to ascertain whether there is a causal connection.

Statistical significance tests are often part of hypothesis testing. Statistical hypotheses parallel research hypotheses; statistical hypotheses are about aspects of populations, while research hypotheses are about the subject of inquiry. Deciding which statistical hypothesis to accept tells the researcher which research hypothesis to accept. The logic of hypothesis testing in general applies to statistical significance tests.

Knowledge is advanced when research questions can be answered. Hypothesis testing, when used correctly, is a powerful method for sorting among possible answers to find the best one. For this reason, it is frequently employed by psychologists in their research.

SOURCES FOR FURTHER STUDY

Giere, Ronald N. *Understanding Scientific Reasoning.* 4th ed. New York: Holt, Rinehart and Winston, 1998. This readable book presents scientific reasoning from the point of view of a philosopher of science, with many examples from all areas of science, including psychology. Chapter 6, on testing theoretical hypotheses, and chapter 12, on causal hypotheses, provide several detailed examples of evaluating data.

Hall, David, Elizabeth Loftus, and James Tousignant. "Postevent Information and Changes in Recollection for a Natural Event." In *Eyewitness Testimony: Psychological Perspectives*, edited by Gary L. Wells and Elizabeth F. Loftus. Cambridge, England: Cambridge University Press, 1984. Discusses the hypotheses pertaining to the effects of postevent information on original memories, and why these hypotheses cannot be tested. Illustrates how questions about the conditions under which recollections change may be answered.

Latan, Bibb, and John M. Darley. *The Unresponsive Bystander: Why Doesn't He Help?* East Norwalk, Conn.: Appleton-Century-Crofts, 1970. Latan and Darley describe why and how they performed their now-classic set of experiments on bystander apathy, clearly laying out for the reader their observations, questions, hypotheses, assumptions, predictions, experimental procedures, and conclusions.

Moore, K. D. *A Field Guide to Inductive Arguments.* 2d ed. Dubuque, Iowa: Kendall-Hunt, 1990. An excellent workbook for learning how to analyze arguments and evaluate evidence. Chapter 4, on hypothetical evidence, provides several interesting exercises on how to generate and test hypotheses.

Stanovich, Keith E. *How to Think Straight About Psychology.* 6th ed. Boston: Allyn & Bacon, 2000. Stanovich tries to undermine the misconceptions that many people have about the contributions of psychology to the scientific study of human behavior. Examples of hypothesis testing abound throughout the book.

Jerome Frieman

SEE ALSO: Animal experimentation; Case-study methodologies; Data description; Experimentation: Independent, dependent, and control variables; Field experimentation; Scientific methods; Statistical significance tests; Survey research: Questionnaires and interviews.

Hysteria

TYPE OF PSYCHOLOGY: Personality; psychopathology; psychotherapy
FIELDS OF STUDY: Biological treatments; classic analytic themes and issues; models of abnormality; personality disorders; social motives

Hysteria is an enigmatic condition that has been described for several millennia in the medical literature. Its manifestations have tended to change from era to era, perhaps reflecting the mores, social expectancies, and medical knowledge of the day. Hysteria as an overarching category has disappeared from modern diagnostic systems, but its symptoms are still reflected in several disorders.

KEY CONCEPTS
• attention seeking
• gender roles
• hypnosis
• psychoanalysis
• psychosomatic complaints
• sexuality
• social expectations
• suggestibility

INTRODUCTION

The concept of hysteria has a rich history that dates back to early civilizations. Ancient Egyptian papyri provide the first medical records of hysteria. Egyptian physicians believed that the somatic and emotional problems of certain unstable women were caused by a migratory uterus. They prescribed the topical use of sweet- or foul-smelling herbs to entice or repel the uterus back to its original position. Interestingly, this theme of sexual etiology has pervaded theories of hysteria throughout the centuries.

GRECO-ROMAN VIEWS

There is considerable continuity between Egyptian and Greco-Roman views of hysteria. Hippocrates (c. 460-c. 377 B.C.E.), often considered the founder of medicine, included the condition in the *Corpus Hippocraticum*, and solidified its connection with the uterus by assigning the appellation "hysteria," which is derived from the Greek term for the organ, *hystera*. The Greeks were the first to connect hysteria with sexual activity; they believed that the condition occurred primarily in adult women deprived of sexual relations for extended periods, resulting in the migration of the uterus. Aromatic remedies were also prescribed by the Greeks, but the recommended remedy was to marry and, if possible, become pregnant. Some skeptics of the day denied the motility of the uterus. For example, the Roman physician Galen (129-c. 199 C.E.) proposed that hysteria was instead caused by the retention of a substance analogous to sperm in the female, which was triggered by long-term abstinence.

THE DARK AGES

As the Middle Ages approached, magical thinking and superstition increased. Some Christian writers, especially St. Augustine (354-430 C.E.), condemned sex as the work of such unholy spirits as incubi, succubi, and witches. Numerous behavioral afflictions, particularly the peculiar and transient symptoms of hysteria, were viewed as the result of witchcraft. Many hysterics became victims of the witch craze, a long and dark chapter in Western history. The *Malleus Maleficarum* (c. 1486; *Malleus Maleficarum*, 1928), a manual whose title means "the witches' hammer," was written by two Dominican monks, Heinrich Kraemer and Jakob Sprenger. This book outlined the "telltale" signs of witchcraft, which were widely used and regarded as diagnostic by Middle Age inquisitors. Hysterical patients became both accusers, who came forth with complaints that spells has been cast upon them, and confessors, who were willing to implicate themselves by weaving accounts of their participation in strange sexual rituals and witchcraft.

THE RENAISSANCE TO THE VICTORIAN ERA

With the arrival of the Renaissance, views on hysteria changed to accommodate natural causes. Medical writers of the day recognized the brain as the source of the affliction. As a result, hysteria soon became a topic of interest for neurologists. In addition, physicians suggested emotional contributions to hysteria, including melancholy (which resembles modern depression). Largely as a result of the writings of physician Thomas Sydenham (1624-1689), hysteria came to be considered an affliction of the mind. At this time, some proposed a male analogue to hysteria termed "hypochondriasis" (though not strictly defined as it is today).

Throughout history, the symptoms of hysteria have reflected prevailing sociocultural norms and expectations. In the nineteenth century, ideal women were physically and emotionally delicate, which was reflected in their greater susceptibility to hysteria and in the nature of their symptoms. Over time, infrequent but spectacular hysterical paroxysms gave way to milder chronic symptoms. Fainting spells, euphemistically called "the vapors," were accepted as a natural reaction of the vulnerable female to emotional distress. Some clinicians of this era considered hysteria a form of "moral insanity" and emphasized hysterical patients' penchant for prevarication, flamboyant emotional displays, and nearly constant need for attention. Others viewed hysterics with a patronizing compassion, as unfortunate victims of the natural weakness of femininity.

HYPNOSIS AND PSYCHOANALYTIC UNDERPINNINGS

Conceptions of hysteria were shaped substantially by the work of French neurologist Jean Charcot (1825-1893). Charcot emphasized the importance of suggestibility in the etiology of hysterical behavior; he found that under hypnosis, some hysterical patients' symptoms could be made to appear or disappear largely at will. Charcot was also the first to assign significance to a pathogenic early environment in producing hysterical episodes.

The young Austrian neurologist Sigmund Freud (1856-1939) began his career by studying the blockage of sensation by chemicals. This interest extended to hysteria (known for its anesthetic symptoms), which brought him into contact with Viennese internist Josef Breuer (1842-1925). Breuer's account of the famous hysterical patient Anna O. and her treatment provided the early foundations of psychoanalytic theory. Breuer found that under hypnosis, Anna recalled the psychological trauma that had ostensibly led to her hysteria. Moreover, he found that her symptoms improved or disappeared after this apparent memory recovery. Freud studied hypnosis under Charcot and extended Breuer's concepts and treatments to develop his own theory of hysteria. He reintroduced sexuality into the etiology of hysteria, particularly the notion of long-forgotten memories of early sexual trauma. Freud himself eventually concluded that most or all of these "recovered" memories were fantasies or confabulations, a view shared by many modern memory researchers.

CURRENT STATUS

The term "hysteria" has long been regarded as vague and needlessly pejorative, and it is no longer a part of the formal diagnostic nomenclature. The broad concept of hysteria was splintered with the appearance of the third edition of the *Diagnostic and Statistical Manual of Mental Disorders* (DSM-III) in 1980 and is currently encompassed by a broad array of conditions, including somatoform disorders, dissociative disorders, and histrionic personality disorder. The separation of somatoform from dissociative disorders in the current diagnostic system is controversial, because these two broad groupings of disorders often covary substantially with one another. Some researchers have argued that somatoform and dissociative disorders should be reunited under a single broad diagnostic umbrella.

Somatoform disorders are a group of ailments in which the presence of physical symptoms suggests a medical condition but in which the symptoms are involuntarily psychologically produced. Somatization disorder, conversion disorder, pain disorder, hypochondriasis, and body dysmorphic disorder are the major conditions in this group. Dissociative disorders are characterized by disruptions in the integrated functioning of consciousness, memory, identity, or perception. Dissociative amnesia, dissociative fugue, dissociative identity disorder (formerly multiple personality disorder), and depersonalization disorder belong to this category. The causes of some dissociative disorders, particularly dissociative identity disorder, are controversial, as some writers maintain that these conditions are largely a product of inadvertent therapeutic suggestion and prompting. This controversy has been fueled by the fact that diagnoses of dissociative identity disorder have become much more frequent.

Histrionic personality disorder captures excessive emotionality and attention-seeking behaviors, which formerly characterized "hysterical personality." This disorder is often a correlate of somatoform and perhaps dissociative disorders.

Two sets of conditions from which hysteria must be distinguished are malingering (feigning physical symptoms to achieve a tangible goal, such as insurance reimbursement or evasion of military duty) and factitious disorder with physical symptoms, better known as Munchausen's syndrome (inducing physical symptoms to assume the "sick role").

The causes of hysteria remain largely unknown. A paucity of behavior-genetic studies leaves the relative contribution of genetic and environmental factors to somatoform and dissociative disorders a mystery. The precise sociocultural expressions of hysteria are also unclear. Many authors have suggested that hysteria has been manifested in a plethora of different conditions over time and across cultures, including dissociative identity disorder, somatoform disorders, purported demonic possession, mass hysteria, and even such religious practices as glossolalia (speaking in tongues). According to these authors, such seemingly disparate conditions are all manifestations of a shared predisposition that has been shaped by sociocultural norms and expectancies. "Hysteria" as a diagnostic label is no longer accepted, but its protean manifestations may be here to stay. At the beginning of the twenty-first century, it is tempting to wonder what guise the hysteria of the next century will assume.

SOURCES FOR FURTHER STUDY

Chodoff, Paul, and Henry Lyons. "Hysteria, the Hysterical Personality, and 'Hysterical' Conversion." *American Journal of Psychiatry* 114 (1958): 734-740. A classic exposition of the primary features of various conditions previously subsumed under the rubric of "hysteria." Includes a good description of the characteristics of the older diagnosis of "hysterical personality," which bears a close re-semblance to the modern concept of histrionic personality disorder.

Kraemer, Heinrich Institoris, and Jakob Sprenger. *Malleus Maleficarum*. Translated by Montague Summers. New York: B. Blom, 1970. A translated edition of the original guide to the identification and persecution of "witches." Frightening and compelling, it offers insight into the mentality of the Inquisition era and the belief in demonic possession as the cause of abnormal behavior. In-cludes an introduction, bibliography, and notes by Summers.

Shapiro, David. "Hysterical Style." In *Neurotic Styles*. New York: Basic Books, 1965. A classic explica-tion of the cognitive and emotional dysfunction of individuals with hysterical traits. Engaging clin-ical anecdotes help illustrate the main concepts.

Spanos, Nicholas P. *Multiple Identities and False Mem-ories: A Sociocognitive Perspective*. Washington, D.C.: American Psychological Association, 1996. A clas-sic exposition of the diverse manifestations of "multiple identity" enactments across cultures and historical periods. Spanos draws upon an im-pressive body of psychological, psychiatric, cross-cultural, and historical data to make the case that dissociative disorders, mass hysteria, speaking in tongues, purported demonic possession, and other putative forms of hysteria are all manifesta-tions of sociocultural norms and expectations.

Veith, Ilza. *Hysteria: The History of a Disease*. Chicago: University of Chicago Press, 1965. A landmark work of its time, in which the author provides an exhaustive history of hysteria, from ancient through psychoanalytic times. It is a useful illumi-nation of the social, historical, and religious cli-mate in which hysteria emerged and evolved.

Katherine A. Fowler and Scott O. Lilienfeld

SEE ALSO: Amnesia and fugue; Breuer, Josef; Freud, Sigmund; Histrionic personality; Hypnosis; Hypo-chondriasis, conversion, somatization disorder, and somatoform pain; Multiple personality; Neurotic disorders; Psychoanalytic psychology and personal-ity: Sigmund Freud; Women's psychology: Sigmund Freud.

I

Identity crises

TYPE OF PSYCHOLOGY: Developmental psychology
FIELDS OF STUDY: Adolescence; adulthood

Identity crises are the internal and external conflicts faced by the adolescent/young adult when choosing an occupation and coming to terms with a basic ideology. Development of a personal identity is a central component of psychosocial maturity.

KEY CONCEPTS
- identity
- identity confusion/diffusion
- identity status
- negative identity
- psychosocial maturity
- psychosocial moratorium

INTRODUCTION

Identity crises are an integral phase in human development. According to ego psychologist Erik Erikson (1902-1994), successful resolution of the identity crisis is contingent on the earlier resolution of the crises associated with infancy and childhood, such as trust, autonomy, initiative, and industry. Further, the extent to which the conflict surrounding identity is resolved will influence how the individual will cope with the crises of adulthood.

According to Erikson's model of the human life cycle, an identity crisis is one of the psychosocial conflicts faced by the adolescent. In Erikson's model, which was published in the 1960's, each age period is defined by a certain type of psychosocial crisis. Adolescence is the life stage during which acquiring an identity presents a major conflict. Failure to resolve the conflict results in identity confusion/diffusion—that is, an inadequate sense of self.

Identity implies an existential position, according to James Marcia, who construes identity as a self-structure composed of one's personal history, belief system, and competencies. One's perception of uniqueness is directly related to the development of this self-structure. A somewhat similar position has been taken by Jane Kroger, who views the identity crisis as a problem of self-definition. The resulting identity is a balance between self and others. Erikson defines identity as the belief that one's past experiences and identity will be confirmed in the future—as exemplified in the choice of a career. Identity is a composite of one's sexuality, physical makeup, vocation, and belief system. Identity is the pulling together of who one is and who one can become, which involves compositing one's past, present, and future. It is a synthesis of earlier identifications. Successfully resolving the identity crisis is contingent on the interactions that the adolescent/young adult has with others. Erikson contends that interacting with others provides the needed feedback about who one is and who one ought to be. These interactions with others enable the adolescent/young adult to gain a perspective of self that includes an evaluation of his or her physical and social self. Identity acquisition is cognitive as well as social.

CONDITIONS FOR IDENTITY CRISIS

From Erikson's perspective, as discussed in a 1987 article by James Cote and Charles Levine, four conditions are necessary for an identity crisis: Puberty has been reached; the requisite cognitive development is present; physical growth is nearing adult stature; and societal influences are guiding the person toward an integration and resynthesis of identity. The dialectics of society and personality, implicit in the last condition, are given the most attention by Erikson, according to Cote and Levine, because the other three conditions are part of normative development. Developmental level of the individual and societal pressures combine to elicit an identity crisis, but Cote and Levine note that timing of this crisis is contingent on factors such as ethnicity, gender, socioeconomic status, and subculture, as well as personality factors (for example, authoritarianism or neuroticism) and socialization practices. The severity of the identity crisis is determined by the extent to which one's identity portrayal is interfered with by the uncertainty inherent in moving toward self-definition and unexpected events.

PSYCHOLOGICAL MORATORIUM

An integral part of the identity crisis is the psychological moratorium, a time during which society permits the individual to work on crisis resolution. During this moratorium, the adolescent/young adult has the opportunity to examine societal roles, career possibilities, and values, free from the expectation of commitments and long-term responsibilities. Although some individuals choose to remain in a moratorium indefinitely, Erikson contends that there is an absolute end to the recognizable moratorium. At its completion, the adolescent/young adult should have attained the necessary restructuring of self and identifications so that he or she can find a place in society which fits this identity.

Based on Erikson's writings, Cote and Levine identify two types of institutionalized moratoria: the technological moratorium, which is highly structured, and the humanistic moratorium, which is less highly structured. The technological moratorium is the product of the educational system, which is charged by society with socializing youth to fit in adult society. Individuals in this moratorium option experience less difficulty in resolving the identity crisis because they move into occupations and societal roles for which they have been prepared with significantly less intrapsychic trauma in accepting an ideology. The school takes an active role in easing this transition by providing vocational and academic counseling for students, facilitating scheduling so that students can gain work experience while enrolled in school, and encouraging early decision making as to a future career.

The identity crisis for individuals in the humanistic moratorium is more stressful and painful and of longer duration than for those in the technological moratorium. The focal concern of the adolescent/young adult in the humanistic moratorium is humanistic values, which are largely missing from the technological moratorium. There is more variability in this concern for humanistic values, which is reflected in the moratorium that is chosen and the

commitments that are made. These conditions elicit an alternation between progressive and regressive states, with the individual making commitments at one time and disengaging at another. The character Holden Caulfield in J. D. Salinger's classic novel *The Catcher in the Rye* (1951) is an example of this type of identity problem. More extreme identity confusion is found among individuals in this moratorium. According to Cote and Levine, social support is often lacking, which hinders formation of a stable identity. Family and community support is especially important for these individuals. Yet these are the adolescents/young adults who, because their lifestyle departs from the societal mold, are often ostracized and denied support. Individuals may promote a cause of some type. Those who choose a humanistic moratorium are more likely to be intellectual, artistic, antiestablishment, and ideologically nonconforming. After a time, some of these individuals accept technological values and roles.

Individuals whose identity seeking is not influenced by technological or humanistic moratoria face a rather different situation. Some remain in a constant state of flux in which choices are avoided and commitments are lacking. Others take on a negative identity by accepting a deviant lifestyle and value system (for example, delinquency or gang membership). In this instance, the negative elements of an identity outweigh the positive elements. This type of identity crisis resolution occurs in an environment which precludes normative identity development (for example, excessively demanding parents, absence of an adequate role model).

IDENTITY STATUS PARADIGM

Erikson's writings on identity crises have been responsible for an extensive literature consisting of conceptual as well as empirical articles. Perhaps the most widely used application is Marcia's identity status paradigm, in which he conceptualized and operationalized Erikson's theory of identity development in terms of several statuses which result from exploration and commitment. By 1988, more than one hundred empirical studies had been generated from this paradigm, according to a review by Cote and Levine. The identity status paradigm provides a methodological procedure for determining identity statuses based on resolution of an identity crisis and the presence of commitments to an occupation and an ideology.

According to the Marcia paradigm, an ego identity can be one of several statuses consisting of achievement, foreclosure, moratorium, or diffusion. An achievement status indicates resolution of the identity crisis and firm commitments to an occupation and an ideology. In a foreclosure status, one has formed commitments but has not experienced a crisis. The moratorium status denotes that an identity crisis is being experienced, and no commitments have been made. The diffusion status implies the absence of a crisis and no commitments. Much of the research has focused on identifying the personality characteristics associated with each of these statuses. Other studies have examined the interactional patterns as well as information-processing and problem-solving strategies. Achievement and moratorium statuses seek out, process, and evaluate information in their decision making. Foreclosures have more rigid belief systems and conform to normative standards held by significant others, while those in the diffusion status delay decision making. Significant differences have been found among the statuses in terms of their capacity for intimacy, with diffusions scoring lowest, followed by foreclosures. Achievement and moratorium statuses have a greater capacity for intimacy.

PARENTAL SOCIALIZATION AND FEMALE IDENTITY

One area of research that continues to attract attention is parental socialization patterns associated with crisis resolution. The findings to date reveal distinctive parental patterns associated with each status. Positive but somewhat ambivalent relationships between parents and the adolescent/young adult are reported for achievement status. Moratorium-status adolescents/young adults also seem to have ambivalent relationships with their parents, but they are less conforming. Males in this status tend to experience difficulty in separating from their mothers. Foreclosures view their parents as highly accepting and encouraging. Parental pressure for conformity to family values is very evident. Diffusion-status adolescents report much parental rejection and detachment from parents, especially from the father. In general, the data from family studies show that the same-sex parent is an important figure in identity resolution.

An interest in female identity has arisen because different criteria have been used to identify identity status based on the Marcia paradigm. Attitudes toward premarital sexual relations are a major content area in status determination. The research in general shows that achievement and foreclosure statuses are very similar in females, as are the moratorium and diffusion statuses. This pattern is not found for males. It has been argued by some that the focal concerns of females, in addition to concerns with occupation and ideology, involve interpersonal relationships more than do the concerns of males. Therefore, in forming a self-structure, females may examine the outside world for self-evaluation and acceptance in addition to the internal examination of self which typically occurs in males. The effect of an external focus on identity resolution in females is unknown, but this type of focus is likely to prolong the identity crisis. Further, it is still necessary to determine the areas in which choices and commitments are made for females.

NEGATIVE IDENTITY

The concept of negative identity has been used frequently in clinical settings to explain antisocial acts and delinquency in youth, as well as gang-related behavior. A 1988 study by Randall Jones and Barbara Hartman found that the use of substances (for example, cigarettes, alcohol, and other drugs) was higher and more likely in youths of identity-diffusion status. Erikson and others have argued that troubled youths find that elements of a negative identity provide them with a sense of some mastery over a situation for which a positive approach has been continually denied them. In the examples cited, deviant behavior provided both this sense of mastery and an identity.

ROLE IN UNDERSTANDING ADOLESCENTS

The identity crisis is the major conflict faced by the adolescent. Erikson's theories about the identity crisis made a major contribution to the adolescent literature. Marcia's reconceptualization of ego identity facilitated identity research and clinical assessment by providing a methodological approach to identity development and the psychological concomitants of identity. As a result, the study of identity and awareness of the psychological impact on the individual become major research areas and provided a basis for clinical intervention.

The concept of identity crises originated with Erikson, based on the clinical experiences which he used to develop a theory of ego identity development. Explication of this theory appeared in his writings during the 1950's and 1960's. Erikson's theory of the human life cycle places identity resolution as the major crisis faced by the adolescent. The success of this resolution is determined by the satisfactory resolution of crises in the stages preceding adolescence.

Identity formation is a major topic in most textbooks on adolescence, and it is a focal concern of practitioners who treat adolescents with psychological adjustment problems. Until the appearance of Erikson's writings, the field of adolescence was mostly a discussion of physical and sexual development. His focus on psychosocial development, especially the emergence of a self-structure, increased immeasurably the understanding of adolescent development and the problems faced by the adolescent growing up in Western society. As Cote and Levine noted, identity is a multidimensional constructconsisting of sociological perspectives, specifically the social environment in which the individual interacts, as well as psychological processes. Thus, a supportive social environment is critical to crisis resolution. The absence of this supportive environment has frequently been cited as an explanation for identity problems and the acquisition of a negative identity.

TEMPORAL CONSIDERATIONS

It is important to realize that identity has a temporal element as well as a lifelong duration. That is, identity as a personality characteristic undergoes transformations throughout the life cycle. While crisis resolution may be achieved during adolescence/young adulthood, this self-structure is not permanent. Crises can reemerge during the life span. The midlife crises of middle adulthood, written about frequently in the popular press, are often viewed as a manifestation of the earlier identity crisis experienced during adolescence/young adulthood.

The outlook for identity crises is difficult to forecast. The psychological moratorium will continue to be an important process. Given the constant change in American society, the moratorium options available for youth may be more restricted, or more ambiguous and less stable. This scenario is more probable for humanistic moratoria as society moves toward more institutional structure in the form of schools taking on increased responsibility for the so-cialization of children and youth. The provision of child care before and after school is one example of the school's increased role. The erosion which has occurred in family structure presents another problem for identity crisis resolution.

SOURCES FOR FURTHER STUDY

Cote, James E., and Charles Levine. "A Critical Examination of the Ego Identity Status Paradigm." *Developmental Review* 8 (June, 1988): 147-184. Critiques the Marcia identity-status paradigm and notes several areas of divergence from Erikson's conceptualization theory of identity. Advances the argument for an interdisciplinary approach to understanding identity, and identifies several questions about identity crises that need to be considered.

_____. "A Formulation of Erikson's Theory of Ego Identity Formation." *Developmental Review* 7 (December, 1987): 209-218. A comprehensive review of Erikson's theory of ego identity and the role of psychological moratoria in the resolution of identity crises. Discusses Erikson's concepts of value orientation stages and the ego-superego conflict over personality control. Offers criticisms of Erikson's work and suggests cautions for the researcher.

Erikson, Erik Homburger. *Childhood and Society*. Reprint. New York: W. W. Norton, 1993. The thirty-fifth anniversary edition. A presentation of case histories based on Erikson's clinical experiences, as well as a discussion of Erikson's life-cycle model of human development. One section of the book is devoted to an examination of youth and identity. Clinical studies are used to illustrate the problems youth face in identity resolution.

_____. *Identity, Youth, and Crisis*. Reprint. New York: W. W. Norton, 1994. A theoretical discussion of ego identity formation and identity confusion, with special attention given to issues such as womanhood or race and identity. Erikson relies heavily on his vast clinical experiences to illustrate the concepts that he discusses. The life cycle as it applies to identity is examined from an epigenetic perspective.

Kroger, Jane. *Identity in Adolescence*. 2d ed. New York: Routledge, 1996. A presentation of identity development as conceptualized by Erikson and others. Each approach is criticized, and the empirical findings generated by the approach are summarized. The first chapter of the book is devoted to an overview of identity from a developmental and sociocultural perspective. The final chapter presents an integration of what is known about identity.

Marcia, James E. "Identity in Adolescence." In *Handbooks of Adolescent Psychology*, edited by Joseph Adelson. New York: John Wiley & Sons, 1980. A discussion of the identity statuses developed by Marcia, based on a paradigm derived from Erikson's conceptualization of ego identity. Reviews the research literature on personality characteristics, patterns of interaction, developmental studies, identity in women, and other directions in identity research. Ends with a discussion of a general ego-developmental approach to identity.

Joseph C. LaVoie

See also: Adolescence: Cognitive skills; Development; Ego psychology: Erik Erikson; Erikson, Erik; Gender-identity formation; Intimacy; Midlife crises; Psychoanalytic psychology; Self.

Imprinting

Type of psychology: Learning
Fields of study: Biological influences on learning; endocrine system

Imprinting is an endogenous, or inborn, animal behavior by which young mammals and birds learn specific, visible physical patterns to associate with important concepts such as the identification of one's mother, navigation routes, and danger. The phenomenon, which relies primarily upon visual cues and hormonal scents, is of high survival value for the species possessing it.

Key concepts
- conditioning
- critical period
- endogenous behavior
- ethology
- exogenous behavior
- imprinting
- pheromone
- plasticity
- visual cues
- vocal cues

Introduction

Imprinting is an important type of behavior by which an animal learns specific concepts and identifies certain objects or individuals that are essential for survival. Imprinting events almost always occur very early in the life of an animal, during critical periods or time frames when the animal is most sensitive to environmental cues and influences. The phenomenon occurs in a variety of species, but it is most pronounced in the homeothermic (warm-blooded) and socially oriented higher vertebrate species, especially mammals and birds.

Imprinting is learned behavior. Most learned behavior falls within the domain of exogenous behavior, or behavior that an animal obtains by its experiences with fellow conspecifics (members of the same species) and the environment. Imprinting, however, is predominantly, if not exclusively, an endogenous behavior, which is a behavior that is genetically encoded within the individual. An individual is born with the capacity to imprint. The animal's cellular biochemistry and physiology will determine when in its development that it will imprint. The only environmental influence of any consequence in imprinting is the object of the imprint during the critical period. Ethologists, scientists who study animal behavior, debate the extent of endogenous and exogenous influences upon animal behavior. Most behaviors involve a combination of both, although one type may be more pronounced than the other.

The capacity for an animal to imprint is genetically determined and, therefore, is inherited. This type of behavior is to the animal's advantage for critical situations that must be correctly handled the first time they occur. Such behaviors include the identification of one's parents (especially one's mother), the ability to navigate, the ability to identify danger, and even the tendency to perform the language of one's own species. Imprinting behaviors generally are of high survival value and hence must be programmed into the individual via the genes. Biological research has failed to identify many of the genes that are responsible for imprinting behaviors, although the hormonal basis of imprinting is well understood. Most imprinting studies have focused upon the environmental signals and developmental state of the individual during the occurrence of imprinting.

MATERNAL IMPRINTING

These studies have involved mammals and birds, warm-blooded species that have high social bonding, which seems to be a prerequisite for imprinting. The most famous imprinting studies were performed by the animal behaviorists and Nobel laureates Konrad Lorenz (1903-1989) and Nikolaas Tinbergen (1907-1988). They and their many colleagues detailed analyses of imprinting in a variety of species, in particular waterfowl such as geese and ducks. The maternal imprinting behavior of the newborn gosling or duckling upon the first moving object that it sees is the most striking example of imprinting behavior.

The maternal imprint is the means by which a newborn identifies its mother and the mother identifies its young. In birds, the newborn chick follows the first moving object that it sees, an object that should be its mother. The critical imprinting period is within a few hours after hatching. The chick visually will lock on its moving mother and follow it wherever it goes until the chick reaches adulthood. The act of imprinting not only allows for the identification of one's parents but also serves as a trigger for all subsequent social interactions with members of one's own species. As has been established in numerous experiments, a newborn gosling that first sees a female duck will imprint on the duck and follow it endlessly. Upon reaching adulthood, the grown goose, which has been raised in the social environment of ducks, will attempt to behave as a duck, even to the point of mating. Newborn goslings, ducklings, and chicks can easily imprint on humans.

In mammals, imprinting relies not only visual cues (specific visible physical objects or patterns that an animal learns to associate with certain concepts) but also on physical contact and smell. Newborn infants imprint upon their mothers, and vice versa, by direct contact, sight, and smell during the critical period, which usually occurs within twenty hours following birth. The newborn and its mother must come into direct contact with each other's skin and become familiarized with each other's smell. The latter phenomenon involves the release of special hormones called pheromones from each individual's body. Pheromones trigger a biochemical response in the body of the recipient individual, in this case leading to a locked identification pattern for the other involved individual. If direct contact between mother and infant is not maintained during the critical imprinting period, then the mother may reject the infant because she is unfamiliar with its scent. In such a case, the infant's life would be in jeopardy unless it were claimed by a substitute mother. Even in this situation, the failure to imprint would trigger subsequent psychological trauma in the infant, possibly leading to aberrant social behavior in later life.

BIRD MIGRATION AND DANGER RECOGNITION

Although maternal imprinting in mammal and bird species represents the best-documented studies of imprinting behavior, imprinting may be involved in other types of learned behavior. In migratory bird species, ethologists have attempted to explain how bird populations navigate from their summer nesting sites to their wintering sites and back every year without error. Different species manage to navigate in different fashions. The indigo bunting, however, navigates via the patterns of stars in the sky at night. Indigo bunting chicks imprint upon the celestial star patterns for their summer nesting site during a specific critical period, a fact that was determined by the rearrangement of planetarium stars for chicks by research scientists.

Further research studies on birds also implicate imprinting in danger recognition and identification of one's species-specific call or song. Young birds of many species identify predatory birds (for example, hawks, falcons, and owls) by the outline of the predator's body during flight or attack and by special markings on the predator's body. Experiments also have demonstrated that unhatched birds can hear their mother's call or song; birds may imprint on their own species' call or song before they hatch. These studies reiterate the fact that imprinting is associated with a critical period during early development in which survival-related behaviors must become firmly established.

HUMAN IMPRINTING

Imprinting is of considerable interest to psychologists because of its role in the learning process for humans. Humans imprint in much the same fashion as other mammals. The extended lifetime, long childhood, and great capacity for learning and intelligence make imprinting in humans an important area of study. Active research on imprinting is continually being conducted with humans, primates, marine mammals (such as dolphins, whales, and seals), and many other mammals, as well as with a large variety of bird species. Comparisons among the behaviors of these many species yield considerable similarities in the mechanisms of imprinting. These similarities underscore the importance of imprinting events in the life, survival, and socialization of the individual.

With humans, maternal imprinting occurs much as with other mammals. The infant and its mother must be in direct contact during the hours following birth. During this critical period, there is an exchange of pheromones between mother and infant, an exchange that, to a large extent, will bond the two. Such bonding immediately following birth can occur between infant and father in the same manner. Many psychologists stress the importance of both parents being present at the time of a child's delivery and making contact with the child during the critical hours of the first day following birth. Familiarization is important not only for the child but for the parents as well because all three are imprinting upon one another.

Failure of maternal or paternal imprinting during the critical period following birth can have drastic consequences in humans. The necessary, and poorly understood, biochemical changes that occur in the bodies of a child and parent during the critical period will not occur if there is no direct contact and, therefore, no transfer of imprinting pheromones. Consequently, familiarization and acceptance between the involved individuals may not occur, even if intense contact is maintained after the end of the critical period. The psychological impact upon the child and upon the parents may be profound, perhaps not immediately, but in later years. Studies on this problem are extremely limited because of the difficulty of tracing cause-and-effect relationships over many years when many behaviors are involved. There is some evidence, however, which indicates that failure to imprint may be associated with such things as learning disabilities, child-parent conflicts, and abnormal adolescent behavior. Nevertheless, other cases of imprinting failure seem to have no effect, as can be seen in tens of thousands of adopted children. The success or failure of maternal imprinting in humans is a subject of considerable importance in terms of how maternal imprinting affects human behavior and social interactions in later life.

Different human cultures maintain distinct methods of child rearing. In some cultures, children are reared by family servants or relatives from birth onward, not by the actual mother. Some cultures wrap infants very tightly so that they can barely move; other cultures are more permissive. Child and adolescent psychology focuses attention upon early life experiences that could have great influence upon later social behavior. The success or failure of imprinting, along with other early childhood experiences, may be a factor in later social behaviors such as competitiveness, interaction with individuals of the opposite sex, mating, and maintenance of a stable family structure. Even criminal behavior and psychological abnormalities may be traceable to such early childhood events.

EXPERIMENTS

Imprinting studies conducted with mammal and bird species are much easier, because the researcher has the freedom to conduct controlled experiments that test many different variables, thereby identifying the factors that influence an individual animal's ability to imprint. For bird species, a famous experiment is the moving ball experiment. A newly hatched chick is isolated in a chamber within which a suspended ball revolves around the center of the chamber. The researcher can test not only movement as an imprinting trigger but also other variables, such as critical imprinting time after hatching, color as an imprinting factor, and variations in the shape of the ball as imprinting factors. Other experiments involve switching eggs between different species (for example, placing a duck egg among geese eggs).

For mammals, imprinting has been observed in many species, such as humans, chimpanzees, gorillas, dolphins, elephant seals, wolves, and cattle. In most of these species, the failure of a mother to come into contact with its newborn almost always results in rejection of the child. In species such as elephant seals, smell is the primary means by which a mother identifies its pups. Maternal imprinting is of critical importance in a mammalian child's subsequent social development. Replacement of a newborn monkey's natural mother with a "doll" substitute leads to irreparable damage; the infant is socially and sexually repressed in its later life encounters with other monkeys. These and other studies establish imprinting as a required learning behavior for the successful survival and socialization of all birds and nonhuman mammals.

BIOLOGY AND BEHAVIOR

Animal behaviorists and psychologists attempt to identify the key factors that are responsible for imprinting in mammalian and avian species. Numerous factors, including vocal cues (specific sounds, frequency, and language that an animal learns to associate with certain concepts) and visual cues probably are involved, although the strongest two factors appear to be direct skin contact and the exchange of pheromones that are detectable by smell. The maternal imprinting behavior is the most intensively studied imprinting phenomenon, though imprinting appears to occur in diverse behaviors such as mating, migratory navigation, and certain forms of communication.

Imprinting attracts the interest of psychologists because it occurs at critical periods in an individual's life; because subsequent developmental, social, and behavioral events hinge upon what happens during the imprinting event; and because imprinting occurs at the genetic or biochemical level. Biochemically, imprinting relies upon the production and release of pheromones, molecules that have a specific structure and that can be manufactured in the laboratory. The identification and mass production of these pheromones could possibly produce treatments for some behavioral abnormalities.

As an endogenous (instinctive) form of learning, imprinting relies upon the highly complex nervous and endocrine systems of birds and mammals. It also appears limited to social behavior, a major characteristic of these species. The complex nervous systems involve a highly developed brain, vocal communication, well-developed eyes, and a keen sense of smell. The endocrine systems of these species produce a variety of hormones, including the pheromones that are involved in imprinting, mating, and territoriality. Understanding the nervous and endocrine regulation of behavior at all levels is of major interest to biological and psychological researchers. Such studies may prove to be fruitful in the discovery of the origin and nature of animal consciousness.

Imprinting may be contrasted with exogenous forms of learning. These other learning types include conditioning, in which individuals learn by repeated exposure to a stimulus, by association of the concept stimulus with apparently unrelated phenomena and objects, or by a system of reward and punishment administered by parents. Other exogenous learning forms include habituation (getting used to something) and trial and error. All learned behaviors are a combination of endogenous and exogenous factors.

SOURCES FOR FURTHER STUDY

Beck, William S., Karel F. Liem, and George Gaylord Simpson. *Life: An Introduction to Biology.* 3d ed. New York: HarperCollins, 1991. Introduction to biology for the beginning student. Contains a clear text, many strong diagrams and illustrations, and beautiful photographs. Contains a thorough discussion of animal behavior, famous experiments, and various types of animal learning, including imprinting, and describes the studies of Konrad Lorenz and others.

Klopfer, Peter H., and Jack P. Hailman. *An Introduction to Animal Behavior: Ethology's First Century.* Englewood Cliffs, N.J.: Prentice-Hall, 1967. An excellent and well-organized introduction to the history of animal behavior research. Presents major themes and models, and cites many important studies. Chapters 3 and 12 discuss instinctive and learned aspects of behavioral development.

Manning, Aubrey, and Marian Stamp Dawking. *An Introduction to Animal Behavior.* 5th ed. New York: Cambridge University Press, 1998. Concise, detailed, and thorough presentation of animal behavior research. Encompasses all major behavioral theories and supporting experiments. Includes a good discussion of imprinting studies, particularly with reference to maternal imprinting, and describes the biological bases behind imprinting and other behaviors.

Raven, Peter H., and George B. Johnson. *Biology.* 6th ed. New York: McGraw-Hill, 2001. A strong presentation of all aspects of biology for the beginning student. Includes excellent diagrams and illustrations. Summarizes the major theories and classic experiments of animal behavior research, including imprinting studies.

Wallace, Robert A., Gerald P. Sanders, and Robert J. Ferl. *Biology: The Science of Life.* 3d ed. New York: HarperCollins, 1991. An outstanding book for beginning students that describes all major concepts in biology with great clarity, using numerous examples, good illustrations, and beautiful photographs. Discusses behavioral research, including studies of maternal imprinting.

Wilson, Edward Osborne. *Sociobiology: The New Synthesis*. Cambridge, Mass.: The Belknap Press of Harvard University Press, 2000. The twenty-fifth anniversary edition. An incredibly comprehensive study of sociobiology, a perspective which maintains that animal behavior is a driving force in animal species evolution. The author, a prominent entomologist, is the leading proponent of this controversial theory, which he defends with hundreds of case studies. Describes the biological basis of behavior during all stages of animal development.

David Wason Hollar, Jr.

SEE ALSO: Defense reactions: Species-specific; Ethology; Father-child relationship; Hormones and behavior; Instinct theory; Learning; Loranz, Konrad; Mother-child relationship; Preparedness; Reflexes; Reflexes in newborns.

Impulse control disorders

TYPE OF PSYCHOLOGY: Emotion; sensation and perception; social psychology; stress

FIELDS OF STUDY: Attitudes and behavior; coping; depression; interpersonal relations; problem solving; social perception and cognition; stress and illness

Impulse control disorders are represented by destructive behaviors resulting from the inability to control urges to act irresponsibly.

KEY CONCEPTS
- destruction
- disruption
- exhilaration
- gratification
- irresistibility
- pleasure
- relief
- spontaneity
- tension

INTRODUCTION

Impulse control disorders are characterized by spontaneous behavior that satisfies a person's urges to feel tension-induced exhilaration. Mental health authorities attribute impulse control disorders to neurological or environmental causes that are aggravated by stress. People with impulse control disorders have an intense craving for instant gratification of specific desires and are usually unable to ignore temptations which tend to cause negative results. Pressure increases these people's impulsive urges until they become irresistible, and they feel pleasure and relief when yielding control to enjoy appealing yet unacceptable activities. They are compelled to engage in destructive, sometimes violent behaviors. Most people with impulse control disorders feel no guilt or remorse for their actions.

People who have impulse control disorders repeatedly indulge in a behavioral pattern of impulsivity, disrupting their lives. Their family and employment roles are often impaired. They frequently face legal ramifications for their recurrent impulsive behavior. People suffering from impulse control disorder often experience associated anxiety, stress, and erratic sleeping cycles.

For centuries, people have been aware of behavior associated with modern impulse control disorders. By 1987, the revised third edition of the American Psychiatric Association's *Diagnostic and Statistical Manual of Mental Disorders* (DSM-III-R) defined impulse control disorders as representing mental disorders which involve uncontrollable impulsive behavior that can potentially result in danger and harm to the affected person and/or other people. According to this classification, individuals with impulse control disorders are unable to resist urges to engage in this behavior despite feeling tension prior to impulsive activity. During the impulsive behavior, the person usually experiences sensations of release, titillation, and then satisfaction.

The 1994 DSM-IV assigned codes to six types of "impulse control disorders not elsewhere classified: pathological gambling (312.31), kleptomania (312.32), pyromania (312.33), intermittent explosive disorder (312.34), trichotillomania (312.39), and impulse control disorder not otherwise specified (312.30). These classifications were retained in the text revision, DSM-IV-TR, published in 2000.

Sometimes impulse control disorders are associated with other mental illnesses, such as bipolar dis-

The categorization of pathological gambling as an impulse control disorder has been controversial, with some psychologists labeling this behavior an addiction or a compulsion. (Raymond P. Malace)

orders, or behaviors including road rage. Patients are often identified with an impulse control disorder while undergoing treatment for another psychological problem. Some mental health professionals attribute behaviors classified as impulse control disorders to types of different mental conditions. Impulse control disorders are distinguished by being primarily characterized by people's absence of control over potentially damaging impulses.

IMPULSES OR ADDICTIONS?

Pathological gambling differs from recreational gambling because it is a recurring behavior in which people, mostly males, continue to gamble self-destructively despite chronic losses and disturbances of their lives. The classification of this type of gambling as an impulse control disorder is controversial. Robert Custer, Henry Lesieur, and Richard Rosenthal wrote various versions of the DSM gambling classifications. In the 1980 DSM-III, compulsive gambling was listed as a separate mental disorder. Seven years later, DSM-III-R included pathological gambling in a description of impulse control disorders.

According to DSM-IV-TR, mental health professionals first assess whether a patient suffered a manic episode that caused an excessive gambling episode, then diagnose pathological gambling if a patient persistently displays a minimum of five of ten designated behaviors. These behaviors include making extraordinarily risky and expensive bets for excitement, gambling in an effort to recoup previous losses, and lying about gambling activities to their family, colleagues, and therapists. Although patients might have repeatedly attempted to quit gambling, they become agitated when trying to do so and fail to stop. The patients might focus all of their attention on gambling, reflecting on previous events and planning for future bets, and scheme how to secure more gambling money. Patients might have been fired from jobs or kicked out of school. Romantic partners might have left them. Patients might ask for financial help to deal with debt or bankruptcy caused by gambling. Some patients might perceive gambling as an escape from reality and unpleasant emotions. Extreme behaviors include criminal activities such as embezzlement to acquire gambling funds. Tax authorities might investigate the financial activities of pathological gamblers.

Some psychological researchers state that gambling is not solely the result of impulsive behavior. They argue that gambling resembles addictions such as alcoholism. Many researchers investigate the role of personality, asking whether specific traits cause compulsive gambling habits or develop because of gambling activities. In 1987, Lesieur and Sheila Blume created the South Oaks Gambling Screen (SOGS) to identify pathological gamblers. This test was translated for international use in treatment facilities.

Eleven years later, M. W. Langewisch and G. R. Frisch presented a study in which impulsivity was not significantly different in nonpathological and pathological gamblers identified according to SOGS scores. Langewisch and Frisch hypothesized that gambling and addictive behaviors are closely related. Professionals who dismiss the classification of pathological gambling as an impulse control disorder stress that many gamblers deliberately research athletes before wagering on sporting events and act more compulsively than impulsively. In 1994, the American Medical Association adopted a resolution that physicians should warn patients that gambling can be addictive. Four years later, the National Institute of Mental Health urged researchers to devise studies focusing on pathological gambling.

RISKY IMPULSIVENESS

In 2002, it was estimated that shoplifters steal approximately $13 billion of merchandise from stores in the United States every year. While many of these thieves are criminals, impoverished people, substance abusers, or teenagers responding to a dare, some thieves have kleptomania. This impulse control disorder is characterized by people submitting to urges to steal items that are not essential to sustain their lives or for the purpose of generating revenues. Instead, kleptomaniacs, usually female, steal to experience thrilling sensations of fear. The threat of being caught, arrested, and prosecuted does not discourage most kleptomaniacs. Occasionally, people with kleptomania experience guilty feelings and discreetly return stolen items. Some mental health professionals state that kleptomaniacs have an addictive-compulsive disorder, not an impulse control disorder.

The DSM-IV-TR describes kleptomania as a pattern of impulsive stealing with the motive to achieve emotional release, then enjoyment. Therapists evaluate whether patients steal due to specific manic episodes or because they suffer from an antisocial personality or conduct disorder. A kleptomania diagnosis is made when patients continually steal unnecessary objects, do not steal because they are delusional, are not motivated by a resentful need to retaliate against businesses, and report feelings of tension, relief, and gratification.

People who have pyromania repeatedly set fires to experience similar emotions. The DSM-IV-TR defines pyromania as recurrent acts of arson for personal enjoyment. Pyromaniacs, usually males, cannot control impulses to spark fires because they are intrigued by the flames, the emergency response to fires, and the resulting destruction. Some children experience a temporary fascination with setting fires which might reveal other psychological problems. Therapists rule out manic episodes, antisocial personality and conduct disorders, delusional behavior, intoxication, and retardation before diagnosing patients with pyromania.

Behaviors associated with pyromania include anxious feelings prior to a deliberate fire setting which culminate in excitement. Patients are usually obsessed with fire and related equipment. They often collect information about disastrous fires, learn about fire fighting techniques, and eagerly discuss fires. Sometimes pyromaniacs indulge in pleasurable emotions by remaining at fire scenes to watch emergency personnel while delighting in the damage they have caused. Pyromaniacs do not set fires to make political statements, commit retaliatory sabotage, seek insurance money, or destroy criminal evidence.

ANGRY IMPULSIVENESS

Intermittent explosive disorder is a violent form of impulsive control disorder. Patients repeatedly act out excessive aggressive impulses and often cause harm to the people and objects they attack. Sometimes property is destroyed. Based on the DSM-IV-TR classification, therapists examine patients for possible medication reactions, medical problems such as Alzheimer's disease or head injuries, and mental conditions such as psychotic, borderline personality, or attention-deficit hyperactivity disorders. Mental health professionals establish an intermittent explosive disorder diagnosis based on whether recurring aggressive behavior exceeds appropriate response to any stimuli and patients seem out of control.

People with intermittent explosive disorder frequently face legal charges of domestic violence, assault, and property destruction. Many patients do not feel guilty and refuse to accept responsibility for their attacks. They usually blame their victims who

---

DSM-IV-TR Criteria for Impulse Control Disorders

INTERMITTENT EXPLOSIVE DISORDER (DSM CODE 312.34)

Several discrete episodes of failure to resist aggressive impulses resulting in serious assaultive acts or destruction of property

Degree of aggressiveness expressed during episodes grossly out of proportion to any precipitating psychosocial stressors

Aggressive episodes not better accounted for by another mental disorder and not due to direct physiological effects of a substance or general medical condition

KLEPTOMANIA (DSM CODE 312.32)

Recurrent failure to resist impulses to steal objects not needed for personal use or for their monetary value

Increasing sense of tension immediately before theft

Pleasure, gratification, or relief while committing theft

Stealing not committed to express anger or vengeance and not in response to delusion or hallucination

Stealing not better accounted for by Conduct Disorder, Manic Episode, or Antisocial Personality Disorder

PATHOLOGICAL GAMBLING (DSM CODE 312.31)

Persistent and recurrent maladaptive gambling behavior as indicated by five or more of the following:

- preoccupation with gambling (reliving past gambling experiences, handicapping or planning the next venture, thinking of ways to get money with which to gamble)
- need to gamble with increasing amounts of money in order to achieve desired excitement
- repeated unsuccessful efforts to control, cut back, or stop gambling
- restlessness or irritability when attempting to cut down or stop gambling
- gambling as a way of escaping from problems or of relieving dysphoric mood (such as feelings of helplessness, guilt, anxiety, depression)
- after losing money, return on another day to get even ("chasing" losses)

- lies to family members, therapist, or others to conceal the extent of involvement with gambling
- illegal acts such as forgery, fraud, theft, or embezzlement to finance gambling
- jeopardizing or losing significant relationship, job, or educational or career opportunity because of gambling
- reliance on others to provide money to relieve desperate financial situation caused by gambling

Gambling behavior not better accounted for by Manic Episode

PYROMANIA (DSM CODE 312.33)

Deliberate and purposeful fire setting on more than one occasion

Tension or affective arousal before act

Fascination with, interest in, curiosity about, or attraction to fire and its situational contexts (paraphernalia, uses, consequences)

Pleasure, gratification, or relief when setting fires, or when witnessing or participating in their aftermath

Fire setting not done for monetary gain, as an expression of sociopolitical ideology, to conceal criminal activity, to express anger or vengeance, to improve living circumstances, in response to delusion or hallucination, or as a result of impaired judgment

Fire setting not better accounted for by Conduct Disorder, Manic Episode, or Antisocial Personality Disorder

TRICHOTILLOMANIA (DSM CODE 312.39)

Recurrent pulling out of one's hair resulting in noticeable hair loss

Increasing sense of tension immediately before pulling out hair or when attempting to resist behavior

Pleasure, gratification, or relief when pulling out hair

Disturbance not better accounted for by another mental disorder and not due to a general medical condition

Disturbance causes clinically significant distress or impairment in social, occupational, or other important areas of functioning

IMPULSE CONTROL DISORDER NOT OTHERWISE SPECIFIED (DSM CODE 312.30)

they claim provoked them. Various forms of stress such as perceived insults and threats and fear of not having demands fulfilled also are offered as justification for intermittent explosive disorder assaults. Researchers have determined that some people with intermittent explosive disorder have irregularities in brain wave activity or chemistry.

SELF-MUTILATION

Trichotillomania is an impulse control disorder characterized by people plucking out their hair uncontrollably to seek an enjoyable release from tension. Some patients remove so much hair that they have bald spots on their bodies. As children, both females and males have been known to have this disorder, but adult females are more likely to suffer trichotillomania than are adult males. Some people with trichotillomania swallow their hair and form hairballs, called trichobezoars, which clog their intestines.

According to DSM-IV-TR diagnostic criteria, mental health professionals can diagnose trichotillomania if other medical and mental conditions are not present, especially any dermatological concerns. Patients have trichotillomania if the act of removing hair or efforts to control plucking create tension which is released when hair is pulled. Therapists diagnose trichotillomania if patient's pleasure in this behavior surpasses any social stigmas for visible hair loss and the patient continues to engage in such hair removal despite its negative effect on the person's employment, social interactions, and health. Infections and inflammations at the distressed site do not deter the person who has trichotillomania. Compulsive skin picking and nail biting are sometimes associated with trichotillomania. Some authorities suggest that trichotillomania is a anxiety or habit disorder, especially in toddlers and infants.

TREATMENT

Psychotherapy and pharmacotherapy are the usual treatments for impulse control disorders. Based on a psychological evaluation, therapists choose treatment methods suitable for each patient and applicable to specific undesirable behaviors. Medication, outpatient therapy, and hospitalization at public or private facilities are options to treat impulse control disorders. Treatment success varies. Many kleptomaniacs are secretive about their behavior and only encounter therapists because of court orders following

arrests. The 1990 Americans with Disabilities Act (ADA) does not recognize impulse control disorders as disabilities.

Some researchers suggest that serotonin reuptake inhibitors (SRIs) can minimize impulses to steal, althought they do not cure kleptomania. Antidepressants and hypnotherapy have helped some people resist trichotillomania impulses. Pathological gamblers often benefit from group support at Gamblers Anonymous in addition to psychotherapy that addresses associated issues such as depression. Therapists use behavior modification techniques to develop alternative behaviors and motivations to replace destructive impulses and responses. Patients learn to revise irrational thinking patterns with cognitive therapy. Anger management methods help some people with intermittent explosive disorder, while neurofeedback aids others to manage stress and develop self-control.

SOURCES FOR FURTHER STUDY

Gaynor, Jessica, and Chris Hatcher. *The Psychology of Child Firesetting: Detection and Intervention.* New York: Brunner/Mazel, 1987. Investigates why some children commit arson and suggests possible treatments to alter dangerous behaviors and attitudes regarding fire which potentially might result in pyromania.

Goldman, Marcus J. *Kleptomania: The Compulsion to Steal—What Can Be Done?* Far Hills, N.J.: New Horizon Press, 1998. Based on case studies and research, the author, a forensic psychiatrist, corrects misconceptions regarding kleptomania, recommends methods to treat this impulse control disorder, and comments on related concerns such as depression and substance abuse.

Hollander, Eric, and Dan J. Stein, eds. *Impulsivity and Aggression.* New York: John Wiley & Sons, 1995. A comprehensive discussion of impulse control disorders as a public health concern in addition to commentary about how to measure and treat impulsivity disorders and legal and ethical concerns associated with impulsive behaviors.

Lesieur, Henry R. *The Chase: Career of the Compulsive Gambler.* Cambridge, Mass.: Schenkman, 1984. Although dated, this text addresses fundamental issues. Written by the leading expert in the field, who was the founding editor of the *Journal of Gambling Studies* and later served as president of the Institute for Problem Gambling.

McCown, William G., and Linda L. Chamberlain. *Best Possible Odds: Contemporary Treatment Strategies for Gambling Disorders.* New York: John Wiley & Sons, 2000. Outlines inpatient and outpatient pathological gambling treatment programs including family therapy and support groups and how to deal with gamblers who suffer addictions and act abusively.

Maees, Michael, and Emil F. Coccaro, eds. *Neurobiology and Clinical Views on Aggression and Impulsivity.* New York: John Wiley & Sons, 1998. Discusses possible causes and treatments for impulse control disorders that are characterized by violent behavior and comments on other mental conditions that often accompany impulsiveness.

Walker, Michael B. *The Psychology of Gambling.* New York: Pergamon, 1992. Walker, the codirector of the University of Sydney's Gambling Research Unit, interprets from a social psychology perspective how some people become pathological gamblers.

Webster, Christopher D., and Margaret A. Jackson, eds. *Impulsivity: Theory, Assessment, and Treatment.* New York: Guilford, 1997. Includes a variety of topics related to impulse control disorders, including psychopathy in children, spousal abuse, impulsivity in incarcerated prisoners, and biopsychology of brain serotonin.

Elizabeth D. Schafer

SEE ALSO: Addictive personality and behaviors; Aggression: Reduction and control; Anger; Bipolar disorder; Domestic violence; Drug therapies; Endocrine system; Endorphins; Misbehavior; Nervous system; Optimal arousal theory; Road rage; Substance use disorders.

Incentive motivation

TYPE OF PSYCHOLOGY: Motivation
FIELDS OF STUDY: Motivation theory

Incentive motivation is a determinant of behavior from without, in contrast to drive motivation, which is a determinant from within. Both jointly determine the quality and quantity of behavior. Each motivation can energize behavior alone, however, and the relative importance of each differs for different behaviors.

KEY CONCEPTS
- achievement motivation
- anticipatory goal responses
- brain reward mechanism
- Crespi effect
- expectancy theory
- intracranial self-stimulation

INTRODUCTION

Motivation refers to a group of variables that determine what behavior—and how strong and how persistent a behavior—is to occur. Motivation is different from learning. Learning variables are the conditions under which a new association is formed. An association is the potential for a certain behavior; however, it does not become behavior until motivation is introduced. Thus, motivation is necessary to convert a behavioral potential into a behavioral manifestation. Motivation turns a behavior on and off.

Incentive motivation is an attracting force, while drive motivation is an expelling force. Incentive is said to "pull" and drive to "push" an individual toward a goal. The attracting force originates from the reward object in the goal and is based on expectation of the goal object in certain locations in the environment. The expelling force originates from within organisms as a need, which is related to disturbances in homeostasis in the body. The two forces jointly determine behavior in a familiar environment. In a novel environment, however, there is not yet an expectation; no incentive motivation is yet formed, and drive is the only force to cause behavior. The organism can be expected to manifest various responses until the goal-oriented responses emerge.

Once the organism achieves the goal, the reward stimuli elicit consummatory responses. Before the organism reaches the goal, the stimuli that antedate the goal would elicit responses; these are termed anticipatory goal responses. The anticipatory responses are based upon the associational experience among the goal stimuli, the goal responses, and the situational stimuli present prior to reaching the goal. The anticipatory responses and their stimulus consequences provide the force of incentive motivation. Incentive refers to the expected amount of reward given certain behavior.

Though drive motivation and incentive motivation jointly determine behaviors, the importance of each differs for different behaviors. For example, bar-pressing behavior for drinking water by an animal in a Skinner box normally requires both drive motivation, induced by water deprivation, and the incentive motivation of a past experience of getting water. Under special conditions, however, the animal will press the bar to drink water even without being water-deprived. In this case, drinking is no longer related to drive. This type of drinking is called nonhomeostatic drinking. Drinking a sweet solution, such as one containing sugar or saccharin, does not require any deprivation, so the behavior to get sweet solutions is based upon incentive motivation alone. Under normal conditions, sexual behavior is elicited by external stimuli, so sexual drive is actually incentive motivation elicited from without.

BEHAVIOR AND INCENTIVES

Two experiments will illustrate how the concept of incentive motivation may be applied to explain behavior. Carl J. Warden of Columbia University conducted a study which is regarded as a classic. A rat was placed in the start box of a short runway, and a reward (food) was placed in its goal box at the other end. The food-deprived animal had to cross an electrified grid on the runway to reach the goal. When the animal reached the goal, it was repeatedly brought back to the start box. The number of times the animal would cross the grid in a twenty-minute period was recorded. It was found that the longer the food deprivation, the more times the animal crossed the grid, for up to about three days without food, after which the number decreased. The animal crossed only about two times with no food deprivation; however, the number increased to about seventeen at three days of food deprivation, then decreased to about seven at eight days without food. When the animal was water-deprived, the animal crossed the grid about twenty times to the goal box containing water at one day without water. When the reward was an infant rat, a mother rat crossed about twenty times. A male rat crossed about thirteen times to a female rat after being sex-deprived (without female companion) for one day. A female rat in heat crossed thirteen times to a male rat. Even without any object in the goal box, the animal crossed about six times; Warden attributed this to a "novelty" reward. The reward variable in this experiment was the goal object, which was

manipulated to fit the source of the drive induced by deprivation or hormonal state (as in an estrous female). The rat, placed in the start box, was induced by the goal.

CRESPI EFFECT

The second study, conducted by Leo P. Crespi, established the concept of incentive motivation as an anticipatory response. He trained rats in a runway with different amounts of food and found that the animals reached different levels of performance. The speed of running was a function of the amount of reward: The more the food in the goal box, the faster the animal would run. There were three groups of rats. Group 1 was given 256 food pellets (about a full day's ration) in the goal box; the animals would run at slightly over 1 meter (about 3.28 feet) per second after twenty training trials. Group 2 was given sixteen pellets, and their speed was about 76 centimeters (2.5 feet) per second. Group 3 was given only one pellet, and the speed was about 15 centimeters (6 inches) per second.

When the speed became stable, Crespi shifted the amount of food. The rats in all groups were now given sixteen pellets. The postshift speed eventually, but not immediately, settled to near that of the group originally given sixteen pellets. An interesting transitional effect of so-called incentive contrast was observed. Immediately after the shift from the 256-pellet reward to the sixteen-pellet reward, the animal's speed was much lower than the group continuously given the sixteen-pellet reward. Following the shift from the one-pellet to the sixteen-pellet reward, however, the animal's speed was higher than the group continuously given the sixteen-pellet reward. Crespi called these the elation effect and the depression effect, or the positive contrast effect and the negative contrast effect, respectively. Clark Hull and K. W. Spencer, two of the most influential theorists of motivation and learning, interpreted the Crespi effect as evidence of anticipatory responses. They theorized that the goal response had become conditioned to the runway stimuli such that the fractional goal responses were elicited. Since the responses occurred prior to the goal responses, they were anticipatory in nature. The fractional goal responses, along with their stimulus consequence, constitute the incentive motivation that would energize a learned associative potential to make it into a behavior.

MANIPULATION OF MOTIVATION

Incentive motivation has been manipulated in many other ways: the delay of reward presentation, the quality of the reward, and various partial reinforcement schedules. In relation to the delay variable, the sooner the reward presentation follows the responses, the more effective it is in energizing behavior, although the relationship is not linear. In the case of partial reinforcement, when the subject received a reward only part of the time, behavior was shown to be more resistant to extinction than when reward was delivered every time following a response; that is, following withdrawal of the reward, the behavior lasted longer when the reward was given only part of the time than when the reward was given every time following the response. The quality of the reward variable could be changed by, for example, giving a monkey a banana as a reward after it had been steadily given raisins. In Warden's experiment, the various objects (water, food, male rat, female rat, or rat pup) placed in the goal box belong to the quality variable of incentive. Another incentive variable is how much effort a subject must exert to obtain a reward, such as climbing a slope to get to the goal versus running a horizontal path.

INTRACRANIAL SELF-STIMULATION

The term "reinforcer" usually indicates any stimulus which would result in increasing the probability or magnitude of a response upon its presentation following that response. When the response has reached its maximum strength, however, a reinforcer can no longer increase it; nevertheless, it has a maintenance effect. Without it, the response would soon cease. A reward reinforces and maintains a response. It is believed that the rewarding effects are mediated by the brain; the mechanism which serves as the substrate of the effects has been studied.

In a breakthrough experiment in this line of study, in 1954, James Olds and Peter Milner reported that a rat would press a bar repeatedly to stimulate certain areas of its brain. (If the bar press resulted in stimulation of certain other areas of the brain, the rat would not repeat the bar press.) Thus, this particular brain electrical stimulation has a rewarding effect. The phenomenon is termed intracranial self-stimulation. The rewarding effect is so powerful that the hungry animal would rather press the bar to stimulate its brain than eat. It has also been shown that animals will press a bar to self-inject cocaine, amphetamine, morphine, and many other drugs. The rewarding effect is so powerful that if rats or monkeys are given access to a bar that allows continuous self-administration of cocaine, they often die of an overdose. It is now known that the neurotransmitter involved in this rewarding effect, as well as in the rewarding effect of food, is dopamine, acting at the nucleus accumbens, a part of the limbic system in the brain. Addictions and drug-directed behaviors can be understood better because of studies related to the brain reward mechanism. This mechanism is defined as the rewarding effect of various stimuli, such as food, cocaine, and intracranial self-stimulation, as related to dopamine activity in the brain. Whether incentive motivation is mediated by the same brain mechanism can also be studied.

ACHIEVEMENT MOTIVATION

In humans, achievement motivation can be measured in order to predict what a subject would choose to do given tasks of different difficulty as well as how persevering the subject will be when he or she encounters failure. Achievement motivation is related to past experiences of rewards and failures to obtain a reward, so it becomes an incentive motivation of anticipating either success or failure to obtain a reward. Fear of failure is a negative motivational force; that is, it contributes negatively to achievement motivation. Those people with a strong fear of failure will choose easy tasks to ensure success, and upon failure they will give up quickly.

Unless an individual anticipates or believes that the effort will lead to some desired outcome, the person will not expend much effort. Expectancy theory states that how much effort a person will expend depends upon the expected outcome of the effort. If the expected outcome is positively correlated to the effort, the person will work as hard as possible. In a classroom setting, effort can be evaluated from a student's attendance, note taking, and discussions with classmates or teachers. The expected outcome would be to earn a particular grade, as well as perhaps to obtain a scholarship, make the dean's list, obtain a certain job, gain admission to graduate school, or gain respect from peers and parents. Unless the effort is perceived to be related to the outcome, little effort will be expended.

If one is expecting a big reward, one would work harder than if the reward were small. An Olympic gold medal is worth harder work than a school gold medal is. Anyone can affect other people's behavior with proper incentive; it can be manipulated to promote learning in students and promote productivity in industry. The way incentive is used to promote productivity distinguishes the free enterprise system based on a market economy from a socialist society of controlled economy which is not based on market force. In a socialist economy, one's reward is not based on the amount of one's economic contribution; it is based on the degree of socialistic behavior. One's political background, in terms of family, loyalty to the party, and "political consciousness," are the things that matter most. It is difficult or impossible to predict, under this kind of reward situation, what kinds of activities will be reinforced and maintained. The expected outcome of an individual's effort or behavior is the incentive motivation; teachers and managers must understand it to promote desired learning and production. For example, an employee will be motivated to perform certain tasks well by a pay raise only when he or she perceives the relationship between the effort and the raise. A student will be motivated to study only when he or she sees the relationship between the effort and the outcome.

RELATIONSHIP TO PLEASURE
The concepts of incentive, reward, and reinforcement originated with the concept of pleasure, or hedonism. The assumption that a major motivation of behavior is the pursuit of pleasure has a long history. Epicurus, a fourth century B.C.E. Greek philosopher, asserted that pleasure is good and wholesome and that human life should maximize it. Later, Christian philosophers asserted that pleasure is bad and that if a behavior leads to pleasure it is most likely bad as well. John Locke, a seventeenth century British philosopher, asserted that behavior is based on maximizing anticipated pleasure. Whether a behavior would indeed lead to pleasure was another matter. Thus, Locke's concept of hedonism became a behavioral principle. Modern incentive motivation, based upon anticipation of reward, has the same tone as Locke's behavioral principle. Both traditions involve the concepts of incentive and of reinforcement being a generator of behaviors.

There is a danger of circularity in this line of thought. For example, one may explain behavior in terms of it resulting in obtaining a reward, then explain or define reward in terms of behavior. There is no new understanding to be gained in such circular reasoning. Fortunately, there is an independent definition of the rewarding effect, in terms of the brain mechanism of reward. If this mechanism is related to pleasure, there could also be a definition of pleasure independent of behavior. Pleasure and reward are the motivating force, and anticipation of them is incentive motivation. Because it attracts people toward their sources, by manipulating the sources, the behavior can be predictably altered.

SOURCES FOR FURTHER STUDY

Bolles, Robert C. *Theory of Motivation.* 2d ed. New York: Harper & Row, 1975. An authoritative book by a productive psychological theoretician; incentive motivation is detailed in several sections.

Crespi, Leo P. "Quantitative Variation of Incentive and Performance in the White Rat." *American Journal of Psychology* 55, no. 4 (1942): 467-517. The anticipatory nature of incentive motivation was first demonstrated in this paper. It is termed the Crespi effect, which includes the elation and depression effects following the incentive contrast.

Green, Russell. *Human Motivation: A Social Psychological Approach.* Belmont, Calif.: Wadsworth, 1994. An introductory textbook on the psychology of motivation, aimed at undergraduates. Covers many theoretical approaches.

Hellriegel, Don, John W. Slocum, Jr., and Richard W. Woodman. *Organizational Behavior.* 9th ed. Pacific Grove, Calif.: Thomson, 2000. A popular text in industrial psychology and personnel management. How to motivate workers with various incentive systems is explained with examples; incentive motivation can be applied in industry to promote productivity.

Kohn, Alfie. *Punished by Rewards: The Trouble with Gold Stars, Incentive Plans, A's, Praise, and Other Bribes.* Boston: Houghton Mifflin, 1999. Argues against teaching based on incentive motivations, debunking the behaviorist basis of incentive theory along the way.

Liebman, Jeffrey M., and Steven J. Cooper, eds. *The Neuropharmacological Basis of Reward.* Oxford, England: Oxford University Press, 1989. Summarizes studies in the area of brain mechanisms of rewarding effects, an area of great interest to many studying incentive motivation.

Logan, Frank A., and Douglas P. Ferraro. *Systematic Analyses of Learning and Motivation.* New York: John Wiley & Sons, 1978. Logan is a well-known researcher in the area of incentive. This book summarizes the relationship between learning and motivation.

Olds, James, and Peter Milner. "Positive Reinforcement Produced by Electrical Stimulation of Septal Area and Other Regions of Rat Brain." *Journal of Comparative and Physiological Psychology* 47 (1954): 419-427. Reports a breakthrough in the area of studying the brain mechanisms involved in the rewarding effects.

Warden, Carl John. *Animal Motivation: Experimental Studies on the Albino Rat.* New York: Columbia University Press, 1931. This is the first research attempting to compare different sources of drive using various reward substances.

Sigmund Hsiao

SEE ALSO: Achievement motivation; Drives; Educational psychology; Motivation; Sex hormones and motivation; Work motivation.

Incompetency

TYPE OF PSYCHOLOGY: Cognition
FIELDS OF STUDY: Aging; cognitive processes; general constructs and issues; psychopathology

Incompetency refers to a state of diminished mental functioning such that a person is judged unable to give voluntary and informed consent to psychiatric hospitalization, or undergo a medical procedure, or participate in research or, in legal contexts, unable to stand trial or waive constitutional rights. Among the conditions that affect mental capacity are mental retardation, mental illness, and the progressive dementias seen in older adults. Although specialized measures of mental capacity are available, no standardized method exists to establish competency.

KEY CONCEPTS
- assessment of mental capacity
- competency
- informed consent
- medical decision-making capacity
- mental capacity
- situation-specific decision-making capacity
- treatment-specific decision-making capacity

INTRODUCTION

The terms "incompetency" and "incompetence" refer to a state of diminished mental functioning that, for example, precludes an individual from giving informed consent to go undergo a particular medical procedure. Other contexts where the issue of incompetency—or its obverse, competency—might arise include competence to consent voluntarily to psychiatric hospitalization, competence to give informed consent to participate in research, and competence in right-to-die issues, such as requesting physician-assisted suicide. In legal contexts, situations requiring determination of whether an individual has the requisite mental abilities for competent decision making include competence to execute a will, competence to stand trial, competence to waive Miranda and other constitutional rights, and competence to waive death sentence appeals.

Psychologists and other health professionals rarely use the terms "incompetency" and "incompetent" because they imply a global deficit that has little practical meaning or application. Alzheimer's disease patients, for example, are at risk for autonomy-restricting interventions, including institutionalization and guardianship. As greater attention is paid to preserving individual rights, increased emphasis is placed on identifying, in functional terms, specific mental tasks and skills that people retain and lose. "Mental capacity" is the term used to describe the cluster of mental skills that people use in their everyday lives. It includes memory, logic and reasoning, the ability to calculate, and the mental flexibility to shift attention from one task to another. Describing a person's ability or mental capacity to perform particular tasks, such as remembering to pay bills or calculating how much change is owed, enables professionals to assess vulnerability more effectively and develop suitable treatment and service plans.

Medical decision-making capacity is defined as the ability to give informed consent to undergo a particular medical test or intervention or the ability to refuse such intervention. Capacity may extend to the question of disclosure of sensitive confidential information or an individual's permission to participate in research. When a legal determination of competency has not been made, decisional capacity is used to describe an individual's ability to make a healthcare decision.

CONDITIONS AND FACTORS AFFECTING MENTAL CAPACITY

Among the conditions that affect mental capacity are mental retardation, mental illness, and the progressive dementias seen in older adults. It should be noted that capacity can and will vary over time, either as a disease process progresses, as in a dementing illness, or as clinical conditions wax and wane, as in a patient with a bipolar disorder. In the case of delirium, for instance, a patient may be capable of participating in treatment decisions in the morning but incapable of making a decision at a later point in that day. A variety of factors, some of which are treatable, may contribute to mental decline. These include poor nutrition, depression, and interactions among medications.

Mental, or decision-making, capacity is also treatment or situation specific. For example, a person may have the ability to agree to a diagnostic procedure, yet be unable to comprehend fully the consequences of accepting a particular medication or surgical intervention. When assessing capacity, one is determining whether an individual is capable of deciding about a specific treatment or class of treatments rather than making a global determination of incompetence. A person will sometimes be found to have the capacity to make some decisions and yet not others, especially when more complex information must be presented and understood.

ASSESSING MENTAL COMPETENCY OR CAPACITY

The Millon Clinical Multiaxial Inventory (MCMI) is often used in forensic evaluations to determine competency to stand trial. The Capacity to Consent to Treatment Instrument (CCTI) tests competence under different legal standards or thresholds. Other widely used instruments include the MacArthur Competency Assessment Tools, the Aid to Capacity Evaluation, and the Competence Questionnaire (CQ), for which versions for pediatric medical patients and children in the juvenile justice system have been developed.

Whereas instruments for measuring abilities thought to be directly related to mental capacity are

available, there exists no standardized method to establish competency, in either medical or legal contexts. A fundamental problem is the lack of standards for assessing capacity. It is important, therefore, to look closely at people in the context of their everyday lives and not decide a priori that someone is incapable of making a decision affecting his or her health or welfare. Some individuals with severe forms of schizophrenia, for example, have demonstrated the ability to give informed consent to participate in research.

THE ROLE OF THE PSYCHOLOGIST

Psychologists are often asked to evaluate a person's cognitive functioning to determine whether he or she is competent, for example, to execute a will or to assign power of attorney. For individuals obviously in mental decline, the role of the psychologist is to determine whether it is appropriate to appoint a guardian to manage the person's financial affairs and to make medical decisions regarding long-term care. To determine treatment decision-making capacity, the psychologist assesses the individual's understanding of the disorder and the recommended treatment, appreciation of the situation of the situation and treatment choices, ability to reason and evaluate options and consequences of choices, and ability to express a choice.

Given the lack of consensus on both the exact criteria and the method for assessing mental competency, it is important that psychologists undertake a broad examination to determine an individual's ability to make decisions affecting his or her own welfare. A competency evaluation begins with a review of the person's medical and psychological records and history, with information being supplied by family members as well as the individual being evaluated. Following the record review, the individual is seen for a clinical interview, which includes several measures of orientation, short-term memory, and reasoning ability.

Following the clinical interview, psychological testing is administered, according to the interview results, for an objective assessment of cognitive functioning. The psychologist then offers an expert opinion, based on the evaluation, regarding whether the person is capable of making decisions regarding his or her welfare and finances. This process is also done retrospectively at times, for instance, to determine if an individual was competent when their last will was executed. The competency evaluation has been characterized as iterative process in which the clinician is both assessing and attempting to maximize the individual's capacity and autonomy.

Psychologists are sometimes asked to determine a person's competency to stand trial. The evaluation might also cover the defendant's competency to plead guilty or to waive the right to counsel. The psychologist's report would include psychiatric, medical, and substance abuse history, as well as results from mental status and psychological testing. A key part of the evaluation is the determination of the defendant's ability to understand the proceedings. Among the specific issues addressed are whether the defendant understands the present charges and overall legal situation and whether he or she can distinguish among various pleas and understands the range of possible verdicts. Competency evaluations are also often required for children in the juvenile justice system.

SOURCES FOR FURTHER STUDY

Grisso, T., and P. S. Applebaum. *Assessing Competence to Consent to Treatment: A Guide for Physicians and Other Health Professionals.* New York: Oxford University Press, 1998. The authors describe the place of competence in the doctrine of informed consent, analyze the elements of decision making, and show how assessments of competence to consent to treatment can be conducted within varied general medical and psychiatric treatment settings. The book explains how assessments should be conducted and offers detailed, practice-tested interview guidelines to assist medical practitioners in this task. Numerous case studies illustrate real-life applications of the concepts and methods discussed. Grisso and Appelbaum also explore the often difficult process of making judgments about competence and describe what to do when patients' capacities are limited.

Sachs, G. A. "Assessing Decision-Making Capacity." *Topics in Stroke Rehabilitation* 7, no. 1 (2000): 62-64. This article reviews several critical aspects of assessing decision-making capacity (DMC) in medical and treatment contexts. Among the topics addressed are the task-specific nature of assessing DMC and the need to use measures that attend to the following aspects of DMC: the expression of choice, understanding of relevant information, appreciation of the consequences of a

decision, and the ability to reason, for instance, to process information and one's preferences in a logical manner.

Schopp, Robert F. *Competence, Condemnation, and Commitment: An Integrated Theory of Mental Health Law.* Washington, D.C.: APA Books, 2001. This book examines the major intersections between legal institutions and the idea of mental illness. Efforts to reconcile involuntary commitment with the right to refuse treatment are reviewed along with a compelling case for requiring as a prerequisite to commitment, a determination of decisional incompetence.

Allyson Washburn

SEE ALSO: Decision making; Dementia; Forensic psychology; Insanity defense; Law and psychology; Mental retardation.

Individual psychology
Alfred Adler

TYPE OF PSYCHOLOGY: Personality
FIELDS OF STUDY: Personality theory; psychodynamic and neoanalytic models

Individual psychology is the personality theory that was developed by Alfred Adler after he broke from Freudian psychoanalytical ideas. Adler emphasized the importance of childhood inferiority feelings and stressed psychosocial rather than psychosexual development.

KEY CONCEPTS
- compensation
- inferiority
- masculine protest
- private logic
- social interest
- style of life

INTRODUCTION

Individual psychology is the name of the school of personality theory and psychotherapy developed by Alfred Adler (1870-1937), a Viennese general-practice physician turned psychiatrist. The term "individual" has a dual implication: It implies uniqueness (each personality exists in a person whose distinctiveness must be appreciated); also, the personality is an indivisible unit that cannot be broken down into separate traits, drives, or habits which could be analyzed as if they had an existence apart from the whole.

The essence of a person's uniqueness is his or her style of life, a unified system which provides the principles that guide everyday behavior and gives the individual a perspective with which to perceive the self and the world. The style of life is fairly stable after about age six, and it represents the individual's attempt to explain and cope with the great problem of human existence: the feeling of inferiority.

ROLE OF INFERIORITY
All people develop a feeling of inferiority. First of all, they are born children in an adult world and realize that they have smaller and weaker

Alfred Adler, the founder of individual psychology. (Hulton Archive)

bodies, less knowledge, and virtually no privileges. Then people start to compare themselves and realize that there are other people their own age who are better athletes, better scholars, more popular, more artistically talented, wealthier, more socially privileged, more physically attractive, or simply luckier. If one allows the perception of one's own self-worth to be influenced by such subjective comparisons, then one's self-esteem will be lowered by an inferiority complex.

Adler believed that since one's style of life is largely determined early in life, certain childhood conditions make individuals more vulnerable to feelings of inferiority. For example, children born into poverty or into ethnic groups subjected to prejudice may develop a heightened sense of inferiority. Those children with real disabilities (learning or physical disabilities, for example) would also be more susceptible to devaluing their own worth, especially when others are excessively critical or mocking.

ROLE OF EARLY FAMILY LIFE
Adler looked inside the family for the most powerful influences on a child's developing style of life.

Parents who treat a child harshly (through physical, verbal, or sexual abuse) would certainly foster feelings of inferiority in that child. Similarly, parents who neglect or abandon their children contribute to the problem. (Adler believed that such children, instead of directing their rage outward against such parents, turn it inward and say, "There must be something wrong with me, or they would not treat me this way.") Surprisingly, Adler also believed that those parents who pamper their children frustrate the development of positive self-esteem, for such youngsters conclude that they must be very weak and ineffectual in order to require such constant protection and service. When such pampered children go out into the larger world and are not the recipients of constant attention and favors, their previous training has not prepared them for this; they rapidly develop inferior feelings.

The impact of the family on the formulation of one's style of life also includes the influence of siblings. Adler was the first to note that a child's birth order contributes to personality. Oldest children tend to be more serious and success-oriented, because they spend more time with their parents and identify more closely with them. When the younger children come along, the oldest child naturally falls into a leadership role. Youngest children are more likely to have greater social skills and be creative and rebellious. Regardless of birth order, intense sibling rivalries and comparisons can easily damage the esteem of children.

INDIVIDUAL INTERPRETATION OF CHOICE

Adler was not fatalistic in discussing the possible impact on style of life of these congenital and environmental forces; he held that it is neither heredity nor environment which determines personality, but rather the way that individuals interpret heredity and environment. They furnish only the building blocks out of which the individual fashions a work of art: the style of life. People have (and make) choices, and this determines their own development; some people, however, have been trained by life to make better choices than others.

All individuals have the capacity to compensate for feelings of inferiority. Many great athletes were frail children and worked hard to develop their physical strength and skills. Great painters overcame weak eyesight; great musicians overcame poor hearing. Given proper encouragement, people are capable of great accomplishments.

DEVELOPMENT OF SOCIAL INTEREST

The healthy, normal course of development is for individuals to overcome their feelings of inferiority and develop social interest. This involves a feeling of community, or humanistic identification, and a concern with the well-being of others, not only one's own private feelings. Social interest is reflected in and reinforced by cooperative and constructive interactions with others. It starts in childhood, when the youngster has nurturing and encouraging contacts with parents, teachers, and peers.

Later, the three main pillars of social interest are friends, family, and career. Having friends can help overcome inferiority, because it allows one to be important in the eyes of someone else. Friends share their problems, so one does not feel like the only person who has self-doubt and frustration. Starting one's own family reduces inferiority feeling in much the same way. One feels loved by spouse and children, and one is very important to them. Having an occupation allows one to develop a sense of mastery and accomplishment and provides some service to others or to society at large. Therefore, those people who have difficulty establishing and maintaining friendships, succeeding as a spouse or parent, or finding a fulfilling career will have less opportunity to develop a healthy social interest and will have a greater susceptibility to lingering feelings of inferiority.

PRIVATE LOGIC

The alternatives to developing social interest as a way of escaping from feelings of inferiority are either to wallow in them or to explain them away with private logic. Private logic is an individual's techniques for coping with the feeling of inferiority by unconsciously redefining himself or herself in a way not compatible with social interest. Such individuals retreat from meaningful interpersonal relationships and challenging work because it might threaten their precariously balanced self-esteem. Private logic convinces these individuals to seek a sham sense of superiority or notoriety in some way that lacks social interest.

One such approach in private logic is what Adler termed masculine protest (because Western patriarchal culture has encouraged such behavior in males and discouraged it in females). The formula is to be rebellious, defiant, even violent. Underlying all sadism, for example, is an attempt to deny weakness. The gangster wants more than money, the rapist more than sex: They need a feeling of power in order to cover up an unresolved inferiority feeling. The prostitute wants more than money; she needs to have the power to attract and manipulate men, even though she herself may be totally dependent on her pimp or on drugs.

USE IN CHILD DEVELOPMENT STUDIES

Adler's theory, like Sigmund Freud's psychoanalysis and B. F. Skinner's radical behaviorism, is a flexible and powerful tool for understanding and guiding human behavior. The first and foremost applications of individual psychology have been in the areas of child rearing, education, and guidance. Because the first six years of life are formative, the contact that children have during this time with parents, teachers, siblings, and peers will influence that child's later decisions in the direction of social interest or private logic. Adlerians recommend that parents and teachers be firm, fair, and, above all, encouraging. One should tell children that they can overcome their disabilities and praise every progress toward accomplishment and social interest. One should avoid excessive punishments, for this will only convince children that others are against them and that they must withdraw into private logic.

After World War I, the new Social Democratic government of Austria gave Adler the task of developing a system of youth guidance clinics throughout the nation. Each child age six to fourteen was screened, then counseled, if necessary. In the 1920's, the rates of crime and mental disorders among young people declined dramatically.

USE IN ELDER STUDIES
A second example of the applicability of Adler's theory occurs at the other end of the life cycle: old age. Late life is a period in which the incidence of mental disorders, especially depression, increases. This can be understood in terms of diminished opportunity to sustain social interest and increased sources of inferiority feeling.

Recall that social interest has three pillars: career, friends, and family. Traditionally, one retires from one's career at about age sixty-five. Elders who do not develop satisfying new activities (especially activities which involve a sense of accomplishment and contribution to others) adjust poorly to retirement and tend to become depressed. Old friends die or move into retirement communities. Sometimes it is harder to see and talk with old friends because of the difficulty of driving or using public transportation as one ages, or because one or one's friends become hard of hearing or experience a stroke that impairs speech. By far the greatest interpersonal loss in later life is the loss of a spouse. When adult children move away in pursuit of their own lives, this may also give an elder the perception of being abandoned.

Conditions that can rekindle old feelings of inferiority abound in later life. Real physical inferiorities arise. The average elder reports at least two of the following chronic conditions: impaired vision, impaired hearing, a heart condition, stroke, or arthritis. The United States is a youth- and body-oriented culture that worships physical attractiveness, not wrinkles and fat. Some elders, especially those who have had the burdens of long-term illness, feel inferior because of their reduced financial resources.

USE IN STUDYING PREJUDICE
A third area of application is social psychology, especially the study of prejudice. Gordon Allport suggested that those who exhibit racial or religious prejudice are typically people who feel inferior themselves: They are trying to feel better about themselves by feeling superior to someone else. Typically, prejudice against African Americans has been greatest among whites of low socioeconomic status. Prejudice against new immigrants has been greatest among the more poorly skilled domestic workers. Another example of prejudice would be social class distinctions. The middle class feels inferior (in terms of wealth and privilege) to the upper class. Therefore, the middle class responds by using its private logic to demean the justification of wealth: "The rich are rich because their ancestors were robber barons or because they themselves were junk bond traders in the 1980's." The middle class feels superior to the lower class, however, and again uses private logic to justify and legitimize that class distinction: "The poor are poor because they are lazy and irresponsible." In order to solidify its own identity as hardworking and responsible, the middle class develops a perception of the poor that is more derogatory than an objective analysis would permit.

The most telling application of the theory of individual psychology to prejudice occurred in the first part of the twentieth century in Germany. The rise of Nazi anti-Semitism can be associated with the humiliating German defeat in World War I and with the deplorable conditions brought about by hyperinflation and depression. Adolf Hitler first blamed the Jews for the "November treason" which stabbed the German army in the back. (This private logic allowed the German people to believe that their defeated army would have achieved an all-out victory at the front had it not been for the Jewish traitors back in Berlin.) All the problems of capitalism and social inequality were laid at the feet of Jewish financiers, and every fear of rabble-rousing Communists was associated with Jewish radicals. Since everything bad, weak, cowardly, or exploitive was labeled "Jewish," non-Jewish Germans could believe that they themselves were everything good. The result of the institutionalization of this private logic in the Third Reich led to one of the most blatant examples of masculine protest that humankind has witnessed: World War II and the Holocaust.

USE IN INTERPERSONAL RELATIONS

A fourth application is associated with management and sales. Management applies interpersonal relations to subordinates; sales applies interpersonal relations to prospective customers. Adler's formula for effective interpersonal relations is simple: Do not make the other person feel inferior. Treat workers with respect. Act as if they are intelligent, competent, wise, and motivated. Give subordinates the opportunity and the encouragement to do a good job, so that they can nurture their own social interest by having a feeling of accomplishment and contribution. Mary Kay Ash, the cosmetics magnate, said that she treated each of her employees and distributors as if each were wearing a sign saying "make me feel important." A similar strategy should apply to customers.

FREUD'S INFLUENCE

The idea of the inferiority complex bears some similarity to the writings of many previous thinkers. Nineteenth century French psychologist Pierre Janet came closest by developing a theory of perceived insufficiency as a root of all neurosis. American psychologist William James spoke of an innate craving to be appreciated. Adler's emphasis on the individual's capacity for compensation (a defense mechanism for overcoming feelings of inferiority by trying harder to excel) and on masculine protest has parallels in the writings of philosopher Friedrich Nietzsche.

Yet the optimistic, simplified, psychosocial approach of Alfred Adler can only be understood as a reaction to the pessimistic, esoteric, psychosexual approach of Sigmund Freud. Adler was a respected general practitioner in Vienna. He heard his first lecture on psychoanalysis in 1899 and was fascinated, although he never regarded himself as a pupil or disciple of Freud. He was invited to join the Vienna Psychoanalytic Society, and did so in 1902, but he was never psychoanalyzed himself. By the end of the decade, he had become president of the society and editor of its journal. As Adler's own theories developed, and as he voiced them within the psychoanalytic association, Freud became increasingly defensive.

Adler came to criticize several underpinnings of psychoanalytic theory. For example, he suggested that the Oedipus complex was merely the reaction of a pampered child, not a universal complex. Adler saw dysfunctional sexual attitudes and practices as a symptom of the underlying neurosis, not as its underlying cause. When Adler would not recant his heresy, the Vienna Psychoanalytic Society was split into a Freudian majority and an Adlerian minority. For a brief period, the Adlerians retained the term "psychoanalysis," only later defining their school as individual psychology.

Freud's influence on Adler can be seen in the emphasis on the importance of early childhood and on the ideas that the motives that underlie neurosis are outside conscious awareness (private logic) and that it is only through insight into these motives that cure can be attained. It is largely in Adler's reaction against Freud, however, that Adler truly defined himself. He saw Freud as offering a mechanistic system in which individuals merely react according to instincts and their early childhood environment; Adler believed that individuals have choices about their futures. He saw Freud as emphasizing universal themes that are rigidly repeated in each patient; Adler believed that people fashion their unique styles of life. Adler saw Freud as being focused on the intrapsychic; Adler himself emphasized the interpersonal, social field.

While Freud's personality theory has been the best remembered, Adler's has been the most rediscovered. In the 1940's, holistic theorists such as Kurt Lewin and Kurt Goldstein reiterated Adler's emphasis on the individual's subjective and comprehensive approach to perceptions. In the 1960's, humanistic theorists such as Abraham Maslow and Carl Rogers rediscovered his emphasis on individuals overcoming the conditions of their childhood and striving toward a self-actualization and potential to love. In the 1980's, cognitive theorists such as Albert Ellis, Aaron Beck, and Martin E. P. Seligman emphasized how individuals perceive and understand their situation as the central element underlying psychopathology.

STRENGTHS AND WEAKNESSES

An evaluation of individual psychology must necessarily include some enumeration of its weaknesses as well as its strengths. The positives are obvious: The theory is easy to comprehend, optimistic about human nature, and applicable to the understanding of a wide variety of issues. The weaknesses would be the other side of those very strengths. If a theory is so easy to comprehend, is it not then simplistic or merely a reformulation of common sense? This may explain why so many other theorists "rediscovered" Adler's ideas throughout the twentieth century. If a theory is so optimistic about human potential, can it present a balanced view of human nature? If a theory is flexible and broad enough as to be able to explain so much, can it be precise enough to explain anything with any depth? Although everything in individual psychology fits together as a unified whole, it is not always clear what the lines of reasoning are. Does excessive inferiority feeling preclude the formulation of social interest, or does social interest assuage inferiority feeling? Does inferiority feeling engender private logic, or does private logic sustain inferiority feeling? At different times, Adler and Adlerians seem to argue both sides of these questions. The Achilles heel of individual psychology (and of psychoanalysis) is prediction. If a given child is in a situation that heightens feelings of inferiority, will that child overcompensate effectively and develop social interest as an adult, or will private logic take over? If it does, will it be in the form of self-brooding or masculine protest?

Although the fuzziness of Adlerian concepts will preclude individual psychology from being a major force in academic psychology, it is safe to predict that future theorists will again rediscover many of Alfred Adler's concepts.

Sources for Further Study

Adler, Alfred. *The Practice and Theory of Individual Psychology*. New York: Routledge, 1999. One in Routledge's International Library of Psychology series, reprinting classic, milestone works on psychology. Adler's own introduction to his work.

Bottome, Phyllis. *Alfred Adler: A Biography*. New York: G. P. Putnam's Sons, 1939. This classic biography was written only two years after Adler's death. It gives much insight into the man and his theory, but the book is a bit too laudatory.

Dreikurs, Rudolf. *Fundamentals of Adlerian Psychology*. 1950. Reprint. Chicago: Alfred Adler Institute, 1989. The author was an Adlerian disciple who became the leader of the Adlerian movement in the United States after World War II. His simple style and straightforward advice are very much in keeping with the style of Adler himself. Dreikurs's own expertise was in the area of child development.

Ganz, Madelaine. *The Psychology of Alfred Adler and the Development of the Child*. New York: Routledge, 1999. Another in Routledge's International Library of Psychology series. A well-organized introduction to Adler's theories.

Mozak, Harold, and Michael Maniacci. *A Primer of Adlerian Psychology: The Analytic-Behavioral-Cognitive-Psychology of Alfred Adler*. New York: Brunner/Mazel, 1999. An introduction aimed at students, with summary and review questions at the end of each chapter.

Sweeney, Thomas. *Adlerian Counseling: A Practitioner's Approach*. 4th ed. Philadelphia: Taylor & Francis, 1998. Provides a practical overview of Adler's individual psychology. Written for practicing mental health professionals.

T. L. Brink

See also: Adler, Alfred; Adlerian psychotherapy; Birth order and personality; Cognitive psychology; Ego psychology: Erik Erikson; Freud, Sigmund; Humanism; Psychoanalytic psychology; Psychoanalytic psychology and personality: Sigmund Freud.

Industrial and organizational psychology

Type of psychology: Social psychology
Fields of study: Group processes; motivation theory; social perception and cognition

Industrial and organizational psychology applies psychological research methods and theories to issues of importance in work organizations. From its beginnings as psychology applied to a few personnel topics, it has expanded to deal with almost all aspects of work, changing as they have.

Key concepts
- experimentation
- fairness in work settings
- field research
- industrial psychology
- organizational psychology
- scientific method

Introduction

Industrial and organizational psychology (often shortened to I/O psychology) is a somewhat deceptive title for the field. Even when industrial psychology alone was used to label it, practitioners were involved with issues and activities far beyond solving industrial problems—for example, designing procedures for selecting salespeople, advertising methods, and reducing accidents on public transportation. "Organizational" suggests the application of knowledge to organizations, but the intended meaning is closer to "the study of forces that influence how people and their activities at work are organized."

In colleges and universities, I/O psychology is a long-recognized discipline. Graduate programs leading to the M.A. and, more commonly, Ph.D. degrees in this field are most typically offered within psychology departments, sometimes in collaboration with departments of business; occasionally they are offered by business departments alone. In most cases, students working toward graduate degrees in I/O psychology first study a wide range of psychological topics, then study in even greater detail those that make up the I/O specialty. The study of research methods, statistical tools for evaluating findings, motivation, personality, and so on forms a base from which psychological testing, interviewing, job analysis, and performance evaluation are studied in depth.

EVOLUTION OF STUDY

Psychologists were certainly not the first to study work settings and suggest changes, or even the first to apply the scientific method to the enterprise. For example, Frederick Winslow Taylor and Frank Gilbreth were industrial engineers who considered workers not too different from cogs in the machines also involved in industry. Their "time and motion" studies sought to discover how workers could most efficiently carry out their parts of the enterprise. Although their conclusions are often now cited as examples of inhumane manipulation of workers for companies' benefits, Taylor and Gilbreth envisioned that both workers and employers were to gain from increases in efficiency. Not surprisingly, most of what industrial engineering studied was appropriated by industrial psychology and remains part of I/O psychology—usually under the designations "job design" and "human factors engineering" in the United States, or the designation "ergonomics" elsewhere.

Early psychologists had an advantage over the others studying and offering advice about work. They were popularly identified as people experts, and for the many problems thought to be based on human characteristics or limitations, their expertise was acknowledged even while it was very modest. The advantage of being expected to make valuable contributions was put to good use, and within the first two decades of the twentieth century, industrial psychology became a recognized discipline with the ability to deliver most of what was expected of it.

Ironically, wars materially aided the early development of industrial and organizational psychology. World War I provided psychologists unprecedented opportunities to try intelligence testing on a very large scale and to develop and implement a very large personnel program. Robert Yerkes directed the intelligence testing of more than one million men between 1917 and 1919, and Walter Dill Scott and Walter Van Dyke Bingham interviewed and classified more than three million men before the war ended.

Testing, interviewing, and classification were also part of industrial psychologists' efforts during World War II, and many other lines of research and application were also pursued. For example, human factors engineering, which emphasized machine design tailored to the people who would use the device, was greatly advanced by the necessity that people be able to control aircraft and other sophisticated weapons.

Following each war, some of the psychologists who had successfully worked together chose to continue to do so. Major consulting firms grew out of their associations and remain a source of employment for many I/O psychologists.

METHODS OF RESEARCH

Industrial and organizational psychology borrowed much from many other areas of psychology during its growth and has retained the strong research orientation common to them, along with many of the research methods each has developed and many of the findings that each has generated. Bringing psychological methods to work settings where experts from many other disciplines are studying some of the same problems results in conflicts, but it also produces a richness of information beyond the scope of any one of the disciplines.

In most cases, the most feasible approach to data collection for I/O psychologists is field research, an approach in which evidence is gathered in a "natural" setting, such as the workplace; by contrast, laboratory research involves an artificial, contrived setting. Systematic observation of ongoing work can often give a psychologist needed information without greatly disturbing the workers involved. Generally, they will be told that data are being gathered, but when the known presence of an observer likely would change what is being studied, unobtrusive methods might be used. Information from hidden cameras, or observations from researchers pretending to be workers and actually engaging in whatever must be done, can be used when justified.

Again studying within the actual work setting, I/O psychologists may sometimes take advantage of natural experiments, situations in which a change not deliberately introduced may be studied for its effect on some important outcome. If, for example, very extreme, unseasonable temperatures resulted in uncontrollably high, or low, temperatures in an office setting, a psychologist could assess the effects on employee discomfort, absenteeism, or productivity.

Still studying within the actual work setting, an I/O psychologist may arrange a quasi-experiment, a situation in which the researcher changes some factor to assess its effect while having only partial control over other factors that might influence that change. For example, the psychologist might study the effects of different work schedules by assigning one schedule to one department of a company, a second schedule to a second department, and a third schedule to a third department. The departments, the people, and the differences in the work itself would prevent the strategy from being a true experiment, but it still could produce some useful data.

An experiment, as psychology and other sciences define it, is difficult to arrange within work settings, but it may be worth the effort to evaluate information gathered by other methods. In the simplest form of experiment, the researcher randomly assigns the people studied into two groups and, while holding constant all other factors that might influence the experiment's outcome, presents some condition (known as an independent variable) to one group of subjects (the experimental group) and withholds it from another (the control group). Finally, the researcher measures the outcome (the dependent variable) for both groups.

Carrying out a true experiment almost always requires taking the people involved away from their typical activities into a setting obviously designed for study (usually called the laboratory, even though it may bear little resemblance to a laboratory of, say, a chemist). The need to establish a new, artificial setting and the need to pull workers away from their work to gather information are both troublesome, as is the risk that what is learned in the laboratory setting may not hold true back in the natural work setting.

Correlational methods, borrowed from psychometrics, complement the observational and experimental techniques just described. Correlation is a mathematical technique for comparing the similarity of two sets of data (literally, to determine their co-relation). An important example of the I/O psychologist's seeking information on relationships is found in the process of hiring-test validation, answering the question of the extent to which test scores and eventual work performance are correlated. To establish validity, a researcher must demonstrate a substantial relationship between scores and performance, evidence that the test is measuring what is intended.

APPLICATIONS IN THE WORKPLACE

Industrial and organizational psychology, as the term implies, focuses on two broad areas; Linda Jewell and Marc Siegall, in their *Contemporary Industrial/ Organizational Psychology* (2d ed., 1990), demonstrate this by their arrangement of topics. Industrial topics include testing; job analysis and evaluation; recruitment, selection, and placement of applicants; employee training and socialization; evaluation of employee job performance; job design; working conditions; health and safety; and motivation. Organizational topics include a company's social system and communication, groups within organizations, leadership, and organizational change and development. Topics of overlap of the two areas include absenteeism, turnover, job commitment, job satisfaction, employee development, and quality of work life.

Testing in I/O psychology most often is done to assess peoples' aptitudes or abilities as a basis for making selection, placement, or promotion decisions about them. It may also be used for other purposes—for example, to judge the quality of training programs. The tests used range from ones of general aptitude (IQ, or intelligence quotient, tests) through tests of specific aptitudes, interests, and personality, although use of IQ and personality tests remains controversial. Aptitude for success in aca demically related activity (as might be related to one's IQ) is often of only modest importance in work settings, but the folk wisdom "the best person is the most intelligent person" can lead to giving IQ tests routinely to applicants. Personality is a trouble some concept within psychology. Tests of it can be useful to clinicians working with mental health is sues but are rarely useful as bases for employment related decisions. When outcomes from personality testing are specific enough to be useful—for ex ample, when they reveal serious personality prob lems—the same information is usually obtainable from reviews of work history or from interviews.

Along with other procedures related to making decisions about people in work settings, testing is of ten targeted as being unfair to some groups—for ex ample, African Americans or women. If the use of a particular test results in decision making that even suggests unfair discrimination, companies must have available solid evidence that this is not the case if they choose to continue using the test.

Job analysis determines what tasks must be carried out in a job. It serves as the major basis for deciding what skills successful job applicants must have or what training to provide unskilled applicants. The evaluation of job performances of individual employ ees must be based on what they should be doing, re vealed by job analysis. Dismissal, retention, promo tion, and wage increases may all be related to job analysis information. It is also a basis for job evalua tion, the determining of what is appropriate pay for the job, although evaluation often must also be based on the availability of applicants, average wages in a geographic area, and other factors.

Recruiting, selecting, and placing refer to sequen tial steps in filling positions. Although some compa nies can let prospective employees come to them, many prefer actively to seek applicants. Recruiting may involve little more than announcing that a posi tion is open or as much as sending trained repre sentatives to find promising people and encourage them to apply for work. At least two considerations make vigorous recruiting attractive. First, it is often possible for companies to reduce training costs greatly by finding already-proficient applicants. Sec ond, when minority-group employees are needed to achieve fair balance in an organization, recruiting can often focus on, for example, African Americans or women.

Although training may be unnecessary if a com pany is able to hire already-skilled people, training is generally advantageous after hiring and period ically over a worker's tenure. Promotion may be based on success in training, or training may follow promotion based on other considerations. Although "training" suggests the development or enhance ment of job skills, it often also includes socializa tion, the bringing of new employees into the "fam ily" of the company and the teaching of values, goals, and expectations that extend beyond carrying out a specific work assignment. Job design, working con ditions, health and safety, and motivation are usu ally given separate chapters in texts, but often in work settings they must be considered as a set. For example, if a job, as designed, forces or even en courages workers to put their health or safety at risk, their working conditions are unsatisfactory, and when they recognize the nature of the situation, their motivation is likely to be impaired.

LEGAL AND ETHICAL REQUIREMENTS

When industrial psychologists of the early twentieth century recommended hiring or promotion, de signed training, or carried out any other of their responsibilities, they had only to satisfy their em ployers' demands. Since the late 1960's, I/O psy chologists have also had to satisfy legal and ethical requirements pertaining to a host of problem areas such as racism, sexism, age discrimination, and dis crimination against the handicapped. More than good intentions are necessary here. The psycholo gists must work to balance the societal demands for fairness in work settings (the basing of decisions about workers' hiring, salary, promotion, and so on entirely on work-relevant considerations and not on race, sex, age, or other personal characteristics) and the practical interests of employers, sometimes hav ing to endure criticism for even the most ingenious of solutions.

For example, if an employer finds the company must increase its number of Hispanic workers, vig orous recruiting is an excellent first step, yet it may prove expensive enough to aggravate the employer. If recruiting is not successful because would-be ap plicants doubt the employer's sincerity, both they and the employer will be unhappy. If recruiting is successful in generating interest, but many inter ested individuals are unqualified, providing them special training could be a reasonable solution. Applicants might feel it degrading, however, to be required to undergo more training than others before them, and/or the employer might balk at the extra cost involved.

The first industrial psychologists needed little more than solid training in their discipline to achieve success. Their successors need, beyond training in a discipline that has enlarged enormously, the talents of diplomats.

SOURCES FOR FURTHER STUDY

Anderson, Neil, Deniz S. Ones, and Handan Kepir Sinangil, eds. *Handbook of Industrial, Work, and Organization Psychology.* 2 vols. Thousand Oaks, Calif.: Sage Publications, 2002. Volume 1 focuses on industrial psychology theories, techniques and methods. Volume 2 offers specific case studies in topics such as motivation, leadership, organizational justice, and and organizational development and change.

Hilgard, Ernest Ropiequet. *Psychology in America: A Historical Survey.* San Diego, Calif.: Harcourt Brace Jovanovich, 1987. Chapter 19, "Industrial and Organizational Psychology," is a definitive review of about eighty years of the field's advancement from a promising application of the new "scientific psychology" to a major subdiscipline of contemporary psychology. An energetic reader could use material in several of Hilgard's other chapters (for example, those on intelligence, on motivation, and on social psychology) to place industrial and organizational psychology in the context of its parent discipline.

Jewell, Linda N., and Marc Siegall. *Contemporary Industrial/Organizational Psychology.* 3d ed. Belmont, Calif.: Wadsworth, 1998. A text for an introductory college course offering excellent coverage of the discipline's topics. Written for students majoring in business as much as for those majoring in psychology. A book that almost anyone can understand, even enjoy.

Rogelberg, Steven, ed. *Blackwell Handbook of Research Methods in Industrial and Organizational Psychology.* New York: Blackwell, 2002. A comprehensive overview of the field, useful to beginners and experts alike. Addresses both practical and theoretical issues of industrial psychology.

Rosenzweig, Mark R., and Lyman W. Porter, eds. *Annual Review of Psychology.* Stanford, Calif.: Annual Reviews. Most volumes of this highly respected se-ries contain a chapter or two on I/O psychology, indexed under "Personnel-Organizational Psychology." Each volume also contains a chapter title index for at least the previous decade, making location of particular topics reasonably easy.

Harry A. Tiemann, Jr.

SEE ALSO: Ability tests; Achievement motivation; Career and personnel testing; Group decision making; Human resource training and development; Leadership; Work motivation.

Inhibitory and excitatory impulses

TYPE OF PSYCHOLOGY: Biological bases of behavior
FIELDS OF STUDY: Nervous system; organic disorders

Two types of processes occur in neurons: those that excite the cell to react to a stimulus and those that inhibit the cell. Cells receive many impulses of both types and must integrate the incoming messages to determine what response should be produced.

KEY CONCEPTS
- action potential
- axon
- dendrite
- depolarization
- excitability
- ion channel
- neurotransmitter
- postsynaptic potential
- resting membrane potential
- synapse

INTRODUCTION

An unstimulated neuron—one which is neither receiving nor transmitting an impulse—maintains a difference in ions on either side of its cell membrane. While many positively charged potassium ($K+$) ions are present within the cytoplasm of a cell, proteins and other large molecules located there carry more numerous negative charges, making a negative net charge inside the membrane. Large numbers of positively charged sodium ions ($Na+$)

are located on the outside of the cell in the intercellular space, giving it a net positive charge. Thus, in a resting neuron, there is a positive charge on the outside of the cell membrane and a negative charge on the inside. This charge difference is called the resting membrane potential. It is usually expressed as -70 millivolts, meaning that the inside of the cell is seventy thousandths of a volt more electrically negative than the outside.

The resting membrane potential is maintained by active transport of ions across the cell membrane. Sodium and potassium ions move across the membrane by diffusion, with sodium leaking into the cell and potassium leaking out. These ions are said to be moving down their concentration gradients, going from an area of higher concentration of each ion to an area of lower ion concentration. Such movement occurs passively, without the addition of energy by the cell. If this movement were allowed to continue uninterrupted, the resting potential would be lost fairly quickly, as the ions would reach equilibrium where they would be at the same concentration on both sides of the membrane. This is prevented from happening by the active transport process of the sodium-potassium pump. Active transport is a means of moving materials across the cell membrane from an area of lower concentration to an area of higher concentration. It cannot occur by diffusion, but requires the input of energy from the cell, released by breakage of a molecule by adenosine triphosphate (ATP), the energy currency of the cell. The sodium-potassium pump is a protein that spans the cell membrane and acts as a channel through which both sodium and potassium are pushed against their concentration gradients by the cell's energy. Much of the ATP made by every cell is used to run this pump and maintain the resting potential, not only in neurons but in all other cells as well. The sodium-potassium pump moves two potassium ions into the cell and three sodium ions out of the cell for each ATP molecule broken.

PROCESS OF INFORMATION TRANSMISSION

The electrical difference between the sides of the cell membrane is particularly important in neurons, since it is through a change in this difference that a message is passed along the surface of a single neuron. In this information transmission, an electrical impulse passes down an excited, activated neuron's axon (the single fiberlike extension of a neuron

that carries information away from the cell body toward the next cell in a pathway) to the "output" end of the cell, the axon terminal. There the electrical impulse causes tiny vesicles or sacs filled with a chemical called a neurotransmitter to move to the cell membrane and fuse with it, emptying the contents of the vesicles into the space between cells, which is called a synapse. The cell that releases its chemical messengers at the synapse is the presynaptic neuron, and the cell which receives the message is the postsynaptic neuron. The message of the neurotransmitter is received by the second cell when the chemical binds to a protein receptor on the surface of the postsynaptic cell, usually on a dendrite (a branching extension of a neuron through which information enters the cell) or the cell body. This message may be interpreted as an excitatory stimulus or as an inhibitory stimulus. Either kind of stimulus causes a change in the properties of the receptor and of the postsynaptic cell to which it belongs, generally by changing the permeability of the cell's membrane.

EXCITATORY STIMULATION

When the stimulus is excitatory, the charge difference on the two sides of the membrane is at first lowered. A threshold level of electrical charge is reached, about -55 millivolts, and an action potential—a rapid change in electrical charges on a neuron's cell membrane, with depolarization followed by repolarization, leading to a nerve impulse moving down an axon—is generated, followed by the firing of the neuron. A self-propagating wave of depolarization results from an excitatory stimulus that causes the neuron to reach threshold. Depolarization can be defined as a shift in ions and electrical charges across a cell membrane, causing loss of resting membrane potential and bringing the cell closer to the action potential. Special proteins called sodium gates open in the cell membrane, forming a channel that allows sodium ions from outside the cell to flow rapidly down their concentration gradient into the cell's interior. As the net charge inside the cell becomes positive, the charge outside the cell becomes negative. There is a sharp rise, then a decline of the charge within the cell, called a spike, that reaches as high as 35 millivolts with the inflow of sodium ions. The action potential that results from this entry of ions acts according to the all-or-none law. A neuron will either reach the threshold and respond completely or will not reach the threshold and will not respond at all; there is no partial response. After sodium ions rush into the cell, the sodium gates close and the potassium gates open, allowing potassium ions to flow out of the cell, restoring the negative charge inside the cell. The sodium-potassium pump then must reestablish the relative ion concentrations across the membrane, necessitating a period in which the cell cannot respond to an excitatory impulse, called the absolute refractory period.

INHIBITORY STIMULATION

When the message imparted by the neurotransmitter is inhibitory, a different response occurs in the postsynaptic neuron. Instead of depolarizing the membrane by changing the membrane potential from −70 to −55 millivolts, the inhibitory message causes hyperpolarization, raising the difference in charge between the inside and outside of the membrane. The interior of the cell becomes more negative, reaching −80 millivolts or more, thus inhibiting the generation of an action potential in that cell. The inhibitory impulses help prevent the chaos that would result if excitatory impulses were firing with nothing to regulate the chain of stimulation. They also help fine-tune sensory perceptions; they can make sensations more exact and sensitive by blocking the firing of neurons around a specific point, such as the precise place on the skin that a touch is felt.

ROLE OF NEUROTRANSMITTERS

Transmission of information in the form of electrochemical messages is the job of the entire nervous system. This information movement can be understood through the study of neurotransmitters. Different parts of the nervous system show the action of many different chemicals that either excite or inhibit the passage of information by means of generation of an action potential in a postsynaptic neuron. The response of the postsynaptic neuron that leads to firing of an action potential is called an excitatory postsynaptic potential (EPSP). If such firing is instead prevented, the response is called an inhibitory postsynaptic potential (IPSP). Together these are referred to as postsynaptic potentials (PSPs).

An important aspect of the generation of these excitatory and inhibitory postsynaptic potentials is that they may be cumulative, with numerous different presynaptic cells sending different messages to the same postsynaptic cell. The messages may all be the same, leading to summation of the information. This would allow a neuron to fire even if each individual excitatory PSP is unable to reach threshold by itself, since the effect can be additive over time (temporal summation, with several messages received from the same cell in a short time) or over space (spatial summation, with several axons sending impulses at the same time). Inhibitory PSPs also have a cumulative effect, but the result of several of these would be to make it harder for the neuron to reach threshold and the development of an action potential. Alternatively, the messages coming into a neuron from several different presynaptic cells might be conflicting, some excitatory and others inhibitory. In this case, the postsynaptic cell would act like a computer and integrate the information from all presynaptic cells to determine whether the net result allows threshold to be reached. If threshold is achieved, the cell fires and a nerve impulse is generated. If threshold is not achieved, the cell does not fire, but it will be brought closer to the action potential by reduction of the voltage difference across the membrane. Since development of an action potential is an all-or-none response, no matter how the threshold is reached the same level of information passage will result. Behavior of an individual organism thus results from the actions of each separate neuron in determining the net balance of incoming information and determining whether an action potential is reached.

FOUR TYPES OF NEUROTRANSMITTERS

Neurotransmitters are the chemical messengers that act in the nervous system to excite or inhibit the postsynaptic neurons. At least four neurotransmitters have been studied in detail: acetylcholine, norepinephrine, dopamine, and serotonin. Other transmitter substances have also been examined, such as the amino acids glutamate, aspartate, gamma-aminobutyric acid (GABA), and glucine. From these studies it has been shown that the interpretation of the message lies within the postsynaptic neuron, since the same neurotransmitter may be either inhibitory or excitatory, depending on the tissues in which it is found.

Acetylcholine, for example, is found in both the brain and the peripheral nervous system. Since the peripheral nerves are more accessible to study, more is known about the activities of acetylcholine there than in the brain. Two types of cholinergic receptors (those for acetylcholine) are found in the peripheral nervous system, called muscarinic and nicotinic receptors. Acetylcholine has an excitatory effect on nicotinic receptors, as in causing the contraction of skeletal muscles, but an inhibitory effect on the muscarinic receptors, as in slowing the heartbeat. This neurotransmitter is also believed to cause excitation of tissues in the brain and in autonomic ganglia. In the cerebral cortex, acetylcholine is thought to be involved in cognitive processes, while in the hippocampus it appears to be linked to memory; in the amygdala, it seems to help control emotions.

Norepinephrine, dopamine, and serotonin are monoamines, neurotransmitters that act by means of a second messenger system to produce a postsynaptic response. In this system, cyclic adenosine monophosphate (cAMP) is produced within the cell when a neurotransmitter binds to its receptor, and the cAMP opens the ion channels (a pathway through the cell membrane, controlled by gates and used for passage of ions during electrical impulse generation) that cause excitation or inhibition to be produced. This causes a longer-lasting effect on the postsynaptic neuron, and the neurotransmitters that utilize this system are apparently involved in long-term behaviors that include memory, emotion, and motivation.

Like acetylcholine, norepinephrine is formed in both the brain and the peripheral nervous tissues, while dopamine and serotonin have been localized to brain tissues only. In the peripheral nervous system, norepinephrine interacts with two kinds of adrenergic receptors on muscle cells, the alpha and beta receptors. Alpha receptors are found on blood-vessel cells, where an excitatory effect results from binding norepinephrine. Beta receptors are seen in the lungs, heart, and intestines, tissues in which norepinephrine has different effects. Binding of the neurotransmitter to beta receptors in cardiac tissue causes excitation, while binding to lung and intestinal receptors inhibits their activities. It is still unclear how the same kind of beta receptor can have different responses in different tissues to the same chemical message.

In the brain, a diffuse system of neurons produces norepinephrine, so its effects are widespread, affecting emotion, learning, memory, and wakefulness. Dopamine is produced by cells found in the substantia nigra, the hypothalamus, and the ventral tegmental areas of the brain, where abnormal levels cause profound behavioral disorders. The related monoamine, serotonin, has distribution and behavioral effects similar to those of norepinephrine. In the upper regions of the brain, the presence of serotonin stimulates higher sensory states and sleep, while reduced levels are associated with severe depression. Since most of the effects of raised or lowered quantities of these mood-altering neurotransmitters seem to cause depression and psychoses, their study has been of great interest. Many of the drugs that have been found to elevate mood clinically act by enhancing or interfering with the action of these neurotransmitters. Through their control of excitation and inhibition of the neural impulse, neurotransmitters control an incredibly complex system of neural interconnections and neuroneffector cell interactions. If this system were under less strict control, behavioral chaos would result, as it does in certain psychiatric and psychological disorders. Applications of knowledge in this area of behavioral research may eventually lead to the ability to control such disorders chemically.

RESEARCH ON SQUID AXONS

Studies on the mechanisms of action of the neuron have been ongoing since the 1930's in giant axons of the squid nervous system. Discovered by J. Z. Young, these axons are so large that a single cell can be dissected out and examined in the laboratory. Much of what is known about the human nervous system's response to excitatory and inhibitory stimuli comes from pioneering work done on these marine mollusks. K. C. Cole and coworkers developed a voltage clamp system of electronic feedback to maintain a constant membrane potential at a chosen voltage level. The axons are penetrated by tiny electrodes and used to measure how electrical transmission occurs in different areas of the neuron across the cell membrane. A later development is the whole cell patch recording, used to examine a small area of the neuron's cell membrane with ion channels more or less intact. A classic series of papers published by Andrew Huxley and Alan Hodgkin in 1952 explained the regulation of electrical conductance along the neural membrane, including movement of ions across the sodium and potassium channels after excitatory stimulation. Huxley and Hodgkin received a Nobel Prize in 1963 for their work on squid axons.

Effect of Drugs and Transmitter Substances

Another way that excitatory and inhibitory responses are studied is with the muscarinic and nicotinic cholinergic receptors, which are inhibited from working by the actions of the drugs muscarine (from poisonous mushrooms) and nicotine (from tobacco). The drugs mimic the action of acetylcholine on these different kinds of molecules on target tissues. Less is known about the effects of acetylcholine on brain tissues, but this area of research is getting widespread attention because of the evidence that the neurotransmitter appears to be related to the development of Alzheimer's disease. Acetylcholine deficiency in the nucleus basilis is a general finding at autopsy in patients with this disease of aging, which is accompanied by loss of memory and intellectual ability and by profound personality changes.

Behavioral disturbances, including depression and mania, are also caused by abnormally high or low concentrations of norepinephrine in the brain. Some of the drugs used to treat depression are able to do so by controlling the levels of norepinephrine and thus the stimulation of excitatory and inhibitory pathways in the brain. Dopamine is associated with Parkinson's disease, in which there is an abnormally low level in the substantia nigra of the brain, and the condition can be treated by increasing the amount of dopamine and by slowing its breakdown in this region. In addition, an abnormally high level of dopamine in other parts of the brain has been associated with causing schizophrenia, suggested by the fact that drugs which block the actions of dopamine also reduce the behavioral aberrations seen in this disease. Since brains of patients with these diseases are studied at autopsy and not during the actions that cause the behaviors, it is difficult to tell what actually occurs at the synapses and whether actions are attributable to inhibition or excitation of particular neurons.

Other transmitter substances include amino acids and neuropeptides, but less information has been gathered on these chemicals, and less is known about their activities in the nervous system and behavior. Glutamate and aspartate are amino acids that are thought to be the main excitatory chemicals in use in the brain, while GABA and glycine are inhibitory. GABA is thought to be the most widespread neuro-transmitter in the brain, particularly in functions involving movement. Neuropeptides include endorphins, but the mechanisms by which they act are less well known. It is thought that certain cells are able to produce and release both a neurotransmitter such as dopamine and a neuropeptide, giving the nervous system more versatility and complexity in its decision-making capabilities. Perhaps both excitation and inhibition may be handled by the same cell at different times in its regulation of behavioral activities.

Sources for Further Study

Carlson, Neil R. *Physiology of Behavior.* 7th ed. Boston: Allyn & Bacon, 2000. An excellent resource for the psychology student on the biological aspects of behavior. The second and third chapters cover communication within and between cells of the nervous system. Emphasis is on research methods in physiological psychology.

Kolb, Bryan, and Ian Q. Whishaw. *Fundamentals of Human Neuropsychology.* 4th ed. New York: W. H. Freeman, 1995. The second chapter of this undergraduate textbook covers the physiology of the nervous system, including the function of the synapse and its excitatory and inhibitory activities. References at the end of the chapter.

Levitan, Irwin B., and Leonard K. Kaczmarek. *The Neuron: Cell and Molecular Biology.* 3d ed. New York: Oxford University Press, 2001. Designed to incorporate neurophysiology into an undergraduate curriculum, this text is very thorough on the concepts of cellular and molecular function of the neuron. Several chapters are devoted to the generation of the action potential, ion channels, and other aspects of intercellular communication. Excellent coverage of research techniques used to study excitation and inhibition. Includes a large bibliography and many diagrams.

Ornstein, Robert Evan, and Richard F. Thompson. *The Amazing Brain.* 1984. Reprint. Boston: Mariner, 1991. An excellent book on the structure and function of the brain for the general reader. Chapter 3 covers neurons and how they work, including the activities at the synapse. Many pictures but no references.

Restak, Richard M. *The Mind.* Toronto: Bantam Books, 1988. Published to accompany the Public Broadcasting Service (PBS) television series of the same title, this well-illustrated book discusses behavior as affected by neurotransmitters in chapters on aging, addiction, and depression. While not involved with inhibition and excitation processes per se, this book does address the behavioral effects of neurotransmitter action on the brain.

Tortora, Gerard J., and Nicholas P. Anagnostakos. *Principles of Anatomy and Physiology.* 9th ed. New York: John Wiley & Sons, 2000. A text for undergraduate college students, this book covers excitatory and inhibitory nerve impulses in chapter 12 on nervous tissue.

Jean S. Helgeson

SEE ALSO: Endorphins; Nervous system; Neurons; Synaptic transmission.

Insanity defense

TYPE OF PSYCHOLOGY: Psychopathology, psychotherapy

FIELDS OF STUDY: General constructs and issues; humanistic-phenomenological models

Legal insanity is a status achieved by convincing the trier-of-fact in a legal proceeding that a defendant did not possess the requisite mind-set, or mens rea, for his or her criminal behavior. It remains one of the most controversial aspects of mental health law, especially to the public. It is an important concept because mental health professionals are often required to evaluate and/or give expert testimony regarding the insanity of a criminal defendant.

KEY CONCEPTS

- civil aspects of insanity defense
- competency determination
- expert testimony
- insanity and criminal culpability

INTRODUCTION

The insanity defense is a legal provision that protects those who are sufficiently incapacitated because of mental illness or defect from being held criminally liable for their acts. It is a legal idea that reflects the humanistic belief of society and the criminal law community that criminal sanctions should be imposed only on those violations of law that are committed willfully, purposefully, knowingly, wan-

tonly, or recklessly, as is usually required by statutory criteria.

The focus of insanity defense is on the mental state of the defendant at the time the crime was committed, not the mental state at the time of trial. A defendant's mental status at the time of trial is the focus of competency evaluation. The competency determination process is concerned with the ability of defendants to understand and participate in their own legal defense.

The insanity defense can be traced as far back as the reign of the English king Henry III (1207-1272), who granted pardons to those he judged insane. By the sixteenth century, the courts in England had so frequently and consistently adopted insanity as a defense that it became a well-established defense in criminal cases whenever the facts of the case permitted. In 1800, Hadfield, a soldier who had suffered very severe head injuries in battle, was acquitted of the crime of attempting to assassinate the king because he was judged to be insane. In 1849, Edward Oxford was also acquitted of attempting to assassinate Queen Victoria on the ground of insanity. When, in 1843, Daniel M'Naghten was also acquitted on insanity grounds after murdering Edward Drummond, a major controversy arose over insanity defense. That controversy led to the first legislative insanity test requiring that the defendant must either not know the nature of the act or not know the wrongfulness of the act.

In the United States, the insanity defense remains established yet controversial. While the Supreme Court has ruled on various occasions that the execution of an insane criminal defendant is unconstitutional, jurisdictions remain divided over procedural, evidentiary, and dispositional aspects of the insanity defense. Fortunately, the number of times and cases in which insanity defense is asserted remains far fewer than the public perceives. The dispute over which mental disease or defect a defendant can use for the insanity defense remains almost as strong as was the case two hundred years ago.

INSANITY DEFENSE TESTS

Over the years, four different insanity tests have emerged, and they remain in use in one form or another in all jurisdictions. The four are the Durham test, the American Bar Association's Model Penal Code test, the M'Naghten test, and the irresistible impulse test. To establish a defense on the grounds of insanity under the Durham test, the defendant's lawyer must clearly and convincingly prove that at the time of the crime, the defendant's mental disease made it impossible for him or her to know the nature and quality of the act he or she was committing. The defendant did not know he or she was doing what was wrong, and the act is a product of mental dysfunctionality.

To establish a defense of insanity under the Model Penal Code test, it must be clearly and convincingly shown that as a result of mental disease or defect, the defendant substantially lacked the capacity to appreciate the criminality or wrongfulness of his or her conduct or to conform to the requirements of law.

To establish a defense of insanity under the M'Naghten test, it must be clearly and convincingly shown that because of his or her mental disease or defect, the defendant was incapable of forming the guilty intent or mind-set required by the crime.

To establish a defense of insanity under the irresistible impulse test, it must be clearly and convincingly shown that the defendant had a mental disease and that his or her action is an irresistible result of the disease.

THE PRACTITIONER AND INSANITY DEFENSE

For mental health professionals, it should suffice to know that all forms and variations of these tests seek to defeat the presumption of the defendant's sanity at the time the crime was committed, either because the crime was a product of mental dysfunction or the dysfunction made it impossible for the defendant to know the wrongfulness of his or her behavior. Critical for mental health professionals is that the legal viability of their expert testimony in any jurisdiction may depend on which test of insanity that jurisdiction uses. Many jurisdictions have made and are making evidentiary changes to streamline and simplify their insanity defense trials to conform with the Insanity Defense Reform Act of 1984, requiring that a defendant bear the burden of establishing his or her insanity by "clear and convincing evidence." Some jurisdictions have gone further, instituting bifurcated procedures in which the defendant's criminal responsibility is determined after a much-simplified determination of guilt or innocence. This makes it possible for an "insane" defendant to be found guilty of a crime and the evidence of insanity considered during the dispositional phase of the case. In such jurisdiction, for example, John Hinckley,

who attempted to assassinate President Ronald Reagan in 1981, would be found guilty of attempted murder because the evidence showed he did commit the act, but before his sentencing, evidence of his insanity would be introduced to determine the nature of his sentencing or responsibility.

In civil cases, defendants are usually held legally responsible for their injury to others or to property. This means that even if the defendant's harmful action is a product of mental disease or defect and/or if, as a result of the disorder, the defendant could not understand the wrongfulness of the action, he or she would still be found liable of the action. The focus of civil actions is generally to compensate the plaintiff for the wrong or loss he or she suffered. However, should a civil case be based on a wrongdoing in which intent is necessary to prove culpability, the mentally disabled defendant may not be found guilty and/or responsible. Mental health professionals need to remember that insanity for civil or criminal defense is defined by law, not by mental health diagnosis. Psychiatric diagnosis is only one of the factors generally taken into consideration in reaching a legal definition of insanity. Mental health expert testimonies about a defendant's sanity or insanity are subject to cross-examination.

SOURCES FOR FURTHER STUDY

Reisner, Ralph. *Law and the Mental Health System: Civil and Criminal Aspects.* St. Paul, Minn.: West, 1985. A textbook on mental health laws and systems. The text carefully and clearly selects, reviews, and presents legal cases that define the landscape of mental health law.

Wulach, James S. *Law and Mental Health Professionals: New Jersey.* Washington, D.C.: American Psychological Association, 1994. A comprehensive review of New Jersey laws and legal procedures that affect mental health professionals.

C. Emmanuel Ahia

SEE ALSO: Forensic psychology; Incompetency; Law and psychology.

Insomnia

TYPE OF PSYCHOLOGY: Consciousness
FIELDS OF STUDY: Sleep

Insomnia is a complaint of poor, insufficient, or nonrestorative sleep; it may be experienced for a few nights or for a lifetime. Daytime functioning is often affected. Insomnia may be caused by an underlying physiological or psychological disorder or by substance abuse, but it can also occur independently of these factors.

KEY CONCEPTS
- chronotherapy
- circadian rhythm
- persistent psychophysiological insomnia (PPI)
- polysomnography
- transient insomnia

INTRODUCTION

Insomnia is defined as a person's perception that his or her sleep is inadequate or abnormal. It may include difficulty initiating sleep, short sleep time, frequent awakenings from sleep, and sleep that is nonrestorative. The daytime symptoms of insomnia include fatigue, excessive daytime sleepiness (EDS), mood changes, and impaired mental as well as physical functioning. Insomnia can be caused by conditions such as stress, anxiety, depression, substance abuse, medical illness, or other sleep disorders, but it may stand alone in some patients, separate from any known underlying disorders. The occurrence of insomnia increases with age; one study estimates that approximately 50 percent of persons between the ages of sixty-five and seventy-nine experience trouble sleeping.

TYPES OF INSOMNIA

The Association of Sleep Disorders Centers (ASDC) recognizes two general types of insomnia. Classified on the basis of the duration of the period in which the person experiences insomnia, these two types are transient insomnia and primary insomnia. Transient insomnia is seen when persons have had a history of normal sleep but experience a period of insomnia which lasts less than three weeks; the patient returns to normal sleep after the insomnia period. The insomnia period is usually tied to a specific experience or situation, and it is believed that there are two common processes that are involved in transient insomnia. The first involves central nervous system arousal and any condition which may cause such arousal, whether it is psychological or environmental. There is no clear physiological disorder as-

sociated with this condition, but some research suggests that individuals who are likely to be aroused by stress may be more vulnerable to this type of insomnia than other people. Some sleep researchers indicate that emotional disturbance may play a role in up to 80 percent of transient insomnia cases.

A second process involved in transient insomnia results from persons having a sleep-wake schedule that is not aligned with their own circadian (twenty-four-hour) rhythms. Biological rhythms control many bodily functions, such as blood pressure, body temperature, hormonal activity, and the menstrual cycle, as well as the sleep-wake cycle. Insomnia can be caused by a sleep-wake cycle which is misaligned with the circadian rhythm, such as that which occurs when persons travel across many time zones or engage in shift work. Circadian rhythm disorders can last for periods of more than six months, in which case the problem would be considered chronic.

Primary insomnia is diagnosed when the patient's insomnia is not secondary to problems such as depression, anxiety, pain, or some other sleep disorder, and it lasts for a period longer than three weeks. Two types of primary insomnia are persistent psychophysiological insomnia (PPI) and insomnia complaints without objective findings. PPI is commonly known as learned, or behavioral, insomnia, as it is caused or maintained by maladaptive learning—that is, by the occurrence of sleep-incompatible behaviors, such as caffeine intake before bedtime. PPI is diagnosed when the patient demonstrates sleep difficulties which are verified in a sleep laboratory and are then traced to their behavioral causes. Figures vary, but approximately 15 percent of those patients diagnosed as having insomnia probably have PPI. One common feature of PPI is excessive worrying about sleep problems. Great efforts are made to fall asleep at night, which are unsuccessful and lead to increased sleep difficulty; however, the patient may fall asleep quite easily when not trying to fall asleep.

THEORIES OF INSOMNIA

One theory concerning how persistent psychophysiological insomnia can develop suggests that some people have a poor sleep-wake cycle, which makes it more difficult for them to overcome sleep-inhibiting behavior. For example, it is possible for persons to become so anxious concerning their poor sleep that even the thought of their own bedrooms causes them stress, which further increases their sleep problems and creates a cycle of increasingly difficult sleep. This cycle would eventually end for persons with normal sleep cycles, but it is much easier for these events to disrupt those who already have the poor sleep-wake cycle suggested by this theory. Although PPI may begin in response to stress or an emotional situation, it should again be noted that in PPI this type of learning or behavior plays the major role in the insomnia complaint.

Most patients with insomnia will exhibit irregular sleep patterns or polysomnographic findings when tested in a sleep laboratory; however, there are those who complain of insomnia yet show no irregular sleep patterns. In the past, these people were viewed as having "pseudoinsomnia," and they were sometimes suspected of poor sleep as an excuse for being lazy. Those who have insomnia complaints without objective findings do not show any physiological or psychological disorder and do not exhibit any sleep-incompatible behaviors, yet they commonly respond to treatment of their insomnia as would a verified insomnia patient.

One study found that insomnia was associated with anxiety, depression, psychiatric distress, and medical illness in 47 percent of the cases. The medical and psychiatric disorders, as well as the pharmacological substances, that can cause insomnia are too numerous to list here. James Walsh and Roger Sugerman note three theories which attempt to explain the occurrence of insomnia in psychiatric disorders that may prove helpful in understanding the process. The first suggests that insomnia results from a psychological disturbance that goes unresolved and leads to arousal that prevents sleep. The second states that neurochemical abnormalities may be the cause of insomnia in psychiatric disorders. The final theory asserts that affective (emotional) disorders may disturb the biological rhythms that control sleep.

DSM-IV-TR Criteria for Insomnia

PRIMARY INSOMNIA (DSM CODE 307.42)

Predominant complaint is difficulty initiating or maintaining sleep, or nonrestorative sleep, for at least one month

Sleep disturbance (or associated daytime fatigue) causes clinically significant distress or impairment in social, occupational, or other important areas of functioning

Sleep disturbance does not occur exclusively during the course of Narcolepsy, Breathing-Related Sleep Disorder, Circadian Rhythm Sleep Disorder, or a parasomnia

Disturbance does not occur exclusively during the course of another mental disorder (such as Major Depressive Disorder, Generalized Anxiety Disorder, a delirium)

Disturbance not due to direct physiological effects of a substance or general medical condition

INSOMNIA RELATED TO [AXIS I OR AXIS II DISORDER] (DSM CODE 307.42)

Predominant complaint is difficulty initiating or maintaining sleep, or nonrestorative sleep, for at least one month associated with daytime fatigue or impaired daytime functioning

Sleep disturbance (or daytime sequelae) causes clinically significant distress or impairment in social, occupational, or other important areas of functioning

Insomnia judged to be related to another Axis I or Axis II disorder (such as Major Depressive Disorder, Generalized Anxiety Disorder, Adjustment Disorder with Anxiety) but sufficiently severe to warrant independent clinical attention

Disturbance not better accounted for by another sleep disorder (such as Narcolepsy, Breathing-Related Sleep Disorder, or a parasomnia)

Disturbance not due to direct physiological effects of a substance or general medical condition

---

DIAGNOSING INSOMNIA

The importance of a greater understanding of the mechanisms of sleep and insomnia can be appreciated by everyone. Everyone knows that when one feels truly sleepy, it is difficult to concentrate, perform simple tasks, or maintain patience with other people. If this situation were to last for a week, a month, or several years, one would at least wish for it to end and at most find it nearly intolerable.

A National Institute of Mental Health survey of Americans reported that approximately 17 percent of a nationally representative sample had experienced "serious" trouble sleeping in the year prior to the survey. Other research suggests that as many as 38 percent of adults in the United States experience trouble sleeping. It is likely that at some time in life, nearly everyone has experienced some difficulty sleeping.

The trouble that many people face when trying to get a good night's rest is not the only problem caused by insomnia. Insomnia may have drastic effects on behavior during the day. Fatigue, excessive daytime sleepiness, mood changes, and impaired mental and physical functioning are all frequently caused by insomnia. Difficulties in the workplace, as well as increased health problems, are also associated with complaints of insomnia, though they are not necessarily caused by insomnia. Insomnia is not a problem that the individual faces only at night.

Diagnosis of insomnia depends on an accurate evaluation of the circumstances surrounding the complaint. The clinician must take many things into account when diagnosing each particular case, as insomnia may be the result of any number of factors in the patient's life. Questions concerning behavior should be asked to determine if the insomnia is caused by sleep-incompatible behaviors. Polysomnographic testing in a sleep laboratory may be necessary in order to determine which type of insomnia the patient has.

TREATMENT OPTIONS

Once properly diagnosed, insomnia may be treated in a number of ways, all of which are dependent on the type of insomnia with which the clinician is faced. While the typical treatment for sleeping problems in the past has been "sleeping pills," and treatment of transient insomnia may still involve small doses of a short-acting drug (such as benzodiazepines) when necessary, merely counseling or educating patients concerning situations that may increase their sleep problems is frequently found to be effective. If the transient insomnia is caused by disrupting sounds in the sleeping environment (such as snoring or traffic noise), devices that mask the noise may be used; using earplugs and placing a fan in the room to mask the noise are two simple examples of this method. If the sleep disturbance is associated with misaligned circadian rhythms, the person's bedtime may be systematically adjusted toward either an earlier or a later hour, depending on what time he or she presently goes to sleep. Strict adherence to the adjusted sleep-wake schedule is then necessary in order for the individual to remain on a regular schedule. This method is referred to as chronotherapy.

Peter Hauri suggests that treatment of persistent psychophysiological insomnia will typically involve aspects of three "domains": sleep hygiene, behavioral treatment, and the use of hypnotics. Methods involving sleep hygiene focus on educating the patient concerning proper sleep habits. Hauri states that the goal is for the patient to avoid all thoughts that may stimulate or arouse the patient. This is done by focusing on or engaging in monotonous or nonstimulating behaviors at bedtime such as reading or listening to pleasant music.

Behavioral methods include performing relaxation therapy, limiting sleep time to a few hours per night until the patient is able to use the time in bed as true sleeping time, and using stimulus control therapy. This method requires the patient to get out of bed whenever she or he is not able to sleep. The process is aimed at reducing the association between the bedroom and the frustration with trying to go to sleep. Finally, the use of hypnotic medications is indicated in patients who have such a need for sleep that they "try too hard" and thus become aroused by their efforts. As with transient insomnia, a small dose of a short-acting drug is suggested in order to break this cycle of frustration. The treatment for patients who exhibit no objective polysomnographic findings is similar to that for patients with any other type of insomnia. Such patients also tend to respond to behavioral, educational, and pharmacological methods.

SLEEP RESEARCH

The discovery of the methods used to monitor electrical activity in the human brain during the late 1920's essentially ushered in the modern era of sleep research. With this development, sleep stages were discovered, which eventually led to a greater understanding of what takes place in both normal and abnormal sleep.

A. Michael Anch, Carl Browman, Merrill Mitler, and James Walsh write in *Sleep: A Scientific Perspective* (1988) that most insomnia research prior to 1980 treated insomniacs as one group, with little attention paid to differences such as duration or causal factors in the subject's insomnia. While this limits the ability to generalize the earlier findings, these authors note that the inclusion of different types of insomnia in studies eventually increased knowledge of the psychology of sleep and insomnia.

With regard to the treatment of insomnia, much has been learned that allows doctors and psychologists to treat the different types of this disorder more effectively. The myth of the "cure-all" sleeping pill has been replaced with a more sophisticated approach, which includes educational and behavioral practices. Medications are still used, but treatment options have increased so that clinicians are not as limited as they once were.

As the study of sleep disorders has developed in terms of scientific sophistication, researchers have been able to learn the importance that sleep holds in day-to-day functioning. They have also discovered how detrimental sleep loss or disruption of the sleep-wake cycle can be. Aiding in the discoveries have been scientific developments in neurobiology, behavioral medicine, physiology, and psychiatry that allow analysis of the mechanisms in normal and abnormal sleep. It is hoped that as scientists gain a further understanding of insomnia through research, they will also understand, more generally, the true purpose of sleep.

SOURCES FOR FURTHER STUDY

Anch, A. Michael, Carl P. Browman, Merrill M. Mitler, and James K. Walsh. *Sleep: A Scientific Perspective.* Englewood Cliffs, N.J.: Prentice-Hall, 1988. A comprehensive work on the field of sleep disorders that also provides a concise history of the science. Chapter 9 covers insomnia, but the entire book is noteworthy for its broad coverage of historical as well as modern research and treatment of sleep and its disorders. A very helpful work for those interested in learning about any aspect of sleep.

Kryger, Meir H., Thomas Roth, and William C. Dement, eds. *Principles and Practice of Sleep Medicine.* 3d ed. Philadelphia: W. B. Saunders, 2000. An extremely thorough collection of articles written by many of the leaders in sleep research and treatment. Section 4 deals exclusively with insomnia and includes further information on many subclassifications of insomnia as well as on the medical and psychiatric illnesses commonly associated with insomnia.

Nicholson, Anthony N., and John Marks. *Insomnia: A Guide for Medical Practitioners.* Boston: MTP Press, 1983. Though the title may sound imposing to those who are new to the study of insomnia, this book is quite easily understood by those with a limited knowledge of sleep disorders. The entire work is devoted to insomnia, and it provides information on diagnosis and treatment of various types.

Poceta, J. Steven, and Merrill Morris Mitler, eds. *Sleep Disorders: Diagnosis and Treatment.* Totowa, N.J.: Humana Press, 1998. Aimed at primary-care physicians, offers case studies and information on sleep disorders and their treatment.

Swanson, Jenifer, ed. *Sleep Disorders Sourcebook.* Detroit: Omnigraphics, 1999. A consumer's guide to common sleep disorders and their treatments, based on government publications. Covers sleep requirements and the costs of sleep deprivation, sleep through the life span, the major sleep disorders, sleep medications, and the relationship between other disorders and sleep.

Alan K. Gibson

SEE ALSO: Aging: Physical changes; Circadian rhythms; Clinical depression; Post-traumatic stress disorder; Sleep; Sleep apnea syndromes and narcolepsy.

Instinct theory

TYPE OF PSYCHOLOGY: Motivation
FIELDS OF STUDY: Biological influences on learning; motivation theory

Until behaviorism, which rejected instincts, became the dominant theoretical model for psychology during the early decades of the twentieth century, instinct theory was often used to explain both animal and human motivation. As behaviorism faded, aspects of instinct theory returned to psychology—modernized, but still recognizable as parts of the oldest theory of motivation.

KEY CONCEPTS

- behaviorism
- instinct
- motivation
- reflex
- scientific method
- tropism

INTRODUCTION

When instinct theory was incorporated into the new scientific psychology of the late nineteenth century, it was already centuries old. In its earliest form, instinct theory specified that a creature's essential nature was already established at birth and that its actions would largely be directed by that nature. A modern restatement of this notion would be that, at birth, creatures are already programmed, as computers are, and that they must operate according to their programs. Charles Darwin's theory of evolution through natural selection, first published in 1859, led to great controversy in the late nineteenth and early twentieth centuries. It also fostered speculation that, if humans were evolved from earlier forms and were therefore more closely related to other animals than had once been believed, humans might have instincts—inherited behaviors—as other animals were observed to have. William McDougall was one of the main early instinct theorists; he suggested a list of human instincts in 1908 that included such varied behaviors as repulsion, curiosity, self-abasement, and gregariousness. Many researchers came up with their own lists of human instincts; by the 1920's, more than two thousand had been suggested.

A computer program can be printed out and studied, but an instinct in the original sense cannot so easily be made explicit. At best, it can be inferred from the behavior of an animal or person after other explanations for that behavior have been discounted. At worst, it is simply assumed from observing behavior. That a person has, for example, an instinct of argumentativeness could be assumed from the person's arguing; arguing is then "explained" by declaring that it comes from an instinct of argumentativeness. Such circular reasoning is unacceptable in scientific analyses, but it is very common in some early scientific (and many modern, popular) discussions of instinct.

VARIATIONS IN THEORY

As is often the case with ideas that have long been believed by both scientists and the general public, instinct theory has separated into several theories. The earliest form was accepted by Aristotle, the ancient Greek philosopher and scientist. He wrote in his *Politics* that "a social instinct is implanted in all men by nature" and stated that "a man would be thought a coward if he had no more courage than a courageous woman, and a woman would be thought loquacious if she imposed no more restraint on her conversation than the good man." The first comment declares an inherent quality of people; the second, inherent qualities of men and women. Very likely, Aristotle's beliefs were based on careful observation of people around him—a good beginning, but not a sufficient basis for making factual comments about people in general.

Aristotle's views were those of a scientist of his day. Centuries later, a scientist would not hold such views, but a layperson very well might. Over the many centuries since Aristotle expressed his views on instinct theory, "popular" versions of it have been more influential than the cautious versions offered by later scientists.

HISTORIC MISINTERPRETATIONS

Modern science reaches conclusions based, to the greatest extent possible, on evidence gathered and interpreted along lines suggested by theories. Traditional instinct theory is especially weak in suggesting such lines; usually it put early psychologists in the position of trying to support the idea that instinct had caused a behavior by demonstrating that nothing else had caused it. Rather than supporting one possibility, they were attempting to deny dozens of others. Even worse, they were forcing thought into an "either-or" pattern rather than allowing for the possibility that a behavior may be based on inherited influences interacting with learned ones.

For example, to try to evaluate the possibility that people are instinctively afraid of snakes, one could begin by finding a number of people afraid of snakes, followed by an attempt to discount all the ways in which those individuals might have learned their fear—that they had never been harmed by a snake, never been startled, never been told that snakes are dangerous, and so on. The task is all but impossible, almost guaranteeing that a researcher will conclude that there are several ways that the fear could have been learned, so there is no need for an instinct explanation. The fact that people who fear snakes can learn not to fear them can be offered as further evidence that they had learned their original fear—not a particularly compelling argument, but a good enough approach for a researcher who wants to discount instinct.

When behaviorism became the predominant theoretical stance of psychology in the 1920's, the problems with instinct as an explanation of motivation were "resolved" simply by sidestepping them. Instincts were discarded as unscientific, and other concepts—such as needs, drives, and motives—were substituted for them. Psychology's dropping of the term "instinct" from its jargon did not eliminate, either for lower animals or for people, the behaviors it had originally labeled; dropping the term did, however, separate even further the popular views of instinct from the scientific ones.

REEMERGENCE OF "HUMAN NATURE" RESEARCH

Instinct theory's purpose in psychology's infancy was the same as it had once been in the distant past: to explain motivation of a variety of species, from the simplest creatures up through humans. Unfortunately, it had also served other purposes in the past, purposes which often proved unwelcome to early behavioral scientists. To declare people superior to other animals, or men superior to women, or almost any target group better or worse than another was not a goal of psychology.

Worse than the heritage of centuries of misuse of the concept of instinct, however, was the accumulation of evidence that instincts (as originally defined, as completely unlearned behavior) were limited to simple creatures and were virtually nonexistent in people. Psychology and related sciences virtually eliminated instinct as a motivational concept for decades, yet they could not avoid bringing back similar notions. The term "instinct" was gone, but what it tried to explain was not. For example, social psychologists, working in the 1940's to find alternatives to the belief that aggression is instinctive in humans, proposed that frustration (goal blocking) is a major cause. When pressed to explain why frustration led to aggression, many indicated that this is simply part of human nature. Some years later, it was demonstrated that the presence of some sort of weapon during a frustrating experience enhanced the likelihood of aggression, apparently through a "triggering effect." Instinct as a concept was not invoked, but these ideas came very close.

Even closer was the work of another group of scientists, ethologists, in their explanations of some animal behaviors. Evaluating what might be thought a good example of instinct in its earliest definition, a duckling following its mother, they demonstrated that experience with a moving, quacking object is necessary. In other words, learning (but learning limited to a very brief period in the duckling's development) led to the behavior. Many other seemingly strong examples of instinct were demonstrated to be a consequence of some inner predisposition interacting with environmental circumstances. A new, useful rethinking of the ancient instinct concept had begun.

INSTINCTIVE INFLUENCES

A 1961 article by Keller and Marian Breland suggested that instinct should still be a part of psychology, despite its period of disgrace. In training performing animals, they witnessed a phenomenon they termed "instinctive drift." (It is interesting to note that although other terms, such as "species-specific behavior," were at that time preferred to "instinct," the Brelands stated their preference for the original label.) Instinctive drift refers to the tendency of a creature's trained behavior to move in the direction of inherited predispositions.

The Brelands tried to teach pigs to place coins in a piggybank; they found that although the pigs could easily be taught to pick up coins and run toward the bank, they could not be stopped from repeatedly dropping and rooting at them. Raccoons could be taught to drop coins in a container but could not be stopped from "dipping" the coins in and rubbing them together, a drift toward the instinctive washing of food. Several other species presented similar problems to their would-be trainers, all related to what the Brelands willingly called instinct.

Preparedness is another example of an instinct/learning relationship. Through conditioning, any creature can be taught to associate some previously neutral stimuli with a behavior. Dogs in Ivan Pavlov's laboratory at the beginning of the twentieth century readily learned to salivate at the sound of a bell, a signal that food would appear immediately. While some stimuli can easily serve as signals for a particular species, others cannot. It seems clear that animals are prepared by nature for some sorts of learning but not others. Rats can readily be trained to press a lever (a bar in a Skinner box) to obtain food, and pigeons can readily be trained to peck at something to do so, but there are some behaviors that they simply cannot learn to serve that purpose.

Conditioned taste aversion is yet another example of an instinctive influence that has been well documented by modern psychology. In people and other animals, nausea following the taste of food very consistently leads to that taste becoming aversive. The taste/nausea combination is specific; electric shock following a taste does not cause the taste to become aversive, nor does a visual stimulus followed by nausea cause the sight to become aversive. Researchers theorize that the ability to learn to detect and avoid tainted food has survival value, so it has become instinctive.

LIMITATIONS AND MISUSE OF THEORY

In popular use, belief in instincts has confused and hurt people more than it has enlightened or helped them. Instinct theory often imposes a rigid either-or form on people's thinking about human motivation. That is, people are encouraged by the notion of instinct to wonder if some behavior—aggression, for example—is either inherent in people or learned from experience.

Once one's thoughts are cast into such a mold, one is less likely to consider the strong likelihood that a behavior has multiple bases, which may be different from one person to the next. Instead of looking for the many possible reasons for human aggression—some related to inherent qualities and some related to learned qualities—one looks for a single cause. Often, intently focusing on one possibility to the exclusion of all others blinds people to the very fact that they are doing so. Searching for "the" answer, they fail to recognize that their very method of searching has locked their thinking onto a counterproductive track.

Instinct theory has been invoked to grant humans special status, above that of other animals. Generally, this argument states that humans can reason and rationally control their actions, while lower animals are guided solely by instincts. At best, this argument has been used to claim that humans are especially loved by their God. At worst, the idea that lower animals are supposedly guided only by instinct was used by philosopher René Descartes to claim that animals are essentially automatons, incapable of actually feeling pain, and that therefore they could be vivisected without anesthesia.

Instinct theory has also been used to support the claim that some people are more worthy than other people. Those with fewer "base instincts," or even those who by their rationality have overcome them, are supposedly superior. Acceptance of such ideas has led to very real errors of judgment and considerable human suffering. For example, over many centuries, across much of the world, it was believed that women, simply by virtue of being female, were not capable of sufficiently clear thinking to justify providing them with a formal education, allowing them to own property, or letting them hold elected office or vote. Anthropologist Margaret Mead, in her 1942 book *And Keep Your Powder Dry: An Anthropologist Looks at America*, reports reversal of the claim that women inherently lack some important quality. Young women in her classes, when told the then-prevailing view that people had no instincts and therefore that they had no maternal instinct became very upset, according to Mead, believing that they lacked something essential. Many minority racial or ethnic groups have suffered in similar fashion from claims that, by their unalterable nature, they are incapable of behaving at levels comparable to those in the majority.

Instinct theory has been used to suggest the absolute inevitability of many undesirable behaviors, sometimes as a way of excusing them. The ideas that philandering is part of a man's nature or that gossiping is part of a woman's are patently foolish uses of the concept of instinct.

SOURCES FOR FURTHER STUDY

Birney, Robert Charles, and Richard C. Teevan. *Instinct: An Enduring Problem in Psychology.* Princeton, N.J.: Van Nostrand, 1961. A collection of readings intended for college students. Contains fourteen articles, ranging from William James's 1887 discussion of instinct to Frank Beach's 1955 "The Descent of Instinct," in which Beach traces the idea of instinct from the time of the ancient Greeks up to the 1950's and concludes that "the instinct concept has survived in almost complete absence of empirical validation."

Breland, Keller, and Marian Breland. "The Misbehavior of Organisms." *American Psychologist* 16 (November, 1961): 681-684. In the process of training performing animals, the Brelands were forced to contend with inherited behaviors of their pupils. This article alerted a generation of psychologists to the possibility that instinct had been inappropriately eliminated from their thinking. The writing is clear and amusing, and the article should be fairly easy to locate; most college and university libraries will have the journal.

Cofer, Charles Norval, and M. H. Appley. *Motivation: Theory and Research.* New York: John Wiley & Sons, 1964. Long regarded as a classic on the topic of motivation, this book includes (in chapter 2, "Motivation in Historical Perspective") thirty-two pages of material that traces instinct through the centuries. Chapter 3, "The Concept of Instinct: Ethological Position," discusses ways the once discredited concept was returning to psychology in the early 1960's.

Hilgard, Ernest Ropiequet. *Psychology in America: A Historical Survey.* San Diego, Calif.: Harcourt Brace Jovanovich, 1987. The material Hilgard covers is often complex, but his clear organization and writing make it accessible to most readers. Material related to instinct in several chapters (for example, those on motivation, comparative psychology, and social psychology) can help a reader gain further background on instinct's place in psychology.

Watson, John Broadus. *Behaviorism.* Rev. ed. Chicago: University of Chicago Press, 1930. The fifth chapter of Watson's popular presentation of the new psychology he was sponsoring ("Are There Any Human Instincts?") nicely illustrates how behaviorism handled instinct. This chapter contains Watson's famous declaration, "Give me a dozen healthy infants, well-formed, and my own specified world to bring them up in and I'll guarantee to take any one at random and train him to become any type of specialist I might select. . . . " Watson's writing is still charming, but his position is today mainly a curiosity.

Weiten, Wayne. *Psychology: Themes and Variations.* 5th ed. Belmont, Calif.: Wadsworth, 2000. Introductory psychology texts all have some coverage of instinct's return to psychology and, more important, describe how several other concepts have been introduced to deal with topics with which instinct was once inappropriately linked. Weiten's text is one of the best: easy and interesting to read, yet strong in its coverage of scientific psychology.

Harry A. Tiemann, Jr.

SEE ALSO: Aggression; Aggression: Reduction and control; Behaviorism; Conditioning; Defense reactions: Species-specific; Drives; Ethology; Imprinting; Learning; Motivation; Preparedness; Reflexes; Taste aversion.

Intelligence

TYPE OF PSYCHOLOGY: Intelligence and intelligence testing
FIELDS OF STUDY: General issues in intelligence; intelligence assessment

Intelligence is a hypothetical concept, rather than a tangible entity, that is used by psychologists and other scientists to explain differences in the quality and adaptive value of the behavior of humans and, to some extent, animals. Its meaning and the theoretical models used to explore it are as varied as the field of psychology itself.

KEY CONCEPTS
- cognitive psychology
- correlation
- factor
- factor analysis
- heritability

INTRODUCTION

The idea that human beings differ in their capacity to adapt to their environments, to learn from experience, to exercise various skills, and in general to succeed at various endeavors has existed since ancient times. Intelligence is the attribute most often singled out as responsible for successful adaptations. Up to the end of the nineteenth century, notions about what constitutes intelligence and how differences in intelligence arise were mostly speculative. In the late nineteenth century, several trends converged to bring about an event that would change the way in which intelligence was seen and dramatically influence the way it would be studied. That event, which occurred in 1905, was the publication of the first useful instrument for measuring intelligence, the Binet-Simon scale, which was developed in France by Alfred Binet and Théodore Simon.

Although the development of intelligence tests was a great technological accomplishment, it occurred, in a sense, somewhat prematurely, before much scientific attention had been paid to the concept of intelligence. This circumstance tied the issue of defining intelligence and a large part of the research into its nature and origins to the limitations of the tests that had been devised. In fact, the working definition of intelligence that many psychologists have used either explicitly or implicitly in their scientific and applied pursuits is the one expressed by Edwin Boring in 1923, which holds that intelligence is whatever intelligence tests measure. Most psychologists realize that this definition is redundant and inadequate in that it erroneously implies that the tests are perfectly accurate and able to capture all that is meant by the concept. Nevertheless, psychologists and others have proceeded to use the tests as if the definition were true, mainly because of a scarcity of viable alternatives. The general public has also been led astray by the existence of "intelligence" tests and the frequent misuse of their results. Many people have come to think of the intelligence quotient, or IQ, not as a simple score achieved on a particular test, which it is, but as a complete and stable measure of intellectual capacity, which it most definitely is not. Such misconceptions have led to an understandable resistance toward and resentment of intelligence tests.

CHANGING DEFINITIONS

Boring's semifacetious definition of intelligence may be the best known and most criticized one, but it is only one among many that have been offered. Most experts in the field have defined the concept at least once in their careers. Two of the most frequently cited and influential definitions are the ones provided by Alfred Binet himself and by David Wechsler, author of a series of "second-generation" individual intelligence tests that overtook the Binet scales in terms of the frequency with which they are used. Binet believed that the essential activities of intelligence are to judge well, to comprehend well, and to reason well. He stated that intelligent thought is characterized by direction, knowing what to do and how to do it; by adaptation, the capacity to monitor one's strategies for attaining a desired end; and by criticism, the power to evaluate and control one's behavior. In 1975, almost sixty-five years after Binet's death, Wechsler defined intelligence, not dissimilarly, as the global capacity of the individual to act purposefully, to think rationally, and to deal effectively with the environment.

In addition to the testing experts (psychometricians), developmental, learning, and cognitive psychologists, among others, are also vitally interested in the concept of intelligence. Specialists in each of these subfields emphasize different aspects of it in their definitions and research.

Intelligence, as measured by tests, involves both genetics and environmental factors such as good schools. (CLEO Photography)

Representative definitions were sampled in 1921, when the *Journal of Educational Psychology* published the views of fourteen leading investigators, and again in 1986, when Robert Sternberg and Douglas Detterman collected the opinions of twenty-four experts in a book entitled *What Is Intelligence? Contemporary Viewpoints on Its Nature and Definition.* Most of the experts sampled in 1921 offered definitions that equated intelligence with one or more specific abilities. For example, Lewis Terman equated it with abstract thinking, which is the ability to elaborate concepts and to use language and other symbols. Others proposed definitions that emphasized the ability to adapt and/or learn. Some definitions centered on knowledge and cognitive components only, whereas others included nonintellectual qualities, such as perseverance.

In comparison, Sternberg's and Detterman's 1986 survey of definitions, which is even more wide ranging, is accompanied by an organizational framework consisting of fifty-five categories or combinations of categories under which the twenty-four definitions can be classified. Some theorists view intelligence from a biological perspective and emphasize differences across species and/or the role of the central nervous system. Some stress cognitive aspects of mental functioning, while others focus on the role of motivation and goals. Still others, such as Anne Anastasi, choose to look upon intelligence as a quality that is inherent in behavior rather than in the individual. Another major perspective highlights the role of the environment, in terms of demands and values, in defining what constitutes intelligent behavior. Throughout the 1986 survey, one can find definitions that straddle two or more categories.

A review of the 1921 and 1986 surveys shows that the definitions proposed have become considerably more sophisticated and suggests that, as the field of psychology has expanded, the views of experts on intelligence may have grown farther apart. The reader of the 1986 work is left with the clear impression that intelligence is such a multifaceted concept that no single quality can define it and no single task or series of tasks can capture it completely. Moreover, it is clear that in order to unravel the qualities that produce intelligent behavior, one must look not only at individuals and their skills but also at the requirements of the systems in which people find themselves. In other words, intelligence cannot be defined in a vacuum.

New intelligence research focuses on different ways to measure intelligence and on paradigms for improving or training intellectual abilities and skills. Measurement paradigms allow researchers to understand ongoing processing abilities. Some intelligence researchers include measures of intellectual style and motivation in their models.

FACTOR ANALYSIS

The lack of a universally accepted definition has not deterred continuous theorizing and research on the concept of intelligence. The central issue that has dominated theoretical models of intelligence is the question of whether it is a single, global ability or a collection of specialized abilities. This debate, started in England by Charles Spearman, is based on research that uses the correlations among various measures of abilities and, in particular, the method of factor analysis, which was also pioneered

by Spearman. As early as 1904, Spearman, having examined the patterns of correlation coefficients among tests of sensory discrimination and estimates of intelligence, proposed that all mental functions are the result of a single general factor, which he later designated g.

Spearman equated g with the ability to grasp and apply relations. He also allowed for the fact that most tasks require unique abilities, and he named those s, or specific, factors. According to Spearman, to the extent that performance on tasks was positively correlated, the correlation was attributable to the presence of g, whereas the presence of specific factors tended to lower the correlation between measures of performance on different tasks.

By 1927, Spearman had modified his theory to allow for the existence of an intermediate class of factors, known as group factors, which were neither as universal as g nor as narrow as the s factors. Group factors were seen as accounting for the fact that certain types of activities, such as tasks involving the use of numbers or the element of speed, correlate more highly with one another than they do with tasks that do not have such elements in common.

Factor-analytic research has undergone explosive growth and extensive variations and refinements in both England and the United States since the 1920's. In the United States, work in this field was influenced greatly by Truman Kelley, whose 1928 book *Crossroads in the Mind of Man* presented a method for isolating group factors, and L. L. Thurstone, who by further elaboration of factor-analytic procedures identified a set of about twelve factors that he designated as the "primary mental abilities." Seven of these were repeatedly found in a number of investigations, using samples of people at different age levels, that were carried out by both Thurstone and others. These group factors or primary mental abilities are verbal comprehension, word fluency, speed and accuracy of arithmetic computation, spatial visualization, associative memory, perceptual speed, and general reasoning.

ORGANIZATIONAL MODELS

As the search for distinct intellectual factors progressed, their number multiplied, and so did the number of models devised to organize them. One type of scheme, used by Cyril Burt, Philip Vernon, and others, is a hierarchical arrangement of factors. In these models, Spearman's g factor is placed at the top of a pyramid and the specific factors are placed at the bottom; in between, there are one or more levels of group factors selected in terms of their breadth and arranged according to their interrelationships with the more general factors above them and the more specific factors below them.

In Vernon's scheme, for example, the ability to change a tire might be classified as a specific factor at the base of the pyramid, located underneath an intermediate group factor labeled mechanical information, which in turn would be under one of the two major group factors identified by Vernon as the main subdivisions under *g*—namely, the practical-mechanical factor. The hierarchical scheme for organizing mental abilities is a useful device that is endorsed by many psychologists on both sides of the Atlantic. It recognizes that very few tasks are so simple as to require a single skill for successful performance, that many intellectual functions share some common elements, and that some abilities play a more pivotal role than others in the performance of culturally valued activities.

Another well-known scheme for organizing intellectual traits is the structure-of-intellect (SOI) model developed by J. P. Guilford. Although the SOI is grounded in extensive factor-analytic research conducted by Guilford throughout the 1940's and 1950's, the model goes beyond factor analysis and is perhaps the most ambitious attempt to classify systematically all the possible functions of the human intellect. The SOI classifies intellectual traits along three dimensions—namely, five types of operations, four types of contents, and six types of productions, for a total of 120 categories ($5 \times 4 \times 6$). Intellectual operations consist of what a person actually does (for example, evaluating or remembering something), the contents are the types of materials or information on which the operations are performed (for example, symbols, such as letters or numbers), and the products are the form in which the contents are processed (for example, units or relations). Not all the 120 categories in Guilford's complex model have been used, but enough factors have been identified to account for about 100 of them, and some have proved very useful in labeling and understanding the skills that tests measure. Furthermore, Guilford's model has served to call attention to some dimensions of intellectual activity, such as creativity and interpersonal skills, that had been neglected previously.

COMPETENCE AND SELF-MANAGEMENT

Contemporary theorists in the area of intelligence have tried to avoid the reliance on factor analysis and existing tests that have limited traditional research and have tried different approaches to the subject. For example, Howard Gardner, in his 1983 book *Frames of Mind: The Theory of Multiple Intelligences*, starts with the premises that the essence of intelligence is competence and that there are several distinct areas in which human beings can demonstrate competence. Based on a wide-ranging review of evidence from many scientific fields and sources, Gardner designated seven areas of competence as separate and relatively independent "intelligences." In his 1993 work *Multiple Intelligences*, Gardner revised his theory to include an eighth type of intelligence. This set of attributes is comprised of verbal, mathematical, spatial, bodily/kinesthetic, musical, interpersonal, intrapersonal, and naturalist skills.

Another theory is the one proposed by Robert Sternberg in his 1985 book *Beyond IQ: A Triarchic Theory of Human Intelligence*. Sternberg defines intelligence, broadly, as mental self-management and stresses the "real-world," in addition to the academic, aspects of the concept. He believes that intelligent behavior consists of purposively adapting to, selecting, and shaping one's environment and that both culture and personality play significant roles in such behavior. Sternberg posits that differences in IQ scores reflect differences in individuals' stages of developing the expertise measured by the particular IQ test, rather than attributing these scores to differences in intelligence, ability, or aptitude. Sternberg's model has five key elements: metacognitive skills, learning skills, thinking skills, knowledge, and motivation. The elements all influence one another. In this work, Sternberg claims that measurements derived from ability and achievement tests are not different in kind; only in the point at which the measurements are being make.

INTELLIGENCE AND ENVIRONMENT

Theories of intelligence are still grappling with the issues of defining its nature and composition. Generally, newer theories do not represent radical departures from the past. They do, however, emphasize examining intelligence in relation to the variety of environments in which people actually live rather than to only academic or laboratory environments. Moreover, many investigators, especially those in cognitive psychology, are more interested in breaking down and replicating the steps involved in information processing and problem solving than they are in enumerating factors or settling on a single definition of intelligence. These trends hold the promise of moving the work in the field in the direction of devising new ways to teach people to understand, evaluate, and deal with their environments more intelligently instead of simply measuring how well they do on intelligence tests. In their 1998 article "Teaching Triarchically Improves School Achievement," Sternberg and his colleagues note that teaching or training interventions can be linked directly to components of intelligence. Motivation also plays a role. In their 2000 article "Intrinsic and Extrinsic Motivation," Richard Ryan and Edward Deci provide a review of contemporary thinking about intrinsic and extrinsic motivation. The authors suggest that the use of motivational strategies should promote student self-determination.

The most heated of all the debates about intelligence is the one regarding its determinants, often described as the "nature-nurture" controversy. The "nature" side of the debate was spearheaded by Francis Galton, a nineteenth century English scientist who had become convinced that intelligence was a hereditary trait. Galton's followers tried to show, through studies comparing identical and nonidentical twins reared together and reared apart and by comparisons of people related to each other in varying degrees, that genetic endowment plays a far larger role than the environment in determining intelligence. Attempts to quantify an index of heritability for intelligence through such studies abound, and the estimates derived from them vary widely. On the "nurture" side of the debate, massive quantities of data have been gathered in an effort to show that the environment, including factors such as prenatal care, social-class membership, exposure to certain facilitative experiences, and educational opportunities of all sorts, has the more crucial role in determining a person's level of intellectual functioning.

Many critics, such as Anastasi (in a widely cited 1958 article entitled "Heredity, Environment, and the Question 'How?'") have pointed out the futility of debating how much each factor contributes to intelligence. Anastasi and others argue that behavior is a function of the interaction between heredity and the total experiential history of individuals and

that, from the moment of conception, the two are inextricably tied. Moreover, they point out that, even if intelligence were shown to be primarily determined by heredity, environmental influences could still modify its expression at any point. Most psychologists now accept this "interactionist" position and have moved on to explore how intelligence develops and how specific genetic and environmental factors affect it.

Sources for Further Study

Fancher, Raymond E. *The Intelligence Men: Makers of the IQ Controversy.* New York: W. W. Norton, 1985. Presents the history of the various debates on intelligence in a highly readable fashion. The lives and ideas of the pioneers in the field, such as Alfred Binet and Francis Galton, are described in some detail.

Gardner, Howard. *Frames of Mind: The Theory of Multiple Intelligences.* New York: Basic Books, 1983. Gardner's description of the talents he designates as "intelligences" and explanation of the reasons for his selections provide a fascinating introduction to many of the most intriguing aspects of the field, including the extremes of prodigies and idiots savants.

_____. *Multiple Intelligences: Theory into Practice.* New York: Basic Books, 1993. Gardner's update of his original theory of multiple intelligences adds an eighth intelligence to the set.

Guilford, Joy Paul. *The Nature of Human Intelligence.* New York: McGraw-Hill, 1967. Guilford describes the foundation of his theory of the structure of the intellect and in the process reviews the history of research into and theorizing about intelligence. This volume is an important contribution to the field.

Ryan, R. M., and E. L. Deci. "Intrinsic and Extrinsic Motivation." *Contemporary Educational Psychology* 25 (2000): 54-67. Reviews contemporary thinking on the subject.

Sternberg, Robert J. *Successful Intelligence.* New York: Plume, 1997. A book aimed at the layperson, describing Sternberg's theory of triarchic intelligence and its practical applications.

_____. *The Triarchic Mind: A New Theory of Human Intelligence.* New York: Viking Penguin, 1988. Sternberg reviews and criticizes the limitations of traditional views of intelligence and presents his own variations on that theme. The book is addressed to a general audience and contains intellectual exercises aimed at enhancing the reader's performance on cognitive tests.

Sternberg, Robert J., Torff, B., and E. L. Grigorenko. "Teaching Triarchically Improves School Achievement." *Journal of Educational Psychology* 90 (1998): 374-384. A review of practical application of Sternberg's theory of triarchic intelligence.

Vernon, Philip Ewart. *Intelligence: Heredity and Environment.* San Francisco: W. H. Freeman, 1979. Presents a thorough and thoughtful review of research on both sides of the "nature-nurture" debate on the development of intelligence. The issue of racial differences in intelligence is also discussed at length.

Susana P. Urbina;
updated by Ronna F. Dillon

SEE ALSO: Ability tests; Cognitive psychology; College entrance examinations; Concept formation; Creativity and intelligence; Giftedness; Intelligence quotient (IQ); Intelligence tests; Logic and reasoning; Mental retardation; Race and intelligence; Stanford-Binet test; Testing: Historical perspectives; Wechsler Intelligence Scale for Children-Third Edition (WISC-III).

Intelligence quotient (IQ)

DATE: The early twentieth century forward
TYPE OF PSYCHOLOGY: Intelligence and intelligence testing
FIELDS OF STUDY: General issues in intelligence; intelligence assessment

Intelligence quotient, referred to as IQ, is a general term used to reflect one's mental or cognitive ability. More specifically, it refers to one's ability to engage in abstract thinking or reasoning, capacity to acquire knowledge, and problem-solving ability. IQ is typically measured by comparing one's performance on a standardized measure of intelligence with the performance of similar-aged individuals.

KEY CONCEPTS
• cognitive ability
• mental quotient

INTRODUCTION

Alfred Binet and Théodore Simon in France designed the first formal test of intelligence, called the Binet-Simon scale, in 1905. Theirs was an age-based test in that items passed by a majority of children at a particular age were assigned to that age level. For instance, if the majority of nine-year-olds passed a particular item, that item was assigned to the nine-year age level.

William Stern first coined the term "mental quotient" in 1912. Mental quotient was derived by dividing mental age, as assessed by performance on a test such as the Binet-Simon, by chronological age, which yielded a ratio. Children with a ratio of greater than 1 were ahead of their age in mental development, whereas children with a ratio of less than 1 were behind their age in mental development.

In 1916, Lewis Terman published the Stanford Revision and Extension of the Binet-Simon scale, subsequently referred to as the Stanford-Binet. With the publication of the Stanford-Binet, Terman changed the term "mental quotient" to "intelligence quotient," and he changed Stern's ratio to a whole number by multiplying the ratio by 100. For example, if a person performed at the seventy-eight-month level on the Stanford-Binet (mental age) and was seventy-two months old (chronological age), his or her intelligence quotient was estimated to be 108.

CHANGE IN IQ SCORE COMPUTATION

Shortly after the publication of the Stanford-Binet, fair criticism began to emerge regarding the age-based format of the tests. The alternative suggested was a points-based test for assessing IQ. Tests that use a points-based format assign points based on correctness, quality, and sometimes swiftness of responding. These points are then converted to standard scores, which are then converted into IQ scores. David Wechsler, in the 1930's, was the first to design an intelligence test based on the points format. Current versions of his scales include the Wechsler Preschool and Primary Scales of Intelligence-III (WPPSI-III), the Wechsler Intelligence Scale for Children-III (WISC-III), and the Wechsler Adult Intelligence Scale-III (WAIS-III); these are the most widely used tests of intelligence. Each of the Wechsler scales actually yields three difference intelligence quotients: Verbal IQ, Performance IQ, and a Full Scale IQ that is a combination of the Verbal and Performance IQs.

INTERPRETATION OF IQ SCORES

IQ scores typically have a mean of 100 and a standard deviation of 15. This means that average intelligence is considered to be any score between 90 and 109. IQs from 110 to 119 are considered to be high average, while scores that range from 80 to 89 are considered to be low average. Scores that fall in the 120 to 129 range are labeled superior, while scores of 130 and above are regarded as very superior. In some instances, individuals who score above 130 are labeled as intellectually gifted. Scores in the 70 to 79 range are considered borderline scores. Those who score below 70 are usually further assessed to determine if a diagnosis of mental retardation is appropriate.

FACTORS THAT INFLUENCE IQ

The environmental factors that seem to impact IQ the most include family income, parental education level, parental occupation, and the home atmosphere, which includes the degree to which the parents press for achievement and language development and the provisions they make for their child's general learning. Although the exact degree to which genetics influences IQ is unclear, estimates are that about 30 to 50 percent of IQ is accounted for by a person's genotype.

USES OF IQ SCORES

One of the primary uses of IQ scores is to assist with the diagnosis and classification of children for special education services. Outside of education, IQ scores have been used to screen applicants for jobs, to help determine the most appropriate job placement within an organization, to assist with vocational counseling, and as part of a complete psychological assessment battery. Relatedly, IQ scores obtained between the ages of three and eighteen have been found to be a significant predictor of educational and occupational success as an adult.

CHANGES IN CONCEPTUALIZATION OF INTELLIGENCE

Early conceptualizations of intelligence were that one primary underlying cognitive ability permeated all other cognitive skills. More recently, researchers have proposed the existence of a number of essential cognitive abilities that should be reflected in the intelligence quotient and have designed tests to measure these different cognitive abilities. For instance,

Jagannath Das suggested that the intelligence quotient should reflect a person's ability to process information simultaneously and sequentially, while Raymond B. Cattell proposed that the two factors that make up intelligence are fluid intelligence and crystallized intelligence. These are two of several possible examples of how the conceptualization of intelligence and the abilities that comprise intelligence have changed.

SOURCES FOR FURTHER STUDY

Block, Ned J., and Gerald Dworkin. *The IQ Controversy*. New York: Random House, 1976. A book of edited critical readings that provides an introduction to some of the crucial issues that confront IQ testing today. Although a bit dated, much of the material is still pertinent for discussion.

Gellman, Ellen. *School Testing: What Parents and Educators Need to Know*. Westport, Conn.: Praeger, 1995. A book written in nontechnical language that describes tests, their purposes, and how scores are used in the educational system. A good overview on all kinds of tests, including IQ tests.

Herrnstein, Richard J., and Charles Murray. *The Bell Curve: Intelligence and Class Structure in American Life*. New York: Free Press, 1994. Perhaps the most controversial book ever published on the topic of IQ. The authors explore race-based differences in IQ and the relationship between IQ and social status.

Hunt, Earl. "The Role of Intelligence in Modern Society." *American Scientist* (July/August, 1995): 356. The author explores various views of the nature and structure of intelligence and provides contemporary explanations for differences in IQ. The author also provides a fair and critical analysis of *The Bell Curve*.

Sattler, Jerome M. *Assessment of Children: Cognitive Applications*. 4th ed. San Diego, Calif.: Author, 2001. The standard text in the field for psychological assessment of children. Although the book covers a variety of topics, it has over four hundred pages devoted to intellectual assessment.

T. Steuart Watson

SEE ALSO: Ability tests; Assessment; Creativity: Assessment; Intelligence; Intelligence tests; Race and intelligence; Stanford-Binet test; Wechsler Intelligence Scale for Children-Third Edition (WISC-III).

Intelligence tests

TYPE OF PSYCHOLOGY: Intelligence and intelligence
    testing
FIELDS OF STUDY: Ability tests; intelligence assess-
    ment

*Individual intelligence tests are used by psychologists
to evaluate a person's current cognitive ability and
prior knowledge. The intelligence testing movement
has a long history, including the development of numerous group and individual tests to measure one
aspect of a person's overall intelligence, which frequently changes over time.*

KEY CONCEPTS
- age norm
- cognition
- intelligence
- intelligence quotient (IQ)
- mentally gifted
- mentally handicapped
- percentile
- performance tests
- sensorimotor tests
- verbal tests

INTRODUCTION

Although means for measuring mental ability date
as far back as 2000 B.C.E., when the ancient Chinese
administered oral tests to determine a candidate's
fitness for carrying out the tasks of civil administration, the modern intelligence test has its origins
in the nineteenth century, when Jean-Étienne-
Dominique Esquirol drew a clear distinction between mentally deranged people ("lunatics") and
mentally retarded people ("idiots"). Esquirol believed that it was necessary to devise a means of
gauging "normal" intelligence so that deviations
from an agreed-upon norm could be ascertained,
and he pointed out that intellectual ability exists on
a continuum extending from idiocy to genius. His
work coincided with studies in Europe and the
United States that were designed to develop a concept of "intelligence" and to fashion a means of testing this capacity. Work done by Sir Francis Galton in
the United Kingdom on hereditary genius, by James
McKeen Cattell in the United States on individual
differences in behavior, and by Hermann Ebbinghaus in Germany on tests of memory, computation,

and sentence completion culminated in the 1905
Binet-Simon scale, created by Alfred Binet and
Théodore Simon. It was the first practical index of
intelligence measurement as a function of individual differences. This test was based on the idea that
simple sensory functions, which had formed the
core of earlier tests, are not true indicators of intelligence and that higher mental processes had to be
included.

THE BINET TESTS

French psychologist and educator Binet founded
the first French psychological laboratory. He was a
pioneer in the study of individual differences in
abilities and introduced intelligence tests that were
quickly accepted and widely used in Europe and the
United States. His work stemmed from a commission from the minister of education in Paris, who
gave him the task of devising a way to distinguish between idiocy and lunacy, as Esquirol had defined
them, and normal intelligence, so that handicapped
students could be given special instruction. Binet
and Simon used many items that had been developed by earlier examiners; the key advances they
made were to rank items in order of difficulty and
to register results in terms of age-based cognitive development. Their scale reflected the idea that intelligence was a combination of faculties—judgment,
practical sense, and initiative—and contained measures related to memory, reasoning ability, numerical facility, and object comparison.

Binet and Simon's work demonstrated the feasi-
bility of mental measurement, assessing intelligence
for the first time in general terms rather than measuring its component parts. Binet revised the test in
1908, and another revision was published in 1911,
the year of his death. Advances in his basic design
led to the development of tests that could be used
for all children (not only those considered mentally
limited) in assessing their "mental quotient," a ratio
adapted by Lewis Terman of Stanford University. It
was obtained by dividing mental age (as determined
through scores on a test) by chronological age. Terman renamed it the intelligence quotient (IQ), and
his 1916 version of the Binet-Simon scale became
known as the Stanford-Binet test, the most common
intelligence test administered in the United States
during the twentieth century. It was revised and updated in 1937, 1960, 1972, and 1986, when a point-
scale format was introduced for the first time.

THE WECHSLER TESTS

Binet's test depended on an age scale; that is, the questions which were answered correctly by a majority of ten-year-old children were assigned to the ten-year age level of intelligence. A more sophisticated version of the test devised by Robert Yerkes depended on a point scale for scoring; this format was fully developed by David Wechsler. While the Binet-Terman method used different tests for different age groups, Wechsler worked toward a test to measure the same aspect of behavior at every age level. The goal of his test was to measure intelligence in a holistic (encompassing the larger whole of personality) fashion that did not depend on the verbal skills that the Stanford-Binet tests required. Wechsler thought of intelligence as a multifaceted complex of skills, the total of an effective intellectual process; he wanted his test to show the way intelligent people behaved as a consequence of an awareness of the results of their actions. He thought that those actions would be more rational, worthwhile (in terms of social values), and meaningful than those of less intelligent people.

Wechsler's first test (the Wechsler-Bellevue Intelligence Scale) was published in 1939, and it awarded points for each answer depending on the level of sophistication of the response. The test consisted of six verbal subjects (information, comprehension, arithmetic, similarities, vocabulary, and digit span) and five performance subtests (picture completion, picture arrangement, block design, object assemblies, and digit symbols). The division into verbal and performance skills permitted the calculation of three intelligent quotients: a verbal IQ based on the sum of the verbal tests, correlated with norms of age, a performance IQ based on the sum of performance tests, and a full-scale IQ derived from the sum of all the answers. The test was standardized on a sample of adults, and it could be used to test individuals who had linguistic or sensorimotor handicaps. The pattern of scores on the separate tests could also be used to diagnose learning disability or, in some situations, clinical disorder or dysfunction.

The original test was limited by the sample used for standardization, but the 1955 Wechsler Adult Intelligence Scale (WAIS) provided a basis for testing adults from the ages of sixteen to seventy-five. Further revision in the standard scale (including the WAIS-R, 1981) updated the test to coincide with changes in cultural experience. In addition, a Wechsler Intelligence Scale for Children (WISC) was designed to cover ages five to fifteen in 1949 and was revised (WISC-R) in 1974 to cover ages six to sixteen. In 1991, another revision (WISC-III) was introduced. Subsequent modifications also led to a test suitable for preschool children, the Wechsler Preschool and Primary Scales of Intelligence (WPPSI) of 1967, which covered ages four to six and a half and included mazes, animal figures, and geometric designs. This test was revised in 1981 (WPPSI-R) to extend its range over three years to seven years, three months. Further adjustments have also been made to account for a candidate's sociocultural background in a test called the System of Multicultural Pluralistic Assessment (SOMPA, 1977).

Recent definitions of intelligence have resulted in further development of testing instruments. Raymond Cattell's proposal that intelligence could be divided into two types—fluid (or forming) and crystallized (fixed)—led to a test that used figure classification, figure analysis, and letter and number series to assess the essential nonverbal, relatively culture-free aspects of fluid intelligence; it used vocabulary definition, abstract word analogies, and general information to determine the skills that depend on exposure to cultural processes inherent in crystallized intelligence. Other theories, such as Jean Piaget's idea that intelligence is a form of individual adaptation and accommodation to an environment, led to the development of a test which measures mental organization at successive ages.

USES OF INTELLIGENCE ASSESSMENT

There was a tendency at various times during the twentieth century to regard intelligence assessment as an answer to questions of placement and classification in almost every area of human experience. The most effective and scientifically valid uses of tests, however, have been in predicting performance in scholastic endeavor, in revealing disguised or latent ability to assist in career counseling, in determining the most appropriate developmental programs for handicapped or mentally handicapped individuals, in locating specific strengths and weaknesses in an individual, in measuring specific changes associated with special programs and forms of therapy, and in comparing a child's mental ability with other children observed in a similar situation to establish a profile of cognitive skills.

One of the most widespread and effective uses of intelligence tests is the determination of possible problems in a child's course of basic education. As reported by Lewis Aiken in *Assessment of Intellectual Functioning* (1987), a typical case involved an eight-year-old boy with a suspected learning disability. He was given the WISC-R test in 1985, and his full-scale IQ was figured to be 116, placing him in the high average classification. This provided an assessment of general intelligence and scholastic aptitude. His verbal IQ was 127, placing him in the ninety-seventh percentile, indicative of exceptional verbal comprehension. This suggested that he could reason very well, learn verbal material quickly, and process verbal information effectively. His performance IQ of 98 placed him in the average category, but the magnitude of the difference between his verbal and performance IQs is very unusual in children of his age. It pointed to a need for additional interpretive analysis, as well as further study to reveal the reasons behind the discrepancy. Close scrutiny of the test results showed that low scores on the arithmetic, digit span, and coding subtests might indicate a short attention or memory span, poor concentration, or a lack of facility in handling numbers. While no absolute conclusions could be drawn at this point, the results of the test could be used in conjunction with other procedures, observation, and background information to determine an appropriate course of action.

INTELLIGENCE AND GUIDANCE

Another common use of an intelligence test is to help an examinee determine specific areas of ability or aptitude which might be useful in selecting a career route. As reported in Aiken, a college senior was given the Otis-Lennon School Ability Test (O-LSAT, Advanced Form R) just before her twenty-second birthday. She planned to enroll in a program in a graduate business school and work toward a master of business arts degree. The O-LSAT is designed to gauge general mental ability, and it includes classification, analogy, and omnibus (a variety of items to measure different aspects of mental functioning) elements. The omnibus includes verbal comprehension, quantitative reasoning, and the ability to follow directions. The examinee was able to complete the test in thirty-five minutes and used the remaining allotted time to check her answers. Her raw score (number of items answered correctly)

was 64 (out of 80), her school ability index was 116—which approximated her IQ—and her percentile rank among candidates in the 18-plus range was 84. These scores were in the average range for college seniors, indicating an overall intellectual ability that could be classified as "high average" in terms of the general population. Of the sixteen items answered incorrectly, a superficial analysis pointed toward some difficulty with nonverbal reasoning, but no conclusions could be reached without further examination in this area. There was no significant pattern of errors otherwise, and the random distribution offered no additional guide to areas of weakness. The initial conclusion that was drawn from the test was that a career in business was appropriate, and that with hard work and the full application of her intellectual abilities, she would be able to earn an M.B.A. at a reputable university.

A particularly important application of intelligence assessment is the identification and guidance of a child with advanced intellectual abilities. In a case reported in Jerome M. Sattler's *Assessment of Children* (1988), a three-year-old boy was tested repeatedly from that age until his sixth birthday. This procedure required the implementation of the Stanford-Binet Form L-M, the WPPSI, and the Peabody Individual Achievement Test (PIAT) for grade equivalents. The Stanford-Binet scores were 127 (at age three), 152, 152, and 159+ (with a linear extrapolation to 163). During his first test he was anxious and did not give long verbal responses, but the range of his scores indicated a very superior classification. He did not cooperate with the examiner on the WPPSI vocabulary and animal subtests (the examiner believed that he was not interested), but his performance at age four placed him in the superior range. On the PIAT, he was consistently above average, earning a grade equivalent above 4.0 at the age of six, with a grade equivalent of 7.4 (his highest score) in mathematics; the average grade equivalent for age six is 1.0.

As Sattler points out, the case illustrates "a number of important principles related to testing and assessment." In the largest sense, it illustrates the way different tests measuring general intelligence may yield different results (although all pointed toward superior mental development). The same test may also yield different scores at different age levels. The child's motivation (among other factors) may also play an important part in his results. More specifically, since the boy showed more interest in read-ing at age three and mathematics at age six, the test could not be considered a useful predictor of later interest, although an interest in solving perceptual-logical problems remained consistent throughout. Finally, since the parents had kept a detailed record of the boy's early development in a baby book, the rich history recorded there was corroborated by the test results which reaffirmed their initial suspicions that the boy was unusually gifted. During his first year in school, he tended to play alone and had fre-quent minor tantrums which affected his perfor-mance in school subjects. When he became accus-tomed to the social process of school life, however, he was able to demonstrate the ability that his par-ents had observed at home and that the initial tests validated.

DEFINITIONS OF INTELLIGENCE

While intelligence tests of some sort appeared in human history as early as the Old Testament book of Judges (7:3-7, 12:6), which indicates that early Jewish society used questions and observations in personnel selection, the intelligence test as it is known today can be traced to Renaissance Europe. In 1575, the Spanish physician Juan Huarte wrote *Examen de Ingenios*, a treatise concerning individual differences in mental ability with suggestions for ap-propriate tests. His work, and that of other investiga-tors and theorists, was the result of the rise of a mid-dle class with aspirations to productive employment. Previously, the aristocracy had controlled every-thing, and fitness for a position was determined by lineage. Once this monarchical rule began to break down, other means were necessary for determining who was fit for a particular occupation and what might be the most productive use of a person's abili-ties. When it became apparent that royal blood was no guarantee of competence, judgment, or mental acuity, the entire question of the origins of intelli-gence began to occupy members of the scientific community. For a time, the philosophy of empiri-cism led scientists toward the idea that the mind it-self was formed by mental association among sense impressions, and sensorimotor tests were particu-larly prominent. As the results of these tests failed to correlate with demonstrations of mental ability (such as marks in school), however, other means were sought to measure and define intelligence. The interest in intelligence testing in the nine-

teenth century was an important aspect of the devel-opment of psychology as a separate scientific disci-pline, and the twin paths of psychometric (that is, the quantitative assessment of an individual's attrib-utes or traits) and statistical analysis on one hand and philosophical conjecture concerning the shape and operation of the mind on the other were joined in experimentation concerning methods of assess-ing intelligence.

From their first applications in France as a diag-nostic instrument, intelligence tests have been used to help psychologists, educators, and other profes-sionals plan courses of action to aid individuals suf-fering from some mental limitation or obstacle. This role has been expanded to cover the full range of human intellectual ability and to isolate many in-dividual aspects of intelligence in myriad forms. The profusion of tests has both complicated and deepened an understanding of how the mind func-tions, and the continuing proposition of theories of intelligence through the twentieth century resulted in an increasingly sophisticated battery of tests de-signed to assess and register each new theory.

MODERN TESTING

In addition, technological developments, particu-larly the growing use of computers, permit a wider use of flexible testing in which the decision about what item or task to present next depends on the previous answer. Computers are also useful in "num-ber crunching," so that such basic components of a test system as norms, derived scores, and reliability and validity coefficients (the basic statistical mate-rial behind the calculation of scores) can be assem-bled more quickly and efficiently. Computers also make it possible to administer tests at multiple sites simultaneously when an individual examiner's pres-ence is not necessary. Nevertheless, the human ca-pacity for judgment and analysis in the interpreta-tion of results remain crucial to test procedures.

Intelligence testing is likely to continue as a pri-mary means of predicting educational or vocational performance, but tests designed to measure the mind in terms of its ability to process information by shifting strategies in response to a changing envi-ronment are likely to become more prevalent. The proliferation of more detailed, separate sets of norms for different groups (age, sex, ethnic origin, and so on) is likely to continue. Also, the relation-ship between intelligence per se and behavioral attitudes that seem to resemble aptitude rather than personality measures is part of the heredity-environment controversy that will continue. Finally, advances in studies on the neurophysiological bases of intelligence will be reflected in tests responsive to a growing understanding of the biochemical aspects of cognition. As an operating principle, though, professionals in the field will have to be guided by a continuing awareness that intelligence testing is only one aspect of understanding a person's total behavior and that the limitations involved in the measuring process must be understood to avoid incorrect or inappropriate diagnoses that might prove harmful to an individual.

Howard Gardner postulated a theory of intelligence which focuses on a symbol system approach that combines both factor analytic and information processing methodology. He included seven dimensions of intelligence: verbal and linguistic, mathematical and logical, visual and spatial, body and kinesthetic, musical and rhythmical, interpersonal, intrapersonal, and environmental. The concept of types of intelligence is not new. L. L. Thurstone developed a test of eight scales named the Primary Mental Abilities test. Edward L. Thorndike identified several types of intelligence: abstract, social, and practical. Sternberg used informational processing and cognitive theory in his model of intelligence and identified three different types of information processing components: metacomponents, performance components, and knowledge acquisition components. He saw metacomponents as the higher-order control processes used to oversee the planning, monitoring, and evaluation of task performance.

SOURCES FOR FURTHER STUDY

Gardner, Howard. *Multiple Intelligences: The Theory in Practice*. New York: Basic Books, 1993. Gardner discusses his theory of multiple intelligences, which takes into consideration the psychological, biological, and cultural dimensions of cognition.

Goldstein, Gerald, and Michael Hersen, eds. *Handbook of Psychological Assessment*. 2d ed. New York: Macmillan, 1990. There are a series of chapters on assessment of intelligence as well as on psychometric foundations of testing.

Herrnstein, R. J., and C. Murray. *The Bell Curve: Intelligence and Class Structure in American Life*. New York: Free Press, 1994. The book presents views of intelligence in today's society which are not widely accepted.

Jensen, Arthur. *The "G" Factor: The Science of Mental Ability*. Westport, Conn.: Praeger, 1998. The author discusses the structure of intelligence.

Kampaus, Randy W. *Clinical Assessment of Child and Adolescent Intelligence*. 2d ed. Boston: Allyn & Bacon, 2001. A good overview of intelligence tests used with children and adolescents.

Sternberg, Robert J., ed. *Handbook of Intelligence*. New York: Cambridge University Press, 2000. The writers discuss the history and theory of intelligence, the development of intelligence and the biology of intelligence.

Leon Lewis and James R. Deni;
updated by Robert J. Drummond

SEE ALSO: Ability tests; Assessment; Career and personnel testing; College entrance examinations; Creativity: Assessment; General Aptitude Test Battery (GATB); Human resource training and development; Intelligence; Intelligence quotient (IQ); Interest inventories; Peabody Individual Achievement Test (PIAT): Race and intelligence; Scientific methods; Stanford-Binet test; Survey research: Questionnaires and interviews; Testing: Historical perspectives; Wechsler Intelligence Scale for Children-Third Edition (WISC-III).

Interest inventories

TYPE OF PSYCHOLOGY: Personality
FIELDS OF STUDY: Personality assessment

Interest inventories are questionnaires that have been developed for the purpose of assessing an individual's patterns of interest in or preference for a variety of activities. Most commonly, the interest inventory is designed to assist a person in making decisions about future educational and career directions.

KEY CONCEPTS
- criterion group
- Holland's typology
- inventory
- reference group
- trait-factor approach
- validity

INTRODUCTION

Since the inception of the interest inventory in the late 1920's, its development in the context of educational and vocational counseling has expanded considerably. The interest inventory is a questionnaire-type device designed to measure the intensity and breadth of an individual's interests. Most often, the specific interests measured by an inventory relate to a variety of vocational and avocational activities. The term "interest" refers to a very specific aspect of human behavior. An interest is an enduring trait, a predilection for a particular activity, avocation, or object. It is a special attitude that engages the individual and motivates him or her to move toward the object of interest.

An interest inventory is distinct from both an achievement test and an aptitude test. An achievement test measures an individual's current ability to perform a particular task. An aptitude test measures potential or capacity for performing that task in the future. An interest inventory, on the other hand, measures a person's liking for a particular task without reference to the individual's actual ability to perform the task or potential for doing so in the future. For example, a high school student may show a high interest in the field of nursing. This interest alone, however, does not mean that he or she has any current nursing skills, nor does it indicate that the student has the mental ability, physical stamina, or emotional makeup for success in the nursing field.

What then is the rationale for examining patterns of interest? First, interest in a particular activity provides some motivation for engaging in that activity. Therefore, when one identifies areas of interest, one is also identifying areas in which a person might have the degree of motivation necessary for following through on that activity. Second, the scores obtained from an interest inventory are helpful in pointing out which groups of persons an individual most resembles. Finally, it has been shown that there is some relationship between a person's domain of interest and the occupational field that that person may eventually choose.

The construction of an interest inventory may be empirically based (that is, based on observation of factual information) or theory-based (based on systematic principles concerning occupational categories). Some inventories have utilized a combination of these approaches. In its development, the empiri-cally based inventory would be administered to various criterion groups of successful persons representing particular occupations. The inventory would also be given to a reference group, a large group representing people in general. The items on the inventory that set apart a particular criterion group from the larger reference group would then become part of the scale for that occupation. A person would be considered to have a high score on a particular occupational scale if he or she has interests that closely match the criterion group's interests.

Other inventories are simply based on occupational theory. One well-known theory that has been utilized in the construction of interest surveys was first set forth in John L. Holland's 1992 publication *Making Vocational Choices: A Theory of Careers*. The theory involved the categorization of occupations into the following six types: realistic, investigative, artistic, social, enterprising, and conventional. Other occupational categories have also been devised and utilized as the bases for interest inventory construction and scoring. Interest inventories also differ on the basis of the format used in the construction of the items. Some inventories ask the individual to indicate the degree of interest he or she has in a particular activity, whereas others use a forced-choice format, asking the testee to make an either/or choice between two activities.

POPULAR INVENTORIES

In their book *Career Guidance and Counseling Through the Life Span* (1996), Edwin L. Herr and Stanley H. Cramer reviewed some commonly used interest inventories. Some of the inventories, such as the well-known Strong Interest Inventory (SII), the Career Assessment Inventory (CAI), and the Vocational Preference Inventory (VPI), yield results based on Holland's six general occupational themes. Others, such as the Career Occupational Preference System (COPS) and the Vocational Interest Inventory (VII), are constructed around Anne Roe's eight occupational groups.

Interest inventories also differ in terms of their intended use. The Interest Determination, Exploration, and Assessment System (IDEAS) was developed for grades six through twelve; the Geist Picture Interest Inventory (GPII) is intended for culture-limited and educationally deprived populations; and the Kuder Occupational Interest Survey

(KOIS) is designed for high school students and adults. The scope of occupations explored is another variable. The Minnesota Vocational Interests Inventory (MVII) deals with skilled occupations, while the COPS, Form P, deals with professional occupations. Some inventories are hand-scored, while others are scored by computer. Tests such as the SII can be computer-administered as well. Some of the inventories are designed to be used in conjunction with the Dictionary of Occupational Titles, published by the U.S. Employment Service, or the Occupational Outlook Handbook, published by the U.S. Department of Labor, Bureau of Labor Statistics, and available on the World Wide Web. The KOIS and the Ohio Vocational Interest Inventory (OVII) are two such examples.

There are various ways to judge the relative value or dependability of these measurement devices. First of all, one must consider the reliability of the inventory. Interests are human traits with a somewhat enduring quality. They are not expected to change radically over a short period of time. The reliability of the inventory is a measurement of how stable scores on the inventory would be if the inventory were administered to the same person over a period of time.

A second consideration in determining the value of an inventory is its validity. Though there are many ways to approach test validity, the aim is to determine if the inventory is really measuring interests as opposed to some other trait. Studies are often undertaken to see if scores on one interest inventory are consistent with scores on another interest inventory which is considered to be a valid measure. Another test of validity involves giving the interest inventory to persons in that occupation to see if their interest scores emerge in the direction expected. Information about the specific reliability and validity of a particular interest inventory are reported in the manual developed for its use.

Of particular concern in evaluating an interest inventory is the possibility of sex-role bias. The extent to which an interest inventory is constructed to perpetuate stereotypic male and female roles is a major issue. The SII, for example, attempted to use both male and female criterion groups for each occupation on the inventory. This posed some problems, such as finding sufficient numbers of males or females in certain occupations. Care was also taken in revisions to eliminate inappropriate references to

gender; for example, "policeman" was changed to "police officer."

INVENTORY USES

Interest inventories are typically used in educational and vocational counseling. Most interest inventories are devised to assist a person in pinpointing possible career options. This entails assessing not only his or her interests in terms of particular careers but also interests related to college majors. Often an interest inventory will be helpful in determining where an individual's interests lie in relation to larger clusters of occupational groupings. Interest inventories are also used by researchers in obtaining information about the vocational interests of specific groups for the purpose of planning and implementing career training programs and noting overall occupational trends.

The following case study serves as an illustration of the practical use and interpretation of the interest inventory. It includes a student profile based on the KOIS and the recommendations that a counselor might make to this student in the light of the results obtained.

"John" is a seventeen-year-old adolescent in his junior year of high school. He is enrolled in a college preparatory program and has often verbalized at least a tentative interest in following in the footsteps of his father, who works in commercial real estate appraisal. His grades in art and drafting classes indicate that he has a propensity for visual thinking and illustration. John would be the first to admit, however, that his interests are very practical in nature, and he is not drawn toward philosophical debates. John's entire class was administered the KOIS through the counseling and guidance department of his school. The tests are computer-scored, and results are distributed to the students during individual appointments with the school counselor.

John's KOIS report form indicates that his results appear to be dependable. His interests in ten vocational activities are ranked in order of his preference for each. As compared with other males, his top interests, which are literary, persuasive, artistic, and mechanical, are average in intensity. The two areas ranked least interesting to John are social service and musical. John's patterns of interest as compared with men in many different occupations are most consistent with auto salesperson, photographer, travel agent, buyer, retail clothier, radio station manager, and real estate agent. Furthermore, John shows an interest pattern most similar to men in the following college majors: business administration, physical education, economics, and engineering.

John's counselor reminds John that the KOIS measures interests, not aptitudes or other personal variables that are part of a successful career match. The counselor observes that John's KOIS profile does accentuate some of the areas of interest to which John has alluded during his high school years. She notes that on the KOIS there were several indications that John might like an occupation related to business and sales.

As a follow-up to the KOIS, the counselor points out that John could benefit from exploring various school programs which offer the college majors that surfaced on his report form. She encourages John to talk to college representatives about his particular interests. She suggests that John look into some of the occupations that appeared on his KOIS report and possibly utilize such resources as the U.S. Department of Labor's Guide for Occupational Exploration in learning about working conditions, employment prospects, promotion opportunities, and related occupational opportunities. The counselor also encourages John to talk with persons working in those general areas of employment that appeared on his KOIS. Exploration of other careers in the same job families as those which appeared on his report form might also prove beneficial. For John, the KOIS is probably the most beneficial in providing him with the impetus for continued career exploration.

The counselor, in perusing all the scores of the junior class members with whom she is working, may note overall patterns of interest appearing in the KOIS report forms. This information may lead her to make certain provisions for those interests in the school's career awareness program, in the type of invited speakers, and in the kinds of college and training program representatives invited to make presentations at the school. While John was given the opportunity to take an interest inventory in high school, there are other situations in which a person may do so. Professional career counselors offer such opportunities to interested parties through college and university career centers and vocational rehabilitation services, in workshops for those planning second careers, and in private practice settings.

Vocational Counseling

Interest inventories can be situated in the overall context of vocational counseling, a field whose origins stemmed from the focus on job productivity and efficiency that arose during the Industrial Revolution. Frank Parsons is credited with laying the foundation for the field of career development. In his book *Choosing a Vocation* (1909), Parsons articulated a conceptual framework for career decision making. He emphasized that career decision making must be based upon a clear understanding of one's personal attributes (such as aptitudes, interests, and resources) as related to the requirements of the job field. Parsons's theory provided the theoretical backdrop for the more scientifically oriented trait-factor approach to vocational counseling which would soon follow.

Getting displaced American workers back on the job was a major impetus in vocational counseling after the Great Depression of the 1930's. During that era, the University of Minnesota became a center for the development of new assessment devices to measure individual differences, and researchers there designed instruments that became part of test batteries used in counseling centers around the country. E. G. Williamson's work in career counseling research led to the publication of the *Dictionary of Occupational Titles* by the U.S. Employment Service in 1939. D. G. Paterson and J. G. Darley were also prominent among those psychologists who developed what is referred to as the "Minnesota point of view," or trait-factor theory.

Trait-Factor Theory

This trait-factor approach has been the basis for many of the interest inventories which have been devised. Attempts were made to match the personal traits (in this case, interests) of the individual with the requirements of particular careers and job environments. The interest inventories have been the most widely used.

The first version of the SII was published in 1927 by Edward K. Strong, Jr., from Stanford University; this inventory has been in use ever since. At that time it was known as the Strong Vocational Interest Blank (SVIB), a project on which Strong worked tirelessly, revising and improving it until his death in 1963. In that same year, David P. Campbell at the University of Minnesota Center for Interest Measurement Research assumed the task of continuing to update Strong's work. Along with Jo-Ida Hansen, Campbell produced the interest inventory that was redesignated the Strong-Campbell Interest Inventory in its fourth (1985) edition.

Probably the most common alternative to the SII is the KOIS, which was first published by G. Frederic Kuder as the Kuder Preference Record. Differences can be noted between the KOIS and the SII in terms of their technical construction and scales.

While many interest inventories have been devised since the idea was first conceived, most of these inventories have focused on interests in career activities and related college majors. The 1970's, however, brought about the notion of inventories designed to measure leisure interests. Richard N. Bolles, in his book *The Three Boxes of Life* (1981), indicated that, in addition to meaningful work, people need to engage in the pursuit of two other "boxes," that of learning/education and that of leisure/playing. This more holistic approach may be more evident in the interest inventories yet to be developed.

SOURCES FOR FURTHER STUDY

Bolles, Richard. *What Color Is Your Parachute?* 32d ed. Berkeley, Calif.: Ten Speed Press, 2001. One of the best selling career books. Filled with useful exercises.

Bringman, Wolfgang. *A Pictorial History of Psychology.* Chicago: Quintessen, 1997. The book contains photographs and biographical sketches of important figures in the history of psychology.

Farr, J. Michael, and Lavern Lidden. *Guide to Occupational Exploration.* Indianapolis: JIST, 2000. The guide provides information on twelve job clusters identified by the U.S. Department of Labor.

Farr, J. Michael, Lavern Lidden, and Lawrence Shatkin. *Enhanced Occupational Outlook Handbook.* 5th ed. Indianapolis: JIST, 2001. The handbook is based on the data provided users by the U.S. Department of Labor.

Gregory, Robert. *Psychological Testing: History, Principles, and Applications.* Boston: Allyn & Bacon, 1996. A good summary of the history of psychological testing, as well as early testing in the United States.

Herr, Edward, and Stanley Kramer. *Career Guidance and Counseling Through the Life Span.* 6th ed. New York: HarperCollins, 1996. One of the most comprehensive books on career counseling.

Kapes, Jerome, and Edwin Witfield, eds. *Guide to Career Assessment Instruments.* 4th ed. Columbus, Ohio: NCDA, 2001. Presents critical review of the widely used tests in the career field and includes interest tests, work values tests, and career adjustment tests.

Sacks, Peter. *Standardized Minds: The High Price of America's Testing Culture and What We Can Do to Change It.* Cambridge, Mass.: Perseus Books, 1999. Reviews current controversies in testing.

Zunker, Vernon. *Career Counseling: Applied Concepts of Life Planning.* 6th ed. Pacific Grove, Calif.: Brooks/Cole-Thomson Learning, 2002. A good developmental perspective on career counseling.

Karen M. Derr;
updated by Robert J. Drummond

SEE ALSO: Ability tests; Career Occupational Preference System (COPS); Career and personnel testing; Career selection, development, and change; Kuder Occupational Interest Survey (KOIS); Strong Interest Inventory (SII); Testing: Historical perspectives; Work motivation.

Intergroup relations

TYPE OF PSYCHOLOGY: Social psychology
FIELDS OF STUDY: Aggression; group processes; prejudice and discrimination

Theories of intergroup relations examine the processes that underlie relationships between individuals belonging to different groups; these theories provide insights into conflict, ethnocentrism, self-esteem, and leadership.

KEY CONCEPTS
- displaced aggression
- ethnocentrism
- in-group
- out-group
- relative deprivation
- social mobility
- superordinate goals

INTRODUCTION

The major psychological theories of intergroup relations include Freudian theory, equity theory, rela-

Despite the potential for conflict, friendships may develop across minority and majority groups. (CLEO Photography)

tive deprivation theory, social identity theory, realistic conflict theory, and the "five-stage model" of intergroup relations. The first three theories are the most reductionist and attempt to reduce intergroup relations to the level of intrapersonal and interpersonal processes. In contrast, social identity theory, realistic conflict theory, and the five-stage model provide explanations at the level of intergroup processes.

Within the general domain of psychology, intergroup theories constitute a subdiscipline of social psychology. The major books that have reviewed intergroup theories have all noted that intergroup relations is still a relatively neglected topic in social psychology. The main reason for this is that social psychology has tended to be reductionist and to seek to explain all social behavior by focusing on processes within and between individuals, rather than within and between groups.

The personal histories of researchers have undoubtably been important factors in the development of intergroup theories. For example, many of the major theories were initiated by researchers who

were themselves outsiders in one way or another and who thus had firsthand experience of prejudice. These include Sigmund Freud (1856-1939), a Jew who lived in Vienna most of his life and had to flee to escape the invading Nazis at the start of World War II; Muzafer Sherif (1906-1988), a Turk who moved to the United States after experiencing political problems in his home country; and Henri Tajfel, a Jewish refugee from Eastern Europe who found a home in England after World War II.

FREUD'S INFLUENCE

Although Sigmund Freud did not develop a formal theory of intergroup relations, his writings on hostility and aggression have had a historic influence on most of the major intergroup theories. Freud presented an irrationalist account of group processes, arguing that conflict arises out of the irrational feelings and emotional needs of in-group members, rather than as a result of differences between the material interests of groups.

Freud proposed that feelings of both love and aversion are involved in emotional ties between individuals. Group members are bound together by the ties of love that link them all with the group leader. The corresponding feelings of hate do not disappear, but are displaced onto out-groups. Freud believed that it is possible for ties of love to bind a number of people together as long as there are some other people left over onto whom hatred can be displaced. The most likely targets for such displaced aggression (aggression that is directed at an object, such as a person or group, which is not responsible for the events that initiated the aggression) would be out-groups that are more dissimilar.

Thus, for Freud, the key to understanding relations between groups lies in the nature of relations within groups, particularly relations between group members and the leader. Freud believed that the only groups worth considering are groups with leaders, because without leadership the group cannot be cohesive and effective in action.

THEORETICAL PERSPECTIVES

Equity theory is also reductionist in its account of intergroup relations, but, in contrast to the Freudian model, equity theory presents a picture of humans as rational beings. The main focus of equity theory is relations between individuals, but it also has implications for intergroup relations. The starting premise is that individuals strive to maximize rewards for themselves, but this "selfishness" is pursued within the norms of justice prevalent in society.

Individuals are assumed to feel distressed when they do not achieve justice in their relationships. Justice is achieved when the ratio of a person's inputs and outcomes is equal to that of the other person in the relationship. When this ratio is not equal, justice can be restored by adjusting the inputs and outcomes, either psychologically or in practice, to arrive at an equal ratio.

What makes equity theory a psychological theory rather than simply a model of economic exchange is that perceived justice is assumed to determine relations between group members. For example, the relations between a minority group and a majority group may in actual practice by very unequal, but the ratio of inputs and outcomes for the two groups may be seen to be equal by both groups; this perceived equality is what determines behavior.

Similar in its emphasis on purely psychological determinants of relations between groups is relative deprivation theory. This theory focuses on the conditions associated with feelings of discontent among disadvantaged individuals and, by implication, groups. Feelings of satisfaction are assumed to be primarily determined not by objective conditions but rather by one's perceptions of one's own situation relative to that of others. Theorists disagree about the exact conditions required in order for relative deprivation to be experienced; however, two generally accepted preconditions for feelings of discontent are that individuals must, first, think they deserve to attain a better situation and, second, believe it possible to do so.

A major European theory, and one that inspired much research since the 1970's, is social identity theory. This theory focuses on groups with unequal power and predicts the conditions in which people will feel motivated, individually or collectively, to maintain or change their group membership or the relations between their in-group and the out-groups. Social identity theory assumes that individuals are motivated to achieve and maintain a positive and distinct social identity. Specifically, this means that individuals will want to be members of groups that enjoy high status and are distinct in some important ways.

Social comparisons between the in-group and out-groups allow individuals to determine the extent to which the in-group provides them with a satisfactory social identity. In conditions in which the social identity of individuals is unsatisfactory and "cognitive" alternatives to the present intergroup situation are perceived, individual or collective forms of action will be taken toward achieving a satisfactory social identity. These actions range from redefining an in-group characteristic, as suggested by the slogan Black Is Beautiful, to direct intergroup confrontation. When cognitive alternatives are not perceived, disadvantaged group members may attempt to improve their social identity by individual mobility, or by simply comparing themselves with other members of the in-group and avoiding comparisons with members of higher-status groups.

INEQUALITY AND CONFLICT

The five-stage model of intergroup relations focuses on how disadvantaged and, to a lesser extent, advantaged group members cope with inequality. It assumes that all intergroup relations pass through the same developmental stages in the same sequential manner. During stage one, group stratification is based on rigid categories such as sex or gender. At stage two, there emerges the concept that individual effort and ability can determine group membership. It is assumed that upward social mobility—the movement of individuals or groups from one social position to another which is higher or lower in terms of status—will be attempted by members of the disadvantaged group, first on an individual basis; this takes place at stage three. When individual mobility is blocked, however, during stage four, talented members of the disadvantaged group will engage in "consciousness raising" in order to try to mobilize the disadvantaged group as a collectivity. At stage five, if the challenge made by the disadvantaged group is successful and the two groups become fairly equal, there will be a healthy state of intergroup competition. If inequality persists, however, then the process of intergroup evolution begins again at an earlier stage in the five-stage cycle.

A rational and materialistic picture of intergroup relations is offered by realistic conflict theory, which addresses how conflicts arise between groups of fairly equal power, the course they take, and their resolution. At a first step, group cohesion and identity evolve as people cooperate in working toward shared goals. Intergroup conflict arises when groups interact and compete for scarce resources, such as territory or status. Conflict can be turned into peace, however, through the adoption of "superordinate goals." An example would be an environmentally safe world, a goal that is beneficial to all humankind but that cannot be achieved without the cooperation of all societies.

The similarity-attraction hypothesis and the contact hypothesis are not major theories, but they should be mentioned in any discussion of intergroup theories. The assumptions that similarity leads to attraction and, by implication, that dissimilarity leads to dislike underlie several of the major theories. The contact hypothesis, in its simplest form, assumes that under certain conditions, liking increases as a result of increased contact between people.

STRENGTHS OF EACH PERSPECTIVE
Intergroup theories have been used to explain a wide range of behaviors involving minority and majority groups, particularly prejudice and conflict. The theories do not necessarily attempt to explain the same events, and, indeed, each of them seems to

have a particular strength with respect to what it can best explain and the problems for which it can provide solutions.

The Freudian model has been used with particular success for explaining hostility against minorities such as African Americans. Feelings of frustration among majority group members are channeled outside the group by the leadership and displaced onto dissimilar minorities. This process intensifies under conditions in which frustration is particularly high. For example, in conditions of economic recession and high unemployment, frustration increases and so do attacks on minority groups.

A solution to conflict, following this line of thinking, is to create "safe" channels for frustration to be expressed. For example, in Japan, some companies have incorporated official exercise sessions for the employees to release their frustrations through sport. Employees can also release tensions by "beating up" dummies who might in their minds represent their boss or a pet peeve at work.

Equity theory is most effective in explaining unequal relationships that from an objective viewpoint seem baffling. For example, one can consider the case of Jane, who is emotionally abused by her boyfriend John. He is always late when they plan to go out, he never buys her presents or even remembers her birthday, and he criticizes her in public. Yet Jane not only puts up with this treatment but also describes her relationship with John as "wonderful." How is this to be explained? From the equity perspective, the answer lies in the subjective interpretation of inputs and outcomes. Jane may see herself as getting much more out of this relationship than an outside observer assumes that she is getting.

An equally puzzling aspect of social life is that unrest and revolution often occur when economic conditions are improving. Relative deprivation theory provides what is probably the best explanation of this by pointing to the role of social comparisons and rising expectations. During periods of economic growth, people have more and so come to expect more. They compare themselves with better-off others. Relative deprivation arises when the economy stops improving but expectations keep rising.

Social identity theory, developed by Henri Tajfel and his students, is particularly effective in explaining the arbitrary nature of the basis for in-group prejudice. In many situations in which social conflict occurs, the differences between the conflicting groups may appear to be rather trivial from the point of view of outsiders. For example, soccer is "only a game," but supporters of opposing teams have sometimes fought to the death to uphold their teams' honor, as in the case of British and Italian soccer fans in Brussels in June, 1985. Both laboratory studies and real-life cases suggest that in order to achieve a distinct and positive social identity for themselves, individuals will exaggerate differences between the in-group and out-groups and will give importance to differences that otherwise might be trivial.

Although social identity theory identifies a range of behavioral options available to disadvantaged group members, from individual acceptance to collective action, it does not specify the priorities people have for the different options. The five-stage model does identify priorities, postulating that people prefer first to improve status individually. Thus, the five-stage model is particularly useful for explaining behavior in Western societies, which are more individualistic than collectivistic.

Among the major intergroup theories, realistic conflict theory, developed by Muzafer Sherif, has had the greatest impact in terms of applications. For example, in the context of education, the concept of superordinate goals has inspired the creation of "jigsaw classrooms," in which students work in small groups to perform a task and each member of the group has information crucial to the group product. Thus, students work in an atmosphere of mutual dependence rather than competition. Research suggests that the jigsaw procedure not only improves the academic performance of children but also can help improve relations between ethnic groups in multiethnic classrooms. In the context of industry, the concept of superordinate goals has been used to help improve labor-management relations. The same concept has also been extended to the area of international relations. For example, world peace and survival are superordinate goals that helped move the superpowers out of the Cold War era.

The contact hypothesis and the similarity-attraction hypothesis have also had important applications. The assumption that contact between members of different groups leads to liking influenced the movement to desegregate schools in the United States. The assumption that people are attracted to others who are similar to themselves has been part of the reasoning for the "melting pot" or assimilation ideology in the United States. The assimilation of ethnic minorities into the mainstream is assumed to create a more homogeneous society, one in which people are more similar to one another and thus more attracted to one another.

ROLE IN SOCIAL MOVEMENTS AND CONFLICTS
Research on intergroup relations has also been influenced in important ways by minority movements such as the "ethnic revival" and the women's liberation movement. As early as the 1940's, African American psychologists highlighted the negative impact of prejudice on African American children. More recently, the Black Power movement and the revival of ethnicity generally have led to a greater focus on psychological research on the treatment of ethnic minorities. Similarly, since the 1960's, there has been a greater concern for women's issues, and this has led to more emphasis on minority-majority relations. For example, the issue of how the majority influences the minority, a major topic in mainstream research, has been turned on its head to become how the minority influences the majority.

Intergroup theories should also be considered in the context of superpower conflicts. From the 1940's until the late 1980's, the United States and the Soviet Union were considered to be superpowers of fairly equal military strength. Not surprisingly, much of the research and several of the major intergroup theories, such as realistic conflict theory, dealt with competing parties of equal strength. The focus on unequal parties came with the more recent theories, particularly social identity theory, developed in the 1970's, and the five-stage model, developed in the 1980's.

Intergroup relations are receiving more attention from psychologists and gaining a more prominent role in mainstream research. This trend is likely to continue, in part as a result of the changing demographic characteristics of North American society, in which the "minorities" will soon become the numerical majority.

SOURCES FOR FURTHER STUDY
British Journal of Social Psychology 23, no. 4 (1984). A special issue of the journal devoted entirely to the topic of intergroup relations. Leading European and North American researchers present

both theoretical discussions and empirical papers. Can be understood by college students.

Hogg, Michael A., and Dominic Abrams, eds. *Intergroup Relations: Essential Readings.* Philadelphia: Psychology Press, 2001. Intended as a textbook for undergraduate students, this volume collects contemporary and classic readings in intergroup relations.

Katz, Phyliss A., and Dalmas A. Taylor, eds. *Eliminating Racism: Profiles in Controversy.* New York: Plenum, 1988. Leading researchers discuss the challenges society faces in the area of race relations. Some limited focus on theoretical concepts such as contact, but most of the issues raised are applied. Literature on "symbolic" racism is discussed in-depth.

Taylor, Donald M., and Fathali M. Moghaddam. *Theories of Intergroup Relations: International Social Psychological Perspectives.* 2d ed. Westport, Conn.: Praeger, 1994. Each of the major intergroup theories is presented and discussed in a separate chapter. A schematic chart of each theory is provided as a simple guide to the reader. Includes suggestions for further reading after each chapter. Can be understood by the college or high school student.

Worchel, Stephen, and William G. Austin, eds. *Psychology of Intergroup Relations.* Chicago: Nelson-Hall, 1986. Presents the work of leading European and American researchers. Many of the chapters are well written and combine theoretical discussions with empirical evidence. Not all theoretical perspectives are presented, but the bibliography is comprehensive.

Fathali M. Moghaddam

SEE ALSO: Cooperation, competition, and negotiation; Crowd behavior; Groups; Prejudice; Prejudice reduction; Racism; Sexism; Social identity theory; Social schemata; Stereotypes.

International Classification of Diseases (ICD)

DATE: 1903 forward
TYPE OF PSYCHOLOGY: Biological bases of behavior; psychopathology

FIELDS OF STUDY: Aging; biological treatments; endocrine system; organic disorders; stress and illness

Development of an international classification of diseases, beginning in the early twentieth century, provided a systematic method of organizing a statistical summary of organic disorders. Many of these illnesses have an impact on the biological basis for behavioral disorders.

KEY CONCEPTS
• alphanumeric coding scheme
• morbidity or mortality statistics
• psychiatric and behavioral disorders
• zymotic

INTRODUCTION

An understanding of the mathematical principles which underlay the existence and spread of disease in populations had its origins within the Royal Society of London during the seventeenth century. Founded in 1662, the Royal Society included among its members John Graunt, a local tradesman. Graunt collected and organized bills of mortality from local parishes, which represented the first complete listing of causes of morbidity and mortality in local populations. Descriptions were simplistic compared with twentieth century data; nevertheless, the principle that information about disease could be statistically compiled would lead to further refinements and increasing accuracy. In 1836, the establishment of the Registrar-General's Office in London provided a central clearinghouse for compilation of such statistics. In particular, under the leadership of William Farr, compiler of statistical abstracts and finally superintendent, the office represented the first complete centralized bureau for analysis of disease in a population.

Farr initially divided diseases into five classes, three of the major groups being zymotic or infectious diseases; developmental diseases, such as those related to age or nutrition; and violent diseases. While some of Farr's conclusions are obviously outdated, the separation of behavioral disease from those with clearly contagious characteristics represented an early attempt to distinguish the two.

The major impetus to categorizing morbidity or mortality statistics was the increasing level of information gathering within individual European countries. The development of the germ theory of disease provided a means of diagnosis for individual illnesses; as noted in several studies of the history of information technology, such growing medical statistics were a part of the larger quantification of everyday life in many of these Western countries.

As noted by information technologist Geoffrey Bowker, the International Statistical Institute (IST) during its 1891 meeting in Vienna established a committee under the auspices of Jacques Bertillon, chief of statistical works in Paris, to develop a system for the categorization of illnesses. At its meeting in Chicago two years later, the committee presented a system which was immediately adopted by the larger institute and which was implemented by most countries. The classification became known as the *International Classification of Diseases*, or ICD; the first system became known as ICD-1. The initial listing included two hundred categories, the number of lines present on the paper used by Bertillon's committee during its deliberations.

PERIODIC REVISION

As further refinements in research into diagnosis or understanding of disease came about, it was quickly clear that the original categories of illness would be insufficient as a universal classification system. Meetings at approximately ten-year intervals addressed such changes, and resulted in significant revisions. The first major revision occurred in 1909 (ICD-2), the second in 1920 (ICD-3), and so on. Following World War I, the League of Nations became the governing body which dealt with the classification system.

At the International Health Conference which met in New York in 1946, the World Health Organization was charged with supervision of the system, including any necessary revisions; the result was ICD-6, which included nonfatal diseases such as those found in psychiatric disorders. In the years since, there have been periodic changes and revisions in that classification system; the ICD-10 was published in 1992. The full name of the publication is now *The International Statistical Classification of Diseases and Related Health Problems*, although the common acronym of ICD is still used. The number of categories has ballooned into some eight thousand.

With development of computer technology, the use of numeric codes became standard in ICD clas-

sification. Among other changes, such a numeric system allowed for the encoding of more than just a single underlying cause of death on death certificates; contributing causes could also now be included. The result was a more accurate rendering of disorders affecting an individual.

ICD CLASSIFICATION AND BEHAVIORAL DISORDERS

ICD classification represents to a significant degree a classification system for causes of death. Its primary function is to track the changes in diagnosis and spread of disease in populations for epidemiological purposes. However, among the illnesses which have been included in the revisions since World War II are those which represent psychiatric and behavioral disorders.

The changes in the coding scheme in ICD-10 represents the most significant revision in the area of mental illnesses. In ICD-9, numeric codes numbered 001-999 were utilized. For the ICD-10 system, an alphanumeric scheme was adopted, which used a letter followed by a two-numeral character (A00-Z99). For example, Alzheimer's disease as a cause of death has been classified as G30 in the ICD-10 coding system. The coding of mental disorders increased from thirty categories in ICD-9 (290-319) to one hundred categories in ICD-10 (F00-F98). Each "family" of disorders represents a particular form or cause. For example, F00-F09 includes only disorders with an organic basis. F10-F19 includes "Mental and behavioral disorders due to psychoactive substance abuse," and so on.

Some of these categories are further subdivided to allow for divisions within the form of the illness. For example, the category F60 represents "Specific personality disorders." The category is subdivided into ten levels on the basis of specific forms or diagnoses of such disorders: F60.0 represents "Paranoid personality disorder," F60.1 represents "Schizoid personality disorder," and so on.

SOURCES FOR FURTHER STUDY

Andrews, Gavin. "Should Depression Be Managed as a Chronic Disease?" In *British Medical Journal* 322, no. 7283 (2001): 419-421. Description of the ICD-10 criteria for repeated depression among subjects.

Bowker, Geoffrey. "The History of Information Infrastructures: The Case of the International Classification of Disease." *Information Processing and*

Management 32, no. 1 (1996): 49-61. Uses the example of the ICD as a prototype for formation of bureaucracies in the handling of information.

_____. "The Kindness of Strangers: Kinds and Politics in Classification Systems." *Library Trends* 47, no. 2 (1998): 255-292. Deals with controversy over and politics associated with present methods of disease classification.

Lilienfeld, David, and Paul Stolley. *Foundations of Epidemiology.* New York: Oxford University Press, 1994. The authors describe concepts of epidemiology in studies of the spread of disease. Background information on ICD is included.

World Health Organization. *The International Statistical Classification of Diseases and Related Health Problems.* Rev. 10th ed. Geneva: Author, 1992. Known as the ICD-10. A summary of changes in classification of disease.

Richard Adler

SEE ALSO: Diagnosis; *Diagnostic and Statistical Manual of Mental Disorders* (DSM).

Internet psychology

TYPE OF PSYCHOLOGY: Learning; origin and definition of psychology; psychological methodologies; psychopathology; psychotherapy

FIELDS OF STUDY: Behavior therapies; cognitive therapies; critical issues in stress; group and family therapies; group processes; interpersonal relations; methodological issues; personality assessment; social motives; social perception and cognition

Internet psychology refers to the study of human behavior taking place on the World Wide Web and related global electronics communications networks.

KEY CONCEPTS
- asynchronous
- boundaries
- bulletin board
- chat room
- on-line learning environment
- psychological distance
- telemedicine

INTRODUCTION

The Internet is an electronic computer-based network facilitating communication among vast numbers of individuals, groups, businesses, and governments. Internet psychology is a new area in psychology that touches upon earlier work in the areas of addiction, communication, learning, teaching, and the provision of therapeutic services. Foundational work in each of these areas of study, based mostly in face-to-face interactions, will provide a standard beside which Internet-related behavior will be compared.

Internet psychology has blossomed both as a result of the large numbers of individuals using the technology and as a result of its unique social interaction features. For instance, in comparison to everyday social interactions, the Internet allows for communication to flow from single individuals to large numbers of other individuals instantaneously. Further, this ability is shared by all individuals on the Internet, whether they are located in major urban areas or in remote locales. The Internet also allows for both asynchronous (meaning not at the same time) and simultaneous communication among individuals. Such features allow individuals to communicate when it is most convenient for them and also in such a way as to reach others whom they might not otherwise meet because of their locales.

One asynchronous Internet-based technology is an electronic bulletin board, an on-line location where information can be posted by individuals so that anyone who later visits the location can see the message posted. The original message poster may then receive a message back, in the form of another message left in the same place or as a private message sent directly to them. What is unusual about an electronic bulletin board in comparison to everyday communication, however, is that other individuals may join in and have other conversations in and around the original conversation without the knowledge of the original poster. For an outsider observing such an interaction, there would be no way to determine the true identity of the individual participants, nor would there be a way for the outsider to know if everyone listed as participating in the conversation has read or otherwise processed the interaction in its entirety. Even more psychologically interesting is that the individuals in the conversation have no way of knowing how many others visiting the bulletin board might be paying attention to their communications and not responding, a practice commonly called lurking.

Similar to bulletin boards, other technologies, such as chat rooms, provide virtual locations where information can be communicated simultaneously, sometimes described as "in real time," and where it is publicly on view. Chat rooms also raise issues about anonymity and uncertainty as to who might be observing one's conversation. Rather than communicating in a somewhat timeless environment, as on a bulletin board, many people may communicate at the same time in a chat room, much like being at a party or large social gathering. The only differences are that no one has immediate physical contact or cues, everyone can see what everyone else is saying, and the conversation is preserved in writing in the chat room for a period of time. Also, to the extent that the conversations are preserved, there may be more time to analyze communications among individuals.

In both of these types of communications, the issue of boundaries, or how information and relationships are defined and limited, also may be perceived as and function in a way that is more fluid than in face-to-face interactions. Further, boundaries may be more vulnerable to intrusion from uninvited others because most communications are publicly observable. In many on-line environments, anyone can communicate with everyone all at once, people can communicate anything they want to, and everyone can respond all at once. As a result, communications can be overwhelmingly positive or negative due to the sheer number of responses one might receive. Also, communications may be jarring because of their content.

This reaction is attributable to another feature of Internet-based communications related to anonymity: psychological distance, the social proximity that individuals feel from others. It is something like a perceived safety or danger zone for interactions that have psychological consequences, such as emotional responses. In Internet-based communication, because of anonymity and because social interactions are computer mediated, where individuals may never see or hear each other, psychological distance can be great and have behavioral consequences in communication. While some Internet users may respond to such an environment by opening up emotionally and allowing themselves to be more vulnerable to others in expressing feelings or

thoughts, other users might become more extreme and aggressive in terms of how they pursue communications and what they express.

These aspects of Internet-based communications are only a few of many that are interesting to psychologists. Other examples include the effect of this type of remote communication on existing social networks and the formation of new social networks; group cohesion in on-line groups; the efficacy of on-line support groups; the development of on-line social skills; the psychological states of individual participants over time; and the relationship between on-line and "real-life" communications.

IMPORTANCE
The Internet affects many different kinds of social behavior, including work communications, organizational behavior, dating behavior, everyday social communications, learning and teaching, and even health care. In terms of positive effects, the Internet allows for many benefits. One major benefit is that individuals in remote locations can participate actively in wide social, learning, and business networks, perhaps more so than they could if they were limited to their own locales. This may lead to increased transmission of new science, learning, and social data into such remote areas. It may also lead to decreased feelings of isolation in the individual participants as well as increased opportunities for such individuals.

One opportunity is Internet-based learning. In an on-line learning environment, individuals in remote locations can access educational opportunities that might otherwise be unavailable to them without traveling great distances. Similarly, such technologies allow for financial savings on intellectual resource acquisition and dispensation, as such resources can be made available to all needing it in one spot on the Internet. This same advantage translates into being able to reach a larger number of trainees than might typically be able to attend training because of time, geographic, and/or financial constraints. Finally, because the learning takes place on-line, where interactions and Web-related behavior can be tracked, new information about how trainees seek information, integrate it, and draw conclusions may be discerned, ultimately contributing to advances in teaching.

Another benefit for individuals in remote locations where health care providers are scarce is Internet-based medicine, such as telemedicine, or medical care provided at a distance. Such technologies can be invaluable in saving lives through prevention and informational or supportive treatments that complement face-to-face medical care. Such services may include health care-related Web sites providing information, assessments, discussion lists for support, chat rooms devoted to individual health care topics, contact information for providers, and even an alternative means of sending messages to health care providers, such as through e-mail. Such Web sites are valuable not only to individual clients but also to their families, treatment providers, and others involved in health care, such as trainees and researchers.

Some of the positive aspects of the Internet also have drawbacks. For instance, rapid and instantaneous communication is good if the information communicated is good. If, on the other hand, it has errors or is vague or phrased in a way that is ambiguous in terms of its social tone, it could create conflict and social discomfort for all receiving the message, as well as for the sender.

Another negative aspect that has received attention is what some call Internet addiction. In this syndrome, individuals are judged as being dependent on their use of the Internet. Such dependence might be characterized by any of the following features: a desire to use the Internet more and more; using it more than intended; feeling a strong desire to cease using it or reduce the time spent using it; reducing or giving up other social behaviors in order to use the Internet; finding that personal Internet use is creating problems in other life activities because they have been neglected; and continued use despite knowledge of psychological or other problems caused or exacerbated by the Internet usage. Finally, "addicted" individuals who do not have access to the Internet may experience feelings of withdrawal. The term "addiction" has been used to describe this condition because many of these features are similar to those defining substance abuse and dependence problems. In terms of the potential scope of the problem, recent reports suggest that as many as 10 percent of college students may experience some feelings of dependence on the Internet.

CONTEXT

The Internet appears to be firmly in place in modern society as a major social, educational, and

health-related resource. In 1998, the Office for the Advancement of Telehealth was established by the Health Resources and Service Administration of the U.S. Department of Health and Human Services. This office is devoted to the advancement of telehealth and Internet-based medicine to improve public health service and research. According to *dotCOMSense*, a free brochure by the American Psychological Association, in 2000 the Internet had more than fifteen thousand sites offering health information. Estimates suggest that each year, more than sixty million people search for health information on-line, including searches for mental health information. In addition, communications technologies improve daily, reaching more homes. By mid-2001, for example, more than half of all households in the United States had a personal computer. In this same time period, many workplaces gained an on-line presence to conduct their business and communicate with their employees. Universities followed suit, using the Internet to host class materials, classes, and even academic conferences.

Understanding the psychology of the Internet remains a critical task. As Internet-based technologies work their way into more settings, the effects of this technology will need to be assessed for their impact on the individuals using the technology and the organizational structures hosting this type of communications network. In addition, it must be kept in mind that the Internet is an international communications medium. Like the telephone and the television, it can spread information anywhere that the technology is installed. Unlike these earlier technological advances, it is capable of transmitting far more information, more rapidly and to more people. The implications of such transmissions remain to be evaluated. As C. A. Bowers suggests in *Let Them Eat Data* (2000), these communications may have costs that are yet to be recognized.

SOURCES FOR FURTHER STUDY

American Psychological Association. *DotCOMSense.* Washington, D.C.: Author, 2000. Outlines the pros and cons of acquiring Internet-based mental health information and advice, as well as guidelines for assessing that information.

Bauer, Jeffrey C., and Marc A. Ringel. *Telemedicine and the Reinvention of Healthcare.* New York: McGraw-Hill, 1999. The history of telemedicine is discussed, along with technical information and commentary on its social and policy implications.

Birnbaum, Michael H., ed. *Psychology Experiments on the Internet*. San Diego, Calif.: Academic Press, 2000. Describes Internet-based strategies used for psychology experiments, highlighting methodological and ethical considerations in such work.

Bowers, C. A. *Let Them Eat Data: How Computers Affect Education, Cultural Diversity, and the Prospects of Ecological Sustainability*. Athens: University of Georgia Press, 2000. Examines computers-based technologies as a means of exporting culture.

Kiesler, Sara, ed. *Culture of the Internet*. Mahwah, N.J.: Lawrence Erlbaum, 1997. Addresses cultural issues related to Internet-based behavior for individuals, dyads, social groups, and even organizations networked over the World Wide Web.

Wallace, Patricia M. *The Psychology of the Internet*. Cambridge, England: Cambridge University Press, 1999. Provides a social science overview on Internet psychology.

Wolfe, Christopher R., ed. *Learning and Teaching on the World Wide Web*. San Diego, Calif.: Academic Press, 2001. Characteristics of on-line learning environments and learners are described, highlighting the importance of a good match between the two.

Young, Kimberly S. *Caught in the Net: How to Recognize the Signs of Internet Addiction*. New York: John Wiley & Sons, 1998. A practical guide with information on how to avoid getting overinvolved on the Internet.

Nancy A. Piotrowski

SEE ALSO: Addictive personality and behaviors; Affiliation and friendship; Attitude formation and change; Consumer psychology; Coping: Chronic illness; Coping: Social support; Coping: Strategies; Coping: Terminal illness; Emotional expression; Groups; Health psychology; Help-seeking; Intimacy; Learning; Media psychology; Self-disclosure; Self-presentation; Social identity theory; Social networks; Social perception; Support groups; Teaching methods.

Intimacy

TYPE OF PSYCHOLOGY: Social psychology
FIELDS OF STUDY: Interpersonal relations

Intimacy describes a special quality of emotional closeness between two people. It involves mutual caring, trust, open communication of feelings and sensations, as well as an ongoing interchange of information about significant emotional events. Self-disclosure is a critical ingredient of intimacy.

KEY CONCEPTS
- difficulties in intimacy
- intimacy and sexuality
- intimacy and well-being
- risk
- self-identity
- vulnerability

INTRODUCTION

Intimacy is the opening of oneself to another person so that the two individuals can share with each other their innermost thoughts and feelings that are usually kept hidden from other people. The word "intimacy derives" from *intimus*, the Latin term for "inner" or "inmost." It denotes a kind of sharing that comes from within and inspires thoughts of closeness, warmth, and shared affection. Intimacy also involves getting close enough to another person that he or she can see not only one's positive qualities and strengths but also one's hidden faults and weaknesses. Authentic closeness between two persons requires that both of them step out of their traditional roles, dispense with their usual facades, and try to become their true selves. Intimacy with another person is, therefore, a combination of individual identity and mutual sharing. In a healthy intimacy, two individuals move into a relationship with each other, sharing common interests without losing their separate identities. Interpersonal exchange in intimate relationships is an end in itself rather than a means to achieving any other goal.

Intimacy, by its very nature, is elusive, subjective, and intensely private. An important basis of intimacy is the sharing of private thoughts and feelings through self-disclosure. Such self-disclosure involves the sharing of both pleasant and unpleasant feelings and emotions. There appears to be something uniquely intimate about sharing personal pain. It is also considered intimate to share feelings of love, caring, attraction, and closeness, as well as well as hopes, joys, accomplishments, and pride. The sharing of joyous experiences and cherished memories is considered to be as intimate as that of unpleasant experiences and long-suppressed secrets. In addition, intimacy refers not just to the act of self-disclosure but also to the interpersonal interaction in which self-disclosure is validated and reciprocated.

Nonverbal behaviors are as important to intimacy as are verbal expressions. Sex is cited as the most frequent example, but other examples include being with another person in an atmosphere of comfort and ease; hand-holding; hugging; sharing excitement, joy, and laughter; and doing things together. Other examples include sharing the touch, taste, and smell of cherished objects. Feeling good in the presence of each other, touching each other in silence, having a quiet dinner together, and silently sharing excitement and anticipation are some other examples that illustrate intimacy.

Intimacy also denotes a special type of feeling that is often described in terms of warmth, closeness, and love. Intimacy can thus refer to individual behavior (such as self-disclosure), to interactions between two partners, to types of relationships, and to specific feelings. Intimate partners experience a unique sense of exuberance, warmth, and vitality. Sometimes they waver, intermittently feeling both closeness and distance. At other times, there can be a simultaneous experience of both closeness and distance.

SELF-IDENTITY

A positive and realistic sense of self is a prerequisite for healthy intimacy. Intimacy requires a full awareness of one's own feelings, thoughts, and values and the ability to bring that awareness into a relationship with another. As one becomes aware of one's own self-identity and self-understanding, one is able to move into a relationship with another individual who also maintains a somewhat similar sense of healthy self-identity. Intimacy involves being able to share worlds while maintaining one's own boundaries. It requires being honest with oneself and one's partner, even during those times when one is not focused on sharing or is in some other way preoccupied.

A person who is aware of his or her own needs and is willing to explore his or her own limitations and potentialities will allow another to do the same. This may, at times, lead to conflicts. Variations in emotional expression, the nature of attention, and the quality of communication are bound to occur in a relationship from time to time and are unavoidable. The truly intimate partners are able to handle such occasional turmoil with graceful acceptance and mutual respect.

Healthy intimacy is notable for an ability to maintain a solid, self-sustained sense of identity while remaining emotionally engaged with another. The sense of self in a person involved in an intimate relationship is very resilient. Such a person is able and willing to differ with another and still maintain his or her unique identity, expressed through thoughts, feelings, values, vulnerabilities, strengths, desires, and fantasies. A person with a healthy sense of self can tolerate multiple, distinct, and coequal realities. Such people can be themselves in the presence of others, and can accept others being themselves.

A less-than-healthy relationship is marked by blurred or indistinct boundaries. In such relationship, a person pays an inordinate amount of attention to the other individual in order to monitor his or her actions and, more important, reactions. Even minor differences can be anxiety producing and/or threatening. One attempts to deny, minimize, or rapidly smooth differences out of existence. Contact with a partner is neither solid nor comfortable because the closeness causes anxiety about losing one's self, whereas separateness creates anxiety about losing the other person. If the self-identity is shaky or insecure, there is an inability to maintain proper boundaries and, in turn, a resistance to really "letting in" another person—whether emotionally or intellectually. In extreme cases, contact with the partner's differing reality is so difficult that it may give rise to an illusion of an alternate reality or a sense of no connection whatsoever.

An alternative to this sort of distortion is to allow both oneself and one's partner to be transparent and visible. When separateness is maintained, the option to know another person exists. One's self is solid enough to withstand the risks that accompany intense emotional involvement—the inevitability of misunderstanding, disappointment, disapproval, conflict, rejection, and even loss. In a paradoxical sense, one can only have as good a relationship as one is willing to lose. This is one of the key dynamics that largely determines how much emotional intensity and intimacy a person is capable of handling.

RISK AND VULNERABILITY

Being intimate with another individual necessitates risk and vulnerability through self-disclosure. Intimacy inherently feels risky because one goes out to the edge of individual expression without being certain how the other person will respond. Whereas closeness affirms and sustains a relationship, intimacy reveals and affirms individuality, and in the process, changes the nature and quality of a relationship. A person who is able to maintain individuality in the midst of togetherness can reap the rewards of both closeness and intimacy. If not, one swings between compulsive togetherness and reactive individuality.

Intimate relationships evolve gradually and naturally. The more valued the relationship, the more there is to lose. One feels more anxiety in being intimate in the sense of being honestly and fully oneself. There is always some amount of tension between closeness and intimacy. The paradox of closeness and intimacy is that the only way to really have either is to be willing at times to sacrifice closeness for the sake of intimacy.

INTIMACY AND SEXUALITY

Although intimacy is commonly thought of in connection with sex, sex is not a necessary component of intimacy. Satisfying intimate relationships in themselves are the most important source of people's happiness. Intimacy is a very important ingredient in the quality of love and sex. A high degree of intimacy between two lovers or spouses contributes to the happiness, emotional stability, and sexual enrichment of both. All activities are more enjoyable and life is richer and more colorful when shared with an intimate partner. Sexual experiences are more pleasurable if the partners know each other intimately, when they are completely open and vulnerable, when they can trust each other to care about each other's feelings, and when they take pleasure in each other's pleasure.

INTIMACY AND WELL-BEING

Humans are social animals, and without intimate relationships they risk loneliness and depression. The availability of intimate relationships is an important determinant of how well people master life's crises. Satisfying intimate relationships are a very important source of most people's happiness. An intimate involvement with a special someone provides a person with a purpose and meaning in life and seems to promote a sense of overall well-being. Intimate relationships have been shown to buffer people from the pathogenic effects of stress. People in intimate rela-

tionships have fewer stress-related symptoms and faster recoveries from illnesses. Intimate partners confide in each other, which has been shown to carry its own health benefits. Individual well-being and intimate relationships appear to be closely intertwined. People in satisfied intimate relationships have been shown to be less vulnerable to the negative outcomes of stress than those who lack such relationships.

DIFFICULTIES IN INTIMACY

People may find it difficult to develop and maintain intimacy in two different ways: They are compulsively searching for intimacy but are unable or unwilling to invest time and energy in developing meaningful intimate relationships, or they are afraid of losing their identity and, therefore, purposefully avoid intimate relationships.

Some people harbor unrealistic expectations about intimacy and closeness. Such people are always looking for instant intimacy, even at the cost of compromising their basic values. They tend to share secrets instantly and pour out their life stories in search of establishing immediate contact and emotional intensity. In doing so, they often end up surrendering their personal boundaries in a relationship. This tendency to lose the sense of self and define oneself through the response of others is called emotional fusion. In such a fusion, the boundaries of self become quite vague, and the person is unable to withstand much pressure or disagreement from another. Holding a distinct, self-defined position can be a very frightening experience for such a person. In such relationships, partners try to merge their internal experiences into a single common reality. As a result, each person's well-being gets inextricably linked to the other's experience and wishes. Both focus on the other, trying to ensure consensus and avoid defining their own reality.

A person with fear of intimacy is basically afraid of losing ego boundaries. There is a lack of interest in and motivation for becoming intimate with others. In most cases, such disturbance in the capacity to form intimate interpersonal relationships stems from early adverse experiences within one's family. Such a person has an active fear of closeness, suffers from self-doubts, and actively distrusts others. He or she has a very low self-image and is easily susceptible to loneliness and depression. Such a person sees himself or herself as undeserving of the love and support of others, is afraid to trust others, and has an unrealistic fear of dependence. When a person is repeatedly unable to share inner thoughts and feelings with a single other person in a sustained manner, he or she may experience emotional isolation.

SOURCES FOR FURTHER STUDY

Brehm, Sharon S., Roland S. Miller, Daniel Perlman, and Susan M. Campbell. *Intimate Relationships*. New York: McGraw-Hill, 2002. Drawing upon psychological, sociological, communication and family studies, the book presents an interdisciplinary perspective on intimate relationships.

Brown, Norman, M., and Ellen S. Amatea. *Love and Intimate Relationships*. Philadelphia: Brunner/Mazel, 2000. The book attempts to explain the mysteries of love, intimacy, and relationships. Includes frank discussion of developmental, interpersonal, and social aspects of homosexual relationships.

Carlson, Jon, and Len Sperry, eds. *The Intimate Couple*. Philadephia: Brunner/Mazel, 1999. A comprehensive collection of articles by experienced professionals in the field. The book provides the most current, cutting-edge theory and research on intimate relationships.

Firestone, Robert W., and Joyce Catlett. *Fear of Intimacy*. Washington, D.C.: American Psychological Association, 2000. The book attempts to explains how difficulties in intimate relationships can be traced to the internal models of self and others and presents clinical vignettes to illustrate self-protective measures that inhibit intimacy.

Prager, Karen J. *The Psychology of Intimacy*. New York: Guilford, 1995. A respected researcher in the field attempts to explore the complex interaction between intimacy and individual development.

Tulsi B. Saral

SEE ALSO: Affiliation and friendship; Affiliation motive; Attachment and bonding in infancy and childhood; Attraction theories; Codependency; Couples therapy; Father-child relationship; Jealousy; Love; Mother-child relationship; Narcissistic personality; Self-disclosure; Self-esteem.

Introverts and extroverts

TYPE OF PSYCHOLOGY: Emotion; personality
FIELDS OF STUDY: Personality theory

The extroversion-introversion dimension has been included in nearly every major taxonomy of personality traits since the middle of the twentieth century. The hypothesized dimension of extroversion is applied to persons who tend to direct their energies outwards and to derive gratification from the physical and social environment. The dimension of introversion is applied to individuals whose primary concerns are their own thoughts and feelings. Most theorists today believe that extroversion and introversion exists not as singular types but rather as a collection of different patterns of behavior in that many individuals exhibit aspects of both.

KEY CONCEPTS
- "Big Five"
- extroversion
- introversion
- libido
- trait

INTRODUCTION

Traditionally, Western philosophy has conceived of two main ways of fulfilling human potential: *vita activa* and *vita contemplativa*. *Vita activa* represented one's being through action, while *vita contemplativa* represented solitary reflection. The term "introversion" first appeared in the seventeenth century in a purely descriptive sense of turning one's thoughts inward in spiritual contemplation.

Theoretical conceptualizations of extroversion and introversion have gradually and consistently evolved since the 1920's. Today, they are found in nearly every widely used personality inventory. Extroverts are often described by adjectives such as adventurous, assertive, sociable, and talkative. Introverts are often described as being quiet, reserved, and unsociable. Although the constructs of extroversion and introversion are intangible and thus difficult to determine, many personality inventories have been developed to attempt to do so. Most individuals could be located at some point on a broad continuum rather than labeled as clearly an extrovert or an introvert.

PERSONALITY THEORIES

The concepts of introversion and extroversion in their modern psychological sense were introduced by Carl Jung in 1910 and were possibly the best-known parts of his system. Jung viewed extroversion-introversion as a bipolar personality dimension along which people can be divided into types, characterized by outward-directedness on one extreme and inward-directedness on the other extreme. Jung did not view introversion and extroversion specifically as personality traits, but rather as different attitudes or orientations. Jung believed that attitudes of extroversion and introversion determine much of people's perception and reaction to the surrounding world.

Extroversion for Jung was the preference for active interaction with others and the environment. Introversion for Jung was characterized by the habitual attitude that preferred introspection and solitary activity. According to Jung, introversion was an orientation inward toward the self.

An important way in which Jung differed from Sigmund Freud was in his conception of the nature of libido. Rather than viewing it exclusively as sexual energy, Jung perceived it as a broad and undifferentiated life energy. In a narrower perspective, libido became the fuel that energized the psyche or personality. It is through this psychic energy that the important psychological activities of perceiving, thinking, and feeling are carried out. As such, the libido could be directed externally toward the outside world (extroversion) or internally toward the self (introversion). Although everyone has the capacity for either attitude, one of them becomes dominant for each individual. At the same time, the nondominant attitude exists and also has the capability of influencing one's behavior. According to Jung, a person is not exclusively extrovert or introvert.

Jung's proposal of extroversion and introversion as two personality types emerged as a single dimension in the analyses of personality as provided by Hans Eysenck in 1947. Eysenck, a German-born British psychologist, is credited with popularizing the terms "introvert" and "extrovert." Eysenck established two dominant factors as being important dimensions of personality, the introversion-extroversion dimension and the neuroticism-stability dimension.

Factor analysis, widely accepted since the 1980's, identified five fundamental dimensions of human personality known as the "Big Five": extroversion, agreeableness, conscientiousness, neuroticism, and openness to experience or intellect. Extensive interest is currently focused on this five-factor model of personality. R. R. Costa and P. T. McCrae, Jr., emphasize the Big Five personality theory in their NEO Personality Inventory, which is an extension of their earlier three-factor model (neuroticism, extroversion, and openness).

PRACTICAL APPLICATIONS

An important issue in life-span development is the stability-change issue, which addresses whether an individual can develop into a different personality type or whether there is a tendency for people to remain older renditions of their earlier years. Costa and McCrae concluded that there is considerable stability in the five personality factors, one of which is extroversion.

Some additional areas of research give interesting practical applications of the extroversion-introversion dimension. First is the question of the heritability of the extroversion-introversion variable. Eysenck believed that individual differences in extroversion-introversion were based in biology, although he had little evidence to support this. Since that time, however, a great deal of research has appeared to support his view for the genetic source of introversion/extroversion. A second question is the potential difference between introverts and extroverts in their preference for arousal. Researchers have found that introverted individuals could be characterized as operating at a near-optimal arousal level and are more sensitive to stimulation. The extrovert, however, is always seeking additional stimulation from the environment. A third area of consideration is the question of whether greater happiness can be predicted for introverts or extroverts. Researchers find that extroverts report higher levels of subjective well-being than do introverts.

SOURCES FOR FURTHER STUDY

Burger, Jerry M. *Personality*. 5th ed. Belmont, Calif.: Wadsworth, 1999. This is a popular selection as a textbook. The author writes in almost a conversational tone, which is unique for books in this area. Discusses each theoretical approach in terms of theory, application, and assessment and then in terms of relevant research.

Friedman, Howard S., and Miriam W. Schustack. *Personality: Classic Theories and Modern Research*. Boston: Allyn & Bacon, 2003. Provides a thorough explanation of personality theories. Includes the unique areas of cross-cultural and gender issues. Includes a chapter on trait approaches.

Hogan, Robert, John Johnson, and Stephen Briggs, eds. *Handbook of Personality Psychology*. San Diego,

Calif.: Academic Press, 1997. Excellent source for information on the historical development of personality theories. Information is thorough and easy to understand.

McAdams, Dan P. *The Person: An Integrated Introduction to Personality Psychology.* 3d ed. San Francisco: Jossey-Bass, 2000. Takes a very basic approach, but includes a section on dispositional traits that is well written.

Pervin, Lawrence A. *Personality: Theory and Research.* 7th ed. San Francisco: Jossey-Bass, 1996. A popular textbook. Includes a chapter on trait approaches to personality.

Lillian J. Breckenridge

See also: Analytical psychology: Carl G. Jung; Eysenck, Hans; Jung, Carl G.; Neurotic disorders; Personality theory.

J

Jealousy

TYPE OF PSYCHOLOGY: Social psychology
FIELDS OF STUDY: Interpersonal relations

Jealousy is the experience of perceiving that one's relationship is threatened; it is influenced by cultural expectations about relationships, self-esteem, and feelings of possessiveness. Jealousy is a common source of conflict, and it can have a destructive impact on relationships.

KEY CONCEPTS
- dispositional
- dyadic
- patrilineage
- possessiveness
- socialization

INTRODUCTION

Jealousy is not a single emotion; it is most likely a complex of several emotions whose central theme is the fear of losing to someone else what rightfully belongs to one. In personal relationships, jealousy focuses on fear of losing the partner; the partner is seen as a possession whose ownership is in jeopardy. Whether the threat is real or imaginary, it endangers the jealous person's self-esteem as well as the relationship. Theorists argue that three elements are central to the emotional experience of jealousy: an attachment between two people, valued resources that are exchanged between them, and an intrusion on this attachment by a third person seen to be supplanting the giver or receiver of resources.

Early theories of jealousy suggested that the jealous person fears losing possession; later conceptualizations, however, have specified that jealousy is a fear not of loss of possession but of loss of control. The intrusion of a third party also threatens the cohesiveness of the attachment, dividing partners into opponents. Insofar as the relationship has been in-

tegrated into each partner's identity, the intruder threatens not only what the jealous person has but also who he or she is. Most researchers conclude that the experience of jealousy is itself a damaging and destructive relationship event. Emotional bonds are reduced to property rights. Jealousy involves the manipulation of feelings and behaviors, and it can erupt in anger or cause depression. The positive aspects of jealousy are few, but they are identifiable: It intensifies feelings, provides information about the partners, can trigger important discussions between them, and can enhance the jealous person's self-concept.

Research on jealousy has several origins. Anthropologists have long observed dramatic cultural variations in the causes and expressions of jealousy. Psychologists have noted that jealousy has no consistent emotional expression or definition: For some people, jealousy is a version of anger; for others, it resembles sadness, depression, or fear. When research on close relationships began to develop in the 1960's and 1970's, jealousy was found to help explain the dynamics of power and conflict in intimacy. Early research produced the counterintuitive findings that jealousy hinders rather than enhances romantic relationships, and that its roots are not in intimacy but possessiveness. Jealousy was eventually found to be an aspect of self-esteem and defensiveness rather than a quality of intimacy or dyadic (pertaining to a couple) communication.

Jealousy is more likely when a relationship is intensely valued by someone; the more important it is, the more dangerous would be its loss. Social norms do not support the expression of some forms of jealousy; for example, most cultures do not tolerate expressing jealousy of one's own children. Inexpressible jealousies may be displaced onto the more tolerated forms, such as a couple's sexual relationship. Sexual attraction or behavior is often the focus of jealousy, even though sexual interaction may not be the most valued aspect of a relationship. For example, one gender difference that has been identified in the experience of jealousy in heterosexual relationships is that while men focus on sexual infidelity or intrusion, women express greater jealousy about the emotional attachment between a partner and a rival.

DISPOSITIONAL FACTORS

Dispositional factors in jealousy include feelings of personal insecurity, a poor self-image, and deficient education. Jealous people appear to be unhappy even before they identify a target for their dissatisfaction. Describing oneself as "a jealous person" is related to a negative attributional style; a self-described jealous person sees his or her jealous reaction as stable and uncontrollable, and thus as less likely to change. Developmental research suggests that jealous emotions originate in childhood when the child's exclusive attachment to the mother outlives the mother's intense bond to the child. Childhood jealousy also manifests itself in rivalry with one's other parent or with siblings, implying that jealousy assumes that love is a finite resource that cannot be shared without diminishment. A common theme in jealousy research is the jealous person's sense of dependence on the threatened relationship, as well as the conviction that he or she is somehow lacking. Before an intrusion appears or is imagined, therefore, a jealous person may already feel inadequate, insecure, and threatened.

Jealousy is also related to possessiveness—the desire to maintain and control a person or resource. Thus the central issue of relationship jealousy is not love but power and control. Relatively powerful people (in most societies, men rather than women) feel less possessive because they feel less powerless. Circumstances can trigger possessiveness: In all types of relationships studied, one partner feels more possessive when he or she fears that the other might have a meaningful interaction with a third person.

CULTURAL VARIATIONS

Cultural and subcultural norms determine the forms and incidences of jealousy. For both men and women, jealousy is related to the expectation of exclusiveness in a relationship. For men in particular, jealousy is related to gender-role traditionalism (adherence to traditional standards of masculinity) and dependence on their partners' evaluations for self-esteem. For women, jealousy is related to dependence on the relationship. With these gender-role expectations, individuals decide whether they are "obligated" to feel jealous when the circumstances indicate a threat to self-esteem or intimacy.

Cultures vary widely in the standards and degree of jealousy attached to sexual relationships. Jealousy is rare in cultures that place few restrictions on sexual gratification and do not make marriage or progeny important to social recognition. In contrast, high-jealousy cultures are those that place great importance on control of sexual behavior and identification of patrilineage (the tracing of ancestry by means of the father's family). Cultural researchers conclude that jealousy is not inborn but learned through socialization to what is valued in one's culture. For example, a cultural norm commonly associated with jealousy is monogamy. In monogamous cultures, alternative liaisons are condemned as wrong, and jealousy is seen as a reasonable, vigilant response. In such contexts a double standard is promoted, separating jealousy from envy, a covetous feeling about material property. While envy and greed are considered unacceptable, jealousy is justified as a righteous defense of intimate territory.

JEALOUSY-INDUCING TECHNIQUES

Despite the negative form and consequences of jealousy in most relationships, it is popularly associated with intensity of romantic commitment. Researchers have found that individuals who score high in measures of romanticism believe that jealousy is a desirable reaction in a partner. Perhaps because jealousy is mistakenly believed to strengthen intimacy (although research indicates that it has the opposite effect), some individuals may seek to induce jealousy in their partners. Researchers have found that women are more likely than men to induce jealousy with an expectation of renewed attention or greater control of the relationship. Five jealousy-inducement techniques have been identified: exaggerating a third person's appeal, flirting with others, dating others, fabricating another attachment, and talking about a previous partner. Theorists speculate that the gender difference in jealousy inducement reflects the imbalance of power in male-female relationships. Provoking jealousy may be an attempt to redress other inequities in the relationship.

VARIATIONS IN REACTIONS

Reactions to jealousy vary by age, gender, and culture. Young children may express rage in tantrums or attack the interloping sibling. Research has identified six common responses made by jealous children: aggression, identification with the rival (for example, crying or acting cute like a new baby), withdrawal, repression or feigning apathy, masochism (exaggerating pain to win attention), and creative competition (with the possible outcome of greater self-reliance).

Gender differences in adult jealous reactions include self-awareness, emotional expression, focus of attention, focus of blame, and restorative behavior. When jealous, men are more likely to deny such feelings, while women more readily acknowledge them. Men express jealousy in rage and anger, while women experience depression and fear (that the relationship may end). Men are more likely to blame the third party or the partner, while women blame themselves. Men engage in confrontational behavior and focus on restoring self-esteem. Women intensify possessiveness and focus on strengthening the relationship. In general, these gender differences reflect different sources of jealousy and different emotional and social implications. For most men, a relationship is regarded as a personal possession or resource to be protected with territorial aggression. For most women, a relationship is an extension of the self, a valued opportunity but not a personal right, whose loss is feared and defended with efforts to secure the bonds of attachment. The focus of post-jealousy behavior is guided by the resource that is most damaged or threatened by the episode: For men, this is the role of the relationship in supporting self-esteem; for women, it is the health and security of the relationship.

Cultural differences in reacting to jealousy range from extreme violence to dismissive inattention. A jealous Samoan woman might bite her rival on the nose, while a New Mexican Zuñi wife might refuse to do her straying husband's laundry. Cultures may overtly or tacitly condone violence incited by jealous passion. Jealousy has been cited as a justifying factor in many forms of social violence: family murder and suicide, spouse abuse, divorce, depression, and criminal behavior. Despite cultural stereotypes of women as more prone to jealousy, a review of murders committed in a jealous rage has revealed women to be the perpetrators in fewer than 15 percent of the cases.

MANAGING JEALOUSY

Researchers have identified positive, constructive approaches to managing jealous experiences. Three broad coping strategies have been identified: self-reliance, self-image improvement, and selective devaluing of the loved one. In the first case, self-reliance involves controlling expressions of sadness and anger, and forging a tighter commitment with one's partner. In the second, one's self-image can be enhanced by making positive social comparisons and identifying and developing one's good qualities. Finally, jealousy can be reduced and the threat eliminated if one convinces oneself that the loved person is not so important after all. These approaches are all popular, but they are not equally effective. Researchers comment that self-reliance works best, selective devaluing is less effective, and self-bolstering does not appear to be effective at all.

LESSONS FROM RESEARCH

Jealousy has gained attention as a social problem because of its implications in criminal behavior and domestic violence. Increases in the rate of domestic assault and murder have warranted a closer examination of the cultural assumptions and stereotypes that support jealous rage and depression. Educational programs to address self-esteem, especially in young children and adolescents, are focusing on jealousy as a symptom of pathology rather than a normal or healthy emotional experience.

Consistent discoveries of cultural differences in patterns of jealous experience have supported the view that jealousy, like many other "natural" relationship phenomena, is learned and acquired through socialization and experience. Thus, jealousy research is contributing to the "demystification" of close relationships—attraction and attachment are not seen as mysterious or fragile processes, but as learned behavior patterns that can be both understood and modified. Jealous individuals can thus be taught to derive their sense of self-esteem or security from more stable, self-controlled sources. Jealousy can be explained as the unhealthy symptom of a treatable complex of emotions, beliefs, and habits. Its contributions to relationship conflict and personal distress can be reduced, and its lessons applied to developing healthier attitudes and behaviors.

SOURCES FOR FURTHER STUDY

Brehm, Sharon S. *Intimate Relationships.* 2d ed. New York: Random House, 1991. This excellent text devotes one chapter to jealousy, reviewing research and putting jealousy in the context of other relationship experiences.

Buss, David. *The Dangerous Passion: Why Jealousy Is as Necessary as Love and Sex.* New York: Free Press, 2000. Using cross-cultural research (thirty-seven countries on six continents), the author suggests that jealousy is an (imperfectly) adaptive behavior that aids in coping with reproductive threats.

Clanton, Gordon, and Lynn G. Smith, eds. *Jealousy.* 3d ed. Washington, D.C.: University Press of America, 1997. An edited collection reviewing gender differences, cultural factors, and other issues in jealousy research.

Salovey, Peter, ed. *The Psychology of Jealousy and Envy.* New York: Guilford, 1991. A collection of essays from a wide range of respected researchers in the field. Covers both theoretical perspectives and practical applications.

White, Gregory L., and Paul E. Mullen. *Jealousy: Theory, Research, and Clinical Strategies.* New York: Guilford, 1989. Includes chapters on romantic jealousy; the origins of jealousy in sociobiology, personality, and culture; gender effects in jealousy; pathological and violent jealousy; and strategies for assessing and managing jealousy.

Ann L. Weber

SEE ALSO: Attraction theories; Emotional expression; Emotions; Intimacy; Love; Self-esteem; Sibling relationships.

Jung, Carl G.

BORN: July 26, 1875, in Kesswil, Switzerland
DIED: June 6, 1961, in Küsnacht, Switzerland
IDENTITY: Swiss psychiatrist
TYPE OF PSYCHOLOGY: Personality; psychopathology; psychotherapy
FIELDS OF STUDY: Evaluating psychotherapy; personality assessment; personality theory

Jung is one of the founders of modern psychoanalytic theory.

As a young boy, Jung, developed an avid interest in superstition, mythology, and the occult. He attended the University of Basel for medical training in 1895. After earning a medical degree in 1900, Jung was employed as an assistant staff physician at the Burghölzli Mental Hospital. In 1902, he wrote his dissertation on occult phenomena and earned a degree in psychiatry from the University of Zurich.

In 1905, Jung was appointed as the senior staff physician at the Burghölzli Mental Hospital and also became a lecturer on the medical faculty at the University of Zurich. He was instrumental in developing the concept of the autonomous complex and the technique of free association. After he met Sigmund Freud in Vienna in 1907, the two men became close friends and worked together on the advancement of psychoanalytical theories. In 1910, Jung was selected as the first president of the International Psychoanalytic Association.

By 1912, Jung believed that Freud was placing too much emphasis on sexual instincts in human behavior. Their friendship ended in 1913. Jung believed not only in the biological drives but also in metaphysical or spiritual aspirations as an integral part of human individuality. In formulating his theory of the collective unconscious, Jung included patterns of human thought that he called archetypes, which developed through heredity and included spiritual yearnings. He suggested that therapy was a way to bring people into contact with their collective unconscious.

Jung also developed a groundbreaking personality theory that introduced the classification of psychological types into introverts and extroverts. He explained human behavior as a combination of four psychic functions, thinking, feeling, intuition, and sensation, and proposed the concept of individuation, which is the lifelong process of "self-becoming." Jung coined the term "synchronicity" as an explanation for extrasensory events that were typically deemed occult. He made significant contributions to the understanding of dreams, as well as the language and importance of myths and symbols.

Jung published many important works, including *Über die Psychologie der Dementia praecox: Ein Versuch* (1907; *The Psychology of Dementia Praecox*, 1909), *Wandlungen und Symbole der Libido* (1912; *The Psychology of the Unconscious*, 1915), *Psychologische Typen* (1921; *Psychological Types*, 1923), and *Synchronizität* als ein Prinzip akausaler Zusammenhange (1952; *Synchronicity: An Acausal Connecting Principle*, 1955). Honorary doctorates were awarded to Jung from many notable universities, including Harvard. In 1934, he founded the International General Medical Society for Psychotherapy and became its first president. He was awarded the Literature Prize of the city of Zurich in 1932, was made an Honorary Member of the Swiss Academy of Sciences in 1943, and was named the Honorary Citizen of Küsnacht in 1960.

SOURCES FOR FURTHER STUDY

Blisker, Richard. *On Jung*. Belmont, Calif.: Wadsworth/Thomson Learning, 2002. Insightful work on the life and contributions of Jung to the development of analytic psychology.

Schoeni, William J., ed. *Major Issues in the Life and Work of C. G. Jung*. Lanham, Md.: University Press of America, 1996. Discusses Jung's life and his contributions to Jungian psychology and psychoanalysis.

Shamdasani, Sonu. *Cult Fictions: C. G. Jung and the Founding of Analytical Psychology*. New York: Routledge, 1998. An accurate, revealing account of the history of the Jungian movement in the development of analytical psychology.

Alvin K. Benson

SEE ALSO: Analytical psychology: Carl G. Jung; Archetypes and the collective unconscious; Dreams; Introverts and extroverts; Personality theory.

Juvenile delinquency

TYPE OF PSYCHOLOGY: Developmental psychology
FIELDS OF STUDY: Adolescence; aggression; substance abuse

Juvenile delinquency refers to crime or status offenses by juveniles; adult criminals typically begin as juvenile delinquents.

KEY CONCEPTS
- crime
- delinquency
- juvenile
- parental neglect
- status offense

INTRODUCTION

Juvenile delinquency refers either to crime or to status offenses by a person defined as not yet being an adult. The age of adulthood varies somewhat from state to state. For example, one is an adult in California at age eighteen, while one becomes an adult under Louisiana law at seventeen years of age. A crime is anything which the criminal laws of the state define as illegal. This is what most people think of when they hear the term "juvenile delinquency." There is a second category of juvenile delinquency, however, known as status offenses. These are actions for which the state holds the youth responsible, although they would not be illegal if the person were an adult. Examples include not attending school, staying out too late at night, and defiance of parents. A juvenile can be sent to a juvenile prison for a status offense. For example, in one instance a youth was sent to a juvenile prison for status offense, fell in with more criminally oriented youth, and participated in the burglary of the home of a woman who did volunteer work with the prisoners. It was rumored that she was well-to-do, although this was apparently not really the case. The youths did not find the money, but in the process of the crime they confronted and killed the woman. Thus, a youth sent to a juvenile facility for a status offense was charged with murder for his part in the affair.

DYSFUNCTIONAL FAMILIES

Studies of juvenile delinquents often try to explain why the youth became a criminal. In many cases, especially with youths from the lower socioeconomic classes but also sometimes with middle-class or upper-class youths, the finding is that the family unit is dysfunctional. That is, the youth does not come from a normally healthy home but from a home in which there is considerable aggression among family members, either verbal or physical. Often the parents are not very supportive of the children but instead show either indifference or constant criticism. Youths who murder have often been physically and psychologically abused by their parents. For example, there is a case of a young murderer who shot and killed a female boarder in his home when he was fifteen years old. The youth had received beatings from his stepfathers. He said that the psychological abuse he suffered was even worse than the physical abuse. He gave an example in psychotherapy of one of his stepfathers telling him, "You are no better than the dog. You can go sleep outside in the doghouse tonight." With that, the adult forced him out of the house.

Many juvenile delinquents have suffered parental physical, sexual, or psychological abuse when growing up, and turning to crime seems to be one way of responding to these abuses. Too few people see the various kinds of abuse as a possible causal factor in choosing a life of crime. There is, however, increasing research supporting this notion. This leads to the idea that early intervention into the home may be a preventative, in that stopping some of this abuse may save some juveniles from becoming criminals. Yet not everyone who suffers such abuse becomes a criminal, so there must be many causes of crime. Some people grow up to be fairly normal despite the abuse, while others suffer various degrees of mental illness instead of becoming criminals or growing up to be normal.

Where there is no obvious physical, sexual, or psychological abuse leading to juvenile delinquency, one often finds that the parents themselves are antisocial. Thus, in a sense, the child grows up following rules of socialization, but in these cases the child is socialized to antisocial choices. For example, parents may violate certain laws, often in a flagrant fashion, such as using cocaine in their child's presence. The child learns that this is the normal, approved way of living within his or her household, and adopts the parents' values. Thus, the road is set for the child to become a juvenile delinquent. When one thinks of crime, one may think of lower-class people, and indeed prisons are primarily filled with people from the lower socioeconomic classes, including many minorities. Middle- or upper-class youths may also be delinquent, but they are more likely to avoid going to prison, either through preferential treatment or by having better attorneys.

PERSONAL RESPONSIBILITY

A totally different view of crime from the one presented thus far puts the blame squarely on the shoulders of the offender. According to this view, people have free will and commit crimes because they choose to do so. They are not seen as victims of family background but as bad people who do bad things. A slightly modified version of this approach would be that there is something in the offender that predisposes him or her toward committing

crimes. It may be brain chemistry that makes a person oriented toward thrill-seeking behavior. Perhaps some people have such a strong need for sensation-seeking that ordinary excitements do not satisfy them, and under the right circumstances, such as a group which encourages them, they will commit crimes. Yet another view that places the responsibility primarily on the individual suggests that many criminals suffer from brain damage or other physical problems which interfere with good judgment.

All these explanations focus on the individual as being responsible for his or her behavior and shy away from seeing the social setting, including the family, as having much to do with the juvenile becoming delinquent. An attempt to explain crime by saying that many criminals possess an extra Y chromosome, giving juvenile delinquency a genetic basis, has been shown to be inadequate. Most criminals do not possess an extra Y chromosome, and those who do seem to have low intelligence. They apparently do not become criminals because of their chromosomal abnormality.

CRIME PREVENTION

Given that society thinks of some juveniles as delinquent, there are two general approaches to the problem. First, society can formulate some way of controlling those juveniles who disobey the law. This approach utilizes the whole criminal justice system: police, juvenile courts, probation officers, prisons, and so on. Second, people can try to help the juvenile via treatment. Some would say that prison or probation is treatment, but what is meant here is the kind of intervention that a social worker, psychologist, or psychiatrist might make.

There are three kinds of prevention. Primary prevention occurs when something bad is prevented from happening before the person shows any signs of a problem. Drug education in the early school grades would be an example. Secondary prevention occurs when professionals work with an at-risk population. For example, helping a youth who lives in a high-crime area where drugs are sold and laws are often violated, but who himself or herself is not delinquent, would be secondary prevention. He or she is at risk of becoming a delinquent, given the environment, but has not become delinquent yet. Tertiary prevention occurs after the problem has already occurred. Treating a disease after a person has become sick is tertiary prevention; so is doing psychotherapy with people who already are mentally ill, or performing some kind of intervention with someone who is already a delinquent.

Unfortunately, most of society's preventive attempts are tertiary prevention, whereas primary prevention would seem to be the most effective, followed by secondary prevention. Psychologists and psychiatrists are typically called upon for tertiary prevention. Social workers offer tertiary prevention as well, but some of the time they may intervene in a primary or secondary fashion, as when they do home visits to assess the problems in a home and devise some strategy for improving the situation. Psychologists and psychiatrists can do primary and secondary prevention, especially if they work with an agency, such as a school, where they try to prevent problems before they occur. It may be too late to change most juvenile delinquents once they reach about sixteen years of age. Primary or secondary preventive efforts would seem the most effective approach. By the time an offender is sixteen, he or she may have a long history of crime and may be dedicated to an antisocial lifestyle. Some sixteen-year-olds can be helped, especially if they are fairly new to crime. Many juvenile delinquents have no sense of how they could be anything other than a criminal. Treatment efforts need to provide them with alternatives and with the skills, via education or job training, to meet these alternatives.

JUVENILE JUSTICE SYSTEM

Once the juvenile has been tried and convicted in a juvenile court (or in a regular adult court, if tried as an adult, as sometimes occurs in very serious cases), the court has three major dispositions it can make. The convicted juvenile may be placed on probation, ordered to make restitution if money was stolen or property damaged, or incarcerated. One would hope that fairness would prevail and that the sentences handed down from jurisdiction to jurisdiction would be similar for similar offenses. Such, unfortunately, is not always the case.

The criminal justice system is plagued with the problem of sentencing disparity. This affects juvenile and adult offenders alike. In other words, if an offender is convicted in one court, the sentence may be very different from that which is handed down in another court for the same offense, and for a juvenile with the same history. History here means that the court, legitimately, takes into account the

previous arrest and conviction record of the juvenile in determining sentence. In one look at sentences given to juveniles by courts in six different sites (five different states and Washington, D.C.), all the offenders were repeat offenders convicted of serious crimes. The sentences handed down in the different sites should have been about the same. They were not. In one jurisdiction, most of the convicted juvenile offenders were incarcerated and none received probation. In the other sites, incarceration was very unlikely, and probation or restitution was frequently employed. Thus, what sentence one received depended upon where one was convicted. This is hardly an equitable application of the law. The jurisdiction that typically used incarceration may be overly harsh, while the other jurisdictions may be overly lenient. Sometimes probation or restitution makes sense in order to give the offender another chance, while sometimes incarceration is necessary for the protection of society. The sentences should fit the needs of society and of the offender, but at times they seem to reflect the bias of the community for either harsh or lenient treatment of convicted juveniles.

THE CONCEPT OF JUVENILES

The idea that juveniles should be treated differently from adults is a fairly modern one. For example, in the Middle Ages people had quite a different conception of childhood. Their art often shows babies who look like small adults. Until quite recently, juveniles were often placed in prison with adults, where they were sometimes subject to rape or other abuse. Some states still place juveniles in adult prisons. Thinking of someone as a juvenile delinquent, instead of simply as a delinquent (criminal), often means that the juvenile receives what are supposed to be special considerations. For example, the juvenile may not be "convicted of a crime" but instead may have a "sustained petition" declaring him or her delinquent. The penalties may be much less than if an adult had committed the crime.

Since juveniles are treated differently, it once was held that the juvenile court was not really a court in the adult sense but a place where the judge's function was to help the youth. One consequence of this thinking was that the adult right to have an attorney was not granted universally to juveniles. Thus, those charged with juvenile delinquency would face the possibility of being convicted and sent to prison but might not have a lawyer during their trial. The United States Supreme Court changed that situation in 1967 in a case known as *In re Gault*, in which it ruled that juveniles are entitled to adultlike protections, including having an attorney. No longer would juveniles be tried and convicted without legal counsel.

It was previously noted that juveniles may receive lesser penalties for crimes than adults; sometimes, however, the penalties are worse. Two examples are status offenses, wherein the offense, such as disobeying parents, would not even be a crime if the juvenile were an adult, and instances in which the juvenile may be confined in a juvenile prison until he or she becomes an adult. In the second case, an adult male who breaks into a warehouse may receive a three-year sentence, while a fourteen-year-old boy may be confined until he is eighteen or perhaps even until he is twenty-one. In this case, the person would have received a shorter sentence had he been an adult. The use of status offenses as a basis for charging or imprisoning juveniles has received much criticism from social scientists as unfair. Those who favor retaining it see it as an effective social control mechanism for what they consider criminal tendencies.

SOURCES FOR FURTHER STUDY

Alloy, Lauren B., Neil R. Jacobson, and Joan Ross Acocella. *Abnormal Psychology: Current Perspectives.* 8th ed. New York: McGraw-Hill, 1998. A very readable abnormal psychology text. The chapter on legal issues in abnormal psychology is of interest. The authors cover the topics of psychological disturbance and criminal law, civil commitment, patient's rights, and power and the mental health profession.

Brown, Stephen E., F. A. Esbensen, and Gilbert Geis. *Criminology: Explaining Crime and Its Context.* 4th ed. Cincinnati: Anderson, 2001. An excellent text that gives a good overview of crime and its various explanations. While not specifically focused on juvenile crime, the book does give a good general explanation of crime from a variety of standpoints, including such things as robbery, the impact of gambling, different theories of crime, and the goals of the criminal justice system.

Hoffman, Allan M., Randall W. Summers, and Andrew L. Cherry, eds. *Teen Violence: A Global View.* Westport, Conn.: Greenwood Press, 2000. A collection of essays providing an overview of juvenile delinquency issues in Australia, Canada, England and Wales, Germany, Israel, Italy, Jamaica, Russia, St. Lucia, Slovenia, South Africa, Spain, Thailand, and the United States.

Karr-Morse, Robin, and Meredith S. Wiley. *Ghosts from the Nursery: Tracing the Roots of Violence.* New York: Atlantic Monthly Press, 1998. Traces the links between childhood development from the womb through the first two years of life and later juvenile delinquency.

Monahan, John, ed. *Who Is the Client? The Ethics of Psychological Intervention in the Criminal Justice System.* Washington, D.C.: American Psychological Association, 1980. This book contains six chapters which deal with working in the criminal justice system. Ethical dilemmas abound, as the professional may have responsibilities both to the agency and to the client (such as a juvenile delinquent).

Russell Eisenman

SEE ALSO: Abnormality: Legal models; Addictive personality and behaviors; Adolescence: Cognitive skills; Adolescence: Cross-cultural patterns; Aggression; Antisocial personality; Child abuse; Law and psychology.

K

Kelly, George A.

BORN: April 28, 1905, in Perth, Kansas
DIED: March 7, 1967, in Waltham, Massachusetts
IDENTITY: American theorist and leader in clinical psychology
TYPE OF PSYCHOLOGY: Personality; psychotherapy
FIELDS OF STUDY: Evaluating psychotherapy; personality theory

Kelly was the founder of the psychology of personal constructs.

George Alexander Kelly was born in Perth, Kansas, in 1905. His early years of education largely consisted of home schooling from his parents and were followed by his earning degrees in a wide variety of fields. He studied physics and mathematics at Park College, Kansas (B.A., 1926), educational sociology at the University of Kansas (M.A., 1928), education at Edinburgh University in Scotland (B.Ed., 1930), and psychology at the University of Iowa (Ph.D., 1931). His first professional position was at Kansas State College in 1931, where he stayed until entering the U.S. Navy in 1943. After the end of the war in 1945, he spent a year at the University of Maryland, and then became professor and director of the clinical psychology training program at Ohio State University. From 1965 to 1967, he held the Riklis Chair of Behavioral Science at Brandeis University.

Kelly's views are not easily assimilated into other approaches to psychology, for he was an independent and original thinker. In his massive two-volume *Psychology of Personal Constructs* (1955) he treated persons as if they were scientists trying to develop a theory (test hypotheses) about the world in which they livid. He tried to understand individuals not from their current environment or past history, but from their subjective or interpretative viewpoint—the hypotheses they had constructed about what was happening to them.

An individual's theory (constructs or interpretations of the real world) was ever-changing, and no one construct was useful for more than a limited range of circumstances or time. For Kelly, individuals were not merely passive victims of the past (as with psychodynamic psychology) or of the current environment (as with behaviorism), but were active and responsible individuals who could change the circumstances they faced by reinterpretating them. Kelly developed a technique for assessing constructs, thereby permitting many applications to personality theory, psychotherapy, business, and education.

Kelly was also a pioneer in developing psychological services for rural areas, a leader in the establishment of psychologists as independent practitioners, and a central figure in the planning of the most widely used clinical training model (the Boulder Model). He died of a heart attack in 1967. The threads of his contributions may be found in the contemporary perspective called constructionism. His influence continues with each issue of the *Journal of Constructionist Psychology*.

SOURCES FOR FURTHER STUDY

Fransella, Fay. *George Kelly*. Thousand Oaks, Calif.: Sage Publications, 1995. This is the most complete source for information on Kelly's life.

Mischel, Walter. "Looking for Personality." In *A Century of Psychology as Science*, edited by Sigmund Koch and David Leary. New York: McGraw-Hill, 1985. An excellent piece which places Kelly in the context of other theorists.

Neimeyer, Robert R., and Thomas T. Jackson. "George A. Kelly and the Development of Personal Construct Psychology." In *Pictorial History of Psychology*, edited by Wolfgang G. Bringman, Helmut E. Luck, Rudolf Miller, and Charles E.

Early. Chicago: Quintessence, 1997. A brief overview of Kelley's life and contributions with many photographs.

Terry J. Knapp

SEE ALSO: Personal constructs: George A. Kelly.

Kinesthetic memory

TYPE OF PSYCHOLOGY: Cognition; developmental psychology; learning; memory; sensation and perception; social psychology

FIELDS OF STUDY: Cognitive development; cognitive learning; cognitive processes; nervous system; social perception and cognition

Kinesthetic memory refers to how muscles remember movements and is an essential for normal motor activity and learning.

KEY CONCEPTS
- body
- cerebellum
- learning
- memory
- motor movement
- muscle
- retention
- sensation
- sequences

INTRODUCTION

Movement is central to sustaining life and fostering learning. Humans learn by kinesthetic, visual, or auditory methods, known as modalities, of processing sensory information. Each learning style engages a specific part of the brain to acquire, process, and store data. Educators develop teaching objectives compatible with students' learning styles. Although the majority of people, approximately 65 percent, tend to learn best with visual memory, and 20 percent learn best through auditory memory, the 15 percent of humans who function best with kinesthetic memory usually retain information longer.

Kinesthetic memories are primarily stored in the cerebellum. This part of the brain has less risk for injury than the neocortex and hippocampus, which are involved in visual and auditory learning processes. Although kinesthetic memory is basic to the motions involved in writing, it is often ineffective for people attempting to comprehend academic topics. Kinesthetic types of learning are more suitable for mastering physical movements in sports and dance and in performance control such as playing instruments or singing.

Kinesthetic memory is fundamental to motor activity. Muscles in people and animals recall previous movements according to how body parts such as joints, bones, ligaments, and tendons interact and are positioned. This innate memory of relationships and sequences is the basis of motor skills such as writing or riding a bicycle. Because the brain relies on kinesthetic memory, it does not have to concentrate on how to move body parts. Instead, the brain can be focused for more complex thought processes and enhancement or refinement of movements.

Proprioception, the unconscious knowledge of body placement and a sense of the space it occupies, benefits from kinesthetic memory. Bodies are able to coordinate sensory and motor functions because of proprioception so that reflexes in response to stimuli can occur. These innate motor abilities help most organisms to trust that their bodies will behave as expected.

People have been aware of elements of kinesthetic memory since the late nineteenth century. Teacher Anne Sullivan used tactile methods to teach Helen Keller words. The blind, deaf, and mute Keller touched objects, and kinesthetic sensations guided her to remember meanings. During the twentieth century, educators recognized the merits of kinesthetic learning to assist students, both children and adults, with reading difficulties. Kinesthetic memory has also been incorporated into physical therapies.

MEASURING MEMORY

Kinesthetic memory is crucial for people to function proficiently in their surroundings. Measurement of kinesthetic memory is limited by clinical tools and procedures. Researchers are attempting to develop suitable tests to comprehend the role of kinesthetic memory in maintaining normal motor control for physical movement. Psychologists Judith Laszlo and Phillip Bairstow designed a ramp device that measures motor development and kinesthetic acuity in subjects' upper extremities but not in specific joints. Kinesthetic acuity is how well people can describe the position of their body parts when their vision is obscured.

Some investigators considered Laszlo's and Bairstow's measurement method insufficient to examine some severely neurologically impaired patients, and it was revised to gauge nervous system proprioceptive deficiencies. Researchers at the University of Michigan-Flint's Physical Therapy Laboratory for Cumulative Trauma Disorders adjusted ramp angles of laboratory devices in an attempt to create a better kinesthetic testing tool.

Kinesthetic studies examine such variables as gender and age and how they affect perception and short- and long-term kinesthetic memory. Results are applied to create more compatible learning devices and techniques which enhance information retention and recollection. Researchers sometimes assess how vibrations of tendons and muscles or anesthesia of joints affects movement perceptions. Studies evaluate how kinesthetic stimuli affect awareness of size, length, and distance.

Kinesthetic memory tests indicate that kinesthetic performance varies according to brain characteristics and changes. Some tests involve tracing patterns at intervals during one week. Subjects are evaluated for how accurate their perceptions and memory of the required movements are from one testing session to the next. Such studies have shown that as people age, their kinesthetic memory capabilities decline. Mental health professionals seek treatment for brain injuries that result in ideomotor apraxia, a memory loss for sequential movements, and ideational apraxia, the breakdown of movement thought.

INTELLECTUAL APPLICATIONS

Some educational specialists hypothesize that people with dyslexia might lack sufficient kinesthetic memory to recognize and form words. Some dyslexia treatments involve strengthening neural pathways with physical activity to reinforce kinesthetic memory. As a result, some processes become instinctive and the brain can concentrate on understanding academic material and behaving creatively.

Teachers can help students acquire cursive handwriting skills by practicing unisensory kinesthetic trace techniques. Touch is the only sense students are permitted to use with this method, which develops kinesthetic memory for future writing. Blind-folded students trace letters with their fingers in a quiet environment. They repeat these hand and arm movements to form letters, then words. Muscular memories of these movements and body positions improve motor control for writing.

Kinesthetic-tactile methods are applied with some visual and auditory learning styles. In 1943, Grace Fernald introduced her kinesthetic method V.A.K.T., which also used visual, auditory, and tactile tasks during stages of tracing, writing, and pronouncing. Margaret Taylor Smith established the Multisensory Teaching Approach (MTA). Beth Slingerland created the Slingerland Approach which integrates all sensory learning styles, including kinesthetic motor skills.

Memorization is a fundamental part of musical activities. Singers rely on kinesthetic memory of throat muscles to achieve their desired vocal range and performance. Musicians develop kinesthetic memory skills by practicing pieces without visual cues to avoid memory lapses due to performance anxiety. Panic or nervousness can disrupt kinesthetic memories unless performers develop methods to deal with their fears or excitement.

Studies indicate that kinesthetic memory provokes signals which influence people's memory. In particular, one study investigated how cues acquired during a learning process affect how people retain memories. Researchers focused on how people interacted with computers, specifically how the use of a pointing device, such as a mouse, and touchscreens affected retention of information viewed on computer screens. Pressing touchscreens, for instance, to control information contributed to increased spatial memory.

BODY INTELLIGENCE

Kinesthetic memory guides children to develop control over their bodies. Jay A. Seitz, of York College/City University of New York, emphasizes that conventional intellectual assessments of children ignore bodily-kinesthetic intelligence. He argues that kinesthetic education, particularly in the mastery of aesthetic movements, is essential to balance traditional Western formal education, which focuses on cognitive linguistic and logical-numerical skills. Many educators consider those skills superior to other means of expressing intelligence. Seitz states that kinesthetic skills such as those developed by dance have significant cognitive aspects which can

enhance academic curricula and children's intellectual growth.

Jean Piaget stressed that movement is an important factor in children's early learning development.
Infants' sensorimotor experiences provide foundational knowledge for speech. Harvard University
professor Howard Gardner built on Piaget's premise
by focusing on how people become skilled in coor-
dinating their movements, manipulating items, and
managing situations competently, what he terms
bodily kinesthetic intelligence.

Kinesthetic memory is one of three main cognitive skills associated with bodily kinesthetic intelligence. Muscle memory allows people to use their
bodies artistically to perform desired motion patterns, imitate movements, and create new nonverbal physical expressions. Motor logic and kinesthetic awareness supplement kinesthetic memory
and regulate neuromuscular organization and presentation in such physical forms as rhythmic movement sequences and posture. Muscles and tendons
have sensory receptors which aid kinesthetic awareness.

Seitz investigated how people use gestures to
think and to express themselves. He emphasized
that movement is the product of intellectual activity and can be recorded in kinesic language such
as choreography, which describes dance sequences.
Seitz conducted a qualitative and quantitative analysis of formal and informal dance classes to determine how children use kinesthetic sense and
memory and motor logic to learn increasingly complicated dance routines. He noted that children
aged three to four years have awareness of movement dynamics such as rhythm and balance.

After being taught simple choreography such as a
butterfly-shaped pattern, children were asked to repeat the pattern five minutes later for a kinesthetic
memory test. They were also asked to demonstrate a
possible final gesture to a pantomime, such as pretending to throw a ball, as a motor logic test. The
children were also shown pictures of people, structures, or items and asked to use their bodies to show
what movements they associated with the images.
All tests were videotaped to assess how children cop-
ied, created, or finished movements or the degree
to which they failed.

Some children who lack motor skill competence
have developmental coordination disorder (DCD),
which was first classified in the fourth edition of

the *Diagnostic and Statistical Manual of Mental Disorders* (1994, DSM-IV). Authorities disagree whether
DCD is caused by kinesthetic or visual perceptual
dysfunction. Some tests reveal that children who
have DCD might not kinesthetically rehearse memories they acquire visually. Laszlo and Bairstow developed kinesthetic sensitivity tests to assess subjects' motor skills in processing information such as
the position and movement of limbs. Kinesthetic
perceptual problems result in clumsy movements.
Therapists advocating the kinesthetic training approach encourage children to practice movements
and develop better body awareness in order to refine motor skills.

THERAPY

Kinesthetic memory contributes to physical fitness
and the prevention of injuries. Researchers in the
fields of kinesiology and biomechanics study how
people move and incorporate kinesthetic concepts.
Many athletes participate in prolates, or progressive
Pilates, which is a kinesthetically based conditioning
program designed to achieve balance of muscle systems and body awareness of sensations and spatial
location. Prolates practitioners view the human body
as a unified collection of connected parts which
must smoothly function together to achieve coordination, flexibility, and efficiency and reduce stress.

This exercise program develops the mind-body
relationship with movement visualization and concentration skills practice so people can instinctively
sense how to fix athletic problems using appropriate muscles instead of repeatedly rehearsing mechanics. Prolates requires participants to achieve
control of their center of gravity during diverse
movements, thus refining kinesthetic memory. Athletes automatically adjust their physical stance when
details about muscles are conveyed to the brain by
proprioceptors, which are enhanced by Prolates.

Aquatic Proprioceptive Neuromuscular Facilitation (PNF) is a movement therapy. This treatment
helps fibromyalgia sufferers learn appropriate
movement patterns to replace damaging behaviors
such as clenching teeth, raising shoulders, and
other excessive and unconscious muscle contractions and tensions that people use to deal with
chronic pain and emotional stimuli. They also learn
more efficient breathing techniques.

Erich Fromm encouraged the use of Visual Kinesthetic Disassociation (V/KD), which is a therapy de-

signed to help patients attain detachment from kinesthetic memories acquired traumatically, through physical abuse or rape. Therapists initiate V/KD by asking patients to act as observers, not participants, as though they are watching a movie, not acting in it, as they recall the traumatic experiences in their imagination. By paying attention to visual and auditory cues, patients gradually release kinesthetic memories. Sometimes, therapists ask the patients to play the scenes backward to reinforce nonkinesthetic memories and develop sensations of being empowered and competent.

SOURCES FOR FURTHER STUDY

Crawley, Sharon J., and King Merritt. *Remediating Reading Difficulties*. 3d ed. Boston: McGraw-Hill, 2000. Provides details of kinesthetic methods used to assist students with memory of words to build vocabularies.

Jamison, Lynette, and David Ogden. *Aquatic Therapy Using PNF Patterns*. Tucson, Ariz.: Therapy Skill Builders, 1994. Based on authors' therapeutic experiences. Tells how kinesthetic memory can be applied to pool exercises to teach patients appropriate muscle movements to ease pain.

Laszlo, Judith I., and Phillip J. Bairstow. *Perceptual Motor Behavior: Developmental Assessment and Therapy*. New York: Praeger, 1985. Describes the authors' kinesthetic test to evaluate psychomotor disorders.

Messing, Lynn, and Ruth Campbell, eds. *Gesture, Speech, and Sign*. New York: Oxford University Press, 1999. Contributors interpret nonverbal movements according to cognitive psychology theories and address how gestures and language, including computer expression and sign language, are interrelated.

Seitz, Jay A. "I Move . . . Therefore I Am." *Psychology Today* 26, no. 2 (March/April, 1993): 50-55. Seitz explains how brain neural systems for thought, emotion, and movement interact so that people use their bodies to think and express themselves kinesthetically in addition to thinking with their minds. He tells how kinesthetic memories aid social interaction and emotional health.

Thompson, Clem W., and Roy T. Floyd. *Manual of Structural Kinesiology*. 14th ed. Dubuque, Iowa: McGraw-Hill, 2001. A classic sport anatomy text which explains how the structure of muscles and joints is related to movement functions and how

to improve muscle performance with kinesthetic methods. Includes a CD-ROM and worksheets.

Wing, Alan M., Patrick Haggard, and J. Randall Flanagan, eds. *Hand and Brain: The Neurophysiology and Psychology of Hand Movements*. San Diego, Calif.: Academic Press, 1996. Focuses on muscular memories used for basic gestures and movements in order to communicate and engage in fundamental and advanced tasks.

Elizabeth D. Schafer

SEE ALSO: Brain structure; Depth and motion perception; Memory; Memory: Animal research; Memory: Empirical studies; Memory: Physiology; Memory: Sensory; Memory storage; Motor development; Sensation and perception.

Kinsey, Alfred

BORN: June 23, 1894, in Hoboken, New Jersey
DIED: August 25, 1956, in Bloomington, Indiana
IDENTITY: American sexologist and zoologist
TYPE OF PSYCHOLOGY: Psychological methodologies
FIELDS OF STUDY: Descriptive methodologies; sexual disorders

Kinsey's survey research in human sexuality revealed the diversity of sexual behavior and helped launch a sexual revolution.

Alfred Charles Kinsey grew up in an extremely restrictive Methodist family. His father forbade dating and Kinsey's keen interest in sexuality may have stemmed from the frustration that this produced.

After earning his a bachelor's degree at Bowdoin College, Kinsey did graduate work in entomology at Harvard. After earning his doctorate, Kinsey was employed at Indiana University as a professor in zoology. In 1938, a group of female students, perhaps at Kinsey's request, petitioned the university to offer a course on marriage and the family. The university president chose Kinsey to teach the course. He later claimed that his study of human sexuality was fueled by the paucity of data that he encountered while teaching the course.

Kinsey began to gather sexual histories from students and, with funding from external sources, established the Institute for Sexual Research, Inc., in

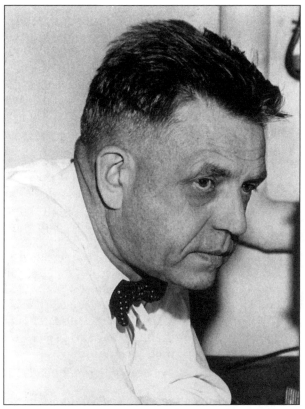

Alfred Kinsey. (Library of Congress)

1942. He and his colleagues then began extensive surveying, questioning several thousand persons over the next few years. The surveys were conducted orally, with the interviewers asking direct, memorized questions in a rapid fashion. Kinsey developed techniques designed to improve honesty and establish rapport with participants; he often altered his speech habits, dress, and behavior to match those of his interviewees.

The surveys became the basis of Kinsey's most famous work, *Sexual Behavior in the Human Male* (1948), which sold nearly 500,000 copies and offended the staid sexual attitudes of the time. The book and its companion, *Sexual Behavior in the Human Female* (1953), presented data and discussion of previously taboo topics such as masturbation, homosexual behavior, and oral sex. Kinsey's research indicated that such behaviors were far more common than expected. For example, he reported that over 90 percent of males and 58 percent of adult females had engaged in masturbation. About half of surveyed females admitted to premarital sex. Critics

validly objected that his sample, while large, was biased, with college-educated whites being overrepresented. Kinsey also endured many personal attacks and threats from conservative groups. The Rockefeller Foundation terminated its funding of his institute in 1954. Kinsey's death may have been hastened by the relentless attacks.

Kinsey is still a controversial figure. There is considerable evidence that Kinsey did engage in several homosexual affairs and that he encouraged his wife to have sexual encounters with other men. To some, these revelations arouse suspicion concerning his data and threaten the integrity of his work. However, many other sexologists have reported findings that generally support Kinsey's work.

SOURCES FOR FURTHER STUDY

Christenson, Cornelia V. *Kinsey: A Biography.* Bloomington: Indiana University Press, 1971. Written by a colleague of Kinsey, this book includes many personal insights.

Gathorne-Hardy, Jonathan. *Sex the Measure of All Things: A Life of Alfred C. Kinsey.* Bloomington: Indiana University Press, 1998. An exhaustively researched effort which argues that Kinsey was a diligent and reputable researcher despite his atypical sexual life

Jones, James H. *Alfred C. Kinsey: A Public/Private Life.* New York: W. W. Norton, 1997. Often questions Kinsey's scientific integrity and the validity of his work.

Charles H. Evans

SEE ALSO: Homosexuality; Sexual behavior patterns; Sexual dysfunction; Sexual variants and paraphilias; Survey research: Questionnaires and interviews.

Kraepelin, Emil

BORN: February 15, 1856, in Neustrelitz, Germany
DIED: October 7, 1926, in Munich, Germany
IDENTITY: German psychiatrist
TYPE OF PSYCHOLOGY: Emotion; personality; psychopathology; social psychology
FIELDS OF STUDY: Anxiety disorders; behavioral therapies; depression; models of abnormality; organic disorders; personality disorders; schizophrenias

Kraepelin developed a classification system for mental illness and identified manic-depressive disorder and schizophrenia.

Emil Wilhelm Magnus Georg Kraepelin was taught the value of hard work by his father, a Prussian schoolteacher. Kraepelin began studying medicine in 1874 at the University of Leipzig, then studied at the University of Würzburg. In 1877, he met experimental psychologist Wilhelm Wundt and studied with him from 1882 to 1883, pursuing a better understanding of the effects of drugs, alcohol, and fatigue on the human mind. Between 1878 and 1882, he assisted Bernhard von Gudden at the psychiatric asylum of Munich County. In 1882, he was appointed as the senior assistant under Paul Flechsig at the psychiatric hospital at Leipzig University.

In an effort to improve his financial situation, Kraepelin wrote his first edition of *Compendium der Psychiatrie* (1883; compendium of psychiatry), which focused on a workable model for classifying mental illnesses. He divided mental disorders into two categories, those caused by external conditions (exogenous), and those related to biological disorders (endogenous). He believed that exogenous disorders, such as fear of spiders and depression, could be treated, while endogenous disorders, such as brain damage and genetic defects, were incurable.

After serving as a senior assistant at the asylum at Leubus (1884), as the head of the ward for mentally ill patients at the general hospital in Dresden, Germany (1885), and as a professor of psychiatry at Dorpat (Estonia) University (1886-1891), he accepted a position as a professor of psychiatry at Heidelberg University. In his sixth edition of the *Compendium* (1899), Kraepelin distinguished between manic-depressive psychosis and schizophrenia. After many years of clinical studies and thousands of cases, he concluded that manic-depressive disorders were treatable but that schizophrenia was incurable. During the same period of time, he also published many papers on the harmful psychological effects of alcohol.

In 1903, Kraepelin accepted a job as a professor of psychiatry at Munich University. In 1909, he and one of his former students, Alois Alzheimer, classified a disorder that became known as Alzheimer's disease. Kraepelin spent a great deal of time designing and preparing the German Psychiatric Research Institution that opened in Munich in 1917. In 1922, he became the director of the institution. Kraepelin's classification system of mental disorders greatly influenced subsequent classifications by other psychiatrists. His fundamental concepts continue to be valid working principles in modern psychiatric research.

SOURCES FOR FURTHER STUDY

Hersen, Michel, Alan E. Kazdin, and Alan S. Bellack, eds. *The Clinical Psychology Handbook.* 2d ed. New York: Pergamon, 1991. Insights into mental disorders, including manic-depressive psychosis and schizophrenias.

McWilliams, Nancy. *Psychoanalytic Case Formulation.* New York: Guilford, 1999. Discusses some of the traits and classifications of mental disorders.

Shrout, Patrick E., and Susan T. Fiske, eds. *Personality Research, Methods, and Theory.* Hillsdale, N.J.: Lawrence Erlbaum, 1995. Contains papers on personality theory, traits, and disorders.

Alvin K. Benson

SEE ALSO: Diagnosis; *Diagnostic and Statistical Manual of Mental Disorders* (DSM); Schizophrenia: Background, types, and symptoms; Schizophrenia: High-risk children; Schizophrenia: Theoretical explanations.

Kuder Occupational Interest Survey (KOIS)

DATE: 1939 forward

TYPE OF PSYCHOLOGY: Intelligence and intelligence testing

FIELDS OF STUDY: Ability tests; intelligence assessment

Career interest surveys such as the KOIS have been developed to assist people in making career placement decisions. KOIS purports to assess self-reported abilities, interests, and other characteristics and correlates them with characteristics or traits of jobs, occupations, college majors, and careers. These selections can outline a direction that an individual can use to make better decisions.

KEY CONCEPTS
- career
- interest inventory
- job choice
- self-efficacy

INTRODUCTION

This Kuder Occupational Interest Survey is an inventory originally developed by G. Frederic Kuder and has been in use since 1939. The earliest version was the Kuder Preference Record-Vocational (KPR-V) survey. This measurement of vocational interest was primarily for use in vocational placement and job choice. Individuals identify items according to most-liked and least-liked preferences. This is accomplished using forced-choice items which differentiate among three activities that might be preferred as a career choice. The goal of the survey is not to suggest specific jobs or occupations, but rather to determine broad interest areas. These are Outdoor, Mechanical, Computational, Scientific, Persuasive, Artistic, Literary, Musical, Social Science, or Clerical. Later, the Kuder General Interest Survey (KGIS) was developed as a revision of the KPR-V, designed for grades 6-12, using simpler language. The KOIS provides scores with reference to specific occupational groups in addition to the broad interest areas noted above. Scores are used to identify 109 specific occupations and 40 college majors.

The scores can also be converted to a common reporting system known as the Holland system (using the R-I-A-S-E-C sequence). The Holland system consists of six concepts, arranged in a hexagon indicating relative positioning: Realistic (R), Investigative (I), Artistic (A), Social (S), Enterprising (E), and Conventional (C). In order to emphasize non-traditional occupations for men and women, a series of new scales have been added to the KOIS.

TECHNICAL ASPECTS

The report received as a result of completing the KOIS is divided into four sections. The first section summarizes the dependability of the results by analyzing their consistency. The report can suggest the dependability of the results for the individual who completed the KOIS. The second section rank-orders interest patterns in comparison to a normative sample of both men and women. This allows either gender to make a comparison directly.

The third section ranks the test taker in relation to men and women who are employed in different occupations and are satisfied with their career choices. The fourth section of the report matches patterns of interest to those of students who have selected different college majors. These sections match interest patterns corresponding to occupations and career choices such as lawyers, personnel managers, and physicians. College major interest patterns include history, English, and political science.

Psychometric properties for the KOIS are very good. For instance, short-term reliability is a property of an instrument which indicates that the score of a test taker will tend to be the same over time (that is, test-retest reliability). Short-term reliability of the KOIS is between .80 and .95, and there is evidence indicating the scores may be stable for as long as thirty years.

Predictive validity is an important concept for career instruments and tests such as the KOIS. Predictive validity indicates that the results of a test score can "predict" the career choice. While the test scores cannot actually predict behavior, it is possible to match up (correlate) a score with career choice, job placement, and college major made by a person at a later date. This type of validity gives credibility to the test. In the case of the KOIS, predictive validity is very high. While job placement and KOIS scores of students in high school match up well, student scores and choice of college major match up better.

CRITIQUE

One useful aspect of the KOIS is how self-efficacy influences confidence for takers' knowledge of themselves when the results of the KOIS are made known to them. Additionally, self-efficacy for specific occupational tasks has been demonstrated. Research indicates that there is a difference between expectations of various groups and the types of occupations, careers, or jobs chosen. This type of information is particularly useful for guidance decisions for high-school and college students. Refinements published in 1985 reflect continuing development of this type of information.

In order for individuals to enter an appropriate career, they must begin to identify specific interests and the relative importance of those interests. Some individuals will need little guidance in making career choices, others will need the guidance of a survey instrument like the KOIS. In the more than seventy-five years since the introduction of the first interest inventory (the Carnegie Interest Survey) millions of people have received important information to use in decision making. Caution is always expressed by the authors of these inventories that no decision should be made solely on the basis of the results determined by one inventory alone. The KOIS is one of eighty interest inventories currently in use.

SOURCES FOR FURTHER STUDY

Anastasi, A., and Susan Urbina. *Psychological Testing.* 7th ed. Upper Saddle River, N.J.: Prentice-Hall, 1997. Provides information about specific test construction, along with explanations of widely used concepts and procedures affecting psychological testing.

Kaplan, R. M., and Dennis P. Saccuzzo. *Psychological Testing.* 5th ed. Belmont, Calif.: Wadsworth/Thompson Learning, 2001. Gives an outline of undergraduate teaching topics such as validity and reliability as well as general information concerning specific tests.

Daniel L. Yazak

SEE ALSO: Ability tests; Assessment; Career and personnel testing; Career Occupational Preference System (COPS); College entrance examinations; General Aptitude Test Battery (GATB); Human resource training and development; Intelligence tests; Interest inventories; Race and intelligence; Scientific methods; Strong Interest Inventory (SII); Survey research: Questionnaires and interviews; Testing: Historical perspectives.

L

Lacan, Jacques

BORN: April 13, 1901, in Paris, France
DIED: September 9, 1981, in Paris, France
IDENTITY: French psychoanalyst and philosopher
TYPE OF PSYCHOLOGY: Psychotherapy
FIELDS OF STUDY: Classic analytic themes and issues; general constructs and issues; personality theory; thought

Lacan was a pioneering psychoanalyst who emphasized the relationship between language and the unconscious.

Jacques-Marie Émile Lacan earned his baccalaureate degree from the Collège Stanislas, a Jesuit school in Paris. He began his clinical training in 1927 at Sainte-Anne's Hospital. Lacan received a diploma in forensic psychology in 1931 and *doctorat d'état* in 1932 for his dissertation on paranoid psychosis and personality.

In 1936, Lacan presented his paper "Le Stade du Miroir" (the mirror stage) at the fourteenth International Psychoanalytical Congress. In this seminal essay, Lacan argued that the child's ego only begins to emerge between the ages of six and eighteen months, when it first sees and identifies with its own reflection in a mirror and begins to conceive of itself as a separate, unified being. The apparent completeness of the reflected image gives the otherwise helpless child a sense of mastery over its own body. The ego is therefore the effect of an alienating identification based upon a lack of completeness in the body of the child. Lacan concluded from this that psychoanalysis should reassess its focus on the patient's ego and turn its attention back to the unconscious because of what he later termed "the falsifying character of the ego."

In the mirror stage, according to Lacan, the child also enters the "language system," characterized by absence, lack, and separation because language names things which are not immediately present ("signifieds") and substitutes words ("signifiers") for them. It is through what Lacan calls the "linguistic chain" that desire seeks to recover its original, though illusory, unity. This is also the beginning of socialization, says Lacan. The child is now exposed to the linguistic world of prohibitions characterized by the figure of the father, or what Lacan calls "the father's 'no.'" Lacan was heavily influenced by structuralist thinkers such as the anthropologist Claude Lévi-Strauss and linguists Ferdinand de Saussure and Roman Jakobson. Lacan's chief claim, based upon his readings of Saussure and Jakobson, is that the unconscious is "structured like a language."

Lacan's *Écrits* (2 vols., 1966-1971; *Écrits: A Selection*, 1977) were based upon transcripts of lectures given over a number of years. The multivolume *Le Séminaire de Jacques Lacan* (20 vols., 1973-1981; *The Seminar of Jacques Lacan*, 1988), edited by Jacques-Alain Miller, contains some of Lacan's most accessible material, including *Quatre Fondamentaux de la Psychanalyse* (1973), translated as *The Four Fundamental Concepts of Psychoanalysis* (1978). Lacan dissolved his École Freudienne de Paris in 1980 and died a year later, leaving behind a body of work which continues to influence psychoanalytic studies, philosophy, and literary and cultural theory.

SOURCES FOR FURTHER STUDY

Dor, Joel. *Introduction to the Reading of Lacan: The Unconscious Structured Like a Language.* New York: Other Press, 1998. A clearly written and accessible introduction. Includes a useful bibliography.

Evans, Dylan. *An Introductory Dictionary of Lacanian Psychoanalysis.* New York: Routledge, 1996. Evans defines over two hundred technical terms in their historical contexts.

Fink, Bruce. *A Clinical Introduction to Lacanian Psychoanalysis: Theory and Technique.* Cambridge, Mass.: Harvard University Press, 1997. A practicing psychoanalyst clearly introduces Lacan in theory and in clinical practice. Includes an extensive bibliography.

Gerard O'Sullivan

SEE ALSO: Analytic psychology: Jacques Lacan; Language; Psychoanalytic psychology; Psychoanalytic psychology and personality: Sigmund Freud.

Language

TYPE OF PSYCHOLOGY: Cognition; language
FIELDS OF STUDY: Cognitive processes, thought

Language is a system of arbitrary symbols that can be combined in conventionalized ways to express ideas, thoughts, and feelings. Various theories and models have been constructed to study, describe, and explain language acquisition, language processing, and its relation to thought and cognition.

KEY CONCEPTS
- displacement
- grammar
- language faculty
- linguistic relativity
- morphology
- phonology
- pragmatics
- semantics
- syntax
- universal grammar

INTRODUCTION

Language is a system of arbitrary symbols that can be combined in conventionalized ways to express ideas, thoughts, and feelings. Language has been typically seen as uniquely human, separating the human species from other animals. Language enables people of all cultures to survive as a group and preserve their culture. The fundamental features of human language make it extremely effective and very economical. Language uses its arbitrary symbols to refer to physical things or nonphysical ideas; to a single item or a whole category; to a fixed state or to a changing process; to existent reality or to nonexistent fiction; to truths or to lies.

Language is systematic and rule-governed. Its four component subsystems are phonology, semantics, grammar, and pragmatics. The phonological system uses phonemes (the smallest speech sound units capable of differentiating meanings) as its building blocks to form syllables and words through phonemic rules. For example, /m/ and /n/ are two different phonemes because they differentiate meaning as in /mēt/ (meat) versus /nēt/ (neat), and "meat" has three phonemes of /m/, /ē/, and /t/ placed in a "lawful" order in English to form one syllable. The semantic system makes language meaningful. It has two levels: Lexical semantics refers to the word meaning, and grammatical semantics to the meaning derived from the combinations of morphemes (the smallest meaning units) into words and sentences. "Beds," for example, has two morphemes, "bed" as a free morpheme means "a piece of furniture for reclining or sleeping," and "s" as a bound morpheme means "more than one."

The grammatical system includes morphology and syntax. Morphology specifies rules to form words (for example, prefixes, suffixes, grammatical morphemes such as "-ed," and rules to form compound words such as "blackboard"). Syntax deals with rules for word order in sentences (such as, "I speak English," but not "I English speak"). Furthermore, the syntax of human language has four core elements, summarized in 1999 by Edward Kako as discrete combinatorics (each word retains its general meaning even when combined with other words), category-based rules (phrases are built around word categories), argument structure (the arguments or the participants involved in an event, labeled by verbs, are assigned to syntactic positions in a sentence), and closed-class vocabulary (the grammatical functional words, such as "the," "on," or "and," are usually not open to addition of new words).

The fourth subsystem in human language is the pragmatic system. It involves rules to guide culture-based, appropriate use of language in communication. For example, people choose different styles (speech registers) that they deem appropriate when they talk to their spouses versus their children. Other examples include the use of contextual information, inferring the speaker's illocutionary intent (intended meaning), polite expressions, conversational rules, and referential communication skills (to speak clearly and to ask clarification questions if the message is not clear).

Language is creative, generative, and productive. With a limited number of symbols and rules, any language user is able to produce and understand an unlimited number of novel utterances. Language has the characteristic of displacement; that is, it is able to refer to or describe not only items and events here and now but also items and events in other times and places.

LANGUAGE ACQUISITION AND DEVELOPMENT

Views on language acquisition and development are diverse. Some tend to believe that language development follows one universal path, shows qualitatively different, stagelike shifts, proceeds as an independent language faculty, and is propelled by innate factors. Others tend to believe in options for different paths, continuous changes through learning, and cognitive prerequisites for language development.

A UNIVERSAL PATHWAY IN LANGUAGE DEVELOPMENT. Stage theories usually suggest a universal path (an invariant sequence of stages) for language development. A typical child anywhere in the world starts with cooing (playing with the vowel sounds) at two to three months of age, changes into babbling (consonant-vowel combinations) at four to six months, begins to use gestures at nine to ten months, and produces first words by the first birthday. First word combinations, known as telegraphic speech (content word combinations with functional elements left out, such as "Mommy cookie!") normally appear when children are between 1.5 and 2.5 years. Meanwhile, rapid addition of new words results in a vocabulary spurt. Grammatical rules are being figured out, as seen in young children's application of regular grammatical rules to irregular exceptions (called overregularization, as in "I hurted my finger"). Later on, formal education promotes further vocabulary growth, sentence complexity, and subtle usages. Language ability continues to improve in early adulthood, then remains stable, and generally will not decline until a person reaches the late sixties.

DIFFERENT PATHWAYS IN LANGUAGE DEVELOPMENT. Although the universal pattern appears true in some respects, not all children acquire language in the same way. Analyses of young children's early words have led psychologists to an appreciation of

---

DSM-IV-TR Criteria for Language Disorders

EXPRESSIVE LANGUAGE DISORDER (DSM CODE 315.31)

Scores from standardized measures of expressive language development substantially below those from standardized measures of nonverbal intellectual capacity and receptive language development

May be manifested by the following:
- markedly limited vocabulary
- errors in tense
- difficulty recalling words
- difficulty producing sentences with developmentally appropriate length or complexity

Expressive language difficulties interfere with academic or occupational achievement or with social communication

Criteria for Mixed Receptive-Expressive Language Disorder or a pervasive developmental disorder are not met

If mental retardation, speech-motor or sensory deficit, or environmental deprivation is present, language difficulties exceed those usually associated with these problems

MIXED RECEPTIVE-EXPRESSIVE LANGUAGE DISORDER (DSM CODE 315.32)

Scores from a battery of standardized measures of receptive and expressive language development substantially below those from standardized measures of nonverbal intellectual capacity

Symptoms include those for Expressive Language Disorder as well as difficulty understanding words, sentences, or specific types of words (such as spatial terms)

Receptive and expressive language difficulties interfere significantly with academic or occupational achievement or with social communication

Criteria for a pervasive developmental disorder are not met

If mental retardation, speech-motor or sensory deficit, or environmental deprivation is present, language difficulties exceed those usually associated with these problems

children's different approaches to language. In her 1995 book *Individual Differences in Language Development*, Cecilia Shore analyzed the different pathways of two general styles (sometimes termed analytic versus holistic) in the four major language component areas.

In early phonological development, holistic babies seem to attend to prosody or intonation. They tend to be willing to take risks to try a variety of sound chunks, thus producing larger speech units in sentencelike intonation but with blurred sounds. Analytic babies are phonemic-oriented, paying attention to distinct speech sounds. Their articulation is clearer.

In semantic development, children differ not only in their vocabulary size but also in the type of words they acquire. According to Katherine Nelson (cited in Shore's work), who divided children's language acquisition styles into referential versus expressive types, the majority of the referential babies' first words were object labels ("ball," "cat") whereas many in the expressive children's vocabulary were personal-social frozen phrases ("Don't do dat"). In Shore's opinion, the referential babies are attracted to the referential function of nouns and take in the semantic concept of object names; the expressive children attend more to the personal-social aspect of language and acquire relational words, pronouns, and undifferentiated communicative formulaic utterances.

Early grammatical development shows similar patterns. The analytical children are more likely to adopt the nominal approach and use telegraphic grammar to combine content words but ignore the grammatical inflections (such as the plural "-s"). The holistic children have a tendency to take the pronominal approach and use pivot-open grammar to have a small number of words fill in the frame slots (for instance, the structure of "allgone [. . .]" generates "allgone shoe," "allgone cookie," and so on). The units of language acquisition might be different for different children.

In the area of pragmatic development, children may differ in their understanding of the primary function of language. Nelson has argued that the referential children may appreciate the informative function of language and the expressive children may attend to the interpersonal function of language. The former are generally more object-oriented, are declarative, and display low variety in speech acts, whereas the latter are more person-oriented, are imperative, and display high variety in speech acts.

Convenient as it is to discuss individual differences in terms of the two general language acquisition styles (analytic versus holistic), it does not mean that the two are necessarily mutually exclusive—children actually use both strategies, although they might use them to different extents at different times and change reliance patterns over time.

THEORIES OF LANGUAGE DEVELOPMENT

With an emphasis on language performance (actual language use in different situations) rather than language competence (knowledge of language rules and structure), learning theories contend that children learn their verbal behavior (a term suggested by the behaviorist B. F. Skinner in 1957 to replace the vague word of "language") primarily through conditioning and imitation, not maturation. Classical conditioning allows the child to make associations between verbal stimuli, internal responses, and situational contexts to understand a word's meaning. It also enables the child to comprehend a word's connotative meaning—whether it is associated with pleasant or unpleasant feelings. Operant conditioning shapes the child's speech through selective reinforcement and punishment. Adults' verbal behaviors serve as the environmental stimuli to elicit the child's verbal responses, as models for the child to imitate, and as the shaping agent (through imitating their children's well-formed speech and recasting or expanding their ill-formed speech).

Nevertheless, learning theories have difficulty explaining many phenomena in language development. Imitation cannot account for children's creative yet logical sayings, such as calling a gardener "plantman," because there are no such models in adult language. Shaping also falls short of an adequate explanation, because adults do not always correct their children's mistakes, especially grammatical ones. Sometimes they even mimic their children's cute mistakes. Furthermore, residential homes are not highly controlled laboratories—the stimulus-response-consequence contingencies are far from perfect.

THE NATIVIST PERSPECTIVE. The nativist perspective, turning to innate mechanisms for language development, has the following underlying assumptions: language is a human-species-specific capacity; language is "unlearnable" because it is impossible for a naïve and immature child to figure out such a complex linguistic system from an imperfect, not very consistent, highly opaque, and frequently ambiguous language environment; and there is a common structural core in all human languages. In 1965, linguist Noam Chomsky posited an innate language-acquisition device (LAD), with the "universal grammar" residing in it, to explain children's rapid acquisition of any language and even multiple languages. LAD is assumed to be a part of the brain, specialized for processing language. Universal grammar is the innate knowledge of the grammatical system of principles and rules expressing the essence of all human languages. Its transformational generative grammar consists of rules to convert the deep structure (grammatical classes and their relationships) to surface structure (the actual sentences said) in the case of production, or vice versa in the case of comprehension. Equipped with this biological endowment, children need only minimal language exposure to trigger the LAD, and their innate knowledge of the universal grammar will enable them to extract the rules for the specific language(s) to which they are exposed.

Evidence for the nativist perspective can be discussed at two levels: the linguistic level (language rules and structure) and the biological level. At the linguistic level, people are sensitive to grammatical rules and linguistic structural elements. For example, sentences in the active voice are processed more quickly than sentences in the passive voice, because the former type is closer to the deep structure and needs fewer transformation steps than the latter type. "Click insertion" studies (which insert a "click" at different places in a sentence) and "interrupted tape" studies (which interrupt a tape with recorded messages at different points) have shown a consistent bias for people to recall the click or interruption position as being at linguistic constituent boundaries, such as the end of a clause. After a sentence has been processed, what remains in memory is the meaning or the gist of the sentence, not its word-for-word surface structure, suggesting the transformation from the surface structure to the deep structure. Around the world, the structure of creolized languages (invented languages), including the sign languages invented by deaf children who have not been exposed to any language, is simi-

lar and resembles early child language. Young children's early language data have also rendered support. In phonology, habituation studies show that newborns can distinguish between phonemes such as /p/ and /b/. Most amazingly, they perceive variations of a sound as the same if they come from the same phoneme, but different if they cross the boundary into a different phoneme (categorical speech perception). In semantics, babies seem to know that object labels refer to whole objects and that a new word must mean the name of a new object. If the new word is related to an old object whose name the child already knows, the word must mean either a part or a property of that object (the mutual exclusivity hypothesis). In the domain of grammar, Dan Isaac Slobin's 1985 cross-cultural data have shown that young children pay particular attention to the ends of words and use subject-object word order, probably as a function of their innate operating principles. By semantic bootstrapping, young children know that object names are nouns and that action words are verbs. By syntactic bootstrapping, they understand a word's grammatical class membership according to its position in a sentence. Even young children's mistaken overregularization of grammatical rules to exceptions demonstrates their success in rule extraction, since such mistaken behavior is not modeled by adults.

THE NEURAL STOREHOUSE. At the biological level, human babies seem to be prepared for language: They prefer the human voice to other sounds and the human face to other figures. Some aspects of the language developmental sequence appear to be universal—even deaf children start to coo and babble at about the same ages as hearing children, despite of their lack of language input, and later develop sign combinations that are very similar to telegraphic speech. Children's language environment is indeed quite chaotic, yet it takes them only four to five years to speak their mother tongue like an adult without systematic, overt teaching. Furthermore, a critical or sensitive period seems to exist for language acquisition. Young children are able to pick up any language or a second language effortlessly, with no accent or grammatical mistakes. After puberty, people generally have to exert great efforts to learn another language, and their pronunciation as well as grammar typically suffers. Reinforced language teaching in postcritical years was not successful in the cases of "Victor" (a boy who had been deserted in the wild) and "Genie" (a girl who had been confined in a basement). Edward Kako's 1999 study, a careful analysis of the linguistic behavior of a parrot, two dolphins, and a bonobo, led him to conclude that no nonhuman animals, including the language-trained ones, show all of the properties of human language in their communication, although he respectfully acknowledges all the achievements in animal language training. Language is unique to human beings.

Although the neural storehouse for the universal grammar has not been pinpointed yet, cognitive neuroscience has delivered some supportive evidence. Infants' brains respond asymmetrically to language sounds versus nonlanguage sounds. Event-related potentials (ERPs) have indicated localized brain regions for different word categories in native English speakers. Research suggests possible specific brain structures that had registered a detailed index for nouns. Brain studies have confirmed the left hemisphere's language specialization relative to the right hemisphere, even among very young infants. Broca's area and Wernicke's area are housed in the left hemisphere. Damage to Broca's area results in Broca's aphasia, with a consequence of producing grammatically defective, halting, telegramlike speech. When Wernicke's area is damaged, speech fluency and grammatical structure are spared but semantics is impaired. This linguistic lateralization pattern and the linguistic consequences of brain injuries are also true of normal and aphasic American Sign Language users.

However, the nativist perspective is not immune to criticism. The universal grammar cannot adequately explain the grammatical diversity in all human languages. The growth spurts in brain development do not correspond to language development in a synchronized manner. The importance of social interaction, contextual factors, and formal education for knowledge and pragmatic usage of complex rules, subtle expressions, speech acts and styles has been neglected in nativist theories.

Dissatisfied with this nature-nurture dichotomy, interactionist theories try to bring the two together. They recognize the reciprocal influences, facilitating or constraining, dependent or modifying, among multiple factors from the biological, cognitive, linguistic, and social domains. For instance, the typical prenatal and postnatal mother-tongue environment will eventually wean the infants' initial

ability to differentiate the speech sounds of any language and, at the same time, sharpen their sensitivity to their native language. Deaf children's babbling does not develop into words as does that of hearing children. Babies deprived of the opportunity of social interaction, as seen in the cases of "Victor" and "Genie," will not automatically develop a proper language. It is in the dynamic child-environment system that a child acquires language.

LANGUAGE AND COGNITION

COGNITIVE DEVELOPMENT AND LANGUAGE ACQUISITION. Cognitive theorists generally believe that language is contingent on cognitive development. The referential power in the arbitrary symbols assumes the cognitive prerequisite of understanding the concepts they signify. As a cognitive interactionist, Jean Piaget believed that action-based interaction with the world gave rise to the formation of object concepts, separation of self from the external world, and mental representation of reality by mental images, signs, and symbols (language). Language reflects the degree of cognitive maturity. For example, young children's immature egocentric thought (unable to understand others' perspectives) is revealed in their egocentric speech (talking to self)—children seem to show no realization of the need to connect with others' comments or to ascertain whether one is being understood. Older children's cognitive achievements of logical thinking and perspective-taking lead to the disappearance of egocentric speech and their use of socialized speech for genuine social interaction. Although language as a verbal tool facilitates children's interaction with the world, it is the interaction that contributes to cognitive development. Piaget gave credit to language only in the later development of abstract reasoning by adolescents.

In L. S. Vygotsky's social-functional interactionist view, language and cognition develop independently at first, as a result of their different origins in the course of evolution. Infants use practical/instrumental intelligence (intelligence without speech) such as smiling, gazing, grasping, or reaching, to act upon or respond to the social world. Meanwhile, the infants' cries and vocalizations, though they do not initially have true communicative intent (speech without thinking), function well in bringing about adults' responses. Adults attribute meaning to infants' vocalizations and thus include the babies in the active communicative system, fostering joint attention and intersubjectivity (understanding each other's intention). Such social interactions help the infants eventually complete the transition from nonintentional to intentional behavior and to discover the referential power of symbols, thus moving on to verbal thinking and later to meaningful speech. Externalized speech (egocentric speech) is a means for the child to monitor and guide his or her own thoughts and problem-solving actions. This externalized functional "conversation with oneself" (egocentric speech) does not disappear but is internalized over time and becomes inner speech, a tool for private thinking. Thus, in Vygotsky's theory, language first develops independently of cognition, then intersects with cognition, and contributes significantly to cognitive development thereafter. Language development proceeds from a global, social functional use (externalized speech) to a mature, internalized mastery (inner speech), opposite to what Piaget suggested.

LINGUISTIC RELATIVITY. Linguistic relativity refers to the notion that the symbolic structure and use of a language will shape its users' way of thinking. The Sapir-Whorf hypothesis, also known as linguistic determinism, is a strong version. According to anthropologist John Lucy, writing in 1997, all the variations of linguistic relativity, weak or strong, share the assumption that "certain properties of a given *language* have consequences for patterns of *thought* about *reality*. . . . Language embodies *an interpretation* of reality and language can *influence* thought about that reality." Many researchers have tested these claims. Lera Boroditsky, for example, in a 2001 study, examined the relationship between spatial terms used to talk about time and the way Mandarin Chinese speakers (using vertical spatial metaphors) and English speakers (using horizontal spatial metaphors) think about time. The findings suggested that abstract conceptions, such as time, might indeed be subject to the influence from specific languages. On the other hand, the influence between language and thought might be more likely bidirectional than unidirectional. Many examples from the Civil Rights movement or the feminist movement, such as the thought of equality and bias-free linguistic expressions, can be cited to illustrate the reciprocal relationships between the two.

LANGUAGE FACULTY AS A MODULE. There have been debates over whether language is a separate faculty or a part of general cognition. Traditional learning theories are firm in the belief that language is a learned verbal behavior shaped by the environment. In other words, language is not unique in its own right. By contrast, nativist theorists insist on language being an independent, innate faculty. Chomsky even advocates that, being one of the clearest and most important separate modules in the individual brain, language should be viewed internally from the individual and therefore be called internal language or "I-language," distinct from "E-language" or the external and social use of language. Nativists also insist on language being unique to humans, because even higher-order apes, though they have intelligence (such as tool using, problem solving, insights) and live a social life, do not possess a true language.

The view of language as an independent faculty has received support from works in cognitive neuroscience, speech-processing studies, data associated with aphasia (language impairment due to brain damage), and unique case studies. Specific word and grammatical categories seem to be registered in localized regions of the brain. Some empirical studies have suggested that lexical access and word-meaning activation appear to be autonomic (modular). As noted, Broca's aphasia and Wernicke's aphasia display different language deficit symptoms. In 1991, Jeni Yamada reported the case of Laura, a retarded person with an IQ score of just 41 when she was in her twenties. Her level of cognitive problem-solving skill was comparable to that of a preschooler, yet she was able to produce a variety of grammatically sophisticated sentences, such as "He was saying that I lost my battery powered watch that I loved; I just loved that watch." Interestingly, Laura's normal development in phonology, vocabulary, and grammar did not protect her from impairment in pragmatics. In responding to the question, "How do you earn your money?," Laura answered, "Well, we were taking a walk, my mom, and there was this giant, like, my mother threw a stick." It seems that some components of language, such as vocabulary and grammar, may function in a somewhat autonomic manner, whereas other parts, such as pragmatics, require some general cognitive capabilities and social learning experiences.

Cognitive psychologists hold that language is not a separate module but a facet of general cognition. They caution people against hasty acceptance of brain localization as evidence for a language faculty. Arshavir Blackwell and Elizabeth Bates (1995) have suggested an alternative explanation for the agrammaticality in Broca's aphasia: Grammatical deficits might be the result of a global cognitive resource diminution, rather than just the damaged Broca's area. In 1994, Michael Maratsos and Laura Matheny criticized the inadequate explanatory power of the language-as-a-faculty theory pertaining to the following phenomena: comprehension difficulties in Broca's aphasia in addition to grammatical impairment; semantically related word substitutions in Wernicke's aphasia; the brain's plasticity or elasticity (the flexibility of other parts of the brain adapting to pick up some of the functions of the damaged parts); and the practical inseparability of phonology, semantics, syntax, and pragmatics from one another.

Some information-processing models, such as connectionist models, have provided another way to discuss language, not in the traditional terms of symbols, rules, or cognitive capacity, but in terms of the strengths of the connections in the neural network. Using computer modeling, J. L. McClelland explains that knowledge is stored in the weights of the parameter connections, which connect the hidden layers of units to the input units that process task-related information and the output units that generate responses (performance). Just like neurons at work, parallel-distributed processing, or many simultaneous operations by the computer processor, will result in self-regulated strength adjustments of the connections. Over extensive trials, the "learner" will go through an initial error period (the self-adjusting, learning period), but the incremental, continual change in the connection weights will give rise to stagelike progressions. Eventually, the machine gives rulelike performance, even if the initial input was random, without the rules having ever been programmed into the system. These artificial neural networks have successfully demonstrated developmental changes or stages in language acquisition (similar to children's), such as learning the past tense of English verbs. As a product of the neural network's experience-driven adjustment of its connection weights, language does not need cognitive prerequisites, or a specific language faculty in the architecture (the brain). Although emphasizing learning, these models are not to prove the tabula rasa (blank slate) assumption of traditional behav-

iorism, either, because even small variations in the initial artificial brain structure can make qualitative differences in language acquisition. The interaction between the neural structure and environment (input cues and feedback patterns) is further elaborated in dynamic systems models. For example, Paul van Geert's dynamic system, proposed in 1991, is an ecosystem with heuristic principles modeled after the biological system in general and the evolutionary system in particular. The system space consists of multiple growers or "species" (such as vocabulary and grammatical rules) in interrelated connections. Developmental outcome depends on the changes of the components in their mutual dependency as well as competition for the limited internal and external resources available to them.

CONCLUSION

As Thomas M. Holtgraves said in 2002, "It is hard to think of a topic that has been of interest to more academic disciplines than language." Language can be analyzed at its pure, abstract, and symbolic structural level, but it should also be studied at biological, psychological, and social levels in interconnected dynamic systems. Continued endeavors in interdisciplinary investigations using multiple approaches will surely lead to further understanding of language.

SOURCES FOR FURTHER STUDY

Blackwell, Arshavir, and Elizabeth Bates. "Inducing Agrammatic Profiles in Normals: Evidence for the Selective Vulnerability of Morphology Under Cognitive Resource Limitation." *Journal of Cognitive Neuroscience* 7, no. 2 (1995): 228-257. Raises caution about the interpretation of agrammatic aphasia as evidence for a grammar module and proposes global resource diminution as an alternative explanation.

Boroditsky, Lera. "Does Language Shape Thought? Mandarin and English Speakers' Conceptions of Time." *Cognitive Psychology* 43, no. 1 (2001): 1-22. Three empirical studies to test the Whorfian hypothesis of language's ability to shape speakers' abstract conceptions.

Chomsky, Noam. *Aspects of the Theory of Snytax*. Cambridge, Mass.: MIT Press, 1965. Explains the innate universal grammar and how the transformational grammar works to map the deep structures to surface structures.

_____. "Language from an Internalist Perspective." In *The Future of the Cognitive Revolution*, edited by David Johnson and Christina E. Erneling. New York: Oxford University Press, 1997. Explains why the author insists on language being modular.

Daniels, Harry, ed. *An Introduction to Vygotsky*. New York: Routledge, 1996. A collection of articles about Soviet psychologist L. S. Vygotsky's theoretical position on thought and speech.

Gleason, Jean Berko, and Nan E. Bernstein, eds. *Psycholinguistics*. 2d ed. Fort Worth, Tex.: Harcourt Brace College Publishers, 1998. Contributors discuss language users' knowledge, the biological bases of human communicative behavior, speech perception and production, word meaning, sentence and discourse processing, language acquisition, reading comprehension, and bilingualism.

Holtgraves, Thomas M. *Language as Social Action: Social Psychology and Language Use*. Mahwah, N.J.: Lawrence Erlbaum, 2002. An interdisciplinary review of the literature that treats language as social action, most relevant to the areas of social psychology, cognitive psychology, and communication.

Kako, Edward. "Elements of Syntax in the Systems of Three Language-Trained Animals." *Animal Learning & Behavior* 27, no. 1 (1999): 1-14. A systematic analysis of the language performance of a parrot, two dolphins, and a bonobo against four criteria of syntax.

Lloyd, Peter, and Charles Fernyhough, eds. *Lev Vygotsky: Critical Assessments, Volume II: Thought and Language*. New York: Routledge, 1999. Vygotsky's views on thought and language (verbal self-regulation, private speech, and play) are introduced, contrasted to Piagetian views, and tested in studies.

Lucy, John A. "Linguistic Relativity." *Annual Review of Anthropology* 26 (1997): 291-312. A review of the history of the linguistic relativity hypothesis and various approaches to testing the hypothesis.

McClelland, J. L. "A Connectionist Perspective on Knowledge and Development." In *New Approaches to Process Modeling*, edited by Tony Simon and Graeme S. Halford. Hillsdale, N.J.: Lawrence Erlbaum, 1995. Discusses the applicability of a connectionist approach to the rulelike progression of behavior.

Matatsos, Michael, and Laura Matheny. "Language Specificity and Elasticity: Brain and Clinical Syndrome Studies." *Annual Review of Psychology* 45 (1994): 487-516. A review of module theories of language and alternative explanations based on clinical studies involving language speakers and signers.

Piaget, Jean. *The Language and Thought of the Child*. Translated by Marjorie Gabain. New York: Meridian Books, 1955. Explains the qualitative differences in children's egocentric speech and socialized speech and their relationship to thought, with child language data.

Shore, Cecilia M. *Individual Differences in Language Development*. Vol. 7 in *Individual Differences and Development*, edited by Robert Plomin. Thousand Oaks, Calif.: Sage Publications, 1995. Discusses the individual differences in phonological, lexical, grammatical, and pragmatic development of young children aged from one to three years.

Van Geert, Paul. "A Dynamic Systems Model of Cognitive and Language Growth." *Psychological Review* 98, no. 1 (1991): 3-53. A dynamic system model analogized to the evolutional system explains how the components in cognitive and language systems mutually support or compete for limited internal and external resources for growth.

Yamada, Jeni E. *A Case for the Modularity of Language*. Cambridge, Mass.: MIT Press, 1991. A case report of Laura, whose vocabulary and grammar seemed to have developed independently of her rather low cognitive abilities, although her pragmatic skills lagged behind.

Ling-Yi Zhou

SEE ALSO: Bilingualism; Brain damage; Brain specialization; Brain structure; Grammar and speech; Linguistics; Nonverbal communication; Speech disorders; Speech perception; Stuttering; Thought: Inferential.

Law and psychology

TYPE OF PSYCHOLOGY: Cognition; social psychology
FIELDS OF STUDY: Cognitive development; group processes; prejudice and discrimination; social perception and cognition

The legal decisions made by juries are intended to be uncontaminated by evidence not presented within the court case. The study of jury behavior and the preconceived ideas that jurors carry into the courtroom reflecting their attitudes, opinions, and personal experiences have been recognized as standard components of trial preparation.

KEY CONCEPTS
- advocacy
- attitudes
- communicative ability
- credibility
- jury research
- memory and retention
- perception
- salience

INTRODUCTION

The study of psychology and law, specifically decision-making by a jury, is a subset of social psychology. A man might be sitting in his living room watching television when, all of a sudden, a police officer knocks on his door, asks him to step outside, and then informs him that he is being arrested on suspicion of burglary. He claims that he is innocent, but six months later he finds himself on trial for this crime and in front of a jury. Should it make any difference to the jury whether he has a good or bad character, whether he is attractive or unattractive, or whether he is white, black, or Hispanic? The U.S. legal system is designed to yield objective, unbiased decisions based on a set of rules and procedures intended to focus on evidence presented at the trial. Yet Clarence Darrow, one of America's most famous lawyers, bluntly saw it otherwise: "Jurymen seldom convict a person they like, or acquit one that they dislike. The main work of the trial lawyer is to make a jury like his client, or, at least, to feel sympathy for him; facts regarding the crime are relatively unimportant." Research in the field of forensic psychology confirms Darrow's 1933 statement by indicating that human beings do not always conform to such idealistic principles as complete objectivity. Though moral character, lifestyle, attractiveness, race, and related factors have little, if anything, to do with the evidence presented in a given case, research shows that they nevertheless affect the outcome of both real and simulated trials.

The field of psychology and law is continually expanding. Research has focused on such topics as jury selection and jury functioning, social influence as it occurs in the courtroom, the deterrence value of capital punishment and the length of jail sentences, the validity of expert witnesses, and the effect of memory on eyewitness identifications. These areas of psychological application to the legal arena provide a wealth of information that not only will make people aware of potential problems within the judicial system but also will, it is hoped, help provide solutions to the make system as unbiased and objective as possible.

JURY PSYCHOLOGY

In trying to persuade a jury, a lawyer must discover jury preferences concerning the verdict or the issue to be decided in the case even before the jury is impaneled. Thus, the *voir dire* examination in which prospective jurors are questioned on their biases or prejudices is of extreme importance. Psychologists have shown in jury research that people decide between alternative explanations of someone else's behavior by using attitudes already established. These attitudes concern the behavior under evaluation and the person being judged. This psychological insight about the importance of prior attitudes is the basis for trial strategy in general and for specific persuasion strategies and techniques in individual cases. The main objective of jury attitude research is to identify attitudes and values that determine which case facts or issues jurors will find most salient, how they will perceive the evidence gathered on those issues, and how those perceptions are likely to influence their decisions about the case. Moreover, in most research on juror decision making, it was found that jurors' decisions tend to be determined by groups or clusters of attitudes related to the decision.

An example of a powerful but supposedly irrelevant variable is the moral character or lifestyle of the person on trial. A study by David Landy and Elliot Aronson in 1969 provided support for this claim when people acting as jurors in a simulated courtroom read facts about a negligent homicide case in which a pedestrian was run over and killed on Christmas Eve. Mock jurors read either positive or negative character descriptions of the defendant. In the positive character case, the defendant was described as a widowed insurance adjuster going to spend Christmas Eve with his son and daughter-in-law. In the negative character case, the defendant was described as a janitor, twice divorced, possessing a criminal record, going to spend Christmas Eve with his girlfriend. Mock jurors were asked to judge whether the defendant was guilty or innocent and, if guilty, to decide how many years he should spend in jail. When the person on trial was described as having a positive character, mock jurors sentenced him to two years in jail; when he was described as having a negative character, they sentenced him to five years in jail. This clearly suggests that the lifestyle and moral character of people on trial do dramatically influence jury decisions.

The attractiveness of the person on trial has also been found to affect the verdict reached by jurors. Michael Efran in 1974 wondered whether physical attractiveness might bias students' judgments of another student who was accused of cheating. He had college students act as school jurors. Students received a photograph of the fellow student and a written description of the cheating case. All students read the same case description. Half had an attractive photograph attached, however, whereas the other half saw an unattractive photograph. Those with the attractive photograph attached judged the student to be less guilty than did those with the unattractive photograph. For those found guilty of the crime, more severe sentencing was recommended for the less attractive photograph group. Evidence that attractiveness affects jury decision is found not only in simulated but also in real court cases. John Stewart in 1980 asked observers to rate the attractiveness of seventy-four male defendants tried in Pennsylvania. When he later examined the court records, he found that the more attractive defendants received the lighter sentences. Once convicted, the more attractive defendants were twice as likely to avoid prison as those who were less attractive.

Although attractiveness often helps, there are circumstances under which good looks can actually hurt a person on trial. In 1975, Harold Sigall and Nancy Ostrove found that when mock jurors judged a woman accused of stealing $2,200 they were more lenient in their sentencing decisions when she was attractive than when she was not. When she was said to have swindled the money by charming a middle-aged man into making a phony investment, however, the beautiful defendant was sentenced more

severely than her less attractive counterpart. Apparently, people react quite negatively toward someone who uses his or her appearance to commit a crime.

The race of the person on trial also seems to affect the jury decision process. Stewart found that nonwhite defendants were more likely to be convicted than were whites for comparable crimes. Further, the convicted were much more likely to be sent to prison if they were nonwhite than if they were white. Louis Cohen, Laura Gray, and Marian Miller in 1990 had white students act as mock jurors in a burglary case. They all read the same burglary case, but the race of the person on trial varied among black, Hispanic, and white. When the defendant was black or Hispanic, a more severe sentence was awarded than when the defendant was white. Although race of defendant should theoretically be irrelevant to a court case, it does, in fact, appear to affect the verdict.

Much of the psychology associated with legal decision making is centered on trial tactics or strategy. The key to courtroom persuasion is understanding what jurors feel, know, and believe, and providing them with information consistent with those predispositions. Jury persuasion is really strategy dependent upon a trial lawyer's ability to conceive, formulate, and convey information with which a jury will agree. This technique demands sophisticated insight into the complexities of human psychology combined with instincts, judgment, and oratory skills. Lawyers must act as advocates, shaping the argument in a fashion most favorable to their position. The ideas or premises jurors bring with them into the courtroom constitute what psychologists call cognitive structures. Cognition pertains to what people know; cognitive structures consist of what people think they know. Jurors are found to be inflexible because their cognitive structures act as a mechanism through which they admit information consistent with what is already there. Therefore, most jurors strive to reach verdicts which do not conflict with the cognitions (beliefs, attitudes, opinions, or values) at the beginning of the trial. Jurors' perceptions of the trial process and their ultimate decisions are largely determined by their preexisting cognitions, which interpret, distort, or reinforce the information presented during the trial. In short, jurors view the evidence presented at the trial through their own value systems and the predisposed beliefs that they bring with them into the courtroom.

ATTITUDES AND VALUE SYSTEMS

The main objective of jury attitude research is to identify attitudes and values that determine which facts or issues in the case the jurors will find most salient, how they will perceive the evidence presented to substantiate those issues, and how those perceptions are likely to influence their decisions about the case. Most psychologists agree that attitudes consist of three components: affect, cognition, and behavior. Affect refers to a person's emotions, feelings, and "gut instincts" about something. Cognition refers to perceiving, thinking about, and interpreting information related to an object, person, or event. Behavior refers to the intention to act in ways that are consistent with an attitude. These three components are closely related. Attitude formation is acquired over time in three ways: It is learned from others, developed through experience, or the product of self-observation. Attitude salience refers to the strength with which attitudes are held. The way to determine what attitudes jurors hold and the salience of these attitudes is to undertake pretrial research focusing on what kinds of jurors hold which attitudes, their composition, and salience.

Attitudes linked to people's key values play a significant role in shaping how they react to events both inside and outside the courtroom, including how jurors think and feel about the entire trial process and their decisions. Most attitudes are developed over a lifetime of experience with parents, friends, colleagues, teachers, books, television, and other direct and indirect sources. Attitudes vary in the intensity with which they are held, depending on how closely they relate to some underlying core value. These attitudes are the best predictors of behavior because people tend to act in ways consistent with their values.

Juror profiles based on demographics such as gender, income, age, education, religion, and political preference are desirable because they are readily observable factors. Attitude and personality, however, are said to be better predictors of juror behavior. Affective jurors decide on an emotional rather than a rational basis. They are impulsive decision makers, who often base their decisions on what they see and hear rather than waiting until all the facts have been gathered. They tend to reformulate in-

formation until it fits into their previously held worldview or set of conclusions based on how they feel about the matter at issue. They often draw conclusions without reviewing the facts or analyzing witness testimony. Affective jurors are generally deeply devoted to religious principles or philosophies of life. They are often not college educated and conduct business based on how they "feel," what they believe, and what "ought to be." Cognitive jurors are orderly and logical decision-makers. They seek information and are organized and fastidious. They are methodical list-makers who seek out facts and information. They are often college-educated physical science majors, who rely on detailed instruction and precision.

KEYS TO PERSUASION

Understanding what jurors feel, know, and believe, and providing them with messages consistent with these predispositions, are keys to persuasion in the courtroom. What jurors see and hear in the courtroom depends on what meaning they attach to the information provided and its relevance according to their value systems. Jurors are not computers or automatons that store information and then later retrieve it verbatim. Rather, jurors store information according to their own ideas of its importance. As a general proposition, it is agreed that jurors tend to remember best the information heard first (primacy) and last (recency). Therefore, jurors tend to retain information presented at the beginning and the end of the trial better than information presented during the middle. Jurors generally argue deductively, from the general to the particular, fitting facts to premises as they are received.

Lawyers attempt to reinforce, change, or create some specific attitude, opinion, or behavior in jurors favorable to the position they are advocating. It is a dynamic process involving the relationship between those who attempt to persuade and their audience. For lawyers to be persuasive, they must adjust their strategies and tactics to the characteristics of the jury.

Jury decisions tend not to be completely objective, and factors irrelevant to the evidence presented in the case are often considered. That is, the character, physical attractiveness, and ethnicity of the defendant, as well as other factors such as attitude similarity between the jurors and the person on trial, all seem to impact the jury's decision-making process, despite the fact that justice should be blind to these extraneous variables.

Although lawyers make use of their clients' attractiveness, dressing and grooming them appropriately for a court appearance, the idea of a trial as a beauty contest is not an appealing one. Means of diminishing the impact of physical attractiveness on legal decisions need to be established. Some researchers have proposed that attractiveness has been found to be less powerful if a sufficient amount of factual information is presented to the jury, if the judge explicitly reminds the jury of the basis on which the verdict should be reached, and if the jury is presented with transcripts of the testimony rather than being directly exposed to those who testify. These same factors should diminish the subjective impact of race as well. These, as well as many other concerns will occupy the thoughts of many in the legal and psychological field until the U.S. legal system becomes more objective, unbiased, and fair.

Words should be free of double or multiple meanings. A. Daniel Yarmey points out that the testimony "Mr. Brown shot Mr. Jones" depends on the witness's perception, memory, and communications process and ability to relate what was seen and heard. Memory and language overlap. In another example, Yarmey points out that a witness who testifies to "seeing a black face" is drawing on questions of eyesight, how much light was present, the witness's distance from the scene, other persons present, physical features, an interpretation of what constitutes "blackness," and other such variable factors. For a jury to accept eyewitness testimony, the credibility of the eyewitness is always at issue. This is also apparent during expert testimony, when the lay jury is asked to determine the relative merit of often technical evidence. Credibility is often a deciding factor, coupled with other considerations. Other factors affecting eyewitness performance include the duration of the event, a stress or fear factor, the age of the witness, the length of the retention interval, postevent information, and the method of questioning. A lawyer who asks a witness to relate "what happened" and then asks questions is often more successful than the lawyer who attempts to draw out facts one by one.

BIBLIOGRAPHY

Hastie, Reid, Steven D. Penrod, and Nancy Pennington. *Inside the Jury.* Cambridge, Mass.: Harvard University Press, 1983. This book emphasizes how the experimental method within psychology creates an invaluable approach to studying the jury deliberation process. It focuses on how juries make decisions as well as on the product of those deliberations. Provides an extremely detailed and scientific approach to the jury process.

Kassin, Saul M., and Lawrence S. Wrightsman. *The American Jury on Trial: Psychological Perspectives.* New York: Hemisphere, 1988. An authoritative review of the entire process of trial by jury, from jury selection to verdict. Includes a review of the history of the jury, of jury research, and of highly publicized trials. The presentation of information about specific trials is very interesting and enjoyable to read.

Landy, David, and Elliot Aronson. "The Influence of the Character of the Criminal and His Victim on the Decisions of Simulated Jurors." *Journal of Experimental Social Psychology* 5 (1969): 141-152. One of the earlier experimental articles examining the impact of irrelevant variables on the jury decision-making process. Both defendant character and attractiveness were manipulated and found to have an effect on the determination of guilt or innocence and the number of years of imprisonment.

Loftus, Elizabeth F., and James M. Doyle. *Eyewitness Testimony.* 3d ed. Charlottesville, Va.: Lexis Law Publishing, 1997. This book provides a comprehensive account of the reliability—or, more appropriately, the unreliability—of remembering people and events from the scene of a crime. Their description of psychological experiments providing evidence for the way people reconstruct memories is both interesting and provocative.

Loftus, Elizabeth F., and Katherine Ketcham. *Witness for the Defense.* New York: St. Martin's Press, 1991. In this book, Loftus continues her exploration into the fallibility of eyewitness testimony. The presentation of her experiences as a consultant in several court cases, such as those of Ted Bundy and Nazi war criminal Ivan the Terrible, makes this extremely interesting and fascinating reading.

Nemeth, C. J. "Jury Trials: Psychology and Law." In *Advances in Experimental Social Psychology,* edited by Leonard Berkowitz. New York: Academic Press, 1981. An extremely complete account of the psychological research completed on a diverse range of topics related to trial by jury. Provides extremely important historical background information on the jury in America, then discusses a number of factors that affect the jury decision process. A fairly technical account of this information.

Taylor, Lawrence. *Eyewitness Identification*. Charlottesville, Va.: Michie, 1982. A text outlining factors in the reliability of eyewitness testimony.

Vinson, Dr. Donald E. *Jury Persuasion: Psychological Strategies and Trial Techniques*. Englewood Cliffs, N.J.: Prentice Hall Law & Business, 1993. An overview of topics from psychology, sociology, and communication science relevant to persuasion in the courtroom. An interesting and readable text geared to the general reader as well as the professional.

Yarmey, A. Daniel. *The Psychology of Eyewitness Testimony*. New York: Free Press, 1979. A textbook and resource book of law and criminology, psychological theories and evidence, and social and cognitive psychology. Uses Loftus as a source.

Amy Marcus-Newhall;
updated by Marcia J. Weiss

See also: Attraction theories; Attributional biases; Eyewitness testimony; Forensic psychology; Group decision making; Juvenile delinquency; Memory; Prejudice; Racism; Social perception.

Leadership

Type of psychology: Social psychology
Fields of study: Group processes

Leadership involves a complex set of interactions between an individual and a group. The conclusion of extensive research on leadership is that good leaders come in many forms; there is no one best type of leader. Effective leadership has been shown to depend on characteristics of the group and its environment as well as those of the leader.

Key concepts
- consideration
- contingency theory
- initiating structure

- leader-matching training
- least-preferred coworker
- transformational leadership

Introduction
Much of the behavior of individuals is shaped and influenced by other people. Someone who has relatively more influence over others than they do over him or her—for better or worse—can be called a leader. This influence can arise naturally through personal interactions, or it may be attributed to a structuring of relationships whereby one person is designated as having power over, or responsibility for, the others.

Consideration Versus Initiating Structure
In general, theories of leadership make a distinction between two broad types of behavior. One type, often called "consideration," revolves around the leader's relationship with the group members. The leader who exhibits this type of behavior shows warmth, trust, respect, and concern for the group members. Communication between the leader and the group is two-way, and group members are encouraged to participate in decision making. The second type of leader behavior concerns "initiating structure." This construct refers to a direct focus on performance goals. The leader who is high in initiating structure defines roles, assigns tasks, plans work, and pushes for achievement.

Over the years, theorists differed in their views on the optimal mix of consideration and initiating structure in their conceptions of the ideal leader. Those advocating a human-relations approach saw leadership success resulting from high consideration and low initiating structure. Others, however, argued for the intuitive appeal of a leader being high on both dimensions. Research soon revealed that there was no single best combination for every leader in every position.

Contingency Theory
One approach to the study of leadership, Fred Fiedler's contingency theory, is founded on the assumption that effective leadership depends on the circumstances. Every leader is assumed to have either a work focus or a worker focus. This is measured by the "least-preferred coworker" scale. By asking people a series of questions about the person with whom they have worked least well, the proce-

dure permits an evaluation of the degree to which one can keep work and relationships separate.

Three characteristics of a situation are deemed important in determining which style will work best. First and most important is the quality of the relations between the leader and members of the group. To assess leader-member relations, a leader is asked to use a five-point scale to indicate extent of agreement or disagreement with statements such as "My subordinates give me a good deal of help and support in getting the job done." After scoring the leader's responses to such items, the leader-member relations are characterized as "good" or "poor."

The second most important feature of a situation is the amount of task structure. A situation is classified as "high" or "low" depending on the leader's rating of the frequency with which various statements are true. The statements ask whether there is a quantitative evaluation of the task, whether roles are clearly defined, whether there are specific goals, whether it is obvious when the task is finished, and whether formal procedures have been established.

According to contingency theory, the third—and least important—characteristic of a situation is the degree of power inherent in the leader's position. Position power is assessed by asking questions such as whether the leader can affect the promotion or firing of subordinates and if the leader has the necessary knowledge for assigning tasks to subordinates. As with the other features, there are two types of position power, strong or weak.

In summary, there are eight possible types of situations, according to contingency theory: every possible combination of leader-member relations (good vs. poor), task structure (high vs. low), and position power (strong vs. weak). These eight combinations vary along a continuum from high situational control (good leader-member relations, high task structure, and strong position power) to low situational control (poor leader-member relations, low task structure, and weak position power). Fiedler notes that the match between situation and leader orientation is critical for effective leadership. He recommends an emphasis on task performance in the three situations with the highest situational control and in the one with extremely low situational control. For the remaining four situations, the theory suggests that a group will perform best if the leader has an employee-oriented style and is motivated by relationships rather than by task performance.

TRANSFORMATIONAL LEADERS

Using an alternative perspective, Bernard Bass conceptualizes leadership as a transaction between followers and their leader. He sees most leadership as characterized by recognizing what followers want and trying to see that they get what they want—assuming that the followers' behavior warrants it. In short, the leader and followers exchange rewards and promises of rewards for the followers' cooperation. A minority of leaders are able to motivate their followers to accomplish more than they originally expected to accomplish. This type of leader is called "transformational." A transformational leader affirms the followers' beliefs about the values of outcomes; moves followers to consider the interests of the team, organization, or nation above their own self-interests; and raises the level of needs that followers want to satisfy. Among those who may be called transformational leaders are Alfred Sloan, for his reformation of General Motors; Henry Ford, for revolutionizing United States industry; and Lee Iacocca, for revitalizing the Chrysler Corporation. Although transformational leadership has been found in a wide variety of settings, the research on its effectiveness has been almost exclusively conducted by Bass and his colleagues.

GENDER AND CULTURAL DIFFERENCES IN LEADERSHIP

There has been much speculation about the differences between men and women in their leadership abilities. Psychologists examine these differences by performing controlled studies. In two field studies of leadership in the United States Military Academy at West Point, Robert Rice, Debra Instone, and Jerome Adams asked participants (freshmen) in a training program to evaluate their squad leaders (juniors and seniors). The program consisted of two parts. First there was a six-week period of basic training covering military protocol, tradition, and skill (such as weapon use and marching). The second part was a field training program covering combat-oriented tasks (such as fabricating bridges, driving tanks, directing artillery fire, and conducting reconnaissance exercises). About 10 percent of the leaders in each program were women. The participants' responses on questionnaires showed the men and women to be comparable in terms of their success as leaders and in the nature of their leadership styles. This conclusion is in agreement with the ob-

The military provides a hierarchical structure in which leadership skills can be tested. (CLEO Photography)

servations of real operational leadership roles at the academy.

Although sex differences in leadership effectiveness appear to be minimal, there appear to be other group characteristics that are important determinants of leadership behavior. For example, in 1981, Frank Heller and Bernhard Wilpert reported different influence styles for managers from different countries. They determined the extent to which senior and subordinate managers involved group members in decisions. At one extreme, managers made decisions without explanation or discussion. At the other extreme of influence, they delegated decisions, giving subordinates complete control. Their data indicated that participation was emphasized in nations such as Sweden and France, but not in Israel. The United States was somewhere in the middle.

LEADERSHIP STYLE RESEARCH

Regardless of the extent to which there are differences among various groups of people, it is clear that there remain individual differences in leadership style. What are the implications for attempts to improve leadership effectiveness if there is no single best leadership style for all situations? One approach is to select the leader who exhibits those characteristics that are most appropriate for the situation.

Another approach, promoted by Fiedler and colleagues, is to engineer the situation to match the characteristics of the leader. That is, people cannot change the extent of task performance or employee orientation in their leadership styles, but they can change the characteristics of their situations. The program to accomplish this uses a self-taught learning process. First the person fills out a questionnaire designed to assess leadership style. Then the characteristics of that individual's situation, leader-member relations, task structure, and position power are measured. Finally, the person is taught to change the situation to mesh with his or her personality. This might involve such tactics as influencing the supervisor to alter position power or redesigning work to modify task structure. A test of this process was conducted by Fiedler and Martin Chemers in 1984 at Sears, Roebuck, and Company. They implemented eight hours of leader-matching training in two of five randomly selected stores. The other stores had equivalent amounts of training discussions. Subsequent rates of the managers on eight performance scales used by Sears showed those who had received the leader-matching training to be superior on every performance dimension.

Assessing Leadership Types

There have been other applications of leadership research that recommend that the leader choose the appropriate behavior. Victor Vroom and Philip Yetton urge leaders to adopt one of four leadership types. The autocratic leader solves the problem independently, with or without information from subordinates. A consultative leader shares the problem with individual subordinates or with the group and obtains ideas and suggestions which may or may not influence the final decision. A group leader shares the problem with an individual, and together they find a mutually agreeable solution, or with a group that produces a consensus solution that the leader implements. A delegatory leader gives the problem to a single subordinate, offering relevant information but not exerting any influence over the subordinate's decision.

Which of the above four types of leadership is advocated depends on the answers to a series of questions about the need for a quality solution, the amount of information available to the leader and subordinates, the structure of the problem, and attitudes of subordinates. The questions are arranged in a decision tree, so that at each step the leader answers "yes" or "no" and then proceeds to the next step. Vroom has developed a training program based on this model. It has several components. First is an explanation of the theory. Trainees practice using the theory to describe leader behavior and deciding how they would handle various hypothetical situations. Then trainees take part in simulated leadership situations and receive feedback on both their actual behavior and the leader behavior that is prescribed by the theory. Finally, there are small-group discussions about the experience. The goal is for trainees to learn how and when to adopt new leadership patterns. Reactions

of participants to the program tend to be highly favorable.

Leader Behavior Research

Concerns about leadership are evident in nearly every aspect of society. Problems such as illiteracy, inferior education, and environmental destruction are routinely attributed to misguided leadership, ineffective leadership, or an absence of leadership. Within organizations, leaders are held accountable for the work of their subordinates and the ultimate success of the organization. Because of its obvious importance, psychologists have pursued the study of leadership with the goal of developing explanations about the factors that contribute to effective leadership.

One popular conception of leadership is that it is a personality trait. If so, people vary in the extent to which they have leadership abilities. It would also be logical to expect that people in positions of leadership will have different personality characteristics from those who are followers. Yet surprisingly, the results of a large number of studies comparing the traits of leaders and followers have revealed only a few systematic differences. For example, those who are in positions of leadership appear to be, on average, slightly more intelligent and self-confident than followers; however, the magnitude of such differences tends to be small, so there is considerable overlap between leaders and followers. One problem in using this evidence to conclude that individual differences in personality determine leadership is that the traits noted may be the result, rather than the cause, of being in a position of leadership. For example, a person who, for whatever reason, is in a position of leadership may become more self-confident.

This research suggests that there are many factors besides personality that determine the ascent to a position of leadership. This is not so surprising if one considers that groups vary in many ways, as do their leadership needs. Thus there is no clear "leadership type" that is consistent across groups. For this reason, psychologists have tended to abandon the study of leadership as a personality characteristic and pursue other approaches. The advent of an emphasis on leader behavior occurred at Ohio State University in the 1950's. Ralph Stogdill, Edwin Fleischman, and others developed the constructs of leader consideration and initiating structure. These constructs have proved to be useful in several theories of leadership and have been important in attempts to improve leader effectiveness, particularly in organizational settings.

In addition to academic settings, applied settings have been important in the history of leadership research. Studies conducted by the oil company Exxon in an attempt to improve leadership effectiveness led to the independent development of the managerial grid by Robert Blake and Jane Mouton. The two important dimensions of leader behavior that emerged from this work are concern for people and concern for production.

SOURCES FOR FURTHER STUDY

Bass, Bernard M. *Bass and Stogdill's Handbook of Leadership.* 3d ed. New York: Free Press, 1990. A complete review of the research of Bass, Stogdill, and others on differences among leaders. Somewhat technical; for advanced students.

_____. *Leadership and Performance Beyond Expectations.* New York: Free Press, 1985. Readable and thorough examination of the work of Bass and others on leadership research and practice. Emphasis on charismatic and transformational leadership.

Smith, Blanchard B. "The TELOS Program and the Vroom-Yetton Model." In *Cross-Currents in Leadership*, edited by James G. Hunt and Lars L. Larson. Carbondale: Southern Illinois University Press, 1979. A description of the work of the Kepner Tregoe organization, based in Princeton, New Jersey, on implementation of the Vroom-Yetton theory.

Yukl, Gary A. *Leadership in Organizations.* 5th ed. Englewood Cliffs, N.J.: Prentice-Hall, 2001. Textbook approach to leadership in the workplace. Suitable for undergraduate college students.

Janet A. Sniezek

SEE ALSO: Behavioral assessment; Crowd behavior; Group decision making; Groups; Human resource training and development; Personality rating scales.

Learned helplessness

TYPE OF PSYCHOLOGY: Learning
FIELDS OF STUDY: Cognitive learning; critical issues in stress; problem solving

The concept of learned helplessness, first observed in laboratory animals, has been applied to humans in various situations; in particular, it has been applied to depression. The idea holds that feelings of helplessness are often learned from previous experience; therefore, it should also be possible to unlearn them.

KEY CONCEPTS
- attribution
- helplessness
- learning
- personality
- self-concept

INTRODUCTION

The concept of learned helplessness originated with experiments performed on laboratory dogs by psychologist Martin E. P. Seligman and his colleagues. Seligman noticed that a group of dogs in a learning experiment were not attempting to escape when they were subjected to an electric shock. Intrigued, he set up further experiments using two groups of dogs. One group was first given electric shocks from which they could not escape. Then, even when they were given shocks in a situation where they could avoid them, most of the dogs did not attempt to escape. By comparison, another group, which had not first been given inescapable shocks, had no trouble jumping to avoid the shocks. Seligman also observed that, even after the experiment, the dogs that had first received the unavoidable shocks seemed to be abnormally inactive and had reduced appetites.

After considerable research on the topic, Seligman and others correlated this "learned" helplessness and depression. It seemed to Seligman that when humans, or other animals, feel unable to extricate themselves from a highly stressful situation, they perceive the idea of relief to be hopeless and they give up. The belief that they cannot affect the outcome of events no matter what force they exert on their environment seems to create an attitude of defeat. Actual failure eventually follows, thereby reinforcing that belief. It seems that the reality of the situation is not the crucial factor: What matters is the perception that the situation is hopeless.

ATTRIBUTIONAL STYLE QUESTIONNAIRE

As research continued, however, Seligman discovered that exposure to uncontrollable negative situations did not always lead to helplessness and depression. Moreover, the results yielded no explanation of the loss of self-esteem frequently seen in depressed persons. To refine their ability to predict helpless attitudes and behavior, Seligman and his colleagues developed a measuring mechanism called the attributional style questionnaire. It involves twelve hypothetical events, six bad and six good.

Subjects involved in testing are told to imagine themselves in the situations and to determine what they believe would be the major cause of the situation if it were to happen to them. After subjects complete the test, their performance is rated according to stability versus instability, globality versus specificity, and externality versus internality. An example of stable, global, internal perceptions would be a feeling of stupidity for one's failure; an unstable, specific, and external perception might consider luck to be the cause of the same situation. The questionnaire has been used by some industries and corporations to identify people who may not be appropriate for certain positions requiring assertiveness and a well-developed ability to handle stress. The same questionnaire has also been used to identify individuals who may be at high risk for developing psychosomatic disorders so that early intervention can be implemented.

Perhaps the primary significance of learned helplessness is its model of how a person's perception of a life event can influence the person's behavior—and can therefore affect his or her life and possibly the lives of others. Seligman believes that the way people perceive and explain the things that happen to them may be more important than what actually happens. These perceptions can have serious implications for a person's mental and physical health.

PERCEPTIONS OF HELPLESSNESS

The human mind is so complex, and the cognitive process so unknown, that perception is one of the most confusing frontiers facing social scientists. Why do people perceive situations as they do—often as events far different from the ones that actually transpired? If a person is convinced that an event occurred the way he or she remembers it, then it becomes that person's reality. It will be stored that way and may be retrieved that way in the future—perhaps blocking opportunities for positive

growth and change because the memory is based on an inaccurate perception.

If children are taught that they are "stupid" because they cannot understand what is expected of them, for example, then they may eventually stop attempting to understand: They have learned that their response (trying to understand) and the situation's outcome are independent of each other. If such helpless feelings are reinforced, the individuals may develop an expectation that no matter what they do, it will be futile. They will then develop a new feeling—helplessness—which can be generalized to a new situation and can interfere with the future. Various studies have indeed shown that many people have been "taught" that, no matter what their response, the outcome will be the same—failure—so there is no reason to bother to do anything.

ROLE IN VICTIMIZATION

One example of this can be demonstrated in the area of victimized women and children. Halfway houses and safe houses are established in an attempt to both protect and retrain battered women and children. Efforts are made to teach them how to change their perceptions and give them new feelings of potency and control. The goal is to teach them that they can have an effect on their environment and have the power to administer successful positive change. For many women, assertiveness training, martial arts classes, and seminars on how to make a strong positive statement with their self-presentation (such as their choice of clothes) become matters of survival.

Children, however, are in a much more vulnerable situation, as they must depend on adults in order to survive. For most children in the world, helplessness is a reality in many situations: They do not, in fact, have much control over what happens to them, regardless of the response they exhibit. Adults, whether they are parents, educators, church leaders, or older siblings, have the responsibility of being positive role models to help children shape their perceptions of the world. If children are allowed to express their feelings, and if their comments are listened to and considered, they can see that they do have some power over their environment and can break patterns of learned helplessness.

A therapist has described "Susan," a client who as a youngster had lived with the belief that if she argued or asserted her needs with her parents they would leave her. She became the "perfect" child, never arguing or seeming to be ungrateful; in the past, if she had, her parents would often get into a fight and one would temporarily leave. Susan's perception was that if she asserted her needs, she was abandoned; if she then begged the parent who remained to tell the absent parent that she was sorry and would never do it again, that parent would return. In reality, her parents did not communicate well and were using their child as an excuse to get angry and leave. The purpose was to punish the other adult, not to hurt the child.

When Susan became an adult, she became involved with a man who mistreated her, both physically and emotionally, but always begged forgiveness after the fact. She always forgave him, believing that she had done something wrong to deserve his harsh treatment in the first place. At her first session with a therapist, she was reluctant to be there, having been referred by a women's shelter. She missed her second session because she had returned to her lover, who had found her at the shelter. Eventually, after a cycle of returns to the shelter, the therapist, and her lover, Susan was able to break free and begin the healing process, one day at a time. She told the therapist repeatedly that she believed that no matter what she did the outcome would always be the same—she would rather be with the man who abused her but paid attention to her than be alone. After two difficult years of concentrating on a new perception of herself and her environment, she began to experience actual power in the form of positive effectiveness on her life. She became able to see old patterns before they took control and to replace them with new perceptions.

Another example of the power that perceptions of helplessness can have concerns a man ("John") who, as a young boy, was very attached to his father and used to throw tantrums when his father had to leave for work. John's mother would drag him to the kitchen and hold his head under the cold water faucet to stop his screaming; it worked. The child grew up with an impotent rage toward his mother, however, and disappointment in his father for not protecting him. He grew up believing that, no matter how he made his desires known, his feelings would be drowned, as they had been many years before. As a teenager, John grew increasingly violent, eventually getting into trouble; he did not realize that his

family was dysfunctional and did not have the necessary skills to get better.

John was never able to believe in himself, even though—on raw rage and little confidence—he triumphed over his pain and terror to achieve an advanced education and black belt in the martial arts. He even developed a career teaching others how to gain power in their lives and how to help nurture the spirit of children. Yet after all this, he still does not have much confidence in his abilities. He is also still terrified of water, although he forces himself to swim.

MIND-BODY RELATIONSHIP

Research has provided validity for the suspected link between how a person perceives and influences his or her environment and the person's total health and effectiveness. There has been evidence that the mind and body are inseparable, that one influences the other even to the point of breakdown or healing. Leslie Kamen, Judith Rodin, and Seligman have corroborated the idea that how a person explains life situations (a person's explanatory style) seems to be related to immune system functioning. Blood samples were taken from a group of older persons who had been interviewed about life changes, stress, and health changes. Those whose interviews revealed a pessimistic or depressive explanatory style had a larger percentage of suppressor cells in their blood. Considering the idea that suppressor cells are believed to undermine the body's ability to fight tumor growth, these discoveries suggest a link between learned helplessness (as revealed by attitude and explanatory style) and susceptibility to diseases.

Studies have also been conducted to determine whether learned helplessness and explanatory style can predict illness. Results, though inconclusive, suggest that a person's attitude and perception of life events do influence physical health some twenty to thirty years later and can therefore be a valuable predictor and a tool for prevention. Particularly if an illness is just beginning, a person's psychological state may be crucial to healing.

NEW RESEARCH DIRECTIONS

The concepts of helplessness and hopelessness versus control over life situations are as old as humankind. The specific theory of learned helplessness, however, originated with the experiments conducted by the University of Pennsylvania in the mid-1960's by Seligman, Steven F. Maier, and J. Bruce Overmier. The idea that helplessness could be learned has opened the door to many exciting new approaches to disorders formerly considered personality or biologically oriented, such as psychosomatic disorders, victimization by gender, depression (the "common cold" of mental disorders), and impaired job effectiveness.

The idea that they actually do have an effect on their environment is of tremendous importance to people suffering from depression. Most such people mention a general feeling of hopelessness, which makes the journey out of this state seem overwhelming; the feeling implies that one is powerless over one's reactions and behavior. Research-based evidence has shown that people do have the power to influence their perceptions of their environment and, therefore, change their reactions to it.

If the research on perception and learned helplessness is accurate, a logical next step is to find out how explanatory style originates and how it can be changed. Some suspected influences are how a child's first major trauma is handled, how teachers present information to be learned (as well as teachers' attitudes toward life events), and parental influence. Perhaps the most promising aspect of the research on learned helplessness is the idea that what is learned can be unlearned; therefore, humans really do have choices as to their destiny and quality of life. Considerable importance falls upon those who have a direct influence on children, because it is they who will shape the attitudes of the future.

SOURCES FOR FURTHER STUDY

Applebee, Arthur N. *The Child's Concept of Story, Ages Two to Seventeen.* Reprint. Chicago: University of Chicago Press, 1989. An innovative approach and eight thought-provoking chapters give this book an edge on some of the classics in this field. The author examines the use of language and how perceptions can be influenced by it. Demonstrates an adult's and child's sense of story, as well as the responses of adolescents. The author shows how perceptions are easily manipulated by skillful use of phrasing. There are three appendices: a collection of analysis and data, elements of response, and a thorough supplementary table.

Bammer, Kurt, and Benjamin H. Newberry, eds. *Stress and Cancer.* Toronto: Hogrefe, 1981. This edited group of independently written chapters presents thirteen different perspectives from a variety of professionals working in the field of cancer and stress. Well written; achieves its goal without imposing editorial constraints. Perception of events is emphasized as a major determinant of healing. Excellent resources.

Coopersmith, Stanley. *The Antecedents of Self Esteem.* San Francisco: W. H. Freeman, 1967. Emphasizes the importance of limits and boundaries of permissible behavior in the development of self-esteem. Discusses the mirror-image idea of humans emulating society as it develops through the parent/child relationship. There are four very helpful measuring devices in the appendix.

Peterson, Christopher, Steven F. Maier, and Martin E. P. Seligman. *Learned Helplessness: A Theory for the Age of Personal Control.* New York: Oxford University Press, 1995. Summarizes the theory and application of the theory of learned helplessness, focusing on personal control as a tool for overcoming the condition.

Seligman, Martin E. P. *Helplessness: On Depression, Development, and Death.* 1975. Reprint. San Francisco: W. H. Freeman, 1992. This easily read and understood book was written by the master researcher in the field of learned helplessness. Covers such areas as anxiety and unpredictability, education's role in emotional development, experimental studies, and how perception influences everyday life. Excellent references. This book is a must for anyone interested in the topic.

Frederic Wynn

SEE ALSO: Causal attribution; Cognitive maps; Conditioning; Depression; Learning; Observational learning; Stress: Theories.

Learning

TYPE OF PSYCHOLOGY: Biological bases of behavior; learning; motivation

FIELDS OF STUDY: Biological influences on learning; instrumental conditioning; Pavlovian conditioning; problem solving

Learning refers to a change in behavior as a result of experience. Learning is studied in a variety of species in an attempt to uncover basic principles. There are two major types of learning: classical (Pavlovian) conditioning and operant (instrumental) conditioning. Exposure to uncontrollable aversive events can have detrimental effects on learning. Consequences can be successfully used to develop a variety of behaviors, including even random, unpredictable performance. Learning produces lasting changes in the nervous system.

KEY CONCEPTS
- classical conditioning
- contingency
- law of effect
- learned helplessness
- operant conditioning
- shaping

INTRODUCTION

Learning has been of central interest to psychologists since the beginning of the field in the late 1800's. Learning refers to changes in behavior that result from experiences. The term "behavior" includes all actions of an organism, both those that are directly observable, such as typing at a keyboard, and those that are unobservable, such as thinking about how to solve a problem. Psychologists studying learning work with a variety of species, including humans, rodents, and birds. Nonhuman species are studied for a variety of reasons. First, scientists are interested in fundamental principles of learning that have cross-species generality. Second, the degree of experimental control that can be obtained with nonhumans is much higher than with humans. These controlled conditions make it more likely that any effect that is found is due to the experimental manipulations, rather than to some uncontrolled variable. Third, studying the learning of nonhumans can be helpful to animals. For example, a scientist might need to know the best way to raise an endangered giant condor so it is more likely to survive when introduced to the wild.

There are two major types of learning. Classical conditioning (also called Pavlovian conditioning, after Russian physiologist Ivan Pavlov) involves transfer of control of reflexes to new environmental stimuli. For example, when a person goes to get a glaucoma

test at an optometrist's office, a puff of air is delivered into the eyes, which elicits blinking. After this experience, putting one's head into the machine elicits blinking. The glaucoma-testing machine now elicits the reflex of blinking, before the air puff is delivered.

Operant conditioning, also called instrumental conditioning, involves the regulation of nonreflexive behavior by its consequences. American psychologist Edward Thorndike was a pioneer in the study of operant conditioning, publishing his work about cats escaping from puzzle boxes in 1898. Thorndike observed that over successive trials, movements that released a latch, allowing the animal to get out of the box and get some food, became more frequent. Movements not resulting in escape became less frequent. Thorndike called this the Law of Effect: responses followed by satisfaction would be strengthened, while responses followed by discomfort would be weakened. The study of operant conditioning was greatly extended by American behaviorist B. F. Skinner, starting in the 1930's.

Starting in the 1960's, American psychologists Martin Seligman, Steven Maier, J. Bruce Overmier, and their colleagues discovered that the controllability of events has a large impact on future learning. Dogs exposed to inescapable electric shock became passive and failed to learn to escape shock in later situations in which escape was possible. Seligman and colleagues called this phenomenon "learned helplessness" because the dogs had learned that escape was not possible and gave up. The laboratory phenomenon of learned helplessness has been applied to the understanding and treatment of human depression and related conditions.

In the 1970's, some psychologists thought the use of rewards (such as praise or tangible items) was harmful to motivation, interest, and creativity. Beginning in the 1990's, however, American Robert Eisenberger and Canadian Judy Cameron, conducting research and analyzing previous studies, found that rewards generally have beneficial impacts. Rewards appear to have detrimental effects only when they are given regardless of how the person or animal does. Furthermore, the work of Allen Neuringer and colleagues has shown that, contrary to previous thinking, both people and animals can learn to behave in random, unpredictable ways.

The changes in behavior produced by learning are accompanied by changes in physiological makeup. Learning is associated with changes in the strength of connections between neurons (nerve cells in the brain), some quite long-lasting. Eric R. Kandel and his colleagues have documented the changes in physiology underlying relatively simple learning in giant sea snails, progressing to more complex behaviors in mammals. Similar physiological changes accompany learning in a variety of organisms, highlighting the continuity of learning across different species.

CLASSICAL CONDITIONING
Classical conditioning was first systematically investigated by Ivan Pavlov beginning in the late 1800's and into the 1900's. Classical conditioning involves the transfer of control of an elicited response from one stimulus to another, previously neutral, stimulus. Pavlov discovered classical conditioning accidentally while investigating digestion in dogs. A dog was given meat powder in its mouth to elicit salivation. After this process had been repeated a number of times, the dog would start salivating before the meat powder was put in its mouth. When it saw the laboratory assistant, it would start to salivate, although it had not initially salivated at the sight. Pavlov devoted the rest of his long career to the phenomenon of classical conditioning.

In classical conditioning, a response is initially elicited by an unconditioned stimulus (US). The US is a stimulus that elicits a response without any prior experience. For example, the loud sound of a balloon bursting naturally causes people to blink their eyes and withdraw from the noise. The response that is naturally elicited is called the unconditioned response (UR). If some stimulus reliably precedes the US, then over time it, too, will come to elicit a response. For example, the sight of an overfull balloon initially does not elicit blinking of the eyes. Because the sight of the balloon predicts the loud noise to come when it bursts, however, eventually people come to blink and recoil at the sight of an overfull balloon. The stimulus with the new power to elicit the response is called the conditioned stimulus (CS) and the response elicited by the CS is called the conditioned response (CR).

Classical conditioning occurs with a variety of behaviors and situations. For example, a person who was stung by a wasp in a woodshed may now experience fear on approaching the building. In this case, the woodshed becomes a CS eliciting the CR of fear because the wasp's sting (the US) elicited pain and fear (the UR) in that place. To overcome the classical conditioning, the person would need to enter the woodshed repeatedly without incident. If the woodshed was no longer paired with the painful sting of the wasp, over time the CR would extinguish.

Many phobias are thought to arise through classical conditioning. One common successful treatment is systematic desensitization, in which the person, through progressive steps, gradually faces the feared object or situation until the fear CR extinguishes. Classical conditioning has also been recognized as the culprit in food aversions developed by people receiving chemotherapy treatments for cancer. In this case, the food becomes a CS for illness (the CR) by being paired with the chemotherapy treatment (the US) that later elicits illness (the UR). Using more advanced principles of classical conditioning learned through research with nonhumans, people are now able to reduce the degree of aversion that occurs to regular meals, thus preventing the person from developing revulsions to food, which would further complicate the treatment of the cancer by introducing potential nutritional problems.

OPERANT CONDITIONING
Operant conditioning (also called instrumental conditioning) involves the regulation of voluntary behavior by its consequences. Edward Thorndike first systemically studied operant conditioning in the late 1800's. He placed cats in puzzle boxes and measured the amount of time they took to escape to a waiting bowl of food. He found that with increasing experience, the cats escaped more quickly. Movements that resulted in being released from the box, such as stepping on a panel or clawing a loop in a string, became more frequent, whereas movements that were not followed by release became less frequent. This type of operant learning is called "trial-and-error learning," because there is no systematic makes to teach the behavior. Instead, the organism makes many mistakes, which become less likely over time, and sometimes hits on the solution, which then becomes more likely over time.

B. F. Skinner, beginning in the 1930's, greatly extended and systematized the study of operant conditioning. One of his major contributions was to invent an apparatus called the operant chamber, which provided a controlled environment in which behavior was automatically recorded. In the operant chamber, an animal, such as a rat, would be able to make an arbitrary response, such as pressing a small lever on the side of the chamber with its paws. The apparatus could be programmed to record the response automatically and provide a consequence, such as a bit of food, to the animal. There are several advantages to this technique. First, the chamber filters out unplanned sights and sounds that could disturb the animal and affect ongoing behavior. Second, the animal is free to make the response at any time, and so response rate can vary over a wide range as a result of any experimental manipulations. This range means that response rate is a sensitive measure to detect the effects of changes the experimenter makes. Third, the automatic control and recording means that the procedure can be repeated exactly the same way in every experimental session and that the experimenter's ideas about what should happen cannot influence the outcome. The operant conditioning chamber is used extensively today in experiments investigating the learning of a variety of species from different perspectives.

One major technique to teach new behavior is called shaping. Shaping refers to providing a consequence for successive approximations to a desired response. For example, to teach a child to tie shoelaces, a parent might start by crossing the laces, forming the loops and crossing them, and having the child do the last part of pulling the loops tight. The parent would then praise the child. The parent could then gradually have the child do more and more of the task, until the whole task is successfully completed from the start. This type of approach ensures that the task is never too far out of reach of the child's current capabilities. Shaping takes place when young children are learning language, too. At first, parents and other caregivers are overjoyed at any approximation of basic words. Over time, however, they require the sounds to be closer and closer to the final, precisely spoken performance. Shaping can be used to teach a wide variety of behaviors in humans and nonhumans. The critical feature is that the requirement for the reward is gradually increased, in pace with the developing skill. If for some reason the behavior deteriorates, then the requirement can be lowered until the person is once

again successful, then proceed again through increasing levels of difficulty. In order for any consequence to be effective, it should occur immediately after the behavior and every time the behavior occurs.

REINFORCERS AND PUNISHERS

In operant conditioning, there are four basic contingencies that can be used to modify the frequency of occurrence of nonreflexive behavior. A contingency refers to the relation between the situation, a behavior, and the consequence of the behavior. A reinforcer is a consequence that makes a behavior more likely in the future, whereas a punisher is a consequence that makes a behavior less likely in the future. Reinforcers and punishers both come in both positive and negative forms. A positive consequence is the presentation of a stimulus or event as a result of the behavior, and a negative consequence is the removal of a stimulus or event as a result of the behavior. Correctly used, the terms positive and negative refer only to whether the event is presented or removed, not whether the action is judged good or bad.

A positive reinforcer is a consequence that increases the future likelihood of the behavior that produced it. For example, if a parent were to praise a child at dinner for eating properly with a fork, and as a result the child used the fork properly more often, then praise would have served as a positive reinforcer. The vast majority of scientists studying learning recommend positive reinforcement as the best technique to promote learning. One can attempt to increase the desired appropriate behavior through positive reinforcement, rather than focusing on the undesired or inappropriate behavior. If the appropriate behavior becomes more frequent, then chances are that the inappropriate behavior will have become less frequent as well, due to the fact that there are only so many things that a person can do at one time.

A negative reinforcer is a consequence that increases the future likelihood of the behavior that removed it. For example, in many cars, a buzzer or bell sounds until the driver puts on the seatbelt. In this case, putting on the seatbelt is negatively reinforced by the removal of the noise. Another example of negative reinforcement occurs when a child is having a tantrum in a grocery store until given candy. The removal of the screaming would serve as a negative reinforcer for the parent's behavior: In the future when the child was screaming, the parent would probably be more likely to give the child candy. Furthermore, the parent is providing positive reinforcement for screaming by presenting a consequence (candy) for a behavior (screaming) that makes the behavior more likely to occur in similar situations in the future. This example should make clear that reinforcement is defined in terms of the presentation or removal of an event increasing the likelihood of a behavior in the future, not in terms of intentions or opinions. Most parents would not consider the behavior inadvertently created and maintained in this way to be "positive."

Positive punishment refers to the presentation of an event that decreases the likelihood of the behavior that produced it. For example, if a person touches a hot stove, the pain that ensues makes it much less likely that the person will touch the stove under those conditions in the future. In this case, the behavior (touching the stove) produces a stimulus (pain) that makes the behavior less frequent. Negative punishment, on the other hand, refers to the removal of an event that decreases the likelihood of the behavior that produced it. For example, if a birdwatcher walking through the woods makes a loud move that causes all of the birds to fly away, then the watcher would be less likely to move like that in the future. In this way, watchers learn to move quietly to avoid disturbing the birds they are trying to observe.

Negative reinforcement, positive punishment, and negative punishment all involve what is called aversive control. An aversive stimulus is anything that an organism will attempt to escape from or try to avoid if possible. Aversive control refers to learning produced through the use of an aversive stimulus. For example, parents sometimes use spanking or hitting in an attempt to teach their child not to do something, such as hitting another child. This type of approach has been shown to have a number of undesirable outcomes, however. One problem is that the appropriate or desired alternative behavior is not taught. In other words, the child does not learn what should be done instead of what was done. Another problem is that the use of aversive stimuli can produce aggression. Humans and nonhumans alike often respond to painful stimuli with an increased likelihood of aggression. The aggression may or may not be directed toward the person

or thing that hurt them. Additionally, the use of aversive control can produce avoidance—children who have been spanked or hit may try to stay away from the person who hurt them. Furthermore, through observation, children who have been spanked may be more likely to use physical harm to others as an attempted solution when they encounter conflict. Indeed, corporal punishment (the use of spanking or other physical force intended to cause a child to experience pain, but not injury, for the purpose of correction) has been linked to many undesirable outcomes for children, some of which extend well into adulthood. Beginning in the 1970's, American psychologist Murray Straus and his colleagues investigated the impact of corporal punishment on children. Their findings indicated that the use of corporal punishment is associated with an increase in later antisocial behavior as a child, a decrease in cognitive development relative to children who are not spanked, and an increased likelihood of spousal abuse as an adult, in addition to several other detrimental outcomes.

LEARNED HELPLESSNESS
As Seligman, Maier, and Overmier discovered, exposure to uncontrollable aversive events can have profound impacts on future learning, a phenomenon called "learned helplessness." In learned helplessness, an organism that has been exposed to uncontrollable aversive events later has an impaired ability to learn to escape from aversive situations and even to learn new, unrelated behaviors. The phenomenon was accidentally discovered in laboratory research with dogs. Seligman and his colleagues found that dogs that were exposed to electrical shocks in a harness, with no possibility of escape, later could not learn to escape shocks in a shuttle box in which they had only to jump to the other side. Disturbingly, they would lie down and whimper, not even trying to get away from the completely avoidable shocks. Dogs that had not been exposed to the uncontrollable shocks learned to escape in the shuttle box rapidly. More important, dogs exposed to the same number and pattern of shocks, but with the ability to turn them off, also had no trouble learning to escape in the shuttle box. In other words, it was the exposure to uncontrollable shocks, not just shocks, that produced the later deficit in escape learning. Moreover, the dogs that had been exposed to uncontrollable aversive

events also had difficulties learning other, unrelated, tasks. This basic result has since been found many times with many different types of situations, species, and types of aversive events. For example, learned helplessness has been shown to occur in dogs, cats, mice, rats, gerbils, goldfish, cockroaches, and even slugs. Humans show the learned helplessness phenomenon in laboratory studies as well. For example, people exposed to an uncontrollable loud static noise later solved fewer anagrams (word puzzles) than people exposed to the same amount and pattern of noise but who could turn it off.

Learned helplessness has major implications for the understanding and treatment of human depression. Although certainly the case with people is more complex, animals that have developed learned helplessness in the laboratory show similarities to depressed people. For example, they have generalized reduced behavioral output. Similarly, early on researchers discovered that learned helplessness in rats could be prevented by treatment with antidepressant medication. Furthermore, exposure to uncontrollable aversive events produces deficiencies in immune system function, resulting in greater physical ailments, in both animals and people. In people, serial combinations of uncontrollable aversive events such as sudden and unexpected loss of a spouse or child, being laid off from a job, or losing a home to fire, can result in the feeling that one is powerless and doomed. These feelings of helplessness can then produce changes, such as decreased interest in life and increased illness, which further compound the situation. Fortunately, there are effective treatments for learned helplessness. One solution already mentioned is antidepressant medication, which may work in part because it overcomes the physiological changes produced by the helpless experience. Additionally, therapy to teach effective coping and successful learning experiences can reverse learned helplessness in people and laboratory animals.

LEARNED CREATIVITY AND VARIABILITY
Beginning in the 1970's, some psychologists began to criticize the use of rewards to promote learning. Tangible rewards as well as praise and attention, they argued, could interfere with creativity, problem-solving ability, motivation, and enjoyment. Fortunately, these concerns were allayed in the 1990's by careful research and examination of previous re-

search, most notably that of Eisenberger and Judy Cameron. Together, they analyzed the results of over one hundred published studies on the effects of rewards and found that in general, rewards increase interest, motivation, and performance. The only situation in which rewards had detrimental effects was when they were offered independently of performance. In other words, giving "rewards" regardless of how the person does is bad for morale and interest.

Furthermore, several aspects of performance previously thought to be beyond the domain of learning, such as creativity and even randomlike behavior, have been demonstrated to be sensitive to consequences. Children can learn to be creative in their drawing, in terms of the number of novel pictures drawn, using rewards for novelty. Similarly, as shown by the work of American psychologist Allen Neuringer and his colleagues, people and animals alike can learn to engage in strings of unpredictable behavior that cannot be distinguished from the random sort of outcomes generated by a random number generator. This finding is particularly interesting given that this novel behavior has been found to generalize to new situations, beyond the situation in which the learning originally occurred. Learned variability has been demonstrated in dolphins, rats, pigeons, and humans, including children with autism. Learning to be creative and to try new approaches has important implications for many aspects of daily life and problem solving.

BIOLOGICAL BASES OF LEARNING
The features of learning do not occur in a vacuum: They often produce lasting, physiological changes in the organism. The search for the physical underpinnings of learning has progressed from relatively basic reflexes in relatively simple organisms to more complex behaviors in mammals. Beginning in the 1960's, Eric R. Kandel and his colleagues started to examine simple learning in the large sea snail *Aplysia*. This snail was chosen as a model to study physiological changes in learning because its nervous system is relatively simple, containing several thousand neurons (nerve cells) compared to the billions of neurons in mammals. The neurons are large, so researchers can identify individual cells and monitor them for changes as learning progresses. In this Nobel Prize-winning work, Kandel and colleagues outlined many of the changes in the

degree of responsiveness in connections between neurons that underlie classical conditioning processes. The same processes have been observed in other species, including mammals, and the work continues to expand to more complex behavior. This research shows the commonality in learning processes across species, and emphasizes the progress in understanding the physical basis that underlies learning.

SOURCES FOR FURTHER STUDY

Branch, Marc N., and Timothy D. Hackenberg. "Humans Are Animals, Too: Connecting Animal Research to Human Behavior and Cognition." In *Learning and Behavior Therapy*, edited by William O'Donohue. Boston, Mass.: Allyn & Bacon, 1998. The authors explain the relevance of work with nonhumans to humans. Includes a discussion of the effects of explicit rewards on motivation and the phenomenon of learning without awareness. This book chapter is clearly written and understandable to the interested nonprofessional reader.

Carroll, Marilyn E., and J. Bruce Overmier, eds. *Animal Research and Human Health: Advancing Human Welfare Through Behavioral Science*. Washington, D.C.: American Psychological Association, 2001. This comprehensive book contains descriptions of the application of research with animals to a variety of human conditions, including anxiety, stress, depression, drug abuse, aggression, and a variety of areas of learning. Also contains a section on the ethics of using animals in behavioral research and a list of additional readings.

Eisenberger, Robert, and Judy Cameron. "The Detrimental Effects of Reward: Myth or Reality?" *American Psychologist* 51, no. 11 (1996): 1153-1166. This journal article in the premier publication of the American Psychological Association provides an analysis of over one hundred studies and finds that rewards generally are not detrimental, but in fact beneficial, to motivation, interest, and enjoyment of a task. Although the article contains advanced statistical techniques, they are not critical to the understanding of the findings.

Mazur, James E. *Learning and Behavior*. Upper Saddle River, N.J.: Prentice Hall, 2001. This best-selling introduction to the topic of learning and behavior assumes no prior knowledge of psychology. The reading is straightforward though sometimes challenging as it covers the basics of classical and operant conditioning, biological bases of learning and behavior, and applications to complex human learning situations.

Overmier, J. Bruce, and V. M. LoLordo. "Learned Helplessness." In *Learning and Behavior Therapy*, edited by William O'Donohue. Boston: Allyn & Bacon, 1998. Scholarly, complete discussion of the history of research in learned helplessness, thorough description of the phenomenon, up to current controversies and debates in this area. Contains information on the physiological underpinnings of learned helplessness and the application of this research to human depression. Includes large reference section with classic papers in this area of research.

Seligman, Martin E. P. *Learned Optimism*. New York: Simon & Schuster, 1998. This book by one of the pioneers in the area describes the basic research underlying the proposed therapeutic approach to address problems with learned helplessness. Contains scales to assess the reader's degree of optimism and scientifically based recommendations to change problematic behavior. Written for a broad audience.

Skinner, B. F. *Science and Human Behavior*. New York: Free Press, 1957. This classic work by Skinner was designed to bring the study of human learning to a wide audience. Describes the application of science to human problems. Reviews basic learning principles before discussing their application to a variety of wide ranging human issues.

Straus, Murray A., and Denise A. Donnelly. *Beating the Devil out of Them: Corporal Punishment in American Families and Its Effects on Children*. New Brunswick, N.J.: Transaction Publishers, 2001. This thought-provoking book by one of the foremost experts on family violence is written for a broad audience. Discusses the prevalence of spanking and other forms of corporal punishment. Outlines the short-term and long-term impacts of spanking on children, including increased aggression, criminality, and depression. Includes a discussion of benefits of alternative child-rearing strategies.

Amy L. Odum

SEE ALSO: Ability tests; Achievement motivation; Assessment; Cognitive ability: Gender differences; Cognitive development: Jean Piaget; Computer models of cognition; Concept formation; Cooperative learning; Dyslexia; Educational psychology; Giftedness; Human resource training and development; Imprinting; Intelligence; Intelligence quotient (IQ); Language; Logic and reasoning; Memory; Mental retardation; Observational learning and modeling therapies; Pavlovian conditioning; Preparedness; Problem-solving stages; Problem-solving strategies; Race and intelligence; Teaching methods; Thought: Study and measurement.

Learning disorders

TYPE OF PSYCHOLOGY: Psychopathology
FIELDS OF STUDY: Child and adolescent disorders

Learning disorders (LD) comprise the disorders usually first diagnosed in infancy, childhood, or adolescence. Because the condition affects the academic progress of approximately 5 percent of all public school students in the United States, it has attracted the attention of clinicians, educators, and researchers from varied disciplines. Substantial progress has been made in the assessment and diagnosis of learning disorders but questions regarding etiology, course, and treatment of the disorder continue to challenge investigators.

KEY CONCEPTS
- disorder of written expression
- dyslexia
- learning disabilities
- learning disorder not otherwise specified
- mathematics disorder
- phonological processing
- reading disorder

INTRODUCTION

Learning disorders (LD) is a general term for clinical conditions that meet three diagnostic criteria: An individual's achievement in an academic domain (such as reading) is substantially below that expected given his or her age, schooling, and level of intelligence; the learning disturbance interferes significantly with academic achievement or activities of daily living that require specific academic skills; and if a sensory deficit (such as blindness or deafness) is present, the learning difficulties are in excess of those usually associated with it. The American Psychiatric Association's *Diagnostic and Statistical Manual of Mental Disorders: DSM-IV-TR* (rev. 4th ed., 2000) specifies four subcategories of learning disorders: Reading Disorder, Mathematics Disorder, Disorder of Written Expression, and Learning Disorder Not Otherwise Specified (NOS). The criteria for the first three specific learning disorders are the same except for the academic domain affected by the disorder. The fourth subcategory is reserved for disorders involving learning the academic skills that do not meet the criteria for any specific learning disorder. Included are problems in all three academic domains (reading, mathematics, written expression) that together significantly interfere with academic achievement even though academic achievement as measured on standardized tests does not fall substantially below what is expected given the individual's chronological age, intelligence quotient (IQ), or age-appropriate education.

A variety of statistical approaches are used to produce an operational definition of "substantially below" academic achievement. Despite some controversy about its appropriateness, the most frequently used approach defines "substantially below" as a discrepancy between achievement and IQ of more than two standard deviations (SD). In cases where an individual's performance on an IQ test may have been compromised by an associated disorder in linguistic or information processing, an associated mental disorder, a general medical condition, or the individual's ethnic or cultural background, a smaller discrepancy (between one and two SDs) may be acceptable.

Differential diagnosis involves differentiating learning disorders from normal variations in academic achievement, scholastic difficulties due to lack of opportunity, poor teaching, or cultural factors, and learning difficulties associated with a sensory deficit. In cases of pervasive developmental disorder or mild mental retardation, an additional diagnosis of learning disorder is given if the individual's academic achievement is substantially below the expected level given the individual's schooling and intelligence.

The term "learning disorders" was first applied to a clinical condition meeting these three criteria in the American Psychiatric Association's *Diagnostic and Statistical Manual of Mental Disorders* (4th ed.,

DSM-IV), published in 1994. Earlier editions of the DSM used other labels such as "learning disturbance," a subcategory within special symptom reactions in DSM-II (1968). In DSM-III (1980) and DSM-III-R (1987), the condition was labeled "Academic Skills Disorders" and listed under "Specific Developmental Disorders"; furthermore, the diagnosis was based only on "substantially below" academic achievement, and the disorder was classified as an Axis II rather than an Axis I or clinical condition. The LD condition is also known by names other than those used in the psychiatric nomenclature, most frequently as "learning disabilities," which is defined as a disorder in one or more of the basic psychological processes involved in understanding or in using spoken or written language, which may manifest itself in an imperfect ability to listen, think, speak, read, write, spell, or do mathematical calculations in children whose learning problems are not primarily the result of visual, hearing, or motor handicaps, mental retardation, emotional disturbance, or environmental, cultural, or economic disadvantage. Learning disabilities is the term used in P.L. 94-142, the Education for All Handicapped Children Act of 1975, and in P.L. 101-476, the Individuals with Disabilities Education Act. Specific learning disorders are also referred to by other names, such as dyslexia (Reading Disorder), dyscalculia (Mathematics Disorder), or dysgraphia (Disorder of Written Expression). Empirical evidence about prevalence, etiology, course of the disorder, and intervention comes mainly from subjects identified as having dyslexia or learning disabilities.

PREVALENCE

Prevalence rates for learning disorders vary, depending on the definitions and methods of determining the achievement-intelligence discrepancy. According to the American Psychiatric Association, estimates range from 2 to 10 percent for the general population, and 5 percent for public school stu-

---

DSM-IV-TR Criteria for Learning Disorders

MATHEMATICS DISORDER (DSM CODE 315.1)

Mathematical ability, as measured by individually administered standardized tests, substantially below that expected given chronological age, measured intelligence, and age-appropriate education

Disorder interferes significantly with academic achievement or activities of daily living requiring mathematical ability

If a sensory deficit is present, mathematical difficulties exceed those usually associated with it

READING DISORDER (DSM CODE 315.00)

Reading achievement, as measured by individually administered standardized tests of reading accuracy or comprehension, substantially below that expected given chronological age, measured intelligence, and age-appropriate education

Disorder interferes significantly with academic achievement or activities of daily living requiring reading skills

If a sensory deficit is present, reading difficulties exceed those usually associated with it

DISORDER OF WRITTEN EXPRESSION (DSM CODE 315.2)

Writing skills, as measured by individually administered standardized tests or functional assessments of writing skills, substantially below those expected given chronological age, measured intelligence, and age-appropriate education

Disorder interferes significantly with academic achievement or activities of daily living requiring the composition of written texts (such as writing grammatically correct sentences and organized paragraphs)

If a sensory deficit is present, writing difficulties exceed those usually associated with it

LEARNING DISORDER NOT OTHERWISE SPECIFIED (DSM CODE 315.9)

---

dents in the United States. The prevalence rate for each specific learning disorder is more difficult to establish because many studies simply report the total number of learning disorders without separating them according to subcategory. Reading disorder is the most common, found in 4 percent of school-age children in the United States. Approximately four out of five cases of LD have Reading Disorder alone or in combination with Mathematics Disorder and/ or Disorder of Written Expression. About 1 percent of schoolage children have Mathematics Disorder, one out of five cases of LD. Disorder of Written Expression alone is rare, it is usually associated with Reading Disorder.

Studies based on referrals to school psychologists or clinics reported that more males than females manifested a learning disorder. However, studies employing careful diagnostic assessment and strict application of the criteria have found more equal rates for males and females. LD often coexists with another disorder, usually language disorders, communication disorders, attention-deficit hyperactivity disorder (ADHD), and/or conduct disorder.

ETIOLOGY

There is strong empirical support for a genetic basis of Reading Disorder or dyslexia from behavior genetic studies. John C. DeFries and his colleagues indicate that heredity can account for as much as 60 percent of the variance in Reading Disorders or dyslexia. As for the exact mode of genetic transmission, Lon R. Cardon and his collaborators, in two behavior genetic studies, identified chromosome 6 as a possible quantitative trait locus for a predisposition to develop Reading Disorder. The possibility that transmission occurs through a subtle brain dysfunction rather than autosomal dominance has been explored by Bruce Pennington and others.

The neurophysiological basis of Reading Disorders has been explored in studies of central nervous dysfunction or faulty development of cerebral dominance. The hypothesized role of central nervous dysfunction has been difficult to verify despite observations that many children with learning disorders had a history of prenatal and perinatal complications, neurological soft signs, and electroencephalograph abnormalities. In 1925, neurologist Samuel T. Orton hypothesized that Reading Disorder or dyslexia results from failure to establish hemispheric dominance between the two halves of the brain. Research has yielded inconsistent support for Orton's hypothesis and its reformulation, the progressive lateralization hypothesis. However, autopsy findings of cellular abnormalities in the left hemisphere of dyslexics that were confirmed in brain imaging studies of live human subjects have reinvigorated researchers. These new directions are pursued in studies using sophisticated brain imaging technology.

Genetic and neurophysiological factors do not directly cause problems in learning the academic skills. Rather, they affect development of neuro-psychological, information-processing, linguistic, or communication abilities, producing difficulties or deficits that lead to learning problems. The most promising finding from research on process and ability deficits concerns phonological processing—the ability to use phonological information (the phonemes or speech sounds of one's language)—in processing oral and written language. Two types of phonological processing, phonological awareness and phonological memory (encoding or retrieval), have been studied extensively. Based on correlational and experimental data, there is an emerging consensus that a deficit in phonological processing is the basis of reading disorder in a majority of cases.

ASSESSMENT

Assessment refers to the gathering of information in order to attain a goal. Assessment tools vary with the goal. If the goal is to establish the diagnosis, assessment involves the individualized administration of standardized tests of academic achievement and intelligence that have norms for the child's age and, preferably, social class and ethnicity. To verify that the learning disturbance is interfering with a child's academic achievement or social functioning, information is collected from parents and teachers through interviews and standardized measures such as rating scales. Behavioral observations of the child may be used to supplement parent-teacher reports. If there is a visual, hearing, or other sensory impairment, it must be determined that the learning deficit is in excess of that usually associated with it. The child's developmental, medical, and educational histories and the family history are also obtained and used in establishing the differential diagnosis and clarifying etiology.

If LD is present, then the next goal is a detailed description of the learning disorder to guide treatment. Tools will depend upon the specific type of learning disorder. For example, in the case of dyslexia, E. Wilcutt and Pennington suggest that the achievement test given to establish the achievement-intelligence discrepancy be supplemented by others such as the Gray Oral Reading Test (GORT-III), a timed measure of reading fluency as well as reading comprehension. Still another assessment goal is to identify the neuropsychological, linguistic, emotional, and behavioral correlates of the learning disorder and any associated disorders. A variety of measures exist for this purpose. Instrument selection should be guided by the clinician's hypotheses, based on what has been learned about the child and the disorder. Information about correlates and associated disorders is relevant to setting targets for intervention, understanding the etiology, and estimating the child's potential response to intervention and prognosis.

In schools, identification of LD involves a multidisciplinary evaluation team including the classroom teacher, a psychologist, and a special education teacher or specialist in the child's academic skill deficit (such as reading). As needed, input may be sought from the child's pediatrician, a speech therapist, an audiologist, a language specialist, or a psychiatrist. A thorough assessment should provide a good description of the child's strengths as well as weaknesses that will be the basis of effective and comprehensive treatment plans for both the child and the family. In school settings, these are called, respectively, an Individual Educational Plan (IEP) and an Individual Family Service Plan (IFSP).

TREATMENT

Most children with LD require special education. Depending upon the disorder's severity, they may learn best in a one-to-one setting, small group, special class, or regular classroom plus resource room tutoring.

Treatment of LD should address both the disorder and associated conditions or correlates. Furthermore, it should include assisting the family and school in becoming more facilitative contexts for development of the child with LD. Using neuropsychological training, psychoeducational methods, behavioral or cognitive-behavioral therapies, or cognitive instruction, singly or in combination, specific interventions have targeted the psychological process dysfunction or deficit assumed to underlie the specific learning disorder; a specific academic skill such as word attack; or an associated feature or correlate such as social skills. Process-oriented approaches that rose to prominence in the 1990's are linguistic models aimed at remediating deficits in phonological awareness and phonological memory, and cognitive models which teach specific cognitive strategies that enable the child to become a more efficient learner. Overall, treatment or intervention studies during the last two decades of the twentieth

century and at the beginning of the twenty-first century are more theory-driven, built on prior research, and rigorous in methodology. Many studies have shown significant gains in target behaviors. Transfer of training, however, remains elusive. Generalization of learned skills and strategies is still the major challenge for future treatment research. As the twenty-first century begins, LD remains a persistent or chronic disorder.

SOURCES FOR FURTHER STUDY

American Psychiatric Association. *Diagnostic and Statistical Manual of Mental Disorders: DSM-IV-TR.* Rev. 4th ed. Washington, D.C.: Author, 2000. Provides a more detailed description of the diagnostic criteria, associated features and disorders, and differential diagnosis. It also describes the course of the disorder and familial pattern, if any, for the specific learning disorders.

Brown, F. R., III, H. L. Aylward, and B. K. Keogh, eds. *Diagnosis and Management of Learning Disabilities.* San Diego, Calif.: Singular Publishing Group, 1996. A multidisciplinary group of contributors provide a comprehensive yet detailed view of diagnosis, assessment, and treatment of learning problems. Because of its clarity and scope, this is recommended as an introductory text.

Lyon, G. Reid. "Treatment of Learning Disabilities." In *Treatment of Childhood Disorders,* edited by E. J. Mash and L. C. Terdal. New York: Guilford, 1998. This chapter gives an excellent description of treatment models and reviews the research on their respective efficacies.

Sternberg, R. J., and Louise Spear-Swerling, eds. *Perspectives on Learning Disabilities.* Boulder, Colo.: Westview Press, 1999. This sophisticated presentation and critique of biological, cognitive, and contextual approaches to learning disabilities is highly recommended for graduate students and professionals.

Felicisima C. Serafica

SEE ALSO: Aphasias; Attention-deficit hyperactivity disorder (ADHD); Brain structure; Cognitive ability: Gender differences; Dyslexia; Education psychology; Forgetting and forgetfulness; Intelligence; Intelligence tests; Language; Logic and reasoning; Memory; Memory storage; Speech disorders; Teaching methods.

Lewin, Kurt

BORN: September 9, 1890, in Mogilno, Prussia (now in Poland)
DIED: February 12, 1947, in Newtonville, Massachusetts
IDENTITY: Jewish refugee to America from Nazi Germany, social psychologist
TYPE OF PSYCHOLOGY: Social psychology
FIELDS OF STUDY: Group process; methodological issues; interpersonal relations

Lewin originated the concept of field theory to explain how human behavior interacts with the environment in which the behavior occurs. He utilized action research, a form of research that integrates the pursuit of knowledge with action on social issues.

Kurt Lewin was born in Prussia to a middle-class Jewish family. The family moved to Berlin, Germany, when Lewin was fifteen years old. He studied the theory of science at the University of Berlin, where he completed his doctorate in 1914 under the influence of Carl Stumpf and the emerging Gestalt psychology, an orientation that focuses on "wholes" rather than the parts that make up the whole. He was injured in combat while serving in the German army in World War I, and wrote "War Landscape" (1917) an initial description of field theory, during his recovery.

He returned to lecture at the Psychological Institute at the University of Berlin. He encouraged social action on important issues such as democracy in government and social organizations. Women were included in his research circle at a time when many scholars excluded them.

Lewin was invited to the United States to present at the International Congress of Psychologists at Yale in 1929. He presented a film that depicted the "field forces" at work on a child learning a new behavior and he interested many psychologists in his ideas. Field theory suggests that behavior is a function of the totality of interdependent facts and circumstances that exist at the time the behavior occurs.

The presentation led to an invitation to serve as a visiting professor at Stanford University in 1930. Adolf Hitler's rise to power and increasing anti-Semitism in Germany led Lewin to accept a temporary appointment at Cornell University and then a faculty position at the University of Iowa and the Child Welfare Research Station, where he stayed until 1945. He published his first major work, *A Dynamic Theory of Personality*, in 1935.

Lewin consulted and conducted research for the United States during World War II regarding public policy issues. He developed "action research," a study of the conditions and effects of types of social action that were used to facilitate social change. He was interested in minority issues and relations between groups of people, which led to the establishment of the Research Center for Group Dynamics at MIT and action research that gave birth to a type of group process known as the "T-group" or "sensitivity group." Such groups used feedback, disconfirmation of a person's existing beliefs, and participant observations to motivate change.

Lewin died in 1947 at the age of fifty-six. The posthumous publication of *Resolving Social Conflicts* (1948) provided a collection of papers he wrote during his time in the United States.

SOURCES FOR FURTHER STUDY

Bargal, David, Martin Gold, and Miriam Lewin. *The Heritage of Kurt Lewin: Theory, Research, and Practice*. New York: Plenum, 1992. An overview of Lewin's work and influence.

Lewin, Miriam A. "Kurt Lewin: His Psychology and a Daughter's Recollections." In *Portraits of Pioneers in Psychology*, edited by Gregory A. Kimble and Michael Wertheimer. Vol. 3. Washington, D.C.: American Psychological Association, 1998. Chapter in a series on key people in psychology, written by Lewin's daughter.

Marrow, Alfred Jay. *The Practical Theorist: The Life and Work of Kurt Lewin*. New York: Basic Books, 1969. Thorough source of biographical information.

Mark Stanton

SEE ALSO: Field theory: Kurt Lewin; Gestalt therapy.

Linguistics

TYPE OF PSYCHOLOGY: Cognition; language
FIELDS OF STUDY: Thought

Linguistics, the scientific study of the structure of language, is a close companion of cognitive psychol-

ogy. The linguist Noam Chomsky changed the way psychologists view language. He sees language as a complex, partly innate system of abstract rules. Linguists and psychologists sometimes disagree about exactly how language is learned and used. They use different kinds of evidence to support their theories of language.

KEY CONCEPTS
- chimpanzee language
- deep structures
- grammatical rules
- Grice's cooperative principle of conversation
- language acquisition
- linguistics
- morphology
- performance versus competence
- phonology
- pragmatics
- semantics
- surface structures
- syntax

INTRODUCTION

Linguistics, the scientific study of the structure of language, is a field in its own right, but it makes contact with psychology at every turn. Linguists address speech perception, language development, and language comprehension, while cognitive psychologists (psychologists who study human thought) study memory for exact wording, the relationship of language and thought, and language disorders, among other topics.

The work of linguists (especially that of Noam Chomsky in the 1960's) has been instrumental in launching American cognitive psychology by drawing attention to the importance of abstract rules that characterize behavior, the distinction between performance and competence, and the distinction between "surface" behaviors and the "deep" structural basis of those behaviors. Prior to Chomsky, it might be said that the best theory of language structure had amounted to the art of drawing diagrams of sentences.

The best psychological account of how people learn language had been B. F. Skinner's behaviorist account. The behaviorists refrained from theorizing about invisible processes within the mind, so they limited their accounts to physically observable events, namely imitation, practice, and reinforcement. They used general principles of learning to account for all behaviors, so their theories applied to mice and pigeons as well as to humans.

CHOMSKY'S THEORY

Noam Chomsky developed a theory of grammar that changed these assumptions forever. Linguistics no longer consisted of mere structural descriptions, but a set of rules with the (theoretical) capacity to generate all and only well-formed utterances of any given human language; linguists hoped to discover rules that were accurate reflections of the process of using language. Chomsky set the standard of "explanatory adequacy" for a linguistic theory, by which he meant that the theory could account for actual psychological processes in the use of language, not merely describe what language is like. Thus, Chomsky's revolutionary ideas about linguistics were also revolutionary ideas about psychology.

He argued that the rules of language are so complex that humans could not possibly learn them, especially not young children with no training in linguistic theory, who are exposed to confusingly faulty examples of language every day. Yet normal four-year-old children across the world effortlessly master all the basic complexities of their native languages, despite the lack of formal (or even much informal) language training. If children do not consciously learn the rules they master, they must have those rules programmed into their brains by genetics.

Chomsky did not claim that any particular language is programmed genetically into human beings. Rather, he claimed that all human languages are more similar to each other than they seem at first glance. All languages share a common core of principles, and it is this core grammar, or set of "linguistic universals," that is thought to be genetically programmed. He suggested that language (in its full complexity) is uniquely human, and the only reason humans are capable of it is that they have genetically engineered language modules in their brains (presumably, he was referring to the famous Wernicke's and Broca's areas in the left cerebral cortex).

Chomsky's claims made a dramatic impact on American psychology. Chomsky's arguments against Skinner's behaviorist account of language learning through imitation, practice, and reinforcement were seized by the scientific community and have become the generally accepted view of language acquisition. Although learning through imitation, practice, and reinforcement can pretty well account for vocabulary acquisition (though there are many who would claim that behaviorism fails in even that area), the acquisition of syntactic structure (correct word order) and of morphology (word formation, such as past tenses and plurals) cannot be understood without referring to the abstract rules underlying those abilities. Research confirms the claim that rule discovery, not rote imitation, and internal organization, not external reinforcement, best account for how young children develop language skills.

Although developmental psychologists have for the most part joined hands with linguists in rejecting behavioral accounts of language learning, the claims that Chomsky made about a genetically programmed core grammar have not fared as well in mainstream cognitive psychology. Most (but not all) psychologists working in the area suggest that what humans have genetically programmed is not anything so rigid as a core grammar, but rather a set of strategies for learning language. Psychologists also cite Katherine Snow's discovery that toddlers are not exposed to confusingly faulty examples of language (as Chomsky claimed), but that, in fact, parents generally use simplified, overly clear and correct language when addressing their young ones. Thus, language is learned through well-designed social interactions (an idea with which the great Russian scholar Lev Vygotsky would have been quite comfortable).

There has been considerable enthusiasm in efforts to disprove Chomsky's claim that language is unique to humans. In fairness to Chomsky, he never claimed that other animals could not communicate, only that those communications were not based upon the complex, abstract, unlearnable, genetically programmed core grammar of human language. No one has ever really challenged that version of Chomsky's claim. There has been immense delight, however, on the part of researchers who have trained chimpanzees and gorillas to communicate with American Sign Language (ASL) or other, artificial, rule-based language systems. Primates have had much more success with these systems than most people would have anticipated. They have learned vocabularies of several hundred words, and have used those words in sentences for personal communication in ways that are unarguably "linguistic." The success has been so impressive and surprising that it is occasionally overlooked that there remain many serious differences between chimp language and human language, not the least of which is the level of complexity: All chimp language has been easily learnable, and no human language is.

The debate between Chomsky and his critics rages on. Chomsky still has some points about language complexity and universals that have been by and large ignored rather than improved upon by current psychological theory. Chomsky in his turn has never felt compelled to modify his theory in the face of psychological research. In many ways, mainstream cognitive psychologists have lost contact with the person who won them their license to defy behaviorist theory.

BASIC LINGUISTIC CONCEPTS

Linguistic theory has come to make several basic distinctions among the various aspects of language that can be studied. Each aspect is a system of rules. The job of each rule system is to create. The rules create (or generate) all the possible (well-formed) utterances of a language. Any structures that cannot be generated by the rules are not well formed, and are therefore considered illegal or anomalous. These rules are not the kind one goes to school to learn. Rather, they are the rules that every speaker of the language already knows. Every time one says something, one uses these rules without even thinking about them, or realizing they are there. In fact, people are so unaware of these rules, which they all use, that it takes a great deal of clever effort for linguistic researchers to figure out what the rules are, and frankly, there still is not agreement on the subject.

PHONOLOGY. Phonology refers to the system of distinctive sounds (or phonemes) used in a language. Phonemes are not to be confused with letters of the alphabet. A letter may stand for a sound (a phoneme), but then, a letter may stand for several different phonemes (the letter *c* stands for the at least three: *c*at, *c*eiling, and an*c*ient) and several different letters can stand for the same phoneme (*c*at, *k*ite, *q*uiche). Every language has a somewhat different set of phonemes. Not many languages other than English have the phonemes for *th* (ei*th*er, e*th*er), but then English lacks the trilled *r* that is common in other languages.

The various sounds of a language can be categorized by their distinctive features, that is, by the characteristics they have that make them recognizably different from other sounds of the language. For example, linguists use the term "plosive" to refer to consonants that are abrupt (such as *b*, *d*, and *k*) not smooth (such as *m*, *s*, and *w*), and they use the term "labial" to describe phonemes made with the lips (such as *b*, *m*, and *w*) and "velar" to describe phonemes made at the back of the throat (such as *k* and *g*). Where English distinguishes between only two labial plosives (*b* and *p*) some languages distinguish between four (they have two different *b*'s and two different *p*'s). That means, where English has only two possible rhymes with the word *dig* that begin with a labial plosive (*big* and *pig*), there are other languages that could have four different rhymes.

Not only does a language's phonology determine which sounds are and are not legal (and distinctive) in the language, but it also determines how sounds can be combined to make syllables. For example, even though all of the sounds in the syllable *ngoh* are completely legal in English, at least in isolation, English phonology does not allow *ng* at the beginning of syllables, nor *h* at the end (though there are languages that allow both).

MORPHOLOGY. Morphology refers to the system of morphemes, (that is, root-words, prefixes, and suffixes). Morphemes such as "book," "hate," "-ful," and "anti-," are the smallest units of language that have meaning. (Phonemes are smaller, but they do not have any particular meaning.) Morphemes are not to be confused with words, because some morphemes (prefixes and suffixes) are less than words, and some words (such as "homework" and "uncooked") consist of several morphemes.

Morphological rules govern how morphemes may be combined to form words. For example, English morphology requires that the past tense morpheme "-ed" not stand on its own, but must appear at the end of a verb (never a noun: talk/talked but not apple/appled). Morphology also specifies exceptions to the rules (such as "make" + "-ed" = "made"). Morphophonemics are rules that govern how sounds change when morphemes are combined ("leaf" + "s" = "leaves").

SYNTAX. Syntax is the language's system of word combination. Syntax governs what words must appear together and what words cannot, as well as the order in which they must appear in. Syntax is close to what most people mean by the word "grammar." The syntax of English allows "The door opened" but not "Opened door the." Syntax does not simply allow and disallow certain word orders; it also specifies the relationship among those words. However, there is not always agreement among theorists about exactly how syntax does this.

For instance, "I opened the door with the key" and "The key opened the door" and "The door opened" refer to essentially the same event, even though all three sentences have a different subject ("I," "the key," and "the door" each take turns "opening"). Some theories of syntax (such as case grammars) attempt to account for these relationships and some theories ignore these relationships as coincidental, or at least as the job of semantics, not of syntax.

Other theories consider the relationships between such sentences as "I kicked the ball" (active voice) "The ball was kicked by me" (passive voice) and "Did I kick the ball?" (yes/no question) to be the responsibility of syntactic theory. Such theories (for example, Chomsky's earlier theories of syntax) suggest that all three of these sentences are derived from the same kernel sentence (or deep structure), namely, "I kick+ed the ball." According to such theories, the deep structure is then transformed into one of the three (surface) sentences by different rules of transformation. Thus, there would be a transformational rule for passive voice, a transformational rule for forming questions, and even a very simple transformational rule for forming active sentences. Chomsky's more recent theories have abandoned relating these three sentences to each other (and so have abandoned the related transformations), yet he uses newly defined transformational rules to account for other things, such as the placement of "did" in "Did I kick the ball?" and "whom" in "Whom shall I give the money to?"

Although the details are still controversial, most syntactic theories claim that word order is governed by at least two kinds of rules: phrase structure rules and transformational rules. The phrase structure rules determine how the deep structure (kernel sentence) is organized, and the transformational rules determine how these deep phrase structures are rearranged to form surface structures (what is actually said out loud). People are not aware of using any of these rules; they just do it.

What is the point in a theory claiming that one or the other set of transformational rules is used by the language? It is hoped that once linguists have settled on the correct set of rules, they will be able to explain such oddities as why, as a person thumbs through Mary's pictures of her children, saying "Who is that a picture of?" is syntactically acceptable, but "Who is that Mary's picture of?" is not. So far, no theory has been able to account for all such examples of acceptable versus unacceptable utterances. This is despite decades of research by the best minds the field of linguistics has to offer (and there are some brilliant minds among them). Yet every normal four-year-old speaker of English knows these rules (not how to state the rules, but how to get these sentences right by following the rules). How is it that average four-year-olds can do effortlessly in a few years what teams of brilliant professionals cannot do in many decades? No wonder Chomsky believed these rules are not learned, but genetically programmed.

SEMANTICS AND PRAGMATICS. Semantics is the meaning system of a language. This includes the meaning both of individual words (for example, "father" means "male parent") and of sentences (take a list of word meanings from a sentence and come up with the point of the statement). Semantic rules state that sentences such as "Colorless green ideas sleep furiously" are nonsense (not well formed). Theories of semantics are fundamental to psychological theories of concept formation, and text comprehension and memory.

Pragmatics is the system of whatever rules of language are not covered by the other systems. It includes the rules of language usage and style. Some sort of pragmatic rule tells us that "Howdy, my lord" is not acceptable, even though it is syntactically and semantically well formed. Conversational rules are pragmatic rules. When a person wishes to end a phone conversation, it is acceptable to say, "Gosh, look at the time" or "Well, it sure has been nice taking to you. Do call again," but it appears as rude to say simply, "Please stop talking." Evidently, yet another rule of pragmatics is at work.

H. P. Grice suggests that pragmatic rules allow more to be said than is actually spoken. According to Grice, anyone who engages in a conversation must agree to be conversationally cooperative, even if one's purpose is to be oppositional and uncooperative. One can be uncooperative in dozens of other ways, but if one is conversationally uncooperative, the conversation simply ends. By conversationally cooperative, Grice means that people try to be clear, succinct, relevant, and (except where they are purposely trying to deceive) truthful. Grice points out that any time people say something that obviously violates this cooperative principle, by being flagrantly unclear, wordy, irrelevant, or untruthful, they are sending an implied message. Sarcasm, for example, is accomplished by saying something obviously false, such as "I simply love being publicly humiliated." This sarcastic comment breaks the cooperative principle of truthfulness. By so doing, it not only lets the hearer know that the speaker hates being humiliated, but it does so better than does the corresponding nonsarcastic statement "I simply hate being publicly humiliated." Grice suggests that when people make such obvious violations of the cooperative principle, the hearer can infer that they did it on purpose, for effect, and can usually even figure out for what effect it was done. By counting on their listeners to figure out why they have done this, speakers can get a point across without coming right out and saying it.

THE SIGNIFICANCE OF AN UTTERANCE

The meaning of a person's statement is not purely a matter of semantics, but of pragmatics as well. Linguists have identified a variety of types of meaning conveyed by language.

Propositional content is the set of claims made by a declarative sentence (and if the sentence is a question or command, the claims made by the corresponding declarative sentence). Thus "You eat cake," "Do you eat cake?" and "Eat cake!" all have the same propositional content, namely the claim that "eating" is performed by "you" upon an object of the type "cake." There can be multiple propositions in a single sentence: "The tall, dark stranger thought the statement I made was clever" includes the propositions that (1) the stranger is tall; (2) the stranger is dark; (3) I made a statement; (4) the statement was clever; (5) the stranger thought so.

The speaker is not committed to the truthfulness of every proposition in the utterance. The stranger may have thought the speaker's statement was clever, but the speaker need not agree. Furthermore, each proposition constitutes a description of some part of the common universe. One of the jobs of semantic theory is to determine the conditions under which such a description would be true (these are called truth conditions). Propositions are understood in terms of their truth conditions, and in terms of their relationships to other propositions.

Thematic structure is a specification of which parts of a conversation are new, or to be emphasized, and which parts are old (given) information that the speaker can safely assume is already understood by the listener. To communicate, the speaker must use both old and new information: new, to tell listeners something they did not already know; old, to help listeners figure out where the new information fits in with what they already know, so they can relate to it. In the following examples, the same sentence is used, but a different word is emphasized. The emphasis indicates that the emphasized material is new, perhaps even unexpected, whereas the unemphasized material is treated as old, already known material.

John ate the cake. (Answers the question, Who ate the cake?)

John *ate* the cake. (Answers the question, What did John do to the cake?)

John ate the *cake*. (Answers the question, What did John eat?)

John ate *the* cake. (Answers the question, Which cake did John eat?)

Presupposition is an assumption that one must make before one can understand the proposition being stated. The assumption is not directly stated, but the statement makes no sense if the presupposition is not made. For example, "Did you ever stop beating your wife?" presupposes that "you" have been beating "your wife," whether the answer to the question is yes or no, and "You left your car unlocked" presupposes "you" have a car.

Entailment is a logical conclusion that must be drawn if the stated proposition is taken to be true. The entailment is not directly stated, nor is it presupposed, but once one accepts the proposition, one must accept the entailment if one is to be logical. "Marty has $10" entails that Marty has more than $3.

Implicature is the conclusion one draws when the speaker conveys it by flagrantly breaking Grice's cooperative principle.

Illocution is the form of a sentence, whether it is declarative (a statement), imperative (a command), or interrogative (a question). Illocutionary force is the direct or implied impact of a statement, regardless of its illocution. For example, the sentence "Could you open the window?" has the illocution of a question, but it has the illocutionary force of a request (something akin to "Please open the window").

SPEECH ACTS AND INDIRECT SPEECH ACTS
Sometimes an utterance is more than just an utterance: It actually does something. When the justice of the peace says, "I now pronounce you husband and wife," the very words cause the couple in question to become husband and wife. When a person says "I promise to stop," that person thereby makes a promise. Any time an utterance does the thing it says it is doing, whether it be promising, commanding, asking, refusing, or whatever, that is a direct speech act. If an utterance accomplishes the same thing, but without coming right out and stating that it is doing so, that is an indirect speech act. "I won't do it again" is an indirect promise, since the speaker never actually said it was a promise.

There are many more kinds of meaning attached to utterances, but these serve as an introduction to the variety that linguists have identified.

EVIDENCE FOR EVALUATING LINGUISTIC THEORY
Both linguists and psychologists have debated about the nature of human language and language processes for decades. Linguists and psychologists use different kinds of data for testing their claims about language. For the most part, linguists use language judgments (of whether a given utterance is acceptable or not) to confirm or refute a proposed rule or rule system. That is, they ask native speakers of a language to judge whether this or that utterance is well formed. Linguists focus on the idealized competence of a speaker and try to avoid performance issues (such as whether an otherwise perfectly good utterance is too difficult to produce or comprehend).

Psychologists, on the other hand, use subjects' performance at perceiving, remembering, interpreting, and utilizing language as clues about human language abilities. They tend to consider idealized rules that overlook actual performance to be less satisfying.

Nonetheless, psychologists are indebted to linguists for proposing an impressive array of linguistic structures and abilities, which psychologists have then taken and tested, using their own methods. Often this endeavor is referred to as testing the psychological reality of a linguistic construct. Basically, the psychology researcher is trying to find out if the rules and structures that linguists have come up with using linguistic research methods will actually make a difference in how long a subject takes to react or how accurately a subject perceives or how well a subject remembers various words, phrases, sentences, or paragraphs. If the pattern of reaction times, or memory errors, is consistent with the proposed linguistic rule (or structure), then that rule (or structure) is said to have demonstrated psychological reality.

Some linguistic rules (such as phrase structure rules) have had demonstrable psychological reality. When researchers presented clicks in the middle of a sentence, participants heard the clicks as if they happened between phrase structure boundaries (say, between the subject and predicate of a sentence) even when the clicks occurred well before (or after) the actual boundary. The fact that people's hearing is altered by the presence of phrase structure boundaries shows that those phrase structures are actually influencing their behavior and are thus psychologically real.

On the other hand, some linguistic rules (such as the passive transformation) have failed to demonstrate any psychological reality. Sentences that were more complex (because they included an extra transformation) took participants no longer to process than simpler sentences. This finding suggests that the so-called complex sentence was not in fact more complex, as far as the research participants were concerned. The supposed extra transformation had no impact on the participants, and is thus concluded to have no psychological reality.

SOURCES FOR FURTHER STUDY

Chomsky, Noam. "Review of B. F. Skinner, *Verbal Behavior.*" *Language* 35 (1959): 26-57. Reprinted in *The Structure of Language: Readings in the Philosophy of Language* (1964), edited by Jerry A. Fodor and Jerrold Katz, and in *Readings in the Psychology of Language* (1967), edited by Leon Jakobovits and Murray Miron. Quite readable. Chomsky's review and criticism of Skinner's book in many ways marked the beginning of the revolution in the field of cognitive psychology and language acquisition.

_____. *Syntactic Structures*. The Hague, Netherlands: Mouton, 1957. Presents Chomsky's earliest theory of language, which revolutionized linguistics. Though this work is dry, it is much more readable than Chomsky's later theorizing.

Davis, Flora. *Eloquent Animals: A Study in Animal Communication.* New York: Coward, McCann & Geoghegan, 1978. A passionate excursion through examples of animal intelligence and communication.

Fromkin, Victoria, and Robert Rodman. *An Introduction to Language.* Fort Worth: Harcourt Brace Jovanovich, 1993. A typical introductory level college textbook introducing phonology, morphology, syntax, semantics, and pragmatics; language change, writing, language development, and the brain; and other related topics about language.

Grice, H. P. "Logic and Conversation." In *Speech Acts*, edited by P. Cole & J. L. Morgan. New York: Academic Press, 1975. Grice introduces his classic theory of the cooperative principle in conversation.

Hudson, Grover. *Essential Introductory Linguistics.* Boston: Blackwell, 1999. This introductory textbook divides linguistics into twenty-eight topics, each covered succinctly in its own chapter, with exercises for students at the end of each chapter.

Searle, John R. *Speech Acts: An Essay in the Philosophy of Language.* New York: Cambridge University Press, 1969. The original theory of speech acts is presented along with many philosophical arguments about the meaning and use of language.

Skinner, B. F. *Verbal Behavior.* New York: Appleton-Century-Crofts, 1957. Nearly five hundred pages, presents the behaviorist account of language, in the words of the master behaviorist, Skinner. Chomsky's review and criticism of this book in many ways marked the beginning of the revolution in the field of cognitive psychology and language acquisition.

Victor K. Broderick

SEE ALSO: Bilingualism; Brain damage; Brain specialization; Brain structure; Grammar and speech;

Language; Nonverbal communication; Speech disorders; Speech perception; Stuttering; Thought: Inferential.

Logic and reasoning

Type of psychology: Cognition
Fields of study: Cognitive processes; thought

Logic and reasoning are essential elements of the human mind and underlie many daily activities. Although humans may not follow the prescriptions of formal logic precisely, human reasoning is nevertheless often systematic. Study of the structures and processes involved in the use of logic and reasoning provides insight into both the human mind and the possible creation of intelligent machines.

Key concepts
- atmosphere hypothesis
- availability
- belief-bias effect
- confirmation bias
- deductive reasoning
- gambler's fallacy
- heuristic
- inductive reasoning
- representativeness
- syllogism

Introduction

Logical and reasoning tasks are typically classified as either deductive or inductive. In deductive reasoning, if the premises are true and a valid rule of inference is used, the conclusion must be true. In inductive reasoning, in contrast, the conclusion can be false even if the premises are true. In many cases, deductive reasoning also involves moving from general principles to specific conclusions, while inductive reasoning involves moving from specific examples to general conclusions.

Cognitive psychologists study deductive reasoning by examining how people reason using syllogisms, logical arguments comprising a major and a minor premise that lead to a conclusion. The premises are assumed to be true; the validity of the conclusion depends upon whether a proper rule of inference is used. The classic example of deduction is:

> All men are mortal.
>
> *Socrates is a man.*
>
> Socrates is a mortal.

A more modern (and more controversial) example of deduction might be:

> Abortion is murder.
>
> *Murder should be illegal.*
>
> Abortion should be illegal.

The second example prompts a distinction between "truth" and "validity." Even though the second syllogism is logically valid, it may or may not be true. Broadly speaking, truth refers to content (that is, applicability of the conclusion to the real world), and validity refers to form (that is, whether the conclusion is drawn logically). It is thus possible to have a valid argument that is nevertheless untrue. For a clearer example, consider this syllogism:

> All dinosaurs are animals.
>
> *All animals are in zoos.*
>
> All dinosaurs are in zoos.

The conclusion is valid but is not true, because one of the premises (all animals are in zoos) is not true. Even though a valid rule of inference was applied and a valid conclusion was drawn, the conclusion is not true. If a valid conclusion has been drawn from true premises, however, the argument is called "sound."

With inductive reasoning, the validity of the conclusion is less certain. The classic example of induction is:

> *Every crow I have seen in my life up to this time has been black.*
>
> All crows are black.

Other examples of induction include a child who begins to say "goed" (from "go") instead of "went," a detective piecing together evidence at the scene of a crime, and a stock analyst who, after observing that prices have fallen during the past two Septembers, urges clients to sell in August. In all these cases, a conclusion is drawn based on evidence observed prior to the conclusion. There remains the possibility, however, that additional evidence may render the conclusion incorrect. It does not matter how many positive instances (for example, black crows, September stock declines) have been observed; if one counterexample can be found (a white crow, a September stock rise), the conclusion is incorrect.

HEURISTICS

The study of induction spans a variety of methods and topics. In this article, most of the consideration of induction involves cases in which people rely on heuristics in their reasoning. Heuristics involve "rules of thumb" that yield "ballpark" solutions that are approximately correct and can be applied across a wide range of problems.

One common heuristic is representativeness, which is invoked in answering the following questions: What is the probability that object A belongs to class B, event A originates from process B, or that process B will generate event A? The representativeness heuristic suggests that probabilities are evaluated by the degree to which A is representative of B, that is, by the degree to which A resembles B. If A is representative of B, the probability that A originates from B is judged to be high; if A does not resemble B or is not similar to B, the probability that A originates from B is judged to be low.

A second heuristic is availability, which is invoked in judgments of frequency; specifically, people assess the frequency of a class by the ease with which instances of that class can be brought to mind. Factors that influence the ability to think of instances of a class, such as recency, salience, number of associations, and so forth, influence availability in such a way that certain types of events (such as recent and salient) are more available. For example, if several people one knows have had car accidents recently, one's subjective probability of being in a car accident is increased.

RULES OF INFERENCE

Before examining how people reason deductively, two rules of inference must be considered: *modus ponens* (the "method of putting," which involves affirming a premise) and *modus tollens* (the "method of taking," which involves negating a premise). Considering P and Q as content-free abstract variables (much like algebraic variables), *modus ponens* states that given "P implies Q" and P, one can infer Q. In the following example, applying *modus ponens* to 1 and 2 (in which P is "it rained last night" and Q is "the game was canceled"), one can infer 3.

1. If it rained last night, then the game was canceled.

2. It rained last night.

3. The game was canceled.

Modus tollens states that given "P implies Q" and ~Q (read "not Q"; "~" is a symbol for negation), one can infer "~P." Applying *modus tollens* to 1 and 4, one can infer 5.

4. The game was not canceled.

5. It did not rain last night.

In general, people apply *modus ponens* properly but do not apply *modus tollens* properly. In one experiment, four cards showing the following letters or numbers were placed in front of subjects:

E K 4 7

Subjects saw only one side of each card but were told that a letter appeared on one side and a number on the other side. Subjects judged the validity of the following rule by turning over only those cards that provided a valid test: If a card has a vowel on one side, then it has an even number on the other side. Turning over E is a correct application of *modus ponens*, and turning over 7 is a correct application of *modus tollens* (consider P as "vowel on one side" and Q as "even number on the other side"). Almost 80 percent of subjects turned over E only or E and 4, while only 4 percent of subjects chose the correct answer, turning over E and 7. While many subjects correctly applied *modus ponens*, far fewer correctly applied *modus tollens*. Additionally, many subjects turned over 4, an error called affirmation of the consequent.

When stimuli are concrete, reasoning improves. In an analogous experiment, four cards with the following information were placed before subjects:

beer Coke 16 22

One side of each card showed a person's drink; the other side showed a person's age. Subjects evaluated this rule: If a person is drinking beer, that person must be at least nineteen. In this experiment, nearly 75 percent of the subjects made the correct selections, showing that in some contexts people are more likely to apply *modus tollens* properly.

When quantifiers such as "all," "some," and "none" are used within syllogisms, additional errors in reasoning occur. People are more likely to accept positive conclusions to positive premises and negative conclusions to negative premises, negative conclusions if premises are mixed, a universal conclusion if premises are universal (all or none), a particular conclusion if premises are particular (some), and a particular conclusion if one premise is general and the other is particular. These observations led to the atmosphere hypothesis, which suggests that the quantifiers within the premises create an "atmosphere" predisposing subjects to accept as valid conclusions that use the same quantifiers.

Influence of Knowledge and Beliefs

Prior knowledge or beliefs can influence reasoning if people neglect the form of the argument and concentrate on the content; this is referred to as the belief-bias effect. If a valid conclusion appears unbelievable, people reject it, while a conclusion that is invalid but appears believable is accepted as valid. Many people accept this syllogism as valid:

> All oak trees have acorns.
>
> *This tree has acorns.*
>
> This tree is an oak tree.

Consider, however, this logically equivalent syllogism:

> All oak trees have leaves.
>
> *This tree has leaves.*
>
> This tree is an oak tree.

In the first syllogism, people's knowledge that only oak trees have acorns leads them to accept the conclusion as valid. In the second syllogism, people's knowledge that many types of trees have leaves leads them to reject the conclusion as invalid.

Biases in Reasoning

A common bias in inductive reasoning is the confirmation bias, the tendency to seek confirming evidence and not to seek disconfirming evidence. In one study, subjects who were presented with the numbers (2, 4, 6) determined what rule (concept) would allow them to generate additional numbers in the series. In testing their hypotheses, many subjects produced series to confirm their hypotheses—for example, (20, 22, 24) or (100, 102, 104)—of

"even numbers ascending by 2," but few produced series to disconfirm their hypotheses—for example, (1, 3, 5) or (20, 50, 187). In fact, any ascending series (such as 32, 69, 100,005) would have satisfied the general rule, but because subjects did not seek to disconfirm their more specific rules, they did not discover the more general rule.

Heuristics also lead to biases in reasoning. In one study, subjects were told that bag A contained ten blue and twenty red chips, while bag B contained twenty blue and ten red chips. On each trial, the experimenter selected one bag; subjects knew that bag A would be selected on 80 percent of the trials. The subject drew three chips from the bag and reasoned whether A or B had been selected. When subjects drew two blues and one red, all were confident that B had been selected. If the probability for that sample is actually calculated, however, the odds are 2:1 that it comes from A. People chose B because the sample of chips resembles (represents) B more than A, and ignored the prior probability of 80 percent that the bag was A.

In another experiment, subjects were shown descriptions of "Linda" that made her appear to be a feminist. Subjects rated the probability that Linda was a bank teller and a feminist higher than the probability that Linda was a bank teller. Whenever there is a conjunction of events, however, the probability of both events is less than the probability of either event alone, so the probability that Linda was a bank teller and a feminist was actually lower than the probability that she was only a bank teller. Reliance on representativeness leads to overestimation of the probability of a conjunction of events.

Reliance on representativeness also leads to the "gambler's fallacy." This fallacy can be defined as the belief that if a small sample is drawn from an infinite and randomly distributed population, that sample must also appear randomly distributed.

Consider a chance event such as flipping a coin (H represents "heads," T represents "tails"). Which sequence is more probable: HTHTTH or HHHHHH? Subjects judge that the first sequence is more probable, but both are equally probable. The second sequence, HHHHHH, does not appear to be random, however, and so is believed to be less probable. After a long run of H, people judge T as more probable than H because the coin is "due" for T. A problem with the idea of "due," though, is that the coin itself has no memory of a run of H or T. As far as the coin is concerned, on the next toss there is .5 probability of H and .5 probability of T. The fallacy arises because subjects expect a small sample from an infinitely large random distribution to appear random. The same misconceptions are often extended beyond coin-flipping to all games of chance.

In fallacies of reasoning resulting from availability, subjects misestimate frequencies. When subjects estimated the proportion of English words beginning with R versus words with R as the third letter, they estimated that more words begin with R, but, in fact, more than three times as many words have R as their third letter. For another example, consider the following problem. Ten people are available and need to be organized into committees. Can more committees of two or more committees of eight be organized? Subjects claimed that more committees of two could be organized, probably because it is easier to visualize a larger number of committees of two, but equal numbers of committees could be made in both cases. In both examples, the class for which it is easier to generate examples is judged to be the most frequent or numerous. An additional aspect of availability involves causal scenarios (sometimes referred to as the simulation heuristic), stories or narratives in which one event causes another and which lead from an original situation to an outcome. If a causal scenario linking an original situation and outcome is easily available, that outcome is judged to be more likely.

EVOLUTION OF STUDY

Until the twentieth century, deductive logic and the psychology of human thought were considered to be the same topic. The mathematician George Boole entitled his 1854 book on logical calculus *An Investigation of the Laws of Human Thought*. This book was designed "to investigate the fundamental laws of those operations of the mind by which reasoning is performed." Humans did not always seem to operate according to the prescriptions of logic, but such lapses were seen as the malfunctioning of the mental machinery. When the mental machinery functioned properly, humans were logical. Indeed, it is human rationality, the ability to think logically, that for many thinkers throughout time has separated humans from other animals (for example, Aristotle's man as rational animal) and defined the human essence (for example, René Descartes's "I think, therefore I am").

As a quintessential mental process, the study of reasoning is an integral part of modern cognitive psychology. In the mid-twentieth century, however, when psychology was in the grip of the behaviorist movement, little attention was given to such "mentalistic" conceptions, with the exception of isolated works such as Frederic C. Bartlett's studies of memory and Jerome S. Bruner, Jacqueline J. Goodnow, and George A. Austin's landmark publication *A Study of Thinking* (1956), dealing with, among other topics, induction and concept formation. The development of the digital computer and the subsequent application of the computer as a metaphor for the human mind suggested new methods and vocabularies for investigating mental processes such as reasoning, and with the ascendancy of the cognitive approach within experimental psychology and the emergence of cognitive science, research on human reasoning has become central in attempts both to understand the human mind and to build machines that are capable of independent, intelligent action.

INVOLVEMENT OF COMPUTERS

In the latter part of the twentieth century, there were attempts to simulate human reasoning with computers and to develop computers capable of humanlike reasoning. One notable attempt involved the work of Allen Newell and Herbert Simon, who provided human subjects with various sorts of problems to solve. Their human subjects would "think out loud," and transcripts of what they said became the basis of computer programs designed to mimic human problem solving and reasoning. Thus, the study of human logic and reasoning not only furthered the understanding of human cognitive processes but also gave guidance to those working in artificial intelligence. One caveat, however, is that even though such transcripts may serve as a model for computer intelligence, there remain important differences between human and machine "reasoning." For example, in humans, the correct application of some inference rules (for example, *modus tollens*) depends upon the context (for example, the atmosphere hypothesis or the belief-bias effect). Furthermore, not all human reasoning may be strictly verbalizable, and to the extent that human reasoning relies on nonlinguistic processes (such as imagery), it might not be possible to mimic or recreate it on a computer.

After being assumed to be logical or even being ignored by science, human reasoning is finally being studied for what it is. In solving logical problems, humans do not always comply with the dictates of logical theory; the solutions reached may be influenced by the context of the problem, previous knowledge or belief, and the particular heuristics utilized in reaching a solution. Discovery of the structures, processes, and strategies involved in reasoning promises to increase the understanding not only of how the human mind works but also of how to develop artificially intelligent machines.

SOURCES FOR FURTHER STUDY

Halpern, Diane F. *Thought and Knowledge: An Introduction to Critical Thinking.* 3d ed. Hillsdale, N.J.: Lawrence Erlbaum, 1995. Presents a brief overview of memory and language, then presents data and theory on performance with different types of deductive arguments, analyzing arguments, fallacies, reasoning with probabilities, and hypothesis testing. The author provides numerous examples and exercises, and the text can be understood by high school or college students.

Holland, John H., et al. *Induction: Processes of Inference, Learning, and Discovery.* Reprint. Cambridge, Mass.: MIT Press, 1989. Presents a broad cross-disciplinary account of induction and examines the role of inferential rules in induction, people's mental models of the world, concept formation, problem solving, and the role of induction in discovery. The authors provide an extensive bibliography of scholarly research on induction.

Johnson-Laird, Philip Nicholas. *Mental Models.* Cambridge, Mass.: Harvard University Press, 1983. Presents an extensive review of data and theory on syllogistic reasoning. The author presents a unified theory of the mind based on recursive procedures, propositional representations, and mental models. The text is very thorough and detailed, and many readers may find it daunting.

Kahneman, Daniel, Paul Slovic, and Amos Tversky, eds. *Judgment Under Uncertainty: Heuristics and Biases.* New York: Cambridge University Press, 1982. Presents a collection of many of the important papers on heuristics, including several papers each on representativeness, availability, causality and attribution, and corrective procedures. Many of the papers are thorough and present detailed information on experiments or theory.

Kelley, David. *The Art of Reasoning.* 3d ed. New York: W. W. Norton, 1998. A well-regarded introduction to classic logic. Thorough and accessible.

Sternberg, Robert J., and Talia Ben-Zeev. *Complex Cognition: The Psychology of Human Thought.* New York: Oxford University Press, 2001. An introduction to cognitive psychology, including explanations of the types of reasoning in theory and in practice. Synthesizes the "normative reference" and "bounded rationality" approaches to understanding human thought.

Weizenbaum, Joseph. *Computer Power and Human Reason II.* New York: W. H. Freeman, 1997. Provides many examples of "computer reason" and argues that some aspects of the mind cannot be explained in information-processing (computational) terms. Makes the case that computers should not be given tasks that demand human reason or wisdom. Written in a very accessible and easy-to-read style.

Timothy L. Hubbard

SEE ALSO: Artificial intelligence; Computer models of cognition; Concept formation; Decision making; Pattern recognition; Problem-solving stages; Problem-solving strategies; Thought: Inferential; Thought: Study and measurement.

Long-term memory

TYPE OF PSYCHOLOGY: Memory
FIELDS OF STUDY: Cognitive processes

The study of long-term memory investigates the mechanisms of information retention and retrieval in relatively permanent storage. Without the capacity for long-term memory, learning would be impossible, as would nearly every facet of human intelligence.

KEY CONCEPTS
- encoding
- episodic memory
- levels-of-processing model
- mnemonics
- procedural memory
- semantic memory

- sensory memory
- short-term memory
- storage

INTRODUCTION

William James, in his famous work *The Principles of Psychology* (1890), was one of the first to make the distinction between short-term and long-term memory, which he called primary and secondary memory. James believed that secondary (long-term) memory was the only true memory, because it possessed two important characteristics that are absent from primary memory: Remembered events seem to belong to the past, and their recollection is brought about by appropriate cues. Another early memory researcher was Hermann Ebbinghaus, who introduced the use of nonsense syllables (meaningless sets of two consonants and a vowel) in investigating the nature of long-term memory. Ebbinghaus systematically studied forgetting of information from long-term memory and found that most forgetting occurs during the first nine hours after learning, and especially during the first hour. After that, forgetting continues, but at a much slower rate. He also discovered that much forgetting from long-term memory is caused by interference from other, previously learned material (proactive interference) or by interference created by learning new material (retroactive interference).

Psychologists today generally propose a three-stage theory of memory: sensory memory, short-term memory, and long-term memory. When information first enters through one of the senses, it is retained briefly (for less than a second, generally) in sensory memory. Even though this information fades very rapidly, through processes such as selective attention, some of the information is processed further. The next processing stage is referred to as short-term, or working, memory. Information is retained in this store for about twenty to thirty seconds, but through the use of rehearsal, items can be maintained in short-term memory indefinitely. Short-term memory has a limited capacity; it can hold about five to nine items at a time.

Information can reach long-term memory by several methods. Items that are particularly meaningful or that have a high emotional content are usually directly encoded into long-term memory. The use of a type of rehearsal called elaborative rehearsal, which involves thinking about how new material relates to information already stored, is also an effective method for transferring items from short-term memory to long-term memory. Unlike short-term memory, storage in long-term memory appears to be relatively permanent, and the capacity of long-term memory appears to be virtually unlimited.

In 1972, Fergus Craik and Robert Lockhart suggested that long- and short-term memory do not necessarily represent distinct stages of memory. They proposed what has come to be known as the levels-of-processing model, which holds that differences in how long or how well something is remembered depend on the degree or depth to which incoming information is mentally processed. The depth of processing for incoming information is related to how much it is thought about, organized, and related to one's existing knowledge. Thus, long-term memory, in their view, simply represents information that has been processed to a greater depth. This model has been very influential and has stimulated a tremendous body of research.

CLASSIFYING LONG-TERM MEMORY

Another influential theorist, Endel Tulving, proposed a classification scheme which distinguishes three aspects of long-term memory: procedural memory, episodic memory, and semantic memory. Procedural memory, also called skill memory, represents knowledge of how to do something. This can involve motor skills, such as knowing how to swing, or cognitive skills, such as reading and writing. Episodic memory is the memory of events from one's personal past. One's recollection of where one was last Saturday night or what one had for dinner yesterday would represent information from episodic memory. Semantic memory represents a person's knowledge of the world not tied to a specific event in one's life. This type of general knowledge includes definitions of words, facts such as the name of the first president of the United States, and relationships between concepts. Although some researchers have questioned the need for these distinctions among types of memory, there is evidence which supports this classification scheme. Many people who suffer from amnesia (partial or total loss of memory), for example, usually are unable to remember specific incidents or facts about their lives (episodic memory), yet their general knowledge (semantic memory) and knowledge of how to do things (procedural memory) remain intact. Also, studies involving monitoring of blood flow patterns in the brain reveal different patterns when one is thinking about personal experiences versus impersonal facts. The frontal region of the brain appears to be more active during retrieval from episodic memory, and the posterior regions have a greater degree of activation during semantic retrieval.

ENCODING, STORAGE, AND RETRIEVAL

Researchers have also attempted to understand the nature of three basic processes associated with long-term memory: encoding, storage, and retrieval. Encoding concerns how information is put into memory; storage refers to the maintenance of information in memory; retrieval refers to the recovery of information from memory. Forgetting can represent a failure of any of these processes. Researchers are interested in the specific mental operations that are involved in each of these operations. Successful encoding of information into long-term memory is usually based on the meanings of the items. This is in contrast to short-term memory, which primarily involves an acoustic coding of information. Acoustic codes can also be used in long-term memory, but the dominant or preferred code involves meaning.

As mentioned above, the capacity of long-term memory appears to be virtually unlimited, and storage relatively permanent, although some storage loss probably does occur. Experimental evidence indicates that storage processes usually require some time for items to be placed in long-term memory. This process is referred to as consolidation. If a disruption (such as electroconvulsive shock) occurs shortly after information is encoded, the information will be lost from storage. Sometimes, information is definitely stored in one's long-term memory but one still cannot recall it (for example, the name of an old friend whom one has not seen for some time). Usually, this represents a retrieval failure. Retrieval of information from long-term memory has sometimes been compared to searching for an item stored in an attic. The success of the search process depends on knowing where to look. The retrieval of information stored in long-term memory is usually initiated by some stimulus, referred to as a retrieval cue. Such cues provide information which can aid in the recall of stored material. Factors associated with encoding can also aid in retrieval. For example, organizing information at the time of encoding will increase the chances of successful retrieval. Re-

trieval will also be facilitated if the context in which information is encoded is similar to that in which it will be retrieved. Many studies have even shown that the psychological state (for example, the drug state or mood state) that one is in during the time information is encoded can act as a retrieval cue at the time of recall. This is referred to as state-dependent memory. Thus, if one was depressed when one learned material, one will more easily recall that material when one is in that same state again.

EYEWITNESS TESTIMONY RESEARCH

Investigations of the nature of long-term memory have led to findings that have proved useful in many areas of psychology and in other fields. Elizabeth Loftus and other researchers have done extensive research on the accuracy of long-term memory in eyewitness testimony. Loftus found that juries tend to rely heavily on eyewitness testimony, but she also found that the reliability of the memories of eyewitnesses was not very high.

When episodic information is stored in long-term memory, it is constantly being affected by material stored in semantic memory, including beliefs, prejudices, expectancies, inferences, and so on. What is stored in memory is not a simple copy of experiences but rather a construction that a person has created based on material already stored in long-term memory. People frequently fill in gaps in their memory with appropriate bits and pieces of their general knowledge of human situations and activities. These changes occur without their awareness; a memory of an event might seem accurate yet may have been changed dramatically. Loftus showed that the memory of witnesses could be affected by the type of question asked or by the specific wording of a question. In one experiment, subjects were shown a film of a traffic accident and then were asked questions about it. A question about the speed of the vehicles was asked in two different ways: "How fast were the cars going when they smashed into each other?" and "How fast were the cars going when they hit each other?" Subjects who were asked the "smashed" question not only estimated greater speeds but also one week later had memories of many details (such as broken glass) that were not in the film.

Another study, done on television station WNBC in New York, allowed viewers to witness a simulated crime in which they could closely see the assailant's face for 3.5 seconds. They were then asked to pick out the criminal from a lineup of six men through a special telephone number. Eighty-six percent of the 2,145 viewers who phoned in either "recognized" the wrong man or decided that the guilty man was not in the lineup. Overall, the performance was at the level that would be expected by chance alone. This type of research has led to modifications in some courtrooms, such as clearer instructions to jurors that are more easily remembered (jurors are usually not allowed to take notes, so they have to rely wholly on long-term memory).

MNEMONIC TECHNIQUES

Understanding the nature of long-term memory has led to the development of many mnemonic techniques: strategies to help improve memory. Two mnemonic systems that are particularly useful for remembering ordered sequences of unrelated items (such as grocery lists) are the method of loci (*loci* is Latin for "places") and the peg-word system. In the method of loci, the first step is to think about a set of familiar geographic locations, such as the rooms in one's house. The next step is to form a mental image of each item on the list in one of these locations, that is, one word in each room in the house. Whenever one wants to remember the list, one takes a mental walk through the house and collects the items in each room.

Use of the peg-word system requires the memorization of a list of words that will serve as memory pegs for the list to be remembered. One popular example of a peg-word list is: "One is a bun, two is a shoe, three is a tree, four is a door, five is a hive, six is a stick, seven is heaven, eight is a gate, nine is a hive, and ten is a hen." Once this list is learned, mental images are created between each new item to be remembered and the previously learned peg word. For example, if the first item on a grocery list is coffee, one might image coffee being poured over a bun. If the second item is milk, one might image a milk carton being kicked by a shoe. This might seem cumbersome, but it works. With both the method of loci and the peg-word system, particularly vivid images seem to produce the best results.

LEARNING TECHNIQUES

The study of long-term memory has also led to the development of techniques for improving the learn-

ing of more complex material. In general, the more that items are elaborated on during the encoding, the more easily they can subsequently be recalled or recognized. This is true because the more connections are established between items, the larger the number of retrieval possibilities. Therefore, if one wants to remember some fact, one should expand on its meaning. Questions about the causes and consequences of an event, for example, are particularly effective elaborations because each question sets up a meaningful connection, or retrieval path, to the event.

The more organized the material is during the process of encoding, the more easily the material will be retrieved later. Massive amounts of information can be stored and retrieved, if only it is properly organized. For example, remembering textbook material can be facilitated by not only outlining a chapter but also sketching a hierarchical tree that pictures the relations between chapter headings and subheadings.

A formal strategy developed for remembering textbook material is the "SQ3R" method. SQ3R stands for "survey, question, read, recite, and review." Before reading a chapter, one should survey, or skim, the material, looking for section headings and key ideas. Next, one should question, or ask oneself what subject will be covered before one reads each section. As one reads the text, one should continue thinking about the question and how topics are connected. Next, one recites to oneself the major points at the end of each section. Finally, one reviews all the material after one has read to the end of the chapter. This method encompasses most of the principles by which material can be effectively encoded, stored, and retrieved from long-term memory.

EVOLUTION OF STUDY

The study of long-term memory has continued in psychology since the pioneering work of William James and Hermann Ebbinghaus in the late nineteenth century. It was clear even during those early efforts that a distinction could be made between the temporary storage of information in short-term, or working, memory, and the relatively permanent nature of long-term memory.

During the early part of the twentieth century, however, the study of memory fell into disfavor during the era in which psychology was dominated by the behaviorist movement. Behaviorists believed that if psychology was to be a science, it had to limit its investigations to phenomena that are directly observable and measurable. Memory was viewed as a subjective element that was not amenable to experimental investigation.

It was not until the development of the computer, around the time of World War II, that the experimental study of memory again achieved respectability in academic psychology. The computer offered an objective model of how information might be stored and processed in human memory. Since that time, developments in computer science and developments in the psychological study of memory have progressed in tandem, with breakthroughs in one area providing insights into the other. The computer model is still very much a part of the study of memory, with new theories of memory often modeled as computer programs. In many ways, the study of memory was responsible for experimental psychology shifting from a focus exclusively on overt behavior to the "cognitive revolution," in which mental functions are studied directly.

The study of long-term memory in the future will likely focus more on understanding how processes related to memory have their physiological basis in the functioning of the brain. Locating where memories are stored in the brain has long eluded psychologists. Most now believe that memory is distributed over the entire surface of the cerebral cortex rather than located at a particular spot. It is also known from the study of amnesiacs that brain structures such as the hippocampus and amygdala appear to be involved in the consolidation of new material in long-term memory. As knowledge of neurotransmitters (chemicals involved in the sending of messages from one brain cell to another) expands, the role that they play in memory may also become more apparent.

SOURCES FOR FURTHER STUDY

Baddeley, Alan D. *Your Memory: A User's Guide.* 2d ed. London: Prion, 1996. A fully illustrated, easy-to-read book about memory written by one of the top-ranking researchers in the field. Discusses all aspects of research on memory. Recommended as a first book on memory.

Bransford, John. *Human Cognition: Learning, Understanding, and Remembering.* Belmont, Calif.: Wadsworth, 1979. By a well-respected researcher. Focuses on the role of memory in complex learning. Contains much practical information that would be useful to students in improving performance in school-related activities.

Hochsler, Christian, ed. *Neuronal Mechanisms of Memory Formation: Concepts of Long-Term Potentiation and Beyond.* New York: Cambridge University Press, 2000. A collection of neurobiological and psychological papers on memory formation, focusing on experiments in long-term potentiation (LTP) and their relevance to actual learning in the human brain.

Loftus, Elizabeth F. *Eyewitness Testimony.* Reprint. Cambridge, Mass.: Harvard University Press, 1996. By a preeminent researcher in the field. Discusses how eyewitness testimony involves a reconstruction of what the person has seen, and the inherent unreliability of such reconstructions. Also discusses how this relates to everyday problems of memory and the ability of people to recall past events accurately.

Neath, Ian. *Human Memory: An Introduction to Research, Data, and Theory.* Belmont, Calif.: Wadsworth, 1997. An up-to-date undergraduate textbook. Describes experimental procedures and theories; covers historical development of the understanding of memory as well as current approaches.

Neisser, Ulric, ed. *Memory Observed: Remembering in Natural Contexts.* 2d ed. New York: Worth, 1999. By one of the early pioneers of the "cognitive revolution." A series of articles which present memory from an everyday, natural perspective, rather than focusing on experimental evidence. Very readable.

Parkin, Alan J. *Memory and Amnesia: An Introduction.* Oxford: Basil Blackwell, 1987. An excellent introduction to the causes, assessment, and explanation of memory disorders such as amnesia. Presents some information on the physiology of memory. Can be easily understood without any previous knowledge.

Oliver W. Hill, Jr.

SEE ALSO: Encoding; Eyewitness testimony; Forgetting and forgetfulness; Kinesthetic memory; Memory; Memory: Empirical studies; Memory: Physiology; Memory: Sensory; Memory storage; Short-term memory.

Lorenz, Konrad

BORN: November 7, 1903, in Vienna, Austro-Hungarian Empire
DIED: February 27, 1989, in Altenburg, Austria
IDENTITY: Austrian ethologist
TYPE OF PSYCHOLOGY: Biological bases of behavior; motivation
FIELDS OF STUDY: Aggression; attitudes and behavior; biological influences on learning

Lorenz was a pioneer in the field of ethology, the study of animal behavior in natural surroundings. His studies support the position that instinct is a major determinant of animal (including human) behavior.

Konrad Lorenz was born in Vienna, the capital of the Austro-Hungarian Empire. He attended an excellent Viennese private school, the Schottengymnasium, where he became fascinated by natural history in general and Darwinist theory in particular. Lorenz continued that interest during summer vacations at the family estate in Altenberg, Austria, where he closely observed instinctive behavior, including imprinting, in greylag geese.

In 1922, Lorenz entered Columbia University in New York and completed his medical studies at the University of Vienna in 1928. He did not immediately practice medicine, however; instead, he worked with a noted comparative anatomist, Ferdinand Hochstetter, at the Vienna Anatomical Institute and in 1933 received his Ph.D. in zoology at the University of Vienna.

In 1939, Lorenz became the chair of the psychology department at the University of Königsberg. In 1941, however, he was drafted into the German army, and from 1942 to 1944 served as a psychiatrist and neurologist in a military hospital. Early in 1944 he was transferred to the eastern front, where Soviet forces captured him. From that point until his release in 1948, he served as a doctor in Soviet prison camps. His experiences in captivity produced a heightened interest in the causes of human aggression and resulted in a key work, *The Natural Science of the Human Species: An Introduction to Comparative Behavioral Research: The "Russian Manuscript" (1944-1948)* (1996).

Following repatriation, Lorenz continued his ethological work with help from the Austrian Acad-

emy of Sciences and, later, in association with the Max Planck Institute. In 1973, his work in genetic programming won international recognition when he became a corecipient of the Nobel Prize in Physiology or Medicine. In 1982, he became a director in the Konrad Lorenz Institute, which was affiliated with the Austrian Academy of Sciences. Lorenz died on February 27, 1989, in Altenburg, Austria

Lorenz's work underlined the importance of instincts and viewed significant aspects of human behavior as refinements of cruder instinctual mechanisms clearly seen in other living creatures. His *Er redete mit dem Vieh, den Vögeln, und den Fischen* (1949; *King Soloman's Ring*, 1952) is a classic on animal behavior, and his *Das Sogenannte Böse* (1963; *On Aggression*, 1966), perhaps his most important work, identifies the instinctual underpinnings of human values. Lorenz's work on fixed action patterns and behavior triggers has gained wide general acceptance. However, his views remain controversial in

Konrad Lorenz. (© The Nobel Foundation)

some quarters, for his deterministic leanings have sometimes been equated with Nazi positions on race.

SOURCES FOR FURTHER STUDY

Evans, Richard I. *Konrad Lorenz: The Man and His Ideas.* New York: Harcourt Brace Jovanovich, 1975. An excellent introduction that contains conversations with Lorenz, several of his essays, and a list of his publications.

Gould, James L. *Ethology: The Mechanisms and Evolution of Behavior.* New York: W. W. Norton, 1982. This work places Lorenz in context of the emerging field of ethology, describes his main experiments, and clearly presents his conclusions.

Nisbett, Alec. *Konrad Lorenz.* London: Dent, 1976. A good general biography of Lorenz, containing a chronology and numerous photographs.

Michael J. Fontenot

SEE ALSO: Animal experimentation; Ethology; Imprinting.

Love

TYPE OF PSYCHOLOGY: Social psychology
FIELDS OF STUDY: Interpersonal relations

Love is a mixture of passion, intimacy, and commitment. Studying these components of love, psychologists have identified how people fall in love, stay in love, and fall out of love.

KEY CONCEPTS

- companionate love
- evolutionary psychology
- intermittent reinforcement
- liking
- passionate love
- perceptual accentuation
- principle of equity
- romantic love

INTRODUCTION

According to psychologist Robert Sternberg, love can be considered to have three main components: passion, intimacy, and commitment. Passion is sex-

ual arousal and an intense desire to be with another person; it is expressed through hugging, kissing, and sexual intimacy. Intimacy is a feeling of closeness and connectedness and is expressed through communication and doing things to support the other person. Commitment is a decision that one loves the other person and wants to maintain that love over time. Commitment is often expressed through fidelity, and the institution of marriage makes one's commitment legally binding.

The amount of love that one feels depends on the strength of these three components. The kind of love one feels depends on the mixture of these components. One might have a commitment to a partner but feel little passion; or, one might be passionately in love but not be able to communicate the deep feelings that go with intimacy. The amount or kind of love one partner experiences in a relationship might not be the same as the other partner's experience. Misunderstandings often result, for example, when one partner thinks the relationship contains commitment and the other partner sees the relationship as only a passionate one. Finally, a loving relationship can change over time. In marriage, the passion may fade over the years, while intimacy and commitment bloom.

PASSIONATE LOVE

Passionate love is the kind of love sometimes described as "love at first sight." It occurs suddenly, and one feels as if one has fallen into love. Passionate love is a state of sexual arousal without the intimacy and commitment components. One knows that one is passionately in love when one is always daydreaming about the other person, longs to be constantly with the other person, and feels ecstatic when with the other person. Passionate love thrives on unavailability. As in unrequited love, either the loved one does not reciprocate the intensity of the lover's affections or the lovers cannot get together as often as they wish. Being loved is reinforcing, and some psychologists say that passionate love may survive only under conditions of intermittent reinforcement, where uncertainty about when one will be reinforced plays a major role. Romeo and Juliet's passionate love, for example, was inflamed by the prohibitions of their feuding families.

In passionate love, partners idealize each other. They engage in perceptual accentuation, or seeing what they want to see. Only the good features of each other are noticed and enhanced. The more the partners live in the illusion of their ideals, the more intense is the passionate love. Passionate love really is "blind."

Most people think of passionate love as being true love, and many people think that passionate love is the only kind of love; they expect passionate love to last forever. Despite their expectations (and wishes), passionate love does not last. Indeed, passionate love appears to last a maximum of two and a half years. After that time, according to Charles Hill, Zick Rubin, and Letitia Paplau, almost one-half of dating couples report having broken up. As partners become more familiar with each other, illusions are shattered and the passion wanes. Unfortunately, some people believe that this is the end of love.

ROMANTIC LOVE

For many people, however, love does persist—in the form of romantic love. Romantic love is passionate love with the added component of intimacy. The romantic ideal, which has existed since the medieval time of courtly love, looks much like passionate love. It contains the belief that love is fated and uncontrollable, strikes at first sight, transcends all social boundaries, and mixes agony and ecstasy. This ideal is very much alive today; it is reflected in romance novels, motion pictures, and advertisements. Psychologists have found that this type of love is a poor basis for marriage, which requires steady companionship and objectivity. If a relationship is to survive, romantic passion is not enough.

Zick Rubin has shown that there is a type of romantic love that contains intimate communication and caring. In his study, loving feelings of dependency, exclusivity, and caring were contrasted with the type of liking that exists in friendship. Men, more than women, tended to blur the distinction between liking and loving. Both sexes, though, often experience liking the person they are in love with. Rubin also noticed that one can tell if two people are "in love" simply by observing them: Partners who are strongly in love exhibit more mutual eye contact than partners who are weakly in love.

Intimacy without passion or a long-term commitment is experienced as liking. One feels closeness, bondedness, and warmth toward the other—as one does in friendship. There is a willingness to let the other person see even the disliked parts of oneself

and a feeling of being accepted when these parts are disclosed. Intimacy includes open communication, acceptance, and the sharing of oneself and one's resources. There is a high degree of trust in intimate relationships.

COMPANIONATE LOVE

When commitment is added to intimacy, one experiences what psychologists Ellen Berscheid and Elaine Walster call companionate love. There is a deep attachment that is based on extensive familiarity with the loved one. Companionate love often encompasses a tolerance for the partner's shortcomings, along with a desire to overcome difficulties and conflicts in a relationship. There is a commitment to the ongoing nurturing of the relationship and to an active caring for the partner, even during rough times. Marriages in which the physical attraction has waned but intimate caring and commitment have increased are characterized by this type of love. When researchers asked couples who had been married for at least fifteen years what kept their relationships alive, they put long-term commitment at the top of the list. The romantic passion that brings a couple together is not the force that keeps them together. Each partner must trust that the other is committed to nurturing support, acceptance, and communication in the relationship.

ATTRACTION

Psychologists have used theories and laboratory studies to answer the basic question, "Why do some people have a happy love life while others have unhappy relationships?" Part of the answer comes from the partner one chooses.

One may think that opposites attract, but psychologist Donn Byrne has shown that people are attracted to those who are similar to them in attractiveness, interests, intelligence, education, age, family background, religion, and attitudes. Researchers have noted what is called a "matching phenomenon" when choosing romantic partners. This phenomenon is described as a tendency to choose partners who are a good match to ourselves in attractiveness and other traits. Studies have shown that those who were a good match in physical attractiveness were more likely to be dating longer than couples who were not well matched, and that married couples are more closely matched in attrac-

Evolution and Love

Evolutionary psychology is a relatively new and growing area of psychological research, which studies the evolution of behavior using the principles of natural selection. Evolutionary psychologists examine behaviors that thrive and survive across different environments and cultures because they are assumed to be adaptive and to lead to the promotion and spread of the genes responsible for the behaviors.

When examining mating preferences and love, evolutionary psychologists make hypotheses based on the theories of sexual selection and parental investment. Individuals choose their partners based on the likelihood that the partner will enable them to pass on their genes. In addition, mating decisions are influenced by the likelihood that the mate will help ensure that their offspring survive and thrive, something which is aided by investment from both parents.

Evolutionary psychologists predict that there should be sex differences in behaviors relating to mating and reproduction. If the goal of behavior is to enhance the chances that one's genes will be passed on and will survive in future generations, the biological differences in men and women will lead to differences in sexual behaviors.

Researchers point to the fact that men are capable of producing trillions of sperm within a lifetime while women produce a limited number of eggs, and these biological differences are assumed to lead to differences in mating behaviors. Men are said to reproduce "widely" and women, "wisely" Also, men predominantly tend to choose mates based on physical features, while women more often choose mates based on the resources their mates can provide. David Buss, a prominent evolutionary psychologist, studied thirty-seven cultures around the world and found a consistent male preference for female traits that signify reproductive capacity, such as youthfulness and a waist at least 30 percent narrower than hips. Likewise, research has found that women across the world tend to prefer men who are at least slightly older than themselves and who have wealth, power, and ambition. An interesting study examined the responses to personal ads placed in newspapers. Researchers found that ads placed by women seeking men got the most responses when mentioning the woman's youth and looks, while men's ads were most successful when they focused on their income and education.

What does this tell us about love? Evolutionary psychologists theorize that feelings of closeness, attachment, and intimacy evolved because they are adaptive. For males to be confident that their children are in fact their own, and for females to be secure in their mate's willingness to continue investing in providing and caring for their children, feelings of love are an advantage.

Michelle Murphy

tiveness than couples who are casually dating. Furthermore, Rubin and his associates have found that dating couples who eventually broke up were less well matched in age, educational ambitions, intelligence, and physical attractiveness than those who stayed together.

Another factor that is extremely important in predicting attraction is proximity. Studies have shown that most people marry someone who lives in the same neighborhood or works at the same job; and it is not simply a matter of physical proximity, but a matter of how often one crosses paths with the potential mate that determines the likelihood of romantic involvement. Overall, people tend to like and be attracted to those who have the potential to reward them. People tend to be attracted to those who are similarly attractive, who share their opinions and attitudes, whom they have grown accustomed to meeting, and with whom they have shared positive experiences.

LOVE IN RELATIONSHIPS

After one finds a partner, whether one is happy or unhappy in love depends on the relationship one creates. According to Cindy Hazan and Philip Shaver, both adults and teenagers re-create the same type of relationship they experienced with their parents during childhood. Secure lovers create an intimate relationship that is neither excessively dependent nor independent. They bring a secure sense of self and an interest in developing the independence of their partner into the relationship. Avoidant lovers are overly independent. They get nervous when their partner gets too close because they do not trust the other person completely. Anxious-ambivalent lovers are too dependent; they often worry that their partner does not really love them or will not want to stay with them. Thus, many lovers end up playing out the script that they were taught as children.

Men often follow a different script from that followed by women when they are in love. Men tend to choose a partner on the basis of physical attractiveness, while women emphasize interpersonal warmth and occupational status. Romance involves both passion and affection; men, however, tend to get hooked into the passion first, while women tend to want the affection as a prerequisite to sex. As the relationship matures, men want the affection as much as the sex, and women get equally excited by sexual stimuli as do men. Who, then, one might ask, are the real romantics? Men agree with more of the statements about romantic love; they fall in love more quickly; and they hold on to a waning affair more so than do women. After the breakup of a relationship, a man feels more lonely, obsessed with what went wrong, and depressed than does a woman.

Indeed, men and women may inhabit different emotional worlds. Men and women both want intimacy, but they express themselves differently. Men are more likely to be doers and women to be talkers. For example, a man will wash a woman's car or bring her flowers to show he loves her, while a woman will tell a man how much she loves him. When asked what causes an emotion such as love, men will say it is something in the world outside themselves, such as seeing an attractive woman. Women, on the other hand, will attribute being in love to positive interactions with others or to internal factors such as moods. These socially learned differences between men and women in their styles of intimacy are often a source of tension between them. Women sometimes want men to talk more, while men will want women to stop talking. Finally, some men will sacrifice intimacy because they fear loss of independence, while some women sacrifice independence because they fear a loss of intimacy.

HISTORY OF RESEARCH ON LOVE

Psychologists have approached the topic of love from a variety of perspectives. In the early 1900's, clinical psychologists looked at love mainly in terms of its sexual component. For example, Sigmund Freud defined love as sublimated sexuality. By the middle of the twentieth century, humanistic psychologists such as Abraham Maslow, Erich Fromm, and Carl Rogers saw love as including the empathy, responsibility, and respect that is characteristic of friendship. Next, there was an attempt to measure love as distinct from friendship, with Zick Rubin creating his liking and loving scales.

Since love involves emotions, motivations, and cognitions, Elaine Walster and Ellen Berscheid drew on the earlier work of Stanley Schachter and Jerome Singer to devise a multifactor explanation of love called the two-factor theory. They theorize that love arises when a person is physiologically aroused and labels that arousal as love. For example, being in a dangerous situation creates physiological arousal, and, if one is with an attractive partner, one could feel that the sweating palms and pounding heart mean that one is falling in love. Researchers have found that men approached by an unknown, attractive woman as they crossed a dangerous bridge were more likely to ask her out and indicate attraction than men approached by the woman while crossing a sturdy, safe bridge. Studies show that watching scary movies, riding on roller coasters, and exercising are all arousing activities which increase the likelihood that people will be attracted to one another.

Social psychologist Donn Byrne tried to explain both the passionate feeling and the friendship feeling as arising from the reinforcement one gets from one's lover. People like, and love, people who give them rewards, whether the reward is sexual gratification or a feeling of being needed.

Although many social psychologists have focused on separate concepts, such as interpersonal attraction, social exchange, and cognitive consistency, to explain love, Robert Sternberg combined all these concepts in his triangular theory of love. Sternberg contends that liking and loving are interrelated phenomena and that there are different types of love that develop from different combinations of liking and loving. Sternberg's theory explains the difference between a partner's love for his or her child and lovers' love for each other.

Historically, conceptions of love have been tied to economic conditions and to social role definitions. One example of these economic conditions is the Industrial Revolution, which moved men out of the fields and into the factories. Women also moved—from the fields into the home. Men's social role was to produce; women's was to love (provide nurturance and intimacy). These roles created societal expectations for the nature of love. Thus, one's expectations determine whether one will be satisfied or disappointed with love. For example, Western society expects a woman to define herself in terms of her relationship with a man; love is closely linked to sex and marriage. Yet women live longer than men, which often means that a woman will be living without a man in her later years. Women can retain society's expectations or can change their expectations so that they can connect with others on a basis other than traditional concepts of love. Psychologists will continue to investigate changing expectations about loving relationships.

SOURCES FOR FURTHER STUDY

Buss, David M. *The Dangerous Passion.* New York: Free Press, 2000. This work, written by a pioneer researcher in evolutionary psychology, details the Darwinian drives that shape the way we experience love. Focuses on the adaptive role of jealousy as seen across time and cultures, theorized to promote fidelity and security in love relationships.

Fromm, Erich. *The Art of Loving.* New York: Harper, 1956. In this classic book, Fromm builds on the theme that immature love is needing to be loved, while mature love is needing to love. The reader learns the qualities that must be developed in oneself before one can maturely love another person.

Jolly, Alison. *Lucy's Legacy: Sex and Intelligence in Human Evolution.* Cambridge, Mass.: Harvard University Press, 2001. Investigates the role of evolution in shaping behavior, particularly in relation to love and sex. Written for a professional audience, but accessible to general readers.

Person, Ethel S. *Dreams of Love and Fateful Encounters.* New York: W. W. Norton, 1988. Written by Dr. Ethel Person, a professor of clinical psychiatry and a practicing psychoanalyst, this book is an illuminating examination of the different forms of love, the pitfalls of romantic love, and gender differences in love. Includes interesting examples from literature and popular culture. Written for a general audience and includes bibliography.

Rubin, Zick. *Liking and Loving.* New York: Holt, Rinehart and Winston, 1973. Rubin discusses how social psychological research answers many questions about love. This book gives hints about what causes two people to be attracted to each other and what may cause them to break up.

Shaver, P., C. Hazan, and D. Bradshaw. "Love as Attachment: The Integration of Three Behavioral Systems." In *The Psychology of Love,* edited by Robert J. Sternberg and Michael L. Barnes. New Haven, Conn.: Yale University Press, 1988. This book contains chapters by all the main social psychologists investigating love. In the chapter by Shaver, Hazan, and Bradshaw, the reader can find out what type of love he or she develops with others—avoidant, anxious-ambivalent, or secure.

Sternberg, Robert J. *Love Is a Story: A New Theory of Relationships.* New York: Oxford University Press, 1998. Noted psychologist in the investigation of love, culls from years of research to promote his theory of love as a "story." The author proposes that people bring their preconceived, unconscious, notions of what love should be to their relationships. Draws on examples of real couples to help illuminate when these "stories" help and hurt relationships. Written for a general audience.

Wright, Robert. *The Moral Animal: The New Science of Evolutionary Psychology.* New York: Pantheon Books, 1994. This popular and scientific book uses findings from evolutionary psychology to examine the unconscious motives that guide choices and actions in daily life, including love and close relationships. Includes detailed notes, bibliography and index.

Beverly B. Palmer;
updated by Michelle Murphy

SEE ALSO: Affiliation and friendship; Affiliation motive; Attraction theories; Emotions; Intimacy; Jealousy; Motivation; Self-actualization; Separation and divorce: Adult issues; Social perception; Social psychological models: Erich Fromm.

M

Madness
Historical concepts

TYPE OF PSYCHOLOGY: Psychopathology
FIELDS OF STUDY: General constructs and issues;
models of abnormality

Throughout history, humans have tried to explain the abnormal behavior of people with mental disorders. From the ancient concept of demoniacal possession to modern biopsychosocial models, beliefs regarding the cause of mental disorder have influenced the way communities treat those variously labeled mad, insane, or mentally ill.

KEY CONCEPTS
- asylum
- biopsychosocial model of mental disorders
- deinstitutionalization
- demoniacal possession
- humoral imbalance
- lobotomy
- madness
- moral treatment
- phenothiazines

INTRODUCTION

People are social creatures who learn how to behave appropriately in families and communities. What is considered appropriate, however, depends on a host of factors, including historical period, culture, geography, and religion. Thus, what is valued and respected changes over time, as do sociocultural perceptions of aberrant or deviant behavior. How deviancy is treated depends a great deal on the extent of the deviancy—is the person dangerous, a threat to self or to the community, in flagrant opposition to community norms, or is the person just a little odd? How the community responds also depends on its beliefs as to what causes aberrant behavior. Supernatural beliefs in demons, spirits, and magic were common in preliterate societies; in the medieval Western world, Christians believed that the devil was in possession of deranged souls. Hence, the mad were subjected to cruel treatments justified by the idea of routing out demons or the devil. For centuries, the prevailing explanation for madness was demoniacal possession.

Prior to the nineteenth century, families and communities cared for the mad. If they were unmanageable or violent, the mad were incarcerated in houses of correction or dungeons, where they were manacled or put into straitjackets. If a physician ever attended someone who was deemed mad by the community, it was to purge or bleed the patient to redress a supposed humoral imbalance. Most medical explanations prior to the advent of scientific medicine were expressed in terms of the four humors: black and yellow bile, blood, and phlegm. Imbalances usually were treated with laxatives, purgatives, astringents, emetics, and bleeding. Understanding moved from the holistic and humoral to the anatomical, chemical, and physiological. Also, views of humans and their rights changed enormously as a consequence of the eighteenth century American and French Revolutions.

During the nineteenth and twentieth centuries, madhouses were first replaced by more progressive lunatic asylums and then by mental hospitals and community mental health centers. In parallel fashion, custodians and superintendents of madhouses became mad-doctors or alienists in the nineteenth century and psychiatrists, psychologists, and counselors of various kinds in the twentieth century. Similarly, the language changed: Madness was variously called lunacy, insanity, derangement, or alienation. The contemporary term is mental disorder. These changes reflect the rejection of supernatural and humoral explanations of madness in favor of a disease model with varying emphases on organic or psychic causes.

Benjamin Rush, one of the founders of the American Psychiatric Association, invented this "tranquillizing chair" in 1811 to help calm the mentally ill. (National Library of Medicine)

EARLY VIEWS OF MADNESS

One of the terrible consequences of the belief in supernatural possession by demons was the inhumane treatment in which it often resulted. An example is found in the book of Leviticus in the Bible, which many scholars believe is a compilation of laws which had been handed down orally in the Jewish community for as long as a thousand years until they were written down, perhaps about 700 B.C.E. Leviticus 20:27, in the King James version, reads, "A man or a woman that hath a familiar spirit . . . shall surely be put to death: they shall stone him with stones." The term "familiar spirit" suggests demoniacal possession, and death was the response for dealing with demons in their midst.

There were exceptions to the possession theory and the inhumane treatment to which it often led. Hippocrates, who lived around 300 B.C.E. in Greece and who is regarded as the father of medicine, believed that mental illness had biological causes and could be explained by human reason through empirical study. Although Hippocrates found no cure, he did recommend that the mentally ill be treated humanely, as other ill people would be treated. Humane treatment of the mentally ill was often the best that physicians and others could do; it has much to recommend it, even in the present.

The period of Western history that is sometimes known as the Dark Ages was particularly dark for the mad. Folk belief, theology, and occult beliefs and practices of all kinds often led to terrible treatment. Although some educated and thoughtful people, even in that period, held humane views, they were in the minority regarding madness.

EIGHTEENTH AND NINETEENTH CENTURY VIEWS

It was not until what could be considered the modern historical period, the end of the eighteenth century—the time of the American and French Revolutions—that major changes took place in the treatment of the insane. Additionally, there was a change in attitudes toward the insane, in approaches to their treatment, and in beliefs regarding the causes of their strange behaviors. The man who, because of his courage, became a symbol of this new attitude was the French physician Philippe Pinel (1745-1826). Appointed physician-in-chief of the Bictre Hospital in Paris in 1792, Pinel risked death at the guillotine. The Bictre was one of a number of "asylums" which had developed in Europe and in Latin America over several hundred years to house the insane. Often started with the best of intentions, most of the asylums became hellish places of incarceration.

In the Bictre, patients were often chained to the walls of their cells and lacked even the most elementary amenities. Pinel insisted to a skeptical committee of the Revolution that he be permitted to remove the chains from some of the patients. In one

Changes and Biases in Contemporary Psychiatric Diagnosis

The *Diagnostic and Statistical Manual of Mental Disorders* (DSM) is an official compendium of disorders published by the American Psychiatric Association (APA). The editions include the DSM-I (1952), DSM-II (1968), DSM-III (1980), DSM-III-R (revision; (1987), DSM-IV (1994), and DSM-IV-TR (text revision; 2000). Each successive manual revised earlier nomenclature (terms) as medical and scientific understanding of mental disorder changed. According to the psychiatrist Edwin R. Wallace, Dv bSM-I had a decidedly psychoanalytical and social psychiatric emphasis and was replete with language that reflected the majority acceptance of Meyerian psychobiology. (Adolf Meyer was an early twentieth century psychiatrist and neuropathologist.) The second manual revised the first DSM and eliminated language that would suggest knowledge of cause. The third manual was an important development in nosology (classification of disease), as there were several methodological improvements. For example, the authors developed explicit criteria sets for each disorder, a multiaxial system for assessment was introduced, and the categories were intentionally described atheoretically. The several axes reflected the belief that a valid diagnosis necessarily entailed consideration of several domains of information. The enhanced operationalization of criteria indicating disorder resulted in a substantial increase in empirical research; hence, the fourth DSM incorporated new knowledge after exhaustive reviews of the literature, reanalyses of extant data sets, and field trials. The APA again claimed an objective and atheoretical stance as to etiology or cause.

There are many critics of the third and fourth DSMs. For example, some esteemed philosophers of science hold that an objective and atheoretical classification system is impossible, that the very process of selecting categories implies valuation and is driven by theoretical orientation. Other critics decry the contemporary emphasis on the biopsychosocial model as neglecting the phenomenological (relating to the perceptions and self-awareness of the patient), the longitudinal and developmental, and relevant social contexts. Some therapists believe that standardized clinical interviews developed for collecting information necessary for DSM assessment interfere with the patient-therapist relationship. Others criticize the DSM on methodological grounds. For example, some would prefer disorders rated on continua, allowing more numeric information instead of classification by category. Even the authors of the DSM-IV-TR point out that within each category or disorder there is tremendous variability and that diagnosis is preliminary to more extensive fact-finding.

Finally, the term "mental disorder" is recognized as being inadequate. The contemporary move towards a more holistic understanding of disease and disorder is a move away from the Cartesian mind/body dualism that has prevailed since the scientific revolution in the seventeenth century. Hence, Allen J. Francis, psychiatrist and chair of the DSM-IV task force, writes in the foreword to *Philosophical Perspectives on Psychiatric Diagnostic Classification* (1994) that the term "mental disorder' is misleading and outmoded.

With each major revision of the DSM, mental disorders are modified, dropped, or added and language is changed. Critics consider the fluidity of the list of disorders and the changing symptoms or criteria as evidence of subjectivity and an ontological problem. In other words, do the disorders exist or are they mere constructions of the community of psychiatrists and researchers? For example, the category "Ego-Dystonic Homosexuality" was dropped from DSM-III-R when homosexuality was no longer seen as pathological, but was regarded instead as a normal variant of human sexuality; on the other hand, a nonpathological category for religious or spiritual problems was added in DSM-IV under "Other Conditions That May Be a Focus of Clinical Attention." (Prior to DSM-IV, religious ideation was typically viewed as pathological and symptomatic of schizophrenia.)

At different times, critics found bias in the diagnostic assessment of homosexuals, religious people, women, African Americans, immigrants, in short, anyone different from mainstream clinicians. They argued that culture determines the form, content, and expression of disease or mental disorder. When the relevant subgroup culture is ignored, symptoms are decontextualized and bias is more likely. For example, the "cultural bereavement" syndrome of Cambodian refugees may appear pathological to Western clinicians, and yet may be a normal Cambodian response to loss in the context of traditional folk religion. In the introductory remarks to the DSM-IV, the APA recognized that bias may stem from a cultural mismatch between the clinician and the patient since what is normal behavior in one culture may be abnormal in the other. The potential for bias is particularly problematic in the assessment of personality disorders because of considerable cultural variation in self-concept, communication, and coping mechanisms. In response to these criticisms of cultural bias, the authors of DSM-IV added descriptive text regarding cultural variation and a glossary of culture-bound syndromes.

Tanja Bekhuis

of the great, heroic acts in human history, Pinel introduced "moral treatment" of the insane, risking grave personal danger if his humane experiment had failed.

This change was occurring in other places at about the same time. After the death of a Quaker in Britain's York Asylum, the local Quaker community founded the York Retreat, where neither chains nor corporal punishment were allowed. In America, Benjamin Rush, a founder of the American Psychiatric Association, applied his version of moral treatment, which was not entirely humane as it involved physical restraints and fear as therapeutic agents. Toward theo middle of the nineteenth century, American crusader Dorothea Dix fought for the establishment of state mental hospitals for the insane. Under the influence of Dix, thirty-two states established at least one mental hospital. Dix had been influenced by the moral model, as well as by the medical sciences, which were rapidly developing in the nineteenth century. Unfortunately, the state mental hospital often lost its character as a "retreat" for the insane.

The nineteenth century was the first time in Western history (with some exceptions) when a number of scientists turned their attention to abnormal behavior. For example, the German psychiatrist Emil Kraepelin spent much of his life trying to develop a scientific classification system for psychopathology. Sigmund Freud attempted to develop a science of mental illness. Although many of Freud's ideas have not withstood empirical investigation, perhaps his greatest contribution was his insistence that scientific principles apply to mental illness. He believed that abnormal behavior is not caused by supernatural forces and does not arise in a chaotic, random way, but that it can be understood as serving some psychological purpose.

MODERN MEDICINES

Many of the medical/biological treatments for mental illness in the first half of the twentieth century were frantic attempts to deal with very serious problems—attempts made by clinicians who had few effective therapies to use. The attempt to produce convulsions (which often did seem to make people "better," at least temporarily) was popular for a decade or two. One example was insulin shock therapy, in which convulsions were induced in mentally ill people by insulin injection. Electroconvulsive

(electric shock) therapy was also used. Originally it was primarily used with patients who had schizophrenia, a severe form of psychosis. Although it was not very effective with schizophrenia, it was found to be useful with patients who had resistant forms of depressive psychosis. Another treatment sometimes used, beginning in the 1930's, was prefrontal lobotomy. Many professionals today would point out that the use of lobotomy indicates the almost desperate search for an effective treatment for the most aggressive or the most difficult psychotic patients. As originally used, lobotomy was an imprecise slashing of the frontal lobe of the brain.

The real medical breakthrough in the treatment of psychotic patients was associated with the use of certain drugs from a chemical family known as phenothiazines. Originally used in France as a tranquilizer for surgery patients, their potent calming effect attracted the interest of psychiatrists and other mental health workers. One drug of this group, chlorpromazine, was found to reduce or eliminate psychotic symptoms in many patients. This and similar medications came to be referred to as antipsychotic drugs. Although their mechanism of action is still not completely understood, there is no doubt that they worked wonders for many severely ill patients while causing severe side effects for others. The drugs allowed patients to function outside the hospital and often to lead normal lives. They enabled many patients to benefit from psychotherapy. The approval of the use of chlorpromazine as an antipsychotic drug in the United States in 1955 revolutionized the treatment of many mental patients. Individuals who, prior to 1955, might have spent much of their lives in a hospital could now control their illness effectively enough to live in the community, work at a job, attend school, and be a functioning member of a family.

In 1955, the United States had approximately 559,000 patients in state mental hospitals; seventeen years later, in 1972, the population of the state mental hospitals had decreased almost by half, to approximately 276,000. Although all of this cannot be attributed to the advent of the psychoactive drugs, they undoubtedly played a major role. The phenothiazines had finally given medicine a real tool in the battle with psychosis. One might believe that the antipsychotic drugs, combined with a contemporary version of the moral treatment, would enable society to eliminate mental illness as a major human

A "centrifugal bed" for spinning mental patients in 1818. (National Library of Medicine)

problem. Unfortunately, good intentions go awry. The "major tranquilizers" can easily become chemical straitjackets; those who prescribe the drugs are sometimes minimally involved with future treatment. In the late 1970's, the makers of social policy saw what appeared to be the economic benefits of reducing the role of the mental hospital, by discharging patients and closing some mental hospitals. However, they did not foresee that large numbers of homeless psychotics would live in the streets as a consequence of "deinstitutionalization." The plight of the homeless during the early part of the twenty-first century continues to be a serious, national problem in America.

DISORDER AND DYSFUNCTION

The twentieth century saw the exploration of many avenues in the treatment of mental disorders. Treatments ranging from classical psychoanalysis to cognitive and humanistic therapies to the use of therapeutic drugs were applied. Psychologists examined the effects of mental disorders on many aspects of life, including cognition and personality. These disorders affect the most essential of human functions, including cognition, which has to do with the way in which the mind thinks and makes decisions. Cognition does not work in "ordinary" ways in the person with a serious mental illness, making his or her behavior very difficult for family, friends, and others to understand. Another aspect of cognition is perception. Perception has to do with the way that the mind, or brain, interprets and understands the information which comes to a person through the senses. There is a general consensus among most human beings about what they see and hear, and perhaps to a lesser extent about what they touch, taste, and smell. The victim of mental illness, however, often perceives the world in a much different way. This person may see objects or events that no one else sees, phenomena called hallucinations.

The hallucinations may be visual—for example, the person may see a frightening wild animal that no one else sees—or the person may hear a voice accusing him or her of terrible crimes or behaviors that no one else hears.

A different kind of cognitive disorder is delusions. Delusions are untrue and often strange ideas, usually growing out of psychological needs or problems of a person who may have only tenuous contact with reality. A woman, for example, may believe that other employees are plotting to harm her in some way when, in fact, they are merely telling innocuous stories around the water cooler. Sometimes people with mental illness will be disoriented, which means that they do not know where they are in time (what year, what season, or what time of day) or in space (where they live, where they are at the present moment, or where they are going).

In addition to experiencing cognitive dysfunction that creates havoc, mentally ill persons may have emotional problems that go beyond the ordinary. For example, they may live on such an emotional "high" for weeks or months at a time that their behavior is exhausting both to themselves and to those around them. They may exhibit bizarre behavior; for example, they may talk about giving away vast amounts of money (which they do not have), or they may go without sleep for days until they drop from exhaustion. This emotional "excitement" seems to dominate their lives and is called mania. The word "maniac" comes from this terrible emotional extreme.

At the other end of the emotional spectrum is clinical depression. This does not refer to the ordinary "blues" of daily life, with all its ups and downs, but to an emotional emptiness in which the individual seems to have lost all emotional energy. The individual often seems completely apathetic. The person may feel life is not life worth living and may have anhedonia, which refers to an inability to experience pleasure of almost any kind.

TREATMENT APPROACHES

Anyone interacting with a person suffering from severe mental disorders comes to think of him or her as being different from normal human beings. The behavior of those with mental illness is regarded, with some justification, as bizarre and unpredictable. They are often labeled with a term that sets them apart, such as "crazy" or "mad." There are

many words in the English language that have been, or are, used to describe these persons—many of them quite cruel and derogatory. Since the nineteenth century, professionals have used the term "psychotic" to denote severe mental illness or disorder. Interestingly, one translation of psychotic is "of a sickness of the soul" and reflects the earlier belief regarding the etiology or cause of mental illness. This belief is still held by some therapists and pastoral counselors in the twenty-first century. Until the end of the twentieth century, the term "neurosis" connoted more moderate dysfunction than the term "psychosis." However, whether neurosis is always less disabling or disturbing than psychosis has been an open question. An attempt was made to deal with this dilemma in 1980, when the DSM-III officially dropped the term "neurosis" from the diagnostic terms.

The contemporary approach to mental disorder, at its best, offers hope and healing to patients and their families. However, much about the etiology of mental disorder remains unknown to social scientists and physicians.

In 1963, President John F. Kennedy signed the Community Mental Health and Retardation Act. Its goal was to set up centers throughout the United States offering services to mentally and emotionally disturbed citizens and their families, incorporating the best that had been learned and that would be learned from science and from medicine. Outpatient services in the community, emergency services, "partial" hospitalizations (adult day care), consultation, education, and research were among the programs supported by the act. Although imperfect, it nevertheless demonstrated how far science had come from the days when witches were burned at the stake and the possessed were stoned to death.

When one deals with mental disorder, one is dealing with human behavior—both the behavior of the individual identified as having the problem and the behavior of the community. The response of the community is critical for the successful treatment of disorder. For example, D. L. Rosenhan, in a well-known 1973 study titled "On Being Sane in Insane Places," showed how easy it is to be labeled "crazy" and how difficult it is to get rid of the label. He demonstrated how one's behavior is interpreted and understood on the basis of the labels that have been applied. (The "pseudopatients" in the study had been admitted to a mental hospital and given a diagnosis—a label—of schizophrenia. Consequently, even their writing of notes in a notebook was regarded as evidence of their illness.) To understand mental disorder is not merely to understand personal dysfunction or distress, but also to understand social and cultural biases of the community, from the family to the federal government. The prognosis for eventual mental and emotional health depends not only on appropriate therapy but also on the reasonable and humane response of the relevant communities.

SOURCES FOR FURTHER STUDY

American Psychiatric Association. *Diagnostic and Statistical Manual of Disorders: DSM-IV-TR.* Rev. 4th ed. Washington, D.C.: Author, 2000. This is the official manual for the classification of mental disorders used by clinicians and researchers in a variety of settings. The manual also is used for educational purposes as disorders are described with respect to diagnostic features, cultural and age considerations, prevalence, course, and familial patterns. The language is accessible to advanced students.

Berrios, German E., and Roy Porter. *A History of Clinical Psychiatry: The Origin and History of Psychiatric Disorders.* Washington Square: New York University Press, 1995. This book addresses the clinical and social history of mental disorders and is a good follow-up for readers interested in studying a particular type of disorder. A major theme throughout involves tracking the interaction between clinical signals of disorder, successive historical periods, and psychosocial contexts. For advanced students.

Frankl, Viktor Emil. *Man's Search for Meaning: An Introduction to Logotherapy.* 4th ed. Boston: Beacon Press, 1992. A powerful book which serves as an example of many publications that emphasize what has been called "moral treatment." Frankl's book is partly autobiographical, based on his experiences as a Jew in a German concentration camp. The book then goes on to develop some ideas related to abnormal behavior.

Freud, Sigmund. *The Freud Reader.* Edited by Peter Gay. 1989. Reprint. New York: W. W. Norton, 1995. This book offers a selection of essays and excerpts meant to give the reader an understanding of the breadth of Freud's seminal work. Topics include the psychosexual theory of human development, his theory of mind, psychoanalysis, and his ideas on the arts, religion, and culture. The editor offers introductions for each selection. Good overview of a historically important thinker.

Grob, Gerald N. *The Mad Among Us: A History of the Care of America's Mentally Ill.* New York: Free Press, 1994. This history of the care and treatment of the mentally ill in America begins with the colonial period and ends with the contemporary period. It is a thoughtful analysis of changing societal perceptions of moral obligation and of the historically varying policies regarding presumed effective care. Documents the contradictory policies of confinement versus community living for the disordered. Also looks at the question of whether the public need for protection overrides the needs of the individual. Written for the general reader.

Porter, Roy. *The Greatest Benefit to Mankind: A Medical History of Humanity.* New York: W. W. Norton, 1997. This is an engaging, scholarly, very readable book that includes a chapter on psychiatry, a short history of mental disorder covering the eighteenth through the twentieth centuries in Britain, Europe, and North America. Good discussions of the asylum movement, degeneration theory and Nazi psychiatry, psychoanalysis, and modern developments. Porter was a social historian of medicine whose scholarship is accessible to the general reader. There is an extensive list of sources for further reading. Very highly recommended.

Robinson, Daniel N. *An Intellectual History of Psychology.* 3d ed. Madison: University of Wisconsin Press, 1995. Although mental illness as such occupies a small part of this book, it is a genuinely important book in helping to understand the philosophical and intellectual currents which have played such a major role in the psychological and scientific understanding of mental illness. A sometimes demanding book to read, it is well worth the intellectual energy for one who wants to understand various intellectual disciplines.

Rosenhan, David L. "On Being Sane in Insane Places." *Science* 179 (January 19, 1973): 250-258. More of a "naturalistic illustration" than a scientific experiment, this article raises provocative questions and puts forth some controversial conclusions. Enjoyable reading that does not require much psychological background on the part of the reader.

James Taylor Henderson;
updated by Tanja Bekhuis

SEE ALSO: Abnormality: Biomedical models; American Psychiatric Association; American Psychological Association; Dix, Dorothea; Lobotomy; Pinel, Philippe; Psychology: Fields of specialization; Psychology: History; Psychosurgery; Psychotherapy: Historical approaches; Schizophrenia: Background, types, and symptoms; Schizophrenia: Theoretical explanations; Thought: Study and measurement.

Masters, William H.

BORN: December 27, 1915, in Cleveland, Ohio

Johnson, Virginia E.

BORN: February 11, 1925, in Springfield, Missouri
IDENTITY: American researchers of human sexual response
TYPE OF PSYCHOLOGY: Emotion; sensation and perception; social psychology
FIELDS OF STUDY: Interpersonal relations; physical motives; sexual disorders

Masters and Johnson were pioneers in the scientific study of sexual arousal and the treatment of sexual problems.

William Howell Masters attended public schools in Kansas City and in Lawrenceville, New Jersey. In 1938, he earned a bachelor's degree from Hamilton College. After receiving his medical degree in gynecology from the University of Rochester in 1943, he began laboratory studies of sexual behavior in 1954 while on the faculty of Washington University in St. Louis, Missouri.

A precocious child, Virginia Eshelman Johnson was allowed to skip several grades during her public schooling. She studied piano and voice, and read extensively. She studied psychology and sociology at Drury College and at the University of Missouri, joining Masters as a research associate in 1957. At that time, scientists knew little about human re-

sponses to sexual stimulation. Masters and Johnson used motion pictures, electrocardiograms, electroencephalograms, polygraph-like instruments, and other scientific equipment to record the human body's physiological responses to sexual stimulations in men and women who volunteered to engage in sexual activity.

In 1964, Masters and Johnson established the Reproductive Biology Research Foundation in St. Louis, Missouri. In 1973, they became codirectors of the Masters and Johnson Institute in St. Louis. Their research stirred up a great deal of controversy. Many critics called them immoral and accused them of dehumanizing sex.

In 1966, the results of their research were published in *Human Sexual Response*, which described the physiological responses during four phases of erotic arousal for males and females. Although written in technical language for physicians and other health scientists, the book became a best-seller. After counseling hundreds of married couples about problems dealing with sexual performance, Masters and Johnson published *Human Sexual Inadequacy* in 1970. It dealt with the treatment of sexual problems, including impotence, premature ejaculation, and frigidity. It is considered by many experts to be the first comprehensive study of the physiology and anatomy of human sexual activity under laboratory conditions. Masters and Johnson were married in 1971.

Homosexuality in Perspective, a report on the clinical treatment of the sexual problems of homosexuals, appeared in 1979. Although they received much criticism for their views, Masters and Johnson claimed an ability to change the sexual preference of homosexuals who wished to change. More controversy was sparked by their 1988 publication of *Crisis: Heterosexual Behavior in the Age of AIDS*, wherein they forecast an epidemic spread of acquired immunodeficiency syndrom (AIDS) among heterosexuals. After their divorce in 1993, Masters and Johnson continued their research collaboration.

SOURCES FOR FURTHER STUDY

Fox, Stuart Ira. *Human Physiology*. 5th ed. Dubuque, Iowa: Wm. C. Brown, 1996. Well-illustrated summary of the function and response of the male and female reproductive systems.

Mader, S. S. *Human Reproductive Biology*. Dubuque, Iowa: Wm. C. Brown, 1992. Addresses the physiology of the human reproductive system and the stages associated with the human sexual response.

Robinson, Paul. *The Modernization of Sex.* Ithaca, N.Y.: Cornell University Press, 1988. Discusses the research of Masters and Johnson and problems dealing with sexual performance.

Alvin K. Benson

SEE ALSO: Gender-identity formation; Homosexuality; Kinsey, Alfred; Sexual behavior patterns; Sexual dysfunction; Sex hormones and motivation; Sexual variants and paraphilias; Survey research: Questionnaires and interviews.

Media psychology

DATE: The 1970's forward

TYPE OF PSYCHOLOGY: Emotion; language; learning; personality; sensation and perception; social psychology; stress

FIELDS OF STUDY: Attitudes and behavior; coping; depression; interpersonal relations; problem solving; social perception and cognition; stress and illness; thought

Media psychology is a field of study which addresses the role of psychology in information dissemination and as a cultural form of entertainment and an influential molder of popular opinion concerning societal psychological issues.

KEY CONCEPTS
- accessibility
- ethics
- expertise
- influence
- information
- media consultants
- newsworthiness
- perceptions
- sensationalization
- technology

INTRODUCTION

Media psychology emerged as an applied psychological discipline concurrently with the rise in popularity of such talk shows as *Donahue* on television and radio in the 1970's. Mental health professionals have contributed their expertise and information to a variety of media, including newspapers, magazines, television, movies, radio, telecommunications, multimedia, and the Internet. Technology advancements have expanded the influence of psychology to more people globally.

Some psychologists serve as media consultants, preparing specific programming or articles about significant issues, such as depression, or topics suddenly newsworthy, such as school violence. Many host or appear on television and radio programs to discuss mental health issues and advise listeners. Other mental health professionals concentrate on media-oriented careers, writing self-help books and screenplays or serving as columnists for national, regional, or local publications. Scholars analyze how the media depict psychological issues, such as mental illness, and influence people's perceptions of themselves and others.

Mental health professionals are concerned with how psychological issues are portrayed in the media. Since the 1950's, newspaper advice columnists such as Dear Abby and Ann Landers have assumed the role of amateur mental health authorities. Culturally, people tend to find such amateur psychological input appealing, accessible, and comforting. Similarly, many talk show hosts who lack professional credentials also often act as if they are psychologically knowledgeable. They unrealistically expect psychology to serve as a sensational entertainment tool to address current media-popular disorders such as anorexia nervosa in an attempt to score high ratings. Hosts have minimal awareness of the complexities and subtleties of the topics they are discussing, nor do they understand suitable therapeutic treatments for their guests.

Professional psychologists worry that such popular psychology is damaging not only to the people involved but also to the mental health profession. From 1953 to 1981, the American Psychological Association (APA) outlined prohibitions in its ethical principles against psychologists offering superficial or sensational services which were unrelated to professional contexts. Some psychologists ignored professional suggestions and began participating in media opportunities before 1992, when the APA loosened its restrictions. New guidelines permitted psychologists to comment about psychological issues or advise people who were not patients in some circumstances understood to be through media outlets.

PROFESSIONALISM

The Association for Media Psychology (AMP) was organized in 1982 and issued guidelines to regulate professional conduct. Five years later, the APA established Division 46 to focus on media psychology issues. Media psychology has many facets. Primarily, the field investigates how media influences human behavior. Division 46's purpose is also to assist mental health professionals and journalists to provide the public with timely, useful, and accessible psychological information which addresses concerns and crises through the mass media.

The division's Web site (http://www.apa.org/divisions/div46), quarterly newsletter *The Amplifier*, and listserv provide forums for professionals to discuss their ideas, research, and concerns regarding media representations of psychology. Those electronic resources also provide contacts for media to consult experts. Two professional periodicals, *Media Psychology* and the on-line *Journal of Media Psychology*, address issues specific to media psychology.

Division 46's goal is to communicate essential information about psychology based on members' experiences in their practices and research. Professionals are urged to utilize media to educate people about psychology. Collaboration with communication experts is encouraged to enhance the delivery techniques of ideas to audiences. Both psychologists and journalists strive to devise informative, accurate, professional, yet entertaining presentations. Mental health professionals participate in workshops specializing in media training and ethics. Outreach programs with journalists help educate them about professional ethics, standards, and credentials so that they will consult a legitimate mental health professional instead of contacting a self-help celebrity who lacks substantial formal training. Division 46 emphasizes the need for mental health professionals to observe the APA's ethical standards and guidelines while interacting with media.

Mental health professionals distribute information in a variety of modes. Some individuals present speeches and participate in public campaigns concerning issues related to mental health such as substance abuse. A public information committee in the APA has functioned since 1979, and the APA public affairs department alerts media to available media psychologists and releases monthly news packages of interesting items related to its research-based journals. The APA science media relations specialist focuses on placing psychological news in science media.

The division specifically seeks to establish theoretical paradigms to study and practice media psychology internationally, such as how mass media influence the public and how effective they are at distributing psychological information. Many researchers design surveys to study how people react to media presentations, such as coverage of the controversial 2000 U.S. presidential election and analysis of the stock market. Media psychologists collaborate with professionals in other psychological fields to examine specific issues, such as how the media portray marriage and family relationships.

At California State University, Los Angeles, Stuart Fischoff, director of the department of psychology's Media Psychology Research Institute (MPRI), initiated the first media psychology classes and laboratory in the United States and developed a master's program specializing in media psychology. The forty-five units required for graduation include sixteen units of broadcasting and communications courses to supplement psychology class work. Each student prepares a thesis investigating some aspect of media psychology.

ETHICS

Radio and television psychology have become subdisciplines of psychology. Audiences seek to be entertained and to acquire advice and information. Many mental health professionals support and encourage this form of media psychology but insist that radio and television psychiatrists should strive to be broadcast educators instead of psychotherapists. They can advise listeners but not diagnose them. The AMP developed ethical guidelines relevant to Federal Communications Commission (FCC) rules for mental health professionals. Prior to a media appearance, professionals should watch or listen to a broadcast to determine what their roles as guests will be and if the show is professionally appropriate and not exploitative and sensationalized. If a professional declines an invitation, he or she should explain to the show's producers what is ethically problematic. Above all else, media psychologists should retain their integrity and standards.

Because media psychology is constantly evolving and expanding in response to new technology and formats, peer discussion is crucial to maintain ethical standards. Some State Boards of Examiners in

Psychology, such as the one in Louisiana, issue opinions that restrict state mental health professionals' participation in media activities to prevent harming the public. State regulations usually require that media psychology professionals base their comments on accurate psychological resources, do not exploit patients, and clarify that they have not established a personal psychological relationship with anybody who receives their information in any form of public delivery. Most important, media psychologists are not to place entertainment over ethical psychological practices.

Mental health professionals participating in media are urged to avoid exploitative relationships. In particular, psychologists on call-in broadcasts must insist that calls are screened off the air before publicly conversing with callers. Also, the screeners should use a process approved by mental health experts, not show producers or hosts, and be adequately trained to refer callers to mental health resources and crisis and support groups as necessary. Professionals must require media to provide callers disclaimers which explain that on-air interaction is not a substitute for therapy and that it is not private and any disclosures will become public information. Also, callers are warned that there may be a delay when they are placed on hold before their call is aired or that their call might not be broadcast because they will be referred to other forms of assistance. The professional should also insist that an on-air disclaimer emphasize that information on the show is presented in a limited format and should not be considered adequate therapy.

In many cases, mental health professionals might be asked about a subject outside of their specialty area, for which they have limited knowledge. They should recognize the limitations of talk show formats and not advise callers to make impulsive, life-changing decisions. Media psychology professionals also need to be alert for callers' and show personnel's unique ethnic, cultural, or special interests, which might influence those people's psychological perceptions, expectations, and agendas.

PSYCHOLOGY VIA MEDIA

Media psychologists strive to tell audiences about psychological topics in concise passages without using complicated jargon. Mental health professionals provide essential psychological assistance during times of crisis, such as the September 11, 2001, ter-

rorist attacks. Media psychologists volunteered with the APA/American Red Cross Disaster Response Network. These professionals helped comfort audiences, especially children, counseled survivors, and suggested how to cope with emotional shocks, tragedies, and trauma. Publicity also addressed people's fear of flying after the hijackings. Media professionals also try to explain the psychological aspects of unbelievable violent actions such as murders and school shootings. Their knowledge can also be used to develop violence intervention and prevention programs for public presentation.

Media used to distribute psychology information range from local to international forums. Information tends to address issues relevant to a broad audience and is often created to be appealing and familiar, such as publicizing the therapeutic role of pets in people's lives. Print is a popular medium, whether in the form of books, pamphlets, or articles appearing in newspapers, magazines, newsletters, or mass mailings. Media psychologists deliver public lectures and perform demonstrations of methods. Often such presentations are recorded on audio or video tapes or broadcast on radio or television programs. Many broadcasts are interactive events between professionals, guests with problems, and audiences. Computer software, CD-ROMs, and the Internet, including chat rooms and message boards, have provided innovative forums to disseminate media psychology information quickly and broadly.

Mental health professionals use media to address their interests and concerns for legislation and community services concerning mental health. Media psychology also has valuable applications to marketing and consumer and political psychology. Psychologists often comment in the media about controversial court trials which involve psychological issues such as battered women, violent children, or mental illnesses. Often, different psychologists present contrasting perceptions of defendants and witnesses during a trial, particularly when assessing the reliability of childhood memories of abuse or trauma. Forensic psychology is appealing to the media and to the public, who want to understand why people might commit shocking crimes but often sensationalize information instead of comprehending psychological data factually and unemotionally. Media psychologists study the role of psychologists in legal reporting. They are concerned about the ethical ramifications of mental health professionals publicly discussing people they have not evaluated and with privacy and confidentiality issues regarding the people being analyzed in the press.

Some media psychologists are celebrities, such as Ruth Westheimer, John Gray, James Dobson, Barbara De Angelis, and Phil McGraw. Others have high-profile positions as consultants on morning news shows or as magazine columnists while also teaching or practicing in their communities. Several serve as staff psychologists for reality television shows. Some media psychologists host regional television shows on local access channels. On *Dr. Carol Goldberg and Company* in New York, viewers learn about the psychology profession during interviews with psychologists who discuss social concerns such as parenting. Professionals address viewer-requested topics during round-table discussions on *Dr. Susan Kastl's Psychology Show* in New Orleans.

EXPERTS VERSUS AMATEURS

Talk shows need psychology professionals to legitimize programs. Media psychologists often encounter disrespect for their expertise, especially on shows such as *Geraldo* and *Jenny Jones*, which encourage tabloid techniques such as ambushes, revenge-seeking, hostility, and exhibitionism. Audiences often prefer receiving psychological advice from flashy, entertaining people who lack academic credentials but offer easy answers and quick fixes. The sensationalism inherent in many public talk show forums encourages an adversarial relationship with mental health professionals. Stuart Fischoff, who frequently appeared as an authority on major talk shows, exposed their exploitative and damaging nature. Fischoff noted that most shows were manipulated to present a biased message which would attract large audiences and that producers expected invited authorities to approve this spin publicly even if it was contrary to their research and beliefs.

According to Fischoff, most talk show formats impede mental health goals. Invited experts are expected to perform by providing entertaining comments in brief, simple sound bites and to summarize complex situations in short time periods averaging thirty seconds. Usually, they can only make general remarks and are often interrupted by hosts or audience members who want to promote their views. Media psychologists only briefly encounter guests and do not develop a therapist-patient relationship in which they acquire sufficient information about

the person for professional analysis. Most guests are not seeking help but want the expert's validation, approval, and acceptance and the exposure to millions of viewers who might identify with them in some way. Some shows, such as *Oprah* and *The Montel Williams Show*, purposefully attempt to educate guests but sometimes succumb to ratings stunts.

Experts are discouraged from engaging in profound, original discourse. Audience members are encouraged to consider themselves equals to psychological experts, and personal experiences are valued more than clinical experiences and academic training. Shows are formulaic, and experts are expected to conform. Many media psychologists appear on talk shows solely for self-promotion. Occasionally guests sue shows for suffering they claimed was inflicted on them, and media psychologists are consulted to evaluate and testify whether the plaintiffs were traumatized.

Media consultants often are frustrated by how some journalists distort and fabricate psychological information. For example, the media often perpetuate stories about syndromes and disorders which lack factual verification by clinical trials and research. Uncritical reporting and hype result when the press is intrigued by sensational descriptions which have no scientific basis. For example, some media depicted psychotherapy negatively in their skewed coverage of false memory syndrome related to childhood abuse described in legal testimony. By concentrating on controversial psychotherapists and clinics, the media caused the public to lose confidence in mental health professionals, sparking a temporary backlash.

Media psychologists urge reporters to aspire to be accurate, fair, and responsible in their coverage of psychological issues. Reporters often do not comprehend who is an expert on a subject and showcase people whose personal experiences are equated with expertise. Media personnel often have insufficient familiarity with social science research methodology to understand why some data or statements are flawed. Psychologists may choose not to appear as experts on media, concerned that they might inadvertently veer from APA principles because of host pressure and editing. Most media psychologists strive to be responsible and to avoid having their comments misused and deceptively presented. In contrast, the nonexperts touting pop psychology often detrimentally influence media and public knowledge through their ignorance, and psychology is often mistakenly comprehended as a pseudoscience because of these amateurs.

MEDIA IMPACT AND DEPICTIONS

Media psychologists research how media impact individuals and society. The role of the media in possibly provoking violence is a controversial topic. Most researchers agree that data analyzed according to accepted methodology reveal that media in the form of television, movies, video games, music, and other modes do not cause people to become violent. Instead, violence is triggered by other factors, mainly environmental, such as peer group pressure. Other media psychologists insist that violence and media are connected and testify to legislative bodies about controlling children's access to violent forms of entertainment. Many journalists ignore the scientific findings and experts' testimony that argue against a media link to causing violence and instead emphasize accounts which suggest that media provokes violence. Other research topics include how stereotypes and clichés in media influence cultural attitudes toward groups such as women and foreigners and processes such as aging.

Media psychology is concerned with how mental health professionals are depicted by popular culture. Psychologists, psychiatrists, and therapists are often characters in television programs such as *The Bob Newhart Show* and *Frasier* and films including *Silence of the Lambs* and *Analyze This*. Soap operas often have a psychiatrist character, Dr. Marlena Evans on *Days of Our Lives* for instance, whose career is pivotal to plots. Therapy and support groups are the focus of plots and settings.

The APA's Division 46 established a media watch committee to monitor how media portray psychologists, psychiatrists, and therapists. The committee's rating system evaluates how television programs emphasize mental health authorities as being professional and ethical, respecting laws and therapist-patient confidentiality, or stress if a character is behaving contrary to professional standards. Media psychologists criticize entertainment which stereotypes psychologists, such as depicting male therapists as extremely competent or evil, while demeaning female psychologists as ineffective and primarily sexual objects.

The Golden Psi Award has been presented to producers of television shows, including *Law & Order,* *Once and Again, The Sopranos,* and *Chicago Hope,* who have responsibly and realistically presented mental health issues and competent, intelligent, and compassionate characters. Descriptions of psychologically related issues on those shows demonstrate accurate knowledge of disorders and comprehension of physiological development and social dynamics relevant to mental health. Characters are identified by their credentials or discredited for not being suitably trained as mental health professionals.

SOURCES FOR FURTHER STUDY

Crigler, Ann N., ed. *The Psychology of Political Communication.* Ann Arbor: University of Michigan Press, 1996. Analyzes how media can be manipulated to alter voters' psychological perceptions of candidates and issues.

Fischoff, Stuart. "Confessions of a TV Talk Show Shrink." *Psychology Today* 28, no. 5 (September/October, 1995): 38-45. A candid account of a media psychology pioneer's dissatisfaction with his experiences on several major national talk shows and his remarks on how the shows are irresponsible, exploitative, and sensationalized.

Fox, Ronald E. "The Rape of Psychotherapy." *Professional Psychology: Research and Practice* 26, no. 2 (April, 1995): 147-155. Former APA president criticizes the press for concentrating on dubious practitioners and inaccurately portraying such mental health issues as false memory syndrome.

Henricks, William H., and William B. Stiles. "Verbal Processes on Psychological Radio Call-in Programs: Comparisons with Other Help-Intended Interactions." *Professional Psychology: Research and Practice* 20, no. 5 (October, 1989): 315-321. Through analysis of verbal responses on a variety of programs, compares the verbal behavior of hosts and callers with psychologists and clients participating in cognitive-behavioral therapy which poses ethical concerns.

Kirschner, Sam, and Diane Kirschner, eds. *Perspectives on Psychology and the Media.* Washington, D.C.: American Psychological Association, 1997. The first volume in the Psychology and the Media series, and the first text focusing on media psychology. Discusses both research and practice concerns and suggests future goals for media psychologists.

Klonoff, E. A. "A Star Is Born: Psychologists and the Media." *Professional Psychology: Research and Prac-*

tice 14, no. 6 (1983): 847-854. Examines how people become publicly identified as psychology experts and media expectations for mental health authorities.

Levy, David A. "Social Support and the Media: Analysis of Responses by Radio Psychology Talk Show Hosts." *Professional Psychology: Research and Practice* 20, no. 2 (April, 1989): 73-78. A study of broadcasts evaluated by APA members concludes that callers benefit from receiving social and emotional support during call-on shows but usually they and the audience do not receive psychologically adequate informational support and guidance.

McCall, Robert B. "Science and the Press: Like Oil and Water?" *American Psychologist* 43, no. 2 (February, 1988): 87-94. Focuses on the differences in how sciences and social and behavioral sciences are covered by media and recommends how psychologists can seek better, more accurate, and objective journalistic comprehension of their work.

Schwartz, Lita Linzer, ed. *Psychology and the Media: A Second Look*. Washington, D.C.: American Psychological Association, 1999. Volume two of the Psychology and the Media series, which explores how media psychology has expanded due to technological advancements.

Elizabeth D. Schafer

SEE ALSO: Disaster psychology; Research ethics; Violence and sexuality in the media.

Meditation and relaxation

DATE: The 1910's forward
TYPE OF PSYCHOLOGY: Consciousness
FIELDS OF STUDY: Prosocial behavior; stress and illness

Psychologists regard meditation and relaxation techniques as possible means for reducing stress, improving mental and physical health, and expanding conscious awareness. Some of these techniques may help psychology fulfill its goals of developing the mental potential of individuals and improving social behavior.

KEY CONCEPTS
• consciousness
• guided imagery
• mindfulness
• progressive relaxation
• self-actualization
• systematic desensitization
• transcendental meditation

INTRODUCTION

Forms of meditation have been practiced in many cultures throughout the ages. Traditionally, meditation techniques have been used to cultivate self-realization or enlightenment, in which higher levels of human potential are said to be realized. Traditional meditation techniques as well as modern techniques of relaxation are often used today for more limited purposes—to combat stress and specific problems of physical and mental health. There is also growing interest, however, in the greater purpose of meditation to achieve higher states of human development.

TECHNIQUES

The various techniques of meditation practiced today derive from diverse sources. Some, such as yoga and Zen Buddhism, come from ancient traditions of India and other Asian countries, having been introduced in the West by traditional teachers and their Western students. Others originate in Western traditions such as Christianity. Some relaxation techniques taught today were adapted from these traditions, whereas others were invented independently of meditative traditions. For example, Edmund Jacobson introduced a progressive relaxation technique in 1910 and advocated its use to the medical profession and the public for more than fifty years. His research found progressive relaxation helpful for a variety of stress-related problems. Jacobson's rather elaborate procedure, which could require up to six months of training, was adapted and shortened by Joseph Wolpe in his book *Psychotherapy by Reciprocal Inhibition* (1958). Later, Douglas A. Bernstein and Thomas D. Borkovec, in *Progressive Relaxation Training: A Manual for the Helping Professions* (1973) further adapted progressive relaxation. These programs require a qualified therapist to teach the relaxation technique. A different approach, autogenic training, derived from self-hypnotic techniques by Johannes Schultz, has been used widely, especially in Europe, since the 1930's.

The approaches of various meditation techniques differ greatly. Most techniques involve sitting quietly with the eyes closed. In some techniques, however, the eyes are kept open, or partially open as in Zazen practice of Zen Buddhism. Other "meditative" techniques, among them tai chi and hatha yoga, involve physical movement. Techniques of meditation may be classified according to the way in which mental attention is used during the practice. In some techniques, one focuses or concentrates attention on a specific thought, sensation, or external object. Such concentration techniques train the mind to ignore extraneous thoughts and sensations in order to remain quiet and focused, as in the Theravadin Buddhist tradition's second stage of practice. Other techniques, such as mindfulness or insight meditation, allow the mind to experience all thoughts and perceptions without focusing on a specific object. In these techniques, the goal is to remain aware of the present moment without judging or reacting to it. Both concentration and mindfulness techniques may be employed in different Buddhist practices. In another approach, contemplative meditation, one thinks about a philosophical question or a pleasant concept such as "love," contemplating the meaning of the thought. This technique is employed, for example, in some Christian practices to produce tranquillity in the mind.

Relaxation techniques take various forms. In progressive relaxation (PR), muscles are consciously tensed and relaxed in a systematic manner. PR is often combined with pleasant mental imagery in a directed manner called guided imagery to produce physical relaxation and a calm mind. Relaxation strategies are often employed in programs of systematic desensitization to reduce stress responses to frightful or anxiety-producing situations. Autogenic training, another major approach to relaxation, employs an adaptation of self-hypnosis to change the body's functioning. This self-regulation can be very effective, as can biofeedback, which uses scientific instruments to reveal specific physiologic information. While observing signals from the instruments, one consciously manipulates bodily functions to achieve more normal states. In clinical settings, biofeedback is more effective when combined with relaxation and psychotherapeutic techniques than when used alone. Relaxation techniques such as

these produce physical and mental relaxation and give the individual some control over physiological processes such as breathing and heart rate. They also result in lower levels of stress hormones such as adrenaline.

Though often confused with these approaches, transcendental meditation, commonly called TM, involves different mechanics. In TM, one uses a sound without meaning, selected for its soothing influence on the mind. This process does not involve concentration, because the sound is used effortlessly. This use of a sound allows one's awareness to shift from the surface level of thinking to subtler levels of the thinking process, and ultimately to transcend thinking and experience a state of silent, restful alertness without thoughts, bodily sensations, or emotions. This inner wakefulness is called transcendental consciousness or pure consciousness. TM is taught in accord with the ancient Vedic tradition of India. Each tradition of meditation has its own understanding of the goals of long-term practice. Though the theme of gaining pure consciousness is shared by several meditative traditions, it cannot be assumed that all techniques of meditation produce the same results.

POTENTIAL BENEFITS

There has been considerable controversy over the years about whether meditation and relaxation techniques differ significantly in the relaxation they produce or in the cumulative effects of their long-term practice. The use of meta-analyses—statistical comparisons of the results of many studies—has produced interesting results in this area. Meta-analyses can reveal trends not observed in individual studies and can control for effects of such variations in methods as sample size, study period, and observer bias by combining results from different sources. Because meditation techniques differ and because most meditation studies have been done on transcendental meditation (TM), these meta-analyses have tended to focus on potential differences between TM and relaxation.

In the mid-1980's, some researchers asked whether simply relaxing with the eyes closed would produce the same level of physiological rest as meditation. A meta-analysis of thirty-one studies showed significantly deeper rest during TM than during eyes-closed rest as indicated by breath rate, basal skin resistance (a measure of stability of the autonomic nervous system), and plasma lactate (a chemical in the blood related to stress).

Individuals practice meditation or relaxation techniques for many different reasons, particularly for relief from anxiety and stress. Both scientific research and anecdotal evidence on some of these techniques indicate that they may produce significant benefits to physical and mental health and to the quality of life as a whole.

APPLICATIONS

People often use relaxation techniques to relieve specific problems. For example, progressive relaxation has been demonstrated to reduce high blood pressure, headaches, insomnia, and anxiety; to improve memory; to increase internal locus of control (being in control of oneself); and to facilitate positive mood development in some people. When used in conjunction with muscle biofeedback, progressive muscle relaxation (PMR) has been effective in treating alcoholism. Autogenic training has also been shown to be effective in many of these areas. These techniques find wide application in psychologists' offices, in hospitals, in schools, and in institutions. For example, medical practitioners teach relaxation techniques to patients for pain management and anxiety reduction, for the control of asthma symptoms, and for treating migraine headaches. Studies have also shown that relaxation improves the concentration abilities of severely mentally handicapped adults and increases academic performance among grade school children.

Of the various meditation techniques, transcendental meditation is the most widely practiced in the West. The standardized method of teaching and uniform method of practicing TM make it particularly suitable for scientific study, and more than five thousand studies have delineated the effects of TM. In a study of health insurance statistics published in 1987 in *Psychosomatic Medicine*, for example, two thousand TM meditators showed 50 percent less serious illness and use of health care services than did nonmeditators over a five-year period. Risk factors for disease, such as tobacco and alcohol use, high blood pressure, and high cholesterol levels, also have been found to decrease among TM meditators. In 1994, psychologist Charles Alexander found that TM proved to be an effective treatment for substance dependance.

There is also some evidence suggesting that meditation is more effective than relaxation techniques.

For example, a meta-analysis of 144 independent findings published in the *Journal of Clinical Psychology* in 1989 indicated that the effect of TM on reducing trait anxiety (chronic stress) was approximately twice as large as that produced by progressive relaxation, other forms of relaxation, or other forms of meditation. This was the case even when researchers statistically controlled for differences among studies in subject expectancy, experimenter bias, or quality of research design.

Although meditation is usually considered an activity that affects only the individual practitioner, studies have been performed which suggest that the influence of meditation can extend beyond the meditator to the environment. Such findings are controversial, with many scientists summarily dismissing the possibility of any correlation between meditation and external events. Respected journals have published such studies, however, because the methodologies used were deemed scientifically sound. More than forty studies have found improvements in social conditions and prosperity when a small proportion of the population involved practices TM. For example, in 1999, British researchers Guy Hatchard, Ashley Deans, Kenneth Cavanaugh, and David Orme-Johnson reported that crime rates in Merseyside, England, dropped by 13 percent when the local TM group grew to a certain size. This drop in crime was sustained for the following four years of the study.

MEDITATION AND THE SCIENCE OF PSYCHOLOGY

The field of psychology was born with the hope that it would someday provide a complete account of human nature. William James (1842-1910), the founder of American psychology, in seeking ways to promote psychological growth, attempted to study elevated states of consciousness and suggested that meditation might be a means to cultivate their development. Few psychologists pursued this direction, however, until advances in bioengineering and the introduction of standardized forms of meditation and relaxation allowed psychologists to study consciousness in the laboratory.

Studies of self-actualization conducted by Abraham Maslow (1908-1970) also renewed interest in meditation. According to Maslow, self-actualizing persons are individuals who display high levels of creativity, self-esteem, capacity for intimacy, and concern for the well-being of the world community.

They seem to have mastered living happily in a complex world. Maslow believed that self-actualization was the pinnacle of psychological development, and he found that some adults spontaneously had "peak" or transcendental experiences. Sometimes these experiences produced abrupt changes in people's self-perception and significantly advanced their psychological development. Recognizing that meditation might produce such transcendental experiences, Maslow strongly encouraged research on meditation as a means for developing self-actualization.

With the recent development of appropriate scientific methods, alternative states of consciousness such as meditation and relaxation have once again become the focus of much research. Currently, meditation and relaxation are the subject of thousands of studies each year. These studies investigate a wide range of psychological variables, from social development and self-actualization to brain activity.

The various types of meditation are based in ancient systems of philosophy or religion and therefore have ultimate purposes beyond those of strictly psychological approaches to personal development. Whereas self-actualization typically refers to the development of one's unique individual self, Vedic philosophy describes the potential for realizing a transcendental self in the growth of "higher states of consciousness" beyond self-actualization. Through repeated transcendence, one is said to experience this transcendental self as a limitless field of intelligence, creativity, and happiness at the source of the individual mind. In higher states of consciousness, the transcendental self comes to be fully realized and permanently maintained in daily life. In the Vedic tradition, the enlightened are said to enjoy freedom from stress and to find life effortless and blissful.

SOURCES FOR FURTHER STUDY

Alexander, Charles N., and Ellen J. Langer, eds. *Higher Stages of Human Development: Perspectives on Adult Growth.* New York: Oxford University Press, 1990. Explores major dimensions of adult growth, including cognitive and moral development, and development of consciousness, with a thorough discussion of Maharishi Mahesh Yogi's Vedic psychology of human development.

Austin, James. H. *Zen and the Brain: Toward an Understanding of Meditation and Consciousness.* Cambridge, Mass.: MIT Press, 1998. Combines neurological research on consciousness with the author's own experiences with Zen meditation.

Gackenbach, Jayne, Harry Hunt, and Charles N. Alexander, eds. *Higher States of Consciousness: Theoretical and Experimental Perspectives.* New York: Plenum, 1992. This collection of original essays by leading researchers on higher states of consciousness and meditation spans a variety of theoretical perspectives.

Jacobson, Edmund. *You Must Relax.* 4th ed. New York: McGraw-Hill, 1957. First published in 1934, this book presents Jacobson's views on the need for relaxation and the technique of progressive relaxation which he developed.

Kabat-Zinn, J. *Wherever You Go, There You Are: Mindfulness Meditation in Everyday Life.* New York: Hyperion, 1994. Presents the basic principles of mindfulness meditation and the philosophy behind Kabat-Zinn's highly successful stress reduction clinic.

Lichstein, Kenneth L. *Clinical Relaxation Strategies.* New York: John Wiley & Sons, 1988. Contains an extensive review and bibliography of relaxation techniques. In his commentary, Lichstein tends to discount any differences in effects that may exist among different forms of practice.

Mahesh Yogi, Maharishi. *On the Bhagavad-Gita: A New Translation and Commentary.* New York: Penguin Books, 1986. This classic text from the Vedic literature describes the steps of growth of higher states of consciousness. The accompanying commentary clarifies many misunderstandings about meditation and discusses the relevance of meditation to modern life.

Murphy, Michael, and Steven Donovan. *The Physical and Psychological Effects of Meditation.* San Rafael, Calif.: Esalen Institute, 1988. A review of research on a variety of meditation techniques, with a comprehensive bibliography covering the years from 1931 to 1988.

Charles N. Alexander and David Sands; updated by Cynthia McPherson Frantz

SEE ALSO: Biofeedback and relaxation; Consciousness; Consciousness: Altered states; Creativity and intelligence; Endocrine system; Nervous system; Self-actualization; Stress: Physiological responses; Stress-related diseases.

MAGILL'S ENCYCLOPEDIA OF SOCIAL SCIENCE

PSYCHOLOGY

COMPLETE LIST OF ENTRIES

Fight-or-flight response
Forensic psychology
Forgetting and forgetfulness
Freud, Anna
Freud, Sigmund
Fromm, Erich

Gender-identity formation
General adaptation syndrome
General Aptitude Test Battery (GATB)
Gesell, Arnold
Gestalt therapy
Giftedness
Gilligan, Carol
Gonads
Grammar and speech
Grieving
Group decision making
Group therapy
Groups
Guilt

Habituation and sensitization
Hallucinations
Health psychology
Hearing
Help-seeking
Helping
Histrionic personality
Homosexuality
Hormones and behavior
Horney, Karen
Human resource training and
    development
Humanism
Humanistic trait models: Gordon Allport
Hunger
Hypnosis
Hypochondriasis
Hypothesis development and testing
Hysteria

Identity crises
Imprinting and learning
Impulse control disorders
Incentive motivation
Incompetency
Individual psychology: Alfred Adler
Industrial and organizational psychology
Inhibitory and excitatory impulses

Insanity defense
Insomnia
Instinct theory
Intelligence
Intelligence quotient (IQ)
Intelligence tests
Interest inventories
Intergroup relations
International Classification of Diseases
    (ICD)
Internet psychology
Intimacy
Introverts and extroverts

Jealousy
Jung, Carl G.
Juvenile delinquency

Kelly, George A.
Kinesthetic memory
Kinsey, Alfred
Kraepelin, Emil
Kuder Occupational Interest Survey
    (KOIS)

Lacan, Jacques
Language
Law and psychology
Leadership
Learned helplessness
Learning
Learning disorders
Lewin, Kurt
Linguistics
Logic and reasoning
Long-term memory
Lorenz, Konrad
Love

Madness: Historical concepts
Masters, William H., and Virginia E.
    Johnson
Media psychology
Meditation and relaxation
Memory
Memory: Animal research
Memory: Empirical studies
Memory: Physiology
Memory: Sensory
Memory storage

CATEGORIZED LIST OF ENTRIES

ABILITY TESTING
Ability tests
Career and personnel testing
College entrance examinations
Confidentiality
Creativity: Assessment

General Aptitude Test Battery
    (GATB)
Giftedness
Intelligence tests
Kuder Occupational Interest
    Survey (KOIS)

Peabody Individual Achievement
    Test (PIAT)
Stanford-Binet test
Strong Interest Inventory (SII)
Testing: Historical perspectives

Reality therapy
Sport psychology
Support groups
Transactional analysis
Virtual reality

CONDITIONING
Behavior therapy
Behaviorism
Conditioning
Learning
Memory: Animal research
Motivation
Operant conditioning therapies
Parental alienation syndrome
Pavlov, Ivan
Pavlovian conditioning
Radical behaviorism: B. F.
    Skinner
Reinforcement
Rule-governed behavior
Taste aversion

CONSCIOUSNESS
Artificial intelligence
Attention
Automaticity
Brain damage
Circadian rhythms
Consciousness
Consciousness: Altered states
Coping: Terminal illness
Denial
Dreams
Hallucinations
Hypnosis
Insomnia
Meditation and relaxation
Self
Sleep
Sleep apnea syndromes and
    narcolepsy

COPING
Aggression
Amnesia and fugue
Anger
Beck Depression Inventory
    (BDI)
Biofeedback and relaxation

Coping: Chronic illness
Coping: Social support
Coping: Strategies
Coping: Terminal illness
Denial
Disaster psychology
Environmental psychology
Grieving
Health psychology
Impulse control disorders
Media psychology
Midlife crises
Multiple personality
Pain management
Parental alienation syndrome
Religion and psychology
Religiosity: Measurement
Social networks
Stepfamilies
Stress
Stress: Behavioral and
    psychological responses
Substance use disorders
Support groups

DEPRESSION
Alzheimer's disease
Battered woman syndrome
Beck, Aaron T.
Beck Depression Inventory
    (BDI)
Bipolar disorder
Children's Depression Inventory
    (CDI)
Circadian rhythms
Clinical depression
Coping: Chronic illness
Coping: Terminal illness
Dementia
Depression
Disaster psychology
Drug therapies
Grieving
Impulse control disorders
Kraepelin, Emil
Media psychology
Mood disorders
Parental alienation syndrome
Postpartum depression
Psychosurgery

Seasonal affective disorder
Social networks
Suicide
Support groups

DEVELOPMENTAL PSYCHOLOGY
Adolescence: Cognitive skills
Adolescence: Cross-cultural
    patterns
Adolescence: Sexuality
Ageism
Aging: Cognitive changes
Aging: Physical changes
Aging: Theories
Attachment and bonding in
    infancy and childhood
Birth: Effects on physical
    development
Birth order and personality
Career selection, development,
    and change
Child abuse
Cognitive ability: Gender
    differences
Cognitive development: Jean
    Piaget
Death and dying
Denial
Development
Developmental disabilities
Developmental methodologies
Erikson, Erik
Family life: Adult issues
Family life: Children's issues
Father-child relationship
Freud, Anna
Gender-identity formation
Gesell, Arnold
Giftedness
Gilligan, Carol
Helping
Identity crises
Juvenile delinquency
Kinesthetic memory
Mental retardation
Midlife crises
Moral development
Mother-child relationship
Motor development
Oedipus complex

Rape and sexual assault
Road rage
Separation and divorce: Adult
  issues
Sexism
Sibling relationships
Sport psychology
Violence and sexuality in the
  media
Violence by children and
  teenagers
Women's psychology: Carol
  Gilligan
Women's psychology: Karen
  Horney
Women's psychology: Sigmund
  Freud

METHODOLOGY
American Psychiatric
  Association
American Psychological
  Association
Animal experimentation
Archival data
Assessment
Beck, Aaron T.
Behaviorism
Case-study methodologies
Complex experimental designs
Confidentiality
Data description
Developmental methodologies
Diagnosis
*Diagnostic and Statistical Manual
  of Mental Disorders* (DSM)
Experimental psychology
Experimentation: Ethics and
  participant rights
Experimentation: Independent,
  dependent, and control
  variables
Eysenck, Hans
Field experimentation
Forensic psychology
Freud, Anna
Grammar and speech
Hypochondriasis, conversion,
  somatization, and
  somatoform pain

Hypothesis development and
  testing
*International Classification of
  Diseases* (ICD)
Kinsey, Alfred
Lewin, Kurt
Motivation
Observational methods
Psychoanalysis
Psychology: Definition
Psychosurgery
Quasi-experimental designs
Religiosity: Measurement
Research ethics
Rorschach, Hermann
Rorschach inkblots
Sampling
Scientific methods
Signal detection theory
Social networks
Statistical significance tests
Support groups
Survey research: Questionnaires
  and interviews
Teaching methods
Virtual reality
Watson, John B.
Within-subject experimental
  designs

MOTIVATION
Achievement motivation
Advertising
Affiliation and friendship
Affiliation motive
Allport, Gordon
Bandura, Albert
Beck Depression Inventory
  (BDI)
Crowd behavior
Denial
Dix, Dorothea
Drives
Eating disorders
Emotions
Evolutionary psychology
Eysenck, Hans
Field theory: Kurt Lewin
Forensic psychology
Helping

Homosexuality
Horney, Karen
Human resource training and
  development
Hunger
Hysteria
Incentive motivation
Industrial and organizational
  psychology
Instinct theory
Jealousy
Learning
Lorenz, Konrad
Love
Masters, William H., and
  Virginia E. Johnson
Motivation
Obesity
Optimal arousal theory
Parental alienation syndrome
Profiling
Psychoanalysis
Reinforcement
Religion and psychology
Religiosity: Measurement
Sex hormones and motivation
Sexual behavior patterns
Sport psychology
Substance use disorders
Support groups
Teaching methods
Thirst
Women's psychology: Carol
  Gilligan
Work motivation

NERVOUS SYSTEM
Artificial intelligence
Beck, Aaron T.
Behaviorism
Brain damage
Brain specialization
Brain structure
Circadian rhythms
Computer models of
  cognition
Defense reactions: Species
  specific
Drug therapies
Endorphins